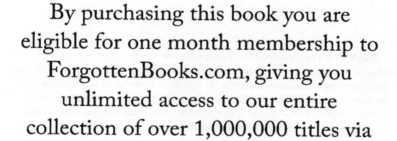

ISBN 978-0-365-22141-8
PIBN 10836817

BRYN MAWR ALUMNAE BULLETIN

ASPECTS OF THE COLLEGE

January, 1933

Vol. XIII   No. 1

Entered as second-class matter, January 15, 1921, at the Post Office, Phila., Pa., under Act of March 3, 1879
COPYRIGHT, 1933
ALUMNAE ASSOCIATION OF BRYN MAWR COLLEGE

Form of Bequest

I give and bequeath to the ALUMNAE ASSOCIATION OF BRYN MAWR COLLEGE, Bryn Mawr, Pennsylvania, the sum of _____dollars.

_____

BRYN MAWR ALUMNAE BULLETIN

OFFICIAL PUBLICATION OF
THE BRYN MAWR ALUMNÆ ASSOCIATION

MARJORIE L. THOMPSON, '12, *Editor*
ALICE M. HAWKINS, '07, *Business Manager*

EDITORIAL BOARD

MARY CRAWFORD DUDLEY, '96
CAROLINE MORROW CHADWICK-COLLINS, '05
EMILY KIMBROUGH WRENCH, '21
ELIZABETH BENT CLARK, '95, *ex-officio*

ELLENOR MORRIS, '27
ELINOR B. AMRAM, '28
PAMELA BURR, '28

Subscription Price, $1.50 a Year   Single Copies, 25 Cents
Checks should be drawn to the order of Bryn Mawr Alumnae Bulletin
Published monthly, except August, September and October, at 1006 Arch St., Philadelphia, Pa.

VOL. XIII   JANUARY, 1933   No. 1

The Academic Committee is performing a real service and fulfilling what has always seemed, to the present writer at least, one of its most significant functions, that of serving as liaison officer between the alumnae and the academic interests of the College, in presenting an account of the Science department, and outlining some of the elements that have gone into its making. The field of science was very definitely one of the fields in which Bryn Mawr pioneered in the early days of women's education. The requirement that every student shall take a year of science makes those long laboratory hours a common experience to all of us. There is not one of the alumnae who does not remember the difficulties of the crowded work space, the lack of equipment, the strange pervasive odour that resulted from the entire lack of a modern system of forced ventilation. On the other hand there is scarcely any one, even the least scientific-minded among us, who failed to realize that those same long hours opened up a new world, with horizons that before we had never even glimpsed. We learned a pleasure in technique, as a thing in itself, and not the least of that pleasure was in the recognition of the admirable technique of the teaching. With the years everyone has, in a measure, come to take for granted the general method, and forgotten how gloriously the foundations were laid, and how revolutionary many of the methods were when they were instituted. The Report recalls many things that we should by no means forget if we are looking forward to a further development of the scientific courses. The second section of the Report will concern itself with present occupations and achievements of former science students. This will be particularly interesting, because it is largely to these women and the excellence of the work that they have done as a result of their Bryn Mawr training, that we owe the three quite extraordinary letters from men at the very head of their respective fields. It is a striking thing that such a man as Dr. Welch, of Johns Hopkins, can say: "I am convinced that Bryn Mawr will render a real national service by improving and enlarging its facilities for educational and research work in science, and by training more young women in the field."

BRYN MAWR SCIENCE

I.

AT THE COLLEGE

A Study Made by the Academic Committee

In planning the future of the College, as part of its fiftieth anniversary, the Directors have voiced the belief that special stress should be laid upon the further development of the scientific courses. They have determined upon this emphasis for two reasons. Science, in the curriculum, from the very beginning of the College up to and including the present, has been second in importance to no other branch of work, whether judged by the eminence of the men and women who have done the teaching, or by the tradition and method of work which they have established and developed, or by the subsequent record of the students who have been in their charge. On the other hand, the physical equipment available to the various science departments is now in such state as to add greatly to the difficulties of maintaining the present standard. It is proposed in this and a subsequent article to give a brief résumé of the situation of the science work of the College from these several points of view, as a background of an anticipated attempt on the part of Bryn Mawr to become a recognized center of scientific training for women. To reach this goal it will be necessary to provide the necessary facilities not only for the present, but for an increased number of students, and to offer even wider fields for advanced work than can now be undertaken.

That the past record of the College justifies a program, may be substantiated by the following excerpts from letters of eminent scientists who have known intimately the work done alike by members of its teaching staff and by its graduates. The fact that they have not been directly associated with the College makes their judgment the more valuable.

Dr. Simon Flexner, of the Rockefeller Institute of Medicine, writes:

"I have followed for many years the work in science at Bryn Mawr College, which has, I think, been outstanding. Besides the excellent work done by the students, no college has, in my opinion, supplied the country with a larger share of able and distinguished scientists through the opportunities given there to teachers and investigators. Bryn Mawr's contributions in these important ways have been notable. I am especially interested that the general facilities for science shall be made more adequate in women's colleges. The world of today is so much run by scientific knowledge and women have now so large a share of political and social power, that it is very desirable that they should come to have an understanding and appreciation of science equal to that of men."

From Dr. William H. Welch, of Johns Hopkins University, comes the strong statement:

"In the great advance in higher education of women marked by the establishment and development of Bryn Mawr College the natural sciences have from the beginning received due recognition, and the remarkable record of the College in their cultivation furnishes a powerful argument for their continued and increasing support, and assures the best possible use of enlarged opportunities and resources.

... At Johns Hopkins Medical School we have had abundant opportunity to appreciate the excellent quality of the preliminary training in the sciences which Bryn Mawr graduates bring to the study of medicine, and we share with Bryn Mawr justifiable pride in the later careers of those graduates.

"The day is long past when argument or discussion is needed regarding the attractions of professional or scientific careers for women or their aptitude and capacity for success, and even high achievement in such careers. It is more pertinent to note the rapidly increasing opportunities and the real need for women well trained in the natural and physical sciences as teachers, assistants, technicians and special workers. Here the supply falls far short of the demand, and I am convinced that Bryn Mawr will render a real national service by improving and enlarging its facilities for educational and research work in science, and by training more young women in the field."

Dr. Robert H. Millikan, of the California Institute of Technology, comments on the plan as follows:

"If it is desirable to have women's colleges and men's colleges, a point on which there would be some difference of opinion but upon which the California Institute and Bryn Mawr both agree *in practice*, it is surely desirable to have these institutions of the highest possible grade, and this they cannot be unless research work is to some extent done by the staffs. Again, among the women's colleges Bryn Mawr certainly stands out preëminently as the women's institution which has succeeded in furnishing opportunities for graduate study and research. . . . If I were charged with the responsibility of placing one women's institution of the country in a position to do *graduate work in the sciences well*, I would choose Bryn Mawr for that institution."

The importance of the graduate section of the College's scientific work upon which Dr. Millikan has laid particular stress is only one of the respects in which the original plan of the Dalton Hall departments may lay some claim to have been a pioneering measure. Certainly without the graduate school it would have been impossible to attract and keep the outstanding specialists whose names are associated with the various departments, such scholars, to name only two, as Florence Bascom in geology or E. P. Kohler in chemistry, of whom more will be said later. In addition to the combination of elementary and advanced work offered by the science section as a whole, the various departments have contributed individually to the development of new methods in the presentation of scientific material. At the opening of the College, the plan of organization of the biology teaching constituted a new departure, but the original plans proved so sound that they still serve as the basis of its present methodology. Because of its early importance, and because Biology is today the largest of the science departments (in 1931-32 it numbered seventy-two graduate and undergraduate students as against forty-odd in each of the other subjects) its work has been selected for discussion in somewhat fuller detail.

It is difficult for the modern American, to whom the laboratory with its technique is almost synonymous with science, to realize that two generations ago its right to a place in a college was hotly contested. At the time when Bryn Mawr was founded, American university life was dominated by the classical tradition of lectures unaccompanied by demonstration or quantitative check. One of the greatest contributions of President Eliot of Harvard to the teaching of chemistry and physics, and one of his greatest struggles, was his establishment of the laboratory method, first at Massachusetts Institute of Technology with Professor Storer at the end of the '60's, and later on at Harvard. The novelty of the departure is clear from what he subsequently wrote of the experiment:

"And I think the most interesting teaching we did during the first two years . . . was to classes of middle-aged teachers, both men and women, who to the number of thirty or thirty-five persons accepted the advertised offer signed by President Rogers to receive such a class. . . . These men and women, anywhere from twenty-five to fifty-five years of age, were, of course, eager to learn the novel method, but they had not the faintest idea how to learn it, how to work themselves with their own eyes and fingers, to make their own experiments and to draw their own inferences. We finally had to give them a series of sheets describing the experiments we wanted them to perform, and describing them in a good deal of detail. Even then these experienced teachers could not grasp the idea of making their own observations without imitating or copying, then describing accurately what they saw, and lastly, drawing the right inference from what they had themselves done and seen. . . . Their idea was to verify the statement made on the sheet of paper; and this remained the supreme difficulty of teaching that class from beginning to end. We had a good deal of the same trouble in teaching the younger students to see for themselves, to record for themselves, and then draw the right inference; but the younger students were more limber at it than these experienced teachers were."

A parallel work in developing new methods of teaching biology was carried out at Bryn Mawr by Edmund B. Wilson. The year after he accepted an appointment as one of the original faculty of the College, he and William Sedgwick brought out an elementary text inculcating the use of the laboratory method as they had become familiar with it while students of Professor Martin at the Hopkins. This text rapidly took the place in biology that Eliot and Storer's *Manual of Chemistry* had come to occupy in the inorganic field. On the basis of this outline, Professor Wilson organized the work of the department, and made certain decisions whose soundness is still accepted today. Perhaps the most important of these related to the question, "whether the beginner should pursue the logical but difficult course of working upwards from the simple to the complex, or adopt the easier and more practical method of working downwards from familiar higher forms." He chose the former (though with certain modifications designed to facilitate the beginner's first approach to the subject), and as a result the general biology course given at Bryn Mawr followed the direct line of development from the single cell to the complex organism in a manner distinctive in American college curricula.

After four years at Bryn Mawr, Professor Wilson was called to Columbia, where he is now Emeritus Professor and recognized not only as an outstanding scientist, but also as the most distinguished scholar on the Columbia Faculty of National Sciences. He was President of the American Association for the Advancement of Science in 1910.

Professor Wilson's work at Bryn Mawr was continued and supplemented by a succession of distinguished biologists. Thomas Hunt Morgan succeeded him as head of the department and served for thirteen years, from 1891-1904; he had gained a name for himself in experimental zoölogy before being called to Columbia in that year. When in 1928 the California Institute of Technology at Pasadena founded the Wm. G. Kerhoff Laboratories of Biological Sciences, it sought, as director, the most distinguished biologist to be found either here or abroad, and selected

Dr. Morgan as a scientist ranking among the most eminent in his field. Dr. Morgan was President of the American Association for the Advancement of Science in 1930, and President of the National Academy of Science the following year. His research was described at that time as "concerned largely with the physical basis of heredity, with the physiological aspect of inheritance. With Morgan's leadership and under the influence of his masterly reasoning and adequately planned experimentation, the hypothesis of the germ plasm as the bearer of hereditary characters has progressively become clearer in the last quarter century."

Though his period of teaching at the College was cut short by a call to the newly founded University of Chicago, to Bryn Mawr belongs the distinction of having brought to America one of the most brilliant of modern biologists, Jacques Loeb. With her usual courage and perspicacity, Miss Thomas, then Dean of the College, singled out this young man, who was attached to a clinic in Zurich, and brought him to Bryn Mawr in 1891 to do his first teaching. Dr. W. J. V. Ousterhout, writing a biographical sketch of Dr. Loeb in 1924, said of his influence in biology:

"It would be difficult to give an adequate account. His conceptions were often so bold and original as to startle conventional thinkers. Fearless in attacking difficult questions of fundamental importance, he showed almost uncanny insight into the most obscure and baffling matters. His discoveries often had a dramatic finality in their unexpected and beautiful solutions of perplexing problems. His results were reached by methods so simple as to compel admiration."

Among Bryn Mawr graduate students who later became members of the Biology Department, Nettie M. Stevens has been outstanding. She received the degree of Ph.D. from the College in 1903, having held the President's European Fellowship and the Resident Fellowship in Biology; from 1904-06 she was Reader, and from 1906 until her death in 1912, Associate in Experimental Morphology. In recognition of her extraordinary abilities in scientific investigation the Directors created for her one of the few research chairs in the United States, and attached to it only a few hours of advanced teaching in order to enable her to pursue original investigation. At the time of her death she was the most eminent scientific graduate of Bryn Mawr and one of the leading biological investigators of her generation. *Science* for October 11th, 1912, contained an article which said in part:

"Modern cytological work involves an intricacy of detail, the significance of which can be appreciated by the specialist alone; but Miss Stevens had a share in a discovery of importance and her name will be remembered for this, when the minutiae of detailed investigations that she carried out have become incorporated in the general body of the subject. . . ."

The independent discovery of Miss Stevens, who, as Dr. Wilson says, was working on parallel lines with him, marks the turning point in the history of the theory of sex determination.

When Dr. Morgan was called to Columbia, Dr. David Tennent was appointed at Bryn Mawr and is the present director of the department. His special field of research is experimental embryology and cytology. In recognition especially of his original work on echinoderns he has been appointed a member of the National Academy of Sciences and of the National Research Council.

The record and the contributions and biological knowledge of the persons associated with this one department, and the technique which they have developed, are alone sufficient to justify an effort to offer it the physical means of maintaining and expanding its work. But the disadvantages under which it suffers are shared, and indeed in some cases shared in greater measure, by the other science departments.

The primary lack in present science equipment is the elementary lack of space. The Geology Department has no lecture room; it is forced to use for this purpose a laboratory so obstructed by pillars as to make the exhibition of charts and maps extremely difficult. Each year about 25 per cent more students attempt to register for the course than this inadequate seating capacity will accommodate, and consequently have to be diverted to other subjects. The department's irreplaceable collection of minerals, of the value of at least $100,000, has no place in which it can be displayed, and is subject to the constant danger of a very grave fire hazard.

The admirable work sketched above has been carried on in spite of lack of space and in the face of other difficulties. The Directors now feel the replacement of plant to be an elementary necessity. But expansion as well as replacement must be arranged if Bryn Mawr is to become the center of advanced scientific work for women suggested by the letters quoted at the beginning of this article.

The contemplated expansion would, however, be definitely planned and restricted. One of the outstanding advantages which the small size of the College has always offered to its students has been the possibility, enjoyed at Bryn Mawr in contradistinction to the larger colleges and universities, of students coming into contact during their elementary years with teachers and scholars of the first rank, and the College has been exceptionally fortunate in the degree to which its greatest scholars have also been great teachers. But the limitations imposed by inadequate facilities have at times reduced the number of students below that which the staff could handle without loss to anyone; and where only two or three post-major or graduate students were doing work in a department, the mutual stimulation which might be derived from a somewhat larger number has been lost. For this reason the new facilities would not be used in increasing the number of fields opened, but in providing in a more satisfactory manner for those already entered upon. As examples of the type of work now done, which could be more adequately offered under expanded facilities, honours work, pre-medical work, and research work may be cited.

———————

Editor's Note: A second section of the Science article, to be called "Bryn Mawr Science. II. Beyond the College Walls," will appear in the February number of THE BULLETIN. It will give some data on the present occupations fo former science students of Bryn Mawr, together with a few of the more striking examples of individual achievement.

INTERNATIONAL UNDERSTANDING AT BRYN MAWR

A Report Presented at the Conference of the International Student Committee,
April 22nd, 1932, by Germaine Brée, Scholar in French, 1931-32

We need hardly tell you with what interest Bryn Mawr students greeted the idea of the Conference. The fact that eight of us are here speaks for itself. We confess to having felt a certain embarrassment when we were confronted with the task of telling you what we have done on our campus to further international understanding. It is easy enough to tell you what we have not done. We have had no official debates or lectures on political and economic subjects. This is partly because, from a practical point of view, such formal discussions are extremely strenuous, and we feel that for foreigners adaptation to new surroundings and work are sufficient in themselves and besides more important, and partly because, whether we be from Germany, America, Russia, New Zealand, etc., we are all subject to the same human failings. However salutary an exchange of ideas on any really vital point may be, the ideal detachment requisite in any debate is, alas, almost impossible to obtain.

But if we seek to avoid as much as possible such subjects as may lead to unpleasant discussions, it does not mean that we have avoided the issues of actual importance in world relations. The formal international political forum *we have not held,* but we have followed all together the weekly reviews of current events by one of our professors, Dr. Fenwick. He is, what we are not all, an expert, competent to deal with the events, and to explain them more dispassionately and more fairly.

Besides, to discuss we must be able to talk to one another. We must, surely, put off the discussion of "World Issues" until we are sure that the words we are using mean to others what they do to us. We must, if we are foreigners in America, learn English, not in a slip-shod manner, but with the desire to get the exact shade of meaning behind a word. If we are American we must do the same abroad. On campus an exchange of lessons has been practised this year with success. We learn more of a nation's thought and spirit through its language than through most anything else; and that is, we think, what we must strive to get. We must, whilst keeping clearly in mind our own national outlook, be able, when necessary, to think as a foreigner thinks, whether we approve or not. In this way we feel that we have accomplished something in Bryn Mawr, and that a great deal has come from doing apparently nothing. It is necessary that we should accept our fellow-students, be they from Asia, Africa, America, Australia or Europe, not as curiosities, but as people like ourselves, without thought of nationality. An hour's work together in the library, groaning over the same reports, or in the laboratory spilling acids and breaking thermometers, a hike or a game of tennis have brought us closer together than many an hour's political debate.

Work together especially is very important; we have had different educations, we use different ways of reasoning. After we have mastered the tongue, it is the way of thinking that we must learn to understand. The foreign students have insight into American culture only in so far as they conform to the American system of education, whilst to an American a report written by a foreigner often throws light on the educational system of another country. Moreover in our leisure time— and almost every day we have managed to spare an hour for tea, even when working

(7)

at top speed—we have talked over music, books, art, even philosophy and religion. If we have been able to do so, it is because first we had got to know each other individually well enough, so that each student was not to the others just the British, Spanish or American student. And in doing so we have each enlarged our interests to take in the culture of other nations, absorbing inevitably at the same time some of the enthusiasm of each student for the culture of her own country; and admiration goes a long way towards understanding. Thus on campus throughout the year a steady current of sympathy has been established, not only between Americans and Europeans, but among the Europeans themselves. They are drawn together by common bonds instead of antagonized by differences. In this the Americans, equally interested in each nation, play an important role in breaking through national egotisms. In the process many petty prejudices have fallen. We are much less ready than last year to generalize, to say with superb confidence— "All Americans are—" or "Of course, Japanese always do so and so."

In fact, we know three things—how different a nation is from its government, how little we know about it, and how apt we are to sympathize with what a friend tells us about it. There is one thing also on which we want to insist; we have. learned that what we need most actually is accuracy. Our misunderstandings are inaccuracies. We need one and all to talk only of what we know, of what we have seen persistently, over and against national and international background, and we must train ourselves to see what is. If we do not know, then let us be quiet until we do, whilst ever ready to interpret events in the light of another nation's understanding.

This does not mean substituting its thoughts for our own. We cannot in our country, or in other countries, have any influence and bring about a more cordial international feeling if we are not sincerely what our countries have made us. Nor shall we have any influence if we do not keep a clear vision both of our country's failings and of the failings and qualities of other countries. We must learn from others to what our countrymen in the majority are blind, and to what in us other nations are·blind. We must from the outset accept this double difficulty as a fact. It is within these limits that we must work if we are to widen them. We shall only get a clear knowledge of these limits when we have as far as it is possible penetrated the working of people's minds. We can so better see with what logic some conclusion has been drawn, some prejudice established, accept it, forgive it if necessary, and never resent it. It is—and we feel this more and more strongly—the acceptance of and sympathy with one's national traits, rather than their suppression that we must seek. It is, I think, this spirit that such a conference as we are having now arouses. We are surer of our aims when we see that we are not scattered and lost units, but part of a strong group; and we see them more clearly because we have troubled to analyze them. If each one of us has made some progress towards adjusting the proportions of her world to those of other students' worlds, between us all, perhaps, we may have come nearer to perceiving the dimensions of the real world.

THE PRESIDENT'S PAGE

A PLEA FOR THE MATURE POINT OF VIEW

It seems to me very necessary this year to emphasize, and if possible to strengthen, any policy of the College which is directed toward making the individual student more mature. Our silly helplessness before a breach of courtesy like the Einstein episode in Berlin, our tragic helplessness before broken laws, our inability to meet by a plan any economic situation which is at all complicated or needs more than the most superficial "once-over," the alternate bravado and panic of the politicians at Washington—such things have brought out a national childishness more alarming I think than any other component in our chaotic thinking. We have lost even our old pioneer claim to "horse sense." It is a moment when any one who is bringing up children or watching the training of young men and women earnestly wants—not to hurry the next generation into bearing its earthly freight, but to make it see at least that there must always be movement in its development, that childish things pass with childish years, steadily and, in the end, wholly.

There is very little to change in the *theory* of Bryn Mawr on this question. The way of its little world has always been sober, and its citizens have never been treated as adolescents. We, its students, and later its graduates, have been given singular independence in our work and our college life. We have met challenge and criticism in the classroom on the ground we were old enough for it. We have often, if not always, been allowed to get what we deserved, and as a consequence, I believe, have later deserved something better. What we need at present, faculty and students alike, is to underline the *practice* of everything which goes to make the student more mature, which brings her into the world of the adult mind, which gives her some of the wisdom dwelt upon so often in the later Old Testament literature, which makes her a woman of the world. The Freshman must be kindly but steadily kept at her hard apprenticeship. She must constantly match herself with the upper-class students in her daily life and in the classroom, she must read not only thoroughly but, to her dismay, quickly, she must learn to take dependable notes by the process of taking undependable ones. She must be helped by faculty, or still better, by more experienced students, to carry on these processes in the midst of the difficulties of what is usually her first independent living, when she is responsible not to handy parents or house-mothers, but to a few vaguely understood rules and a busy executive committee of older students whom she does not know. All her difficulties are a part of a Bryn Mawr tradition which its undergraduates believe valuable, and as the younger student surmounts them she comes into the adult student world of an equally treasured Bryn Mawr tradition.

There she and the older students as well must be helped to learn that life is not some new and different existence awaiting them at the close of a little period of martyrdom as heaven awaited the primitive Christian. They must make Sophia Bains' discovery: that what they are living through is life, that its experiences are the only experiences that are to be theirs. This learned, the student is both richer and poorer—poorer because she knows the over-exciting experiences of other people are definitely not her own; richer because everything that is her own is for her use, the hard, the disagreeable, the laborious, as well as the work or the play to which she looks forward eagerly.

A faculty which prizes the qualities of maturity will teach its students the possibility of a clear recognition of differences, and the danger of lumping together good and bad, better and best, the disadvantages of poor standards, the danger of muddy thought. And in its method of teaching it will follow the example of the skilled teacher of physical exercise who does not push too hard his pupil in swimming or tennis or fencing, but always offers him the new instruction and help at precisely the farthest point he has reached in his previous training, and keeps his pupil never over-worked but forever on his toes!

Maturity in its application of wise opinion rather than childish chatter will not solve America's difficulties; intelligence, knowledge and much more must be applied to them. But as it is the only way of meeting one's personal life which to the right-minded person is endurable in the end, so it is the only way of taking one's part in national life. We cannot be contented with the child's directed and controlled choice.

"He hath set fire and water before thee:
Thou mayest stretch forth thine hand unto whichsoever thou wilt.
Before man is life and death;
And whichsoever he liketh, it shall be given him."

BRYN MAWR—AN ADVENTURE IN EDUCATION

An Address delivered over the radio by Millicent Carey McIntosh in the series arranged by the Seven Women's Colleges

The opening of Bryn Mawr College was an adventure. In 1885 a little band of thirty-six undergraduates and eight graduate students gathered in the suburbs of Philadelphia, in the College built and endowed with the money left by Dr. Joseph Taylor to found an institution of higher learning for women. Brought together to teach them were their president, Dr. James Rhoads, their dean, Miss M. Carey Thomas, afterwards president for nearly thirty years, and a band of brilliant young scholars, culled largely from the recently opened Graduate School of Johns Hopkins University. These included Woodrow Wilson, Paul Shorey, known and loved by all students of Greek, and Edmund Wilson, afterwards professor and now professor-emeritus of Biology, at Columbia University.

The world was exciting for these pioneers, and the flame of knowledge burned bright. Even this first group worked for difficult entrance examinations, and from the beginning the pursuit of learning was the chief end of their lives. They were taught by scholars who were in the height of their youth and enthusiasm, who while they prepared classes for undergraduates, at the same time were encouraged to do research in their own fields by the fact that they also taught graduate students. From the earliest years, advanced work was available to undergraduate students, who as Juniors and Seniors could work in groups of two or three with their professors. The world was a thrilling place during the late '80's to those who had ears to hear and ambition to learn. The theories of Darwin and Huxley, the poetry of Swinburne, the painting of the Pre-Raphaelites, the plays of Ibsen—all were grist to their intellectual mill, and they made the most of it and of their able teachers.

The development of Bryn Mawr College was an adventure—to those who took part in it and to those who cared for the education of women. With the leadership of Miss Thomas there came into its faculty a group of young men and women whose names have since become famous in Bryn Mawr itself and in universities all over the country. Attracted by the hard entrance examinations, many able girls were prepared to enter, and well-known girls' schools in the East began to steer their children toward the College, until the undergraduate body reached its present limit of 400. The Graduate School became known as a place where women scholars could work for the Ph.D., and gradually increased in numbers until it reached its present figure of 101. Money was given for foreign fellowships, and in 1916 arrived the first of a group of distinguished foreign women who have come to contribute to the life of the College an international outlook, and European standards of scholarship; and to take back to their own country the American point of view and American methods of work. Women trained at Bryn Mawr began to go out into the various professions: into teaching, into executive positions, into medicine and science, into public life.

During all this time, the watchword of the College was freedom. From the beginning, under the influence of the Quaker Trustees, the students were allowed independence. Freshmen have always been allowed to choose courses they wish and sit side by side with upper classmen under heads of departments. Self government was established a few years after the founding of the College, and rules have always been changed to embody the most liberal point of view as to the conduct women should have. And yet, with all its freedom, Bryn Mawr has no license; for with its small numbers it is possible to exercise a wise supervision over the lives of the students and to take an interest in their individual welfare.

The Bryn Mawr of the present is still an adventure. In 1922, Miss Thomas reached the age of retirement, and Miss Marion Park, an A.B. and Ph.D. of the College, became President. In the ten years of her administration, the College has developed along the lines which it has always held. The advanced work of its early years slipped almost imperceptibly into Honors Work for able students. A new curriculum, in which there are fewer hours of lecture, more opportunity for independent study, and more time for specialization, has been in operation now for three years. With a library equipped for graduate students, a student body so small that every undergraduate can come in close contact with her professors, and a group of teachers chosen partly because of their ability to teach graduates, Bryn Mawr offers fine opportunities for the real student.

The fall is the time of year when every daughter of Bryn Mawr thinks back wistfully to her undergraduate days, remembering how the smell of leaves is wafted up from the hockey fields; and the double row of great maples reflects in burnished gold the slanting rays of the afternoon sun. In the cloisters of the library the fountain is playing and from the battlements above the ivy flames a vivid scarlet. Bryn Mawr is eternally to us a setting for youth and strength, for ambition and honest, hard work, for clear thinking and daring idealism.

So with pride in her past, Bryn Mawr looks forward with hope and confidence to the adventure of the future.

THE UNDERGRADUATE POINT OF VIEW

A Speech delivered at the Council by Rebecca Wood, 1933,
President of the Undergraduate Association

In trying to present the undergraduate point of view, one must accept the obvious qualification that there is never an absolute consensus of opinion among the students on any one subject or a uniform manner of looking at problems and activities in and out of College. But I do think that this year, within the College itself, there is far more group interest, group thinking and participation in organized group activity than there has been for a long time—certainly a more serious attitude toward the academic work; and what is more, a very conscious appreciation in the students of the value of themselves as a group, and a group of which each individual is a responsible and functioning member.

A few years ago I was under the impression that the attitude of the undergraduates towards the running of the College and even toward their own organizations was a very passive one, and that the burden of responsibility was carried by outstanding individuals. The rest of the student body were too apt to take what the College had to offer, do a certain amount of work in return, get their diversion and carry their interests elsewhere, and consider that the responsibility ended with the academic work and the payment of their bills. What we did not realize was how interesting the College itself can be: and that the mechanism of College itself is not an inflexible and out-of-date affair, the inconveniences of which one complains about among one's friends, and endures; but that the students themselves form an important part of this ever-changing mechanism, and that it is a very pliable affair when approached through the channels of organization and administration.

But more recently, through the activities of the Curriculum Committee, the College Council, the editorials in the *News,* and various Undergraduate Committees, all sorts of ends have been accomplished which the students desired, and they are beginning to realize that their opinion, when properly voiced (that is, through the proper channels, and not just at random in the smoking rooms) has a very immediate effect on the actual workings of the College. I think that such adjustments as the cutting down of required subjects two years ago; the cutting down of classes after May Day last year, in order to allow students to catch up work in the last week before finals; the procuring of the privilege of radios with ear-phones in the halls; of permission to dance after the theatre until 2 o'clock hereafter, and such adjustments as adding a week to the year's calendar instead of taking away our Thanksgiving vacation to make up for the late opening of College; or the postponing of quizzes the day after Election—all are combining to prove to the students that the administration, the faculty, and the self-government, etc., are very flexible and generously responsive bodies, when requests for adjustments are logically presented. And this, of course, makes the students feel their own responsibility.

Along with this growth of consciousness of the students as a functioning body there is this year especially, I think, a growth of interest in College activities. Whether it is a result of May Day, in which co-operation and organization established all sorts of new contacts, and aroused the interest in campus activity; or whether serious conditions outside have made the students feel less secure as individuals (with no money to spend outside); and more secure as a working body with all sorts of possibilities for creating and enjoying a life of satisfying activity within the College; or whether it is just another step in the steady trend toward more serious thinking and more active interests, which has been developing in the College for many years—whatever be the reason, there is certainly more interest in the academic work and more "college spirit" than there has been for a long time.

I notice this especially in the number of students who come to the Undergraduate Association with suggestions for speakers, exhibitions of paintings, etc.; in the requests of students that certain matters be brought up at the College Council, recognizing it as a valuable means to action; in editorials and letters to the *News* which have come to bear directly and significantly on College problems, such as the quota system in the halls, criticism of numerical marks, the upkeep of the campus, grounds, etc.; and, of course, in the general discussions in the smoking room, not only of the recently flaming political questions, but of courses being studied—problems in anthropology are rampant in Pembroke just now—and on College activities in every field. Upperclassmen, who were afraid of appearing conscientious before (and in this attitude I'm afraid they influenced the younger students as well), have now suddenly begun trying out for choir, for hockey teams, for all sorts of activities they never deigned to go into before partly because they considered that the more popular girls had enough social interests and could get their fun outside of college, whether the type of popular girl is changing so that she can now admit a serious and somewhat conscientious side, or whether the depression has confined girls to the campus so that they desire to create activity there, or whether College activities have raised their standards so that they automatically invite more interest, I do not know; probably it is a combination of all these factors. That the standards of activities have been raised in the estimation of the students, I do know. The choir established its proud identity last year by broadcasting in competition with other women's colleges; it also made Victor records of the same program for private sale; it is illustrating Dr. Vaughan Williams' lectures on *Nationalism in Music* this year; and we are very excited about singing in the *Parsifal* program with the Philadelphia Orchestra under Dr. Stokowski in the spring. The interest in Dramatics is always current, but this year the Players' Club has been revived and enlarged by quite a group of students discovered through the acting in May Day, so that the Players' Club is putting on one-act plays once a month now; and the Varsity Dramatics will put on two big plays this year; one of these will be either a melodrama, or *The Royal Family of Broadway* or *Little Women*, presented with Haverford in December, and there is a possibility of presenting *The Trojan Women* in the spring, out of doors at night, which will provide interesting experiments in out-of-door lighting. One of the small one-act plays is to be a Christmas play just before vacation, and the players hope that this may become a tradition in the College, like a Christmas party and the carolling. There is also considerable interest being shown in the make-up class sponsored by the Players' Club, in which one is taught by an expert the fine art of cosmetics; and, of course, an even more widespread interest in the talks and informal discussions they are arranging.

Then there is always the Glee Club, which draws an enthusiastic membership of practically everybody who can carry a tune, with either sweetness or gusto, for the production of the Gilbert and Sullivan opera in the spring. We shall be especially enthusiastic to return to it this year, whether it be *Patience* or *The Gondoliers*, on account of the necessary omission of a performance last year because of May Day.

Another College activity which has raised its standard of organization and enjoyment is that of social entertainment within the College: chiefly the undergraduate dances, after the varsity play in the fall, and after the Glee Club concert in the spring. The tone of these entertainments is raised by the fact that we have abandoned those crowded tea dances in Rockefeller, held in the trying hours before a performance, for the much pleasanter arrangement of a formal dance held in a specially decorated gymnasium after the evening performance, and lasting until two o'clock. This gives the actors or singers a chance to enjoy themselves likewise (after the paint of the performance has been scraped off), and I think it is significant that there is a growing interest in making these entertainments at College more formal and more attractive, rather than getting all one's social diversion on weekends, and in Philadelphia.

Incidentally, the Undergraduate Association has just purchased a very good piano (for twenty-seven dollars!) which is not to be used for practicing, but is to be at the mercy of any student at any hour of the day, for the pleasure of herself or her friends, and is now in the May Day room for that purpose.

I hope that the alumnae do not think that the interest in athletics has suffered in the least for its not being required in one's last two years of College. Perhaps the personality of Miss Applebee accounted for more Junior and Senior class teams than these at present in the various sports, and perhaps there once was more interclass hostility and excitement over games; but I think Miss Petts, and the report submitted by Elizabeth Baer on Physical Education at the Council last year, both vouch for a genuine interest in sports; and I know myself that there are always Junior and Senior teams in every sport, though I think whatever collegiate furore may have existed in athletics before has now been supplanted by a sane desire for vigorous exercise and a non-partisan interest in and appreciation of good teamwork.

I have suggested possible explanations for the more serious and enthusiastic point of view of undergraduates towards work and other activities, as due to the depression, or May Day, or the general more serious trend in all colleges; but I think that the interest in academic work was increased by the cutting down of required work two years ago, whereby the students are being made to take a minimum of courses that might not interest them, and so have a much wider field for subjects that really fascinate them, which is really true in a great many cases now. And the more thrilled they are about their work, the more they talk about it in the smoking rooms and to their friends, so that other students have a clearer idea of the type of study covered by various courses, before choosing their own.

But it is certainly true that students who are in College now are not there just to fill up a space of several years without actually idling, as has been the case at times before. If they are there now, it is at the cost of some sacrifice on the part of themselves and their families—primarily because they do want to work, want to learn, want to do things; and, because they know that in these times and under these circumstances they are lucky to be there at all, they are making the most of every opportunity to live a full, active and interesting life within the campus itself.

REPORT OF THE ALUMNAE COMMITTEE OF SEVEN COLLEGES

The fourth year of work by the Alumnae Committee of Seven Colleges has been marked by two new developments. The Committee was established by the Presidents on the theory that the needs of the colleges, in order to be met, must be more widely known. In other words, the task of keeping the colleges by one means and another, before the public mind, has been the object of this Committee. It was not anticipated that outside agencies would help in this, and it has therefore been one of the gratifying developments of this year that the Central Hanover Bank and Trust Company has come to the Committee requesting full information on the needs of each of the seven colleges. The bank also asked that revised statements of these needs be sent in every six months in order to keep the information up-to-date. This bank is one to which many people turn for advice on wills, and its purpose in requesting information is the desire to have the facts ready for anyone interested in leaving money to the women's colleges. It is part of a comprehensive plan the bank has made, of surveying all the fields of giving in this country, in order to have available complete data on what philanthropies are the most needy. In education, the women's colleges present one of the best "cases."

This use of prepared statements on the pressing needs in the seven colleges and on plans for development may be termed "applied publicity." Chicago has a definite plan to extend its use. Under the aegis of the old Chicago Dinner Committee, three prominent lawyers gave a luncheon to lawyers and trust company officers of that city this autumn to explain the needs of the colleges and how Chicago may help. This plan will be followed in cities where there have been dinners in honor of the Seven Presidents. In other cities where it seems advisable committees will be set up for this purpose.

The second new development of the year has been the formation of the Advisory Council. Only men have been asked to serve on the Council, and several of them are financiers of international reputation. These men have made public their endorsement of the needs of the women's colleges, citing these needs separately and specifically. The gathering together of such a Council has been no small task, but it has been perhaps the most gratifying work the Committee has attempted. Endorsement from such distinguished citizens will do much to draw public attention to the plight of the women's colleges.

It is pleasant to report that a previously unknown friend left four of the seven colleges, Vassar, Smith, Wellesley, and Bryn Mawr, equal shares in a $200,000 estate. This illustrates what the Committee hopes to accomplish on a larger scale, namely to interest new friends as well as increase the benefactions of old friends and alumnae. The Committee has felt that its bequest program was more important than ever in these years of financial stringency. Wills are still being made, and though the sums left may be smaller, the donors are using greater care and consideration.

A seven-college radio series has been another important piece of work of the year. This is the third series brought about by the committee, but the first to illustrate the actual work done in the colleges. The seven college choirs and glee clubs gave the series on seven successive Monday afternoons, and these concerts were broadcast on the national network of the Columbia system. A gratifying amount of newspaper publicity resulted from this series of concerts. There followed another unexpected result. After hearing the Barnard students sing, a listener-in sent $250 to be used in the music department of Barnard College. Out of this radio series has grown a plan for a music, festival of the seven colleges which promises to be one of the most important events which the committee has attempted.

The year marked the death of one of the best friends of the Seven Colleges, the Honorable Mr. Dwight W. Morrow. In his will, Mr. Morrow put into practice the thing for which he had pled—that the women's colleges be given parity with men's colleges. He left equal sums to his wife's college, Smith, and to his own college, Amherst. This was widely commented upon in many editorials in newspapers, and the *Woman's Home Companion,* which has long been in sympathy with the work of the committee, published an excellent editorial.

It has been the privilege of the committee this year to assist Ruth E. Finley, author of "The Lady of Godey's, Sara Josepha Hale," in collecting material for her chapter on the early days of Vassar. In this chapter the point was made that the present situation of the women's colleges is relatively the same as it was in the early days of higher education for women. The same necessity exists for the creation of a sentiment in favor of gifts and bequests for women.

Increasingly, writers and editors turn to this committee for material on colleges and on the college woman. Material is frequently used in articles which are not devoted wholly to a discussion of the seven colleges and which the committee cannot, therefore, claim distinctly as its achievement. Such publicity helps, however. Scarcely a week passes that the committee does not have a chance to supply material for this kind of publicity in magazines and newspapers.

In the June number of *Scribner's* you have found an article by **President Neilson,** under the title, "Are American Colleges Wasteful?" Four other magazine articles dealing with various aspects of our colleges are completed and they await only the editor's announcement, which out of courtesy must precede any announcement by this committee. Two others are in the process of being written for magazines, and a seventh for the magazine section of a Sunday newspaper which is syndicated widely. A series of articles based on visits to the seven colleges has appeared in *Needlecraft.* In the January issue of *Scribner's* is appearing an article, "College Girl, 1932-1933," written by Mrs. Eunice Fuller Barnard.

There are many activities of the committee which may be called "lesser" activities, but which may at any time turn into more important ones. One of these was a recent meeting with a group of women who control a sum to be given every year to the advancement of music. This group more than a year ago made a tour of the seven colleges, and since that time has given sums to various music departments of the seven colleges.

On the last day of the fiscal year, April 30th, at the invitation of the Radcliffe undergraduates, the committee went to Radcliffe College to attend a second undergraduate conference on publicity. The first such meeting was held last year at Barnard at the suggestion of the Barnard students. The purpose of these confer-

ences is to acquaint the undergraduates in each of the seven with the material prob-
. lems which each college faces, in order that they may graduate as informed alumnae.
To this end, then, two undergraduates were selected from each college to meet the
Alumnae Committee at Radcliffe.

It was evident that the idea of student interest in the committee had gained
real momentum during the year, and that the students have a much deeper appreciation of·what it means to finance education for women. After a delightful speech
of welcome by President Comstock, the conference considered what the students
should do, and what they should not do. It was made plain to them that this is not
a money-raising committee. Finally, a definite charge of making their own student
bodies conscious of the needs of their own college first, and then of all seven, was
laid on them. This they were asked to do through their own publications, and not,
of course, through any others. Statements of the work of the committee will be sent
to them from time to time, but these statements, as well as all the copy they write,
they were asked to refer to their publicity director before using. This will avoid
mistakes in policy peculiar to each college, and will ensure closer co-operation
between the publicity office and the undergraduates.

The students themselves proposed what may prove to be the most fruitful
result of the meeting. This was a plan for an assembly or convocation in each
college last fall, which was addressed on "needs" by their own president and a
visiting president from one of the other colleges.

The committee hopes that the enthusiasm of the students and their fresh, eager
interest will continue. They have asked that an undergraduate's conference with
the Alumnae Committee be held every year, and that the two delegates attending
from each college shall include one who attended the year before.

It is impossible to suggest in a short summary of a year's work with what
great pleasure each task has been undertaken and with what zest difficulties have
been met. Each of the committee feels that the work is beginning to have a real
significance. In quarters where there was indifference three or four years ago, the
committee is now received with deepest interest and respect. To one who has seen
and experienced this change, it is a concrete, tangible thing.

Respectfully submitted,

FRANCES FINCKE HAND, 1897.

ANNUAL MEETING

The annual meeting of the Alumnae Association will be held in the Auditorium
of Goodhart Hall, on Saturday, February 11th, 1933, at 9.45 a. m. At one-thirty p. m.
the meeting will adjourn to Pembroke Hall, where the members of the Association
will be the guests of the College at luncheon. President Park will speak, and after
the meeting tea will be served in the Common Room, Goodhart Hall.

On Friday evening there will be an informal dinner in Rockefeller Hall at
seven o'clock. Professor Rhys Carpenter, former Director of the American School at
Athens, who has returned to the College after seven years' absence, will speak about
recent archaeological discoveries in Greece. Tickets for the dinner, at $1.10, may
be obtained from the Alumnae Office. Cheques should be made payable to
Bertha S. Ehlers, Treasurer,

CAMPUS NOTES

By Janet Marshall, 1933

In the tremendous stir that a recent editorial caused in the *News,* on the appearance of the undergraduates, it was very illuminating to note that not one ripple of the waves of storm that raged in the newspapers of the whole Eastern Seaboard, and even over the radio, was reflected on the campus. Deans of other colleges came forth with announcements that their co-eds were not poorly dressed, sloppy, and even a little unwashed, as the *News* accused Bryn Mawr students of being; tabloids produced sketches of just what they thought we looked like; and over Thanksgiving the average student was asked about fifteen times if all this was really true. Just how little the limelight means to the College was evidenced by the fact that the only comment one heard before vacation on this subject was to the effect that "such an awful stir" was being made about nothing. And just how little influence the editorial page of the *College News* has on the actual life and manners of the student-body was shown quite clearly after vacation when the group streamed back in all their finery, only to appear an hour after arrival in the same offensive articles of clothing.

While there need be no excuse for what amounts to a nearly ideal reaction to newspaper publicity, the indifference to the *News* criticism ought to be explained. It is not, we feel, so much that no one reads or discusses the articles and editorials in the *News,* for they are being read more generally and commented on more heatedly than they have been in a long time. It is rather that this was a strange time for such an editorial to appear, since on the whole Bryn Mawr students are looking cleaner, neater, and more attractive this year than they have for at least four years, and judging from reports one hears, for more than that. This is not to say that the campus costume has approached what dress-shops advertise as the ideal campus costume, but the fad for the *outré* in dress, the habit of wearing cast-off finery instead of sports clothes, and above all, the old idea that to be queer in one's clothes and messy in one's person indicated genius, all of these are fancies that have happily passed. The worst that can be said now is that too many students simply do not care how they look until Friday at one o'clock—and even this change is something.

We spoke last time of the rebirth of spontaneous student activities, especially in the fields of the arts. The movements, far from dying out, seem to be gathering steam as they go. The newly formed Art Club is holding sway in the basement of the gym, and those who venture into its sacred precincts are startled with the really fine sketches, oils and water-colors that hang in various states of completeness on its walls. As soon as more equipment can be procured, the members are hoping to foster some of the crafts, such as metal-work, design, and pottery. The Players Club had produced two one-act plays, *Helena's Husband,* by Philip Moeller, and *Saint's Day,* by Tom Prideaux, the latter performance being a real première. They have brought down two most successful speakers: Claude Hamilton, Chairman of the Pulitzer Prize Committee, who spoke on "Cyrano and Rostand," and Alexander Wyckoff, who spoke on stage lighting and costuming. The ambitious attempts of the group have already brought up against certain barriers in equipment and gen-

eral facilities, especially in the matter of lighting, and they are now in the process
of providing in so far as they can the modern equipment that they need.

It is really amazing that of all the splendid speakers that have addressed the
College this fall, by far the greatest enthusiasm was created by John Avery Lomax'
more or less informal talk on "Cowboy Songs." Not only was he encored time and
again with great enthusiasm, but he has been invited to return in the near future
and sing, recite and comment on "The Negro Spirituals," of which he has a really
exhaustive collection. It is the first time in the memory of the present senior class
that a speaker has been recalled at the purely spontaneous request of the students.
It may be that the interest aroused in folk-music by Dr. Vaughn Williams' lectures
has contributed to this enthusiasm, for here, as many students have said, is the real
folk-music of America, even more than in the Kentucky mountain songs, where much
of the material is preserved almost perfectly from the English traditions that the
settlers took into the mountains with them. It is, in any case, a sign of some new
sensitiveness or some new source of stimulation that the Bryn Mawr audience, often
so apathetic, is finding something to applaud with vigor.

Along with all the nice things about the campus this year, and despite the
world outside, it really is a nice year, come a few developments which do not make
the college hall a more pleasant place to live in, though they may make it more
stimulating. One of these is the growth of a really belligerent group of minorities.
In the past there have been small and more or less coördinated groups working at
the different student activities unopposed by the great majority, which was perfectly
willing to let those who wanted to settle any questions they pleased. The freshman
class, for instance, is usually the only class that undergoes any really tremendous
political agitations when the time to elect a president comes around, and even they
often lack the vigor of their prep-school days in this respect. This year, while it
has seen no great rise in the numbers of those interested in the administration of the
classes, has seen a whole new group come into other student groups, dramatics in
particular. The old system of an interested and experienced oligarchy running this
and other activities stands in great peril at present. A spirit of democracy, which
may or may not be practical in the production of artistic work, is nevertheless crying
for a voice. Next year may see an entirely new system, and for the present things
are in a stimulating but rather bewildering state of chaos.

HELEN CHAPIN SPEAKS ON RECENT FINDS IN BUDDHIST ART

On Wednesday evening, November 30th, an interested group of students, faculty and friends gathered in the music room of Goodhart Hall to hear Helen Chapin,
1915, tell of her "discovery" of an extraordinary Chinese Buddhist scroll painting
about a year ago in Peking.

Shortly after graduation from college, and while on the staff of the Museum of
Fine Arts in Boston, Miss Chapin became interested in Buddhism as it was developed in China and Japan, and especially in the identification of Buddhist deities in
the art of those countries. Little research has been done in this field, and for a
foreigner to undertake the task of solving problems of Buddhist iconography, the
obstacles seem almost insurmountable. With characteristic determination and

dogged perseverance Miss Chapin set about laying the foundation for her work. In seven years of residence in Japan and China, full of unremitting study, she has acquired a command of the languages which might be envied by a life-long student of Chinese or Japanese. In those countries she lives as a native, stopping at the native inns, eating native food. She is well known in the East, and in Japan was affectionately dubbed "The Chapin," after she had gained some attention by going to live for several months in Yakushi-ji monastery where she attended all Buddhist services and learned all the monks themselves knew about their images and scriptures. One Japanese archaeologist told me with pride that "The Chapin" spoke Japanese so well that when he talked with her over the telephone he could hardly believe he was not speaking with a native Japanese. She is equally at home in China, reading and speaking the language as few foreigners can.

In her search through original sources Miss Chapin was naturally interested in the opening of certain old collections of books and pictures which have remained until recently sealed up in some of the storage rooms of the Imperial Palace at Peking, and so was invited a year ago to be one of two foreigners who were privileged to be present at the examination of some works of art which had just been brought out. Among the paintings Miss Chapin noted one as particularly important, and it was of this that she spoke at Bryn Mawr, as she believes that the discovery of this scroll will throw light on many hitherto obscure problems of Buddhist iconography.

The scroll is fifty-one feet long and on it is depicted the whole Buddhist pantheon in full colors and gold. Most of the figures have beside them small labels establishing their identity beyond any doubt. At the end of the scroll are three long annotations, the earliest by a monk of the Ta Li Kingdom in 1240, the latest by Emperor Ch'ien Lung (1736-1795), which give all the information one might desire about the painting, and which Miss Chapin has translated. Thus we learn that the artist was a Chan master (a Zen Buddhist teacher) of the Ta Li Kingdom (on the western border of China) and that this was painted in the 13th century. Miss Chapin showed many interesting slides illustrating parts of the painting and told, to the great entertainment of her audience, some of the Buddhist tales connected with personages depicted.

Miss Chapin's learning and enthusiasm are inspiring to the student of Buddhist art as affording a glimpse of a most fascinating field of study. She is known as a writer in the *Art Bulletin* and recently an article of hers appeared in the *Ost Asiatiche Zeitschrift*. We hope also that some day we may hear more about her personal experiences and adventures, which have been so unusual, and see some of the lovely slides she has taken to illustrate her travel talks.

HELEN FERNALD,

*Curator of Far Eastern Art at the
University of Pennsylvania Museum.*

THE ALUMNAE BOOK SHELF

LIONS, GORILLAS AND THEIR NEIGHBORS, *by Carl and Mary L. Jobe Akeley.* Dodd, Mead and Co., New York, 1932. $2.50.

" 'When we find a good tree we'll stop for lunch,' Carl had said. Then as his eyes wandered to and fro among the trees in search of shade, 'Do you see that lion over there?' "

For the Akeleys, lions instead of hot-dog stands, spoil a picnic ground, and Mrs. Akeley has the same agonizing, exhausting thrill watching her husband take close pictures of the fourteen lions that we have felt watching ours on the tennis court. In Africa life is tuned a pitch higher, but there are enough familiar notes for us to respond to—we can still identify ourselves with the heroes and have the adventure.

And adventures there are. In this recent book, which comprises four stories from the notes of Mr. Akeley, and eight by his wife, the Akeleys tell of their dramatic experiences with the wild animals of Africa. They throw every possible light on the subject, from interesting scientific explanations to appropriate anecdotes of other explorers. The tales move along as some sparkling conversation might.

Mr. Akeley writes with a swinging style but he senses the dramatic moment always—stops and holds it for us. And with his jogging anecdotes he creates a feeling of suspense. Even though everything has gone wrong all day, although the day is nearly over—something is about to happen.

Mrs. Akeley's style is more detailed, or, rather, her observation covers a wider field. She is telling of this one great adventure, her first trip to Africa, and she never blurs the image with reminiscences of former hunts. When everyone in camp is restive because the wily buffaloes stay hidden, Mrs. Akeley enjoys her surroundings. She tells the color of the marshes, the kinds of birds she saw, and incidents about the quail family that strolled through her tent. In the beginning, when the responsibility of the work had not yet fallen upon her, her attitude toward it was, naturally, freer than her husband's.

Throughout the book one feels Mr. Akeley's definite personality. "I have never respected the leopard." "I have always felt that the lion is a gentleman." His theories and the joy he had in proving them, his conviction of the need for game laws, his scorn of the big game hunters who kill merely for excitement, color all his stories. We know his sense of humour, his quick sympathy. We feel the eagerness and intensity of his search, and above all, his spirit of steel that carries on past physical endurance.

This same courage characterizes Mrs. Akeley, and, because she has written the most, her mood is the strongest undercurrent. When she alludes to the tragic death of her husband on Mt. Mikeno, she marks the climax of the book. The whole atmosphere turns cold and bleak. There can be no more gay reminiscences. Her style becomes objective. "Have you ever seen a real gorilla?" Her following stories are full of interesting and scientific facts about the Pygmies and African Life. But the joy is gone. In my opinion, Mr. Akeley's splendid chapter on leopards should have come earlier in the book. I can see why Mrs. Akeley put it almost at the end, why she wanted his ideas to be our final impression, but I feel that she broke the sombre atmosphere unnecessarily and spoiled what was a good contrast in mood and setting with the beginning. This is, of course, a minor criticism.

Lions, Gorillas and Their Neighbors is particularly good for boys and girls who are likely to think of hunting simply as a stuffed moose's head and "How I Got Him." As an adventure story it holds its own against the movies and it becomes part of our background. Long after we have forgotten how we learned it, we shall still know that the waves of heat sweep over African plains, that the hippopotamus carries its baby on its back, and that somewhere there are islands of pink flamingoes in a greenish blue lake. The experiences of the Akeleys become our own.

ELIZABETH MALLETT CONGER, 1925.

GUARIENTO DI ARPO, *by Anne FitzGerald.* Reprinted from the MEMOIRS OF THE AMERICAN ACADEMY IN ROME, 1931.

Miss FitzGerald's monograph on Guariento di Arpo proves beyond doubt that careful study of an archaic, provincial master outside the main current of development may well bring reward. Having neatly summarized the meagre biographical material and the few early references to the artist, the author reconstructs the personality of an attractive painter. She assigns without reservation to the master only two paintings in fresco, two panels, and a series in both mediums, accepting with caution but few other attributions: yet she arrives at a convincing estimate of Guariento: a graceful painter, a resourceful decorator with a good sense of color and of composition.

After stating the various conflicting opinions on attribution and chronology, Miss FitzGerald frequently establishes confidence in her own decision through careful analysis and precise observation. It is unfortunate that she sometimes lapses into such awkward phrases as "those as to which there seems to me to be no question"; unfortunate, too, that she treats at disproportionate length the iconography of the painted cross. In connection with her account of the evolution of this type, one is tempted to question whether she does well to assume that the appearance of the Father and the Dove above the Crucified is the result of confusion with an Ascension scene rather than revival of the older iconography of the Trinity found in the twelfth century. But these are trifling faults, counting little against the clarity and precision of the whole.

Clearly and ingeniously Miss FitzGerald settles the heated controversy on the "Paradiso" of the Palazzo Ducale in Venice. The problem—whether it was painted in monochrome or in color—is complicated by the fact that Sansovino used both "dipinta" and "colorisse" in a description of the fresco, and again by the fact that the work is much the worse for a fire which may have destroyed size and colors. The author finds a satisfactory interpretation of the ambiguous passage, observes indubitable vestiges of color, and adduces good external evidence that the fresco was once of gay and brilliant appearance. She is singularly fortunate in bringing to this problem a thorough knowledge of the methods and mediums of the fourteenth-century painters. For reconstruction of a great Trecento fresco and of the personality of its author, students and mediaeval Italian painting are indebted to her.

DELPHINE FITZ DARBY, 1923.

LYDIA SHARPLESS PERRY

In the old gym in the fall of 1904 a chaotic class meeting of the entering Class of 1908 elected Lydia Sharpless captain of the class hockey team, a position which she held for all four college years. She was a member of the basketball and track teams as well, and always took a prominent part in all athletics, in which her social instinct, sense of fun, her spirit of fair play and balanced judgment made her a valued leader.

To an ever-widening circle of her class and in the college she was a leader, also in all the best things of college life, furthering them with an unselfish and whole-hearted loyalty. The daughter of Isaac Sharpless, then president of Haverford College, and of Lydia Cope, she united in her inheritance fine traditions of quiet Quaker scholarship, integrity and service. Born and bred on the Haverford campus, college life was to her a native element. She loved the sports, the friendships, the world of thought. With an inquiring and speculative turn of mind, however, went a just balance, a strong sense of actuality, a breadth of humor which kept her feet on earth and in paths that lead to practical accomplishment.

The life which in college showed so many sides and interests, always subject to the central control of a strong personality, broadened and deepened with the years. Graduated in 1908, she spent a year at home doing part-time work in a Philadelphia settlement, then taught for a year at Wykeham Rise, a girls' boarding school in the Connecticut hills. During this year she became engaged and was married in January, 1911, to Harvey C. Perry, of Westerly, R. I., and the rest of her life was spent in this typical and beautiful New England town.

Small town life was never small to her. She was always opening doors to new and vivid interests, to many and varied friendships. A favorite hobby was local history, research into the sea-faring and farming life of the neighborhood in pioneer days. The beautiful country about their home was thoroughly explored, the rocky hills and pastures and woods roads were intimately known to them and to their friends. Their "back lot" became a miniature wood, planted with trees and shrubs brought back from their wanderings, and filled with birds, known to the whole family by sight and note, and attracted there by home-built feeding trays and bird houses. The need for good milk for the children led to raising thoroughbred Ayrshires, building a model barn, and an interest in line with Mr. Perry's business in improved dairying on the impoverished farms of the nearby countryside. The Perrys studied farm problems, belonged to the local Grange, and counted their farm neighbors among their many friends. Domestic life for the Perrys was never humdrum, but interesting, creative, and generously shared. Lydia gave herself to the ordinary small town activities, the library, the girl scouts, the college club, the town meeting, in a way that made them larger, touched with her intelligence, helpfulness, and her never-failing sense of humor and sound judgment.

With all her wide range of interests, Lydia's home was the centre of her life. It was an ideal environment for children, whom Lydia loved and understood and allowed to grow in their natural way. She had three, the eldest of whom, Edith, died at the age of four in the infantile paralysis epidemic of 1916. Charles Perry is now a student at Haverford, and Sylvia at Westtown, the Quaker boarding school where Lydia prepared for college. As these children grew to adolescent independence the Perrys adopted a baby boy. Lydia said, "We have a good home for children to grow up in and I want something real to do." Through her years of motherhood ran a current of ill health and suffering at which she never protested or complained, and which she never allowed to influence her mental attitude. It might have been someone else's body that often lay perforce inert, the head on the pillow was unchanged, full of interest in her family and friends, in the world of thought and of affairs.

Perhaps it was this always vital interest which gave her strength to accomplish and enjoy and share in spite of ill health. Home and family and friends and local interests and hobbies and reading and world affairs—she cared and thought about and was alert to them all. Then, too, she loved travel and could get and give the utmost from a few days in Boston or New York, or a week's motoring among colonial homes in Virginia. One summer was spent in Germany just after the war when her husband was helping there in the child-feeding reconstruction work of the American Friends' Service Committee. More friends, some of them German, wider interests, quiet, unceasing work toward better international understanding grew out of this experience. Ten years later another summer was spent abroad with their children, renewing German contacts and friendships, and enjoying England and Scotland.

On her return from this trip, her ill health became such as even her courage could not ignore. Long weeks in hospital, slight gains at home, a very gradual losing ground followed for three years. Yet her fortitude, her interests beyond herself, in people and ideas, even her whimsical humor never failed. After three long months in a Philadelphia hospital, where her room was often filled with her friends, she said: "Well, at any rate, this winter has been a great social success." To how many of these friends, widely scattered, diverse, her life is a memory so precious, vivid, inspiring, that it even transcends one's sense of loss!

EDITH CHAMBERS RHOADS, 1908.

THE LOUISE HYMAN POLLAK LIBRARY FUND

The death of Louise Hyman Pollak has left her friends with a keen sense of deep and lasting loss. There were many gleaming facets to her personality. Her interest in the college which was hers, in the city in which she lived, in education, cultural and political, in charity and in social service, was combined with a great capacity for friendship, with an understanding loyalty for those with whom she worked and played.

In order that the memory of her vivid life shall not fade, the Bryn Mawr Club of Cincinnati is establishing a Bryn Mawr Library Fund in memory of Louise Hyman Pollak. The income from this fund will be used to purchase for the college library books on such subjects as especially interested her, and each volume will bear a book-plate inscribed with her name.

CLASS NOTES

Ph.D.'s

Class Editor: MRS. M. A. PARRISH
Vandalia, Mo.

1889

No Editor appointed.

1890

No Editor appointed.

1891

No Editor appointed.

1892

Class Editor: EDITH WETHERILL IVES
(Mrs. Frederick M. Ives)
145 E. 35th St., New York City.

1893

Class Editor: S. FRANCES VAN KIRK
1333 Pine St., Philadelphia, Pa.

1894

Class Editor: ABBY BRAYTON DURFEE
(Mrs. Randall Durfee)
19 Highland Ave., Fall River, Mass.

1895

Class Editor: ELIZABETH BENT CLARK
(Mrs. Herbert Lincoln Clark)
Bryn Mawr, Pa.

1896

Class Editor: ABIGAIL C. DIMON
1411 Genesee St., Utica, N. Y.

1897

Class Editor: FRIEDRIKA HEYL
104 Lake Shore Drive, East, Dunkirk, N. Y.

Believe it or not—just as I was collecting pencil and pad preparatory to jotting down items of news for the '97 notes, the postman brought the December BULLETIN. In looking through it I am not sure whether I felt more humiliated by seeing Abba Dimon's full page of '96 notes—with no '97 notes following—or by reading in the proceedings of the Council in Chicago that it was urged "in an effort to have Class Editors realize their responsibility, that each month the name and address of each Class Editor be printed in the proper order even if there is no news for that particular class." It is a question, I think, whether a Class Editor's conscience is not stabbed quite as effectively by an awful blank as by seeing

her name in print. However, if the BULLETIN can spare the space to post, each month, the forty odd names, I am all for it! Our classmates, as well as the Class Editor, may be spurred on to action.

I ought not have waited until Mary Hand Churchill's little son was nearly a year old before telling you that Frances Hand had a grandchild.

Elizabeth Higginson Jackson's older daughter, Betsy, a Senior at Bryn Mawr, won an award last May because her work in Biology was the most distinguished work in Science done by anyone in the Junior Class. Congratulations! She and her brother, Charles, who is now at the Harvard Law School, both studied at Harvard this summer. The younger Jackson daughter, Peggy, is all prepared for college, but is having a bit of society before she enters next fall. She made her debut in November.

Mary Campbell and her father had a very happy summer in England and Scotland where there were gatherings of the Campbell clan. Arthur Babson and Edith Campbell were with them part of the time. The Campbells are now living at the Parkside Hotel, Gramercy Park.

Grace Albert spent her summer in England and France and seems much refreshed by the change and rest. She wrote of seeing Alice Cilley Weist in Paris. Alice, by the way, seems to be a very satisfactory kind of foreign representative. One is constantly meeting people, not only Bryn Mawr friends, who are most enthusiastic about having met her at the Women's University Club in Paris. She and her daughter Helen are both in Boston this winter, or near Boston.

Clara Vail Brooks' daughter, Margaret, was married in September to John C. Juhring, Jr., in Woodstock, Vermont.

Florence Hoyt's sister, Margaret, bought an old car this summer and they had a wonderful time tripping through New England and visiting friends.

Eleanor Brownell and Alice Howland spent the summer at their New Mexico home on the outskirts of Santa Fé. The little adopted daughters are old enough to ride ponies in the horse show.

When sending in your news items will you please note the change in the editor's address? She is not at Bryn Mawr. Wyndham, where as warden she was looking forward to welcoming you, was not opened. So she is holding the position of warden, in absentia, and is at present at home. The name of the street, by the way, has been changed, but the house is the same. Apropos of the house, if you will forgive a still more personal note, a little girl, visiting here, asked me whether I had lived in this house very long. I assured her that I had, that I was born here. She was rather surprised, and surprised me a little. Looking up at me suddenly and then around the room, she exclaimed, "Why the house doesn't look as old as that!"

That was a few years ago, but I am still able to drive my faithful old Plymouth. In October and November my sister, Mrs. Nichols, and I drove about two thousand miles to New England and to Bryn Mawr. I wish I could tell you of the glorious New York State country from Lake Erie through the Wyoming and Genesee valleys to Ithaca, through the lovely Cherry Valley to Albany, where we spent the night with Elizabeth and Mary Kirkbride, and of the trip through the Berkshires, in the rain, to Boston. There were a few happy days with Elizabeth Higginson Jackson, in Dover, and a chance to hear of her trip last spring to Egypt and to Constantinople where she enjoyed so much seeing Gertrude Frost Packer's daughter and her husband. There was a friendly visit with Rebekah Chickering, who shifted her English classes at the Abbott Academy and came in town for luncheon with us. And I should love to tell you of our run up to Cornish, N. H., to spend the night with Frances Arnold, of the charm of her meadow house which she was getting ready for the winter.

The first week in November I spent in Bryn Mawr having delightful visits with Marion Park, and Margaret Lord, and with Sue Blake, and seeing other friends on the campus and in the neighborhood.

Sue Blake has had another article accepted by a scientific journal. She plans to spend part of her Christmas vacation at a convention of scientists in Atlantic City.

This brings me quite up to date and I wish you all a very happy New Year—and I promise never to write such a personal epistle again.

1898

Class Editor: EDITH SCHOFF BOERICKE
(Mrs. John Boericke)
Merion, Pa.

1899

Class Editor: CAROLINE TROWBRIDGE RADNOR-LEWIS (Mrs. Herbert Radnor-Lewis)
140 E. 40th St., New York City.

1900

Class Editor: LOUISE CONGDON FRANCIS
(Mrs. Richard S. Francis)
414 Old Lancaster Rd., Haverford, Pa.

1901

Class Editor: HELEN CONVERSE THORPE
(Mrs. Warren Thorpe)
15 East 64th St., New York City.

The class wishes to extend its deep sympathy to Corinne Sickel Farley whose husband died on the first of July. Her daughter is teaching in the Junior High School in Philadelphia and is working for her M.A. in French at the University of Pennsylvania.

1902

Class Editor: ANNE ROTAN HOWE
(Mrs. Thorndike Howe)
77 Revere St., Boston, Mass.

1903

Class Editor: GERTRUDE DIETRICH SMITH
(Mrs. Herbert Knox Smith)
Farmington, Conn.

1904

Class Editor: EMMA O. THOMPSON
320 So. 42nd St., Philadelphia, Pa.

1905

Class Editor: ELEANOR LITTLE ALDRICH
(Mrs. Talbot Aldrich)
59 Mount Vernon St., Boston, Mass.

Florance Waterbury has just held an exhibition of "Still Life and Other Paintings" at the Montross Gallery, in New York City. It was given a very favorable criticism in the *New York Times* under the caption "An Escape from Realism." . . . "Calm and delicate beauty characterizes her work. . . . Here is peace, with a touch of poetry. Delicacy so frequently connotes triviality to some persons, that one hesitates to apply the word to Miss Waterbury's paintings. These still lifes are far from trivial. Hers is the capacity to make of flowers and objects of art, painting of distinction. This she accomplishes with sublety and poetic color."

Catherine Utley Hill writes from Geneva: "I left New York in November, 1931, to rest in the south, then went to Maine for Christmas. Hearing that Egypt was cheap, I sailed from New York in January, and was there eight weeks. After that, Palestine, Syria, Transjordania, Rhodes, Istambul, Greece, Italy, Vienna, the Tyrol and here to stay put—economize, talk international relations and attend the League of Nations Assembly. I have been helping on the American Committee. I attended Helena Dudley's funeral here. I shall leave soon for Paris, London and—home? I've had a marvelous time even if I'm poor! Last November I finished my work with the Fruit and Flower Guild and resigned. Since the crash, gardens and beautifications cannot be pressed when bread is needed. So now I am ready for another job."

Margaret Fulton Spencer is in Paris. She writes: "Architecture being at a standstill, I have rented my house for a year—perhaps longer—and brought my two girls over here to school and to study music, while I go on with my painting. We have an apartment for the winter at 24, rue Saint Sulpice, and I have my old studio nearby again, and am concentrating on figure work from models, something for which I have previously not had much time. I hope, of course, to go on with architecture as soon as times are better, and while here, plan to study manoirs, chateaux and gardens, as we brought along our Buick so that we might get out into the byways. If any of you could look us up, our permanent address here is Bankers' Trust Co., Place Vendome, Paris."

1906

Class Editor: LOUISE CRUICE STURDEVANT
(Mrs. Edward W. Sturdevant)
3006 P Street, Washington, D. C.

Helen Davenport Gibbons writes the following interesting letter, from Berne, about herself and family: "Christine, after four years of musical studies in Paris, is now teaching French at the Dwight School in Englewood, and is going to New York a time or two per week for singing lessons. Floyd is a Senior at Princeton. Mimi spent a few months in Princeton during the late winter and returned to Paris in May to continue her study of dancing with Bereska. Hope passed her matriculation examinations in July and is exempt, on account of her good record from Previous and Responsions, of Oxford and Cambridge. She passed the highest in French from her school, bringing back the notation 'Distinction. She has now returned for further work at Malvern Girls' College, in Worcestershire, England."

1907

Class Editor: ALICE HAWKINS
Taylor Hall, Bryn Mawr, Pa.

Anna Haines will be in Pittsburgh this winter working for the Public Health Nursing Association. We wonder whether she finds conditions more or less lurid there than among the striking miners of Kentucky. You may remember that she says that she left Boston because her "protoplasm could not stand the high osmotic pressure of the cultural media." Minnie List Chalfant's second daughter is a Freshman at Carnegie Technology, studying art. Eleanor, her elder, is doing outstanding work as a Senior at Bryn Mawr.

At the Council meeting in Chicago your editor was charmed to see Mary Fabian, Helen Roche Tobin, Harriot Houghteling Curtis, and Peggy Ayer Barnes. One of Helen's daughters is at the Baldwin School preparing for Bryn Mawr. Harriot looked wonderful—evidently it agrees with her to be kept on ice in Labrador. Her husband is due a furlough this winter and expects to join Harriot in Boston.

A few weeks ago Ellen Thayer paid one of her too rare visits to the campus, staying with Eunice Schenk, who was able to collect Tink Meigs, Anne Vauclain and A. Hawkins to greet her. Our Dean entertained the group by telling about P. Barnes' lecture on her own remarkable career as delivered to the Philadelphia intelligentsia. The society reporter who wrote up the affair went into ecstasies over Eunice's clothes, particularly her hat, which was "made interesting by a diamond pin." As some of us had seen Eunice hastily remove this creation from her own knitting needles just in time to don it for the lecture, adding one of Woolworth's best shiners, the story was well received. Peg then went on to speak in Brooklyn, staying with E. Pope Behr. Before she began, she took a look at her audience and was agreeably surprised at its size. She mentioned this to her introducer—not Popie—and was crushed to be told "the course is required," a credit course for public school teachers.

Brooke Peters Church has just published the book on which she has been working for years —*The Israel Saga*. More of this anon.

1908

Class Editor: HELEN CADBURY BUSH
(Mrs. Helen Cadbury Bush)
Haverford, Pa.

1909

Class Editor: HELEN B. CRANE
70 Willett Ave., Albany, N. Y.

1910

Class Editor: KATHERINE ROTAN DRINKER
(Mrs. Cecil Drinker)
71 Rawson Rd., Brookline, Mass.

1911

Class Editor: ELIZABETH TAYLOR RUSSELL
(Mrs. John F. Russell, Jr.)
333 E. 68th St., New York.

Marion Scott Soames is spending the winter in Wales and the spring in Dinard. Her permanent address is in care of the Natl. Prov. Bank, Wreyham, Wales.

Margaret Friend Lowe spends her time chauffing her four children to different schools and tries to keep peace in the family. Her eldest hopes to enter B. M. in the fall of 1933.

Harriet Couch Coombs, besides running her family, which consists of one husband, one grandmother, five boys, one honey-bear, and at least six snakes, which Harriet recommends as perfect pets, organized a troupe of colored girl scouts last spring. After that she took all the family and the menagerie to Maine for the summer.

Willa Browning's main interests outside her family are gardening and knitting. From personal observation we are able to state that she is an authority on the latter.

Sophie Blum Arnold has moved back to New York. Her daughter Augusta goes to the Brearley school and is headed for B. M.

1912

Class Editor: GLADYS SPRY AUGUR
(Mrs. Wheaton Augur)
820 Camino Atalaya, Santa Fé, N. Mex.

1913

Class Editor: HELEN EVANS LEWIS
(Mrs. Robert M. Lewis)
52 Trumbull St., New Haven, Conn.

1914

Class Editor: ELIZABETH AYER INCHES
(Mrs. Henderson Inches)
41 Middlesex Rd., Chestnut Hill, Mass.

1915

Class Editor: MARGARET FREE STONE
(Mrs. James Austin Stone)
3039 — 44th St., N. W., Washington, D. C.

1916

Class Editor: LARIE KLEIN BOAS
(Mrs. Benjamin Boas)
2736 Broderick St., San Francisco, Cal.

1917

Class Editor: BERTHA CLARK GREENOUGH
203 Blackstone Blvd., Providence, R. I.

Virginia Litchfield Clark died very suddenly early in November, in Arizona, after an illness of only a few days. Her few months of married life had been extremely happy ones. "Ginger" had been living in California for a number of years, and few of us had seen her lately, but we understand that her painting and her teaching of art had occupied most of her time until her marriage in June. We wish to express our deepest sympathy to her family.

Marian Tuttle received her Ph.D. from Cornell in June, and is now living at 78 West Fifth St., Oswego, N. Y. She received her M.A. from Yale and taught at Wheaton College prior to studying at Cornell for two "glorious, but nerve-racking years."

Eleanor Dulles was married, in Washington, December 9th, to Mr. David Blondheim, Professor of Romance Languages at Johns Hopkins. Dooles expects to keep her own name, and to continue her work at Bryn Mawr and at the University of Pennsylvania. Just before her marriage she polished off the book on which she had been working for the last three years— *The International Bank at Work*—published by Macmillan.

1918

Class Editor: Not yet appointed.

Helen Walker has handed in her resignation as Secretary and Class Editor for 1918. Her successor is as yet undetermined. Eager applicants please apply to Ruth Cheney Streeter.

As her swan song the retiring editor offers the following bits of news—all that has been voluntarily sent her during the past sixteen months.

Molly Cordingley Stevens has a daughter, Amy, born in June.

Margaret Timpson adopted a little girl in 1931. Timmie now has abandoned her habit of annual and extensive travels, because she cannot bear the thought of leaving her little responsibility. The snapshot of the chubby little tot quite explains Timmie's feeling.

Helen Walker had a telephone chat with Irene Loeb Cohn when she was in St. Louis last May. Irene was well and full of news of her two girls.

The Council meeting in Winnetka gave Helen Walker a glimpse of two of 1918. Marjorie Strauss Knauth was one of those delegated to H. W.'s care from the time of the arrival of the eastern group till the luncheon at the Casino. Chicago offered its dankest, chilliest weather to the guests. After inspecting, together with the entire delegation, three frigid specimens of the structurally interesting, but aesthetically nauseating architecture of the 1933 Century of Progress, Strauss delighted Helen's soul by suggesting an escape to the Art Institute where the collection of Modern French Art was a welcome relief.

Because of the twenty-two miles between Helen's home and the scene of the Council gatherings in Winnetka, together with a conflicting and unusually seductive symphony program, the Class Editor attended only the Council luncheon on Thursday and the dinner on Friday, thereby missing all the valuable discussion of class editors. However, the next incumbent may apply to Marjorie, who perforce drank it all in.

During the dinner at the Indian Hill Club, Helen Walker spied a familiar nose and chin in a far corner of the dining room. Could it be? Yes, it was Cattie Holliday Daniels, with whom she later had ten short minutes' chat over the coffee. Cattie was natural as ever, and apparently not a day older than when she lived in Rockefeller Hall.

Helen Walker is now a member of the Chicago Society of Miniature Painters and has five of her miniatures on view in their current exhibition.

Helen Edwards Walker, who has been our Class Secretary for so many years, writes that she really must ask to be relieved of the job on account of the heavy responsibilities she has at home. When she first broached the subject last spring, I hoped she would forget about it after a good vacation, but she still feels that it is too much for her to carry, so Charlotte and I have accepted her resignation with great regret and with many thanks for all the hard work she has done for the class. There was one bit of good news in her letter. She had a fall recently which, instead of having bad results, seems to have knocked into place a vertebra which has troubled her for a long time; so she feels better now than she has for years. Helen is getting quite famous as a painter of miniatures, having contributed to an exhibition last month at the Grant Studios, in Brooklyn. The miniature she sent was copied from a sketch of my small daughter, so altogether it was a 1918 affair.

We hope to announce the name of the temporary Class Secretary, who will act until our next reunion, in the next issue of the BULLETIN.

And, by the way, don't get worried about that next reunion. It doesn't come until the spring of 1934, in spite of the fact that 18+15 usually makes 33. Let's hope the depression will have lifted a bit by that time, so that we can all come back with free minds.

RUTH CHENEY STREETER.

1919

Class Editor: MARJORIE REMINGTON TWITCHELL
(Mrs. Pierrepont Twitchell)
Setauket, L. I., N. Y.

Dorothea Chambers Blaisdell announces the arrival of Ann Lang, on August 7th. Ann is named for a number of her New England ancestresses, the first Ann Lang Blaisdell appearing in the annals in 1708. Nesbitt (otherwise known as Nibbs) was four in December. Mr. Blaisdell is beginning his third year in the Department of Government at Williams College. Lucretia Garfield Comer's husband is head of the department. Ruth Hamilton was at the Institute this summer. Besides Ruth, "Nan Rock is all of '19 I have seen for a year. I wish they would remember I live between the Mohawk and the Taconic Trails and stop off on motor jaunts which must bring some this way."

Frannie Clarke Darling and B. Sorchan Binger and their husbands spent ten days in the Adirondacks together in the summer. Catherine Taussig Opie and her husband stayed with B. while in America this summer. Mr. Opie is a Don at Oxford, so their address for some time will probably be "Cotuit," Pullen's Lane, Headington, Oxford, England, where they have just made over a lovely old house.

Helen Spalding is in New York for the winter, at 396 Bleeker Street. She visited Class Editor for a week-end in the fall and the two had a great time reminiscing, not having seen each other for, well, we'll not mention the number of years—since 1919.

The class extends its deepest sympathy to Marion Moseley Sniffen whose husband died in August after a long illness. She is back in Chicago now.

Louise Wood leaves for France early in January to stay until June with a small group of girls. They will live in an apartment in Paris and follow a course of study which includes French, History, History of Art, and Modern European Problems.

1920

Class Editor: MARY PORRITT GREEN
(Mrs. Valentine J. Green)
433 E. 51st St., New York City.

1921

Class Editor: WINIFRED WORCESTER STEVENSON
(Mrs. Harvey Stevenson)
Croton-on-Hudson, N. Y.

Barbara Schurman came to New York in October on a flying trip from Paris where she and her husband, Vladimir Petropavlosky, are spending the winter. He is an engineer, and their permanent home is in China.

Grace Lubin is now Mrs. J. E. Finesinger, and her address is 310 Riverway, Boston, Mass.

Dorothy Wyckoff received her Ph.D. in Geology from Bryn Mawr last June.

Katherine Walker Bradford and her husband are spending a month in England, returning just before Christmas.

Helen Farrell gave up her real estate activities a couple of years ago and has gone in for photography. Some of her pictures are on exhibition at the Women's City Club, New York.

1922

Class Editor: SERENA HAND SAVAGE
(Mrs. William L. Savage)
106 E. 85th St., New York City.

1923

Class Editor: RUTH McANENY LOUD
325 E. 72nd St., New York City

In what Dorothy Burr describes as the "meatier" section of the BULLETIN—November issue—she gave a delightful and graphic picture of how and where she digs. Before coming back to her winter's work, she had apparently abandoned herself to Europe, in the grand manner—"Everything from a convent in Brittany to Geneva, where I danced with Poles and heard world news just before it was published, to more solid hours in the Louvre and Berlin Museum and lots of cheese and radishes and sour milk with the Mommsen family. I also took in a bit of Holland and Dalmatia on the way back."

Katherine Raht is teaching history again, this time at Foxcroft, in Virginia. She was in New York some six weeks ago, and one got an impression of tweeds and good country mud, and delight in an excellent job. Last summer Ratz played in stock in Gloucester, Mass., such impressive parts as *Fanny* in *The Royal Family*, the mother in *Lady Frederick*, and *Boucy* in *Let Us Be Gay*.

Florence Harrison Dunlop has been taking a correspondence course from Columbia, in writing, and has been doing Junior League work.

Elizabeth Ericcson is teaching at Miss Lee's school, in Boston.

Helen Wilson Collins lectures and writes articles on gardens, and also contributes poetry for children to such as the *Parents Magazine*. We wish we knew more about this.

Margaret Longyear Lutz writes from Palo Alto, California: "I received my A.B. from Mills College in 1923, and my M.A. from the same college in 1927, in the Department of Geology and Geography. On September 12th, 1927, I married Ralph Haswell Lutz, Professor of Modern European History at Stanford University and Director of the Hoover War Library. Since then I have made my home on the Stanford University campus. I have accompanied my husband on two interesting European collecting trips for the library; in 1928 and 1931. I have one child, Katherine May Lutz, born June 29th, 1929."

1924

Class Editor: DOROTHY GARDNER BUTTERWORTH
(Mrs. J. Ebert Butterworth)
8024 Roanoke St., Chestnut Hill, Pa.

Splendid response has been made to the November questionnaires, although the majority of the class are mainly occupied with formulas, strained vegetables and the usual details related to the rearing of three or four young hyenas—still the old spirit of research is alive. We have some illustrious classmates who manage homes and offices, and even travel occasionally.

Molly Angell McAlpin is sending out an appeal for the Alumnae Fund. Make out your contribution to the Alumnae Fund and send it to Taylor Hall, Bryn Mawr. Molly was married December 4th, 1926, to William R. McAlpin; lives in Rye, New York; has two children, Sylvia, aged four and one-half; Billy, aged one. Besides being the usual housewife, according to the census, she does social work, mainly with the Henry Street Visiting Nurse Association. Outside of a honeymoon to Egypt and Italy she now confines her travels to Maine and back for the summers.

Those who think they are overworked please listen to this report from Bobby Murray Fansler. On July 9th, 1924, she was married to Thomas Fansler. Three girls, Ruth Murray, almost six, Cynthia, nearly two, and Katharine, born October 6th, only partly occupy Bobby's time. While on leave of absence from the Metropolitan Museum she is acting as Art Adviser to the President of the Carnegie Corporation of New York, for one year. She spends her summers on a farm in Columbia County, New York, where eventually she hopes to stay permanently.

Quoting from Katherine Conner's letter: "I was married April 15th, 1929, to Anthony W. Brackett, Harvard '20, war veteran, investment banker, yachtsman, jack-of-all trades, now trying rural rusticity near Concord, Mass., and reviving bicycle polo, as bicycles are cheaper than horses and right now the game is more active than investment banking. We have one child, Anthony, Jr., known as Toby, born August 10th, 1930. I am not occupied outside the home, but very much so in it, running 'round trying to catch pennies that are about to fly out the window."

Kitty Prewitt Dabney was married to Edward Dabney, November 19th, 1929. She lives in Lexington, Kentucky, where she is mainly occupied with a daughter, Elizabeth Prewitt, born August 22nd, 1931.

A child prodigy has been produced by Elsa Molitor Vanderbilt. Elsa Molitor, called Molly, at the age of three and one-half can print her own name. Elsa says that her second girl, Nancy Spencer, born July 18th, 1930, is a pure and unadulterated imp. In addition to house duties Elsa writes stories and plays bridge. Her husband is in the advertising business, plays the piano and writes songs on the side.

1925

Class Editor: ELIZABETH MALLETT CONGER
(Mrs. Frederic Conger)
325 E. 72nd St., New York City.

1926

Class Editor: HARRIOT HOPKINSON
Manchester, Mass.

1927

Class Editor: ELLENOR MORRIS
Berwyn, Pa.

This department is notoriously slow in keeping up with the birth rate. We now learn that Bina Deneen House has a little girl, born last March. The House family lives in Cincinnati.

Helen Klopfer has received an M.A. degree from the University of Pennsylvania. Her field is economics, and her thesis was: "Grain Prices in Philadelphia, 1801-1860."

Madeleine Pierce Lemmon's twin daughters are getting to be distinguished horsewomen. Nancy and Jane are only three this winter, and for two years in succession they have taken first and second prize for horsemanship in a lead rein class in one of our local shows.

Gladys Jenkins Stevens, who lives on Long Island, comes over to Philadelphia occasionally to visit her family. Her sister, Hope, is a debutante this year, and Glade, looking just as pretty and exactly the same as she did in College, received with her at her coming out party.

1928

Class Editor: ALICE BRUERE LOUNSBURY
(Mrs. Richard Lounsbury)
424 E. 52nd St., New York City.

1929

Class Editor: MARY L. WILLIAMS
210 E. 68th St., New York City.

The class wishes to extend its deepest sympathy to Winifred Trask Lee whose husband, Howard M. Lee, was drowned November 25th.

Lucy Brown Barry is living in Cambridge, Massachusetts, with her husband and two children, a boy and a girl. Her husband is Professor of Psychology at Tufts College, Medford, Massachusetts; last summer they attended the International Psychological Congress at Copenhagen.

Becky Wills Hetzel has a daughter, Helen Wills Hetzel, born November 7th. We hasten to add that she was named for her grandmother, and not for Mrs. Moody, in spite of Beck's athletic interests.

Marcella Kirk Homire and her husband have settled, after considerable wandering, in a "slightly slummy" part of Croton-on-Hudson, where they have a house large enough to accommodate them and three children, also "any heavily muscled African who can be persuaded to endure us." She says that everyone in Croton is committed heart and soul to the progressive school, and wishes somebody with a dime and a daughter would come along to help reclaim some more of her slum.

The class wishes to extend its deepest sympathy to Juliet Garrett Hughes, whose mother died in October.

1930

Class Editor: EDITH GRANT
2117 Le Roy Place, Washington, D. C.

Lorine Sears is married to Mr. Harold Stein and living in New Haven.

Harriet Simeral is now Mrs. Charles Samstag Bunch and lives in Hot Springs, Arkansas.

A closely written post card from Olivia Stokes says that she has been having a most interesting trip and was expecting to be in Cairo by Christmas. She sounded very remote indeed, writing from Elizabethville, in the Belgian Congo.

Edith Fisk spent last summer working with the Wharf Players in Provincetown and is now looking for a job on the New York stage.

Hazel Seligman is also connected with the theater now. She is working at the business and executive end of the Commonwealth Theatre, which recently started off in New York with the production of "Carrie Nation." Her energies are not confined to this, however, as she is also finishing her courses for her doctor's degree in economics at Columbia, and hopes to get off to Hawaii in January.

Through a misreading of handwriting, Kate Hirschberg's new name was printed as Kobe instead of Kohn. Moral: Send in all information typed.

1931

Class Editor: EVELYN WAPLES BAYLESS
(Mrs. Robert N. Bayless)
New Britain, Conn.

The Class Editor was married in Philadelphia, on December 17th, to Mr. Robert Nelson Bayless, of Springfield, Ohio. Mr. Bayless, who is an accountant, attended Wittenberg College and the Harvard Business School. Mr. and Mrs. Bayless are living in New Britain, Conn.

Class Editor: JOSEPHINE GRATTON
182 Brattle St., Cambridge, Mass.

Alice Hardenbergh writes: "We trudged the streets of Liverpool looking for bicycles within our means till we finally got a couple for 35 shillings. We shipped all our wordly goods, except tooth brush, pyjamas, and as many guide books and maps as we could carry, on to Dolly Tyler. We spent five and a half days cycling and going slowly, doing about 151 miles in all! And think of the ground we ate up in the good old Buick — but England would seem too minute that way; we'd be all across it and back between breakfast and supper. Spent nights at Chester, Denbigh, Llangollen, Shrewsbury, Lichfield, and Warwick. Wales was lots of fun, if a bit steep. Denbigh is a sweet little town on the top of the longest and highest hill in Wales (at 6 p. m. after a wet and windy day anyway). But we were blessed with a heavenly day (one of the three or four really sunny ones), next day and came over the pass (quite a bit of walking managed to slip into this cycling trip), really not exhausted. In Llangollen we were just old pals with our nice host and hostess (we stayed in sort of dollar-a-night places like ours in Virginia, and found some delightful middle-class English), when they found there really was a place in America that had all the queer names that existed around there.

"Their former house was named Bryn Mawr, so we went in for a Welsh evening, starting our letters home 'Anwil Taur yr Maur,' which in good old English means dear Ma and Pa. They couldn't speak Welsh themselves, but knew what lots of words were and their child took it in school. Next day we went over a big pass (all of 1200 feet, I think), and climbed the mountain at the top on one side, and got a heavenly view of hills in every direction, with rain on one side and sun on the other. Coming down was almost too much for even us, who welcomed any kind of down grade with open arms. It was a long-twisting, hair-pinny downhill, and the good old bikes got so much momentum we were wearing our brakes out (have to pinch them on the handle bars and my hand was numb), and even so tearing down. No gear shift—cost $3.50 extra— not necessary. By the time we got to Stratford it was freezing cold and windy and rainy, so there being nothing but one hundred long weary miles between us and Cambridge, we succumbed, and took a five-hour train ride instead of a three-day bike ride. But it was swell fun, and we arrived dirty and messy, but quite triumphant, all the English people on the boat having prophesied we'd never even start, and thinking us mad."

Announcing..

A SERIES of twelve Staffordshire dinner plates by Wedgwood . . .

The Bryn Mawr Plates

The Views

LIBRARY CLOISTER
MERION HALL
PEMBROKE ARCH
LIBRARY ENTRANCE
THE OWL GATE — ROCK-
    FELLER
WING OF PEMBROKE EAST
RADNOR
SOUTH WING OF LIBRARY
TAYLOR TOWER
GOODHART
DENBIGH
PEMBROKE TOWERS

SPONSORED by the Alumnae Association, these plates are being made expressly for us by Josiah Wedgwood & Sons, Ltd., of Etruria, England. They are dinner service size (10¼ inches in diameter) and may be had in blue, rose, green, or mulberry.

THE DESIGN has been carefully studied under the supervision of the Executive Board of the Alumnae Association. The College seal dominates the plate, balanced by medallions of Bryn Mawr daisies. The background in true Victorian fashion is a casual blanket of conventionalized field flowers. This border, framing twelve views of the campus, offers a pleasing ensemble reminiscent of the Staffordshire ware of a century ago.

THE PRICE of the plates is $15 per set of twelve (postage extra). A deposit of $5 is required with your order, balance due when the plates are ready for shipment. All profits go to the Alumnae Fund.

BRYN MAWR ALUMNAE ASSOCIATION, BRYN MAWR, PENNSYLVANIA

Please reserve for me................sets of Bryn Mawr plates at $15 per set. I enclose $5 deposit on each set and will pay balance when notified that the plates are ready for shipment.

Color choice ☐ Blue   ☐ Rose   ☐ Green   ☐ Mulberry

SIGNED..

ADDRESS..

Make checks payable and address all inquiries to Alumnae Association of Bryn Mawr College Taylor Hall, Bryn Mawr, Pennsylvania

SCHOOL DIRECTORY

The Saint Timothy's School for Girls

CATONSVILLE, MARYLAND
Founded September 1882

COLLEGE PREPARATORY
AND
ELECTIVE COURSES

MISS LOUISA McENDREE FOWLER
Head of the School

WYKEHAM RISE
WASHINGTON, CONNECTICUT

A COUNTRY SCHOOL FOR GIRLS

FANNY E. DAVIES, LL.A., *Headmistress*
Prepares for Bryn Mawr and Other Colleges

ROSEMARY HALL
College Preparatory
(With supplementary but not alternative courses)

CAROLINE RUUTZ-REES, Ph.D. }
MARY E. LOWNDES, M.A., Litt.D } *Head Mistresses*

GREENWICH · · CONNECTICUT

BANCROFT SCHOOL FOR GIRLS

32nd Year. Complete College Preparation.
Individual Attention to carefully selected group in
Boarding Department of Progressive Day School.
Summer and Winter Sports. Dramatics, Art,
Music. *Address*

HOPE FISHER, *Principal*, Worcester, Mass.

LOW-HEYWOOD
On the Sound ~ At Shippan Point
ESTABLISHED 1865

Preparatory to the Leading Colleges for Women.
Also General Course.
Art and Music.
Separate Junior School.
Outdoor Sports.

One hour from New York

— Address
MARY ROGERS ROPER, *Headmistress*
Box Y, Stamford, Conn.

The Ethel Walker School
SIMSBURY, CONNECTICUT

Head of School
ETHEL WALKER SMITH, A.M.,
Bryn Mawr College

Head Mistress
JESSIE GERMAIN HEWITT, A.B.,
Bryn Mawr College

THE
SHIPLEY SCHOOL
BRYN MAWR, PENNSYLVANIA

Preparatory to
Bryn Mawr College

ALICE G. HOWLAND }
ELEANOR O. BROWNELL } *Principals*

 ## MISS BEARD'S SCHOOL

A complete educational program for girls. City and country advantages.

LUCIE C. BEARD, Headmistress
Orange, New Jersey

The Kirk School
Bryn Mawr, Pennsylvania

Boarding and day school. Preparation
for Bryn Mawr, Mount Holyoke, Radcliffe, Smith, Vassar, Wellesley, and
other colleges Individual instruction.
Special one-year intensive course for
high school graduates. Outdoor sports.

MARY B. THOMPSON, *Principal*

1896   **1933**

BACK LOG CAMP

(A camp for adults and families)

SABAEL, P. O., NEW YORK
ON INDIAN LAKE, IN THE ADIRONDACK MOUNTAINS

*B*ACK LOG CAMP offers none of the usual "attractions" of a summer resort, such as golf, motor boating, arranged programs, dancing, and visiting celebrities, It is a large tent camp, inaccessible to automobiles, but easy to get to, situated far from all other camps in a very wild part of the Adirondack Preserve. A fleet of fine canoes and rowboats always at the service of the guests without extra charge, and innumerable trails, many of our own making, enable Back Loggers to penetrate to isolated parts of the woods seldom visited by the usual run of summer visitors. That's what Back Log does: it runs the woods.

What strikes most newcomers is the personal, friendly atmosphere of the Camp. It is owned and run by a large family of brothers and sisters and their children (and one grandchild), college graduates and Philadelphia Quakers, and the note of the Camp is a cheerful sobriety that marks that religious body.

Send for a new fully illustrated booklet to

LUCY HAINES BROWN   **WESTTOWN, PENNSYLVANIA**

Reference: **Mrs. Anna Hartshorne Brown (Bryn Mawr, 1912),**
Westtown, Pennsylvania

Issued November 1st

THE NEW INTERNATIONAL LAWS OF CONTRACT BRIDGE

AUTHORIZED EDITION

Now in effect in the United States and all over the world

IMPORTANT CHANGES   NEW COUNT

NEW PENALTIES   NEW PREMIUMS

Bound in Cloth 50 cents
At all booksellers and stationers

Authorized American Publishers

THE JOHN C. WINSTON COMPANY
WINSTON BUILDING   PHILADELPHIA, PA.

I *really don't know if I should smoke...*

...but my brothers and my sweetheart smoke, and it does give me a lot of pleasure.

Women began to smoke, so they tell me, just about the time they began to vote, but that's hardly a reason for women smoking. I guess I just like to smoke, that's all.

It so happens that I smoke CHESTERFIELD. They seem to be milder and they have a very pleasing taste.

the Cigarette that's Milder

the Cigarette that Tastes Better

BRYN MAWR ALUMNAE BULLETIN

February, 1933

Vol. XIII   No. 2

Entered as second-class matter, January 15, 1921, at the Post Office, Phila., Pa., under Act of March 3, 1879

COPYRIGHT, 1933

ALUMNAE ASSOCIATION OF BRYN MAWR COLLEGE

Form of Bequest

I give and bequeath to the ALUMNAE ASSOCIATION
OF BRYN MAWR COLLEGE, Bryn Mawr, Pennsylvania,
the sum of........................dollars.

BRYN MAWR ALUMNAE BULLETIN

OFFICIAL PUBLICATION OF
THE BRYN MAWR ALUMNÆ ASSOCIATION

MARJORIE L. THOMPSON, '12, *Editor*
ALICE M. HAWKINS, '07, *Business Manager*

EDITORIAL BOARD

MARY CRAWFORD DUDLEY, '96   ELLENOR MORRIS, '27
CAROLINE MORROW CHADWICK-COLLINS, '05   ELINOR B. AMRAM, '28
EMILY KIMBROUGH WRENCH, '21   PAMELA BURR, '28
ELIZABETH BENT CLARK, '95, *ex-officio*

Subscription Price, $1.50 a Year   *Single Copies, 25 Cents*
Checks should be drawn to the order of Bryn Mawr Alumnae Bulletin
Published monthly, except August, September and October, at 1006 Arch St., Philadelphia, Pa.

VOL. XIII   FEBRUARY, 1933   No. 2

More and more, everyone interested in the whole question of unemployment has come to feel that the significance of the employment and placement bureaus has never been sufficiently emphasized, and that their scope is something wider than the mere recommending of a person for a job. Intelligently and efficiently managed they can certainly reduce annual turn-over to a minimum by filling a position with some one with exactly the right qualifications for that particular place. Perhaps even more important for us, however, is the point which Dean Manning emphasizes in her article on the Bureau of Recommendations at Bryn Mawr, namely, that of vocational guidance. At a place like Bryn Mawr, a Liberal Arts college, where there are no vocational courses as such, there is a very real need to be met. A clearing house of information about the best opportunities for sound professional training and advancement in all of the fields, both new and old, now open to women, has become a necessity and an obligation on the part of the college, not only for its alumnae, but for its undergraduates. Sound advice, fairly early in a student's college life, very often can spare her a waste of time and money and effort in those first few years after graduation before she really finds herself, and certainly can help her in college to steer her course a little more directly toward a definite objective. For a number of years now the College has been arranging, under various auspices, sometimes departmental, a series of meetings, addressed usually by an alumna eminent in a chosen field and followed by conferences with any students who are especially interested in entering that field. The range of the subjects covered has been very diversified, and the lectures have been of great value not only to the undergraduates but to the younger alumnae who have been able to hear them. It is interesting to note that the responsibility for these conferences has been given to the Bureau of Recommendations, which now will be able to coördinate information in a way that was impossible before, and consequently will itself be better equipped both to place applicants and to give professional advice.

THE BUREAU OF RECOMMENDATIONS

By Helen Taft Manning

Dean of the College

The Bureau of Recommendations at Bryn Mawr has had a somewhat checkered and uncertain career. Since its beginnings under Marion Reilly it has been a part of the Dean's office, and until two years ago the typing and record keeping were handled by the Dean's secretaries. The directorship was changed very often, however. The duties were usually performed by one of the wardens of the halls, and owing to the frequent changes in the appointments to those positions it was necessary to readjust the work of the Bureau about every two years. There have been in all eight or nine people concerned in the direction of the Bureau of Recommendations since it was reorganized by Dean Schenck in 1917. Some of the directors have had a very marked success in making placements, but the result of so many changes has been to make the work uneven and unsystematic. There was always a difficulty in carrying on the work when it had to be done by the regular staff of the Dean's office where the other work is seasonal and where in such busy times as the periods of registration in the fall and spring, the routine is so heavy as to make it impossible to attend to such unexpected calls as often occur in the work of the Bureau.

There was at one time a serious question in the minds of a good many of us whether the Bureau of Recommendations could ever be of sufficient service to Bryn Mawr alumnae to justify its existence and the annual expenditure of approximately twelve hundred dollars by the College on its maintenance. In recent years, however, I have become convinced that the Bureau must be maintained and that it is discreditable to the College if it is not maintained in an efficient manner. In the first place, such bureaus are maintained by all first-class colleges and do a work for their alumnae and for the student body, both in collecting references and in giving advice, which no other bureaus in the country are ready to do. The Coöperative Bureau for Women Teachers in New York, which is maintained in part by the support of the women's colleges, can do very little in placing beginners in the teaching field and can therefore be of small use to college Seniors. The schools which are willing to take on students recently graduated, either as apprentice teachers or as inexperienced teachers, prefer to write directly to the colleges. In the second place, the Coöperative Bureau reports that it seldom or never hears of openings for teachers in the colleges. Appointments in the colleges are made as a rule by application to the heads of departments in those institutions which have graduate schools. It is absolutely essential in every college which has a graduate school that there should be a central office where members of the faculty and the students themselves may obtain information and where recommendations may be on file to be sent with the least possible delay to the institutions where there are vacancies.

Moreover, the whole subject of vocational guidance is being regarded everywhere as an essential part of the whole educational program, and we must recognize that we do owe it to students, recently graduated, to give them what advice we can as to the best opportunities for professional training and advancement. The Bureau of Recommendations, which serves as a clearing house for such information as is available about opportunities not only in the teaching field but in other fields of work, is in a better position than any other office in the College to give such advice and to arrange for conferences. The justification for the existence of the Bureau must rest in the final analysis on the fact that so many letters arrive at the College from institutions and organizations in search of candidates for a variety of positions, and also from alumnae who wish to be informed of opportunities for professional advancement. Such correspondence cannot be neglected; yet it is only in a few cases that the President or Dean from her personal knowledge can make intelligent suggestions.

It was for these reasons that it seemed absolutely essential to me two years ago when I was running the Bureau myself, after the resignation of Miss Helen Crane, that someone should be appointed who would be able to carry on the work with continuity over a number of years. We were very fortunate in obtaining the services of Mrs. James Crenshaw, whose experience in secretarial work in two schools has given her the kind of information she particularly needs in running the Bureau, and whose acquaintance with Bryn Mawr alumnae and with Bryn Mawr undergraduates is extensive, to direct the Bureau on the basis of devoting to it a quarter of her time during the college year. She has working under her a part-time secretary, who is in charge of the correspondence during most of the summer months. Mrs. Crenshaw has studied the work of the personnel bureaus and vocational advisers in the other women's colleges, and is this year handling the vocational conferences for the Bryn Mawr undergraduates.

Her report for the year 1931-1932 showed the following calls to the Bureau and placements made by the Bureau:

Total calls to the Bureau 118
    Calls for teachers 59   of which 12 were from colleges and 47 from schools.
    Full-time positions 36   permanent or for the summer.
    Small or temporary positions .... 23 ·   substitute teaching, typing, reading aloud, etc.

Placements made by the Bureau 31
    Teaching positions 12   of which only one was in a college and 11 were in schools.

Of the schools at which the Bureau was able to place teachers, four were in Bryn Mawr, one in Wayne, Pa., two in Massachusetts, one in New York, one in Virginia, one in Washington, and one in Kentucky.

The miscellaneous positions which were filled included one as librarian at the Great Neck (New York) Library, one as research assistant at the Philadelphia General Hospital, and one as reader on the *Atlantic Monthly*.

The placements made by the Bureau last year in comparison with the year before, when it was being very inefficiently run by myself, show an increase of about 40 per cent. The proportion of placement to calls, considering the number of applicants for every kind of position last year, speaks extremely well for the work of Mrs. Crenshaw.

SOME NOTES ON GERMAN WOMEN'S ATTITUDE TOWARD DISARMAMENT

By Mary Goodhue Cary, 1915

Up to the present the German women have not been very active in a public way on the subject of disarmament. Their apparent tardiness has been due to their absorption in their political and economic troubles internationally and to their lack of political experience. There are splendid women in various departments of the government, but the rank and file of the German women are not politically minded. Besides this handicap, the war and its results tore them into little groups of Left and Right, so that when you go to one women's organization, its leaders will almost always tell you that the other clubs working along similar lines are all wrong, and that you cannot get the true German point of view from any group but theirs!

So it is really to their credit that so many groups have now begun to educate their members on the work and purpose of the Disarmament Preparatory Commission and the Geneva Conference. Disarmament petitions are being circulated for signatures, and I secured a page of names from very simple working people, some of them ex-soldiers, and some of them long-unemployed men and women, but all glad to put down their signatures in favor of something that would assure the people of a lasting peace.

It was to give the American women living in Berlin a chance to hear the German point of view in these matters, that the International Relations Committee of the American Women's Club, of which I am a member, invited Frau von Velsen to speak to us. She is the President of the *Staatsbürgerinnen Verein,* an organization somewhat like our League of Women Voters, working to educate women in an understanding of civil affairs and to teach them to take their rightful part in the government. They are trying now to concentrate on advocating general disarmament. They have the coöperation of the Trade Unions, the Catholic Women, and the National Council of Women, which is a very strong and influential body of working and professional women. They are circulating disarmament resolutions printed in blue, because Frau von Velsen is a great admirer of Mrs. Catt, and the latter uses blue for her color in peace work. She explained that there has been little public demonstration or street parades in favor of disarmament in Germany, as owing to the government's orders, made to keep down political riots, such things are forbidden by the police.

Frau von Velsen's thesis was this: Germany was disarmed under the Versailles Treaty, and Marshall Foch himself reported to the French Chamber of Deputies in 1925 that he was satisfied that there had been an actual fulfillment of the treaty stipulations. At the same time in the Versailles Treaty the Allies promised to disarm "to the lowest point consistent with national safety." To this end the League Council appointed the Preparatory Disarmament Commission, which has drawn up a Draft Convention for the Geneva Conference to work on. Now in this Draft Convention, in article 53, there is a statement that no previous treaties can be upset by anything that the Geneva Conference may do. The French members succeeded in having the following added, "the maintainance of such provisions (existing

(4)

treaties) being for them (the High Contracting Parties) an essential condition for the observation of the present Convention." This means that the war guilt clauses of the Versailles Treaty, the continued inferior position of Germany in military equipment, and other provisions which place Germany in an unequal position with other nations, will still be recognized.

So Frau von Velsen told us that the German women of her organization had drawn up their resolution, which is being signed and which they will present at Geneva, to the effect that there must be an equality between the armed and unarmed powers, and that they reject the Draft Convention of the Disarmament Conference. This is not a strange point of view for these women to take, as the German Government Delegation has reserved the right to reject the Convention on the grounds of unfairness. Frau von Velsen further said that the Germans do not expect much from the Geneva Conference. If Germany does not receive there promises of "security," she will be forced to obtain them in some other way, possibly by withdrawing from the League of Nations.

A more hopeful and constructive program for the future was expressed at a recent meeting of the World Peace League for Mothers and Teachers. This League was started in France by a mother who lost her only son in the war. It has now 50,000 French members and branches in about ten German cities, as well as in Holland, Belgium and other European countries. True to the German tradition, the meeting opened and closed with music, the tender, rich notes of a 'cello in a Schubert movement putting us all into the mood for a magnificent challenge to our womanhood given by Frau Dr. Bäumer, who is a permanent government adviser. She called on German women to realize that a new world order is being ushered in by the Geneva Conference. Nations were coming together to disarm permanently, and we women must create the atmosphere for this new peace machinery to survive in. We must create new means to break down international misunderstandings. The old way of giving our sons to settle matters must never be used again, but instead we must use all our mother love and all our educational technique to create international understanding that will reinforce the new method of coöperation. We mothers and teachers must live in this spirit, we must believe it to the depths of our consciousness. We must forward every means for the coöperative life of nations and give up our isolated nationalism. If the Disarmament Conference goes no further than limiting guns and tanks, and does not achieve something that expresses these spiritual desires of the people, it may as well not meet. The German women are not concerned merely with restoring Germany's military position to an equality with other nations. All nations must be on an equal footing in order to express the will of the people, who want real coöperation on a basis of equality. Frau Dr. Bäumer regretted that the German delegation to Geneva has no representative of the women, the workers, or the churches who could really express the desires of the German people.

ANNOUNCEMENTS

The second section of the Science article, prepared by the Academic Committee, and scheduled for this number, will appear in the April BULLETIN.

Commencement will be held Tuesday, June 13th.

THERA

By Pamela Burr, 1928

On the *mappa mundi* in the Doge's Palace, the island of Thera appears, and though larger than life and not in the least natural, can still be recognized as one of the Cyclades. It was, I decided at a glance, an island to explore when I went to Greece.

On a memorable evening I set sail from the Piraeus with two friends on a Greek cattle steamer bound for the outer islands. Our plans were vague. The island, we had been told, boasted a hotel that was certainly unhygienic and a French convent that was probably inhospitable. Preferring an inhospitable convent to an unhygienic hotel, we decided to throw ourselves on the nuns' mercy. This was difficult. Of course, we could memorize the two Greek words in our phrase book for *French Convent*. But if our Greek suceeded in bringing us to the doors of the Convent, would our French admit us there? And did any one of us possess the eloquence equal to coping with a Mother Superior? From my knowledge of Mother Superiors, based on *The Cradle Song* and *The Abbot*, I doubted it. We promptly forgot our misgivings, however, when we turned into the harbor of Thera, and saw that the island of the *mappa mundi* was only less extraordinary than the island of reality.

Thera, in shape, is like "the hornèd moon with the star in her nether tip"; the star, in this case, is a wee volcano, its triple craters rising as from a giant coal heap of black lava. In erruption it broke away from the main island, and now, like a sulky dwarf, it squats apart across a narrow channel, malignantly regarding the miracle it created: a cliff rising to some hundreds of feet which resembles a rampart weathered into rounded Norman towers. By some bizarre fluke of nature, these rocks are streaked with lateral bands of black and red, out of which mouthe dark caves cut with the fantastic regularity of a dream. A white zigzag path leads audaciously up to the white town which crowns the top like an illustration for the *Arabian Nights*.

We were rowed in, nosing through the pumice stones which floated on the top of the water porous as dried gray sponges. These are scattered all over the island so that it is impossible to go anywhere on foot. Beyond the town, the fields, bare to the sea, look as if some mythical dragon after uprooting every tree had strewn dried bones all over the ground, spattered with poppies as with drops of blood.

There on the wharf the animals waited to take us up to the town, the mules kicking back the flies, the donkeys regarding us with a mournful myopic gaze, drawing back their lips from their teeth to admit a sound which resembled nothing so much as a cow trying to low with a very bad cold. We repeated our two Greek words over and over like a charm. They certainly worked like one. Before I knew what was happening, a muleteer seized me and lifted me onto his mule. Scarcely had I settled myself sideways on the saddle of wooden slats, or placed my feet in the improvised stirrup of rope, when a second muleteer, rushing forward, pulled me off the mule to place me firmly on his donkey. Not until I had been snatched from two mules and several donkeys did I realize this was only the island's effective way

(6)

of soliciting the stranger's trade! Since the mule on which I then found myself could certainly understand me better than the muleteer, I uttered a cry which started us up the path at an appalling speed that I was powerless to control. He had no reins and the more I tried to stop him, the faster he went. All I could do, like the prince in the *Arabian Nights,* was to cling to the wooden peg in which my saddle terminated, and go willy nilly where my beast wished. By half an inch we missed a woman with a shawl over her head leading a goat on a leash. She smiled. We diverted a young donkey, laden with sticks, from the path of duty. He left us, only under force, lamenting down the path with his nose firmly fixed in a wicker basket. A thundering of hooves heralded the approach of four riderless, bridleless horses stampeding down at us, driven before the menacing, wand-like whip of a man who galloped after them.

At last we turned up a cobblestoned street under a white archway, and ascending three steps, we stopped before a large gray door. So, when they joined us, did the muleteer and my friends. So did the donkey who brought our baggage. So did the little boys who followed the donkey, and so did the yellow dog who followed the little boys. The muleteer smote on the door, and stood listening.

"You go," murmured my friends.

I found myself in a vestibule painted white, where a wooden gate rang a sepulchral bell as it opened on a courtyard. Here I sat down to wait for the Mother Superior, and though I bravely reviewed a few French irregular verbs, I could not feel eloquent enough to ask her for shelter nor godly enough to remain. At last she came, ducking gravely through the door so as not to disarrange her widespread cap of a Sister of Charity.

"Ma mère," I began at once, "Nous sommes trois jeunes filles toutes seules."

To this introduction she listened with troubled attentiveness and without humor. Sometimes they took travelers, she told us, but none had come this year, and she feared we would not like it, because, as she phrased it, "vous no pouvez pas sortir le soir avec des hommes." Unlike the Mother Superiors of fiction, she was young and pretty, with a line of perplexity which deepened between her eyes the longer we stayed. Though she treated us with exhaustive kindness, she could not disguise her uneasiness in our presence, nor her dread, less of our morals than of our scorn. I learnt later that she had enough to worry her here even without us. Still in her twenties, she had been sent to rule over a convent which sheltered, in addition to nine nuns of four nationalities, a charity school and an old ladies' home. And on this remote island there was no money and little sympathy for Roman Catholicism. If at the end of a year she did not make a success of it, the church had threatened to abolish the convent. It looked as if other forces beside the church would accomplish this before a year, since the nuns were over eighty and the building falling to decay. She told us this with misgiving. We should not stay here, for were we not used to shower baths and electric lights?—"Ce n'est pas une jolie maison."

No, it was not pretty, but seen in the dusk of that first evening, it was romantic beyond one's dreams. Perhaps circumstances enchanted our first endless excursion through courts and passages to our room. Certainly no electric torch would have cast the shadows of the Mother Superior's lantern, which was of a type reserved by the Metropolitan Opera for the jailors of the condemned. I remember a courtyard where heads of lettuce, planted in neat rows, unfurled their leaves; darkness descending half way down stairways to settle there; a flag-stoned passage, as long as the Hudson Tunnel, which led to an exterior staircase mounting through crumbling walls to a parapet and the stars. Here rabbits and pigeons were kept behind wire. A nun stood among them scattering grain, her cap perched on her head like a starched butterfly, her eyes following us as we vanished around the corner. With gravity and concern, our guide paused to caution us against the cords hung above the parapet for the washing, before she opened the door which led through a disused kitchen to our room.

What a night in Maeterlinck I spent there! I had thought those congeries of courts and passages empty; now I learnt they were a rabbit-warren to shelter the curious. Everyone, from the shyest child to the slyest old woman, wanted a sight of us. Dinan, not yet five, spent a daring evening on the parapet outside our window, which was, we were informed, quite proper, "seulement un enfant qui vous regarde." An old woman who chose to eat her supper just outside our door was not in the least confused when I found her there. She showed me her gums, nodded, and crowed triumphantly when she discovered that I spoke Italian even worse than she. She had descended to eat her meal here, she explained, because her room-mate, an idiot, "piange, piange, tutto il giorno," and did I know her grandson who worked in San Francisco? Cleverer than she, another old hag invented the pretext of making our beds. I still see her distended shadow cast on the white vaulted ceiling lowering over the room like a witch as she overturned the straw mattress in which worms wriggled.

When I had extinguished the lamp, and propped the stone to hold the broken window open on the Aegean, I scorned the idea of sleep beneath the shroud of the mosquito netting and the protection of the palm leaves dying behind holy paintings. Why waste time on sleep when I could listen to the wind and sea in such surroundings? But, beyond this resolution, I remember nothing more until dawn, when there came a sudden outburst of sound: bells ringing, footsteps hurrying, and voices whispering as suddenly suppressed into the well-regulated murmur of the responses.

The next morning a little girl came to take us to breakfast. Indeed, we were royally conducted to all our meals, for would three mad Americans be equal to mastering the complexities of that convent? We ate in the reception room, on stiff chairs covered with linen slips, facing the painted figure of the Virgin from whose fingers the gilt rays reigned down to bless the slab of crystals which ornamented the dresser. Always a nun came, not to eat with us, but to sit bolt upright and to inquire if we liked that soup, why had we not drunk as much today as yesterday, and if the squab was to our taste, why had we left that unpicked bone? So we really liked everything from the soup to the *yaorti*? Then we should have exactly the same meal tomorrow for supper and as long as we stayed.

Our luncheon they put up for us whenever we explored another surprising corner of the island. One by one the pigeons were killed, cooked, and, with their thin arms crossed on their chests, handed us in a paper parcel, together with a bottle of wine, copious nuts and candies, and striped blankets to soften the wooden saddles of the mules.

When we returned we always found the Mother Superior waiting to hear our adventures, to her right a colored picture portraying Hell as a place of lively discomforts, to her left a map of France. I noticed that, though the borders of Hell were carefully protected by tape, the map was far more worn, and I could follow the track of her finger passing over the well-known route to Lyons, where she lived. Here we told her of picnics in the background of a Persian Miniature: of strange rock-shapes rising abruptly from fields recklessly sown with a variety of tiny flowers, of white towns with the square white roofs of the East, white stairways, white arches, and white cats glaring over white walls with round, yellow eyes. Here we told her of our first and last glimpse of the Church of Perissa. From the ancient Acropolis we looked down on it, lonely, inaccessible, fronting a beach of black volcanic sand, a small white church with a large blue dome. Flattened into artificiality by the great height from which we saw it, it had no more dimensions than a medallion in an oriental rug.

Here I told her I must leave. Plans of a sort that never worry nuns claimed me. I was to go back alone, leaving my friends now making reckless statements about taking the veil. When I broke the news the Mother Superior looked at me as if I were damned, but, with a shrug, "Voilà les Américaines!" From her I found out that the boat, which made the tour of the islands, arrived at four if it did not come at five; though never expected before six, it often appeared at two and left at two-fifteen. But how did one *know?* I demanded, trained by years of telephoning steamboat agencies. One waited.

Two o'clock found me following this advice, my duffel bag and bottle of boiled water beside me. At three, the convent servant, a Greek who spoke French, was sent up to the parapet to watch for the first sight of my boat. At four the nuns said good-bye, with requests for postals to be sent from France. At five, the servant appeared, and replied to all questions by rolling his eyes upward:

"Le bateau ne vient pas."

At six the moon shone green on the white walls outside, and the malarial mosquitoes, entering through the broken shutter, wove a dance above our heads. At seven the servant reappeared. I deluged him with questions and impatience. He protruded his under-lip, cut the air in a semi-circle with the thumb of his right hand, and returned to the parapet. At eight the wind began to blow, and a nun, entering to light the lamp, told me that the boat never comes until midnight, when the wind blows, and then is likely to put up in the harbor of Naxos for four or five days.

"I don't think I'll—" I began, "I don't think—"

But I never finished the sentence which would have given me another night beneath the mosquito-netting. A clatter on the cobblestones outside interrupted me.

"Les mules!" cried the Mother Superior, rising.

Then the servant, flinging wide the door, proclaimed, "Le bateau!"

Seizing my duffel bag in one hand, and the bottle of boiled water in the other, I obeyed the summons. But as I descended alone in the moonlight, the water gurgling as my mule jolted downward step by step, I experienced little regret at leaving. For was this not one of those rare moments in life when my departure had been worthy of my arrival?

BALKAN IMPRESSIONS

By Cornelia B. Rose, Jr., '28

Kipling probably was responsible for it. Do you remember in *The Light That Failed* the Nilghai who was constantly predicting "trouble in the Balkans in the spring"? The rather romantic ambition to visit the Balkans at that season which was stirred by this phrase, was achieved this year.

After a month in Berlin and two in Vienna, we set out for Budapest just as the lilacs were coming into bloom. Hungary, of course, is not exactly a part of the Balkans, but it belongs to the region of Southeastern Europe and shares its problems. It is said that everyone succumbs to Hungarian charm, and we were no exceptions to the rule. We listened sympathetically to tales of how the Czechs had taken Hungarian land; how the Roumanians, asked to save the country from the Bolshevists after the war, had turned on the Hungarians and looted everything they could lay their hands on, in addition to getting a large share of their territory; and of how the Jugoslavians cut them off from the sea. In Vienna we had become used to hearing speeches beginning, "Before the war . . . " but this dislike and fear of neighboring countries was new. The Hungarians are intensely nationalistic. This feeling was characteristically expressed when a professor of history said to me, "Those new countries created after the war will not last. Those people have never made good statesmen and don't know how to run a country. Their machinery will break down, and then there will be a place in the world once more for Hungarian idealism." One should in justice remark that there is some question about just how "idealistic" was the Hungarian treatment of minorities before the war.

We were in Bucharest only a short time and had only a limited experience from which to judge the Roumanian attitude. But we met less expressed hatred of neighbors there—quite understandably, of course, since Roumania profited greatly after the war at her neighbors' expense. We did find, however, many perplexing problems of internal organization. In Bucharest there is a small "upper class" of people, most of whom have been educated in France and speak French as their everyday language. This group is quite out of touch with the great mass of peasants, who, until recently, have lived a completely self-sufficient life, coming in contact with the city only when they had surplus produce to sell. The level of culture varies from one part of Roumania to the other, from the Germans and Hungarians in the western part to the Russians and Bulgarians in the eastern part, and the fusion of all these elements is a difficult process.

From Bucharest we made a flying trip—literally—to Istanbul, where the sights and sounds and smells excited us because they were so different from anything we had known before. The story of the Turks is inextricably interwoven with that of the Danubian peoples, and no fair estimate of the present problems can be made without taking this fact into account. And then on to Sofia, by means of the famous Orient Express, which didn't quite live up to our expectations. A train with a world-wide reputation should not have to back down a hill three times before it can make a fairly moderate grade, as that train did! Sofia with its yellow brick streets, its modest royal palace in the center of the town, its imposing Eastern Orthodox Cathedral, very new, its ox carts rumbling down the main street, its "crushed strawberry" opera house with black and gold trimmings, looks like an overgrown village. And this is just what it is. Fifty years ago it was a small Turkish settlement of about 3,500 inhabitants; now it is well on its way to a population of 300,000. Here again we found border hates. The Bulgarians do not like the Roumanians, because they took the "granary of Bulgaria" after one of the Balkan wars; they do not like the Turks, nor the Greeks, but above all, they hate and fear the Jugoslavians. The Macedonian problem is a constant source of irritation between these two countries, and the presence of bands of *comitadjis* excuses many outrages on both sides.

Belgrade we found intensely interesting as an example of a city built almost entirely since the war. A few years ago none of the streets were paved, and the houses that were left after the bombardments of the war were, for the most part, decrepit Turkish huts. Now there are broad, well-paved streets with impressive government buildings, and well-kept parks with extensive rose gardens, all blooming at the time of our visit. The Jugoslavians have no love for the Bulgarians, whom they have not forgiven for their "treachery" after the first Balkan war, but they hate the Hungarians, and most of all they fear the Italians. Moreover, they, too, have serious internal problems, for the Croations distrust the Serbs, and the Dalmations and Montenegrins and the various other groups each have their own pet grievances.

Several outstanding impressions remained after we had completed the circle and returned to Vienna. There was a sense of having been in touch with colorful, semi-oriental, wholly vital groups of people with whom a more intimate acquaintance promised rich rewards. Then there was a feeling of depression because of the intense mutual enmities so generally betrayed. We remembered the warning we had been given before we set off. "Those people are all propagandists; they will all try to sell you their own country and make you dislike the others." It was true. It had been easy to believe the Hungarians, because they were the first to speak to us. But when one had heard the same tune played on many different harps, one became rather critical of the technique. Each group of people that we met were charming and always most cordial in their hospitality. Each city was of special interest. But we learned that there were some topics one had to avoid in order to keep the conversation on a friendly basis. Intelligent, cultured people completely lost their heads when one of these dangerous subjects was mentioned.

Each of these countries, Hungary, Roumania, Bulgaria, Jugoslavia, is tasting a new independence and defending it jealously. Any suspected encroachment upon this independence raises a storm of protest. Thus, the so-called "Tardieu Plan" for a Danubian economic understanding met with no response among them, each nation seeking only what it would lose by such an arrangement and not what it might gain. Each nation feels that so far as possible it must be autarchic. Intelligent people admit that perhaps this fostering of industries which can produce only at high cost those things which might be imported more cheaply from a neighboring country is wasteful, but counter with the query, "What can we do when we go to war if we cannot manufacture these things for ourselves?" This attitude is so universal that it necessitates a revision of the opinion I have held: that if economic difficulties could be ironed out, the political difficulties would cease to exist. Now I see that with this constant fear of war—and the acceptance of the coming of war as inevitable—political problems must be re-solved before the world càn follow a sane economic policy.

Quarrels between Bulgaria and Jugoslavia, or Jugoslavia and Hungary, or Hungary ánd Roumania, in themselves would, perhaps, not be so important. But the larger powers each has made a move to take these nations under its respective wings. Italy considers Bulgaria and Hungary her protegés; France lends money to Jugoslavia, Roumania and Czechoslovakia. This means that any open break between opposing groups would have reactions far beyond the importance of the immediate cause. It means that another Sarajevo episode could again involve the whole world in war if not checked before the matter went too far and the nations' "honor" became involved. And since there are numerous points of friction which might burst into flame at any time, there is constant potential danger of war.

Looking back, I feel that although I have had a glimpse into the problems and perplexities of this region, I found very little light cast on the solution of them. It is regrettable that knowledge of and interest in the Balkans is not more widespread. It is possible that the safety of the world depends upon a proper understanding and a helpful adjustment of the difficulties of these people. As it is, we are still bound to feel with the Nilgai, that "there might be trouble in the Balkans in the spring."

ANNUAL MEETING

The annual meeting of the Alumnae Association will be held in the Auditorium of Goodhart Hall, on Saturday, February 11th, 1933, at 9.45 a. m. At one-thirty p. m. the meeting will adjourn to Pembroke Hall, where the members of the Association will be the guests of the College at luncheon. President Park will speak, and after the meeting tea will be served in the Common Room, Goodhart Hall.

On Friday evening there will be an informal dinner in Rockefeller Hall at seven o'clock. Professor Rhys Carpenter, former Director of the American School at Athens, who has returned to the College after seven years' absence, will speak about recent archaeological discoveries in Greece. Tickets for the dinner, at $1.10, may be obtained from the Alumnae Office. Cheques should be made payable to Bertha S. Ehlers, Treasurer.

MEETING OF THE BOARD OF DIRECTORS OF THE COLLEGE

The Board of Directors of the College met in Bryn Mawr, at President Park's home, on Thursday, December 15, 1932. All the Alumnae Directors and the three Almunae Directors-at-large were present. The next meeting of the Board will be held in Philadelphia on March 15th. If members of the Association have suggestions which they would like brought before the Board, they are urged to communicate with the Alumnae Directors.

"PRINCIPAL WOMEN OF AMERICA" AND BRYN MAWR'S DAUGHTERS

Edith Edwards, 1901, sent the following information, gleaned from the book, Principal Women of America, which is said to be the first compendium of its kind published in England. The Editors of The Bulletin do not hold themselves responsible for its sins of omission.

. This thin volume, the first of a series, published at the Mitre Press, in London, in early summer, bears as sub-title "A directory giving short biographical sketches of the most important ladies in the United States of America." The book contains 1500 biographies. Of these, Bryn Mawr's daughters can claim something under forty.

The graduates! The Bryn Mawr type! The list opens with the class, the outstanding class, of '97, with Cornelia Bonnell Greene King, Mrs. Paul King, and with Miss Edith Edwards. There follows Miss Katharine Riegel Loose, 1898; two brilliant personalities of our campus days from the ranks of 1900, Edna Fischel and Grace Jones, now Mrs. George Gellhorn, and Mrs. C. F. W. McClure. And Louise Atherton Dickey, 1903 (Mrs. Samuel Dickey), Sally Porter Law McGlannan, also 1903, Mrs. Robert Walcott (Mary Richardson, 1906), and Mrs. George Fred Miller (Margaret Duncan, 1908). Younger women are: Mrs. Rollin T. Chamberlin (Dorothy Smith, 1909); Mrs. O. M. Sayler (Lucie Reichenbach, 1910); Mrs. G. B. Myers (Margaret Hobart, 1911). Mrs. Alexander Meiklejohn (Helen Everett) and Mrs. John T. McCutcheon (Evelyn Shaw) are from the youngest classes mentioned, 1915 and 1914 respectively. If I may be forgiven a gossip's comment, we may seem to shine with a reflected glory. But you will admit that we are highly representative.

Ten ladies who did not toil so hard as students, have still made the grade. These are Mrs. Margaret Scruggs Carruth, 1913; Mrs. Wm. S. Culbertson (Mary T. Hunter, G. S. '10-'11), of the American Embassy at Santiago, Chile; Mrs. David Friday, Mrs. Arnold van Couthen Huizinga (Faith Mathewson, '96). We all remember Blanche Harnish, '98! Also Mrs. John A. MacMurray (Lois Goodnow, 1916), another diplomat's wife. And the list ends with Mrs. William Francis Reinhoff, Jr. (Francis Young, 1923), Mrs. Dorothy Godfrey Wayman, 1914, editor of the *Falmouth Enterprise,* and Mrs. Ralph Wyckoff (Laura Laidlaw, 1926).

Of graduate students there are some fifteen: Isabel Ely Lord, our librarian of the old library; Miss Drinkwater, graduate scholar, now Dean of Women, Carleton College, Minn.; Miss Louise Dudley, a Doctor of Philosophy of Bryn Mawr College and now head of the English Department at Stephens College, Columbia, Mo.; Mrs. Mabel E. Goudge; Miss Mary K. Isham, a Fellow in Philosophy, and Mrs. C. E. Magnusson (Elva Cooper), Fellow in Mathematics; Mrs. James M. Leake, Mrs. John Shapley (Fern Rush, Ph.D.), Mrs. Frank D. Watson, Ph.D., and Winifred Warren Wilson (Mrs. G. A.), Ph.D. Mrs. J. P. Whitman was a Foundation Scholar in Semitic Languages. And let us be glad to record two members of the faculty of Bryn Mawr College, Dr. Bascom and Dr. Susan Kingsbury, to whom is attributed the organization of the Carola Woerishoffer Graduate Department of Social Economy of Bryn Mawr College, the first graduate school of this type, and the planning and organization of a Summer School for women-workers in industry.

DIGGING IN ALASKA

By Frederica de Laguna, 1927

When I promised to write something for the BULLETIN about my archaeological work in Alaska, I was finishing a long report on the first two seasons' work, and I thought it would be easy to extract a few bright morsels for this article. But the hurry of sending the ponderous manuscript off in one direction and of getting my little party started for Alaska in the opposite direction made this impossible. Neither the voyage up from Seattle nor the first days in camp were conducive to literary effort, and now that I can pause for breath I find to my dismay that the summer is half gone, and those wise reflections I would have humbly offered you are as elusive as ever. Here, surrounded by the absorbing minutiae of camp life and excavation, there is no time for, and no vantage point from which to catch a broad view over what we are doing and the problems we are trying to solve. There is only the recurrent daily routine of digging, washing, cataloging, shellacking and mending specimens, getting meals and washing up after them, until it is time to crawl reluctantly into our sleeping bags, while the northern sky is still flushed with the tardy sunset.

From our rocky point we look out across sheltered waters with many little islands—some dark with timber, others bare and green, where gulls and puffins nest in the abandoned refuges that the natives built against surprise attacks by boat—across to the mountains, still covered by snow. Between our island and the large one opposite us there is a rock-infested channel leading out into the open inlet, beyond which stand the beautiful snow-capped volcanoes of the Alaska Peninsula, the same chain that make the Aleutian Islands farther west. Augustine is a perfect cone, rising by itself from the water—it is like a delicate Japanese silk painting of Fujiyama. Farther north, hidden by our island, but springing into view, majestic and immense, whenever we go out in the boat, are Iliamna and Redoubt volcanoes, with many lesser peaks between, and beyond them again other volcanoes, almost out of sight in the north. Behind us on the mainland is one of the remnants of the great glacier that once covered all this country. Arms of it come down the valleys to the fjords, and these arms are named, but the great inland ice that feeds them is still one of the largest unnamed glaciers in the world.

Cook Inlet, reaching from the Gulf of Alaska almost two hundred miles into the interior, has been a meeting place of peoples. Along its shores today live a branch of the mighty Athabaskan nation, whose home is the interior, and who here only have gained access to the sea. Along the mouth of the Inlet, on Kodiak Island to the south, Prince William Sound to the east, and the Alaska Peninsula to the west, live the southernmost Eskimo, those dauntless sea-otter hunters and whalers whom the Russians found so hard to subdue. On the Aleutian Islands live their cousins. Southeastern Alaska belongs to the Tlingit Indians, whose rich culture with its pattern of a privileged nobility, slavery, warfare, elaborate festival and potlatch, and its highly stylized art, has permeated and remolded the culture of the primitive Athabaskan Indian and the peaceful Eskimo. Cook Inlet is at the crossing place of these several cultural influences, and Kachemak Bay is its finest and most

(14)

sheltered arm. Yukon Island, where we are digging now, is the strategic point in the bay.

Here, on a narrow shingle bar, five villages have been built, one above the other, and now all but the last, a tin-can Indian settlement of fifty years ago, have been buried under the beach by the sinking land. All that remains of the older villages is the vast kitchen-midden of rotted shells, built up from God knows how many clam and mussel bakes and over how long a period of time, into the twelve-foot pile through which we are slowly scraping our way. The layers, alternately striped white or black with strata of shells or charcoal, show where houses and graves were dug. It has been our fortune to find many human remains, some scattered among the animal bones, some decently buried with a little cache of grave goods, and others piled in horrid confusion in a little hole, the teeth missing, the limbs partially dismembered, and the bones marked by the stone knife with which the flesh was cut from them and the brain scooped out. The fragile skulls have always been crushed in by the weight of earth, and I would gladly trade the lot for one perfect skull that might tell us with certainty who were these first inhabitants. That the Athabaskan Indians who live here now are but recent immigrants is evident from the archaeological evidence, and their culture still bears the deep imprint of their former life in the interior, but partially modified by what they have learned of the sea from the Eskimo who lived here before them. The culture of these earlier inhabitants was a rich mixture of both Eskimo and Indian, showing contact with the peoples of Arctic America and Siberia, southern British Columbia, and even Neolithic Japan. Perhaps it will be impossible to discover exactly who were the first comers; it may be that the line between Eskimo and Indian can not be drawn sharply after all, and the whole problem needs refomulation. This is a pioneer field and we are only beginning the exploration. Probably ours will not be the great rewards. Some day, however, the archaeologist will stumble here upon the trail of the first Americans, who pressed south along the west coast from Bering Strait.

A quotation from a letter of a slightly later date follows:

"We have found quite a lot of good stuff, but, to my mind, the most interesting thing we have done is the copying of cave paintings. These are the first Eskimo rock paintings I have ever heard of. They are on over-hanging rocks, in most lonely places. These shelters are said to have been used by the whalers in pre-historic times. These whale-killers were medicine men of a very special kind. They used to steal human bodies to make poison of the fat for their lances. After a body had been dismembered and the fat cooked from the bones in a secret rite, the bones had to be kept and fed as if they were alive, otherwise the skeleton would go after the whaler and eat him. Sometimes part of the body was kept for a charm. Some of the bodies were mummified and preserved in caves. The natives suggested that these paintings were made by the whalers as part of their magic ritual, but since none of the Indians here today know much about the old Eskimo, one can't be sure. The painting are made in red silhouette, and are so badly weathered that it is difficult to trace them. They represent whales, bears, seals, birds, men in kayaks and in larger skin boats. Other figures are just blobs, others conventional symbols it is impossible to interpret. Some of the representations may be half human, half animal. We had a very hard time to find these caves. In no case did we have a guide, but had to go to the caves by report alone, and, of course, they were in the most out-of-the-way spots."

CAMPUS NOTES

By JANET MARSHALL, 1933

The week before College ended for the Christmas vacation, Varsity Dramatics presented the fall three-act play, which was, this year, *The Royal Family*, by George Kaufmann and Edna Ferber. The production was a difficult one from the point of view of staging and direction, and not an easy one from the point of view of acting. The staging was most successful, despite the difficulties of creating a stage large enough for the requisite number of people in the crowded scenes without making it look more like the Grand Central Terminal than a New York apartment, and of building a balcony six feet from the floor, a very firm set of stairs leading up to it, and an off-stage balcony firm and wide enough to hold some twelve or thirteen characters at one time. Lois Thurston, of the Class of 1931, came back to College for the week preceding the play and assisted in the building of the set, her experience with the set of the *Constant Nymph* being excellent preparation for the problem of that for *The Royal Family*. The direction problem, which has been a great one in the last few years, found a happy solution, this time in the selection of Mrs. William Flexner (Magdalene Hupfel, '28) as director. Mrs. Flexner was active in Dramatics in her college years and is living on the campus now; all in all, she seems to have been the perfect solution to the question of professional or student direction. Varsity Dramatics hopes to be able to train some competent directors through the one-acts, which are still to be student-directed, but the general verdict at present seems to be that, so long as a person like Mrs. Flexner is available and interested, the productions will benefit more by her services than the students would by the experience of directing themselves.

The play as a whole was fairly successful. It was extremely well received by excellent audiences two nights in Bryn Mawr, and one night in Atlantic City, where it was taken at the very beginning of Christmas vacation. The greatest criticism of it seems to be that Dramatics is missing unparalleled opportunities for real experimental work in turning every year to second-hand Broadway productions for its big plays. The one-act plays done by the Players' Club have shown a tendency to do more unusual things, and many people were disappointed when the choice of the big play was so conventional. There is, however, a division among those who criticize the choice, as to whether it was too difficult or too easy a play. It will be interesting to observe in the next choice what the verdict of those who worked on the production is. It may be that Ibsen or Chekov or Maeterlinck will appear on the Goodhart stage before the year is out.

Just before the vacation broke the thread of campus activities, an important question was brought up for discussion in the Athletic Board's meetings, and, unusually enough, caught the interest and attention of a large part of the campus. It is the old question of required athletics as against competitive sports. There is a rumor which has struck terror to many hearts that, due to the lack of interest in general health-care and exercise in particular, the powers-that-be are meditating the institution of required athletics in one form or another four hours a week for all four undergraduate years. There is no doubt that such a step would meet with tremendous opposition from the student body, but there is a surprisingly large number of individual students who may be heard declaiming loudly that they think it would be an excellent idea. The idea is, that while they object to being pushed into anything or required to attend any extra classes, they admit freely that they are in sad need of a little regular outdoor exercise.

The Athletic Board made a valiant attempt to gather student opinion so that they might attempt to find a solution which would allow more individual freedom. Some thought, and still think, that the encouragement of competitive sports, either through the creation of a number of teams in each sport, with a winning place on Varsity held out as an inducement, or the institution of a series of awards and trophies for individual sports like tennis and swimming, or even the renewal of the old emphasis on class competition might stimulate enthusiasm. Others, the athletic faculty included, feel that this type of synthetic stimulation lost its great effect at the end of prep school days and has no place in a college program. They also doubt that the most advantageous forms of exercise and sport would profit most under such a system, and feel that there is too great a tendency to place the emphasis on certain undesirable aspects of sports when competition is over-stressed. It is on a principle of discouraging the competitive aspects of sports that the athletic faculty is working at the moment, and it is an interesting commentary that the most popular athletic activity in College now, the class in natural dancing, is one in which competition is at a minimum. If the undergraduates can work out their own salvation in this matter, much credit will be due them, because it is a difficult job to make any large group of individualists want to do anything all together and at the same time.

THE ALUMNAE BOOK SHELF

TOWER WINDOW, by *Mary Owen Lewis*. David McKay Co., Philadelphia. $1.50.

Mary Owen Lewis, 1908, has done an interesting volume of verse in "Tower Window," and has written with nice feeling and subtlety of the variety of subjects passing before the pane of glass that is in reality the poet's eye. With sensitive appreciation she has described impressions brief as they are sharp, and has set down with genuine freshness of observation many visual experiences. It is safe to prophesy that Miss Lewis is a lover of the rain, for she is at her best when writing of it. *Morning Rain* and *Wet Summer Night* convey fully her delight in the sight and sound of rain-fall. She is less happy when describing urban subjects. *Game of Titans*, while suggested, is too crowded with images, and *Underground Rhythm* suffers likewise from a too general meaning.

In *Narcisse*, on the other hand, Miss Lewis is at her best, and many of her poems, *Facing on the South*, have rich color and reality. In her quintets, tankas and hokkus she is always imaginative and able to utter the one phrase that suggests the many unsaid. *Window Arrangement in Color* is quoted for its economy and success:

> "Negress with your hands
> Dropped at rest beside a vase
> Of fading tulips,
> How your deep enduring eyes
> Recreate the years of pain."

CLASS NOTES

Ph.D. and Graduate Notes

Editor: MARY ALICE HANNA PARRISH
(Mrs. J. C. Parrish)
Vandalia, Missouri.

Lily R. Taylor, Ph.D. 1912, head of the Latin Department of Bryn Mawr, has been appointed Annual Professor of the School of Classical Studies at the American Academy in Rome for the year 1934-35. According to the Trustees of the Academy, "Miss Taylor's appointment is particularly notable because she is the first woman upon whom the honor has ever been conferred."

In the Syracuse, N. Y., newspapers of December 29th appeared a large picture of Mary Swindler, Ph.D. 1912, Professor of Classical Archaeology at Bryn Mawr, with the caption, "Eminent Scholar Attends Meeting of Archaeological Institute of America." Four small pictures of male archaeologists were also shown.

At the meetings of the Modern Language Association of America, held in New Haven December 29-31, Florence Whyte, Ph.D., Instructor in Spanish at Mount Holyoke College, read a paper entitled "Charles V. and the Dance of Death."

At another section of these meetings, Grace Frank, Associate Professor of Romance Philology at Bryn Mawr, read a brilliant paper on *"Aoi* in the Chanson de Roland." Mrs. Frank was elected Chairman of this section—Mediaeval Literature and Linguistics—succeeding Mr. David S. Blondheim, of Johns Hopkins, husband of Eleanor Dulles, Bryn Mawr 1917.

Edith Fishtine, who hopes to take her Ph.D. in June, is now Assistant Professor and head of the Department of Spanish at Simmons College.

Kathryn Wood has an article in the *Revue de Littérature Comparé* (July-September, 1932), entitled "The French Theatre in the XVIIIth Century, According to Some Contemporary English Travellers."

1889

No Editor appointed.

1890

No Editor appointed.

1891

No Editor appointed.

1892

Class Editor: EDITH WETHERILL IVES
(Mrs. Frederick M. Ives)
145 E. 35th St., New York City.

1893

Class Editor: S. FRANCES VAN KIRK
1333 Pine St., Philadelphia, Pa.

1894

Class Editor: ABBY BRAYTON DURFEE
(Mrs. Randall Durfee)
19 Highland Ave., Fall River, Mass.

1895

Class Editor: ELIZABETH BENT CLARK
(Mrs. Herbert Lincoln Clark)
Bryn Mawr, Pa.

1896

Class Editor: ABIGAIL C. DIMON
School of Horticulture, Ambler, Pa.

As THE BULLETIN goes to press, word has just been received of the death in Boston on January 22nd of Dr. Caroline Latimer.

Elizabeth Hopkins Johnson spent a short time in New York before going to Arizona for the winter. While she was in New York, Marion Taber, '97, gave a tea for her, and Mary Hill Swope a luncheon.

Florence King has just moved to a housekeeping apartment, 40 East 83rd St., New York. It is the first one she has had since 1917, and she hopes to remain in it.

Mary Mendinhall Mullin is spending the winter at 8 Bedford Court, Wawaset Park, Wilmington, Delaware. She took a motor trip this summer with her younger son, Arthur, during his two weeks' vacation. They passed through Scarsdale, calling upon Beth Fountain, '97. At Sandwich they spent the day with Elizabeth Wing. She writes: "Asa Wing's house is very quaint. It is where he was born and died, and is the oldest house thereabouts. Elizabeth has a very interesting collection of sandwich glass and old whale oil lamps." They then pushed on to Provincetown where they viewed the eclipse from the sand dunes "in a panoramic view over the bay and ocean and sand." On their return they drove over the Bear Mountain Bridge, which was constructed by Lucy Baird's brother, Howard.

Virginia Ragsdale writes: "Mother is frail, but holds her vigor remarkably well considering that she is nearly ninety-two. She continued until the last year or so to supervise the work on her farm, but she has now turned all responsibility over to me. So at present I am not only nurse and companion to her, but housekeeper, gardener, and farmer as well. Of course, we lead a very quiet life, varied frequently with visits from the grandchildren and great-grandchildren. The number of the latter continues to grow—it is fourteen at present. They are a source of interest and pleasure to both of us."

An Associated Press item of December 6th reports: "A group of women gathered at the home of Mrs. Gerard Swope (Mary Hill Swope) adopted today a resolution asking the recall of George S. Massersmith, consul general in Berlin, 'because of his ignorance' in the incident of Dr. Albert Einstein's visa."

Clara Colton Worthington says: "You see, I am still in Wilmington, and am now a voter in this state, but much of my heart is still in the west, as Bill, the younger boy, is married and living there. . . . After being out of any club work for years I am in it again, at least up to my waist, as I am chairman of the Public or Foreign Affairs group of the local A. A. U. W., and vice-chairman of the International Relations group in the New Century Club of Wilmington. It is an ironical sort of thing for me to be doing, for I have had much trouble with my eyes—vision and eyes O. K., but a strong photophobia which prevents my reading more than head lines. . . . I have a grand time with my A. A. U. W. group and this year started a second group off with a fine leader. It really takes the place of newspapers for me, as they do all the work and I reap the benefits."

Abba Dimon is now assistant to the Director of the Pennsylvania School of Horticulture for Women, at Ambler, Pa.

1897

Class Editor: FRIEDRIKA HEYL
104 Lake Shore Drive, East, Dunkirk, N. Y.

1898

Class Editor: EDITH SCHOFF BOERICKE
(Mrs. John Boericke)
Merion, Pa.

1899

Editor: CAROLYN TROWBRIDGE (BROWN) LEWIS
55 Park Ave., New York.

We must confess that '97 has nothing on us so far as remorse, conscience, and all that is concerned, so here's to the results of a noble example.

There'll be a real '99 reunion at the wedding, February 11th, of Dorothy Fronheiser Meredith's daughter, Catherine, to John Mason Brown. The fortunate bridegroom is the nephew of Mary and Margery Brown, of Baltimore, a graduate of Harvard, '23' formerly an instructor at Yale (that's where Dorothy's son is studying to be a medico) and is now dramatic critic of the *New York Evening Post*. Here's a community of interest, the best of foundations for a successful marriage, for Catherine, after finishing at Rosemary Hall, Greenwich, made her bow to society, and continued her studies at the American Laboratory Theatre.

Katherine Hepburn, Kate Houghton Hepburn's daughter, has made a quick ascent up the dizzy ladder of sucess, apparently just by being herself, "the something new and different" as vital to the screen as to any other industry. Fortunately the youth of today has an "idol" whom they can emulate with much benefit to themselves. Her splendid work in *A Bill of Divorcement* took the honors right out of the hands of Billie Burke and John Barrymore.

Jean Clark Fouilhoux's Anita danced the old year out and the new in while visiting her parents in New York, and then returned to Bryn Mawr for the mid-years. Alice Carter Dickerman's Honora, who is Anita's roommate, isn't returning next year, we hear, but Anita is going on to capture the elusive sheepskin.

Did you see our Guffey's name—Emma Guffey Miller—in the list of prominent Democrats suggested by the *New York Times* as members of President-elect Roosevelt's cabinet? And the rest of it—"famous as a convention orator having thrilled the Madison Square Convention, because she, of pioneer Presbyterian American stock, vigorously seconded Smith's nomination." It went on to say that she had been active for Roosevelt, also in peace movements. Emma writes she's going to Washington March 4th; if she has to go in the Ford station wagon, she'll be there.

Marion Ream Vonsiatsky leaves the 15th of this month for Arizona where she is planning to spend two months or so before joining her husband for a year of travel in the Old World. We haven't discovered whether Russia is on the itinerary.

Sibyl Hubbard Darlington was in New York for a few weeks around the holidays with her very pretty young daughter, returning to California for the New Year.

From Mollie Thurber Dennison comes the happy news that her third daughter, Mary, is engaged to David Stickney, of Cleveland. The

"Class Baby," Helen Dennison Smith, has just been chosen by Dr. Miriam VanWater to have charge of all the music at the Massachusetts Reformatory for Women. Besides her classes there five days a week she is carrying on her studies at Radcliffe. Her sister, Buff, has turned her talents to a nursery school for her two children and eight of their little friends, and she is also having much success in amateur theatricals. This prompted Mollie to add, "I almost shouted right out when I saw Katherine Hepburn; she is so much like her mother."

Percival Sax, Jr., and wife have taken a. novel way to beat the depression. They have gone to Europe to stay until it is over or until jobs become more plentiful. They have been in Germany, visiting his mother's relatives, and are now in the South of France.

1900

Class Editor: LOUISE CONGDON FRANCIS
(Mrs. Richard S. Francis)
414 Old Lancaster Rd., Haverford, Pa.

1901

Class Editor: HELEN CONVERSE THORPE
(Mrs. Warren Thorpe)
15 East 64th St., New York City.

1902

Class Editor: ANNE ROTAN HOWE
(Mrs. Thorndike Howe)
77 Revere St., Boston, Mass.

1903

Class Editor: GERTRUDE DIETRICH SMITH
(Mrs. Herbert Knox Smith)
Farmington, Conn.

The class extends its sympathy to Dorothea Day Watkins, whose husband died quite suddenly of heart failure in December.

Martha R. White is spending the winter in Santa Fé, New Mexico.

Gertrude Dietrich Smith has been elected a member of the Connecticut General Assembly, to represent the town of Farmington. She spent the Christmas holidays in Santa Fé with Margretta Stewart Dietrich.

1904

Class Editor: EMMA O. THOMPSON
320 S. 42nd St., Philadelphia, Pa.

The class is distinguished this year with three daughters in the Freshman class—Sara Palmer Baxter's daughter, Barbara; Eleanor McCormick Fabyan's daughter, Eleanor, and Hope Woods Hunt's daughter, Sophie Lee.

Sadie Briggs Logan's daughter, Constance, is at the Northampton School for Girls, doing excellent work and devoted to the school. Sadie and her husband have moved from the big city house to a cozy two-floor apartment at 152 Russell Street, Worcester, overlooking a beautiful park. Sadie writes that she enjoys the apartment immensely.

Bertha Brown Lambert sends word that her address for 1932-33 is 1090 Funa, Funabashi, Tokio-fulsa, Japan.

Daisy Ullman says that it was a great pleasure to have the Council meet in the mid-west, and most interesting to see people at the big meetings whom they have not seen for many years. Daisy entertained four of the class at a luncheon at Winnetka: Eloise Tremain, Evelyn Holiday Patterson, and Alice Shiedt Clark.

Buz (Anne Palmer Lloyd) returned just before Christmas from a month's trip to California. She spent some time at Hollywood and found it very satisfactory. Her daughter, Nancy Palmer, is a Sophomore at the University of Wisconsin.

1905

Class Editor: ELEANOR LITTLE ALDRICH
(Mrs. Talbot Aldrich)
59 Mt. Vernon St., Boston, Mass.

Elma Loines sailed for Florida just before Christmas. She and her mother will be at the Virginia Inn, Winter Park, for three months, or so. The husband of Elma's niece teaches at Rollins College, and various relatives are there fore-gathered. She "hopes to get in much reading, a little writing, and some star gazing."

Rachel Brewer Huntington's address is now 38 Kildeer Road, Hamden, Connecticut. She says they came home from their European trip to find the name of the street changed and the post office transferred—the easiest moving she ever did!

1906

Class Editor: LOUISE CRUICE STURDEVANT
(Mrs. Edward W. Sturdevant)
3006 P Street, Washington, D. C.

1907

Class Editor: ALICE HAWKINS
Taylor Hall, Bryn Mawr, Pa.

Esther Williams Apthorp's new address is 226 Center Street, Milton, Mass. Her two boys are attending Milton Academy.

Also at Milton are two others of interest to 1907. This item was gleaned from an interesting letter from Dorothy Forster Miller: "My eldest boy is a Freshman at Harvard this year—got in very well, with honors in three out of four subjects (New Plan) and highest honors in one out of the three. There were 51 in Bleecker's class at Milton and 48 went to Harvard. He was slated for Yale, but you can understand why he changed. Our second boy, Henry, is still at Milton—in Edward Barnes' class, and they are good friends, which is quite amusing. Susan is at the Brearley." Dorothy goes on to boast of her own recently discovered prowess as a cook, assisted by Susan, "an angel of goodness and efficiency." The results of this combination are so enthusiastically admired by her husband and sons that she fears she may never escape.

Mary Tudor Gray, after many years in California, has now returned to New England to live. Her address is 20 Highland Road, Cambridge, Mass.

Grace Hutchins is still in New York. She is a Research Worker for the Labor Research Association.

Blanche Hecht is doing volunteer work at the Polyclinic Hospital in New York, in the Neurological Clinic. She helps also at the Heckscher Foundation.

In *Shorter Modern Poems, 1900-1931,* compiled by David Morton, published by Harper, is a poem by Hortense Flexner King entitled *Return from Captivity.*

Esther Reinhardt is head of the English Department at the Olney High School, Philadelphia.

1908

Class Editor: HELEN CADBURY BUSH
Haverford, Pa.

Virginia McKenney Claiborne went to the Council meeting in Chicago in November in her capacity of Alumnae Director. She also spoke for the Academic Committee.

The David McKay Co. has published a new book of poems by Mary Owen Lewis called *Tower Window* (see page 17). These poems have appeared in many periodicals, but it is interesting to have them collected into book form. Mayone is a spirited lecturer as well as a poetess.

Nellie M. Seeds writes: "I am taking a year off and trying to write up into some kind of organic form the educational material that I have been collecting during the five years that I was directing the Manumit School. My son, John, has gone to Russia to do structural steelwork in the big new plant at Magnitogorsk, in the Urals."

Jacqueline Morris Evans writes: "My two oldest sons (19 and 17) took part last summer in an interesting and worth-while experiment in promoting international friendship. Under the leadership of Dr. Kenneth Appel, of the Institute of the Pennsylvania Hospital, and Mr. Donald B. Watt, formerly of Syracuse University, they spent six weeks with a group of about 20 American boys in a camp at Valangin, Switzerland. Here they worked and played with a group of French and German boys. Some time each day was spent on language work, and lively discussions of international questions were held; also opportunity was given to each boy to develop any special hobby that appealed to him. Two boys, for example, took butterfly nets with them and caught some rare specimens on their trips. Some delightful hikes, lasting several days at a time, were arranged over the mountain passes. The simple, wholesome out-of-doors life together was the beginning of what I hope will prove to be some lasting friendships. The group reached Velangin by way of France and came home through Germany, first by the Black Forest, then in canoes down the Neckar, with Heidelberg students, and finally with a visit to Hildesheim before sailing home from Hamburg."

It is interesting that next summer girls are to be included in the group.

1909

Class Editor: HELEN B. CRANE
70 Willett St., Albany, N. Y.

1910

Class Editor: KATHERINE ROTAN DRINKER
(Mrs. Cecil Drinker)
71 Rawson Rd., Brookline, Mass.

1911

Class Editor: ELIZABETH TAYLOR RUSSELL
(Mrs. John F. Russell, Jr.)
333 E. 68th St., New York City.

May Egan Stokes, to quote her note, "is taking a very small graduate course at the University of Pennsylvania this winter in Mediaeval French, keeping my hand in until I can gird my loins for another B.M. Seminar."

Lois Lehman spent last summer in Vichy and Paris, but has returned to Geneva.

Florence Wyman Tripp is living at 125 E. 72nd St. this winter. She is singing at the Town Hall in the Adesdi Chorus. Her children are Peter, aged 12; Jean, 18, and Kathleen, 19, who is studying sculpture at the American Academy of Design.

Margery Hoffman Smith is making a tour of the East on behalf of the Portland Art Museum, of which she is a trustee. This fall she costumed the Junior League production of the "Golden Goose," and taught a class in practical problems of interior decorating, specializing in lacquering glass.

Dorothy Coffin Greeley helped produce the show given this fall by the Winnetka Puppeteers. She has four children, two girls and two boys, and is very interested in child psychology, in theory and (we suspect) in practice. Her oldest son is a Freshman at Harvard, and won his numerals for playing in the Harvard-Yale freshman game.

Helen Parkhurst has returned from her Sabbatical to New York and to Barnard as associate professor. She addressed the meeting of Philosophical Association held at B. M. in the Christmas vacation.

Jeanette Allen Andrews reports that horses are still her "hobby," although she did "solo" in a plane last spring. She has a daughter, Josephine, aged 18, a son, Allen, 15, and another daughter, Jean, 9.

Margaret Hobart Myers is teaching her own four children and four others this winter. She lectured on religious drama at the Sewanee Summer School and "staged a lovely out-of-doors pageant, with a cast of sixty people, including lots of bishops, deans, canons, and lesser clergy." This winter she is continuing her courses in drama at the Theological School, but was able to leave all these activities for a week's motor trip through Mississippi in November.

Margaret Prussing Le Vino has sold a story to M-G-M, in which she confidently hopes that Greta Garbo will appear as "Christina of Sweden."

1912

Class Editor: GLADYS SPRY AUGUR
(Mrs. Wheaton Augur)
820 Camino Atalaya, Santa Fé, N. Mex.

1913

Class Editor: HELEN EVANS LEWIS
(Mrs. Robert M. Lewis)
52 Trumbull St., New Haven, Conn.

TWENTIETH REUNION

Have you got anything on four wheels that will go? Get it out and give it a preliminary run or two, and promise it a trip to Bryn Mawr in June. If your family asks you what makes you think the old thing will go, tell them it *has* to, because you are going to your 20th reunion. If they look at you and say, "Oh, mother, how old you must be!" spank them, and put them to bed. Deal in like summary manner with any obstacles which may be offered by a job or lack of a job, and begin brushing up on "Cocky-Hockey Basketball."
Dates: June 10th to 13th.
Reunion manager: Elsie Maguire, 3813 Spruce St., Philadelphia, Pa.

There will be no special costume, and all expenses will be cut to a minimum, as befits this brave new world.
Further details will follow, but don't wait for them to make up your mind. Make it up now and come.

KATHARINE PAGE LORING.

1914

Class Editor: ELIZABETH AYER INCHES
(Mrs. Henderson Inches)
41 Middlesex Rd., Chesnut Hill, Mass.

REUNION

Remember that we have a reunion this year. Class supper is on June 10th, commencement on June 13th. Headquarters is in Pembroke West. Come early and stay late!

1915

Class Editor: MARGARET FREE STONE
(Mrs. Janes Austin Stone)
3039 44th St., Washington, D. C.

Mildred Justice lost her father early in November, after a short illness.

Mildred Jacobs Coward and her husband spent ten days visiting friends in Florida in December.

Eleanor Freer Karcher writes: "Home, husband and offspring take up all my time. However, as aftermath of all my choir training I have three musical children: Freer, the eldest, plays the banjo, Barbara the piano, and Archie the violin. We make a grand noise when we get started."

REUNION

This is to remind you that Reunion is coming from Friday, June 9th, to Tuesday, June 13th, Commencement Day. Rock has been reserved for us to sleep, meet talk and eat in. Please plan ahead to come if you possibly can, as we seldom see Bryn Mawr and one another, and it is such fun when we do. Full details will follow later. Best wishes to you all.

KITTY McCOLLIN ARNETT.

1916

Class Editor: LARIE KLEIN BOAS
(Mrs. Benjamin Boas)
2736 Broderick St., San Francisco, Cal.

1917

Class Editor: BERTHA CLARK GREENOUGH
203 Blackstone Blvd., Providence, R. I.

Mildred Willard Gardiner writes that she is enjoying a happy, busy, "middle-aged" existence. Her son, Jeffy, is "a big boy, almost 4, already in his second year of school. It seems funny to think of two more years before he *starts first* grade! I never stepped inside a school until I was 9. I'm still faithful to my old interests—psychology and tennis, but the former is decidedly in the lead now as the pounds and years accumulate."

Elizabeth Emerson Gardner returned with her husband from Europe in time for Christmas with their children.

Since the last BULLETIN we have learned more of the work which Virginia Litchfield Clark has been doing since college, and have been tremendously impressed by the versatility of it. From the Italians she had studied *jesso* and had made perfectly lovely boxes. She had recently developed the art of wood-block cut: ting and had done illustrations for an anthology of California poems and stories, also for a book on California homes and gardens, put out in a set on California by the Powell Publishing Co., of Los Angeles. She had also worked in the Japanese print technique. Her embroidery was very beautiful, for she had studied stitches from Elizabethan embroideries, ancient tapestries, and other sources. Recently she had been adapting these stitches to designs of her own, expressing the California landscape feeling. The summer before she was married she spent at the bottom of the Grand Canyon, where she did a series of beautiful water-colors of the rocks and river. It was while there that she met Owen Clark, whom she later married, and it was there that the first months of her married life were spent. The friend at Scripps College, to whom we are indebted for this information, also tells us that Ginger had hoped to develop the western feeling even more in her art under the influence of the grandeur of the southwestern scenery. At the time of her death they were building a house on a grape-fruit ranch in Yuma, which her husband owned.

Ginger was a joyous person, brimful of vitality, who made warm friends wherever she went. Her artistic appreciation of all beauty made her a grand companion, and her spirit is one that does not die.

1918

Class Editor: MARGARET BACON CAREY
(Mrs. Henry R. Carey)
3115 Queen Lane, East Falls, Philadelphia.

As announced last month, Helen Walker has felt it necessary to give up her job as Class Secretary, and Charlotte Dodge Devine and I regretfully accepted her resignation. From the throng of eager applicants for the position we have selected Peg Bacon to hold the fort until our next class meeting. We hope you will all encourage Peg by writing her at once

lots of unsolicited news. See her address above.

We seem to be afflicted with an epidemic of resignations. Charlotte has gone and done it, too. If there were any one left for me to resign to, I'd feel like following the example of the rest of the class officers, but I didn't think quick enough. I told Charlotte that I didn't believe the class would know what to do without her, since she has held some official position ever since our freshman year. But she was adamant, and refuses to stay longer than to help me choose her successor. We hope to announce that appointment in the next BULLETIN.

RUTH CHENEY STREETER.

1919

Class Editor: MARJORIE REMINGTON TWITCHELL
(Mrs. P. E. Twitchell)
Setawket, N. Y.

Helen Tappan was married on the 3rd of December to Mr. Walter Thrall Sheldon, in New York. Mr. Sheldon is a brother of Harriet Sheldon, 1914. Helen is living at 333 E. 53rd Street, New York.

Marj. Martin Johnson writes that after twelve years in Canada they are now settled, temporarily at least, in Allenwood, Plainfield, Vt. All the family but the two youngest ride horseback. Vermont rural schools are famous for their excellence; so Marj. is for the first time satisfied with the children's schooling. She is active in the Little Theatre there, and says the change from city life is a very welcome one. "Feeny (J. Peabody) visited me this summer. She is president of the New Haven Junior League. Helen Huntting Fulton I saw a lot of in Montreal. She is back in Minneapolis now after a thyroid operation at the Mayo's. Franny Day Lukens and her lively children called."

Angela Moore Place has her daughter in Miss Chapin's School, in New York, her older boy at Lawrence Smith School, and the baby at the Dalton School. Angela says she does not care for co-education. Georgia Bailey Seelye and her two children spent a week with Angela in the summer. Betty Dabney Baker has a farm in Millbrook, too, in the summer.

Faf. Branson Keller's daughter is in the Shipley School.

A classmate's trip in an aeroplane still seems notable enough to mention. Buster Ramsey Phelps flew to Boston for a week-end last year.

Helen Karns Champlin's husband was exchange professor the first semester this year at the University of Puerto Rico. Helen herself taught General and Educational Psychology in the university to teachers in service. Carolyn was at school at Santurce, a few miles away. Helen writes: "The San Ciprian hurricane was a terrific experience. . . . Our roof was the only one in the immediate neighborhood that stayed completely on, and at times during the frightful night it seemed as though the house . . . would certainly give way before the violence of the 130-mile gale. Then we were days without water, and weeks without electricity. . . . Our experiences . . . are proving valuable and interesting, but we shall be glad to return next month to a cold and vigorous North. . . . We expect at present to take our car from here to Santiago de Cuba, drive the length of Cuba to Havana, cross to Key West, spend some time in Florida . . . and then drive North to Penn State College for the second semester."

1920

Class Editor: MARY PORRITT GREEN
(Mrs. Valentine J. Green)
433 E. 51st St., New York City.

From Miriam O'Brien comes the following: "Yes, I am going to be married on January 27th to Robert Lindley Murray Underhill, of Ossining, N. Y., A.B. from Haverford and Ph.D. from Harvard. (Then I shall be a cousin of Dorothy Griggs Murray.) We expect to live at 130 Warren St., Newton Center, Mass. Yes, indeed, Bob is a mountain climber, and has done a great deal, both in the Alps and in the west here. He has made a lot of first ascents, which means climbing peaks that have never been climbed before.

"And here is some more news: We have a nice little luncheon club here in Boston of Martha Lindsey, Martha Chase, Isabel Arnold Blodgett, Dorothy Griggs Murray, Mary Hoag Lawrence, Mad Brown, and me. We eat together at our different homes every few weeks. Martha Lindsey has a grand job, being the head of Hathaway House of the Milton Academy Girls' School—she chaperones the girls to dances and to church, does the marketing and just everything. It's most impressive. The other day in the market she said to the clerk: 'I'll take two of those little squashes there.' 'Madam,' said he, 'those are Casaba melons.'"

Isabel has a new daughter, Katharine Blodgett, born July 4th.

Martha Chase is giving a course on old silver at Miss Sackett's School of Interior Decorating, where she graduated. She also lectures on old glass, etc., and is most learned.

Marguerite Eilers Beer sent us an announcement of the birth of her son, Andrew Eilers Beer, on November 15th, 1932.

In the *New York Tribune* of December 3rd we saw a picture of Polly Chase Boyden (and eight others) labeled: "Failed to See President in Behalf of Hunger Marchers," and, quoting from the paper, "A group of socially prominent women from New York City and elsewhere, who came here as private citizens to assert the 'constitutional rights of the hunger marchers.'"

Millicent Carey McIntosh was elected a life trustee of Bryn Mawr College at the quarterly meeting of the directors and trustees held on December 15th.

1921

Class Editor: WINIFRED WORCESTER
(Mrs. Harvey Stevenson)
Croton-on-Hudson, N. Y.

Eleanor Collins was married on June 25th to Mr. Charles J. Darlington. He graduated from Swarthmore in 1915 and is a chemical engineer in the du Pont plant at Deepwater Point, N. J. They are living in Woodstown, N. J., where Eleanor has a young people's discussion group and has started a children's club.

1922

Class Editor: SERENA HAND SAVAGE
(Mrs. William L. Savage)
106 E. 35th St., New York City.

1923

Class Editor: RUTH MCANENY LOUD
325 E. 72nd St., New York City.

Louise Affelder Davidove wrote from Paris at Christmas time saying that she and her husband had just completed another six months' study trip through Russia and Central Europe. They expect to be at home again by the beginning of February.

Irene Lemon is again teaching History and Social Studies at Horace Mann, in New York.

Nancy FitzGerald still has her job in the Brookline Public Library; this is her third year there. In the January BULLETIN you read Delphine Darby's review of Nancy's *Guariento Di Arpo*, apparently a very excellent and scholarly monograph on the Italian painter. Her amazing varsatility has now produced the new *Schnauzer Book*, the most complete work to date on that breed, some one hundred pages, with copious illustrations. "It really was fun to do, though an appalling job, as it was like pulling teeth to get some of the material." In addition to being their Boswell, she has been Secretary of the Schnauzer Club of America for the past year.

Lucy Kate Blanchard has also "gone to the dogs," Nancy writes. She is raising pointers and English setters, which her husband trains for shooting and field trials, and which her twins are learning to handle.

1924

Class Editor: DOROTHY GARDNER BUTTERWORTH
(Mrs. J. Ebert Butterworth)
8024 Roanoke St., Chestnut Hill, Pa.

Eloise Requa, who is in charge of the Library of International Relations in Chicago, writes that she travelled all last summer, visiting Harriot Hopkinson, Carrie Remak, Bee Pitney Lamb, Irene Wallace Vogel, and the Institute of Politics at Williamstown. She says that the Council meeting in Chicago was great fun, that Miss Park's tales of College were wonderful, and everyone enjoyed seeing Miss Park and Mrs. Collins.

A note from Margaret Dunham informs us that she was married, May 1st, 1929, to John Tileston Edsall, and has lived ever since in Cambridge. Her son, Lawrence, born June 6th, 1930, has a mop of brown curls, dark blue eyes, and is wildly enthusiastic over everything. Margaret went to Europe on her wedding trip, but has not travelled since. She spends her summers on a farm in Vermont, gardening and enjoying other country pleasures. Her spare time is occupied with reading, going to concerts, and enjoying the companionship of many friends.

It is pleasant to hear from those who spent only freshman year with us, but haven't forgotten old friends.

Elizabeth Rust was married, May 23rd, 1925, to Stanley Nöel Brown. Her main items of interest are Henry B. R. Brown, aged 7; Stanley, Jr., aged 5, and Fitzhugh, born May 12th, 1932. Elizabeth and her family of boys live in Pittsburgh.

One of the most charming and unexpected replies came from Blanche McRae. Blanche came to college freshman year from far-off Vancouver. The next year she stayed home and was married to Richard Plunkett Baker. She has two daughters, Jocelyn, almost 10, and Audrey, aged 8. She says that every time she thinks about it they make her feel at least 105. At present Blanche is President of the Vancouver Junior League, which takes a tremendous amount of time, otherwise her great occupation is golf. Her trips last year were in the interests of the Junior League. At the conference in Los Angeles she caught a glimpse of Jean Palmer. Two years ago the Bakers visited Paris and Vienna. Blanche expects to be greyheaded before she takes another trip like it.

No world flights, deep sea diving, or even a divorce—to enliven our column—are being planned by Pamela Coyne Taylor. She no longer has a regular job, but is fully occupied in the home, especially on rainy days, with Pamela, born August 12th, 1930, and Emily Newbold, born May 14th, 1932.

1925

Class Editor: ELIZABETH MALLETT CONGER
(Mrs. Frederic Conger)
325 E. 72nd St., New York City.

Because we haven't written anything for two months, you doubtless think we don't know any news. You probably say to yourself, "Poor thing—such a very sheltered life!" As a matter of fact, we're practically omniscient. We know, for instance, that Tommy Tomkins Villard had a little daughter, Mariquita Serrano Villard III, on December 16th (and by telephone we can talk about this for hours—Butterfield 8-4061). But Tommy isn't in our class. And we know that Bobby Loines Dreier had a son, Marc Russell, early in December—our second grand nephew—and we have lots of information about his charms, but Bobby doesn't belong in our class. We know, too, that Helen Hill Miller had a son, Andrew Pickens Miller, on December 21st, but Helen isn't in our class either.

Now you know how it is. We do get about after all; in fact we ride on the bus twice a day. But unless we get the jump on all the other editors, we just can't publish at all.

Our own latest scoop is Adele Pantzer's marriage a year ago. Dady was married in the Little Church Around the Corner, last January, to Mr. J. Schurz Westendarp, and is now living at 1334 Riverside Drive, New York. Telephone: Wadsworth 3-4004.

We beat this information out of Carrie Remak by sheer blackmail. Carrie, by the way, has a puppy, but we can't mention him because we feel the BULLETIN is cold to puppies. It frowns even on picket fences.

Peggy Pierce Milholland had a daughter on December 10th. The Milhollands are living now at 269 S. 21st St., Philadelphia.

A life-saving post card from Baldie (E. Baldwin) tells us of Franny Briggs Leuba's young son. Roger Hamilton Leuba II. was born on November 23rd. Briggy is blooming and loves the life at Yellow Springs where Clarence teaches. Baldie finishes her internship at the Presbyterian Hospital this June.

Kay McBride received her Ph.D. at Bryn Mawr last June, and her thesis was about the psychology of aphasia—at least we think it was. Kathy is going on with her work on aphasia in Philadelphia this winter.

Mary Lytle Seddon writes, in a delightful letter, than her permanent address is Moor House, Stanmore, Middlesex, England. She saw Kay Fowler Lunn several times before Kay's return to Africa, and the two British husbands have become good friends. Mary writes: "I should hate to miss any of '25 who may be passing by and '25's lantern is shedding a ruddy glow through the window to welcome them."

Emily Watts Tracy had a son, Earnest B. Tracy, Jr., on January 3rd. ' ·

1926

Class Editor: HARRIOT HOPKINSON
　　Manchester, Mass.

The other day, December 22nd, to be exact, we were passing through New York, and with some slight suspicions, called up Deirdre O'Shea Carr. The voice that answered was not Deirdre's, but her rather sleepy husband's, who announced, not without pride, that Deirdre had that very night presented the world with a son, weight seven and a half pounds! Both doing well, and young Mr. Carr very handsome.

Not that this is the only recent baby for the class—Miss Mariquita Villard appeared on December 16th to join her parents; Mrs. Villard being the former Tommy Tomkins, to whom we offer our most joyful felicitations.

Betty Burroughs is taking a year off from teaching school in Washington. This year she is going on with her painting, which she has studied before in the summers, and is working now at the Grand Central School, in connection with the Grand Central Galleries, in New York.

Jean Loeb Whitehill is extremely busy in Philadelphia. She is Executive Secretary of the Maternal Health Centre, and spends almost all her time working at and for the clinic, which proves intensely interesting. Also, the Whitehills have moved, and are now living at 1414 Spruce Street.

Delia Johnston is now teaching at the Shipley School, and while her husband is abroad is living at 408 Berkeley Road, Haverford.

We saw Angela Boyden while we were in Chicago. She is living in Lake Forest, and while she comes in town for current events lectures and concerts, she *says* she feels very countrified. If true, it seems to agree with her.

H. Hopkinson, although still affiliated with the Library of International Relations in Chicago, is leaving it for a few months and is going to Egypt, sailing the middle of January. But for goodness' sake, don't let this discourage you all from sending news about yourselves for the BULLETIN. What *has* been discouraging you lately, by the way?

We have a couple of engagements to announce this month, so let's begin with them right away. Rex FitzGerald is going to marry Walter Beckman Pedersen, of Long Island. He will graduate next June from the Harvard Divinity School, and plans to enter the Unitarian ministry. Rex, as we doubtless have mentioned ere now in these columns, got her Ph.D. in Vienna last year.

The other is Via Saunders; be big-minded about this, '25, and let *us* announce that the end of January she is marrying James Agee. He is a poet, and on the staff of *Fortune*, working under Archibald MacLeish. Via herself has been working on *Symposium*, and, of course you all know what this is. They'll live in New York.

Franny Jay has got herself an apartment all by herself, on East End Avenue. She cooks beautifully in her kitchen, and also spends time in a green-house. This is because she is taking a course in Horticulture at Columbia, preparatory to gardening again next summer in the country.

Winnie Dodd is teaching again this year at Brearley.

Folly von Erffa and her husband have moved to 50 Trowbridge Street, Cambridge. They spent the summer abroad, visiting Folly's new German in-laws, and now that they are back, she is continuing work on her Bible research, which is to lead to another publication in the not distant future. In so far as the casual observer can comprehend, she is separating one strand · of the Old Testament from all the others, according to author and date, and will thus produce a small and unmixed version.

1927

Class Editor: ELLENOR MORRIS
　　Berwyn, Penna.

On December 27th Elizabeth Norton was married to Mr. William Potter, in Cambridge, Mass. Nortie still has her job in the History of Art Department, and until the Christmas holidays was living in Low Buildings. She and her husband, who is an architect, have an apartment at Bryn Mawr Gables.

1928

Class Editor: CORNELIA B. ROSE, JR.
　　424 E. 52nd St., New York City.

The class wishes to extend its sympathy to Ruth Elting, ex-'28, one of whose brothers died at Christmas time as the result of an appendicitis operation.

Well, here we are back again. And first of all, we want heartily to thank Alice Bruère Lounsbury for carrying on so manfully what is, as we know better than anyone, a very tough job. In fact, her November budget was so good that we felt we could rest on her laurels awhile.

Preparatory to our taking up the keys of office again, we wish to make a plea that you all co-operate in sending in news.

Maly Hopkinson Gibbon supplies the name of Betty Brown Field's daughter, born last February, Leila, and she also tells us that

Cal Crosby Field has a daughter, born last April. Allie Talcott Enders has a son, Tom, born November a year ago. Maly adds not a word about herself.

Louise Gucker was married the 15th of last June to Mr. Robert Alan Page, and is now living in New York City, at 111 E. 10th St. They spent the summer in New England. Recently Louise saw Diza Steck in Philadelphia. She is still teaching Math and Science at the Agnes Irwin School.

Bertha Alling Brown says that her present occupation other than housekeeping and feeding the husband and dog is being an off-stage noise in the Junior League play and revising a list of 5000 for invitations for the Arden Shore Charity Ball.

Jo Young Case, whose daughter, Josephine Edmonds Case, was born on October 10th and reported in the last notes, is now living in Plainfield, N. J. All the news we have of Barby Loines Dreier comes from her Christmas card. But since is was mailed in Winter Park we presume that she did not come up for the holidays, and that her second son, Mark Russell Dreier, whose name was on the card, was born in Florida.

Your editor contacted with very few Bryn Mawrters while abroad—surprisingly few considering the number known to be there. Of our own classmates, we saw only Frances Bethel Rowan in Berlin, whom Liz Bethel and her mother were to visit just after we left Berlin in September, and Ruth Elting, who returned on the same boat after a summer spent with Martha Gellhorn, ex-'30, in Spain and southern France. We tried to see the Countess Eleanor Davico (Eleanor Speiden) while at Lake Como, but found that she had just left for the United States. Did anyone see her while she was here?

After our return we fleeted through Philadelphia and Bryn Mawr and saw that Pol Pettit was growing fat and rosy over her hospital work; that Maud Hupfel Flexner was comfortably established in Dr. Huff's old house on Faculty Row, and learned that she was to take a hand in coaching Varsity Dramatics this winter; discovered that the years do not change Peg Barrett at all, and that Ginny Atmore is working as hard as ever at her plum puddings. We heard a rumor, too, that Betty Stewart is working in Cambridge in a book store.

One of the surprises we received on our return to this country was the discovery of the meteoric rise of Kate Hepburn Smith. We have been showered with the amusing publicity that is appearing about her in the papers and the movie magazines. At present she is in Hollywood making a picture and is scheduled to take the part of Jo in a movie version of *Little Women*. Certainly all her work in *A Bill of Divorcement* was excellent, and if this keeps up, 1928 will have a place in the sun.

1929

Class Editor: MARY L. WILLIAMS
210 E. 68th St., New York City.

1930

Class Editor: EDITH GRANT
Pembroke West, Bryn Mawr, Pa.

We wish to correct an error appearing recently among these notes, with apologies to Harriet Ropes for using a bit of rumor grown inaccurate on its way to our ears. She is not working in the Fogg Museum, as we stated, but is a volunteer assistant in the Decorative Arts Department of the Museum of Fine Arts in Boston. She is also treasurer of the Volunteer Service Bureau. Harriet further informed us that she is engaged to Mr. Edward Clarke Cabot, of Boston. He has been studying geology at Harvard.

Eleanor Latané Bissell has a daughter, Marie Truesdale Bissell, born December 14th. We congratulate Eleanor on being the first graduate of 1930 to have two children.

Edith Grant is to be Assistant Warden of Pembroke second semester.

1931

Class Editor: EVELYN WAPLES BAYLESS
(Mrs. Robert N. Bayless)
New Britain, Conn.

1932

Class Editor: JOSEPHINE GRATON
182 Brattle St., Cambridge, Mass.

"Jenks" Smith writes from the Folger Library in Washington: "Washington is great fun. The job couldn't be more fun, in fact it's much more fun than job. People keep dropping in on me and Shakespeare."

Kay McClelland has "found the lure of the classroom too strong" for her, and as a result is taking a course in Accounting and Finance at the Oklahoma City University. Sally Black enrolled at the University of Illinois this fall, but left after about six weeks, visited Kay on her way to and from Texas, and on December 3rd sailed on the "Rex" to spend the winter in Italy.

A letter from Margo Reinhardt Pyle tells that her husband is a corrosion engineer for the Sun Oil Company, Wilmington. Margo is taking a business course, as are also Adele Nichols and Tommy Thomas. Ginny Speed, we have heard, is going to Palm Beach in January to study with Madame Homer. Maysie Hansen is in Los Angeles, working at present, but after

Christmas she will be job hunting—she refuses to spend her time at Secretarial School. Ellen Shaw is private secretary to the superintendent of schools of Lower Merion Township.

Elizabeth Pleasants has announced her engagement to Francis Haynes Jencks, of Baltimore.

We wish to correct our erroneous statement made in the November issue of the BULLETIN. Eleanor Stonington was said to be studying at a nursery school; in reality she is working at the University School of Nursing.

A. Hardenbergh writes from Cambridge:

"The town *is* the university and the citizens the students. They are a young and healthy-looking lot, all garbed in the universal costume of mussy grey flannels and heavy checked brown coat and scarf wound round the neck when its cold, and always the little black short gown sort of hanging back of their shoulders, as though they wished they hadn't it on. (Which they probably do.) The buildings are beautiful, every bit as nice as expectations, though I have many yet to see. Classes are held all over town, so that to get anywhere on time (and they, classes, all begin and end simultaneously) a bicycle is necessary. Hence it is much as your life's worth to try to cross the street between classes. Dolly almost had her neck broken the other day because she was thinking of something else and the cyclist didn't ring his bell. But it's fun when you're on one with the rest, and we all have them.

"Any one seems to be able to go to class with impunity, so I've gone to a couple or so every day, sampling every kind and hearing famous people like Quiller-Couch and Trevelyan that we studied once. Dolly's tutor, or whatever you call him, is very good—heard him on *Lord Jim* the other day. The classes are not so very big (about 25-50) except for some of the popular lectures, but no questions or discussions. That's all in their interviews, I guess.

"The three of us hopped on our bikes and went to Ely, where is the best cathedral I've yet seen, and came back to find the town lit up and noisy with fire crackers—Guy Fawkes Day. The whole town was abroad in the evening and the paper this a. m. says six were arrested for shooting off fire crackers too near people! We saw their methods of discipline—proctors (older men) in cap and gown walk the street all evening, flanked on either side by "bull dogs," men fleet of foot and tough of fist, in high silk hats, who run after anyone without a cap and gown and beat anyone up who is misbehaving. The procession moved around from group to group, all raising their hats (caps rather) whenever confronted by the proctor. We longed for a little chase or pummelling, but all was quiet. However, we were well hooted at when we walked out of a restaurant where we couldn't get any service. I guess they'd been pledging Guy Fawkes quite loyally."

Kindly mention BRYN MAWR ALUMNAE BULLETIN

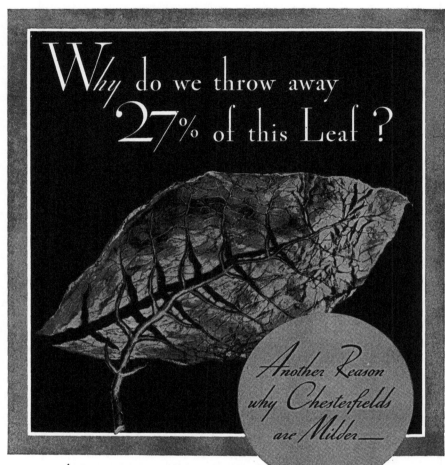

Why do we throw away 27% of this Leaf?

Another Reason why Chesterfields are Milder—

A LEAF of Bright Tobacco or of Kentucky Burley has in it about 27% in weight of stem.

The stem is woody. It does not contain the same ingredients as the tobacco. It does not burn like tobacco.

This 27% in weight of stem, therefore, is removed from the tobacco used in Chesterfields.

Everything is done that can be done to make Chesterfield milder and taste better.

BRYN MAWR
ALUMNAE
BULLETIN

THE ANNUAL MEETING

March, 1933

Vol. XIII   No. 3

Entered as second-class matter, January 15, 1921, at the Post Office, Phila., Pa., under Act of March 3, 1879
COPYRIGHT, 1933
ALUMNAE ASSOCIATION OF BRYN MAWR COLLEGE

Form of Bequest

I give and bequeath to the ALUMNAE ASSOCIATION

OF BRYN MAWR COLLEGE, Bryn Mawr, Pennsylvania,

the sum of.............................dollars.

Bryn Mawr Plates

THE first finished samples of the Bryn Mawr plates have arrived, but we have not yet been able to secure from the Wedgwood Company a definite date when delivery may be promised. Apparently all the other colleges had to submit to the same sort of delay, but in the end they have all been satisfied. The sample plates are even more attractive than we had dared to hope. Please be patient, and rest assured that everything possible is being done to hasten delivery.

*Forty years ago
. . . today's White Star
captains in the making*

SEAMANSHIP

—the foundation of
White Star's perfect service

A glorious tradition of the sea—White Star service!
The perfect service that begins with perfect seamanship . . . expert knowledge that "paves the waves" and
gives you every opportunity to enjoy the grand good
time that's so much a part of White Star travel.

That's why scores of seasoned travellers have
crossed with White Star 50 times over . . . "50 Timers"
—those constant travellers who are never more happy
than when enjoying White Star's perfect service.

You will find, on White Star liners, the strictest attention to every detail of your comfort. Swift, unobtrusive
care for all your wants is a matter of deep, personal
pride with every man who wears the White Star insignia.

Seamanship — Service! That's why scores of
travellers are glad to call themselves "50 TIMERS"
—via White Star Line.

TOURIST CLASS IS "TOP"
CLASS ON THESE GREAT
RED STAR LINERS
*Minnewaska, Minnetonka,
Pennland* and *Westernland*—the
former two *were* exclusively
First Class, the latter two *were*
popular Cabin liners. *Now,*
for the low Tourist rate, you
may have the finest on the
ships. Fares from $106.50,
one way; $189 round trip.

**For full information and reservations apply to your
local agent or to your own Graduate Travel Service.**

WHITE STAR LINE

RED STAR LINE · I. M. M. COMPANY

Main Office: No. 1 Broadway, New York

Offices in other principal cities. Agents everywhere

UTMOST OCEAN SERVICE
through your
local agent

*It costs no more to enjoy the service
that makes the "50 TIMERS"*
MAJESTIC *(world's largest ship)*
OLYMPIC   **HOMERIC**
*De luxe express service from New York
to England and France*
GEORGIC *(new)* **BRITANNIC** *(new)*
Largest British motor liners
ADRIATIC   **LAURENTIC**
*Cabin service from New York and Boston
to Ireland and England*

White Star Liner Majestic, world's largest ship

BRYN MAWR ALUMNAE BULLETIN

OFFICIAL PUBLICATION OF
THE BRYN MAWR ALUMNÆ ASSOCIATION

MARJORIE L. THOMPSON, '12, Editor
ALICE M. HAWKINS, '07, Business Manager

EDITORIAL BOARD

MARY CRAWFORD DUDLEY, '96
CAROLINE MORROW CHADWICK-COLLINS, '05
EMILY KIMBROUGH WRENCH, '21
ELLENOR MORRIS, '27
ELINOR B. AMRAM, '28
PAMELA BURR, '28
ELIZABETH BENT CLARK, '95, ex-officio

Subscription Price, $1.50 a Year   Single Copies, 25 Cents
Checks should be drawn to the order of Bryn Mawr Alumnae Bulletin
Published monthly, except August, September and October, at 1006 Arch St., Philadelphia, Pa.

VOL. XIII   MARCH, 1933   No. 3

To almost everyone at the Annual Meeting the announcement, under the head of new business, that President-Emeritus Thomas no longer intended to make the Deanery her home, but offered it, subject to the approval of the Trustees, to the alumnae as a completely equipped Alumnae House, making them a gift of all its beautiful contents, came as a complete surprise. The first reaction, I think, was, paradoxically enough, one of loss. No one who has ever shared in Miss Thomas' gracious hospitality, with those beautiful rooms as her appropriate setting, can think of the Deanery without her moving through it and illuminating it with her presence. Following close on the first impression came, of course, warm pride and gratitude, and a realization of the sense of confidence and affection that Miss Thomas must feel for the alumnae to make them both the actual and spiritual inheritors of the beauty that she cares for so much and gathered around her during the years she lived on the campus. There was not one student, graduate or undergraduate, while Miss Thomas was in residence, who was not touched in some degree, during her college life, by the mellow, ordered charm of those rooms, made for gracious living; or by the green peace of the garden, filled with the faint sound of trickling water. Because of all this, no one can think of the offer quite coolly or dispassionately, and consequently the admirably worded Resolution carried in the minutes of the meeting was particularly valuable. It expresses so truly the sense of deep appreciation that we all feel, but ensures that between now and June we shall have time to think out exactly what the offer means, in all its financial aspects, not only to the alumnae, but to the College, since what concerns the one cannot help concerning the other. The special meeting to be called at Commencement time will inevitably be more representative than the Annual Meeting, from the point of view of geographical distribution, and it is imperative that as many alumnae as possible should be there to discuss what will be one of the most eagerly awaited reports in the history of the Alumnae Association, that of the especially appointed Ways and Means Committee,—a report which soon will appear in THE BULLETIN.

(8)

ANNUAL MEETING OF THE ALUMNAE ASSOCIATION OF BRYN MAWR COLLEGE

SATURDAY, FEBRUARY 11, 1933

There is on file in the Alumnae Office a full stenographic report of the Annual Meeting. The following minutes are much condensed.

The meeting was called to order in the Auditorium, Goodhart Hall, at 10.11 A. M., with Elizabeth Bent Clark, 1895, President of the Association, presiding. About 100 members attended the meeting.

After it was voted to omit the reading of the minutes of the last meeting, Mrs. Clark presented the report of the Executive Board for the past year. (Page 11.) As the meeting was slow in assembling, it was thought best to change somewhat the regular order of the program, and, accordingly, it was

M. S. C. that the reading of the Treasurer's report and of the report of the Chairman of the Finance Committee and of the Alumnae Fund be postponed until a quorum is present.

Ellen Faulkner, 1913, then read the report of the Academic Committee, and added some interesting statistics about the subsequent careers of students who had studied Science at Bryn Mawr. She was followed immediately by Elizabeth Y. Maguire, 1913, Chairman of the Scholarships and Loan Fund Committee, and then by Dr. Marjorie Strauss Knauth, 1918, Chairman of the Committee on Health and Physical Education. These three reports were accepted without discussion, and will be printed in the April issue of THE BULLETIN, which will carry also the Academic Committee's second article on Science at Bryn Mawr.

Marjorie Thompson, 1912, Editor of THE ALUMNAE BULLETIN, gave a short report on the magazine and its aims. In reply to the request for criticism, Emma Cadbury, 1897, spoke of her enjoyment of the Class Notes, especially when far from Bryn Mawr, and said that she wished there could be even more of them. Another member said that she would like to have THE BULLETIN review scientific as well as literary publications.

Alice Sachs Plaut, 1908, Corresponding Secretary of the Association, read a thoughtful and interesting paper on the Council Meeting held in Chicago and Winnetka in November, emphasizing the value of the Council to the residents of the District where the Council is held and to the visiting Council members. She spoke of Miss Taylor's plea that the Scholarship Committees should remember the Graduate School in their search for able students, and of "Miss Lawther's request that all alumnae consider themselves Councillors-at-large, especially in out-of-the-way places where there is little alumnae organization, where the mere mention of Bryn Mawr may evoke forgotten memories and bring about a rebirth of interest in campus and buildings, and in the spirit of learning which hovers over them. . . . . The habit of housing the visiting Council members among the alumnae of the neighborhood is a valuable one for guest and hostess alike. Old bonds are renewed, new ties are born, and husbands are privileged to see how adaptable and interesting, how self-effacing and how fascinating Bryn Mawr alumnae can be. And small daughters around the house will surely be seized with a burning desire to go to Bryn Mawr."

At the ·conclusion of Mrs. Plaut's report, Mrs. Clark announced that, since a quorum was now present, she would ask for the report on the finances of the Association. (See pages 14 to 17.) Bertha S. Ehlers, 1909, Treasurer of the Association, said that instead of giving the usual report, she had had prepared two charts which show graphically the receipts and disbursements of the Association money. She then commented on them in some detail, and answered a few questions, explaining that only the amount of money which actually passed through the books of the Association is illustrated on the charts, and that gifts made directly to the College do not appear on them. Miss Ehlers then presented for the consideration of the Association the budget for the year 1933, amounting to $16,195.00. It was *M. S. C. that the Budget for 1933 be approved as presented.*

Lois Kellog Jessup, 1920, Chairman of the Finance Committee and of the Alumnae Fund, next presented her report (page 18), which was formally accepted by the Association, including the recommendation that the sum of $7,000 be raised in 1933, over and above the requirements of the Association budget, and that this be considered a contribution to the College for academic needs.

Mrs. Jessup was followed by Elizabeth Lewis Otey, 1901, who reported on behalf of the Alumnae Directors. (See page 22.) Mrs. Clark spoke of the regret of the Association that Mrs. Otey's term is drawing to a close.

Taking up the next business of the meeting, the Association approved the two amendments to the By-laws necessitated by the acceptance at the last Annual Meeting of the recommendation that the Alumnae Directors be elected at a separate election to be held in the spring instead of in February. As notice of the proposed alterations, involving only slight changes in the numbering and wording in several of the sections of Articles VI. and XII., had been mailed to all of the members, the amendments were adopted without discussion.

Closely connected with these amendments was the report presented by Josephine Goldmark, 1898, Chairman, of the Special Committee on Alumnae Representation on Governing Boards of Colleges. (See page 20.) Two recommendations were offered by the committee, and it was decided to act on them singly. The question was then put to the Association, and after some discussion, it was *M. S. C. that the five-year term for Alumnae Director be retained.*

Then followed a long discussion about the proposed method of securing from the country at large suggestions for Alumnae Directors. (See page 21.) Miss Goldmark said that she thought the Council had been hasty in objecting to this, and that the committee wished to make the recommendation again. The sense of the meeting was all along favorable to the general scheme of having the District Councillors send in for the consideration of the Nominating Committee the names of those who would be suitable candidates for this office, but the point at issue was the clause, "Assurance of the willingness of the suggested alumnae to be candidates should be first secured." Caroline Morrow Chadwick-Collins, 1905, said that she did not think the Council action had been hasty and that she still thought this proceeding unnecessary in a small organization like Bryn Mawr's. She added that, in her opinion, confusion and embarrassment would be avoided by leaving this matter entirely to the Nominating Committee. Eleanor Little Aldrich, 1905, a former Chairman of the Nominating Committee, said that she agreed with Mrs. Collins, and that, because the same names are suggested to the Nominating Committee year after year, it would cause some difficulty if these people had already been asked if they would be willing to serve, and then were never approached by the Nominating Committee. Mrs. Collins said that she believed that many people might reply in the negative to an inquiry from the Councillor, who would give favorable consideration to a direct request from the Nominating Committee. Dr. Knauth said that she was of the same opinion. All the members of the committee present, Miss Goldmark, Mrs. Francis, Miss Martha Thomas and Miss Hawkins, spoke in favor of the recommendation with this clause included, because they had found that this procedure is usual in other associations, where in some cases the written consent of the suggested person is necessary before the name is considered by the Nominating Committee. Finally, by a large majority, it was

M. S. C. that this recommendation be amended, omitting the words "Assurance of the willingness of the suggested alumnae to be candidates should be first secured."

M. S. C. that the recommendation as amended be accepted.

Speaking for the last of the Association Committees on the program, Elizabeth Nields Bancroft, 1898, the new Chairman, said: "There is no report for the Nominating Committee other than the ballot prepared under Emily Cross, 1901, and presented to the Association in the November issue of THE ALUMNAE BULLETIN; and again on the ballots mailed to each member with the notices of the Annual Meeting." Josephine Young Case, 1928, Recording Secretary of the Association, then read the results of the nomination and elections as follows:

Nominated to the Directors of the College as the choice of the Association for:

Alumnae Director for the term of years 1933-38:
GERTRUDE DIETRICH SMITH, 1903

Elected Councillor for District II. for term of years 1933-36:
HARRIET PRICE PHIPPS, 1923

Elected Councillor for District V. for term of years 1933-36:
JEAN STIRLING GREGORY, 1912

Mrs. Clark then said that under New Business she had the great pleasure of announcing that President-Emeritus Thomas had made an extraordinarily generous offer to the alumnae. She wishes to transfer the Deanery to the Association, to be held on the same terms as those granted her by the Trustees of the College in 1907, and to be used as an Alumnae House. To this end she will make a gift of all its contents, so that it will be completely equipped. Miss Thomas wishes that she could endow the house now, but since that is impossible, she plans to make provision in her will for adequate endowment, and meanwhile has suggested a plan whereby the alumnae can finance it themselves for the next five years. The announcement evoked great enthusiasm, and a rising vote of thanks was offered to express to Miss Thomas the Association's appreciation of her generosity. Mrs. Clark explained to the Association the terms of the offer and the proposed method of financing the proposition, and said that no official action could be taken until after the next regular meeting of the Board of Directors of the College on March 16th. After a number of questions had been answered, Louise Fleischmann Maclay, 1906, offered the following resolution of thanks:

"Resolved, That though Miss Thomas' decision to discontinue making the Deanery her home is news we deeply deplore, her generous offer to the Alumnae Association of a completely equipped Alumnae House is a mark of confidence and affection for which our appreciation can never find adequate expression. In order that all alumnae may share in accepting this gift, I move: that a Ways and Means Committee be appointed by the Chair to present a plan to the Alumnae in June at a meeting especially called to pass upon this delightful and unusual project."

M. S. C. that this resolution be adopted.

M. S. C. that the President of the Association write a letter of thanks to Miss Thomas, expressing the appreciation of the alumnae, and embodying this resolution of Mrs. Maclay's in the letter.

Meeting adjourned at 1.15 P. M.

BY-PRODUCTS OF THE ANNUAL MEETING

The annual meeting week-end was particularly pleasant. An unusual number of people were back so that the events were not the neighborhood gatherings that they sometimes are. Friday night before the dinner in Rockfeller there was a kind of pleasure and excitement in the air as one greeted unexpected people, and when we trooped into dinner we seemed to be a vast gathering, and certainly were a festive one. All the people who had never been at one of these dinners before seemed to think that it was their own discovery, and that they were clever to have found out about it. The only thing that one wonders about is that even more people do not make a point of coming. After we had had coffee and cigarettes in front of the fire in the hall, Dr. Rhys Carpenter spoke delightfully on the adventure of archaeology. Perhaps he thought that by talking about the water supply at Corinth, or the luck of the dig, bad as well as good, or the problem of disposing of the countless worthless things turned up, of which the archaeologist is nevertheless trustee in perpetuity, he could make us see it as a very prosaic business, but he went about it in the wrong way, for to describe all these difficulties with such inimitable lightness and humor and charm gave them a glamor of their own.

The next morning not quite so large a company of eager alumnae met in the auditorium of Goodhart. The arrangement of doing all the business before lunch is certainly worth trying again. Everything seemed to move smoothly, without undue haste, but also without prolonged discussion. Additional business has always seemed rather an anticlimax after Miss Park's speech at the luncheon, to which people come especially because they are eager to hear what Miss Park and Miss Park alone could tell them about the College on this occasion, when she talks so frankly of her hopes and plans. The tea in the Common Room was the last event of the day. It gave an opportunity that used to be lacking, to discuss at leisure and rather intimately all the things of significance and interest that came out in the course of the meeting. As one saw groups of friends making their way across the snowy campus to the Common Room, which always has a welcoming charm, one realized that there would be a delightful conclusion to a pleasant and interesting and significant week-end.

PRESIDENT PARK'S ADDRESS TO THE ALUMNAE

The campus news comes this year in a compact bundle, with no violent colors or grotesque shapes among its parts. Fewer students than usual by about eight have registered, but the drop is visible nowhere except in the dark windows of Wyndham —certainly not in the Library or on the stairways of Taylor Hall. At the moment the lovely peace of the mid-year recess reigns. It has been well earned, we think, by study and interested work, and we shall all be satisfied with the First Semester record!

You have probably read in THE BULLETIN the diary of the music, the plays, and the games of the autumn. To single out a few details: the lovely singing of the choir in the difficult folk-songs which Dr. Vaughan Williams used as his illustrations, the clever stage set of the Varsity Play, the excellent hockey and the half-professional dancing, the good reporting of the *News*, and the poetry in the *Lantern*—they have all proved the increase in *skills* of the ordinary undergraduate. The alert schools and the way of the world no less are behind her natural cleverness and efficiency, and the result makes her genuinely interesting to live with.

I think all the alumnae should be delighted with the work the faculty is accomplishing. First of all, of course, in the steady round of the class-room and laboratory, but also in the academic world outside.

Four faculty books have come out this fall:

The Influence of the Commons on Early Legislation, by Professor Gray.

The Bank for International Settlements at Work, by Dr. Eleanor Lansing Dulles.

Municipal Rule in Germany, by Dr. Roger H. Wells.

Tragedia Josephina, by Dr. Joseph E. Gillett.

They all happen to be unusually handsome and well-set-up volumes, and their contents are highly praised by the press. Miss Swindler's beautiful volumes of the *American Journal of Archaeology* follow one another regularly, and the last born always excels the rest, and Professor Carpenter's remarkable paper on "The Lost Statues of the East Pediment of the Parthenon" takes up the whole of the last number of *Hesperia.* Professor Taylor has been appointed Visiting Professor of the American School of Classical Studies in Rome for 1934-35—the first appointment of a woman which has been made, although Bryn Mawr has been represented there before by Professor Tenney Frank and Professor Carpenter. Not only has Dr. Carpenter come back to his teaching in Archaeology, but Professor Anna Pell Wheeler returns to full work in Mathematics next year, which, at the invitation of the Department of Mathematics at the University of Pennsylvania, includes a joint Seminary for the students of the University and of Bryn Mawr. Professor Ernst Diez is returning to his courses in Oriental Art after what he terms an "exile" in Cleveland. On the other hand, we lose with this year Professor Leuba, Professor Wright and Professor Crandall, of whose work I shall speak formally later in the year, but whose empty places in the College we lament.

Our steady round has had, and is to have, its usual illumination of outside visitors—this year an unusually lively parade of musicians, poets, novelists and critics.

Dr. Vaughan Williams for six weeks lectured and taught the music class as the Mary Flexner Lecturer.

The Curtis Institute Quartette and Mr. Alwyne are each giving the College a present of a concert, in February and March, respectively.

Of the two most distinguished representatives, I should suppose, of traditional and untraditional poetry, Mr. Yeats has been here, and Mr. T. S. Eliot comes in April. Miss Sackville-West speaks this week, and Mrs. Pearl Buck later on, brought by the Chinese Scholarship Committee. Frank Lloyd Wright on Modern Architecture is matched by Professor Rhys Carpenter on Ancient Architecture. Professor Grierson, of the University of Edinburgh, and Professor Paul Hazard have spoken each inimitably on his inimitable countryman—Burns and Voltaire. Mr. Beebe, under the auspices of the Cosmopolitan Club of Philadelphia, took us to the depths of the sea, and Mr. Picard, although he did not make a formal address, lent the interest of his presence to the campus. Frances Perkins and Mary Van Kleeck lead off at the Conference on Unemployment February 17th. And newest of all, and as yet known only for a matter of hours, is the name of the first lecturer on the Anna Howard Shaw Foundation. The capital sum making this possible was given, as you know, in 1920. It has been allowed to accumulate, and the result makes it possible for us to alternate, at least once in two or three years, the Anna Howard Shaw Lectureship in Politics or Government with the Mary Flexner Lectureship on the Humanities. This glorious alternation begins next year, and as an acknowledgment of the gratitude the College owes for this new gift to President Thomas and to Caroline Slade, who welded it together out of their admiration and love for Miss Shaw and for the College, I have asked them to choose the first speaker. They have asked that Miss Jane Addams be invited to give the first two of the six lectures, and Miss Addams has at once, and with great interest, accepted. The series will deal with International Affairs, to be treated in public lectures and in conferences and round tables at the College. It will begin the first of October, and Miss Addams will, I hope, give two lectures and be for two weeks in residence—so that many students may remember her almost as a friend!

The graduates of Bryn Mawr have given to the College in the last decade gifts remarkable for their number, but no less for their skilful direction. The undergraduates would say, if they could be persuaded to listen to the catalogue, that there was not a flop among them. Goodhart Hall, used all day and, one might almost say, all night long; shelves full of books in every department of the Library; microscopes in Dalton; special courses such as that in Playwriting; various single lectures and the annual Horace White Lectures in Greek; the reorganization of the Graduate School with its particular Dean and hall, the large and miraculously constant annual fund which has made it possible for Bryn Mawr to call or to keep valuable professors and associate professors—these are skilfully directed gifts.

And crowning all other gifts, the graduates of Bryn Mawr have deliberately and officially sent back to her a number of students which mounts each year, the Regional Scholars, a so-to-speak guaranteed group, intelligent, competent, right-minded girls, who with notably few exceptions have gone out after four years intelligent, competent and right-minded women. This gift is first of all to

Bryn Mawr, but second and permanently a gift to the communities in which those scholars will live, where they will earn their living and marry and bring up their children. Students are the college. Without them it is stone and lime, paper and binding, speakers without hearers. Buildings, books, professors are important: the gift of students is the most important of all. To perfect it the alumnae have poured out not only a steady stream of money, but more important, time and judgment.

Now in this spring and for the immediate future beyond this spring I hope the alumnae of Bryn Mawr will set about enlarging this gift of students. I am not asking any increase in the number of Regional Scholars; I am asking increase in the number of girls, hand-picked by the same interested experts for just the same outstanding qualities which have made the Regional Scholars a distinguished group, but different from them in not needing scholarships. In the past the alumnae have used their competent heads and their competent organizations to make the good of Bryn Mawr and the good of the girl, who cannot enter Bryn Mawr without financial help, click. I hope now that they will bring under their selective eyes and the spell of their tongues another set of girls who have the same combinations of intelligence, competence and outstanding morale.

Like the other women's colleges, Bryn Mawr has on its list of applicants at present fewer names than at the same time last year. The fall is discouraging, but not alarming. But it demands clearly a readaptation of our old, somewhat laissez-faire methods of assembling students for the College, an enlistment of the coöperation of alumnae which has never before been called for in this connection and which the alumnae with their instinct of non-interference have not offered. Deans and presidents can blow their bugles on selected high hills, and catalogues can march out in solid gray ranks with every outgoing train, but the school, the parent and the girl herself listens to some pleasant, convincing voice of the less involved civilian and catches fire from some unofficial argument. Such were we as girls in school! Such will next year's freshmen be! The College needs its usual income from students' fees. It needs, in fact, as far as need goes, more than that to balance its heavy scholarship outgo, over and above all that the alumnae can contribute. But it needs still more all the intelligence and high-mindedness and ability it can put its fingers on. The College asks its alumnae to aid it in its search and to send for each Regional Scholar at least her counterpart in a student who pays her way. On its side the College recognizes a special situation. The Plan B arrangement of examinations opened a wider possibility for entrance to Bryn Mawr, whether one thinks in terms of schools or of individual girls, and it makes a late choice of college more possible. As to the courses required in preparation for its work, the College stands by its preference for the definite preparation which it has found satisfactory.

With lean years ahead for the world, however, I should like to experiment by admitting each year a few students who have not studied exactly the subjects which are at present required, but who have excellent records in school and on College Board examinations. Especially in this Philadelphia community I should like to make possible this year for girls who may in good faith have prepared for other colleges but whose resident college expenses elsewhere are hard to meet, that training for a useful and independent life which I believe Bryn Mawr can give. The faculty has such a plan under consideration.

REPORT OF THE EXECUTIVE BOARD

During a year—that of 1932—which will undoubtedly appear in the history of this country as one of *utter* depression, not only financial, but also mental and spiritual, the record of the Bryn Mawr Alumnae Association is one to which every alumna may turn with pride and joy—pride in the very real achievements of the year that has passed, and joy in the good faith and loyalty of its members that is an earnest of yet better things to come.

Towards the end of the year, even though our expenditures had been reduced to a minimum, it seemed improbable that the $7,000 promised to the College for the purpose of maintaining academic salaries, and of extending honours work, would be forthcoming. The prospect was not bright, yet the Finance Committee hesitated to send out a special appeal to the ever-generous alumnae. The appeal was not sent; yet the year ended, after all obligations had been met, with a balance of several hundred dollars.

And here may I make a plea to the alumnae that we should, under no consideration, fail in our pledge to the College. Salaries must not be allowed to shrink. Honours work must not cease. Only by salaries, thus supplemented by our pledge, can competent professors and instructors be retained and our high standard of scholarship continue.

Quite naturally, never in the life of the College have the demands upon the Scholarships and Loan Fund been so numerous, so urgent, and so well-justified as during the past year. And yet the supply fell so far short of the demand that the problem seemed quite insoluble. How to make a hundred dollars suffice where a thousand was needed seemed beyond human power—even that of the canniest financier. But Elizabeth Maguire, working indefatigably with her able and faithful committee, proved capable of the task, and many a brilliant scholar was saved to the College by a partial scholarship, or by a small loan in time of need. Nor can sufficient praise be given to the Regional Scholarships Chairmen, who in all parts of the country have found it unusually difficult to raise the necessary funds. The success of their efforts against fearful odds is evident in the result.

The Committee on Health and Physical Education, composed of a number of experts well known in the world of medicine and of science, stands ever ready to help when called upon by the College for advice or suggestions.

In the beginning of the year the Academic Committee was fortunate in being able to discuss with President Park the manner in which the committee could best serve the College. From this conference two important plans developed: one, that of admitting in the year 1936 a few selected students under special conditions, without the formality of entrance examinations. The second plan was that of assembling information in regard to the special phases of academic work at Bryn Mawr, with a view to keeping the alumnae more closely in touch with the College, and for purposes of publicity when needed. Already a most interesting article on Science has appeared in the January BULLETIN, soon to be followed by another one.

It was with great regret that the Executive Board heard from Emily R. Cross, Chairman of the Nominating Committee, that it was necessary for her to resign

(11)

because of her rather unexpected departure for Europe, for an indefinite stay; but we are most fortunate in having as her successor Elizabeth Nields Bancroft, who is one of our most loyal and devoted alumnae. Before Emily Cross resigned, she and her committee prepared a ballot which was presented to the Association. The committee welcomes suggestions from all interested members.

As you remember, at our last Annual Meeting the Special Committee on Alumnae Representation on Governing Boards of Colleges presented several problems of such vital interest that it was decided that action in regard to them should be held over until the next meeting in order that they might have proper consideration. Of the faithful work of this committee I shall say no more, as Josephine Goldmark, its able Chairman, will later report in detail the findings of the committee.

The work of the special Anniversary Committee is held in abeyance; but under the leadership of Louise Fleischman Maclay, an enthusiastic committee is ready to proceed with their well-developed plans for the Anniversary Drive as soon as world conditions seem more favorable to such activity.

Our Association now numbers 2,784, of whom 470 are life members. There have been only eight resignations, a matter, I think, in view of present conditions, of congratulation. 88 were dropped for non-payment of dues, 18 members have died, and 116 new members were added to our list. Of these, 84 are from 1932, 8 were graduate students, 9 former members of 1932, 7 members of other classes who received their degrees in 1932, and 8 who have resumed their membership in the Association.

I shall now read the list of changes during the year in the officers and members of the various committees:

New	*Succeeding*
Alumnae Director	
Louise Fleischmann Maclay, 1906	Margaret Reeve Cary, 1907
Councillor for District III.	
Vinton Liddell Pickens, 1922	Alletta Van Reypen Korff, 1900
Academic Committee	
Anne Kidder Wilson, 1903	Formerly ex-officio
Louise Dillingham, 1916	Virginia McKenney Claiborne, 1908
Mary H. Swindler, Ph.D., 1912	Marion Parris Smith, 1901
Helen Hill Miller, 1921	Frances Browne, 1909
Finance Committee	
Lois Kellogg Jessup, 1920, Chairman	Florence Lexow, 1908
Bertha Ehlers, 1909	Margaret Brusstar, 1903
Elizabeth Higginson Jackson, 1897	Elizabeth Bent Clark, 1895
Helen Riegel Oliver, 1916	Louise Watson, 1912
Scholarships Committee	
Julia Langdon Loomis, 1895	Emma Thompson, 1904
To be appointed	Margaret Reeve Cary, 1907
Mary Gardiner, 1918	Margaret Gilman, 1919

Committee on Health and Physical Education
Dr. Isolde Zeckwer, 1915..Marion Moseley Sniffen, 1919
Dr. Bettina Warburg, 1921..Ida Pritchett, 1914

Nominating Committee
Elizabeth Nields Bancroft, 1898, Chairman............Emily Cross, 1901
Katharine Walker Bradford, 1921 ....Frances Childs, 1923
To be appointed..Eleanor Little Aldrich, 1905

Fiftieth Anniversary Committee
Frances Fincke Hand, 1897 (additional member)

Committee on Alumnae Representation on Governing Boards of Colleges
Louise Congdon Francis, 1900............................Eleanor Riesman, 1903
Frances Day Lukens, 1919............................Lois Kellogg Jessup, 1920

We are very proud of the fact that one of our younger alumnae, Millicent Carey McIntosh, 1920, is now a Trustee of the College, elected to that important position by the Board of Trustees.

For the first time in many years we shall, unfortunately, have Margaret Reeve Cary in no official position. As President of the Alumnae Association, as a member of the Scholarships Committee, and as Alumnae Director, she has never failed to aid us by her wise counsel and unfailingly good judgment. Even though, for the present, it may be in an unofficial capacity, we trust that she will help us. We are fortunate in having Louise Maclay as our new Alumnae Director.

In the retirement at the close of the last academic year of Dr. William B. Huff, the College lost a distinguished Professor of Physics, and it is fitting that we should here record our sincere appreciation of his invaluable services and devotion.

To all officers of the organization, to all Chairmen and members of committees, I feel that I cannot sufficiently express my gratitude for the assistance so unstintingly given in developing the policies and in carrying on the work of the Association.

We wish to express our heartfelt thanks to the alumnae who, by their well-executed plans and their boundless hospitality made the Council Meeting in Chicago not only a remarkable success, but also a most delightful occasion.

I shall now ask you to rise and remain standing while I read the names of those members of the Alumnae Association who died during the year. And, while we are standing, let us pay tribute to the memory of Dr. Arthur Leslie Wheeler, who was associated with the College for so many years, and who died suddenly at Princeton, New Jersey, last spring.

Helena S. Dudley, 1889
Anne Emery Allinson, 1892
Annie Laurie Logan Emerson, 1893
Margaret Nichols Smith, 1897
Margaret W. Browne, 1900
Elise M. Gignoux, 1902
Amy Sussman Steinhart, 1902
Marjorie Canan Fry, 1904
Florence Robins, 1904

Katharine Huey, 1907
Winifred Matheson, 1907
Lydia Sharpless Perry, 1908
Louise Hyman Pollak, 1908
Margaret Doolittle, 1911
Dora Levinson Kramer, 1915
Virginia Litchfield Clark, 1917
Rebecca Hickman Wyman, 1919
Mary Wyckoff Simpkin, 1927

ELIZABETH BENT CLARK, 1895.

1932 RECEIPTS
$ 47,881

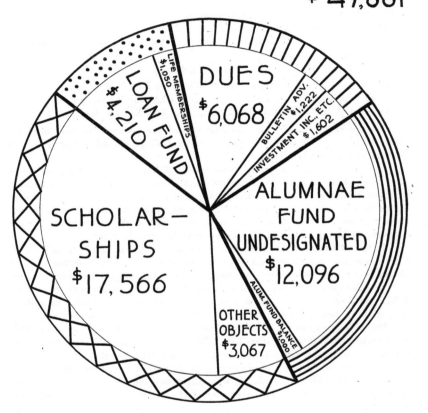

CURRENT INCOME
PERMANENT TRUST FUNDS
ALUM. FUND UNDESIGNATED
ALUM. FUND DESIGNATED

1932 DISBURSEMENTS
$ 51,616

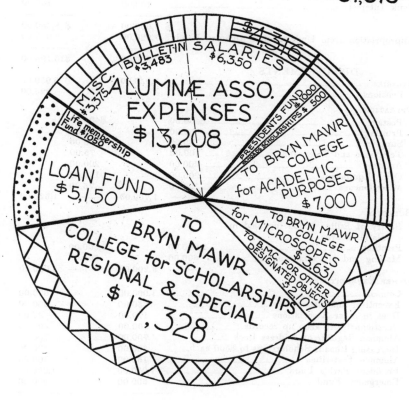

$4,316

MISC. $3,375

BULLETIN $3,483

SALARIES $6,350

ALUMNÆ ASSO. EXPENSES $13,208

Life membership Fund $1050

PRESIDENTS FUND $1800

ROADS SCHOLARSHIPS $500

TO BRYN MAWR COLLEGE for ACADEMIC PURPOSES $7,000

LOAN FUND $5,150

TO BRYN MAWR COLLEGE for MICROSCOPES $3,631

TO B.M.C. FOR OTHER DESIGNATED OBJECTS $2,107

TO BRYN MAWR COLLEGE for SCHOLARSHIPS REGIONAL & SPECIAL $17,328

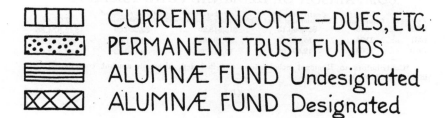

CURRENT INCOME — DUES, ETC.
PERMANENT TRUST FUNDS
ALUMNÆ FUND Undesignated
ALUMNÆ FUND Designated

BUDGET FOR 1933

	1932	1933
INCOME		
Dues	$ 6,250.00	$ 6,000.00
Bulletin	1,300.00	1,000.00
Income, Life Membership Fund Investments	1,000.00	900.00
Income, Rhoads Scholarships Fund Investments	50.00	50.00
Bank Interest	400.00	400.00
	$ 9,000.00	$ 8,350.00
Appropriation from Undesignated Alumnae Fund	7,820.00	7,845.00
	$16,820.00	$16,195.00

DISBURSEMENTS

		1932	1933
SALARIES		$ 6,950.00	$ 6,950.00
Pensions			325.00
OPERATION			
Postage	$400.00		$400.00
Printing	550.00		500.00
Supplies	150.00		125.00
Telephone and Telegraph	100.00		75.00
Auditors	200.00		200.00
Office Equipment	200.00		150.00
Miscellaneous	100.00		75.00
		1,700.00	1,525.00
BULLETIN			
Salary of Editor ($600 included in salaries above).			
Printing	2,600.00		2,500.00
Mailing and Miscellaneous	600.00		500.00
		3,200.00	3,000.00
OTHER EXPENDITURES			
Council		1,000.00	600.00
Executives and Committees		650.00	600.00
Dues in other Associations		170.00	95.00
Questionnaire to keep up records		300.00	300.00
Alumnae Register or Address Book		700.00	700.00
Increasing Rhoads Scholarships to $500 each		500.00	500.00
Alumnae Festivities		150.00	100.00
President Park's Fund		1,000.00	1,000.00
Emergency Fund		500.00	500.00
		$16,820.00	$16,195.00

COMPARISON OF ALUMNAE FUND RECEIPTS

Year	*No. of Contributors	Contributions to Undesignated Fund	Contributions to Scholarships & Loan Fund	Other Designated Contributions	TOTAL
1932	948	$12,096.13	$18,548.20	$2,230.53	$32,874.86
1931	1164	15,453.11	19,291.62	6,241.00	40,985.73
1930	1068	12,504.66	15,911.98	9,150.42	37,567.06

*Contributors to Regional Scholarships not included, although amount contributed is incorporated in figures given.

REPORT OF THE TREASURER

For many years it has been the custom of the Alumnae Association to publish in THE BULLETIN the entire report of the professional auditors, which covers every technical phase of Association finances. As an innovation we propose to omit this unless the members of the Association express a desire to see it in print. The books of the Association were audited as usual for the year 1932, and the report is on file in the Alumnae Office, where it may be seen by anyone who wishes to look at it, and, if there is a real request for it, it can be printed later.

As a substitute for this we are printing reproductions of two charts made for the Annual Meeting, which show, in a form more easily understood by the majority of our members, the story of our finances. When these are studied in connection with the budget, we believe that the whole situation can be grasped.

At first glance it may seem that we spent more money than we had, but this can be easily explained by the fact that in some cases we paid over to the College in 1932 money actually collected in 1931. In business parlance it might be said that we do about a $50,000 business—that is, about that much money passes through the Association books during the year. This money falls into three classes: first, general funds, in which we include the Undesignated Alumnae Fund; second, trust funds, i. e., money which we are holding for special purposes, and in this group is our Life Membership Fund; and third, Circulating Funds, i. e., Designated Contributions, which we receive and record and pay out as soon as possible for the named purpose. The divisions on the charts are supposed to indicate fairly accurately the proportions of these classes.

It may be noted that the Association expenditures for 1932 were $2,116 less than the budgeted figure, in spite of the fact that the Council was held at a distant point. However, not all of this can be considered actual saving, since nothing was spent for the publication of a Register or for Office Equipment, although the budget had included $900 for those two items.

In the proposed budget for 1933 there are a number of reductions and no increases, with the exception of the addition of an item of $325 for Pensions. After careful investigation we came to the conclusion that the salaries paid to employees of the Association are moderate, and somewhat lower in each case than those paid to holders of similar positions in the College and in outside organizations where continuity of service is valuable. The item for pensions was added in an endeavor to give the Association employees the same privilege available to those of the College.

In presenting the budget, I wish to remind you that it does not include the $7,000 pledge to the College. It includes only the income and expense account, but does not include that gift for academic purposes which has really become an obligation of the Association.

A more detailed summary and analysis of contributions to the Alumnae Fund will be published in the April issue of the BULLETIN. In this number also will appear the report of the Scholarships and Loan Fund Committee, which gives the statement of the Loan Fund. The list of securities owned by the Association remains the same as that published in the BULLETIN of March 1932.

BERTHA S. EHLERS, 1909, *Treasurer.*

ANNUAL REPORT OF THE FINANCE COMMITTEE

The personnel of your Finance Committee has undergone no change since the last Annual Meeting with the happy exception of one addition: Elizabeth Higginson Jackson, of the Class of 1897, has joined the committee to fill the vacancy made by Elizabeth Bent Clark, now an ex-officio member of the committee.

The other members of the Finance Committee during the year 1932 have been as follows: Bertha S. Ehlers, 1909 (ex-officio); Caroline Chadwick-Collins, 1905, Director of Publicity; Louise Watson, 1912; Lilian Davis Philip, 1920, and Josephine Stetson, 1928. We are exceedingly regretful that Louise Watson's term expires today, but we are fortunate to be able to fill her place with such a valuable person as Helen Riegel Oliver, of the Class of 1916.

When, on December 5th, the Executive Board of the Alumnae Association held its last meeting for the year 1932, we were confronted by figures which led us to believe that the Association might fall short of its pledge to the College by about $500. We were regretful, but not surprised. A letter was composed which was to arrive in the Christmas mail of many a generous alumna, a letter calculated to turn those last needed dollars our way, so that our books for 1932 should not balance in the red. But on December 14th I received a letter from the Alumnae Office telling me that our Christmas greeting would not be necessary, that, without having made any special appeal, we were actually over the top! An achievement for this year of grace, 1932, which seems to me an extraordinary testimonial to the work of the Class Collectors and to the intelligence and generosity of our alumnae body.

I do not forget for one minute that we are indebted to the Finance Committee of 1931 (of which Miss Lexow was the able Chairman) for a handsome nest-egg of $1,000; but I feel that it augurs well for the future of our pledge to the College that, without bringing any extra pressure to bear on anyone, we should have been able to meet our obligations this past year.

At this point I should like to stop and analyze very briefly some of the figures which Miss Ehlers has given you. In the first place, I want to point out to you how carefully every possible item of expense in the "overhead" of the Association has been pared to the bone during the past year. The running expenses of the Association seem, in some miraculous way, always to fall short of their budgeted allowance. At the end of 1931 we had spent approximately $1,000 less than the budget allowed. At the end of 1932, however, in spite of the increase in the cost of holding our Council Meetings in Chicago instead of in the East, we show a saving of a little over $2,000!

This, of course, means that our office staff, Miss Hawkins, Miss Franke and Miss Broome, seizes every opportunity of striking a good bargain. Sometimes they seem to me to be closely akin to the proverbial French peasant who is said to bite every sou before dropping it into his sock.

If we glance down the balance sheet we find such items as this: Postage, $33 less than in 1931 (this in spite of the rise in postal rates); printing $138 less; supplies $74 less; office equipment $257 less (in other words, not a dollar spent on office equipment in 1932), and so on. Obviously, we have in Taylor Hall a trio of hard-headed bargainers!

And now to take a look at the other side of the picture—our income from the alumnae body. During the year 1932 the number of contributors to the Alumnae Fund (exclusive gifts to Scholarships on which Miss Maguire has reported) was 216 fewer than in 1931. *But* (and this to me is the most heartening of facts) the average gift has decreased by only $2.70—from an average of $18.99 in 1931 to $16.29 in 1932. From this it is obvious that we must make a concerted effort during this next year to increase our number of contributors. Everyone will be urged to give *something*, no matter how small the amount.

In conclusion, I might say that in the financial history of the Alumnae Association, 1931 appears to have been a fat year, flanked on either side by two lean years. But, because of the fact that we have even further and more drastic economies in view for the coming year, and the fact that the Alumnae, without, as far as I know, any undue pressure brought to bear on them, are rallying to the needs of the College, we have no reason to think that the seven lean years of Joseph's prophecy are in store for us.

It would have been possible a year ago, at our last Annual Meeting, to draw a convincing picture of the economic and financial depression; to point out the increased demands which unemployment and similar needs were placing upon the members of every community. We might have amply satisfied our conscience in voting to reduce our pledge to the College. But the Association courageously maintained the figures of the previous year, and you have already heard of the response. The same arguments could be advanced today, perhaps even more effectively. But a reduction in the amount of the pledge would be a confession of defeat in advance; it would run counter to our experience of this past year; it would be a serious blow to the budget of the College. It was with high confidence in the continued loyalty of the alumnae, despite the many other demands upon them, that your Finance Committee and Executive Board at their last meetings unanimously voted in favor of maintaining the amount of the pledge.

Madam President, I wish to submit the following recommendations, which have been passed unanimously by the Finance Committee and have been approved by the Executive Board:

First, that the sum of $7,000 be raised in 1933, over and above the requirements of the Association budget.

Second, that the objective of this Alumnae Fund for 1933 be a contribution to the College for Academic Needs.

My next two recommendations are really only a matter of form. They refer to the balance on hand on December 31st, 1932, but the last Annual Meeting actually authorized expending this money (should there be such) as follows:

Third, that the Treasurer be authorized to pay to the College the sum of $7,000 promised in 1932.

Fourth, that the sum of $279.68, representing the balance on hand after the $7,000 is paid to the College, be appropriated as follows: $200 be reserved by the Association toward the publication of an Alumnae Register or Address Book, and the remaining $79.68 be set aside for office equipment.

Lois Kellogg Jessup, 1920, Chairman.

REPORT OF COMMITTEE ON ALUMNAE REPRESENTA-
TION ON GOVERNING BOARDS OF COLLEGES

At the last Annual Meeting of the Alumnae Association, this committee recommended, among other things, that the term of the Alumnae Directors of the College be kept, as at present, five years. Two recently retiring Alumnae Directors had recommended that the term be increased to ten years, on the ground that the Directors were elected for life, and that the short term of the alumnae handicapped them. As the report was given late in the day, there was no time for discussion and the recommendation was laid on the table. The committee was continued for another year.

After further consideration, the committee still remains of the opinion that the present term be retained, and while giving due weight to the argument urged in favor of the longer term, still thinks that its disadvantages outweigh its advantages.

In proposing that the five-year term of office be lengthened to ten years, it is urged that Alumnae Directors need sufficient time to orient themselves in the work of the Board, and are not likely to be useful members for the first year or so. While there is undoubted truth in this argument, the disadvantages of a ten-year term seem to the committee to outweigh any advantages which may accrue.

In particular we think that lengthening the term of office will increase the difficulty of obtaining the right type of alumna to serve as Director. Besides the four regular annual meetings of the Board, Directors are expected to give sufficient time to sub-committees to which they may be assigned. It is highly desirable for them to spend time on the campus before or after meetings in order to be in touch with College affairs. Women of the calibre desired as Directors are usually busy and carry other responsibilities. Various Alumnae Directors, at Bryn Mawr and at other colleges, have stated that they would be less willing to serve for ten years than for five, or might, indeed, find it impossible to undertake the work for the longer period of time.

One of the great advantages of the present five-year term is that it affords many different alumnae an opportunity to participate in, and thus to become well acquainted with, the work of the Board of Directors of the College. A larger number of alumnae have this experience than there would be if the term were ten years.

We, therefore, recommend that the present five-year term be retained.

Second. Our committee commented last year on the fact that Bryn Mawr differs from most of the other women's colleges in its method of nominating Alumnae Directors. In our Association the burden of finding suitable candidates to serve falls entirely upon the Nominating Committee. In other college Alumnae Associations, nominations are sent in by regional branches or clubs. The number of candidates to be voted upon is then reduced to two or three names, which appear upon the printed ballot.

Our Nominating Committee consults a large number of representative persons and has been untiring in its own inquiries and efforts. We question, however, whether some system similar to those used in other women's colleges might not arouse more interest in the election of Alumnae Directors, as well as assist the Nominating Committee in its difficult task.

There are more than twenty local organizations of Bryn Mawr alumnae throughout the country.. These meet at least once during the year, and have some sort of officer. They may be clubs, branches or Regional Scholarship Committees. In every case they have at their head one or more of the best informed and most influential alumnae of the locality. The committee thinks that it would strengthen the Association as a whole, and that it might stimulate the work of the local organizations to know that, at a regular time, they are expected to discuss and to present suggestions for candidates for Alumnae Directors. Since all local bodies are supposed to be under the jurisdiction of the District Councillors, it seemed appropriate that these suggestions for the Nominating Committee should be collected through the Councillors.

Accordingly, in our report for the Council in November, we recommended a systematic procedure for this purpose. We stipulated that assurance of the willingness of the suggested alumna to serve should first be secured.

At the Council meeting, however, it was voted that the Councillors and subcommittees be consulted as to whom they consider good material for Alumnae Directors, but that the person herself be approached only by the Nominating Committee.

It was argued that persons who might be asked whether they would serve, if invited by the Nominating Committee, would take offense if subsequently not invited. But obviously, if suggestions are to be sent in by twenty different branches, all cannot be accepted as candidates. The Nominating Committee must choose from among them, considering the geographical distribution of the Directors in office, the type of person needed at any particular time, and various other factors.

It seems to us to imply a wholly undue sensitiveness on the part of Bryn Mawr alumnae to expect them to take offense under such circumstances and refuse to serve on another occasion. On the contrary, it seems to us an honor to any one to be asked to have her name considered as candidate; and we believe that the matter can be so presented to the person in question.

Obviously, also, it will not facilitate the work of the Nominating Committee if the proposed candidate has not been asked whether she will consent to serve.

We believe that the motion quoted was passed by the Council without sufficient consideration of the factors involved, and we again recommend, this time to the Association as a whole, the following procedure:

We recommend that soon after the Council meeting each year, printed forms, giving the essential information about qualifications for Alumnae Director, be sent to each Councillor, who should see that each local organization in her district secures from its members—either at a meeting or by mail—suggestions for candidates for Alumnae Director. Assurance of the willingness of the suggested alumnae to be candidates should first be secured,* and the suggested names forwarded by the Councillors, not later than January 1st, to the Alumnae Secretary, who will send them on to the Chairman of the Nominating Committee. This will give the Nominating Committee time to pass on these before nominations must be published in the April issue of THE ALUMNAE BULLETIN.

*This clause later stricken out by vote of Association. See page 6.

We recommend further that organizations of ten members or less be asked to send in one nomination for each vacancy to be filled. Larger organizations, one nomination for each fifty members.

The committee is of the opinion that efforts should be made to widen, if possible, the geographical distribution of Alumnae Directors. On account both of the time and the expense involved, it is not feasible to have Directors from too great a distance from Bryn Mawr—probably not more than a 36-hour journey away. Local organizations must bear this limitation in mind in suggesting candidates, and cannot, therefore, limit themselves to nominations from their own localities.

We feel, also, that local groups, in recommending candidates, should try to secure people who are able to spend a little time on the campus, so as to familiarize themselves with its problems as much as possible.

Trial of this proposed plan—which involves no change in the by-laws—would enable us to test it and learn whether it will, as we hope, be an aid to the Nominating Committee and a stimulus to the local groups.

JOSEPHINE GOLDMARK, 1898, *Chairman.*

REPORT OF ALUMNAE DIRECTORS

The Agenda of the Board of Directors in the past year has already in large measure been made known to you through the pages of THE ALUMNAE BULLETIN. Gifts of money, books, bequests, microscopes for Dalton, scholarships, academic appointments, retirements, the reports of the President, of the Dean of the Graduate School, and of the Dean of the College, have all passed in review. This fact, therefore, confines the Directors' report to such matters as constitution of the Board, officers, standing committees, meetings, etc.

The Board, consisting of 24 members—13 trustees, President Park, 5 Directors-at-Large, and 5 Alumnae Directors—has had one addition and one change in the last twelve months. It is a source of pride to this Association that Millicent Carey McIntosh has been elected a trustee since your last gathering, and as you know, Margaret Reeve Cary, Alumnae Director, has been followed by Louise Fleischmann Maclay. With the happy abundance of good material in Bryn Mawr, regret at the loss of one able officer is tempered by the succession of another. Last year, you will recall, a Nominating Committee was appointed to make recommendations to the Board. It reported the following slate, for which the Directors instructed the Secretary to cast the ballot:

For President, Rufus Jones.
For First Vice-President, Charles J. Rhoads.
For Second Vice-President, Caroline McCormick Slade.
For Treasurer, J. Henry Scattergood.
For Secretary, Agnes Brown Leach.
For Assistant Secretary, Richard M. Gummere.

The committee, recognizing that it has no jurisdiction in the matter of the Committee Chairman, "respectfully suggested that in choosing Chairmen of Standing Committees the President and the Board give serious consideration to the appointment of members of the Board of Directors who are not trustees, to the Chairmanship of the committees, especially of the Executive Committee and the Library Committee."

Three Alumnae Directors (Mrs. Otey, Mrs. Frantz, Mrs. Claiborne) are on the Executive Committee; none on the Finance; two (Mrs. Maclay, Miss Waterbury) on Buildings and Grounds, two (Mrs. Claiborne and Miss Waterbury, who is Chairman) on the Library Committee; none on Religious Life. Of the four other daughters of Bryn Mawr, Caroline Slade McCormick, Frances Fincke Hand, Susan Follansbee Hibbard and Millicent Carey McIntosh, three Directors and one trustee, three are on the Executive Committee, one (Mrs. Slade) is Vice-Chairman as well as Second Vice-President of the Board, two (Mrs. Slade, Mrs. Hibbard) are on the Finance Committee, two on Buildings and Grounds (Mrs. Hand and Mrs. Hibbard), the latter serving as Chairman of Sub-Committee on Halls.

Pursuant to the policy adopted several years ago of fewer meetings, the Board met four times, March 17th, May 19th, October 20th, at the Provident Trust Company in Philadelphia, and December 15th at the President's House, where we enjoyed the gracious hospitality of President Park. There were meetings of the committees in between, the Executive Committee twice, the Finance Committee perhaps oftener, with typewritten reports of the meeting circulated among other Board members.

There is discussion at present of efforts to mitigate the effect of the austerity of the stately board room of the Provident Trust Company on the meetings of the Board. The seating arrangements around the long table promote neither hearing nor easy discussion. One rather hesitates to lift a feeble voice in that atmosphere, a situation for Bryn Mawr graduates as uncomfortable as it is unique.

As a retiring Director, aware of the necessary limitation of directorships and Boards, I want to say that wherever and whenever possible, Alumnae Directors want to represent alumnae opinion. Accordingly they welcome the recommendation that the Executive Board of the Alumnae Association meet with Alumnae Directors some time during the year. More *rapport* with the Alumnae Association would certainly fortify and encourage the Directors. It is also very desirable that the Alumnae Directors meet together before Board meetings. The practice of lunching together at the College Club before the meeting, which rather lapsed last year, will be resumed. The policy of the committee work has helped the situation, and no doubt when the moratorium is off, the Committee on Financial Policies of the College will be further benefitted.

I should like to add my deep appreciation of the honour the Alumnae conferred on me in appointing me to this office.

ELIZABETH LEWIS OTEY, 1901,
Alumnae Director.

Caroline McCormick Slade, 1896, has been appointed Chairman of the Special Ways and Means Committee to consider the offer of the Deanery for an Alumnae House.

THE ALUMNAE BOOK SHELF

TINY GARMENTS, *by Cornelia Otis Skinner, Drawings by A. Winter.* Farrar & Rhinehart.

In *Tiny Garments,* Cornelia Otis Skinner inveighs against the sentimentality, superstition, and general "hush-hush" which still surround that ancient function of having a baby. In words well chosen for their humorous content she recounts her own experiences before the birth of her red-headed Dicky. Her story will have a delirious appeal for all who have gone through those long nine months, and it should teach those who have not to be less awestruck about woman's "great function." Miss Skinner with one sweep does away with the tender whimsicality which has so long surrounded the pregnant woman. With bitter rapier thrusts she unmasks the instinct of women friends who offer advice, for, as she says, "Nothing is dearer to a woman than a nice long obstetrical chat."

The horror of those sweet little gifts which start pouring in more and more profusely is well described in the author's diatribe against baby blankets. And so it goes. Nothing is omitted. Pre-natal influence and the eternal visits to the doctor's office—even the arrival there of a solitary husband,—all these are described with Miss Skinner's characteristic wit and candor.

Tiny Garments by the very subtlety of its humor must of necessity lose its quality in any review. To be enjoyed it must be read—preferably aloud to a group of intimates, and I can guarantee not only half an hour of delight in the reading, but a flock of reminiscences to all mothers which, looked upon with Miss Skinner's lack of solemnity, should provoke endless mirth.

SOPHIA YARNALL JACOBS, 1923.

AN OPEN LETTER

Bryn Mawr, Penna.,
February 19, 1933.

To the Editor of the ALUMNAE BULLETIN.

Dear Madam:

May I take this opportunity to correct a mistake which was made in the Campus Notes of last month? The term *Natural Dancing* was used to describe the kind of dancing which is taught at Bryn Mawr, and it should have been *Duncan Dancing.* I feel strongly on this point, as we tried Natural Dancing here for two years and found it too inaccurate in its technique to be educational, while the dancing which is "the most popular activity in College now," is that of the Elizabeth Duncan School in Salzburg and is based upon such correctness of movement from the point of view of the development of the body that its technique is used in the Body Mechanics Class to prevent and correct poor posture. In fact, this sort of dancing has been most carefully selected from among the various types now prevalent in this country and in Europe, because it does follow with precision the laws which govern the movement of the body and therefore has the proper effect on its development.

JOSEPHINE PETTS,
Director of Physical Education.

CAMPUS NOTES

By JANET A. MARSHALL, 1933

One day a few weeks ago the leaders of various campus activities were asked by Mrs. Collins to lunch with Mrs. Barnes, a special correspondent of the *New York Times*, who wished to see and question some of the students in order to get first-hand material for the articles she is going to write on co-educational and women's colleges in America for that paper. The luncheon, while it was for the purpose of informing the guest of honor, was marvelously instructive to the students who attended. There are few of us, leaders or followers, in college who are well in touch with activities in which we do not participate. The general impression a student received there, listening to the various heads talk about the activities they directed, was one that I have stressed here before, but that came home to me then with renewed strength: that there is hardly an activity on campus that is not undergoing a sort of rejuvenation. From the Bryn Mawr League, which reports that while its chapels are not startlingly well attended but that at least one-half of the student body is doing some sort of social work through its channels, down to the Glee Club, which began the year by assisting Dr. Vaughan Williams in his Flexner Lectures on *Folk-Music*, and which is to sing this spring in the great chorus of *Parsifal* when Stokowski conducts it in Philadelphia on March 31st, April 1st and 3rd, and intends to wind up the year with a production of Gilbert and Sullivan's *Patience* in May, all of the organizations are feeling a new stimulus from somewhere.

Questions by the correspondent on subjects of campus conversation brought forth some interesting new light, when it became evident that one of the favorite topics of conversation was international relations, as embodied in the newly formed International Club. This is a brand-new organization, and like the Liberal Club, is an off-shoot of the ever-growing interest in the Current Events lectures that Dr. Fenwick gives in the Common Room on Tuesday nights. The purpose of the club is to stimulate discussion on related topics, to keep up an active contact with other similar college groups through a common periodical to which they all contribute, and to bring to Bryn Mawr competent lecturers on international relations. Their program is already drawn up and is as ambitious as their membership is startling, for the first begins with John A. MacMurray lecturing on China on February 15th, and the membership of the club, which is hardly a month old, is already well over forty. How much more interest will be stimulated by the lectures one can only guess.

Both amusing and interesting was another phase of the questioning around the table when Mrs. Barnes asked each undergraduate present, separately, what would be her ideal life once she was out of college, barring all obstacles such as an economic depression. Oddly contrasting to the militant independence of women students a generation ago was the composite answer, for there were only a few dissenting voices in the chorus of those who wanted to get themselves a job—of no particularly professional and certainly no scholarly kind—work at it for a few years, and then get married and have, on the average, about three children. There was not a feminist in the group, and only one who was not definitely looking forward to marriage as the greatest influence and occupation in her future life. Also, as Mrs. Barnes pointed out, there was hardly a girl present who·was making an effort to fit herself for the task of training the children she so definitely expected. There were in the group two professional aspirants, and two creative aspirants, one teacher to be, and innumerable social workers. The only really modern aspect of these planned lives was that all of the mothers wanted one interest so well developed that when their children no longer needed them they would not be left high and dry without an occupation or an interest. Independence, financially, was desired by comparatively few, although most of them wanted to prove to themselves before marriage that they could be financially independent if they ever had to be.

The one really striking thing about all this, beside the strange lack of what is considered the modern woman's point of view, was that there was evidently very little correlation between what activities most of the students represented and the lives they had planned for themselves. The one architect of the group was there representing a purely executive campus function, while the representative of the Glee Club is a budding professional archaeologist. This I think is significant. Most of us seem to have drifted a bit in college; many of those present were not sure, although they were Seniors, of just what they did want to do; but all of those who spoke so hazily of the future were and are doing concrete and unusually active work on an unusually stimulated and active campus. In other words, while few of us seem to have thought out clearly what is ahead of us in this chaotic time, our energies are peculiarly engaged in whatever problem presents itself at the moment, and we are genuinely feeling ourselves out, almost without knowing it.

A fine example of this is the playwriting class, conducted by Miss Minor White Latham, of Barnard and Columbia. It is a study in the practical business of writing plays, according to a standard which is that of the best, without being the most aesthetic, modern theatre. The numerous sketches and short plays that keep the members feverishly busy are put on each week before the rest of the class, and the author is required to sit out in front and watch her play live or die on the ultimate question of "Will it go on the stage?" One would hardly think that a number of people would be found to whom the subject would be of immediate interest, especially when it requires so much time and effort—of which the college girl has so little to spare. But it is one of the most popular courses on the campus. To be sure, when Miss Latham once asked the individual members of the class why they were taking the course, few of them could say with any honesty that they had any intention of becoming playwrights. Her method, however, demands that they treat the course as if they did harbor just that intention, or not treat it at all, and, as I have said, the course is highly successful. Perhaps it is that this unbounded energy is just the normal energy of youth, flying from one thing to another without much direction. I think rather—and this is only a guess—that there are two comparatively new ideas in the conscious or unconscious mind of the typical student. One idea produces international clubs, for the student feels that she must fit herself to become a citizen of the world; the other produces specialized activities, for the student feels that if she is to preserve herself in the chaos that awaits her outside of college, she must have an interest besides matrimony and social life.

CLASS NOTES

Ph.D. and Graduate Notes

Editor: MARY ALICE HANNA PARRISH
(Mrs. J. C. Parrish)
Vandalia, Missouri.

1889
No Editor appointed.

1890
No Editor appointed.

1891
No Editor appointed.

1892

Class Editor: EDITH WETHERILL IVES
(Mrs. F. M. Ives)
145 E. 35th St., New York City.

Kate Claghorn is doing research work in Berlin.

Helen Clements Kirk and Dr. Kirk are spending the winter at Winter Park, Florida.

Grace Pinney Stewart, who has spent the past two years traveling or visiting with her son and his wife in Chicago, returned to New York in the fall.

Helen Robins has been spending the winter with Jane and Mary Mason in Germantown. She sailed for her home in Siena on February 11th.

Elizabeth Winsor Pearson's oldest son, Theodore, was married last summer to Louise Mott Sanford, of the Class of 1924.

Edith Hall and her sister Florence have bought and rebuilt a house on Lambert Ridge Road, near New Canaan, Connecticut, where they are living, and which they expect to make their permanent home.

1893

Class Editor: S. FRANCES VAN KIRK
1333 Pine St., Philadelphia, Pa.

1894

Class Editor: ABBY BRAYTON DURFEE
(Mrs. Randall Durfee)
19 Highland Ave., Fall River, Mass.

1895

Class Editor: ELIZABETH BENT CLARK
(Mrs. Herbert Lincoln Clark)
Bryn Mawr, Pa.

1896

Class Editor: ABIGAIL CAMP DIMON
School of Horticulture, Ambler, Pa.

Please note the new address of your Class Editor. She is, since the Christmas holidays, Assistant to the Director at the Pennsylvania School of Horticulture for Women, and expects to enjoy it greatly. There are forty students, and the position is not unlike that of Warden at Bryn Mawr. Remember the address and come to see her and the school when you are in the neighborhood.

Gertrude Heritage Green writes that in the fall she drove her automobile into a tree with dire results. Fortunately she was alone, and her worst injury was a very badly splintered nose. Early in January, more than two months after the accident, she was just out of bandages and beginning to use her eyes again.

Tirzah Nichols and her sister Louise built a house last summer on Airedale Road, Rosemont, moved in on October 1st, and expect to spend the rest of their days in it. Their sister, Elizabeth Nichols Moores, '93, is keeping house for them.

1897

Class Editor: FRIEDRIKA HEYL
104 Lake Shore Drive, East, Dunkirk, N. Y.

1898

Class Editor: EDITH SCHOFF BOERICKE
(Mrs. John Boericke)
328 Brookway, Merion Station, Pa.

After seeing that awful blank following my name as Class Editor in the January BULLETIN, I sent a hasty letter to each member of the class, with very meager results so far. It seems as though the Editor is almost compelled to make up news; however, this is authentic, that she and Mr. Boericke have just announced the engagement of their daughter Edith to Mr. Andrew Fell McCandless, who is working at Round Mountain, Nevada, in the same mine with Edith's brother Fred. Fred was married last October. My daughter hopes to be married in the summer, if her parents can plan to go out with her.

Hannah Carpenter continues painting, and has had an exhibition of her water colors in Providence.

Louise Warren is in Bridgeport, wishing she could come to the Alumnae Meeting, and longing for class news.

Florence Wardwell spends six months abroad every year, and gets involved with Child Welfare during her six months at home, and is on the Republican State Committee and its Executive Committee in New York. She is sailing early in February for Italy, France and England.

Helen Williams Woodall and her husband spent twenty days in London and Conway, Wales, last August, and thoroughly enjoyed the drives and walks in North Wales, and later the familiar sights of London. They stayed at their farm in Maryland until Thanksgiving.

Blanche Harnish Stein's husband, stated clerk of the General Synod of Reformed Church in the United States, has recently been elected President of the Classis of Philadelphia at its 98th annual session at Norristown. Her oldest son is a Congregational minister at Sandusky, Ohio, married, and having two children. Her daughter Caroline teaches preparatory English at Moorestown Friends' School. James, Jr., is again at child-feeding work under the U. S. Government and the Friends' Service Commission, lately taking charge of the work in Hopkins County, Kentucky. Eleanor and George are in medical work, the former an interne at the University of Pennsylvania Hospital, and the latter assisting Dr. Hartman at the Keystone Hospital of Harrisburg. ·

Elizabeth Holstein Buckingham's daughter Katharine was married in November to Mr. Frederick Vinton Hunt, and they live in Cambridge, Mass. I hope that Mr. Hunt is an architect, so that she can help him, as she graduated in that department at M. I. T., and had a studio in Washington last winter.

1899 .

Editor: CAROLYN TROWBRIDGE BROWN LEWIS
    (Mrs. Radnor Lewis)
    55 Park Ave., New York.

1900

Class Editor: LOUISE CONGDON FRANCIS
    (Mrs. Richard S. Francis)
    414 Old Lancaster Rd., Haverford, Pa.

1901

Class Editor: HELEN CONVERSE THORPE
    (Mrs. Warren Thorpe)
    15 East 64th St., New York City.

1902

Class Editor: ANNE ROTAN HOWE
    (Mrs. Thorndike Howe)
    77 Revere St., Boston, Mass.

1903

Class Editor: GERTRUDE DIETRICH SMITH
    (Mrs. Herbert Knox Smith)
    Farmington, Conn.

1904

Class Editor: EMMA O. THOMPSON
    320 S. 42nd St., Philadelphia, Pa.

The class wishes to express its sympathy to Harriet Southerland Wright, whose father, Rear Admiral William Henry Hudson Souther-land, died in Washington, D. C., on January 30th.

The class will also wish to send sympathy to Ruth Wood Smith, whose mother died February 7th, after a short illness.

Edith McMurtrie's striking portrait of Mrs. Arthur Willson is hung in the Annual Exhibition of the Academy of Fine Arts in Philadelphia.

Recently Mrs. Rufus Jones (Elizabeth Cadbury, '96) spoke at the College Club in Philadelphia on "Women of the Orient," and during her talk referred enthusiastically to Michi Kawai's school. Bertha Brown Lambert is spending the winter with Michi.

1905

Class Editor: ELEANOR LITTLE ALDRICH
    (Mrs. Talbot Aldrich)
    59 Mount Vernon St., Boston, Mass.

Gertrude Hartman has published a new history—*These United States and How They Came to Be*—which is a sequel to her other book.

Louise Johnston Baker's eldest daughter was married in October at the Presbyterian Church in Bound Brook, New Jersey, to Herbert Budd Gillespie, a graduate of Lawrenceville and a former student at Princeton. He is now in the credit department of the Bank of Manhattan, New York City, and they are living in Plainfield, New Jersey.

Anne Greene Bates writes that she is "interested mainly in sending a daughter to Bryn Mawr and in raising scholarship funds for the daughters of other persons."

Julia Gardner's postal reads: "Same name, same house, same job."

Theodora Richards Ellsworth's daughter Cheryl expects to graduate in June from the Wisconsin Library School and College of Arts and Sciences.

Natalie Fairbank Bell: "I haven't much to report, as I was laid up rather flat for three months this fall with arth- and neu-ritis. I get around now a bit, but am really enjoying myself reading and seeing friends at home—as long as I have a decent excuse not to be civic!"

Isabell Ashwell Raymond at last breaks her silence, remarking, "Even if one is doing nothing of interest except to oneself, it does not seem fair to enjoy so much the 1905 news and not make at least a gesture toward coöperating." (Cheers from the Editor; other classmates, please take notice!) Her letter, from Litchfield, Connecticut, follows: "Dr. Raymond retired from New York practice in 1927 and we took the two boys and two younger girls for a summer in England and a winter in French schools at Toulouse. Keenly interesting! I could write reams on varying educational points of view in the different countries— as a matter of fact, I did give a lecture on it after coming home and got some of it out of my system! It would all have been an unqualified success had not our eldest boy developed a dangerous infection the day we were sailing back by a long Mediterranean cruise. Somehow or other he finally pulled through, but regained his strength only last spring, which meant preparing at home for Yale, where both he and his brother are now. It has been interesting to compare the results of his "free type" of study with that of the other boy's conventional boarding-school life. The school boy finds it far easier to handle college. . . . Our two girls are at Wykeham Rise, Washington, Connecticut, and love it."

Ella Powel McLean writes: "I have three young ones fast growing up. John is a Junior at Cornell Medical here in New York after having won his M.E. at Stevens Tech. William, the second, also has his M.E. from Stevens, and now hopes for his M.S. at Harvard, where he is spending his second year as instructor in the Engineering Department. My baby is just 18 and is a Freshman in Skidmore College at Saratoga Springs. She wanted a Home Economics course, so although I took her to Bryn Mawr for last May Day and she loved the place, she stuck to her idea and is now very happy."

1906

Class Editor: LOUISE CRUICE STURDEVANT
(Mrs. Edward W. Sturdevant)
3006 P St., Washington, D. C.

1907

Class Editor: ALICE HAWKINS
Taylor Hall, Bryn Mawr, Pa.

The class will wish to extend its heartfelt sympathy to Virginia Hill Alexander, whose husband died in Philadelphia on January 25th after a short illness. Virginia has two children, Julian, Jr., aged 16, and Louisa, aged 11.

At President Park's luncheon in Pembroke after the Annual Alumnae Meeting on February 11th, eight of the class huddled together, eating and talking busily. Active participants were Margaret Reeve Cary, Katharine Harley, Helen Lamberton, Edith Rice, Dorothy Forster Miller, Lelia Woodruff Stokes, Eunice Schenck, Alice Hawkins.

Tink Meigs had attended the meeting earlier. We quote the criticism of her course which appeared in the *College News* of January 25th. Miss Donnelly and your Class Editor agree that in all their experience on the campus, no such spontaneous praise of the handling of any course has ever appeared before. It is a unique and heartening experience.

"The cry of a great many Bryn Mawr students has been most happily answered this year by the addition to the college curriculum of a class in Experimental Writing.

"The class meets once a week, taking up at each discussion a different type of writing, essays formal and informal, description, biography, historical narrative, short story and novel construction. Reading from contemporary authors in these varying types of prose is assigned for each week, and each student turns in a composition of her own in prose or in poetry as she chooses. Both the original papers and the reading are discussed in class for the purpose of formulating the requirements necessary for each type of writing.

"The purpose of this course is three-fold, to give the student practice, to awaken her to thoughtful criticism, and, above all, to enable her to find that field of writing for which she is best suited. The requirement of a paper every week in an assigned form trains the student to write facilely and with whatever material she may have at hand, and prepares for a journalistic career or for the day when her publisher may tell the popular author what her next book must be in order to satisfy the demand of her public. Critical reading and discussion of popular contemporary authors helps one more than anything else to discover what one likes or dislikes in current literature and for what tangible reasons. Finally, by uncurbed experiment and by comparing the results, the writer finds her limitations and her ability, and starts herself in the field where she is most likely to succeed. In this experimenting and first venture, the student is helped by the actual experience and impartial judgment of Miss Meigs, who corrects the papers and discusses with each student her progress and her failures in frequent interviews.

"The class, although new this year, is attended by twelve students. It is encouraging to know that so many people who have the definite intention of writing will have gained valuable experience and training by the end of the second semester, when each student has completed a long piece of work in that field in which she has chosen to specialize. We cannot voice loudly enough our appreciation to the college for initiating this course, and to Miss Meigs for consenting to struggle with such eager but untrained material."

1908

Class Editor: HELEN CADBURY BUSH
Haverford, Pa.

Eleanor Rambo read a paper before the Ohio Classical Conference at its tenth annual meeting in Marietta, Ohio, *On Homer's Similes and Epithets.* The *Classical Journal* printed *On Homer's Similes* in the October number. Similarly in the November issue are to be found notes *On Homer's Epithets.*

Dorothy Dalzell, who teaches modern languages, is doing only part-time work this year.

Ina Richter sent the folder for *La Loma Feliz*, her country school for delicate children. The school is in the foothills overlooking Santa Barbara. The folder opens upon a picture of six little children all smiles and wind-blown hair, and closes most impressively with a . list of some thirty-five non-resident consultants.

Margaret Morris Hoskins and her 10-year-old Sally are living in New Haven. "Sally is in a good school with children of other professors and it is a more congenial atmosphere for her than that of a New York suburb. I find the commuting rather restful! I am working hard at my same old problem of ductless glands. It's a woman's work, all right—at least, it's never done. In my spare time I'm fooling with various arts and crafts—landscape in pastel, and just at present, metal work. I had a half year's leave last winter, so we went to London in December. Crossed on the *American Merchant* with the now famous Captain Stedman. By the way, I was at the University College for two terms, learning the technique of blood chemistry. It was an interesting experience, as I hadn't worked· in a chem. lab. since 1907 and was practically starting from the bottom. During the spring holiday we went to France and Holland. In the summer we hired a Morris-Cowley and drove through Devon, Cornwall, and Wales—altogether a most successful jaunt."

Mabel Frehofer writes:

"Of course, I enjoy telling about my interesting experiences abroad last year. Here is the response to your request—but it is hard to be brief about it. In addition to my fellowship from Bryn Mawr I had an unexpected grant of money (part salary) from Goucher, which is the explanation of my sudden change of plans. With very little knowledge of the German language in the beginning (after all, one can't converse in scientific German), I found my hands more than full at first, learning grammar and vocabulary, and scientific progress exceedingly slow because of misinterpretations and misunderstandings. I did research in radioactivity with the element polonium (discovered and named by Mme. Curie), the rays of which can break down certain light atoms, such as aluminum. The Kaiser Wilhelm Institute near Berlin proved to be a delightful place to work. A number of the Fellows from foreign countries go there every year, and I greatly enjoyed my associations with them, even though we did talk English too much and German less than was good for us. However, I lived with a German family who took wonderful care of me, and who liked to hear me talk about the wonders of America.

"The director in charge of the research in the physics of radioactivity is a very intelligent and capable woman who has done much excellent work in this field,—Professor Dr. Lise Meitner, a Viennese, who has stayed in Berlin since her university days there. It was a great pleasure and privilege to me to be working in her beautiful laboratory under her guidance.

"Yes, to be sure there were vacations, and I visited the institutes for radioactivity in Vienna and at Cambridge, had a trip into Italy, and flew from Venice to Vienna to save time. After the Kaiser Wilhelm Institute closed in August, I returned home by way of Denmark, Sweden, Norway and England."

1909

Class Editor: HELEN B. CRANE
70 Willett St., Albany, N. Y.

1909 can still point with pride to two hardy athletic perennials. This is Florence Ballin's news: "I meant to write you last spring to say how sorry I was to miss Reunion. But having 'gone broke' with the rest of the world, I turned tennis 'pro' and couldn't leave my young baby; it needed nursing. I hardly dared leave the house for fear I'd miss a phone call and a possible pupil! Considering the year, I did very well and hope to be still busier this year. I teach anywhere that I can get a pupil; last year I went to various clubs that had no 'pro,' where someone wanted lessons, and also taught at various 'Courts to rent' here in the city. Tilden kindly proffered his backing and turned over a 14-year-old boy for me to coach the day after I told him my plans! If you mention my new job in Class Notes, maybe I'll get some B. M. grandchildren! I taught classes all fall—Packer School children—and the principal said he was indebted to my friend who sent me there. So, in answer to your question, you see that I still play tennis!"

And Lacy, who spent Christmas in Geneva, writes: "I've had a wonderful experience of two months' visiting in Greece, with trips to the islands and in Jugoslavia on the way home. Rome and work again after Christmas."

The class extends deepest sympathy to Alta Stevens Cameron, whose father died in December after a long illness. Alta says in her note: "We did all enjoy the Council meeting—a table of 1909 seated Grace Dewes, Antoinette Hearne Farrar, Mary Herr, Dorothy Smith Chamberlin, Bertha Ehlers and myself; also Grace, as President of the Chicago Bryn Mawr Club, was a great success."

On January 26th, Hono Goodale Warren was married to Reginald H. Carter. We hope to have more details later.

1910

Class Editor: KATHERINE ROTAN DRINKER
(Mrs. Cecil K. Drinker)
71 Rawson Road, Brookline, Mass.

Frances Stewart Rhodes has lived for more than five years in New York, where her husband is connected with the Public Health Service. Her daughter, now twenty-one years old, is showing her medical inheritance by working on a volunteer job in the laboratory of the same hospital in which Dr. Stewart works. Frances reports her own activities as being largely domestic.

Frances Hearne Brown lives in Hubbard' Woods, Ill., and has four children, two boys and two girls. The oldest, Antoinette, 1910's Class Baby, is a Freshman at Bryn Mawr and lives in Denbigh, as her mother did. The youngest, Frances, aged 10, is also "Bryn Mawr minded." One of the boys goes to college next year.

Janet Howell Clark writes: "I am still teaching as Associate Professor of Physiological Hygiene at the School of Public Health of Johns Hopkins University, and last summer I pursued both business and pleasure in Europe by going to an International Light Congress in Copenhagen and an International Physiological Congress in Rome. My daughter (Ann Janet) and I sailed early in June, and did much climbing in Switzerland and walking in the Black Forest before we started attending congresses. In Copenhagen I saw a great deal of very interesting work at the Finsen Institute, and found that a delightful young daughter of 14 is a most desirable asset for a scientific mother. We treasure a clipping from a Danish newspaper which spoke of how 'Miss Clark went to all the parties, while her mother gave papers at meetings.' We hurried from Copenhagen to Rome for the Physiological Congress. There we saw Mussolini and had an audience with the Pope, but as A. J. developed dysentery, we saw rather little of the Congress itself."

The class wishes to extend its very genuine sympathy to Marion Wildman McLaughlin, whose husband died last May, and to Betty Tenney Cheney, whose father died early this winter.

A letter sent last May to Edith Klett Cunning, in Klamath Falls, Oregon, was returned to the Alumnae Office, marked "Deceased." Your Editor wrote several months ago to Edith's husband, Mr. George Cunning, in an effort to check this bare post-office statement, but has never received a reply. Edith spent only one year at Bryn Mawr—our Sophomore year—and never came back afterwards, but she was so hearty, so vigorous, so alive both physically and in spirit, that she remains unforgotten even after twenty-five years.

1911

Class Editor: ELIZABETH TAYLOR RUSSELL
(Mrs. John F. Russell, Jr.)
333 E. 68th St., New York City.

The class extends its deepest sympathy to Florence Wood Winship upon the death of her husband, Dr. Herring Winship. Dr. Winship's work as county physician made him widely known in all parts of Georgia, and his death is a great loss to the community.

Warm sympathy also goes to Agnes Wood Mosser, whose mother died on February 7th.

Alice Channing has written "Employment of Mentally Deficient Boys and Girls," a publication of the U. S. Children's Bureau.

Charlotte Claflin helped to write a report on "Children on the Stage" and spoke over the radio station WKBW on January 4th on "The Child and the Movie." All this is part of her job in the Children's Aid Society in Buffalo, N. Y.

Ruth Tanner Vellis and her husband are sailing early in February for Northern Africa, where they will spend the spring. After that they expect to be in Greece, with headquarters at the Hotel Acropole Palace in Athens. They will return to New York in the fall.

1912

Class Editor: GLADYS SPRY AUGUR
(Mrs. Wheaton Augur)
820 Camino Atalaya, Santa Fé, N. M.

Lorle Stecher Weeber is now on the faculty of the University of Hawaii in Honolulu. She is an assistant professor of psychology and education. Since graduation she has been associated with psychological work in Temple University, Columbia University, and the University of Iowa. Her husband, Charles F. Weeber, is an official of the Hawaiian Dredging Co. Lorle joined the staff of the island university in 1931. The University of Hawaii has a teaching and research faculty of 200 members.

1913

Class Editor: HELEN EVANS LEWIS
(Mrs. Robert M. Lewis)
52 Trumbull St., New Haven, Conn.)

1914

Class Editor: ELIZABETH AYER INCHES
(Mrs. Henderson Inches)
41 Middlesex Road, Chestnut Hill, Mass.

Katherine Annim has one boarder and eighteen country day pupils in the school she and her husband started last year in Richmond,

Mass. They are so interested in the work they are planning a summer session.

Helen Porter Simpson has a new daughter named Elizabeth Carroll, we think, born October 16th. Her family now consists of one boy and two girls. She is living at 935 Park Avenue, New York City.

Elizabeth Shattuck took a chance on an opera box for the Grenfell Mission and won, luckily for some of her classmates. She is reported as doing so much philanthropic work and so much entertaining, as well as giving a great deal of time to her two boys, that she amazes her friends.

Edwina Warren Wise is living in Beverly Farms this winter, while her husband is doing some writing until it is time to open his summer tutoring school.

Marion Newberry and her husband made a flying trip home last summer and took Alice Chester, husband and two children back with them. They apparently had a wonderful time in Switzerland and walking in the English Lakes with all their children. Marion looks just the same and loves living in England. She now writes of "Cake Balls" and "Hunt Balls" contract, and many Xmas parties where parents and infants all join in Up Jenkins. Apparently the depression is far more noticeable there than here, but it is not discussed so much and people find life most enjoyable, even in a simple way.

Lina Newton has just sailed for the South of France, and expects to remain there until spring, and then perhaps go down to Florence. She and Ida Pritchett and Mary Shipley Allinson were the only members of 1914 at the Annual Meeting.

1915

Class Editor: MARGARET FREE STONE
(Mrs. J. A. Stone)
3039 44th St., N. W., Washington, D. C.

Mildred Jacobs Coward, our industrious class collector, has just sent me some letters from various members of the class, and the one from Mary Goodhue Cary deserves to be transmitted in full. Mary's husband is in Germany under the auspices of the American Friends' Service Committee and has the family with him, and, of course, they have been having some very interesting experiences. Here is the letter:

"Dec. 7, 1932.

"Dear Mildred:

"Just this minute I am 'bummeling' along on a train from Magdeburg to Berlin after a two-day visit to a very clever school principal and his wife who are Quakers and wanted Dick to give some addresses to a sort of Rotary Club and a group of teachers and Socialists. So I have had that mixed pleasure of hearing him

tell these trustful Germans about American politics and then in the next talk give them as honest a picture as possible—can one ever do it satisfactorily?—of what Americans think of Europe.

"We expect to stay in Berlin for the year 1933-34 with a flying trip home to touch base in the coming spring. The children are firmly entrenched in the German school system, with music lessons and teeth straightening added, so they won't come for the visit.

"Last summer we economized and spent three weeks on the Baltic in a fishing village. Our landlady had a tiny brick cottage with a barn a few steps behind, and while we were there the cow had a calf, the cat had kittens, a new pig was bought and christened 'Dornröschen' by our Ellen, eight rabbits had to be fed and exercised, the hens watched to see where they laid their eggs, besides two swims a day on the perfect beach and moonlight sails to the accompaniment of our landlord's accordion music. A successful vacation, taken by and large!

"In September I was in Nuremberg on a visit to our Quaker group and quite unexpectedly met Myra Jessen and Ingeborg on their way to the steamer after a satisfactory summer in Freiburg at the University. Myra and I had a thorough rehash over our coffee in the cloisters of the Meistersängers' Church—St. Katarina —while Ingeborg listened indulgently, and I hope not too attentively!

"Aside from that, no 1915 has crossed my path. There should be a European reunion or Alumnae Council meeting in Berlin or Paris every so often. It would help us a lot from both points of view. Why take orals and never suffer for them?

"I've been interested in the formation of a Federation of American Women's Clubs in Europe. There are six affiliated clubs, and we are beginning some studies in international problems and hope also to collect and exchange information on education and social service trends in the various countries. In Berlin the American women are so few that we are all in one club—no university group—with the result that it is an experience of a lifetime to handle a committee of such a motley crew, but very worth while as a study in feminine complexes.

"Germany is going through a political mess, but it doesn't affect the real intelligence, patience and wisdom of the people. This Nazi movement is just the symptom of the external pressure, economically and geographically, on the German. Of course, the word 'commonsense' can't be very well translated into German and it doesn't fit into their mode of thinking after several centuries of being told what and how to do things by their parents, teachers, army officers and government officials. But they can produce and play and sing heavenly music and invent clever things and go in for out-door sports superbly and generally organize and carry things through as well as any other 'civilized' nation.

"So it is no hardship to find my lot cast here. I've just finished reading Margaret Ayer Barnes' *Years of Grace*, and cheer that we are living in an age that can still see the funny side of life in spite of its hopelessness judged from our comfortable 1915 standards. Let's hope when the grandchildren want to go for winter sports to the Antarctic and study art on the Amazon that we'll be open-minded.

"With all good wishes for Christmas and 1933,

Yours sincerely,

MARY GOODHUE CARY."

In the *Evening Public Ledger* for November 21st there was a notice of the death of Dr. Henry John Doermann, Alice Humphrey's husband. He was President of the University of Toledo, where they had been since December, 1927.

Ethel Robinson Hyde writes that she is spending all her spare time working for Neighborhood House, a settlement house in Detroit, her home. She is serving her second year as President of the Board of Directors. She says: "We feed fifty school children daily, who are suffering from malnutrition. We distribute clothing, helping the mothers to fit the clothing and remake it for their particular families. And at present we are sold heart and soul on 'recreational facilities for boys as a crime prevention' and show Saturday movies, offer gym classes, boxing lessons, shop work, games including ping pong, pool, checkers, etc. —and all this boys' club work is *volunteer* service."

Miriam Rohrer Shelby's boys are now nine and five and a half. The older one is in fourth grade, and Miriam is President of the Parent-Teacher Association in his school. Besides that and her family duties, she still has time for a new hobby, genealogy. She writes: "I always did like puzzles, and that is the most fascinating form a puzzle can take, it seems to me."

Susan Brandeis Gilbert continues to practice law with her husband in New York under the firm name of Gilbert and Brandeis, although she now has three children. Louis Brandeis Gilbert, age 6, attends Horace Mann School, "one of those schools that have taken progressive methods and worked them into the old-fashioned schooling so that you have a school which I might call 'moderate,' that is, with the advantages of progressive education

and the advantages of the old-fashioned school." Alice Brandeis Gilbert, four and a half, is in the kindergarten of the Oberlin School. Frank Brandeis Gilbert, the third child, was born December 3rd, 1930.

Isabel Smith is the Dean of Scripps College, Claremont, California. She describes the college thus: "It is one of the Claremont Colleges in the small collegiate town of Claremont, not far from Los Angeles. I think that this is the only place in the country where a group of colleges is being built up on the Oxford scheme. Scripps has made a remarkable start, and scarcely a semester passes without three or four of the country's well-known educators stopping in to see us. The East is gradually becoming aware of the fact that a new and promising liberal arts college for women with excellent academic standards has sprung up on this far coast. It is a kind of miniature Bryn Mawr—only 200 students, all of whom are in residence on the campus. The curriculum is very stimulating and the faculty as fine as one could hope to find anywhere."

1916

Class Editor: LARIE KLEIN BOAS
   (Mrs. Benjamin Boas)
   2736 Broderick St., San Francisco, Calif.

1917

Class Editor: BERTHA CLARK GREENOUGH
   203 Blackstone Blvd., Providence, R. I.

Mary Worley Strickland has a daughter, born the 1st of August. Her other child, John is just 2 years old.

Thalia Smith Dole has a son, Jeremy Haskell Dole, born on the 26th of last December. Her younger daughter Jennifer, who is not quite 2, is very cunning. She is just beginning to talk. Diana, who is now about 13, is doing excellent work at school and seems to have considerable talent for drawing. Her main joy in life consists in riding horseback. The Doles are spending this year in Concord, Massachusetts, in a most attractive old house.

Anne Wildman Murray and her husband returned to Springfield the 1st of January after several months spent in Virginia and Maryland.

Caroline Shaw Tatom sang over the radio with a group during November and December. What really keeps her busy, however, is the placing of the unemployed in her district. She is in charge of this work and says that, as we can all imagine, it is a "heart-breaking job."

Dorothy Shipley White's step-son, William Wilson White, was married to Mary Lowber in Philadelphia December 27th.

Caroline Rogers' brother, Samuel Dale Stevens, died in North Andover early in January after a long illness. Our deepest sympathy is extended to her and her family, and to his wife, Molly Cordingly, ex-'18.

Those of you who are addicted to *Vogue*, will no doubt have seen the snapshot of Princess Constance Pignatelli di Montecalvo with her bewitching smile on board the new Italian liner, *S. S. Rex*.

1918

Class Editor: MARGARET BACON CAREY
(Mrs. Henry Reginald Carey)
3115 Queen Lane, East Falls Post Office, Philadelphia, Pa.

To encourage you all to be generous with news of yourselves, until the present Editor has had time to send out helpful questionnaires, she will give a brief personal history, and a few random items of interest she has picked up.

Elsbeth Merck Henry lives nearby in Germantown. In spite of two large daughters and a very cunning young son, she has time for a variety of activities (this is a leading remark, Elsbeth) and looks exactly as she did in college.

Helen Hammer Link spent a night in Germantown recently. Her . daughter, Helen Stuart, is taller than Hen and was here looking up boarding schools for next year. Hen's husband is Headmaster of Sewickley Academy, near Pittsburgh.

Sydney Beleville Coale and I meet frequently at school collecting our children. Her son Ned and my second are in the same class at Germantown Friends'.

Four children—Henry, 11; John, 8; Bill, 6; and Alida, 4—keep me busy, mentally as well as physically, especially since the death of my husband a year and a half ago. For the last three months we have been living in a hotel (a method of existence not to be recommended with active children) while our house has been enlarged. We now boast a guest room which has the latch string out. Altering a house is a very exciting business, as one never knows what will appear when a wall is torn down or a floor taken up.

We have high hopes that, encouraged by these random remarks, some of you will send voluntary contributions to fill in the blank under 1918.

1919

Class Editor: MARJORIE REMINGTON TWITCHELL
(Mrs. Pierrepont Twitchell)
Setauket, N. Y.

A letter from Helene Johnson van Zonneveld tells us of her Elizabethan cottage in Kent, not far from London. "It used to be the keeper's lodge on a big estate, and we have all the pleasure in our proprietor's beautiful gar-dens and park, with none of the expense! I enjoy immensely living in England and find it very restful after Paris. . . . I have given up my business for the time being, but have a very nice girl representing me in Paris." Helene was married last March 3rd very quietly in Paris, "the only real excitement being that my sister and brother-in-law (who live in Paris but were in America for a visit) arrived ten minutes before the ceremony at the *mairie*, as their boat was delayed. . . . My husband is in the oil business. He is four years older than I am, has been married before, and has a terribly nice young son of 14, who is in school in England, lives with us, and of whom I am already very fond."

Winifred Perkins Raven has been laid up in bed for a year and a half, but is on the mend now. She says they have lived in Hanover, N. H., for twelve years, "but have worked in four trips to Europe, one for fourteen months and one for seven. Two years ago we built a house."

Ruth Woodruff during Christmas vacation saw Enid MacDonald Winters and her four children, who "had taken Christmas on high with many pets to show, as well as toys eminently suited to their ages, especially to their ears. Enid seems to be quite serene in the midst of it all." Ruth is Dean of Women at the University of New Hampshire, and also teaches two classes of Economics. She helped with their May Day last year, Last summer she went to England, Holland, Switzerland and Germany.

Your Editor took a step into politics last month, appearing before the town board of incidentally the largest township in New York State to urge the passage of an ordinance to license the sale of non-intoxicating liquors, with right of inspection of premises at all hours by special officers.

1920

Class Editor: MARY PORRITT GREEN
(Mrs. Valentine J. Green)
433 E. 51st St., New York City.

Margaret Ballou Hitchcock took pity on us and wrote us a long and newsy letter, from which we gather that she is still teaching three days a week at Mrs. Foote's school, is working on two or three committees, and living what she calls "a routine domestic life."

Leita Harlan Paul, Ballou says, has for the last year had a young nephew and niece living with her, but still is the snappiest looking person in New Haven. She is a badminton fiend and one of the champions of the town.

We were very sorry to hear that Dolly Bonsal Winant's husband died several months ago. The class send their love and sympathy to her.

Katherine Cauldwell Scott, who is living in Ridgewood, N. J., has two daughters, aged 4 and 6, whom she was already instructed in the arts of swimming and tennis.

M. K. Cary is technician at the New Haven Hospital and is doing good work with the Department of Pediatrics. She has a boat and sails winter and summer in Long Island Sound.

"Dear 1920:

"Those of you who shared in sending me the class wedding present have probably wondered why you have not heard from me. The present arrived the day before my wedding, and touched me so much that I could hardly be torn away from it to see my relations! Then it was taken away from me by a committee of the class, who felt I should have something useful as well as very ornamental, as this was.

"In October the present arrived, a lovely old Sheffield tray, which I use practically every day for my tea service. I hoped at that point to write letters to all the people whose cards were enclosed in the original present, but when I tried to do so, found that the cards were mislaid.

"So may I take this way of telling you that your present is deeply appreciated and continually used; that it is one of my most valued possessions, and always will be. In fact, my tea served on your tray is one of the pleasantest of many pleasant aspects of my married life. Yours with affection and gratitude."

MILLICENT CAREY MCINTOSH.

1921

Class Editor: WINIFRED WORCESTER
(Mrs. Harvey Stevenson)
Croton-on-Hudson, N. Y.

1922

Class Editor: SERENA HAND SAVAGE
(Mrs. William L. Savage)
106 E. 35th St., New York City.

1923

Class Editor: RUTH MCANENY LOUD
325 E. 72nd St., New York City.

Virginia Corse Vitzthum with her brand-new son has recently returned to Haiti, but we have no details as regards the baby's weight or disposition, or color of hair.

Agnes Clement Robinson has been spending a vacation at Nice. She broke her ankle some four months ago in a fall from a horse, and it has unfortunately been very slow to mend. She writes that although she believes strongly in progressive education for the young, she has a daughter who goes to school in Oxford in a "horrid grey uniform" and loves it.

1924

Class Editor: DOROTHY GARDNER BUTTERWORTH
(Mrs. J. Ebert Butterworth)
8024 Roanoke St., Chestnut Hill, Pa.

Bess Pearson's engagement to Mr. Thomas Horrocks, of Philadelphia, has been announced.

Martha Cooke Steadman has a second son, born October 1st, 1932, in Honolulu. Martha has recently moved into a lovely, rambling old house where she has plenty of room to spread out. Dorothea, Martha's sister, gave a tea for Vinton Liddell Pickens, of '22, who with her husband is on the way to the Orient.

At 11.30 every weekday morning, over WOR, may be heard Mrs. Stevens, who is no other than Mary Rodney Brinser, who has changed her allegiance from Macy's to Bamberger's.

Elsie Parsons Patterson, 320 E. 72nd St., New York City, is associated with a firm which manages artists, lecturers, etc., primarily for radio. Elsie is divorced, has two boys—Rufus, 11, and Herbert, 8—works very hard and travels whenever time, opportunity and bank account permit.

Mrs. Redington Fiske, Jr., none other than Juliette Longfellow, was married May 24th, 1924. She has two daughters, Julia, aged 8, and Lucy, aged 4. Her numerous occupations outside the home include a part-time job selling children's clothes, sewing for charity, studying architecture, exercising and dancing classes, and work on the Horticultural Committee of her local Garden Club. Juliette lives in New Canaan, and "times being hard," she does not travel.

For years no word has been received from Louise Kirk. Here is her history up to date: She was married October 24th, 1924, to Dr. Julius Lane Wilson, now connected with the Winchester Hospital of West Haven, Conn. She has three children—Octavia, aged 7; Hugh Hamilton, aged 5, and Mary Louise, 2. Though quite busy in the home managing the children and occasionally her husband, she finds time to travel to Saranac for winter sports, last year to Tryon, North Carolina, for golf, and is looking forward to attending a medical conference in Toronto this spring, as well as another in Poland two years hence. Last summer the Wilsons designed and helped build a house (in the country) which, if not architecturally perfect, has plenty of room to take care of the present and possibly future family. It also has accommodations for increasing litters of Scotties. Louie says it's grand to paint the walls as they wish, instead of writing reams of requests to invisible heads, who always send "No" as an answer.

Another one with three children to keep her well occupied is Betty Price. Betty was married May 19th, 1925, to Archibald M. Richards, present address, 1105 Park Avenue, New York City. The family so far consists of Peter, aged 7; Elizabeth Price, aged 5, and Susan, 2. With no time for travel, Betty says she does read a book now and then.

Doris Hawkins was married in December, 1928, to Schuyler F. Baldwin, Haverford, 1926. She is having the "time of her life" taking care of her two babes. Gordon, born in September, 1929, and Beryl, born in February, 1932. The Baldwins have kept on the move, living in Binghamton, Detroit, and now are managing the Hotel Wellington, New York City. Doris invites any of '24 to look her up while in New York.

1925

Class Editor: ELIZABETH MALLET CONGER
(Mrs. Frederic Conger)
325 E. 72nd St., New York City.

1926

Class Editor: HARRIOTT HOPKINSON
Manchester, Mass.

1927

Class Editor: ELLENOR MORRIS
Berwyn, Pa.

1928

Class Editor: CORNELIA B. ROSE, JR.
434 E. 52nd St., New York City.

The class wishes to express its sincerest sympathy to Virginia Atmore and her sister, Molly Atmore, '32, whose father died suddenly on January 28th. Many of us who had the pleasure of knowing Mr. Atmore and counting him as a friend feel his death as a personal loss.

As the result of a recent visit to Betty Brown Field, we hasten to correct a statement in last month's notes. Her daughter's name is not Leila, but Lila, a plump and most engaging person. Betty is studying psychology at Columbia and living in a house at 217 East 48th Street, New York City. Her husband has just left for a four months' stay in Hawaii in connection with his work at the International Institute of Pacific Relations.

Your Editor's address as given above is not a misprint; she has moved next door to the building in which she formerly stayed with Al Bruère Lounsbury. In addition to having found a temporarily permanent home, we have landed a job with Douglas W. Clinch & Co., "specialists in foreign investments," doing research on conditions in foreign countries.

1929

Class Editor: MARY L. WILLIAMS
210 E. 68th St., New York City.

Honor (Scott) Croome writes: "After leaving Bryn Mawr in 1926 at the end of Freshman year (please note I did not flunk out), I went to Paris for a year and found it an over-rated place. Then, being seized with a passion for politics, I settled down to take a degree at the London School of Economics, where I spent three years, made a lot of amusing acquaintances, got engaged (a common fate), helped run the local Labour Party (which included orating on soap boxes in Charing Cross Road). and duly graduated in 1930. After which I messed about and traveled for some months, wrote an elementary textbook (*The Approach to Economics*), of which there may some day, perhaps, be an American edition, taught English to an extraordinarily dense collection of Bolsheviks at "Arcos," which is the Russian trading organization in London, and finally landed a job as Research Secretary of the New Fabian Research Bureau, a Socialist organization which hunts up facts and figures, and goes in for national planning. After nine months of this I got married. My husband, John Lewis Croome, was a year senior to me at the School of Economics, and is now a civil servant. That gave me a chance to see just how strenuous running a house and simultaneously holding down a job can be. I got sacked last month owing to financial stringency and was thoroughly glad of it."

1930

Class Editor: EDITH GRANT
Pembroke West, Bryn Mawr.

Agnes Howell is engaged to Mr. Barton Lee Mallory, Jr.

Peggy Martin was married in Watertown, Connecticut, on February 25th, to Mr. John Harwood, Jr., of Boston.

Anne Wood was married on December 11th to Mr. Joseph C. Harsch. They are living in Washington, D. C.

On December 17th, Kit Wooster-Hull, ex-1930, married Mr. William Stanley W. Edgar, Jr., in New York, where they are now living.

Marjorie Park Swope is continuing her study of architecture at Columbia.

Sylvia Knox is in New York working for *Common Sense*, a radical publication.

We are newly installed as warden in Pembroke West and intend to take some courses during the second semester.

The class extends its sympathy to Harriet Ropes on the death of her father.

The *St. Louis Globe-Democrat* for January 31st featured a picture of Erna Rice and carried a leading article about the journalistic adventure she is engaged in, with five other young men and women:

"Last March *St. Louis Review* made its appearance as an outlet for their quixotic enthusiasm and protest against any feeling of local provincialism. .It was started by its editors as a fortnightly experiment for three months, frankly to see if it found any public response for local self-expression, and its immediate success has launched it as a permanent publication. It is the voice of youth raised in local pride and urging the development of individuality that is both authentic and robust.

"There is no reason why cities like St. Louis and Baltimore, Detroit and Denver, should not develop their own institutions and stand culturally on their own feet, as independent of New York as, for instance, Munich is of Berlin; or Barcelona of Madrid; or Florence of Rome, *St. Louis Review* declares in its December issue.

"'What we can develop in the way of social and cultural institutions may never exert any marked influence on the country at large, but it is bound to confer upon our lives a dignity that they cannot have as long as we feel ourselves to be in the inferior position of provincials. Chicago is freeing herself from this self-imposed stigma. Its achievements in the fields of education, architecture and city planning, to mention just a few, are characteristic and notable.

"'This acceptance of our city, and consequently ourselves, as second-rate, is responsible for our toleration of the smoke horror, which is destroying the form and beauty of our city and affects the health and disposition of all the citizens. We shrug our shoulders and say that it is too bad that the soft coal beds are just across the river. It also explains why such an organization as our symphony orchestra, which in point of view of age is first in this country, is periodically on the point of going out of existence due to lack of endowment and public support.

"'And so it goes. St. Louis is not unique in its provincialism, but it is a nearly perfect example of the psychology of the hinterland. Its submission to mediocrity is the result of being nurtured on a tradition that creates no regional awareness, but a snobbery toward all local activity.'

"None of which sounds like the traditional young intellectual who is wont to look with disfavor on the scenes of his childhood."

Annie Leigh Hobson Broughton has a daughter, Margaret Shannon, born on Valentine Day.

1931

Class Editor: EVELYN WAPLES BAYLESS
(Mrs. Robert N. Bayless)
301 W. Main St., New Britain, Conn.

Last fall Bobsy Totten was married to Clarence E. Turney, of Fairfield, Iowa. Mr. Turney is Assistant to the Secretary of the Treasury, and he and Bobsy are living in Washington now after their honeymoon in Bermuda. He builds boats on the side. The wedding was at 8 at night, and only Bobsy's immediate family were present, but there was a small reception afterwards at 2110 R Street.

Margaret Scott received her M.A. in Education at the University of Pennsylvania, and was granted a Studley Scholarship at Boston University, where she is now studying for a Doctor's Degree in Religious Education.

Mr. and Mrs. Zeben have announced Sadie's engagement to Mr. Werner Buehne, of Berlin.

Dot Jenkins is on the point of announcing her engagement to Edwin M. Rhea, son of Mrs. Andrew L. Ralston, of Pittsburgh. Mr. Rhea, who was Rhodes Scholar at Oxford for three years, is now Secretary to the Chief Justice of the Pennsylvania Supreme Court. They plan to be married in June.

Mary Drake Hoeffel is still in San Diego—1746 Montecito Way. Kenneth has orders to shore duty in Northwestern University beginning next June, and Mary hopes to be able to go on with her English while there.

1932

Class Editor: JOSEPHINE GRATON
182 Brattle St., Cambridge, Mass.

Betty Young sends news from New York City. She spent the summer playing leads in a stock company—*The Red Barn Theatre*, in Locust Valley, Long Island. During the winter she is with an organization in New York called the *Actors and Authors, Incorporated.* Monica Brice, Betty says, is studying at Columbia; and Charlotte Einsiedler and Grace Holden are in New York also.

Denise Gallaudet, while living at the College Inn, is working at the Tea Room. She is also working for Leopold Stokowski on the concert performance of *Parsifal* for this spring.

Leonore Bernheimer has opened a shop in Philadelphia at 10 South 18th Street. She is selling hand-made jewelry and novelties—her own work—and is doing extremely well.

Word from abroad tells that A. Lee Hardenbergh and Dolly Turner spent three heavenly weeks on skiis in S. Anton, Austria. They seem to have enjoyed themselves thoroughly, and declare S. Anton to be the most beautiful place ever seen. Dolly has returned to Cambridge, and A. Lee is going on to Vienna and Paris.

Kindly mention BRYN MAWR ALUMNAE BULLETIN

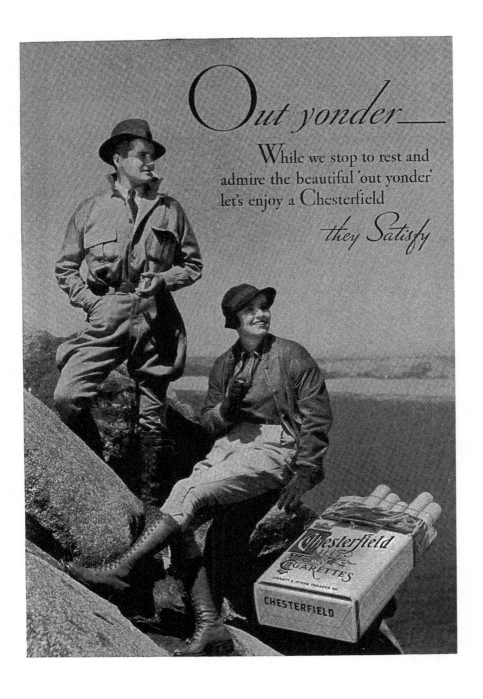

Out yonder—

While we stop to rest and
admire the beautiful 'out yonder'
let's enjoy a Chesterfield

they Satisfy

BRYN MAWR ALUMNAE BULLETIN

BRYN MAWR SCIENCE

April, 1933

Vol. XIII   No. 4

Entered as second-class matter, January 15, 1921, at the Post Office, Phila., Pa., under Act of March 3, 1879
COPYRIGHT, 1933
ALUMNAE ASSOCIATION OF BRYN MAWR COLLEGE

Form of Bequest

I give and bequeath to the ALUMNAE ASSOCIATION

OF BRYN MAWR COLLEGE, Bryn Mawr, Pennsylvania,

the sum of..........................dollars.

BRYN MAWR ALUMNAE BULLETIN

OFFICIAL PUBLICATION OF
THE BRYN MAWR ALUMNÆ ASSOCIATION

MARJORIE L. THOMPSON, '12, *Editor*
ALICE M. HAWKINS, '07, *Business Manager*

EDITORIAL BOARD

MARY CRAWFORD DUDLEY, '96
CAROLINE MORROW CHADWICK-COLLINS, '05
EMILY KIMBROUGH WRENCH, '21

ELLENOR MORRIS, '27
ELINOR B. AMRAM, '28
PAMELA BURR, '28

ELIZABETH BENT CLARK, '95, *ex-officio*

Subscription Price, $1.50 a Year   *Single Copies, 25 Cents*
Checks should be drawn to the order of Bryn Mawr Alumnæ Bulletin
Published monthly, except August, September and October, at 1006 Arch St., Philadelphia, Pa.

VOL. XIII   APRIL, 1933   No. 4

At the time that this Editorial is being written the general situation all over the country gives an added point to Miss Park's plea that the alumnae should enlarge their gift of students to the College, not of Regional Scholars, but of girls who are just as carefully selected for "intelligence and high-mindedness and ability," to use Miss Park's own phrase, and who, in addition, will not need scholarships. Such girls, if they are chosen as carefully and discriminatingly as the alumnae have chosen their scholars in the past, will not only enrich and give added significance to the intellectual life of the College, but by the very fact that they do not need assistance themselves, will help to ensure the girls, just as able and intelligent, who do need such help, the certainty of having it. Miss Park went on to say in her speech to the alumnae at the time of the Annual Meeting, "The College asks its alumnae to aid it in its search and to send for each Regional Scholar at least her counterpart in a student who pays her way." In the past the relation between the number of girls who needed scholarship aid and those who were independent of it, more or less automatically adjusted itself, and all the alumnae needed to concern themselves about was quality in the girls that they sent. Now with all economic balances upset, the ratio between scholarship girls and non-scholarship girls has to be consciously adjusted so that it in some measure approximates the old relationship, and the College can continue to be able to help all the able students within its walls who need such help. All of this must be borne in mind in reading the stirring Report of the Scholarships Committee, which appears in this issue. Last spring the committee and the College together accomplished what quite literally seemed the impossible. It gives one a sense of quick pride to realize that the College once more was able to say that no worthy student who needed help failed to receive it, but unless each alumna in each Regional District takes very seriously her own position of serving as an ambassador from Bryn Mawr to the countless potential students, the College may find that it is faced with a problem that neither it nor the Scholarships Committee can solve as triumphantly as they did the one they faced last spring.

BRYN MAWR SCIENCE

II

IN THE FIELD

The discussion of the Dalton departments published in the January Bulletin sketched only part of the story of Bryn Mawr Science for it dealt chiefly with the research which has been done on the campus and the technique of science teaching developed there. Because the primary function of college science is to train its students for their future work, this second article is an attempt to survey some of the results of Bryn Mawr scientific teaching as they show in the subsequent careers of its graduates.

The success which Bryn Mawr has achieved as a scientific training center is due in large measure to the two-fold interest of her faculty in research and in teaching. In this connection, mention has already been made of Dr. E. P. Kohler. His wide experience with students gives special value to his impressions of the science work of Bryn Mawr students, as stated by him in a recent letter to President Park, which will be quoted below. For the first twenty years of his career he taught Chemistry at Bryn Mawr, and in 1912 was called to Harvard. During his Bryn Mawr years, Professor Kohler originated the lines of inquiry on unsaturated compounds and carried on the fundamental experiments which have served as a basis for his later work and equipped him to be an ideal director of a research laboratory. He also evinced the preëminent qualities of a teacher which account for the widely diversified enrollment in his present course on Theoretical Organic Chemistry at Harvard attended not only by advanced undergraduate students but also by graduates of extensive training in widely scattered fields. These same qualities make him a particularly useful member of the Research Council of the National Academy of Science in selecting its fellows and promoting their research work.

Dr. Kohler wrote to President Park regarding the proposed new science building and additional endowment for scientific work as follows:

"During my twenty years at Bryn Mawr I gradually came to the conclusion that, with adequate facilities, the institution would represent almost ideal conditions for the training of women for scientific work. And after nearly twenty years at Harvard, I find myself still of the same opinion.

"It is not always easy to give satisfactory reasons for one's faith. While I was at Bryn Mawr I was, doubtless, impressed by the enthusiasm of our graduate students, their single-minded devotion to their work, and the promptness and regularity with which they began their own independent researches after they left. After twenty years in an environment which most men would regard as one that would be more likely to develop enthusiasm for research, I find it a difficult problem to account for the fact that despite better opportunities, the number of my Harvard "doctors" who are actively engaged in research is relatively very much smaller than that of my Bryn Mawr graduates.

"The answer, I think, must be sought in the conditions under which graduate work is carried out at Bryn Mawr, . . . the ability and enthusiasm of the scientific faculty, the close collaboration of instructor and student, the freedom from distraction, including that of a multiplicity of attractive courses which kill individual initiative without providing an adequate equivalent. But, whatever the reason, the fact is that Bryn Mawr has been extraordinarily successful in training women for science."

(4)

Science has always had a prominent place in the Bryn Mawr curriculum, for every student as a prerequisite for an A.B. degree must take at least one full unit in science. Fifteen per cent of the graduates have taken this degree[1] with a major in science, and twenty-two per cent of those taking the Ph.D. degree have taken it in science. Thus a total of approximately 425 undergraduates and graduate students have done intensive work in Dalton Hall.[2]

Of this number, obviously, many have subsequently taken up professions not necessarily of a scientific nature. It would be impossible in a brief article fully to evaluate the assistance which familiarity with the scientific method has given to these students, but many have commented on the great benefit they received therefrom. Also the work of the large group of Bryn Mawr graduates who are science teachers in the secondary schools of the country is not included here beyond noting that Bryn Mawr women are heads of the science departments in five of the large private schools which prepare for Bryn Mawr.

Turning to the special group of students who are the subject of this paper, a concrete idea of the effect of their training can be presented by summarizing, as far as possible, the work which they are carrying on. In order to secure current information, a questionnaire was sent to each one last summer, and, in large part, the data used here has been obtained from this source, but when no replies were received the material was supplemented by personal interviews and by the college records. As to publications of the science students, both in college and in the field, an impressive and relatively complete list of books, reprints from scientific journals, government publications, and the like, is on file at the College.

The information which the committee has gathered deals only with persons living[3] and engaged in their professions. It includes data on 81 physicians, 47 teachers of science in colleges and universities, and 48 research workers in academic, commercial or government positions,—that is a total of 176 persons.

The committee was impressed, in dealing with the histories of these graduates, by two aspects of women's participation in professional life which emerged quite definitely from the record. First, the changing attitude toward work by women placing it more and more as a matter of course on an equal footing with that of men, and second, the variety of positions held by graduates of more recent years strikingly indicate the increase in opportunities for women.

Of all the scientific fields, medicine has been selected by the largest number of former Bryn Mawr students, namely 81. It is noteworthy that only about one-fourth have gone to schools exclusively for women, while three-quarters attended coeducational institutions. Of the latter the largest number studied at Johns Hopkins and at Columbia, respectively 16 and 10. But the complete list shows a wide distribution of medical schools attended in different parts of the country; viz., University of Pennsylvania, eight; Cornell, five; New York University, Texas, Rush, Yale and foreign schools, two each; Boston University, University of California, Cincinnati, Minneapolis, Michigan, Ohio State and Virginia, one each. Thus the records bear

[1] The total number of degrees given by the College: 2636 A.B., 311 M.A., and 153 Ph.D.
[2] Psychologists are not included because Psychology is not one of the Dalton Departments.
[3] Two who have died should be mentioned because of their special contributions: Nettie M. Stevens, who was for eight years an associate in experimental morphology at Bryn Mawr, and Anne H. Strong, a pioneer in her field, who for seven years was head of Public Health Nursing at Simmons College.

out the fact that Bryn Mawr students are entering a large number of coeducational institutions of first rank. Reports received from two of the leading schools indicate that many have ranked high in their work, in some instances even attaining first or second place in their classes.

These Bryn Mawr physicians and surgeons have entered a number of general and special fields, including public health, internal medicine, psychiatry, pediatrics, gynaecology, obstetrics, disease of eye, ear, nose and throat, pathology, bacteriology and anatomy. By far the largest number, however, have specialized in pediatrics.

The attainment of Bryn Mawr women in medicine is even more definitely brought out when one reviews the number of teaching positions in medical schools which they now hold. Of the twenty-eight such positions, nineteen, or two-thirds, are in coeducational institutions. Bryn Mawr women are on the faculties of Johns Hopkins, Columbia, Cornell, Yale, Rush, Tufts, Vanderbilt, Universities of California and Pennsylvania medical schools. Five are holding positions of professorial rank (associate or assistant professors) in these schools, five are instructors, and nine are clinical assistants or associates.

On the other hand, nine former Bryn Mawr students are now on the faculties of women's medical schools, three holding the rank of professor and six of associate professor or instructor.

Several students who have not taken an M.D. degree nevertheless hold positions in medical schools or in research institutes, such as Johns Hopkins, Rockefeller and Wistar Institutes, and Washington University, St. Louis. Their specialties include biology, otology, anatomy, optics, genetics and pharmacology.

Besides doing this teaching, many of the physicians are engaged in clinical research in pediatrics, pathology, child hygiene, infant and maternal mortality studies, as well as in public health problems and the organization of clinics.

In still other fields nine Bryn Mawr women physicians are acting as house officers of hospitals, two are resident physicians, and seven are internes. The latter are in residence in the Medical Centre, New York City, the New Haven Hospital, the Philadelphia General and in the St. Charles Hospital, Madrid, Spain. Further, six of our physicians are in administrative jobs in hospitals, in school medical work and as admitting physician to a clinic; two are attending physicians in women's colleges; and thirty-four are in private practice (in many cases combined with one of the above-mentioned appointments). Finally, one of the Bryn Mawr physicians, after experience in various hospitals, is managing editor of an important journal.

In scrutinizing the histories of this group of Bryn Mawr M.D.'s, it is abundantly clear that they have not wasted valuable training by shortly thereafter abandoning their profession. Indeed, on these lists there are many who, even after marriage, have for many years continued an active career.

Leaving the medical profession and turning to the science teachers and research workers in universities and colleges, Bryn Mawr graduates are to be found not only in this country and Canada, but scattered over the rest of the world, from England to China. Of the thirty-three scientists of professorial rank in the colleges, twenty-four have taken their doctorates, 14 at Bryn Mawr (the only women's college, besides Radcliffe, giving this degree), and ten at the following colleges: Breslau, Germany; Cornell, Columbia, Ohio State, and three each at Johns Hopkins and Yale.

Fourteen of the above are biologists who hold positions in twelve different colleges as far removed as to geographical location as Yenching University at Peiping, and Dalhousie, Canada.[4] Only six of these colleges are attended by women only, Bryn Mawr being one. The specialties of these scientists include cytology, experimental zoölogy and embyrology, anatomy, genetics and botany. There are besides, two instructors in biology, one in botany in Birmingham University, England, and the other in graduate zoölogy at Johns Hopkins.

Of chemists of professorial rank there are eleven, eight holding full professorships in women's colleges, namely Barnard, Mount Holyoke, Connecticut, Queens, Wilson, North Carolina for Women, Mills, St. Mary in the Woods, and three holding associate professorships at Barnard, Wellesley, and University of Missouri.

Research is employing many of the women trained in the biology and chemistry departments in interesting fields, namely a total of twenty-four, among whom may be mentioned four research workers and technicians on bacteriological problems at Harvard, Fifth Avenue Hospital, Johns Hopkins, and University of Wisconsin, respectively; two on cancer at the Rockefeller Institute and Sheffield University, England, two on genetics at the Carnegie Institute, two on biochemistry at Agricultural Station, University of Tennessee, and Columbia respectively, and one on blood chemistry at Yale. There are besides a number on executive staffs of research institutions.

In Physics, two Bryn Mawr graduates have achieved international reputations. One is Professor of Physics at Mount Holyoke and the other is associate professor at the School of Hygiene at Johns Hopkins, where she carries on research work on the physiological effects of ultra-violet light, X-rays and radium, and also prepares students for the Public Health Certificate and the Doctorate of Science. Among her students are Rockefeller fellows representing some twenty different countries. Of the four other women holding academic appointments in Physics, one is a professor at Rockford and three are associate professors at Goucher, Smith and Lingnan University, China. Two who specialized in Physics are instructors at Bryn Mawr and at McGill University. Of research workers there are three, one in spectroscopy and two in perimetry; one of the latter is an optical expert who has had a unique experience in applying tests to aviators.

As indicated in our first paper on the Dalton departments, discussion of the geologists begins with an account of Dr. Florence Bascom, Ph.D., Johns Hopkins, who is undoubtedly the foremost American woman geologist today. She created the Geology Department at Bryn Mawr, serving at the College from 1895 to 1928, for twenty-two of those years as full professor. Soon after coming to Bryn Mawr she became attached to the U. S. Geological Survey and spent her summers in the field working out the areal geology of various localities in Pennsylvania and Maryland. Her field work was supplemented by microscopic study and became the basis of many U. S. Geological Survey publications and maps. She was a pioneer in the investigation of the very complex history and structure of the Pre-Cambrian of the Piedmont Belt.

---

[4] Besides these two, the list consists of the following women's colleges: Albertus Magnus, Bryn Mawr, Elmira, Milwaukee-Downer, North Carolina for Women, Skidmore; and co-educational colleges: California-Christian, University of Missouri, Oberlin, and Southern California.

One of Dr. Bascom's first students, who gives graduate courses at Columbia and is also head of the Geology Department at Barnard, had the distinction of being the first woman to teach in the Columbia Graduate School. Among the others one has returned to her native state of California to be dean and head of the Geology Department of Scripps College, three are lecturers and instructors, and one a research worker in crystallography.

Besides these, three of Dr. Bascom's students have followed her into the U. S. Geological Survey, where two hold positions as geologists and one as assistant geologist. All three are authors of folios and maps based on field work in different parts of the country, and published in technical journals and by the government. One of them has also contributed to the guide-book published by the Geological Survey for the International Geological Congress to be held in America in 1933.

Among the younger graduates holding government positions, one holds an exceptional engineering position, as far as women are concerned, with a large public utility corporation; another is working for an important Sanitary Water Board on chemical examination of water. Another branch of the government in which Bryn Mawr is represented is the United States Children's Bureau. Three physicians hold appointments here, two as medical officers making special studies in the field of growth and development, one as director of the Child Hygiene Division.

Graduates of Bryn Mawr are also working in commercial fields. One, an analytic and consulting chemist for the paper industry, has just finished a three years' study of the permanence of rag papers and is now working on a case before the German American Claims Commission developing evidence on the genuineness of certain documents. One is a technician in one of the largest electrical companies; another is testing pharmaceutical products for a large drug firm.

Two Bryn Mawr geologists are working for private companies in far corners of the earth, one is employed in Peru by an oil company, and the other is working for a gold mining company in Sierra Leone, West Africa.

Turning for a moment to the present students of the science departments, there is every reason to believe that they are consistently upholding the traditions of the College. Several recent biological students will hold positions next year in the graduate departments of Yale and Harvard, and next year, too, there will be three Bryn Mawr students in the Johns Hopkins Medical School. Both graduate students and undergraduates working in the Bryn Mawr laboratories have published in scientific journals reports on their researches.

An interesting exchange of scientific students from abroad continues. Foreign scholars from the Universities of Berlin, Nancy, Madrid and Melbourne have come to study in the Bryn Mawr graduate school in the past few years. One student who took her doctorate at Goettingen and later taught in Russia has been a research scholar at Bryn Mawr for the past two years working in the field of relativity. On the other hand, European fellowships have recently enabled some of our scientific students to study in the Universities of Berlin, Copenhagen and Oslo.

As stated in the first of these articles, the Directors of the College have selected the further development of the Dalton departments as the subject for particular stress in connection with the fiftieth anniversary of Bryn Mawr. Because of this, the Academic Committee has collected material on the outstanding aspects of Bryn Mawr Science, on the departments as they have been and are conducted on the campus, and on the subsequent careers of their graduates in the teaching and practice of medicine, in academic life, in government bureaus, and in industrial concerns.

It presents this *résumé* of the more popular phases of its findings to the alumnae and does so with a double purpose. In the first place, it is hoped thus to open a series of articles presenting the work of different departmental groups at Bryn Mawr which, it believes, may prove of general interest. In addition, the committee desires to present the data contained in this paper to support the President and the Board of Directors of the College in their effort to make Bryn Mawr even more preëminently equipped as a scientific training center for women. The achievements described here bear unmistakable evidence to the fact that scientific training at Bryn Mawr has fitted women to take their places matched with men in the present-day world of affairs. This training will be all the more needed in the economic changes that are undoubtedly facing us in the near future.

ELLEN FAULKNER, 1913, *Chairman.*

THE BRYN MAWR ROOM AT THE CITÉ UNIVERSITAIRE

Applications for the Bryn Mawr room at the Cité Universitaire in Paris for the French academic year, November 15th, 1933-July 1st, 1934, should be made before May 1st to President Park.

The cost of a room including service amounts to approximately twelve dollars a month during the academic year. During the summer, the charge is from four to five dollars weekly. Meals are served in the building on the cafeteria plan. The minimum expenditure for food is fifteen francs daily, and the average between twenty and twenty-five.

The following classes of applicants will be considered in nominating the occupants of the Bryn Mawr room:

(1) Holders of Bryn Mawr degrees (A.B., M.A., Ph.D.).

(2) Other present and former students of the Bryn Mawr Graduate School.

(3) Members of the Senior class.

A careful plan for the year's work should be submitted, and if the candidate is not at the time of application a student at Bryn Mawr College, at least three people competent to estimate her work should be referred to. Application may also be made before May 1st to President Park for the use of the Bryn Mawr room for a period of not less than two months during the summer. This application should be accompanied by a plan of work and academic references.

The American House is part of the great international system of student houses being established on the site of the old fortifications of Paris opposite the Parc Montsouris. It can accommodate two hundred and sixty students, one hundred and thirty men and one hundred and thirty women. There are large common living-rooms and libraries, an auditorium and seventeen studios for students of art and music.

PRELIMINARY REPORT OF THE WAYS AND MEANS COMMITTEE

APPOINTED BY THE PRESIDENT OF THE ALUMNAE ASSOCIATION TO CONSIDER PLANS FOR THE DEANERY AS AN ALUMNAE HOUSE

The Ways and Means Committee report that the problem which they were appointed to solve has been met by President-Emeritus Thomas herself.

In order to make immediately available her gift of the furnishings and equipment of the Deanery, appraised in 1929 at $180,000, Miss Thomas is making a further gift of $20,000 to pay the expenses of running the Deanery as an Alumnae House for four years.

The committee at its first meeting had decided that the Deanery could be run on a simple scale with an appropriation of $5,000 a year, and that if this sum could be guaranteed they would recommend the acceptance of the Deanery as an Alumnae House.

In view of the difficulty of carrying through any financial plan at this time, even on the proposed basis of well-secured loans, and because of her deep conviction of the value to the College of an Alumnae House, Miss Thomas has made this additional gift.

The Board of Directors of Bryn Mawr College at its meeting on March 16th voted unanimously to transfer to the Alumnae Association the rights and privileges in the Deanery granted to Miss Thomas and Miss Garrett in 1907.

The Committee will continue to draw up detailed plans to propose for the operation of the Deanery.

Meantime these generous gifts need only the formal acceptance of the Alumnae Association at its special meeting in June to bring to reality the Deanery as an Alumnae House.

> CAROLINE McCORMICK SLADE, *Chairman;*
> ELIZABETH BENT CLARK, *ex-officio;*
> MARTHA G. THOMAS,
> FRANCES FINCKE HAND,
> CAROLINE CHADWICK-COLLINS,
> LOUISE FLEISCHMANN MACLAY,
> MILLICENT CAREY McINTOSH,
> LOIS KELLOGG JESSUP.

The next meeting of the Board of Directors of the College will be held in Philadelphia on May 18th. If members of the Association have suggestions which they would like brought before the Board, they are urged to communicate with the Alumnae Directors.

REPORT OF THE COMMITTEE
ON HEALTH AND PHYSICAL EDUCATION

The committee has had no meeting since last year, following the policy of its previous Chairman, Dr. Marjorie Murray. It maintains its advisory position, and is glad to add Dr. Isolde Zeckwer, '15, and Dr. Bettina Warburg, '21, as new members to fill the places of Marion Moseley Sniffen and Ida Pritchett, whose terms expired in February. There have been no calls on its fund of advice this year.

A program for the organization of the health and physical education departments was presented by this committee in 1923 after much study. These recommendations have in part been adopted by the College, and others will be adopted when circumstances permit, as the departments and the Dean find it possible. The present organization is a sensible and satisfactory one to work with. It is well described in Dr. Wagoner's report in the ALUMNAE BULLETIN of February, 1930. Changes which have occurred since then have from time to time been reported to you.

The Chairman has had informal conferences with Dr. Wagoner, Miss Petts and Dean Manning, and is glad to give you information in answer to some of your questions a year ago.

You asked about over-work. Campus opinion has not upheld your fears, and the medical report shows an excellent record. The therapeutic record shows 237 admissions to the Infirmary last year, with a total of 585 infirmary days, which averages less than 2½ days per patient, against 4½ days each in 1927-28 for 220 admissions. It is interesting to note that the largest number of admissions came from the Senior Class.

Sixteen consultants were called on for 68 consultations. Emphasis on preventive work has prompted the practical isolation of cases of common cold. Other preventive efforts include: 165 medical interviews, 154 medical supervision visits, 248 ultra-violet treatments, 137 vaccine treatments, and 104 medical excuses for colds. This constitutes 37 per cent of the 2755 office visits this year.

You asked about under-exercise. From Miss Petts' report in 1928 you know the change in policy. At present, two hours a week of supervised exercise is required in the first two years, plus one hour of body mechanics one year and one hour of hygiene the other. No exercise is required in the last two years. The effect of this decrease in required hours may be seen in the present schedule of sports. Of 96 Seniors, only 9 are not exercising regularly, and of 83 Juniors, 8 are not exercising regularly. Miss Petts feels that there is a genuine interest in exercise which she believes is fostered by the attempt to teach the students to become expert in some exercise which will give them enjoyment, not only at College, but throughout life. I am glad to report that water polo is dead at Bryn Mawr.

The epidemic of infantile paralysis in Philadelphia this fall postponed the opening of College for one week. The health department and the Freshman Class felt the brunt of this in the elimination of Freshman Week during which medical examinations are disposed of before classes begin. Quarantine was maintained until the case incidence had dropped to normal limits.

MARJORIE STRAUSS KNAUTH, 1918, *Chairman.*

(11)

SUMMARY OF ALUMNAE FUND FOR 1932

Class	No. in Class	No. of Contributors	Percentage of Class	Undesignated Contributions	Designated Contributions	Total Contributed
Ph.D's....	111	25	22.5	$195.50	$100.00	$295.50
M.A's.....	109	8	7.3	20.00	......	20.00
Grad. Students (A. A. members)	65	7	10.7	76.00	......	76.00
1889......	28	9	32.1	67.00	334.75	401.75
1890......	8	..	....	......	......	......
1891......	15	1	6.6	10.00	......	10.00
1892......	22	11	50.0	111.00	......	111.00
1893......	36	13	36.1	117.00	......	117.00
1894......	39	8	20.5	95.50	......	95.50
1895......	32	15	46.8	190.00	100.00	290.00
1896......	62	29	46.7	348.00	10.00	358.00
1897......	71	16	22.5	327.00	225.00	552.00
1898......	55	18	32.7	152.50	210.00	362.50
1899......	60	17	28.3	184.50	......	184.50
1900......	65	20	30.7	309.00	......	309.00
1901......	84	27	32.1	253.00	10.00	263.00
1902......	74	14	18.9	311.52	......	311.52
1903......	110	26	23.6	393.50	300.00	693.50
1904......	92	19	20.6	225.00	......	225.00
1905......	115	38	33.0	511.50	953.42	1,464.92
1906......	72	27	37.5	1,215.25	547.50	1,762.75
1907......	114	38	33.3	234.00	100.00	334.00
1908......	98	41	41.8	385.00	35.00	420.00
1909......	99	29	29.2	486.00	......	486.00
1910......	86	26	30.2	315.40	......	315.40
1911......	85	34	40.0	509.00	......	509.00
1912......	94	28	29.7	693.00	225.00	918.00
1913......	104	25	24.0	318.68	100.00	418.68
1914......	106	25	23.5	166.00	......	166.00
1915......	125	16	12.8	146.00	10.00	156.00
1916......	104	18	17.3	183.00	......	183.00
1917......	112	19	16.9	207.00	......	207.00
1918......	94	15	15.9	363.50	......	363.50
1919......	119	29	24.3	258.50	30.00	288.50
1920......	106	31	29.2	356.00	......	356.00
1921......	134	37	27.6	288.00	25.00	313.00
1922......	97	19	19.5	391.50	24.86	416.36
1923......	103	14	13.5	194.00	5.00	199.00
1924......	116	16	13.7	134.00	......	134.00
1925......	111	13	11.7	121.28	......	121.28
1926......	125	22	17.6	254.00	......	254.00
1927......	125	19	15.2	106.00	......	106.00
1928......	115	19	16.5	212.50	......	212.50
1929......	107	14	13.0	92.00	......	92.00
1930......	127	20	15.7	222.00	......	222.00
1931......	116	17	14.6	142.00	......	142.00
1932......	128	16	12.5	205.00	......	205.00
	4,175	948	....	$12,096 13	$3,345.53	$15,441.66

Total Class Collections for 1932..................................... $15,441.66
Group Contributions for Scholarships............................. 14,550.00
Special Scholarships... 2,071.22
Miscellaneous... 30.00
Total Contributions through Alumnæ Fund....................... $32,092.88
Donations to Loan Fund.. 781.98
Total Contributed in 1932...................................... $32,874.86

ANALYSIS OF ALUMNAE FUND FOR 1932

Payments on Music Endowment and Auditorium pledges............ $81.86
Furnishings for Goodhart Hall (Payments on pledges)............. 61.92
Marion Reilly Memorial Fund................................... 10.00
Portrait Fund, Class of 1898................................. 210.00
Microscope Fund... 499.75
Reunion Gifts—Pledged in 1931—Classes 1905, 1907 and 1908 for
   Microscope Fund and Special Scholarship.................... 1,019.50
Endowment Fund for Library Books, Class of 1906................ 547.50
Special Scholarships... 3,016.22
Regional Scholarships.. 14,550.00

District I....................................	$3,150.00	
Special Grants..............................	550.00	
District II:		
New York.........................	$2,000.00	
New Jersey.......................	1,250.00	
Eastern Pennsylvania...............	1,800.00	
Western Pennsylvania	700.00	
		$5,750.00
District III:		
Baltimore........................	$750.00	
Washington.......................	500.00	
Richmond	100.00	
South..........................	500.00	
		$1,850.00
District IV....................................	800.00	
District V.....................................	1,300.00	
District VI....................................	400.00	
District VII:		
Northern California for academic	$500.00	
year 1931–32 .... $200.00		
" 1932–33 .... 300.00		
Southern California................	250.00	
		$750.00

President Park's Fund... 1,000.00
Rhoads Scholarships... 500.00
Alumnæ Association Expenses................................. 4,316.47
Surplus:
  *Appropriated for Academic Purposes.............. $6,000.00
  Appropriated for Register or Address Book 200.00
  Appropriated for Office Equipment......... 79.66
                        6,279.66

                          $32.092.88
Donations to Loan Fund:...................................... 781.98

   Total Contributed in 1932............................... $32,874.86

---

  * $1,000.00 appropriated from 1931 Surplus to complete 1932 pledge of $7,000.00 for academic purposes.

REPORT OF THE SCHOLARSHIPS AND
LOAN FUND COMMITTEE

Last year at this time, when I made my first report for the Committee on Scholarships and Loan Fund, we were in the midst of a period of tremendous financial distress. There had been no sign of an upward turn at that time, and even to the most optimistic eye the future looked ominous. At such a time it was inevitable that the colleges of the country should be suffering from depleted incomes from their invested funds. The parents of students were having great difficulty in paying college fees, and were uncertain of their ability to pay future fees. The alumnae and friends who ordinarily made generous contributions to college coffers were feeling the pinch of poverty, and could, by no means, be counted on to help at such a time.

Last March the Central Committee found itself confronted with 89 scholarship applications for 1932-33, about one-third more than in 1931-32. The funds at the disposal of the committee had lessened somewhat, the most serious losses being in the Bookshop profits and in the money available from the Parents' Fund. The problem confronting the committee was how to apportion these inadequate resources to the very best advantage. It was decided to give to students with outstanding academic records the full amount of scholarship help they required, and then to distribute the remaining money as far as it would go in smaller amounts. This meant that the leading students in every class were well provided for, and that the middle ones were given rather less scholarship help than they really needed. And there were found to be twenty students who were well worth helping, and who would have been helped in any ordinary year, who could not return to College in 1932-33 unless they were given adequate financial assistance.

It was estimated that from $3,500 to $5,000 would be needed for grants and loans to these and to other students, the fund to be a flexible one, administered by the Dean, with the Central Committee coöperating. President Park and Dean Manning both spoke in Chapel about the matter. It was pointed out that if twenty students, many of whom were actively connected with undergraduate organizations, could not come back, it would be a serious loss to the life of the College. The Dean wrote an article on the subject for the ALUMNAE BULLETIN, to let the alumnae know of the seriousness of the situation, and I wrote a letter to the *College News* for the information of the undergraduates. The Dean then appealed to a certain number of parents who were in a position to help their daughters' friends. She also tried to interest individual alumnae in the matter. The response was immediate, and was immensely gratifying to us all. Contributions began to come in, and continued all through the late spring and summer.

As a direct result of this special effort the parents of students gave $2,350, alumnae members of the faculty $210, other alumnae $1,000, and outside friends of the College $125. Two scholarships awarded for merit irrespective of financial need were returned by their winners and there were other refunds to the extent of $512.98. Other gifts, for which the special effort was indirectly responsible, were $500 from the alumnae of the Girls' High School, Philadelphia, for a special student, and two other generous donations. Miss Hoyt, the donor of the Mary Helen Ritchie

Prize, said that the accumulated principal and interest of that prize, amounting to $1,284.09, might be transferred to the Loan Fund. Helen Lovell Million, Fellow in Greek, 1887-88, sent the Loan Fund $433.38, money raised by the sale of a life insurance policy. The grand total received as a result of the special effort is $7,063.45.

Thus the twenty needy students were given the necessary help; several other brilliant students who applied for help later in the summer were assisted, and as far as we know practically every *worthy* student who needed further financial help has received it. We want to express our great admiration for Dean Manning's resourcefulness and energy in carrying through the plan for the fund. Though we may rejoice over the response to the appeal, we must not lose sight of the seriousness of the situation. If this money had not been raised last spring and summer there would now be empty rooms in all the college halls; many students able to pay part of their fees could not have paid all without the help which has been given them by the special fund. And it is quite evident that this year at least $5,000 must again be raised.

Here is a statement of the scholarship help, from all sources, given in the year 1932-33: 125 students received scholarships, grants or other aid (exclusive of the special $100 room-rate) to the amount of $53,060. Some of this money is from college funds and endowed scholarships, some from donations, and $16,750 of it was secured by the Regional Scholarships Committees. $16,050 of this money is for scholarships, and $700 is for loans to Regional Scholars. We are more than grateful to the Regional Committees for the splendid and unceasing work which made possible such a total.

In this sum of $16,750 are included not only the regular Regional Scholarships, but also some special scholarships for students who for various reasons were not chosen as Regional Scholars. The New England Committee especially has given help in this way to girls in whom it is interested, and of its $3,700 sent in this year, $2,800 is for regular Regional Scholarships and $900 is for special scholarships. New York has one special scholar in addition to its Regionals, Western Pennsylvania has one, and District V. has one. We are including also in this sum two loans from Women's Clubs to Regional Scholars from their towns. The New Jersey Committee secured these loans, and it is an idea to be commended to the attention of the other Regional Committees. A scholarship given by the Colonial Dames is also included.

As for Regional Scholars for 1932-33: there are 45 in College, as many as there were last year, and as usual most of them are distinguishing themselves academically. Fifteen of them hold named scholarships in addition to their Regionals. Every year it becomes more and more apparent that by the selection and continued support of this distinguished group of students the alumnae are doing a piece of work of inestimable value to the College.

Perhaps I may say a word here about the two new scholarships which have been given to Bryn Mawr in the last year. The friends and family of Amy Sussman Steinhart, 1902, have established a scholarship in her memory, the income of $5,000. It will probably be a competitive scholarship, given to a western applicant. The other scholarship is to be named for Louise Hyman Pollak, 1908, who left life insurance of $5,000 to the College.

One of the results of the campaign for the Special Fund was that people became aware of the disastrously low state of the Loan Fund, and came forward with much-needed help. Some contributions were marked definitely for the Loan Fund, and the Mary Helen Ritchie prize money and Mrs. Million's fund are a god-send. The Loan Fund did not actually receive their gifts until 1933, and therefore they do not appear in our statement below, which is for the calendar year 1932. Nevertheless the Loan Fund is again taking its place as a real factor in helping worth-while students who need extra financial assistance.

The statement from January 1, 1932, to January 1, 1933:

Balance on hand, January 1, 1932		$1,219.59
Receipts:		
Payment on Loans	$2,501.89	
Interest on Loans	249.04	
Interest on Bank Balances	18.47	
Donations	1,441.48	
Loans to Loan Fund	200.00	
		$4,410.88
Total		$5,630.47
Disbursements:		
Loans to Students	$4,150.00	
Repayment of Loans to the Loan Fund	1,200.00	
Tax on Checks	.50	
		$5,350.50
Balance on hand, December 31, 1932		$279.97

Since the Alumnae Meeting is later than usual this year we want to bring the Loan Fund statement up to date:

Balance, January 1, 1933		$279.97
Receipts, January 1 to February 10, 1933:		
Payment on Loans	$137.20	
Interest	73.14	
Donations	2,138.47	
		2,348.81
Total		$2,628.78
Disbursements:		
Loans to Students	$450.00	
Repayment of Loans to Loan Fund	300.00	
Tax	.02	
		750.02
February 11, 1933, Balance		$1,878.76

In spite of this apparently large balance at the moment, we must pay off $700 more loans to the Loan Fund in 1933, and there will not be much more than usual in the balance when this is done. We have paid back $1,000 worth of these loans by alumnae in 1932, and $300 worth thus far in 1933. We have taken special pains to pay them back at exactly the date they were due. If there are any alumnae who want to take the places of those who have lent money to the Loan Fund and have had it returned to them, I need hardly say how grateful we should be for their help.

In comparing our Loan Fund statement for 1932 with the one for 1931, we note that in 1931 there were donations of $2,014.50, as compared with $1,441.48 in 1932. This falling off in donations is explained by the fact that in 1931 we had our $1,000 from the Parents' Fund, and in 1932 this sum was not given to the Loan Fund. In 1931, $5,561 was lent to 30 students, as compared with $4,150 lent in 1932 to 29 students. On the other hand, $2,204.97 was repaid to the fund in 1931, and $2,501.89 has been repaid in 1932.

Though less money has been borrowed in 1932 than in 1931, because of the fact that there was less to borrow, you will realize that the Loan Fund is nevertheless a large and increasingly complicated business. The bills are usually sent out on January 1st and July 1st of each year, and this year for the first time bills have been sent out on October 1st to the people who failed to make any payment in July. The bills are accompanied in some cases by letters when it seems necessary to stimulate repayments, and sometimes we get very pathetic replies from people who declare that they cannot repay even their interest, but who assure us that they will go on with their payments as soon as possible. The borrowers who are keeping up their payments of both principal and interest are many; there are some who are behind on their repayments, and there are a very few who show no disposition to pay anything on their debts.

The amount of money due to date: Principal $3,476.65

Interest 1,180.38

Of this, $840 of principal and $207.08 of interest may probably be regarded as hopeless, so we may call $2,636.65 the collectible amount of principal now due, and $972.58 the collectible amount of interest. We hesitate to call any debt absolutely hopeless, because last year one person in this category paid her whole amount of indebtedness, to our great delight.

	No. of Students	Principal	Interest	Total
Past due Loans	13	$2,365.91	$524.49	$2,890.40
Active	44	13,661.25	657.83	14,319.08
Not yet due	27	6,725.00		6,725.00
	84	$22,752.16	$1,182.32	$23,934.48

When we consider what financial difficulties there are everywhere, we feel that the Loan Fund's statement is not only not disheartening, but even more encouraging than might be expected.

ELIZABETH Y. MAGUIRE, 1913,

Chairman.

THE PRESIDENT'S PAGE

Further excerpts from Miss Park's speech at time of the annual meeting.

Bryn Mawr seemed to most of its graduates, I think, a reasonably efficient as well as a pleasant little world, profitable to its own temporary denizens and to many outside, a justification of generous endowments and gifts of the past. It had definiteness and solidity, and it made a definite and solid contribution, however small, to the great world around it.

The best part of that contribution was not learning, not new method, but the kind of woman which the college turned out; for however much the individual varied, the type of training was safeguarded. Students came by the then unusual selective apparatus of the entrance examination. A curriculum of wisely chosen content was presented to them, and presented skilfully. Books and apparatus, the presence of older students and of the scholars on the faculty, underlined the undergraduates' daily work, and process and type were justified. The Victorian and post-Victorian periods of, on the whole, increasing well being, increasingly liberal views and a growing social conscience, needed and appreciated the intelligent well-trained independent woman whom Bryn Mawr turned out with her honest, if at times exaggerated, faith in her standards and her powers. The education fitted the time.

Bryn Mawr is still making a contribution, and still a definite and solid contribution in its graduates, and I believe its training and its graduates are again adapting themselves to an immediate need. In 1914 the tradition of the Victorian age broke abruptly, and for almost twenty years we have lived in an abnormal world—first in the shadow of war, then briefly in war itself, and since 1918 in mounting confusion. Our values have been contorted every moment of every day. The young person going out into American life needs, as never before, intelligence, sound training and independence; but something more—resourcefulness and courage. What idea in that earlier formula hampers it for immediate use now? The rigidity of its mould, I think. Its traditional origin affected its content, and it affected no less the relation of its acquirer or its possessor toward it. She was to be of different stuff from her surroundings—as rock to sand, as water springs to the desert, as leader to followers. At the moment another picture of education seems to be more to be emphasized—that which sees education as a common food from which we draw, that common nourishment to become in each individual her own fabric.

From this view of education the individual, her formal training ended, turns to a world not of a different substance from herself, but one in which she must use to best advantage what is common to all. She needs a preparation, practical, spiritual, which will make her able to deal with the common possibilities, make them her own and enlarge them. This means that those of us who have the formalities of admission and curriculum in charge must have as an end not a fixed programme, however carefully chosen its balance and however established its variety, but an elastic and adaptable plan which will meet the needs of the particular student and leave in her as infrequently as possible unproductive areas which one may compare to the particles of shell or sand which the shellfish walls off and leaves untouched forever! It is because Bryn Mawr has become more elastic in its various requirements and devices that I feel more satisfied today. The college is interested in finding two equally good ways toward an end. It recognizes that the kind of brain a student brings is more important than the exercise that brain has learned to perform. So it has varied and is varying and increasing the points of view from which it surveys its applicants. Once the individual girl is in college, the work is fitted earlier and more directly to her liking. As she proceeds with it she can carry it further herself with informal rather than formal direction from the older scholar. Her own life is less academic, though I think no less intellectual. It is interpenetrated far more by the life outside. And difficult as that situation often is for the administration of the college, I believe that later on it will make the college graduate more ready to insist that her ordinary life should be interpenetrated by the abstract, the intellectual and the spiritual.

COLLEGE SCHEDULE FOR APRIL, 1933

Tuesday, April 11th—Auditorium at 4 and at 8.20: Motion picture, *A nous, la liberté,* for the benefit of Scholarships. Admission, 50 cents.

Thursday, April 13th—Auditorium at 8.20: Dr. Morris Cohen, Professor of Philosophy at City College, will speak on *Philosophy of History.*

Sunday, April 16th—The Cloister at 5.00. Miracle Plays by the Bryn Mawr Players.

Wednesday, April 19th—Auditorium at 8.30: Mrs. Pearl S. Buck, lecture on *The Chinese Sense of Humor,* under the auspices of the Chinese Scholarship Committee. Admission, $1.00 and $1.25. Tickets may be obtained from the Director of Publication, Taylor Hall.

Friday and Saturday, April 21st and 22nd—Auditorium at 8.20: The Varsity Players' presentation of *Lady Windermere's Fan.* Admission $1.25 and $1.50.

Sunday, April 23rd—Music Room at 7.30: Musical Service; address by the Reverend Andrew Mutch, D.D., Minister of the Bryn Mawr Presbyterian Church.

Friday, April 28th—Auditorium at 8.20: Ann Elizabeth Sheble Memorial Lecture by T. S. Eliot.

Sunday, April 30th—Music Room at 7.30: The Reverend Henry Sloane Coffin, D.D., President of the Union Theological Seminary.

Commencement will be held this year
on Tuesday, June 13th.

HOLIDAY IN RUSSIA
THOUGHTS OF A CASUAL TOURIST

By Marguerite Bartlett Hamer, 1913
Assistant Professor of History, University of Tennessee

"He that would bring home the wealth of the Indies must carry with him the wealth of the Indies," wrote "the wisest of mankind" centuries ago. A first visit to the United Soviet Socialist Republics might be thrilling to the visitor if he could have in mind the story of a nation's rise from autocracy, superstition, serfdom, actual slavery. By political revolution, and social upheaval, the U. S. S. R. came into being, dedicated to the elevation of the proletariat. Russia is today a living, acting embodiment of a new social order in the making. It is well to keep this fact in mind when drawing analogies between this new world and the aged social order of our western world.

Thus entrenched, the tourist is ready to visit the Soviet Republics. His Soviet hosts are ready to receive him. Already before the frontiers are reached, interpreters have boarded the train and are on hand to assist foreigners through the customs, to aid them in changing money, or rather in not changing money, for even in its own home the ruble is not welcome. Only foreign money is acceptable at the Torgsins, government stores for tourists. Kodaks are admitted, but are noted on the owner's passport, together with all undeveloped films, which may not be exported from Russia and are developed and printed for the tourist at a nominal price by the U. S. S. R. I still await the delivery of prints which were to be mailed from Moscow. Diaries, dictionaries, postcards, and printed material generally are so many objects of solicitude on the part of customs officials until suspicions are set at rest by the ever-present interpreters.

Every newcomer into Russia is sure to be impressed by the guides. They correspond to no other institution in any other country of which I know. They make of sightseeing a fine art, a glorified profession. They are at once companions, students, teachers, hosts, guardians, and even ministering angels to tourists in distress. They flatter the visitor with stimulating questions: How do the American people feel about prohibition, disarmament, the negro problem. Their broad interests, familiarity with political and social problems of the wide world, personal appreciation of art treasures, stamp them as the logical heirs of the old *intelligentsia*, sharing their common scorn of the aristocracy and corresponding devotion to the proletariat.

Unlike their prototypes of other days, the Soviet guides are the faithful employees of the government. They have passed rigorous civil service examinations, and are ready and able to expound the virtues of the U. S. S. R. Western visitors cannot escape learning that Soviet Russia represents the fulfillment of the Revolution, the millenium, the glorified realization of a plan, or of plans, for the second Five-Year Plan is already under way, anticipating, among other ends, the annihilation of all social inequalities. Through charts, statistics no end, the benighted western world is encouraged to profit by Russia's example. As a last parting fling the walls of the customs house on a Russian frontier bordering Poland proclaims

in five languages to an unsympathetic world: "Proletarians of the world, unite!"
The United States of America having failed to recognize the U. S. S. R. is a beloved
object of attack. In a Rogues Gallery confined to Soviet enemies I recognized the
unaggressive features of our President Hoover. I found the United States listed
among the most militaristic nations of the world. My attempted defense of the
American people against the charge of militarism withered before the spirited retort
of my Russian friend: "Your government is militaristic and the people are not,
then they should revolt."

For the further edification of foreigners, the Soviet guides love to draw contrasts between the social inequalities of the old regime and the prevailing equality
of opportunity for all. Gorgeous czaristic palaces serve to show the ease that
marked the life of the rulers in contrast with the poverty of the enslaved proletariat.
The czar's palatial rooms contrast with the modest quarters of Stalin and the two
poor little rooms proudly pointed out as the dwelling place of Lenin and his wife.
So the tourist is permitted to tread where the saints have trod. He may tread also
the pearl inlaid floors of the palace of Catherine the Great, note the walls magnificent even yet in yellow satin damask, Wedgwood plaques, silver, gold, tapestries,
Gobelins, and rare paintings, the gifts of foreign sovereigns to Russia's czars. Not
far away the tourist sees also a photostat of an old newspaper advertisement: A
horse, a pig, and a young girl are to be sold on a given day.

Just as cruel inequalities in czaristic society are emphasized, so, too, the
church, the capstone of the old regime, comes in for the taunts of the guides. They
take sly delight in pointing out the throne of the czar still undisturbed in a great
cathedral in Leningrad, in deriding the still preserved relics of the late Czarina:
her sacred dead fish, her beloved icons, her favorite family portrait in which an
angel from high heaven is pictured conversing with the Romanoffs, who, like the
Cabots of Massachusetts, spoke only to God, with an exception in each case:
Rasputin and the Lowells respectively.

The fall of the church with its attendant sacraments doomed the wedding ceremony. Soviet law recognizes only civil marriage. I witnessed several marriages at
Moscow. The betrothed take seats before a table opposite a clerk who records the
customary details: previous marriages, divorces, age, residence, health. The divorce
procedure differs merely in being even simpler. Only the aggrieved party need
appear. Notice is served on the party of the second part. A divorce may be granted
the day after the marriage and no cause need be assigned. However, as my inter-
preter explained, "It is not allowed to a man that he 'spoil' (ruin) a girl."

The U. S. S. R. has made sightseeing as nearly as possible enjoyable. The
guides are not only cultured, but charming and friendly young women. I have
known them to retain their poise and good humor for days on end, even under the
duress of questions leveled at them by tourists from almost any part of the
U. S. A. For the comfort of the visitors, the guides have at their command a fleet
of handsome touring cars, the property of the Soviet government. Interspersed with
sightseeing is a program of entertainment. The tourist is virtually the guest of the
U. S. S. R. At the modest rate of ten dollars a day he receives not only hotel
accommodations and meals, but is treated to a glamorous performance at the opera,
or to a movie, where he may see again the clergy satirized and the old nobility held

up to scorn, as in one picture called "The Crippled Landlord." Here a nobleman ·
has "spoiled" a peasant girl, who therefore drowns herself. Her dripping form is
spread on the beach exactly at the moment that her despoiler rides by accompanied
by an aristocratic bride. These were the bad old days.

The movie or opera may be ended, but not Soviet entertainment. Our gentle
guide carries her charges back to the hotel, where, still under the auspices of the
U. S. S. R., a sumptuous meal is served at two in the morning, the good old Russian
hour for dinner. The food itself is splendid. It was no fault of the delicious soups
that I never succeeded in finishing a portion. The flies were too quick for me.
Screens, I hope, are included in the Second Five-Year Plan. I might make several
suggestions; but in Russia I soon forget material details.

That the U. S. S. R. is a government that caters to its workers is everywhere
obvious. The guides, for example, are given six weeks vacation at government
expense. Workers take vacations at public rest clubs. One which I visited in
Leningrad was a mansion converted into a boarding house. Rows of cots made an
incongruous showing in their setting of frescoed ceilings and ornate walls. In
another Workers Club at Moscow, recreation rather than rest was the Soviet object.
Here workers played chess, read books and pamphlets, or enjoyed from a roof
garden a view of the Moskva. For the more energetically inclined, broad open spaces
furnished opportunities for folk dancing in which any improvised leader was free
to spring from the crowd and direct the dance.

More strictly athletic development is made possible in Moscow at a govern-
ment-built stadium, where track events of many types are the order of the day.

In raising the masses to levels of greater happiness, the Soviet Republics have
not neglected the children. The notorious wild boys of Leningrad are no more to
be seen begging and stealing on the streets. They have been collected and placed
in boarding schools far removed from the city. My guide informed me that I was
the first foreigner ever to visit any one of these schools. Certainly the one that
I saw was no showplace. At first the general atmosphere of dire poverty crowded
out all but materialistic considerations. Buildings were dilapidated, work shops
inadequate, the boys scarcely clothed at all. The young men who instructed them
were clad only in the briefest of dark blue or black shorts without even a pretense
at footgear. But first impressions of gloom gave way to something more joyous.
The spirit of contentment on the part of the youngsters, the geniality of the
instructors proved contagious. I enjoyed seeing the several plots of ground for
vegetables and flowers which each boy individually cultivates. Finally, when I took
my leave, I carried away several bouquets of flowers, the individual gifts of these
several youngsters, children but lately rescued from city slums.

This is all that I know of the religion that is taught the younger generation
of the U. S. S. R. Churches of several denominations among them, even a Chinese
temple, do exist and hold services. The mass in a Roman Catholic Church in
Moscow is celebrated just as in any other Roman Church in western Christendom.
Yet many of the magnificent cathedrals have fallen upon luckless days. While
walking one morning in the broad streets of Leningrad I selected as my objective
the Byzantine dome of a distant church. Eager anticipation hastened my footsteps.
Closer sight changed glamour to gloom. The lovely building was serving as a

warehouse. Packing boxes lined the interior and rested against doors overlaid in metal which represented New Testament scenes. A jagged fragment had been torn from its place and was creaking in the morning breeze. Words in such languages as I know, wild gestures, a few kopeks and the jagged scrap of cathedral door was mine. After surviving at least four customs inspections it has come at last to rest in a fitting frame and now graces the wall of my study.

It would be a mistake to suppose that foreigners in Russia are not free to roam at will as fancy directs. I have walked along carefree and unobserved for hours along the narrow cobblestone streets of Moscow, and struggled across Leningrad's broad Nevski Prospekt. The streets are universally clean, but dotted with great puddles of water. The passers-by are energetic, hurrying on with no regard for a stranger. The tramways, always filled to overflowing, furnish the main means of transit. Droshkys stand idle at ten rubles (five dollars) the hour, for hire, not sale, nor could a driver be importuned to take less. No Russian street scene would be complete without at least one drunkard staggering by to end his zigzag course in the gutter, there to remain unmolested, evidently a not uncommon sight.

Almost any type of person excepting well dressed may be seen in the busy streets of a Russian city. Surely in the Soviet Republics there are neither riches nor poverty. The men are invariably clad in plain black shirts gathered at the waist and falling over loose pantaloons. For the women any kind of skirt reaching to the knees suffices, with cotton stockings or none at all. Flat-soled shoes are the unvarying type. Instead of a hat, a 'kerchief is tied at the back of the head. In Moscow the rough black shirts, often as not, yield to white ones. Once at a park I saw a silk shirt trimmed in colored embroidery.

Clothes do not matter in Russia. Everyone has something more interesting with which to engage his thoughts. There is no unemployment in the Soviet Republics. I saw no beggars on the streets or along country roads. All this was in delightful contrast to neighboring Poland, where ragamuffins lounge about the churches or street icons, pestering passers-by. In Russia every sixth day is a holiday for someone. No one general day of idleness is observed by all. The names of the days of the week are forgotten, along with other relics of the old régime. Monday is no more noted than Sunday, nor Sunday more than Monday.

What may be the state of the Russian soul I cannot, of course, pretend to say. I think of country houses with ornately carved windows that are bright with fresh flowers. I think of the ballet, the music, and especially of the sight of lovers walking hand in hand along twilight streets, and then I would inquire, "What is wrong with Soviet Russia?"

The College Library would like to have a collection of Year Books, which are completely absent from the shelves. Copies of these in good condition would be welcome, and may be sent to the Alumnae Office, Taylor Hall, Bryn Mawr.

CAMPUS NOTES

By JANET MARSHALL, 1933

Of especial interest just now are the spring plans for Varsity Dramatics, which include three plays instead of the usual one: a version of an Easter miracle play to be given out of doors, a modern-dress production of *Lady Windermere's Fan*, and a Greek tragedy to be given at night outside of Goodhart on the evening of Garden Party. Also, the old custom of playing with Princeton actors in the male parts is being revived. Varsity Dramatics sponsored a most successful venture here this month when they invited the famous Jitney Players to present *Murder in the Red Barn*, a good old 1840 "melodramer," in Goodhart. The Players invited the company here with some misgivings, as it is almost impossible to fill Goodhart this season with anything like a price of admission to scare off impecunious undergraduates. This is unfortunate, as the program in Goodhart has been unusually fine this year, including such men as Yeats and Alfred Adler, the psychologist. Free lectures and concerts draw audiences that show all too clearly the reasons for the slim attendance at pay-affairs. There is plenty of interest and enthusiasm, but there is a sad lack of means.

Another performance in Goodhart that attracted a great deal of attention was the lecture given by Victoria Sackville-West on D. H. Lawrence and Virginia Woolf, under the auspices of the Undergraduate Board. Miss Sackville-West is a person of great personal charm and she proved tremendously popular. There were some critics on the campus who complained of the lack of scholarly material in her lecture and took issue with the critical opinions she expressed—or denied even that they were critical opinions, but the large majority of the students, while they were forced to admit that her lecture was put across mainly on her personality, did not feel that this was a fault.

Two other lectures which should have been of unusual interest were Dr. Perry Dunlap Smith's lecture on Progressive Schools and the problems of teachers in them, and Dr. Rhys Carpenter's lecture on *When the Greeks Began to Write*. The first was very sparsely attended, and although Dr. Smith is considered one of the foremost authorities on progressive schooling, none of our prospective teachers seemed overwhelmingly interested in progressive methods. It may have been the time of day, or the unusual pre-quiz hustle in College that prevented more from attending, but it is odd that more discussion should not have been raised among those who did attend. One can only conclude that Bryn Mawr teachers have no intention of becoming factors in the new educational movements—for all that they are fervent individualists in college.

Dr. Carpenter's lecture met with a more enthusiastic reception, but in this case it was only from the comparatively small group of classical scholars who knew what he was talking about. Those who did attend and who understand were most enthusiastic. It was an unusual opportunity, even in a college community, to be allowed to hear from the lips of the leader in a most important line of classical research, the statement and proofs of a theory as vitally important as the new theory concerning the dating of the rise of the Greek alphabet. Dr. Carpenter is an extremely charming speaker and is very popular as a lecturer with his college classes, but his field is likely to seem very specialized to the uninitiated, and many students who would undoubtedly have enjoyed his lecture steered clear of it because they did feel that it was outside their ken. As usual, the outside world knew more about the importance of such affairs than the student body, and the audience from the graduate school and the neighborhood was larger and of course more intelligent than the undergraduate audience.

The two ever-present college problems of numerical against letter grades, and of the "quota" system in assigning students to halls have been discussed in the editorial columns of the *News* all year and are now being discussed in committees of the Undergraduate Association. The first is a question of whether or not numerical marks are really fair, or whether their very definiteness does not defeat their purpose of enabling the administration to make accurate comparisons between the work of any group of students. From the point of view of the students themselves, the vaguer type of grading as represented by the old "credit and merit" system is preferable, because it discourages invidious comparisons and decreases the interest in grades as such. From the administration's point of view it is a question of the real accuracy of number-symbols for effort and achievement. The "quota" question is a very old and very complex problem. As things stand now, certain percentages of each class are assigned to each hall and the ruling is enforced with absolute inflexibility. This works out inconveniently in so very many individual cases that it is a serious obstacle to many types of interclass friendships and contacts. No one wants to live apart from her friends, but if she is so unlucky as to make her friends in different halls, she is up against a serious problem in trying to move to them or have them move to her. There is a good deal less moving on the campus than might be desired, anyway, because the dangers of the chaotic general draw are such that no student feels at all secure, when she gives up her room and goes into the draw with the intention of moving to another hall, from the horrible prospect of finding herself out of her own hall, unable to get into the hall of her first choice, and deposited some place where she never did want to go. On the other hand, without the quota there is considerable danger of class-halls.

Both of these are complex problems and ones which affect everyone in College, but while most of the students have an opinion, it is amazing to see how apathetic most of them are in the matter of concerted and constructive action. It is all the more amazing when it is recalled how very constructive student reformers have managed to be in the not-far-distant past. Much of the apathy is caused, I think, by the great amount of necessary red tape involved in making any change; but surely some of it is just another reflection of that lack of "college spirit" on which Bryn Mawr seems to pride itself. Another contributing factor is, doubtless, a difficulty which seems especially acute this year, that of constructive coöperation between the scattered and very individualistic leaders of campus thought and activity. While they are full of opinions and some excellent constructive criticism, they have so far been unable to hit upon a plan that is practical and which suits any majority group. Perhaps next month, when the committees have turned in their reports, all this will have to be recanted; it is a consummation devoutly to be wished. If we can learn to coöperate in our creative activities, and I should certainly say we had, we should be able to learn to coöperate in affairs of ordinary business.

THE ALUMNAE BOOKSHELF

THE ISRAEL SAGA, *by Brooke Peters Church*. The Macmillan Company, 1932.

In the *Israel Saga*, a book of some 300 pages, it is not the King James version of the Bible which interests Brooke Peters Church, nor the influence of its uniquely magnificent English on all subsequent writings in our tongue. The English text is for her merely a means of penetrating to the Hebrew, in which alone her enthusiasm seems to live—an enthusiasm potently inherited from the distinguished Biblical scholar who was her father. The detailed intricacies of the "higher criticism," which sorts out the interwoven strands composing the accepted text and labels them with cold anonymity J, E, P, Sm, Sl, will scarcely ever interest a lay reader except in broadest summary; and they are consequently seldom offered to the general public. In the *Israel Saga* we encounter them throughout. Anyone who has ever tried to master them will ever afterward experience great difficulty in shaking free of them and viewing the Old Testament externally; and Mrs. Church has clearly fallen victim to this difficulty. The consequent emphasis on textual source analysis seems to me the only drawback to an otherwise completely successful work.

Particularly effective are the introductory chapters on the historical and mythological background, written with maturity of judgment and great clarity. The succeeding analysis of the various books of the Old Testament gains by having all religious sentiment set aside for the moment as irrelevant to the task in hand. Literary value for Mrs. Church does not depend on poetical but on dramatic quality, not on beauty of thought or expression but on vividness and power of plot and characterization. This attitude, as unfamiliar as it is stimulating, no doubt results from the deliberate disregard of the Bible as English and unfamiliarity with it as Hebrew, thus eliminating the more obvious and immediate resources of language and bringing into prominence the more remote factors of thought and meaning, of dramatic purpose and formal structure.

Recently I have by chance been re-reading Eduard Meyer's chapters on the Hebrew people and their religion. Turning from them to Mrs. Church's book, I have felt only the more strongly how extremely well read she is, how judicious in presenting her material, how skilful in constructing a critical narrative which is worlds removed from a mere popular revamping of Bible stories. The *Israel Saga* springs from a serious and successful attempt to look at the Old Testament with an accurately informed and independently thoughtful mind, and to record the resulting observations in exceptionally lucid English.

RHYS CARPENTER,
Professor of Classical Archaeology.

THESE UNITED STATES AND HOW THEY CAME TO BE. A history for young readers, *by Gertrude Hartman*. The Macmillan Company, $5.

It can be said without qualification that this is a good book. It is very decidedly an excellent history, told with sincerity, accuracy and an extraordinary care as to the selection of details. Any single narrative of American history from the time before Columbus to the present day must, of necessity, pass with great

(26)

rapidity over a vast number of events. It is the method of this account, however, to give in each period some special episode, set forth with all the vividness of intimate description, and yet to slight nothing, apparently, of the connecting intervals. We read of the tremendous welcome accorded to Columbus by the whole of rejoicing Spain when he returned from his great discovery, of Balboa's first going to sea as a stowaway in a barrel, of Drake, on the darkest of stormy nights, making his attack by torch light on the Spanish treasure houses at Nombre de Dios.

It is not merely the picturesque period of discovery which had been made to sound so alluring, but the whole march of settlement and progress in our country. The chapter, New Homes for Old, is not narrative at all, but an absorbing review of life exactly as it was lived at the time before the Revolution. Very little has been made of wars and military detail; a great deal is said of the steady advance of real history during the eras of peace. It is true that the people stand out rather less than the events, in this account, and that such men even as Washington and Lincoln are dwarfed by the magnitude of the whole American panorama.

The illustrations are delightfully chosen, and are large and varied, but always appropriate collection from many sources. There are a great many of these old prints in which the ladies and the horses have preternaturally slim ankles and everybody appears as very stately and noble. There is an inimitable picture of the Spanish Armada, taken from a tapestry in the House of Lords. Some particularly important scenes are shown through reproductions of mural paintings by Howard Pyle and Albert Herter, in which the beauty and excitement of those great moments are captured forever.

Mention must be made also of the chapter headings, "First Families of America"—these being the red ones—"For England and the Queen," "Gold! Gold!! Gold!!!," "Thenceforth and Forever Free," "Towering Cities and the Busy Hum of Men." Many an indifferent young mind will be lured by this book into an interest in our own history, and many an appreciative one will be stimulated by it, for this is the true stuff of the American adventure.

CORNELIA L. MEIGS, 1907.

IMPRESSIONS OF SACKVILLE-WEST

Written by an alumna to an English friend

At last I know why the British are the greatest colonizers in the world. They are thoroughly nice people, but they *dare* to be anything. I wish you could have heard Miss V. Sackville-West's lecture on D. H. Lawrence and Virginia Woolf. She had crammed Lawrence from the Letters and Aldous Huxley's preface. She may have read a few of the books, but I am more inclined to believe that she had other source books and had made a compilation. Virginia Woolf she apparently knows, but she must have been told that little "whimsy"-Winnie the Pooh-Barrie-ish stuff would please an American audience, and she gave an awful and repelling picture of that fastidious queen of the super-lettered. I will say to her credit that she did not enjoy lecturing. She ended as nearly on the hour as it was decent to do.

CLASS NOTES

Class Editor: MARY ALICE HANNA PARRISH
(Mrs. J. C. Parrish)
Vandalia, Missouri.

1889

No Editor appointed.

1890

No Editor appointed.

1891

No Editor appointed.

1892

Class Editor: EDITH WETHERILL IVES
(Mrs. F. M. Ives)
145 E. 35th St., New York City.

1893

Class Editor: S. FRANCES VAN KIRK
1333 Pine St., Philadelphia, Pa.

1894

Class Editor: ABBY BRAYTON DURFEE
(Mrs. Randall Durfee)
19 Highland Ave., Fall River, Mass.

1895

Class Editor: ELIZABETH BENT CLARK
(Mrs. Herbert Lincoln Clark)
Bryn Mawr, Pa.

1896

Class Editor: ABIGAIL CAMP DIMON
1411 Genesee Street, Utica, N. Y.

Lucy Baird is teaching this year at the Shipley School and living at Low Buildings.

Polly McKeehan Core is at 64 Oxford Street, Cambridge, Mass., this year, while her daughter, 17 years old, attends the Sargent School of Physical Education. After her husband died in 1927 Polly took an apartment in Washington, D. C., which she expects to make her permanent home.

Mary Gleim is still Field Secretary for the Cas' Alta School in Florence, Italy.

Laura Heermance spent a few days in January with Hilda Justice. Laura is living in her old house in New Haven and enjoys the companionship in her home of an old friend, a librarian.

Anna Hoag entertained several of her college contemporaries at dinner on Sunday after the Alumnae Meeting. The large house is full again this winter. John and his wife occupy a housekeeping apartment on the second floor, and Clarence's mother, 95 years old, but youthful in mind and spirit, with a companion, takes two rooms, so Anna and Clarence have betaken themselves to the third floor. Anna keeps busy cooking and looking after the house and is flourishing under her active life.

The Nation of January 25th prints a remonstrance in verse by Edith Wyatt, "concerning free speech and freedom of religious belief" and "addressed to a certain school of American literary critics." Another poem by Edith, "In Praise of Obscurity," appeared in the *Saturday Evening Post* of February 18th.

The Class of '96 are sorry to learn of the death of Dr. Caroline Latimer on January 22nd, in Boston. Since leaving Baltimore several years ago she had made her home in a Boston hotel, where, because of ill health, she lived very quietly, writing a little from time to time as she was able.

Though her classmates had lost touch with her of late, we all, especially those of us who spent our first two years in Radnor, remember her with warm affection. Her caustic and yet sympathetic comments on life and affairs in and out of college helped us to see things in their true proportions, and association with her unusual mind and character was one of the stimulating experiences of our undergraduate life.

1897

Class Editor: FRIEDRIKA HEYL
104 Lake Shore Drive, East, Dunkirk, N. Y.

Does everyone know that '97 is having its 36th reunion in June? A special letter is going out to each one from the committee in charge of arrangements, but M. Campbell has asked me to let you know at once that the class supper will be held on Saturday, June 10th, in the Common Room, so that you may all be able to plan for that date. We are to live in Pembroke West.

Sue Blake, Emma Cadbury, Marys Campbell, Converse and Fay, Elizabeths Jackson and Towle, and Mabel Searle attended the alumnae meetings at mid-year.

During the week following, Sue Blake, at her home in Merion, gave a small tea for Emma Cadbury, who was her guest. Emma is now with her brother, Benjamin Cadbury, in Moorestown, N. J. We are hoping that she will in a later issue tell us something about her interesting activities in this country.

Elizabeth H. Jackson's daughter Margaret, who plans to enter Bryn Mawr next fall, is spending a few months in Paris learning more French. She sailed in February in company with Gertrude Frost Packer's daughter, Mrs. Cedric Seager, and her husband and infant daughter, who are on their way back to Instanbul after visiting the Packers in Winchester, Mass.

Before M. Campbell returned from England in September, she had the pleasure of attending the wedding of Lydia Tierney's daughter Anna, and the reception at Lydia's home in London.

Out along the shores of Lake Erie, still piled high with snow hills, the sap is surging up into the maple syrup buckets; the crows are flapping over the wet fields; the stars of Bethlehem are peeping up, dark green, through the gray grass—but very, very meagre news has dripped into the Class Editor's bucket since the beginning of the year. Not. one peep— not even a caw—has come from 97 per cent of the class. Awake! Spring is here! R. S. V. P.

1898

Class Editor: EDITH SCHOFF BOERICKE
(Mrs. John J. Boericke)
328 Brookway, Merion Station, Pa.

Alice Gannett writes from Cleveland that her settlement is busier than ever before in its history. The attendance has doubled in two years since the depression, and they are interested in helping the men try out various forms of community organization—one, beautifying the park near the settlement with a lovely garden on which the Neighborhood Improvement Association did all the supervision of work. The other is a barter scheme which they are discussing with interest, but as yet with no tangible results. Alice is also tremendously interested in the Unemployment Insurance bill now in the Ohio Legislature. She went to a hearing on it in Columbus, and they have hopes of its passing.

As usual, '98 had a little group at the Alumnae meeting on February 11th, headed by Marion Park, whose late address has already been published. Others present were: Betty Bancroft, whose daughter is Warden of Merion Hall; Ullericka Oberge, still teaching at Miss Wright's School; Mary Calvert, Mary Bright, Helen Woodall, Esther Thomas, Blanche Stein, Josephine Goldmark, Bertha Wood, and your Editor.

1899

Editor: CAROLYN TROWBRIDGE BROWN LEWIS
(Mrs. Radnor Lewis)
55 Park Ave., New York.

1900

Class Editor: LOUISE CONGDON FRANCIS
(Mrs. Richard Francis)
414 Old Lancaster Rd., Haverford, Pa.

The members of our class at the Alumnae Meeting were Emily Palmer, Lois Farnham Horn, Ellen Baltz Fultz, Renee Mitchell Righter and Louise Congdon Francis.

Emily Palmer has given up her position as Head Worker in the settlement and come back to Philadelphia for a hard-earned rest. Emily lives in the same house she did when we were in College. She and Mary Kilpatrick are the only members of the class who have not changed their address.

Johanna Kroeber Mosenthal has changed her address very recently. She has only one child at home and so has moved to the Hotel Volney, 23 East 74th Street. Johnny writes that it is economical and sensible, but she is not very enthusiastic about hotel life. Joan is planning for Vassar next fall. Barbara graduates from there this June. Joseph is a blissful sophomore at Yale.

Clara Seymour St. John has been vacationing in Florida after pneumonia.

Julia Streeter Gardner has under her wing this winter her year old grandson. His mother is in a sanitarium in Brookline and his navy father is at sea.

Two daughters of our classmates will graduate from Bryn Mawr this June—Barbara Korff and Anna Martin Findley.

Although it is a long time since we have any of us seen Mary Kirkbride Peckitt, I am sure the members of the class will sympathize with her in the death of her father, Dr. Kirkbride.

Edna Fischel Gellhorn and Dr. Gellhorn have just been on an Eastern tour visiting their sons. Walter Gellhorn has just accepted a very interesting position at Columbia as Associate Professor in the Law School. His chief interest is governmental work. He will go to Columbia from the Solicitor General's Office in Washington. Incidentally, while Edna was in Philadelphia she spoke to the Bryn Mawr undergraduates on "Women in Politics."

1901

Class Editor: HELEN CONVERSE THORPE
(Mrs. Warren Thorpe)
15 East 64th St., New York City.

1902

Class Editor: ANNE ROTAN HOWE
(Mrs. Thorndike Howe)
77 Revere St., Boston, Mass.

1903

Class Editor: GERTRUDE DIETRICH SMITH
(Mrs. Herbert Knox Smith)
Farmington, Conn.

1904

Class Editor: EMMA O. THOMPSON
320 S. 42nd St., Philadelphia, Pa.

Hope Woods Hunt is very busy this winter enjoying running her farm at Kendal Green, Massachusetts. Every Tuesday she conducts a class on International Current Events. Hope is Chairman of International Co-operation under the League of Women Voters. Her greatest interest and enthusiasm, however, is in her *Poetry Readings.* Already she has given a number of very successful readings at women's clubs and girls' schools.

On Saturday evening, March 4th, the Freshman Class of '36 presented the play "Heavenly Bodies." In the front row of seats I discovered Sara Palmer Baxter and Patty Rockwell Moorhouse enjoying the play immensely and especially thrilled by the fair Barbara Baxter arrayed in great splendor as Cleopatra and looking very beautiful and distinguished. Another famous individual in splendid armor with great helmet and shield appeared as Mars. This war-like gentleman proved to be Eleanor Fabyan, daughter of Eleanor McCormick Fabyan. Sophie Hunt, daughter of Hope Woods Hunt, was very efficient in taking care of the scenery. We are all so glad that Sophie is out of quarantine.

At an after the play celebration in Doreen Canaday's room (Doreen is the daughter of Marian Coffin Canaday, '06, and was the General Manager of the play), I discovered Eleanor Fabyan again, this time looking very like her mother.

Sara Palmer Baxter and her husband are visiting Patty Moorhouse for a few days.

1905

Class Editor: ELEANOR LITTLE ALDRICH
(Mrs. Talbot Aldrich)
59 Mount Vernon St., Boston, Mass.

The Class extends its deepest sympathy to Florance Waterbury on the death of her mother, February 25th.

1906

Class Editor: LOUISE CRUICE STURDEVANT
(Mrs. Edward W. Sturdevant)
3006 P St., Washington, D. C.

Ethel Bullock Beecher's two boys are both in college, one at Michigan, one at Yale. Carol, B. M. 1931, is teaching the second grade at the school for the children of the construction engineers at Hoover Dam, Nevada, and feels like a pioneer.

Elsie Biglow Barber is still running her big farm in Anne Arundel County, Maryland. She is also president of the Board of Managers of the Annapolis Hospital, on the altar guild of her church, and is deep in many other activities.

Annie Clauder is teaching Social Science and Ancient History at the Gratz High School in Philadelphia. Her thesis on American Commerce as affected by the Wars of the French Revolution and Napoleon has just been published. She is much interested in Christian-Socialism, Disarmament, and Interracial Co-operation. She is studying a little amateur astronomy.

Alice Colgan Boomsliter has been ill since September and has been forced to give up her manifold activities. Her three children are all students at the University of West Virginia. She saw Ida Garrett Murphy, Helen Wyeth Pierce, and Peggy Coyle Rahilly when she was in Philadelphia at Christmas. Ida is still deep in child welfare work for the League of Women Voters; Helen still keeps her pupils in music in spite of the depression, and Peggy is active in Democratic politics.

Phoebe Crosby Allnut resigned her position at Carson College last June. She had been there eighteen years. She spent last summer in Gloucester, Mass., studying Modern Art under Ralph Pearson, of the Design Workshop in New York. She became so interested that she is now giving all her time to it, going to New York one day a week to work with Mr. Pearson and giving weekly classes in creative design, drawing, painting, and clay modeling to a group of people who include Virginia Robinson.

Louise Cruice Sturdevant expects to sail for Shanghai, China, to spend two and a half years, on June 7th. She has been giving a class in short story writing to a group of Junior League girls this winter.

Ethel deKoven Hudson spent last summer cruising in the Mediterranean on a friend's yacht. She also visited her mother in her apartment in Venice and spent several weeks in Paris.

Augusta French Wallace returned from Europe late in September. She and "Cruice" had a marvellous spring together in Paris. Young Augusta made a brilliant record at the Sorbonne, finishing first in the Vassar group, third in the group from Delaware College, and fourth of all the American students. She has been a debutante this winter in Louisville and thoroughly enjoying it, but is thinking of studying at Columbia next winter to get her degree.

Margaret Scribner Grant is living in Washington. Her address is the Shoreham Hotel. She and Elsie and "Cruice" have had numerous informal reunions.

1907

Class Editor: ALICE HAWKINS
Taylor Hall, Bryn Mawr, Pa.

1908

Class Editor: HELEN CADBURY BUSH
Haverford, Pa.

1909

Class Editor: HELEN B. CRANE
70 Willett St., Albany, N. Y.

Catherine Goodale Warren was married on January 26th, in San Francisco, to Reginald H. Carter, an Englishman who has lived in Honolulu at various times. Hono's address is still 247 Dowsett Ave., Honolulu. We all send her our felicitations.

Early in February Scrap Ecob made one of her trips in this direction which brightened our personal outlook considerably. In an exclusive interview granted to the Editor she said: "Conforming to the necessities of the times, the New York State Committee for Mental Hygiene is placing less emphasis on mental hygiene resources (visiting teachers, etc.), and giving more time to a program of professional education in the subjects.

Eliot O'Hara, husband of Shirley Putnam, has just completed the third long painting trip he has made without his family. To Russia and Labrador he has now added South America, four months of it. As usual, he has found that a traveler who comes with a landscape brush in hand is welcomed almost as a guest. Like the moujiks of the Caucasus the sheep-ranchers of the Straits of Magellan even refused any pay for board and lodging. Mr. O'Hara has been invited by the Corcoran Gallery of Art in Washington to show his South American watercolors there from March 30th through April 23rd. This summer the four O'Haras will again be at Goose Rocks Beach, near Kennebunkport, Maine, where Mr. O'Hara will have his school of watercolor painting, as well as his general exhibition of watercolors by different artists.

Scrap also passed on the news that Georgina Biddle is off on a West Indies cruise, which we'll hope to hear about later.

A brief card from Lacy Van Wagenen says that she saw Gladys Stout Bowler, who is chaperoning her young daughter at school at some spot (illegible to us) in Switzerland. "After Christmas Sally Jacobs and I were together visiting a pupil of mine, now starting my work in Paris most successfully." It is nice to have even this casual mention of Sally; as far as we are concerned.

Mary Goodwin Storrs, as we mentioned earlier, is in Foochow, busy teaching "three classes of one each" in her own home, and occasionally substituting for her husband in teaching English to Chinese boys. Some of their Chinese friends from Shao-wu are also in Foochow, because of the Communist invasion. "Most of these people have lost pretty much all of their goods, except what they had on their persons when they fled. A number saved some bedding, and a few had boxes and baskets of clothes and valuables. But businesses are ruined and land, while it is still there, is of no present use to them. The Reds arrived at harvest time, and the rice was left to rot in the fields. So Shao-wu, a granary for this city, is itself going hungry.

"The pastors are planning to go up, without their families, and work wherever they can. Curiously, you may think, the people are eager for them. Communism looked like a way out. But experience seems to show that as its campaign is conducted in China it has all the destructive features and none of the constructive ones which are being developed in Russia. It has become as militaristic, they say, as militarism. Where, then, is the road to happiness?

"But in China, Communism is much less centralized than in Russia. When a Christian village is taken over, the 'workers' can live and run their institutions much as they choose. So even now some of our churches and schools are carrying on within the Red lines."

1910

Class Editor: KATHERINE ROTAN DRINKER
(Mrs. Cecil K. Drinker)
71 Rawson Road, Brookline, Mass.

1911

Class Editor: ELIZABETH TAYLOR RUSSELL
(Mrs. John F. Russell, Jr.)
333 E. 68th St., New York City.

Helen Emerson Chase and her husband took a holiday in Jamaica this winter, instead of skiing in Canada.

Margery Hoffman Smith has prolonged her stay in New York in order to take a course at the Art Students League in *tempera* painting which interests her especially.

Kate Chambers Seelye's Christmas letter was full of interest. "About the end of November a pet cat of the family died, of bubonic plague. The following weeks were filled with fumigation, floorwashing, rug-beating, vaccinations, and inoculations." No one else came down with the disease although several of the family "went to bed with crumbling of muscles, creaking of joints, and croakings of voice after the inoculations." During the isolation period the family made plans for next summer and in June the seven Seelyes hope- "to pile into some kind of a car and start across Europe." The five Seelye children are Dorothea, 15; Mary Averett, 13; Talcot, 10; Muriel, 7; and Katherine, 3.

1912

Class Editor: GLADYS SPRY AUGUR
(Mrs. Wheaton Augur)
820 Camino Atalaya, Santa Fé, N. M.

1913

Class Editor: HELEN EVANS LEWIS
(Mrs. Robert M. Lewis)
52 Trumbull St., New Haven, Conn.

1914

Class Editor: ELIZABETH AYER INCHES
(Mrs. Henderson Inches)
41 Middlesex Road, Chestnut Hill, Mass.

1915

Class Editor: MARGARET FREE STONE
(Mrs. J. A. Stone)
3039 44th St., N. W., Washington, D. C.

1916

Class Editor: LARIE KLEIN BOAS
(Mrs. Benjamin Boas)
2100 Pacific Ave., San Francisco, Calif.

Happy is the country that has no history, but not so the class and certainly not the Class Editor. News has been filtering through very slowly to the west—hence the lack of space 1916 has occupied in the BULLETIN.

From far-off Austin, Texas, Caroline Crowell, who is a physician in the health service at the University of Texas, writes: "As for what I am doing,—just trying to convince some five thousand female and male students that every time they get a blister they've not got blood poisoning; and calming anxious mothers as to morality and health of the University of Texas. If you are a mother, come not near me."

We wish more of our classmates would follow the heartening example of Elinor Hill Carpenter, who has written most entertainingly of country life in Pennsylvania. "After a year in Italy and five years in Greece, we have returned to America, accompanied by a Dobermann Pinscher, an Italian servant and his Greek wife; and bought ourselves a hundred and fifty-acre farm, five miles north of Downingtown. Our life is a quaint combination of·continental and American style (trilingual housekeeping, a cold house, and late dinners, combined with local farm club meetings, lots of hot water and all electrical devices) in our one hundred and seventy-five year old microscopic house. Eventually we hope

to convert the one hundred year old stone barn into a somewhat more spacious residence. I am as yet undecided as to whether to try my hand at raising dogs, alfalfa, or the more decorative subjects. As I am still too Near-Easternly suspicious of my fellow man to be very gregarious, I spend most of my time landscaping the place, or hunting rabbits and pheasants, with the dog, Jerry, from whom, plus the brook, the place takes its name, 'Jerry Run.' Some day I hope the more tolerant and self-sufficient of my classmates will pass this way, preferably when the weather is warm and the roads are open."

Ruth Lautz Cunningham is now living at 542 Michigan Ave., Evanston, Ill., and would love to see any one of 1916 who is passing through Chicago. She writes: "I have a niece, Lautz by name, who will enter Bryn Mawr in the fall. She·lives with us during her vacations, so my husband and I really belong to the group of frantic parents and guardians of the 'younger generation.'"

1917

Class Editor: BERTHA CLARK GREENOUGH
203 Blackstone Blvd., Providence. R. I.

Our deepest sympathy is extended to Lucia Chase Ewing whose husband died of pneumonia on February 8th at their home in New York.

Elizabeth Emerson Gardner has a second son, Walter Richmond Gardner, Jr., born in February.

Despite the statement contained in this column in December, Isabella Diamond is still living at 5521 Colorado Ave., Washington. D. C., where "I am having lots of fun, and which I am not even thinking of leaving—so long as my job lasts! Since it concerns income tax, I'm sure all payers thereof will consider my chances excellent." The Editor offers her humble apologies for having moved Issy's place of residence erroneously!

1918

Class Editor: MARGARET BACON CAREY
(Mrs. H. R. Carey)
3115 Queen Lane, East Falls Post Office, Philadelphia, Pa.

In spite of high hopes for a volume of news this month, your Editor has nothing to offer; partly because she knows nothing herself, partly because no one has been charitable enough to send unsolicited items, and partly because letters have so far failed to raise any class list on which to begin work. Please all take warning from the present dearth and write to the above distressed woman, and don't say, "I am doing just what I have been for the last ? years and have no news"—we have had no class notes for so long that anything can be called news.

1919

Class Editor: MARJORIE REMINGTON TWITCHELL
(Mrs. Pierrepont Twitchell)
Setauket, N. Y.

Mary Ramsay Phelps is president and treasurer of the newly-formed Bryn Mawr Club of Delaware. Frances Tatnall, '31, is secretary. They organized in order to raise money for their Regional Scholarships, and have sent in to the committee $300. Buster has been spending the winter at "Cat Island Plantation," Georgetown, S. C., where she has been tutoring nieces and nephews, keeping house for a family of twelve over the Christmas holidays, helping run the rice plantation, making a lovely garden of camellias and other winter flowers in an oval clearing in the pine woods. She and her husband returned in February to Delaware for the spring nursery work.

Liebe Lanier Boiling is connected with the Centaur Book Shop in Philadelphia.

Margaret Fay Howard has been living in Pittsburgh for the past two years, after four years in Akron. Her address is 6121 Jackson Street, Pittsburgh, 6, Pa. Her son is four and a half. They spend the summers with Margaret's mother in Wisconsin.

Hazel Collins Hainsworth has been in Wyandotte, Mich., this winter where her husband has been supervising the building of a new chemical plant. She's been studying European History every morning among her many other activities.

1920

Class Editor: MARY PORRITT GREEN
(Mrs. Valentine J. Green)
433 E. 51st St., New York City.

1921

Class Editor: WINIFRED WORCESTER
(Mrs. Harvey Stevenson)
Croton-on-Hudson, N. Y.

Elizabeth Taylor is a Regional Director of the Junior Leagues of America, and as such gets more free carfare than anyone we know. She spent February in New York, coming from Chicago where she saw all the Lake Forest contingent of our class. On her way home she was to stop at about eleven cities to inspect their Junior Leagues—she has twenty-nine under her jurisdiction.

Marian Walton (Mrs. James Putnam) is having an exhibit of sculpture at the Weyhe Galleries in New York. Another sculptor, though a far more amateur one, is Chloe Garrison Binger, who took it up only last year and is exhibiting what looks to me like a very good head at the Junior League.

Helen Weist, after thirteen years with the Dalton Schools in New York, broke away last year and has been working in Boston since then.

Nancy Porter Straus wrote at Christmas time that it looked as though her whole family might move east, as her husband has a job, the nature of which I couldn't possibly decipher. I should like more information.

1922

Class Editor: SERENA HAND SAVAGE
(Mrs. William L. Savage)
106 E. 85th St., New York City.

The class extends its sympathy to Cornelia Baird Voorhis on the death of her father who died suddenly in January; and to Ray Neel on the death of her brother, Walter Neel, who died of pneumonia in February.

Cornelia Baird Voorhis has a job on the magazine *Babies Just Babies.* She runs a shoppers' column.

Barbara Clarke has gone to Bermuda for a three weeks' sketching trip.

Mary Douglas Hay is going to Mexico in the spring with Mary Palache Gregory, '24, and her husband.

Nancy Jay Harvey has a new daughter, her second child. She was born in February and is named Phoebe.

Jeannette Palache has gone to Haiti to visit Virginia Corse Vitzthum von Eckstaedt who lives there with her husband and new son.

Harriet Stevens Robey recently published an article in the January number of the *Junior League Magazine* entitled "It Can Be Done." She gives a cheerful, entertaining picture of how to live on an income that has been cut almost in half.

1923

Class Editor: RUTH McANENY LOUD
325 E. 72nd St., New York City.

1924

Class Editor: DOROTHY GARDNER BUTTERWORTH
(Mrs. J. Ebert Butterworth)
8024 Roanoke St., Chestnut Hill, Pa.

In spite of snow-blocked roads, '24 turned out nobly for the Alumnae Meeting in February. Mrs. Clark presided most graciously, and after the main business was finished, announced Miss Thomas' offer of the Deanery for the use of the Alumnae. Among those attending the meeting in Goodhart Hall, and later on luncheon in Pem. were Buck Buchanan Bassett, Betsy Crowell Kaltenthaler, Beth Tuttle Wilbur, Mary Woodworth and your editor. While enjoying luncheon and President Park's talk on

Bryn Mawr, present and future, we glimpsed many familiar faces from '22 and '23·

Betty Ives Bartholet, who was married only last May, is now settled in her apartment at 170 East 78th Street, New York City. On the outside Betty indulges in squash and work for the unemployed. She says that Olivia Fountain is being kept busy with architectural pursuits.

Margaret Vaughan Smith was married June 9, 1928, to Dr. Francis W. Davison, who is now Associate in the Eye, Ear, Nose and Throat Department of the Geisinger Hospital in Danville, Pa., and also wielder of a bronchoscope for some hundred-mile radius. She writes: "My first baby, Joan Dudley, was born March 7th, 1930, and her little brother, Richard Alvin, arrived last April 29th. By some miracle she has the curly hair. I have no occupation outside the home except contract, which sometimes brings in a nickel or so, and the nearest I ever get to traveling is exclaiming over the cheapness of the various tours advertised in the Sunday papers."

Although she usually comes all the way from Collingwood, Ontario, to spend Christmas with her mother in Merion, this year Buck paid an extended visit. Accompanied by her husband, F. Alvin Bassett, and her young son, Buck arrived for the holidays, but as a result of a series of colds, stayed on till late in February. When last seen at the Alumnae Meeting she was clutching tickets and making a frantic attempt to start back to Canada. While there Buck is active on Church, School and Civic Committees, mostly occupied with Girl Guides and Brownies. None of these, says Buck, are for profit.

Ruth Tubby sent in a grand, detailed letter. She lives in Westfield, New Jersey, drives sixteen miles to work as head of the Children's Department of the Montclair Public Library. Her interesting job includes supervisory work of the school libraries, book buying and story telling. Last spring she was sent to the meeting of the American Library Association in New Orleans. With her mother she drove down, enjoyed the dogwood in Atlanta and the summer flowers in New Orleans. Last summer a year ago, Ruth drove all 'round France, through the Pyrenees, into Switzerland for a week and Germany for three days. She says, via Leila Barber, that Kay Neilson is studying in Germany this winter and working on her Ph.D. thesis.

As these notes go to press, I am scouring up the guest room in preparation for a flying visit from Bee Constant Dorsey. As most of you know, Bee has entirely recovered from a serious illness lasting almost a year—and we are all delighted to have her in the East again for her usual spring visit.

1925

Class Editor: ELIZABETH MALLET CONGER
(Mrs. Frederic Conger)
325 East 72nd St., New York City.

Dot Lee Haslam's second son arrived February 15th and narrowly missed being a Valentine and birthday present at the same time. Dot's birthday was the 14th, and the baby came at 6 the next morning—no sense of the dramatic.

And Peggy Boyden Magoun writes to tell of the arrival of a daughter, Margaret Boyden Magoun, 2nd, on December 28th. The Magouns are back in Cambridge at last, 4 Berkeley Place, after their year abroad. Peg says, "The trip was great fun, and it was especially nice actually settling down and keeping house and sort of seeing how it was all done. Strasbourg, where we were for the whole academic year, was terribly interesting, being a combination of French and German that I hardly realized was possible. We had a grand summer in Garmisch in the Bavarian Alps—with Munich only an hour and a half away, when we got discouraged with the rain!"

Tibby Lawrence Mendel, another expatriate, came home for Christmas, but is probably half way up an Alp now. Tibby is working on her thesis while in Rome this winter. In good Italian surroundings she writes in pure French for the Sorbonne.

Elaine Lomas also is in Rome finishing her law course. Virginia acted in a stock company last summer, but is now enjoying life in New York—818 Madison Avenue.

May Morrill Dunn is studying music in Chicago, so that she will be able to teach it. Her address is 66 Belleview Place.

In Toronto Jean Gregory is working for an M.A. in history.

Helen Herrmann has an apartment of her own at 333 East 41st Street. Helen is reading for a Ph.D. in economics, which information we cudgeled out of her.

Crit and Chet D'Arms like Vassar. (Crit is Crit Coney and she has no right to like Vassar, and Chet is her husband, whose real name is more formal, and he teaches Latin.)

Leila Barber, too, is still at Vassar, brightening the art department.

Alice Parker as usual leads a gay life in Washington and continues to be a bad correspondent (we hear).

Rachel (Foster) and John Manierre, having rented their house for the winter, are living at 596 Maple Avenue, Winnetka, with Rachel's mother. The two children are blooming.

Dorry Fiske continues to adorn a pinnacle of Harper's and likes it.

And speaking of pinnacles, somehow reminds me of thumbtacks (so agile is the human brain!) and that brings us to our own job. We're still teaching History of Architecture and Painting at the Spence School. Our bulletin board stretches for miles and miles, covered with modern pictures. In vacations we visit our son, who is staying with his grandparents in North Carolina. He's a real Southerner—sets on the po'ch, eats co'nbread and likes his religion with a lilt.

1926

Class Editor: HARRIOT HOPKINSON
Manchester, Mass.

Mary Tatnall Colby has a son, James Gordon Colby, born on February 14th.

Frances Waite was married on March 2nd to Mr. Norman Bel Geddes.

1927

Class Editor: ELLENOR MORRIS
Berwyn, Pa.

Mary Cruikshank, now Mrs. O. H. Kyster, Jr., is living in the Philippines—Fort Mills, Corregidor, is the latest address if you are writing. She hopes eventually to return to this vicinity, Fort Monroe being the next post in order.

Marian Pilton Myers is also in the Philippines, but at Manila. Her husband is in the Navy on the destroyer *Bulmer.*

Jan Seeley is an athletic instructor at William Smith College, Geneva, New York. Now don't get excited, girls; contrary to the name, it is a female institution! Jan was at Bryn Mawr for a week-end this winter, and she says that she is having a fine time.

Corinne Chambers has a job with the Cavendish Trading Company in New York, and has an apartment with Puppy McKelvey.

Lucylle Austin had Peggy Brooks Juhring and husband here for the week-end of the Philadelphia Junior League Cabaret. We glimpsed Peggy several times on the very crowded dance floor and beamed and winked, but didn't get close enough for any news value. Lu Austin, by the way, is the pillar of the Junior League, being Chairman of the Women's Committee of the Children's Heart Hospital, our special charity. Bryn Mawr is also represented on the Committee by Carrie Remak and Dot Lee Haslam, of '25, and by your editor. We are all awfully useful because we help to second motions! What a debt we owe our training at Bryn Mawr.

1928

Class Editor: CORNELIA B. ROSE, JR.
310 East 55th St., New York City.

Please note that your wandering editor has moved again. This time we hope to stay put until June 1. Perhaps if we can stay in one place long enough we may hear some news.

Mary Gaillard is living at 322½ East 50th Street, New York, with Edith Morgan Whitaker's sister, Lillian. Gaillard is still doing bacterial research at the Fifth Avenue Hospital.

1929

Class Editor: MARY L. WILLIAMS
210 E. 68th St., New York City.

1930

Class Editor: EDITH GRANT
Pembroke West, Bryn Mawr.

We have heard that Marcella Palmer Blanchard has a son of the name of Bruce, born in Manila, on December 26th.

It has just come to our notice that Miriam Lobb, ex-'30, was married last November 26th to William J. Geggis, Jr., and is living in Wayne, Pa. Mr. Geggis is a chemical engineer for the Atlantic Refining Company. Blanche Thrush was one of Miriam's bridesmaids.

Sylvia Carafiel is studying law at Washington University in St. Louis, and expects to graduate this spring.

1931

Class Editor: EVELYN WAPLES BAYLESS
(Mrs. Robert N. Bayless)
301 W. Main St., New Britain, Conn.

1932

Class Editor: JOSEPHINE GRATON
182 Brattle St., Cambridge, Mass.

On February 22nd, Elizabeth Gill announced her engagement to William Hamilton Lathrop, of Philadelphia.

A letter from Grace Holden tells of an apartment she and Charlotte Einsiedler have at 210 East 13th Street, New York City. Grace was modeling and selling in Macy's Debutante Dress Department until she decided to take a business course. Charlotte has spent her time playing the piano and writing. They are always glad to receive company, and according to report they cook Hamburgers "marvelously."

Enid Saper, so Grace says, is taking a business course, and Monica Brice has just finished one.

Patricia Stewart is teaching Latin and Ancient History at the Howard Seminary in Bridgewater, Massachusetts. She seems to enjoy it except when she must sit in the parlor on Sunday afternoons and chaperone the young ladies and their young men.

Susan Hardin has a position as social secretary in New York. She is working for Miss Miller, with whom Denise Gallaudet was abroad last summer.

We wish to extend our love and sympathy to Ruth Milliken, who recently lost her mother.

SCHOOL DIRECTORY

The Saint Timothy's School for Girls
CATONSVILLE, MARYLAND
Founded September 1882

COLLEGE PREPARATORY
AND
ELECTIVE COURSES

MISS LOUISA McENDREE FOWLER
Head of the School

WYKEHAM RISE
WASHINGTON, CONNECTICUT

A COUNTRY SCHOOL FOR GIRLS

FANNY E. DAVIES, LL.A., *Headmistress*
Prepares for Bryn Mawr and Other Colleges

Miss *Beard's* SCHOOL

PREPARES girls for College Board examinations. General courses include Household, Fine and Applied Arts, and Music. Trained teachers, small classes. Ample grounds near Orange Mountain. Excellent health record; varied sports program. Established 1894. *Write for booklet.*

LUCIE C. BEARD
Headmistress
Berkeley Avenue
Orange   New Jersey

LOW-HEYWOOD
On the Sound ~ At Shippan Point

ESTABLISHED 1865

Preparatory to the Leading Colleges for Women.
Also General Course.
Art and Music.
Separate Junior School.
Outdoor Sports.

One hour from New York

Address

MARY ROGERS ROPER, *Headmistress*
Box Y, Stamford, Conn.

The Ethel Walker School
SIMSBURY, CONNECTICUT

Head of School
ETHEL WALKER SMITH, A.M.,
Bryn Mawr College

Head Mistress
JESSIE GERMAIN HEWITT, A.B.,
Bryn Mawr College

ROSEMARY HALL
Greenwich, Conn.
COLLEGE PREPARATORY
Caroline Ruutz-Rees, Ph. D.
Mary E. Lowndes, M. A., Litt D.
Head Mistresses
Katherine P. Debevoise, Assistant to the Heads

THE SHIPLEY SCHOOL
BRYN MAWR, PENNSYLVANIA

Preparatory to
Bryn Mawr College

ALICE G. HOWLAND   } *Principals*
ELEANOR O. BROWNELL

The Kirk School
Bryn Mawr, Pennsylvania

Boarding and day school. Record for thorough preparation for the leading women's colleges. Four-year college preparatory course. One-year intensive course for high-school graduates. Resident enrollment limited to thirty girls. Advantage of small classes and of individual instruction when desirable. Informal home life. Outdoor sports.

MARY B. THOMPSON, *Principal*

Announcing ..

A SERIES *of twelve*
Staffordshire dinner
plates by Wedgwood . . .

The
Bryn Mawr Plates

The Views

LIBRARY CLOISTER
MERION HALL
PEMBROKE ARCH
LIBRARY ENTRANCE
THE OWL GATE — ROCK-
   FELLER
WING OF PEMBROKE EAST
RADNOR
SOUTH WING OF LIBRARY
TAYLOR TOWER
GOODHART
DENBIGH
PEMBROKE TOWERS

SPONSORED by the Alumnae Association, these plates are being made expressly for us by Josiah Wedgwood & Sons, Ltd., of Etruria, England. They are dinner service size (10¼ inches in diameter) and may be had in blue, rose, green, or mulberry.

THE DESIGN has been carefully studied under the supervision of the Executive Board of the Alumnae Association. The College seal dominates the plate, balanced by medallions of Bryn Mawr daisies. The background in true Victorian fashion is a casual blanket of conventionalized field flowers. This border, framing twelve views of the campus, offers a pleasing ensemble reminiscent of the Staffordshire ware of a century ago.

THE PRICE of the plates is $15 per set of twelve (postage extra). A deposit of $5 is required with your order, balance due when the plates are ready for shipment. All profits go to the Alumnae Fund.

BRYN MAWR ALUMNAE ASSOCIATION, BRYN MAWR, PENNSYLVANIA

     Please reserve for me................sets of Bryn Mawr plates at $15 per set. I enclose $5 deposit on each set and will pay balance when notified that the plates are ready for shipment.

     Color choice ☐ Blue ☐ Rose ☐ Green ☐ Mulberry

SIGNED..

ADDRESS..

*Make checks payable and address all inquiries to Alumnae Association of Bryn Mawr College
Taylor Hall, Bryn Mawr, Pennsylvania*

Bryn Mawr Plates

THE first finished samples of the Bryn Mawr plates have arrived, but we have not yet been able to secure from the Wedgwood Company a definite date when delivery may be promised. Apparently all the other colleges had to submit to the same sort of delay, but in the end they have all been satisfied. The sample plates are even more attractive than we had dared to hope. Please be patient, and rest assured that everything possible is being done to hasten delivery.

1896   *1933*

BACK LOG CAMP

(A camp for adults and families)

SABAEL P. O., NEW YORK

ON INDIAN LAKE, IN THE ADIRONDACK MOUNTAINS

QUESTIONNAIRE

Ques. Where is Indian Lake?
Ans. About 150 miles from Albany, in a real wilderness.
Ques. Can you drive to it?
Ans. To the lower end of the Lake; not to the Camp.
Ques. What do the Campers live in?
Ans. Mostly in tents very comfortably equipped. There are two cottages.
Ques. Who goes to the Camp?
Ans. People like yourself. Single men and women; whole families.
Ques. Who runs the Camp?
Ans. A large family of Phila. Quakers, college graduates.
Ques. What sort of life does the Camp offer?
Ans. Terribly boring to the sort who never come; fascinating to those who love the woods.
Ques. Is the food good?
Ans. Absolutely.
Ques. Have the rates been reduced?
Ans. Yes.

Letters of inquiry should be addressed to

LUCY HAINES BROWN · **WESTTOWN, PENNSYLVANIA**

Reference: **Anna Hartshorne Brown (Bryn Mawr, 1912),
Westtown, Pennsylvania**

Issued November 1st

THE NEW
INTERNATIONAL LAWS
OF CONTRACT BRIDGE

AUTHORIZED EDITION

Now in effect in the United States and all over the world

IMPORTANT CHANGES   NEW COUNT

NEW PENALTIES   NEW PREMIUMS

Bound in Cloth 50 cents

At all booksellers and stationers

Authorized American Publishers

THE JOHN C. WINSTON COMPANY

WINSTON BUILDING · PHILADELPHIA, PA.

BRYN MAWR ALUMNAE BULLETIN

BRYN MAWR WOMEN

IN

NATIONAL AND INTERNATIONAL AFFAIRS

May, 1933

Vol. XIII   No. 5

Entered as second-class matter, January 15, 1921, at the Post Office, Phila., Pa., under Act of March 3, 1879
COPYRIGHT, 1933
ALUMNAE ASSOCIATION OF BRYN MAWR COLLEGE

Form of Bequest

I give and bequeath to the ALUMNAE ASSOCIATION OF BRYN MAWR COLLEGE, Bryn Mawr, Pennsylvania, the sum of.............................dollars.

Sketched by Wallace Morgan in the "Club Leviathan"—its smartest supper club afloat

Ended All too Soon

—each glorious day on the LEVIATHAN

"The end of a perfect day"— how delightful to discover a day that's perfect from start to finish...how doubly delightful to know that there's another day ahead that will be as full of gay good times! On the LEVIATHAN, as on all United States Liners, you will find travel that's joyously different — good times that are *planned* in the American manner, *by* Americans—and enjoyed *with* fellow Americans.

You'll find on the ships that fly your own flag swift, understanding service by stewards who speak your own language . . . delicious treats prepared by chefs who know how to suit your own exacting taste. Yes, on United States Liners you'll find every privilege any ship can offer, *plus* the enjoyment of the American standard of living— highest in the world. For full information see your local agent. He knows travel values.

Services to GERMANY, Ireland, England and France

• • •

LEVIATHAN—*America's largest ship*

• • •

MANHATTAN WASHINGTON*
The modern "Yankee Clippers." Fastest Cabin Liners in the world.
*Maiden voyage May 10
President ROOSEVELT
President HARDING

And four staunch American Merchant Liners . . . one class only . . . very moderate rates.

CONSIDER THIS
Eighty-five cents of the dollar paid for freight and transportation on American ships is spent in America . . . It's "good business" to have the fun of traveling under your own flag.

The official GRADUATE FLEET *in over fifty colleges*

FOLLOW THE TREND TO AMERICAN SHIPS

UTMOST OCEAN SERVICE
through your local agent

U. S. LINES

AMERICAN MERCHANT LINES
ROOSEVELT STEAMSHIP CO., Inc.—*Gen. Agents*
No. 1 Broadway, New York   Agents everywhere

BRYN MAWR ALUMNAE BULLETIN

OFFICIAL PUBLICATION OF
THE BRYN MAWR ALUMNÆ ASSOCIATION

MARJORIE L. THOMPSON, '12, *Editor*
ALICE M. HAWKINS, '07, *Business Manager*

EDITORIAL BOARD

MARY CRAWFORD DUDLEY, '96
CAROLINE MORROW CHADWICK-COLLINS, '05
EMILY KIMBROUGH WRENCH, '21

ELLENOR MORRIS, '27
ELINOR B. AMRAM, '28
PAMELA BURR, '28

ELIZABETH BENT CLARK, '95, *ex-officio*

Subscription Price, $1.50 a Year   *Single Copies, 25 Cents*
Checks should be drawn to the order of Bryn Mawr Alumnae Bulletin
Published monthly, except August, September and October, at 1006 Arch St., Philadelphia, Pa.

VOL. XIII   MAY, 1933   No. 5

At the Council Meeting and at the Annual Meeting, a Report for the BULLETIN is always submitted, but such a Report concerns itself more with what has been done than with why certain things have been done, and for the most part the statement of policy is limited to the two fundamental aims of the BULLETIN: first, to keep the alumnae in touch with the College, and second, to keep them in touch with each other. A good part of each Bulletin Meeting is given over to argument back and forth as to the best way to accomplish this end. We have a definitely limited budget, which is only elastic enough to allow us to add extra pages over and above the usual 36 when it seems really necessary. The certain regular departments that we have worked out as best suited to accomplish our two-fold purpose always take up a fairly large proportion of the space. And in addition, twice a year, after the Council and after the Annual Meeting, a number of the reports must be carried to keep the alumnae, as a whole, in touch with the work of the Association. Any change in college policy, such as the experimental change in methods of admissions, or in the budget, we feel always should have right of way, to keep the alumnae as a group in touch with the College itself. All of this means that there is not much leeway in the matter of space, and that the problems of selection and proportion facing the Editorial Board must be solved with the utmost nicety and care. Now that the BULLETIN has a public of over 2,800 alumnae and is used by the College itself as a means of publicity, it ceases to be a kind of round-robin and is the organ of a large and disparate group, in which things and persons beloved and familiar to one college generation mean very little to another. That explains why, time and again, the BULLETIN has to say regretfully that it cannot print long and intimate articles about some one known to a single alumnae group, either in point of time or place, no matter how beloved by that group. The only way to make the BULLETIN fill the significant place that it should, we feel, is to try for as universal an appeal as possible. How well we succeed depends on the sympathetic and intelligent co-operation of each alumna.

RECOLLECTIONS AND REFLECTIONS OF A DEMOCRATIC CAMPAIGNER

EMMA GUFFEY MILLER, 1899

Member of the Democratic National Committee for Pennsylvania

Mrs. Miller's political experiences have been unique. She made seconding speeches for Al Smith in '24 and '28, and for Franklin Roosevelt in '32, and in the convention which nominated Smith for the Presidency, she herself received a vote and a half for President, the first time a woman was so honored in a nominating convention. In the letter she sent with her manuscript she said: "As requested, I have written a political article . . . you may not wish to publish it, for I could not avoid making it personal and partisan."

It is difficult to write of the recent campaign without referring to the previous campaigns in which women have had a part as voters. As a resident of Illinois I had voted under the laws of that state in 1916, but my real political activities began in my native commonwealth of Pennsylvania, where we had returned just before the adoption of the 19th amendment, known to most women as the Suffrage Amendment.

My family (Guffey) had been ardent and active Democrats since the days of Jefferson, but I felt there were other reasons than heredity why I should enroll as a Democrat in 1920.

Those of us who had worked for suffrage had argued passionately, if ignorantly, that when women were enfranchised they would use the ballot both intelligently and unselfishly, not for their own advantage, but for all mankind. Therefore, it seemed to me that in our first campaign all thinking women should support the Democratic party for these reasons: it was offering the world a means of permanent peace and international understanding; its declarations in regard to tariff and taxation would make for wider opportunity and more equitable distribution of wealth, and finally, history having shown that the Republican party had utterly failed to solve the reconstruction problems of the Civil War, it was not to be supposed that the same party would do any better after the World War, since its leaders were so similar to those who had undone the plans of Lincoln.

Hence most of the women speakers made campaign pleas along those lines, but with no apparent effect, for the Democrats suffered a crushing defeat. However, our first campaign taught us one thing, that women were no more motivated by altruism or a sense of historical perspective than men, and in the future the same arguments could be used for both sexes.

Meeting an old friend at the recent inauguration who thought we had motored to Washington, she inquired, "How long did it take you to get here?" and I replied, "Twelve years," because the political arguments which had failed in 1920 were receptively and enthusiastically received in 1932.

The intervening campaigns of 1924 and 1928 were memorable for two things, indifference and bigotry. In 1924 the Democrats centered their attack on the corruption of the Harding administration, which the Republicans generally ignored, but the voters remained indifferent and preferred promises of prosperity and the suggestion that the administration would grant business a free hand rather than a "clean up" in government. In 1928 came the weighty pronouncement on the one hand that prosperity was a permanent attribute of the Republican party, and on the other rose a tremendous wave of bigotry and intolerance against a candidate because of his church membership. It was a distinct shock to us Protestant speakers to discover how widespread religious bigotry was, and of the use that was being made of it by other Protestants. There is undisputed proof that the so-called endorsement of Prohibition in 1928 was merely a cloak for bigotry. This made many political leaders believe that it would be useless for a Catholic to seek the Presidency as long as the 18th Amendment is in the constitution. Happily its end is in sight.

Though once more we Democrats were defeated, many believed that the Republican party's hold on government would be of short duration, for every student of politics could see very definite cracks showing through the smoothness of the financial plaster. For example, during the eight years of the Wilson administration there were but 600 bank failures, or an average of 75 a year. In the next eight years the average was 600 a year. Surely this must mean that Republican leadership was financially inept or financially careless, but the public remained oblivious to all warnings and the campaign of 1928 was fought around personalities and religion.

Looking back on that campaign, when I spoke in thirteen states and traveled many thousands of weary miles in all kinds of weather, there is another fact which stands out in equal significance to the intolerance everywhere displayed—the complete devotion of millions of Americans to the Democratic candidate, Governor Alfred E. Smith. There was something particularly touching and inspiring in the whole-hearted love poured out to this typical American. The campaign seemed to focus on his personality. Audiences were interested in hearing mainly about "Al," and when his defeat came, thousands of his devoted admirers suffered actual grief for some time to come, at least until the market crash of 1929, when they seemed to feel a sort of vindication.

The Sunday following the election of 1928 I was in New York and called Mrs. Franklin D. Roosevelt on the phone for some hope and encouragement for the future of our party, and asked if I might come up and talk things over. She readily assented and I went to the house which has since become so famous, 49 East 65th Street, but I found I had gone to the wrong place, for Mrs. Roosevelt was just as discouraged as I was and just as blue! When I referred to her husband's election as something to be thankful for, Mrs. Roosevelt replied, "Oh! Franklin and I have scarcely thought about it; we are so depressed over the Governor's (Smith) defeat." In speaking of the fearful intolerance encountered during the campaign, Mrs. Roosevelt said; "If we had ever realized it was so deep-seated, we never would have asked Governor Smith to make the fight."

Out of the vast desert of defeat of 1928 there was left but one oasis: the election of Franklin D. Roosevelt as governor of New York. As soon as he took office the eyes of the country were turned on him as a probable Democratic candidate for President in 1932, and his overwhelming reëlection in 1930 intensified that interest.

In the celebrated Madison Square Garden convention of 1924 Mr. Roosevelt had put Governor Smith in nomination by his renowned "Happy Warrior" speech, and it had been my privilege to second that nomination.

It was during this long-drawn-out convention that I received a vote and a half for President, the first and only woman thus honored in a nominating convention since women had become "people." While I appreciated this signal distinction it came about from different motives. A young man in the Massachusetts delegation liked my seconding speech for Governor Smith so much that he decided that for one ballot he would leave his candidate and vote for me. At the time this attracted a good deal of attention, and later, when a Vermont delegate was being urged to change his vote from McAdoo to Smith, he remarked, "Well, I won't go over so sudden like; I'll vote one ballot for that Pennsylvania woman who got a vote the other day." Having, as it were, used me as a bridge, he crossed over to the other side.

In 1928 our convention met in Houston, Texas, and there Mr. Roosevelt and I enacted the same roles as in 1924, he making the nominating speech for Governor Smith and I following with a seconding speech.

Thus Franklin Roosevelt was no stranger to me. For years I had marveled at his physical courage, delighted in his sense of loyalty and justice, and wondered at his mental grasp when dealing with problems of government and administration. Even more appealing to me was his full endorsement of Jefferson's creed: "Man over money, human rights over property rights, equal and exact justice to the rich and poor, with special privilege to none."

For some time after his reëlection to the governorship he gave no signs of being a candidate for President, but early in 1932 Governor Roosevelt agreed to enter the race. Immediately from all over the country came an eager response from enthusiastic Democrats and liberal Republicans. The interesting fact, as we look back on that period, is that almost all the Roosevelt support came from the poorer districts, from the great agricultural sections, from scattered villages and county-seat towns. There was practically none from the strongholds of wealth. Recent revelations and developments in banking and financial circles show the reason for this.

To the Roosevelt delegates at our Chicago convention it was perfectly evident that our candidate was not popular with "big business." The boxes at the convention were, as is the custom, sold to the public in order to meet expenses, and it was enlightening to see how many were occupied by representatives of "special privilege."

I shall never forget a "set to" I had with one of these boxholders, a fellow-Bryn Mawrter, who was entering the hall at the same gate the night we went into that famous all-night session. We greeted each other cordially, and then noticing my Roosevelt ribbon pinned beside my delegate's badge she "sniffed" and said, "Oh! he won't be nominated. We are going to name ————," mentioning one of the lesser candidates. Suddenly all the blood of a thousand free-will ancestors reddened my face as I "snapped" back, "Excuse *me*, but this is a Democratic convention and *we* are going to name the candidate." Twenty-four hours later we did.

I had been asked to second Governor Roosevelt's nomination, but as that long session drew on and it seemed as if the speeches would never end, our strategy committee decided to cut out all further seconding speeches.

I left the platform and returned to my delegation, and told my friends there that I was relieved from speaking. Immediately the chairman of the delegation announced that would never do, as Roosevelt had more delegates in Pennsylvania than in any other state and their voice must be heard. I then endeavored to make a trade with another speaker, a delegate from my state who was going to second another candidate. I agreed to forego my speech if he would omit his, but he would not listen to such an idea, saying as mayor of his city he could not afford to disappoint the home folks. Thus, somewhere between four and five o'clock in the morning, in a much-curtailed speech beginning "Today the Democratic party faces a new era" and ending with "Be right with Roosevelt," I seconded the nomination of the present occupant of the White House.

After experiencing three national conventions I am sure of one thing, that there are always too many speeches, but no speech, unless it be by a delegate who hopes the lightning will strike him in case of deadlock or party split, ever changes many votes. Delegates are pretty well set before they go to a convention, and oratory does not affect their voting although it may influence outsiders.

Another positive feeling I have in regard to conventions is that we are prayed over too much and the Lord is over-much advised. The very fact that a minister is invited to open a political convention with prayer seems to give him the opportunity he has long desired and he becomes very personal. He seems to take it for granted that the delegates are all very wicked and he gives plenty of warnings as to the result of sin and corruption, then he usually follows with an exposé of all our country's troubles, and ends by telling God just how they should be solved. I have heard more than one person say, after sitting through days of such prayers, "Well, no more church-going for me; these preachers have disgusted me with their propaganda."

Radio has now brought political conventions not merely to our door, where the newspaper is dropped, but right to our bedside. Though I spoke at a very lonely hour there must have been many people tuning in, for frequently since, both Democrats and Republicans have said to me, "I heard you seconding Roosevelt; I never went to bed at all that night." Later in the summer a San Francisco lawyer wrote for a copy of my speech and asked for permission to use my ideas in the California campaign, so the whole country must have stayed awake.

If the convention was so interesting to those listening over the radio, think what it must have been to us who were there working constantly to keep our lines intact. Despite the propaganda against him, Governor Roosevelt had such a preponderance of delegates that it was scarcely to be considered that any coalition could defeat his nomination. Nevertheless, until the withdrawal of Mr. Garner the opposition never gave up hope, and even after the leaders knew the "jig was up," the lesser fry were still circulating about the floor trying to "steal" Roosevelt delegates at the very moment Chairman Walsh was presenting Mr. McAdoo, who made the withdrawal announcement amidst approving cheers from the delegates and jeers from the packed galleries.

It is mere repetition to relate many of the exciting and thrilling moments of those days in Chicago, but no one who was fortunate enough to be present can ever forget that impressive moment when Franklin D. Roosevelt faced Senator Thomas J. Walsh for his notification. Somehow it seemed like a crowning achievement for Senator Walsh; his long fight for honesty in government, for the rights of the people against greed and graft, for the supremacy of law over chicanery, seemed to reach fulfilment as the grim but gratified veteran spoke to the young and active crusader as the herald of a new day.

Many people said that moment had for them a spiritual significance like that of a church consecration. It certainly was the quietest time I ever felt in any such gathering, and to those of us who had long been working for the nomination of Governor Roosevelt it came like a benediction.

Then came the candidate's speech of acceptance, which was so universally acclaimed that almost without exception the delegates who had been opposed to his nomination now acknowledged that Roosevelt would be a real leader and at once offered their unstinted support.

Then the campaign started, for we took our candidate's advice and went to work at once. Instead of my speaking engagements beginning late in September or October, as was the usual time, they began in August and never ceased until the Saturday night before election.

It was an intensely interesting campaign. The only difficulty was, there was not sufficient time to tell it all! Speakers were bubbling over with information, and audiences were keen to hear everything a speaker had to say. You did not have to tell of the candidate, for they seemed perfectly familiar with Roosevelt's private and public life. What they wanted to hear was issues. No difference how much the "other Roosevelts" might explain their distant relationship, it is said there were people who would have "F. R. a son of T. R." I do know of one instance where a Swedish-American Republican, when handed a picture of "Franklin," joyfully exclaimed, "My, my! Don't he look like his Papa!"

Another story from a vastly different source exhibits a similar lack of intelligence. When it was seen that Roosevelt's nomination could not be stopped, a "grande dame" sitting in a box was heard to say, "Now I suppose he will win, but when the Democrats get to Washington, will they know how to entertain?" Shades of Dolly Madison and Harriet Lane Johnston! Memories of Frances Folsom Cleveland and Edith Bolling Wilson!

In the recent campaign our audiences wanted to listen to discussions of public questions, which they at last seemed to realize had some connection with their private lives. Therefore, all I had to do was to go back to 1920 and talk internationalism in the light of our lessened world trade and influence; to argue for lower tariff and increased commerce as against the prohibitive Smoot-Hawley tariff and shrunken exports; to plead for lower taxes through government economy; to denounce special privilege through tax refunds and to decry the bureaucratic tendencies of our government during the last three administrations.

One of the curious anomalies of the campaign was that when we Democrats wanted to show up government extravagance and the downright senselessness of many departments we went straight to Republican sources for our material. A book entitled "The Wonderland of Bureaucracy," by Hon. James M. Beck, a zealous and active Republican member of Congress, furnished us with more ammunition than we could use. It is a splendid book.

As the campaign progressed it soon became evident to the experienced political prognosticator that the only question to be decided was the size of the Democratic majority, yet we campaigners kept on working because the public wanted to hear more. With the exception of Pennsylvania the straw vote analysis was practically correct, for the election was a landslide.

Perhaps I may be forgiven for gloating somewhat over our victory, particularly since my home city of Pittsburgh and its county, Allegheny, were carried by a Democratic Presidential candidate for the first time since the Civil War. To be a Democrat in Pennsylvania during the last generation has been considered somewhat *outré*, but to be one in Pittsburgh is to be branded as a pariah by many of the well-known "high-hat" Republicans. I have met Republicans in Dallas, Texas, who did not hesitate to declare their party affiliations; I have met Republicans in Richmond, Virginia, who were not afraid to mention their party choice, but once a Texas, Virginia, Maryland or any other southern Democrat enters the business or social confines of Pittsburgh, sensing what is good for himself, he changes his political coat over night from white Democrat to black Republican.

We are accustomed to hear of political coercion in different parts of the country, but the one great point of pressure for high and low alike in Pittsburgh, is the protective tariff. Contradict that theory as an employer and you are court-martialed and degraded; reject a tariff candidate as a wage-earner and you are fired! The customary coercion was attempted in the last election in this section, but for once it failed, as I heard many working men declare, "If we can't vote as we like, then we may as well lose our jobs and join the bread line."

Under the day of the New Deal, when crooked banking is exposed and corrected, when doubtful financial deals are uncovered and regulated, when criminal practices are stopped and punishments meted out, when government is again administered without fear or favor, let us hope that within the "Holy Experiment" of William Penn every citizen may be permitted to vote for the candidate of his choice, that people of all classes will no longer be fearful of showing their political colors and no longer be scornful of the label, Democrat.

For twelve years I have been speaking before all sorts of audiences and meeting all types of voters, from the wife of the ward leader to the Phi Beta Kappa college professor who "Like the Colonel's lady and Judy O'Grady are sisters under the skin," with one great difference—the uneducated sister is almost without exception the more intelligent politically.

After wide experience in four Presidential campaigns and numerous state and local elections I wish I could state that I believed college men and women exhibited much learning, acute information and an admirable grasp of governmental questions and showed political independence as well, but alas! such is not the case.

This may be due to a lack of academic freedom in many institutions of learning, especially state controlled colleges, or to a complete indifference to public affairs in most colleges and universities, but if our country is to advance politically to the heights to which we all aim, then one of the first requirements is a display of deeper interest in and wider knowledge of political questions and government problems by the men and women who have had advantage of our much-vaunted higher education.

BRYN MAWR PLATES

The first finished samples of the Bryn Mawr Plates have arrived, but we have not yet been able to secure from the Wedgwood Company a definite date when delivery may be promised.

THE COLLEGE BUDGET

In the report of the Advisory Council of Men for the Seven Women's Colleges, the phrase occurs, "In the way of women, their colleges are so managed that one dollar is made to do the work of three." This is almost literally true. In the present condition of general economic uncertainty, Bryn Mawr College has found it both wise and necessary to continue the policy of last year. Although the budget for 1932-33 was accepted on the principle of "cutting to the bone," as President Park said, yet further drastic reductions have been necessary for 1933-34.

1932-1933

The total estimated income of the College	$868,877.00
The total estimated cost of running the College	825,722.00
Estimated surplus	$43,155.00

This estimated surplus was achieved by a 10 per cent. cut on all executive, library, physical instruction, secretarial and clerical salaries above $2,500, and a 5 per cent. cut on salaries between $1,500 and $2,500, also by reducing to a minimum all the work on the buildings and grounds. No cut was made in any teaching salary or appropriation.

This surplus has already been drawn upon to the extent of $32,100 and will be further reduced by all sorts of items, so that it is impossible to say how much, if any, of the surplus provided for will be unused.

1933-1934

The budget for 1933-34 was drawn up on the same basis as that of 1932-33, namely, to show a safe estimated surplus.

FIRST BUDGET PREPARED IN FEBRUARY, 1933

In the first budget presented to the Executive Committee the estimated income of the College, based on the funds producing income on February 1st, was	$819,546.00
The estimated cost of running the College was	808,315.00
Estimated surplus	$11,231.00

Even from the first it had seemed wise to estimate an amount to cover possible reduction in room rents and vacancies and after discussion this amount was fixed at $20,000, leaving for estimated income $799,546. This resulted in an estimated deficit of $7,968. Even without this $20,000 reduction the first estimated surplus of $11,231 did not seem a sufficient margin of safety for the income of the College might shrink. Therefore it seemed wise to obtain an estimated saving of about $45,000. The different committees therefore—Executive, Building and Grounds, Library and Religious Life—were asked to make further reductions.

As every reduction in 1932-33 had been made on the non-teaching side of the College, it was necessary both to meet this estimated deficit and to secure a sufficient estimated surplus to make cuts on the teaching side of the College.

SECOND BUDGET PREPARED IN MARCH, 1933

(Accepted at the Board of Directors' Meeting, March 17)

The estimated income of the second budget...$799,546.00

The estimated cost of running the College.. 763,434.00

Estimated surplus $36,112.00

This saving was arrived at as follows:

Executive Committee

The budget of the Executive Committee as presented first was $645,344. This was reduced to $606,563 in the following manner:

A 10 per cent. cut in all teaching salaries over $2,500 and a 5 per cent. cut in salaries between $1,500 and $2,500, yielding a saving of $22,495. President Park insisted, over the protests of the Executive Committee, on taking a 10 per cent. cut in addition to the 10 per cent. cut which she took in 1932-33, yielding a saving for 1933-34 of $1,250.

A cut of 10 per cent. in the maids' and porters' wages.

In addition, all general expenses, such as printing, office expense, telephone, publicity, entertaining and even appropriations for the laboratories and departments have been reduced.

In view of the fact that fewer applications for foreign scholarships had been received for next year, a saving was effected through temporarily discontinuing the five foreign scholarships at $1,000 each and substituting for them five graduate scholarships at $400 each, also temporarily discontinuing two Friends' Scholarships at $400 each, thereby saving $3,800. This decision was taken after consultation with Dean Schenck and with her approval. As the Foreign Scholars are a source of pride and intellectual stimulus to the College, it is hoped that this substitution is merely a temporary expedient.

Building and Grounds Committee

The budget of this committee was reduced from $116,085 to $111,735 by eliminating four large pieces of work which seemed reasonably safe to postpone.

Library Committee

The budget of this committee was cut 10 per cent., reducing it from $15,460 to $13,960.

Religious Life Committee

The budget of this committee was cut 10 per cent. reducing it from $2,500 to $2,250.

The expenses of the Treasurer's Office, estimated at $3,925, and the interest on the debt of the College, estimated at $25,000, stood.

Thus has the College planned to meet the existing economic situation and while making possible reductions in room rents for able students unable to pay the full amount, yet has insured itself as far as is reasonably possible against any deficit for the year 1933-34.

FRANCES FINCKE HAND, 1897.

WORKING FOR PEACE

By EMILY G. BALCH, 1889

Miss Balch will lecture at Bryn Mawr next year on the Howard Anna Shaw Foundation

Having been invited to write for the BRYN MAWR ALUMNAE BULLETIN an article on my efforts on behalf of peace, and asked to make it quite informal and not to spare the first person singular, I am trying to do just this.

When the World War broke out in 1914 my reaction to it was largely a sense of tragic interruption of what seemed to me the real business of our times—the realization of a more satisfactory economic order.

To that problem I had given myself unreservedly from my undergraduate days—first as student and then as teacher (though always also as student), and also as sharing in efforts to change conditions in the desired direction, as occasion offered.

Now all the world was at war, one hardly knew for what—for reasons of ambition, prestige, mutual fear, of frontiers and colonies. None of the war aims seemed very relevant to progress, in any important sense.

For some time I had been interested in the peace movement, as expressed, for instance, in the Hague Congresses and the growing provision for arbitration, and had taken these up with my students as practical social problems, but I had not come to the conviction, which later I gradually but inevitably reached, that there is no half-way house and that resort to war can and must come to an end.

At first the war seemed almost incredible. Returning from isolation in the country, I was surprised to find that people generally, like myself, were condemning Germany. I had thought that it was the other way 'round. I was reading Tolstoy, but could not (and cannot) accept the use of physical force as in itself the criterion of right and wrong, though in deep sympathy with his position as a whole.

In the spring of 1915, Jane Addams persuaded me to secure a leave of absence from Wellesley College, where I was professor of economics, to go with her and a really remarkable group of some fifty other American women to an International Congress of Women at the Hague. Women from twelve countries, belligerent and neutral, took part. They organized a Women's International Committee for Permanent Peace, with Jane Addams as International Chairman and headquarters at the Hague. A carefully considered set of policies was approved and we were later much interested to learn that President Wilson had been studying them, that he had asked Miss Addams for a second copy, as the one which he had (which he drew from his pocket) was dog's-eared, and to find much that it contained embodied in his famous fourteen points.

One outcome of the Congress was that a delegation was sent to the various governments to urge upon them a policy, which I still think was a promising one, and one that came near to being tried; namely, an agreement by neutral powers to offer continuous mediation. The greater part of this interviewing of statesmen was done by Miss Addams and Dr. Aletta Jacobs, of Holland. I was sent with another delegation to the Scandinavian countries and Russia, and later to England, where we saw Sir Edward Grey; and to Washington, where President Wilson called me to him to report. I left filled with the greatest admiration for him personally, but bitterly disappointed that he practically vetoed the plan. The war went on, more and more furiously, for over three years longer. The story of these efforts is best told in Miss Addams' book, *Women at the Hague.*

In 1916 came Mr. Ford's efforts to shorten the fighting. * * * I did not go on the peace ship, but when Mr. Ford set up in Stockholm a commission of international lawyers, experts, and peace-workers, I accepted an invitation to join them. * * *

I returned to the United States in the summer of 1916 to find a powerful Preparedness Movement in full swing and a steady pull toward war. The college year 1916-1917 bringing to me the freedom of a Sabbatical year, I went to New York, where I led a very active life, as things turned out, for three years. Besides some following of lectures at Columbia I carried on a private class in current affairs and prepared a book, *Toward the Great Settlement.* The book is still of some value for its collection of various proposals as to the possible peace terms which had been put forward in different countries and by different groups, as a basis for a negotiated peace. The most important feelers for peace do not, however, appear in it, as, being secret, they were unknown at the time.

Besides all this, I worked with various peace groups. I was a member of the Committee Against Militarism, which was active till the United States joined the war. This included Miss Lillian D. Wald, Paul V. Kellogg, Rabbi Wise, Max Eastman, and others, with Charles Hallinan in its Washington office, where he did brilliant work toward stemming the rising tide of military feeling in the United States. I also worked in the organization led by the brilliant and beautiful Crystal Eastman, but I was especially identified, as the situation developed, with a younger and more adventurous group which was doing what it could toward preventing the United States entering the war. At one time we ran huge anti-war broadsides in the New York papers on this issue. These would include an appeal for dollar contributions to pay for more advertisements. One morning our office at 70 Fifty Avenue was flooded, with long queues down the corridor, with women bringing their dollar bills, and we had to borrow waste-paper baskets to hold the dollars that came by mail. We took a delegation to Washington, where disgusted soldier-boys painted our office door yellow and drummed their heels on the corrugated-iron roof of the hall where we were trying to hear our speakers.

When in the spring of 1917, as my Sabbatical year was drawing to a close, the United States entered the war, I felt that my return to Wellesley the next year would be embarrassing to the college and to me, and that it would be better for my students for classes to continue as they were for another year. I therefore asked for, and received, a year's leave of absence without pay. At the end of this year my existing appointment expired, and much as I grieved that the well-known liberality of Wellesley College should have been over-strained by me, I could not be surprised when, after much discussion and much friendly advocacy of my reappointment, the trustees decided against it.

This left me at 52 with my professional life cut off short and no particular prospects. It was naturally with great appreciation that I accepted from Mr. Villard an invitation to join the staff of the *Nation*. I worked for the most part in the most modest capacities, but I remember one day when Mr. Villard came in and, telling me that Austria-Hungary had collapsed, asked me if I could write a leading article on the subject before the paper went to press in two hours' time. From studies which I had made on the spot for my book, *Our Slavic Fellow-Citizens*, I knew well the component parts of that conglomerate empire. I was especially interested in the effect of the change on the nationalities, but I was blind, as were the responsible statesmen who framed the peace settlement, to the fact that, monstrous as the Hapsburg empire might appear politically, it was a functioning economic organism, and that to tear it apart without further concern was to create chaos and entail the hideous suffering of the post-war years, especially in Vienna.

It is needless to say that to me, as to everyone else, the war years brought pain, although it happened that I had no poignant personal anxiety nor bereavement, nor personal hardship or danger. It is a hard thing to stand against the surge of war-feeling, against the endlessly reiterated suggestion of every printed word, of the carefully edited news, of posters, parades, songs, speeches, sermons. In spite of a consciousness at times as clear as Luther's *Ich kann nicht anders*, at other times one staggered. To the question, "What if Germany wins and militarizes the world?" I had no answer ready. Bitterest of all was the sense that if America kept out of the war it would be largely, perhaps mainly, not for noble reasons, but from greed for profits. Conscience was uneasy, as well it might be. Where is the line dividing inner integrity from fanatical self-will?

I do not know whether what held me should be called a religious faith, or an irresistible set of the inner self, or fanaticism. My support, in my belief that one must not resort to war for any purpose, came largely from friends whom I revered and who felt as I did. Conscientious objectors, too, whose sufferings for their convictions in England and here were known to us (those on the continent we could not then know of) shamed me and encouraged me. So did the courage of men like Bertrand Russell and Romain Rolland.

A drawing toward the Society of Friends which I had felt for some years grew into a definite desire to become one of them, but to do so, if possible, not through one of the groups into which the Society separated in the United States, at the time of the Unitarian controversy, but in England, where no division took place. This I was able to do after the war, being received as a member of London Yearly Meeting. It was not alone their testimony against war, their creedless faith, nor their openness to suggestions for far-reaching social reform that attracted me, but the dynamic force of the active love through which their religion was expressing itself in multifarious ways, both during and after the war.

The women who met at the Hague in 1915, having decided to meet again as soon as the ending of war conditions should permit, called a second Congress in Zurich in May, 1919. The Peace Conference was sitting in Paris, and Miss Addams came to Zurich with an advance copy of the Covenant of the League of Nations, not yet made finally public. It was decided to continue our common work, but under a new name: The Women's International League for Peace and Freedom. We were much the same group as before, with the addition of Frenchwomen who had been prevented from coming to Holland in war-time.   *   *   *

I was offered and accepted the position of paid International Secretary and opened our new headquarters in Geneva. We settled there some little time before the League of Nations itself arrived, and during the three years that I served there I had the most interesting opportunity to see its development in its earlier and more idealistic phase before power.politics had sensed its importance and sought to use it for its own purposes.

In other respects these first post-war years were painful and disappointing—confused and disheartening to the last degree. Peace was a by-word. The reaction against war, which we had thought would make itself felt as soon as peace was made, did not do so at once, though it did come later and is now a swelling tide.

There was, however, great exhileration in the sense of active and organized comradeship with women working for peace all over the world. I recall in one day receiving letters from Iceland, South Africa and Fiji. An American correspondent wrote me that she had worked as a young woman against slavery, then for woman suffrage, and, both of these causes being won, was now working to end war. I thought of Galileo's *e pur si muove*—things do move, in spite of everything!

In 1922 my health obliged me to give up my work for peace for a time, but I was soon able to take it up again, being active both on the international executive of the W. I. L. P. F. and in the United States Section, where I have served in various capacities. Miss Addams has been International President from the beginning, since 1929, in a nominally honorary capacity. Much of her experience can be found in her book, *Bread and Peace in Time of War,* to me the most interesting of her writings. * * *

I began by saying that the war broke upon me as an interruption of a social development that I believed was in process and for which I was working. I did not, however, return to my old social reform efforts after the war, partly because I had dropped behind in that work and become specialized in another, but also because, while the work of social building still seems to me the largest, the effort to prevent war, if that be possible, has an emergency claim.

Yet more and more it becomes evident that the political nationalistic tension is all intermingled with the social-economic unrest. If France and Germany fear one another, and territorial problems like those of "the Corridor" and Hungary are danger points, not less certainly is there a threat of conflict between left-wing Revolution and right-wing Fascism, and between these and evolutionary social-economic democracy.

We live in a terribly explosive world and no one can foresee the future. Yet we all are building it, part consciously, part unconsciously.

As I see it, we need, for one thing, to establish a substantial "peace" structure, capable of controlling the danger of war between states. We already have the beginnings in treaties, courts, conferences and the League of Nations—but it is not yet nearly so tough or so genuine as it needs to be.

There is also the still more difficult work of trying to deal with the sources of trouble—the injustices, stupidities and inadequacy of the system (or lack of system) from which the peoples of the world are trying to escape by different paths.

And fundamental to all else is the need that men should grow to understand and practice patience and tolerance, and come to substitute for the clumsy, uncertain, cruel tool of violence, the methods of reason and coöperation.

NEW PLANS OF ADMISSION

Bryn Mawr, Mount Holyoke, Smith, Vassar, and Wellesley announce changes in admission plans to be used experimentally beginning in 1933, in addition to the present plans of entrance.

PLAN C.

Candidates shall be allowed to take at the end of the junior year the Scholastic Aptitude Tests and two examinations (not English) from the groups now required by Plan B. On the basis of the results of these examinations, the Scholastic Aptitude Tests, school records, and recommendations from the principal, provisional acceptance may be given. Final acceptance will depend upon the results of the remaining two examinations which are to be taken at the end of the senior year and upon the school records of that year.

A candidate who is not provisionally accepted at the end of the junior year, may apply for admission by examinations to be taken in the senior year under any College Board examination plan acceptable to the college she wishes to enter.

Candidates wishing to enter by Plan C should make application to the Board of Admission on or before May 1 of their junior year in secondary school.

PLAN D.

Admission under this plan is on the basis of the school records and recommendations and the Scholastic Aptitude Tests. To be considered for admission by Plan D a candidate must have ranked, during the last two years of her school course, among the highest seventh of a graduating class containing at least seven students. She must have covered the equivalent of a standard four-year high school course which satisfies in general the requirements for approval under Plan B. Unqualified recommendation of the candidate by her school principal or headmistress is essential.

Since all admission is on a competitive basis, candidates for entrance by Plan D cannot be guaranteed admission. They may become eligible for admission subject to the same conditions as candidates applying for entrance by examination. As heretofore, final selection of all candidates is made by the Committee on Admission on the consideration of all evidence, both personal and academic.

Bryn Mawr and Vassar announce that candidates from schools remote from the college and from schools where the course of study has not been specially designed to meet the College Entrance Examination Board examitions may use this plan. Ordinarily candidates from the larger endowed academies and private preparatory schools must enter by examination.

Mount Holyoke, Smith, and Wellesley announce that candidates from any school may be considered for admission by this plan. These colleges, however, will feel free to consider the geographical distribution of students in the entering class and the proportional representation from public and private schools.

(16)

REGULATIONS GOVERNING THE ADMINISTRATION OF PLAN D.

1. Candidates are eligible to apply for admission without examination other than the Scholastic Aptitude Tests, only in the year in which they first graduate from a secondary school.

2. Candidates must register with the College Entrance Examination Board to take the Scholastic Aptitude Tests.

3. Applications should state specifically:
   (a) The number of pupils in the graduating class.
   (b) The applicant's exact numerical rank in the class.

4. Applications must be filed in the office of the Secretary of the Board of Admission. on or before May first in the year in which the candidate first graduates from a secondary school.

SCHOLASTIC APTITUDE TESTS.

All candidates for admission by any plan are now advised to take the Scholastic Aptitude Tests at the end of the junior year in secondary school.

March 22, 1933.

ANNOUNCEMENT BY THE COMMITTEE ON ENTRANCE EXAMINATION AT BRYN MAWR

The Committee on Entrance Examination of Bryn Mawr College wishes to announce that it is willing this year to consider the applications of candidates who are highly recommended by their schools but whose preparation is somewhat irregular when judged by the standard of the fifteen required entrance units listed on page 30 of the 1932 Bryn Mawr College Calendar.

The Committee regards this policy as experimental. It is made possible during the present year by the limitation of the number of candidates due to the difficulty which many students find in meeting the expenses of a residence college. Bryn Mawr is always interested in giving special consideration to students of exceptional ability, and the Committee on Entrance Examination can do so this year without injustice to students who have undertaken the school courses regularly prescribed.

The Committee, therefore, hopes that schools will report to the Director of Admissions the case of any pupil who can be highly recommended and who would be interested in making application for admission to Bryn Mawr College next autumn, but whose preparatory work does not entirely cover the fifteen prescribed matriculation units. If the candidate has covered high school courses in subjects not included in the prescribed fifteen units, such work should also be reported to the Committee.

March, 1933.

COLLEGE SCHEDULE FOR MAY, 1933

Friday, May 5th—Auditorium at 8.20: Dr. Evarts B. Greene, Professor of History at Columbia University, will give the Mallory Whiting Webster Memorial Lecture in History on "American Horizons in the Days of Washington."

Wednesday, May 10th—Auditorium at 8.20: Skit by the Faculty for the benefit of an entrance scholarship for 1933-34.

Friday and Saturday, May 19th and 20th—Auditorium at 8.20: "Patience," presented by the Glee Club. Reserved seats for Friday, $1.75 and $1.50; for Saturday, $1.75 and $2.00, may be secured at the Office of the Director of Publication.

THE PRESIDENT'S PAGE

THE EXPERIMENTAL CHANGES IN ENTRANCE REQUIREMENTS

Two statements announcing experimental changes in its entrance requirements have been sent out by Bryn Mawr and appear in this number of the BULLETIN. One is an adjustment of a present plan; the other two are new to our experience, and neither of the latter, if retained, will ever affect many students. All are definitely announced as experimental, and the experiments will be closed if in the judgment of the Committee on Entrance Examination they fail of their purpose. This purpose is definite: to bring to Bryn Mawr students who have shown a high degree of ability but who are not able or, at any rate, likely to come to the College under the present requirements.

These experiments are both possible and, I think, desirable. They are possible because in a state of things common to all colleges the list of applicants for entrance for 1933-34 is shorter than the corresponding list last year. The College Entrance Examination Board, for instance, is preparing for a drop of 15 per cent in those taking examinations. At the same time more upper class students than usual will probably be obliged to withdraw. It seems certain, therefore, that other students can be admitted this summer in addition to those who have completed the usual preparation and who for several years have filled the freshman class full and provided in 1929, 1930 and 1931 long waiting lists. In 1932 almost all qualified applicants for admission could be accepted. The experiments are, I believe, advisable because a full college not only furnishes a better business basis but is far more interesting and stimulating.

Plan C is an adjustment of Plan B, adopted by Bryn Mawr in 1932, and it has been worked out in prolonged discussion by the five women's colleges announcing it. It offers the college a preliminary view of the girl a year before she enters, such as was offered by the first division of examinations taken under Plan A, and by making review courses in the fourth year unnecessary the student can add, if she wishes, something to her college equipment. I believe Plan C has certain advantages of both Plan A and Plan B, and I suspect it will remain among entrance plans and be often chosen. It is a two-year plan and probably will not bring students into next year's class at Bryn Mawr.

Plan D was devised in 1923 by Harvard to extend the geographical distribution of its student body and has been in use since then at Harvard and Radcliffe. After experimenting with a form similar to that announced by Mount Holyoke, Smith, and Wellesley, and finding it unsatisfactory, Harvard and Radcliffe limited the wider plan to that announced by Bryn Mawr.

This plan will bring relatively few students to Bryn Mawr, I think, because relatively few students from "schools remote from the college and from schools where the course of study has not been specially designed to meet the College Entrance Board examinations" will be able to present the fifteen units of subject matter required by Bryn Mawr. It may make it possible, however, to add a few exceptionally able girls to the Bryn Mawr student body. Alumnae Regional Committees in the west and south have insistently called our attention to it as the means which Radcliffe has used to get good students from good but far-away schools.

I am ready to experiment with this plan carefully limited, for I should like to discover whether without cutting down quality the variety of students in college can be increased. President Comstock reports favorably on Radcliffe's experience. I think it may be successful at Bryn Mawr; on the other hand, it may prove to affect such small numbers that it is not worth while to break with our up-to-this-time unbroken allegiance to the entrance examinations.

The various plans, A, B, C, D, are concerned only with methods of entrance. Subject requirements in all of them remain unchanged. The Committee on Entrance Examination has, however, proposed that this year slight irregularities in subject matter be accepted in the case of students exceptionally well recommended by their schools. This arrangement is made primarily for girls in Philadelphia and the neighborhood who have prepared themselves to enter other colleges, but under present conditions can get a college education only if they can attend Bryn Mawr as non-residents and this seems a service to the community which we would do well to perform. But this proposal of the Entrance Committee may also make it possible for good students elsewhere whose work shows only a *slight* variation from Bryn Mawr requirements to make a late decision to enter Bryn Mawr this year. Permission to use this plan is given to the committee only for this year.

PLANS FOR COMMENCEMENT WEEK

Ten classes are scheduled to hold reunions this year. At the time of going to press the following arrangements had been made:

Class	Class Supper	Reunion Headquarters	Reunion Manager
1894		Pembroke East	Anna West West
1895			Edith Pettit Borie
1896	Valley Forge	Merion	Emma Linburg Tobin
1897	Common Room	Pembroke West	Mary Campbell
1913	Wyndham	Wyndham	Elizabeth Maguire
1914	Pembroke	Pembroke West	Lillien Cox Harman
1915	Rockefeller	Rockefeller	Adrienne Kenyon Franklin
1916	Denbigh	Pembroke East	Helen Robertson
1931	Picnic	Denbigh	Virginia Shryock
1932	Picnic	Denbigh	Molly Atmore

The Class Suppers or Class Picnics will be held Saturday evening, June 10th. At noon on Sunday there will be a special meeting of the Alumnae Association to pass on the project of the Deanery as an Alumnae House. This will be followed by the Alumnae Luncheon at 1.15 P. M. in Pembroke, at which President Park and representatives of the reuning classes will speak. Sunday afternoon the Association will have a tea for the graduating class. The Baccalaureate Sermon will be preached that evening by Rabbi Wise. On Monday two picnic luncheons have been planned, one for the Classes of 1894-97, and one for 1913-1916. The Alumnae-Varsity Tennis Tournament will take place that morning, and the Senior Garden Party will be held on the campus that afternoon. Commencement will be held in the Auditorium of Goodhart Hall at 11 o'clock on Tuesday, June 13th. President Woolley, of Mount Holyoke, will deliver the address.

CAMPUS NOTES

By JANET MARSHALL, 1933

This is the in-between-time at College when not very much of anything is happening and when a very great deal has either just happened or is just about to happen; what I have to say must, therefore, consist mainly of little scraps about various activities and problems. One of the most pleasant of the scraps of news is that of the Glee Club's spring activities and plans. The choir, which may be said to form the nucleus of the Glee Club, has distinguished itself twice this year, first in connection with Mr. Vaughan William's lectures and then, this past month, by its participation in the performance of *Parsifal* at the Academy of Music in Philadelphia, under the direction of Leopold Stokowski. This last was an undertaking of such magnitude that only very experienced and fine choirs could be asked to participate, and the honor to Bryn Mawr of Mr. Stokowski's invitation was very great. It was, however, an honor which involved a tremendous amount of very hard work for every member of the choir, and it is really remarkable that after all of this, they should have the courage and the time to do anything else this spring. The temporary abandonment of the tradition of a Gilbert and Sullivan opera every spring was seriously considered for just this reason, but in the end it was decided to go on with it, and the operetta, *Patience,* was chosen. The date is set for the early part of May and rehearsals have already begun, although there has as yet been no public announcement of the cast. If the opera is as successful as the Glee Club performances have been in the past, it will be the climax of a very unusual and active year for the musical organizations of the College.

Another project of which we have spoken before is coming to what seems a successful fruition. The Athletic Board's plan for reviving the College's interest in sports by means of class teams and class rivalry seems to have worked well. So far the plan has only been tried in two sports, swimming and basketball, but the increase in the number of participants in both was amazing. Two class swimming meets were held, with cups and medals for individual performances and for class performances; the Freshman class was finally awarded the cup, with the Seniors running a fairly close second, while a really remarkable grandstand attendance for Bryn Mawr cheered their respective classmates. It remains to be seen what effect this plan will have on spring sports, but since the general interest in athletics usually rises the minute the tennis courts are opened, it is probable that the plan will be even more effective then.

The one really vital issue on the campus this month has been the vote on whether or not the *College News* should be put on a basis of automatic subscription and thus become the official organ of the Undergraduate organization as it is the official organ of the Administration. So hot a debate has not been heard in an Undergrad meeting for a long time, nor have the columns of the *News* been filled with as many letters. The great points of the argument were that on one hand, the *News* was supported by a comparatively small group of subscribers and read by a much larger group that enjoyed its advantages without paying for them, while on the other hand it was a very poor policy to force students to pay for something for which they did not want to pay. After several weeks of debate and inquiry the matter was finally put to a vote whose results have not yet been announced.

The question of the quota has been settled, for this year at least, by a recommendation of the committee of the College Council created to investigate the problem and its possible solutions. It has been decided that the question is much too complex to be dealt with in a high-handed fashion, and that most of the proposed schemes have in them greater flaws than those of the present system. Consequently the quota is being left much as it always has been, with the exception of certain minor changes which have the general effect of making it more pliable. Pembroke, for instance, used to be treated as two halls in the matter of hall-draw and will now be treated as one. The matter of vacancies created by students dropping out has also been dealt with, and students within the same class who wish to exchange halls will now be permitted to do so, without regard to the state of the quota in the halls concerned. The whole aim of the group that raised the question of quota reform was to make the present system more elastic, and while they did not accomplish any radical changes, the system has been made far more flexible and they seem to be well satisfied.

An editorial which appeared recently in the *College News* seems to me to be of some interest to the alumnae and I shall quote from it here at some length. "There is a rumor current on the campus to the effect that some of the courses and lectures offered this year as especial gifts of interested alumnae and friends may be discontinued next year. We feel that before any vital decisions are made in this matter it would be well to take occasion to express what we feel to be the attitude of the majority of students about the courses and lectures which are especial gifts. Two excellent examples of especially endowed features of the curriculum and lecture program are the lectureship which this year will bring T. S. Eliot to speak at College, and the endowment that has brought Miss Minor White Latham, of Barnard and Columbia, here as a lecturer in a course on playwriting. This type of gift to the College, we feel sure, is one of the most valuable of all gifts, and certainly one of the most generally appreciated. Scholarship gifts and endowments may be more worthy—if indeed there can be a scale of relative values placed on gifts to an institution—but scholarship gifts touch directly only one person. Gifts of lectureships and courses touch every one who chooses to attend the lecture or to take the course." The writer goes on to give an appreciation of the playwriting course, which has been so very popular, and concludes thus: "We have discussed this course at length because it is one of the few that we know are given by outsiders. We wish to thank the donor on behalf of the members of the class and on behalf of the student body as a whole. If we knew more definitely which other courses in College were offered in the same way, we should like to express our appreciation in the same manner. Since we do not, we can only say that we do thank these unknown friends of the College and that we do appreciate in an unusually forceful way their thought and their gifts. We can also say only very vaguely, hoping that this editorial may come to the right eyes, that on behalf of the student body we hope very much that these gifts will not be discontinued, but that the privileges which have been so deeply enjoyed by the present student body will be extended to those who have not enjoyed them and to incoming classes."

THE ALUMNAE BOOK SHELF

THE BANK OF INTERNATIONAL SETTLEMENTS, *by Eleanor Dulles.* Macmillan, $5.00.

Miss Dulles, it seems evident, enjoyed herself in gathering the materials for her book, *The Bank of International Settlements at Work.* She found her subject congenial; she was interested in its theoretical bearings and in the special character of the Bank's technique. She was penetrated, moreover, by the sense of the momentousness of the historic occasion. The Bank of International Settlements was one of the unforeseen, if inevitable, outcomes of the Treaty of Versailles; it was devised by the Young Plan to ease the payment of reparations and to make possible the departure of the foreign commissioners from Germany. Something new under the sun, founded because of a special necessity, the Bank might, once in being, accomplish much more than its immediate narrow tasks. The imagination of its possibilities seems to have raised high in Miss Dulles a sense of excitement and it is in this atmosphere that I feel she has constructed her book. Her material is admirably complete; her knowledge of the history of banking theory is evident. To her professional equipment she added a quickened imagination but the result is not the heightened effectiveness one might have expected, but the heaviness which results from a confused design. Miss Dulles remained too close to her subject. She wished to record with the minuteness of a devout chronicler every fact of the pre-history and infancy of the possible future great Bank of Banks. This might not have been harmful had Miss Dulles been content to separate the history of the institution from the technical discussion of its activities. Unfortunately, she attempted to reproduce reality; to unfold together the events and the problems in their simultaneousness and their incompleteness. But the purpose of exposition is to be clear and focused; it must depart from the methods of life. I hope Miss Dulles will go back for her next model to the old masters, say Adam Smith, and away from the new with their habit of portraying the flux of things.

The Bank of International Settlements at Work might have been better reading but I think it an important work. It shows the Bank formulating its policies cautiously in the midst of national rivalries and differing economic outlooks, able, probably because of its caution, to emerge at the end of two years sound financially and with an established position. On the Bank converged during this period the shock of opposing opinion in all that matters most to banking policy. The inflationist and the deflationist fought their still unsettled battle. The expansionist who would have used the Bank to finance trade for Germany in unexploited territory (one wonders what hinterland Dr. Schacht had his eye on) was opposed by those who held that a sufficient first task was presented by the transfer ·problem and the development therefrom of more centralized clearing for the foreign exchanges. Those who have professional economic interests will be most grateful to Miss Dulles for isolating clearly the new problems which have risen since the war as to the functions and weapons of central banks; for showing the possible influence of a more developed forward market on the range of prices of the foreign exchanges, and for raising in the special international setting of the Bank the question of the gold standard and its possible substitutes. For those to whom such things are of moment this book is rich in content. It is equipped with an admirable bibliography, historical appendices, and index.   ESTHER LOWENTHAL, 1905.

Songs and Sonnets, 1915-1932, *by Rebecca McDoel Hickman Wyman.* Privately printed, 1932.

The collection of Songs ond Sonnets, written by Mrs. Wyman in the last half of her too short life, and printed by her mother after Mrs. Wyman's death last year, contains ideas and images so diverse that the reader is amazed and delighted and saddened. With real regret one feels that the delicate and subtle poems are not to be followed by many others, for they promise even more than they fulfil. Amazement gives place to comprehension on reading *Inheritance,* which explains the combination of ancestral influences that shaped the poet's mind.

> "O Puritan who pulled the Maypole down,
> O Huguenot with faith-enkindled face,
> O English earl who kept a bawdy clown,
> O red upstanding Scot whose pride of race
> Gave you a bloody plaid to keep you warm,
> What woman did you mate with?"

Potent for good or ill, sure to cause unrest and conflict and passionate desire for proof of Life's enigmatic offerings, is this extraordinary heritage: the soul descended from these resolute spirits would find delight in seed time and harvest, lonely woodland paths and jostling crowds, perfume of moonlit gardens and sound of the tireless sea.

Color and light and sound are charmingly suggested . . .

> ". . . . In that Tuscan night of unreality
> There seemed to be
> The piercing scent of red clove pinks—"

> "The gorse was tarnished with shadow."

> "Into the window from far down the lane
> Drifted piano-music, loved and played
> By one whose hands made Chopin live again."

That is good. Chopin needs special hands, and gets them all too seldom.

But music was loveliest for Mrs. Wyman, flowers were gayest and sweetest when she shared them with one she loved.

> "I am a tree bent in the hurricane,
> I am a stone rubbed smooth by ocean's hand,
> I am a star that vanished, the moon that wanes
> When night is over.
> You are the wind, the sea,
> The sun, lighting dark lands,
> You are my lover."

Perhaps her eager hands had grasped their fill of beauty, and her eyes had grown weary of looking on the changing world, but the pictures she has left are so delightful that the reader is grateful for the loving care which has preserved them.

BEATRICE McGEORGE, 1901.

CLASS NOTES

Ph.D. and Graduate Notes

Editor: MARY ALICE HANNA PARRISH
(Mrs. J. C. Parrish)
Vandalia, Missouri.

1889

No Editor appointed.

1890

No Editor appointed.

1891

No Editor appointed.

1892

Class Editor: EDITH WETHERILL IVES
(Mrs. F. M. Ives)
145 E. 35th St., New York City.

1893

Class Editor: S. FRANCES VAN KIRK
1333 Pine St., Philadelphia, Pa.

1894

Class Editor: ABBY BRAYTON DURFEE
(Mrs. Randall Durfee)
19 Highland Ave., Fall River, Mass.

1895

Class Editor: ELIZABETH BENT CLARK
(Mrs. Herbert Lincoln Clark)
Bryn Mawr, Pa.

1896

Class Editor: ABIGAIL CAMP DIMON
1411 Genesee St., Utica, N. Y.

1897

Class Editor: FRIEDRIKA HEYL
104 Lake Shore Drive, East, Dunkirk, N. Y.

"Alice in Wonderland," playing in New York, must have felt a particularly sympathetic response from the section of the theater where, on March 18th, the following appreciative group gathered to renew their youth: M. Campbell, E. Bowman, E. Fountain, J. and P. Goldmark, F. Hand, E. H. Jackson, Alice Jones MacMonnies, Aimée Leffingwell McKenzie, M. Taber, Emma Linburg Tobin and Elizabeth Nields Bancroft. E. H. Jackson writes that May Campbell got up the dinner and theater party, and M. Campbell writes that it was given in honor of E. Bancroft and E. H. J. and that the latter invited each and every last one of them to the theater.

The MacMonnies gift to the French nation in commemoration of the Victory of the Marne was unveiled last fall.

Marion Taber is still working hard in New York contributing her loyal interest to the State Charities Aid.

The McKenzies are very enthusiastic about their university life in Princeton, where they have built their own house. Aimée finds time to do translating of French books into English.

Frances Hand has been appointed to serve on the committee to arrange for the Fiftieth Anniversary of the College.

A large part of May Campbell's Spring holiday was taken up in getting out the class reunion letters. Many of you no doubt definitely decided even before her persuasive letter reached you, to be back at Bryn Mawr this year for the Special Meeting of the Alumnae Association in June. Not one of the class if she can possibly make it, will miss this history-making occasion.

1898

Class Editor: EDITH SCHOFF BOERICKE
(Mrs. John J. Boericke)
328 Brookway, Merion Station, Pa.

A member of our class who lives abroad recently wrote a very sad letter, Sophie Bertelsen, of Copenhagen, Denmark. After losing her father last October both Sophie and her husband had influenza in December, and Mr. Bertelsen's attack, made worse with the added complication of heart trouble, resulted fatally February 2d. His loss was felt deeply in the whole community, as he was loved by all who knew him. I am sure that all of Sophie's classmates will join in deepest sympathy to her and her family. Sophie's oldest daughter, '98's class baby, has a second daughter, born last July. Her two little girls are named Birgitte and Elsebeth. Sophie's son, who finished his law course two years ago, received almost immediately a position in Denmark's foreign office, and at present specializes in the League of Nations. Last fall he was down in Geneva about a month, together with their delegation at the meetings there. Her younger daughter will finish school next June.

1899

Editor: CAROLYN TROWBRIDGE BROWN LEWIS
(Mrs. Radnor Lewis)
55 Park Ave., New York.

It is with much regret that we announce the death of Etta Lincoln Davis which occurred some months ago after a long illness. Etta took her A.B. at Bryn Mawr and later attended Radcliffe where she took her A.M. She was a constant reader and student, particularly along philosophical lines, and she taught for a time, spending a year in Honolulu. Etta was always with us at reunions and her quaint humor and clever observations enlivened many a gathering. The class extends its deepest sympathy to her brother and aged mother who survive.

"Guffey" writes that she is descending the political scale; after being mentioned with a hundred and fifty-nine others for a cabinet post she was lately written up as a candidate for governor of Pennsylvania. She dabbles in play writing; her first effort, a country play, won first prize last year in the Twentieth Century Club, Pittsburgh, contest. This year she won an honorable mention with a "triangle play." She attended the inauguration and returned to Washington in April for the W. O. N. P. R. convention, looked after some chores for her constitutents and finished up with tea at the White House. Now she has gone "high brow," having been appointed a trustee of the State Teachers College at Slippery Rock by Governor Pinchot.

1900

Class Editor: Louise Congdon Francis
(Mrs. Richard Francis)
414 Old Lancaster Rd., Haverford, Pa.

The class will all sympathize with Edith Fell in the loss of her mother. Mrs. Fell died at Holicong early in April.

1901

Class Editor: Helen Converse Thorpe
(Mrs. Warren Thorpe)
15 East 64th St., New York City.

1902

Class Editor: Ann Rotan Howe
(Mrs. Thorndike Howe)
77 Revere St., Boston, Mass.

The class will want to express its sympathy through this column to Lucille Porter Weaver, whose husband died suddenly in November. Lucille has a married daughter living in Philadelphia and a son a senior at Princeton—these two the eldest of seven.

Ruth Miles Witherspoon has a son in McGill and two others in the University of Rochester.

Frances Allen Hackett has a granddaughter (Ed. Note: *Can* we have been out of college 30 years?) and sons at Princeton, Dartmouth and Williams, playing no favorites.

Mirabile dictu, we have a letter from Jean Crawford, from which we quote herewith: "We met, seven of us, for the Alumnae Luncheon at Pembroke Hall, on Saturday, February 11th. To omit married names, Fanny Cochran, Edith

Orlady, Eleanor Wood, Mary Ingham, Emily Dungan, Marion Haines and myself were there. All looked strong and healthy, and some of us rather more buxom than of yore. From the meeting we gleaned that Eleanor Wood is living in her old apartment in New York City, Edith Orlady is spending the winter at the College Club, Philadelphia, ready poised to dash at any moment up to Harrisburg or Huntington for various and sundry meetings of importance connected with School Boards, State Reformatories, Tuberculosis Institutions, etc. Only two of Marion Haines' children are at home this winter. Of the absentees, Catharine and Marion are abroad studying music and languages at Munich, Betsy is at Smith College and Samuel Emlen, Jr., is at the Harvard College Business School.

"Eleanor, Fanny Cochran's older adopted child, is at boarding school, while Virginia, the younger one, is at home with Fanny. Mary Ingham is active as usual at Foreign Policy Luncheons and all meetings of a political nature, while Emily Dungan is usually to be met at Philadelphia Orchestra Concerts, Opera and Musical Events. We all missed Anne Todd. who rushed off on a Caribbean Cruise with her sister, Mrs. Brinkerhoff, of New York."

Grace Douglas Johnston, after some rather radical surgery in the fall, is now entirely restored to her usual form. She and Harriett Spencer Kendall foregathered with Anne Rotan Howe in New York for a few days early in February, after which hilarious occasion the Howes sailed on a six weeks' cruise to Brazil. Harriett's youngest child is a freshman at Bennington's, Anne's a freshman at Harvard.

Ethel Clinton Russell's daughter, Nancy, came out in Buffalo this winter.

The Alumnae Office sends a new address for Irma Silverman Schoenthal: 1227 Bennington Avenue, Pittsburgh, Pa.

Irene Sheppard, who was appointed Secretary of the Board of Missions of the Presbyterian Church in the U. S. A. in 1925, went to South America in November to visit Presbyterian Missions in Columbia and Venezuela. From her office at 156 Fifth Avenue, New York, she keeps in constant touch with missionaries in twelve stations in the Cameroon, West Africa, and with twenty-five stations in six countries in Latin America. From 1908 to 1924 she was with the Y. W. C. A., spending ten years of that time in Buenos Aires and Valparaiso. The Board of Foreign Missions says, "Her keen judgment and sympathetic attitude have played no small part in the success of the missionary enterprise in those countries. Because of her personal experience in Latin America, Miss Sheppard understands the missionary's problem, and it has been said of her that no matter how late the hour, she is always willing and ready to give her support and sympathy to those missionaries who seek her advice when on furlough in this country."

Jane Brown has recently been around the world, and is gadding again this winter, we hear.

Mrs. John A. Lafore (Nan Shearer) and Mrs. A. J. Barron (Elizabeth Congdon) were on the list of those who had passed the examination for flower show judging in Pennsylvania published in the March 15th issue of *Horticulture*.

1903

Class Editor: GERTRUDE DIETRICH SMITH
(Mrs. Herbert Knox Smith)
Farmington, Conn.

1904

Class Editor: EMMA O. THOMPSON
320 S. 42nd St., Philadelphia, Pa.

Word has come from Sue Swindell Nuckols that on April 3rd, 1933, her youngest son, Samuel Nuckols, who was just seventeen years old, was instantly killed in an automobile accident in Albany. He was being driven by his friend when the car skidded on a wet car track and crashed into a tree. Her son was President of the Senior Class of his school, the Albany Academy, and also Captain of the Cadet Battalion.

It is difficult, almost impossible, to tell Sue how shocked and grieved we are.

1905

Class Editor: ELEANOR LITTLE ALDRICH
(Mrs. Talbot Aldrich)
59 Mount Vernon St., Boston, Mass.

Theodora Bartlett is still in New York and has three classes—15 to 45 in number—of women doing various bits of modern history with a view to making foreign news more understandable. One is doing "Germany Since 1800," another "History of American Relations with England" and the third, "India." Theodora was in India two years ago. (And never mentioned it to us, which shows how hard is the life of a class editor!) She says that this is by all odds the most interesting work she ever did but she needs more classes.

Gladys King Johnston and her husband are living with her mother and brother, so her address is once again the one so familiar to us all, 16 Stuyvesant Place, New Brighton, Staten Island.

Florance Waterbury's one-man show of her paintings was held at the Present Day Club in Princeton from March 7th through March 19th.

The Class wishes to extend love and sympathy to the family of Alberta Warner Aiken, who died of pneumonia on April 3rd.

1906

Class Editor: LOUISE CRUICE STURDEVANT
(Mrs. Edward W. Sturdevant)
3006 P St., Washington, D. C.

1907

Class Editor: ALICE HAWKINS
Taylor Hall, Bryn Mawr, Pa.

Tink Meigs' life of Louisa Alcott is called "Invincible Louisa." It is scheduled for publication by Little Brown on May 10th.

Harriot Houghteling Curtis and her husband have just returned from a short trip to Vienna, where Dr. Curtis spent most of his furlough. They are due back in Newfoundland for the summer.

Minnie List Chalfant's daughter will graduate in June. Minnie is planning to spend a week with her in Merion Hall between her last examination and Commencement Day.

Julie Benjamin Howson expects to bring her daughter, Joan, to spend a week-end at College this spring. This procedure is recommended to all 1907 mothers of sub-Freshmen.

Edith Rice has just become a member of the Alumnae Scholarships and Loan Fund Committee. Edith is head of the Modern Language Department at the Kensington (Philadelphia) High School.

Lelia Woodruff Stokes and her husband have acquired a beautiful country estate in Maryland, not far from the great Conowingo Dam. The old house has been delightfully modernized and overlooks rolling meadows bordering Deer Creek. On the place was standing an old mill, which has again been harnessed to the creek and now supplies all the heat, light and power needed for the large family connection and many friends who enjoy Lelia's hospitality. The two eldest boys are at Haverford, and the other three children at Germantown Friends' School. They are all keen naturalists, helped on by the remarkable course in Nature Study which Margaret Reeve Cary has given at that school for a great many years. Early in April Calvert Myers Beasley and Alice Hawkins enjoyed a week-end at "The Mill" and lent four rather inexpert hands to such pleasant enterprises as making a wild garden along the brook or transplanting seedlings from cold frames.

The class wishes to extend warm sympathy to Katharine Harley whose mother died in March.

1908

Class Editor: HELEN CADBURY BUSH
Haverford, Pa.

1909

Class Editor: HELEN BOND CRANE
70 Willett St., Albany, N. Y.

Evelyn Holt Lowry has responded nobly to the editorial postcard. She writes from her new home, Vineyard Lane, Greenwich, Conn., which is her address from September to June. In the summer she visits her mother in Washington, Conn. As to her family: "My daughter, Marion, 12, attends the Greenwich Academy. She is a lively, not to say buxom, young lady with red hair and a great interest in dramatics and tap dancing. However, in spite of these she intends to become a trained nurse. Philip, just past 15, is at the Romford School in Connecticut, aiming at Princeton. Stamps and astronomy are his chief interests, and he hopes to pursue a career in the direction of astrophysics. Since mother built this house, my own time has been consumed in landscape gardening—the actual physical labor—and I have gotten a surprising thrill out of shovelling dirt, laying flagstones and building a stone wall. . . . What I learned from watching the masons I am putting to use now in walling in my flower-garden-to-be. My other activities are a budding garden club out here and the treasurership of the Yorkville Speedwell Unit—a New York boarding babies' society—and, up to this month, the Bryn Mawr Club. But being president and living in the country didn't work too well, and, the Club being safely ensconced in its new quarters and going well, I have resigned from the office. Scrap (Ecob) is the assistant treasurer.

"Anne Whitney comes out for week-ends occasionally. She is still living with my mother in New York and continues as Health Education Director of the American Child Health Association. She is in demand for speeches all over the country and makes many trips to deliver them. Last month she and a member of her staff motored to South Carolina, where the Association is doing a job in rural schools, I think. Now she is busy arranging a Health Conference which meets in Ann Arbor in the early summer."

Georgina Biddle's cruise seems to have been full of interest. "In Havana everyone in the streets looks sad because their friends are either being murdered or starved by their so-called President. In Jamaica the color problem seems on the way to being solved by the paler brown people being socially as well as racially absorbed in the white race. . . . Then Panama, which no one had told me was really beautiful—high blue hills sloping down to Gatun Lake, bananas planted all over the lower slopes and dead trees (not beautiful but picturesque) all around the edges of the lake and through the lake itself. As a pacifist I was pained to see everything extremely well run under the absolute dictatorship of the U. S. Army! Perhaps it was not because it was the Army but because it was dictatorship (pro tem only)."

Aristine Munn has been getting into the headlines recently as "Savior of the pugs." It seems that the breed was vanishing in this country, and Aristine imported a number, collected a kennel of 35 and began showing them. "Young fanciers gave them scarcely a glance; judges had even forgotten how to judge them. But older folks, whose memories reached back to the '80's and '90's, recalled with deep sentiment how the very first dogs they ever owned were pugs, etc. . . . Dr. Munn has given up her practice in New York and has retired with her pugs to a farm near West Long Branch, N. J. She came to town recently and collected five blue ribbons at the Westminster Kennel Club Show."

1910

Class Editor: KATHERINE ROTAN DRINKER
(Mrs. Cecil K. Drinker)
71 Rawson Road, Brookline, Mass.

1911

Class Editor: ELIZABETH TAYLOR RUSSELL
(Mrs. John F. Russell, Jr.)
333 E. 68th St., New York City

The class sends its deepest sympathy to Elsie Funkhauser upon the sudden death of her mother in Washington, D. C.

Ruth Roberts McMillen has written voluntarily to us (others please note and copy this splendid example). Ruth's three children are two daughters, aged two and fifteen, and a son, Tom, who has just been elected president of next year's senior class at Hotchkiss School. Tom expects to go to Princeton in 1934.

We omitted Kate Chambers Seelye's probable address for next winter. It will be 96 Maynard Road, Northampton, Mass. Laurens Seelye will give some courses at Smith College, and the Seelye family will be there until the summer of 1934, when they will start on a tour of the U. S.

Your editor, in spite of tremendous family complications, like the loss of a valued nurse and spring vacations, persists in indulging her weakness for amateur theatricals and has a small part in the forthcoming Junior League play, *Mr. Dooley, Jr.*

1912

Class Editor: GLADYS SPRY AUGUR
(Mrs. Wheaton Augur)
820 Camino Atalaya, Santa Fé, N. M.

Beth Hamilton Hurd stopped in Santa Fé on her way to California and managed to see the

Editor as well as all of Santa Fé and Taos in one day.

Alice Stratton is now at the Philadelphia Home for Incurables. Mary Peirce and Marjorie Thompson saw her recently and she was gay and very welcoming. She would love to see any of the class when they come to Bryn Mawr, or to hear from them.

Carlotta Welles Briggs is in New York this spring with her baby and his nurse, and may be here part of the summer, but Christine Hammer, from whom this information came, did not give her address.

The class will join in sending love and sympathy to Gertrude Llewellyn Stone, whose mother died recently while on a trip to the West Indies. She had gone to recuperate from a mastoid operation. Everyone who knew Mrs. Llewellyn will feel a sense of personal loss.

1913

Class Editor: HELEN EVANS LEWIS
 (Mrs. Robert M. Lewis)
 52 Trumbull St., New Haven, Conn.

The first two unsolicited contributions to the class notes to be received by the present editor arrived simultaneously the morning mail of March 7th. One said, "My dear Helen, can't we have some 1913 notes? Yours very sincerely, Katherine Schmidt Eisenhart." The other said, "Governor and Mrs. C. Douglass Buck announce the marriage of Miss Marion Irwin to Dr. Winthrop J. Y. Osterhout on Monday, February 27th, 1933, at 'Buena Vista,' Wilmington."

The Class Editor has decided that her role demands the combined talents of a detective and an archaeologist. She has sat peacefully for a year (or is it two?) pursuing a policy of watchful waiting for the letters that never came. Now is the time for a new deal. If you don't want what you do to be reported in the class notes don't do it.

To return to Iki. It seems that she had added to a career distinguished in science a husband even more distinguished in science. Dr. Osterhout was formerly a professor at Harvard and is now a Member of the Rockefeller Institute for Medical Research.

Dorothea Baldwin McCollester is teaching Mediaeval History at the Nightingale-Bamford School in New York. She has two boys, nine and seven, and a daughter of three and a half.

Katherine Page Loring is spending the winter in Chocorua, N. H. Her oldest daughter, Alice Page, goes to the Tamworth High School; Kate is at boarding school, and Katherine is teaching young Charley at home. (These last two items were gleaned by the help of mutual non-Bryn Mawr friends.)

Margaret Scruggs Carruth has lately published, in collaboration with her mother, a book,

"Gardening in the Southwest," and has illustrated the book with drawings in line and color. Margaret has been a national officer in the National League of American Pen Women.

Olga Kelly spent a week at Miami, recovering from an attack of grip, and returned to Baltimore in time to attend a dinner given by various eminent Johns Hopkins doctors to her distinguished father on his 75th birthday.

Eleanor Bontecou is established in a delightful cottage outside of Washington. She is definitely better after her long illness and is busy doing beautiful weaving on a hand loom, working out all of the traditional old patterns. However, she will turn from folk-lore to a discussion of the latest political news of Washington, and back again, in a way that seems miraculous to anyone to whom both weaving and the political scene seem hopelessly intricate.

1914

Class Editor: ELIZABETH AYER INCHES
 (Mrs. Henderson Inches)
 41 Middlesex Road, Cambridge, Mass.

I am sure that the class will be very sorry to hear of the sudden death of Mrs. Charles Cox, Lill Harman's mother, last month, and will wish to send Lill their love and sympathy.

Eleanor Allen Mitchum writes cheerily of feeling most healthy and satisfied with life in spite of doing much more housework than usual. She plays golf regularly on a club team and feels as if she were back in college. She is treasurer of the "Infant Shelter," which cares for sixty children under five, and has been raising dogs.

Evelyn McCutcheon writes that she and her family are having a splendid time in Tucson, Ariz., this winter. They motor, ride and visit different ranches, and have two boys in school there. The oldest boy is at Milton and spends many week-ends with Helen Shaw Crosby.

1915

Class Editor: MARGARET FREE STONE
 (Mrs. J. A. Stone)
 3039 44th St., N. W., Washington, D. C.

1916

Class Editor: LARIE KLEIN BOAS
 (Mrs. Benjamin Boas)
 2100 Pacific Ave., San Francisco, Calif.

1917

Class Editor: BERTHA CLARK GREENOUGH
 203 Blackstone Blvd., Providence, R. I.

Just as the BULLETIN was about to go to press without any '17 notes the following arrived from Caroline Stevens Rogers.

Having put in a strenuous winter with her brother's long illness and death in January,

Caroline is again absorbed in, as she puts it, "the ordinary suburban life, spending much time over my children's education." (Her four children range in ages from three to eight). "With my next-door neighbor I am still running a kindergarten (with a highly-trained teacher), an outgrowth of my original nursery school; am also on an executive committee that runs an elementary school of 20 pupils, a conservatively progressive school. Have tried to become more civic minded since the children have grown out of the nursery by working on the District Nursing Association Committee and by giving rummage sales for a charity nursery school. All civic duties seem to pall, however, in comparison with a thrilling family life, recently made more interesting by the addition of a pony which runs away very often. The children are being taught to ride bareback by my greatly beloved cook who used to be a cowpuncher and who now can cook and serve as easily as he can rock the baby."

1918

Class Editor: MARGARET BACON CAREY
(Mrs. H. R. Carey)
3115 Queen Lane, East Falls P. O., Phila.

A long (and spontaneous) blessing on her head!) letter from Helen Whitcomb Barss says, "Because it is pleasant to hear news of 1918 again, I'd like to do my bit. I see a good deal of a number of Bryn Mawr people, but they are all either much older or appallingly younger than we. You know, of course, that Molly Cordingly Stevens' husband died a couple of months ago. Until this winter I have seen her fairly often as we belong to the same Folk Dancing Class. Several springs we have had a picnic luncheon at her house and danced on her lovely grassed terrace. I, myself, do none of the travelling that always sounds so alluring. However, if the bank commissioner permits, I am going to Bermuda for a week or so to try to get rid of persistent bronchitis. (I mention the cough only because it seems faintly immoral to be considering unnecessary galivanting at the moment.) As for activities, I am at present President of the local League of Women Voters, and I occasionally lead discussion groups on International Affairs; and I look after my two children, and give tea and chaperonage and occasional advice to twenty boys who live in the dormitory above us, and to any others of the 650 who may apply."

To Molly Cordingly Stevens the class extends its deep sympathy, especially those few of us who have been through the same experience.

A letter from Helen Walker, enclosing the old class minutes, etc., fails to give any news of herself, and is extremely discouraging about the job of Class Editor!

Early this week your editor was hurrying along 50th Street (N. Y. C.) and nearly ran into Peppy Turle. We both recognized each other, and stopped for a word, but the editor was so surrounded by family-in-law that she did not gather any concrete news—except that Peppy lives below Al Newlin.

1919

Class Editor: MARJORIE REMINGTON TWITCHELL
(Mrs. Pierrepont Twitchell)
Setauket, L. I., N. Y.

Helen Prescott Churchward writes, "I am keeping my nose to the grindstone and am thankful I have the job which I took out of boredom when the income therefrom was not needed. Last summer we took about ten days off and had a wonderful trip south through Oregon to Crater Lake, west to Crescent City, California, and then up the Oregon coast."

Betty Dabney Baker seems to spread herself over a great number of activities—active in the Parent-Teachers' Association of the Dalton School in New York, where Barbara and Joan go to school. "Also along educational lines is my committee work with the Child Study Association. For two years I had a committee to investigate and give information about schools at the Junior League. I have resigned that, but am still doing other work at the League. One of my main interests in the last two years has been in music. I became interested in the way music was being taught to children and decided my own musical education needed thorough overhauling. I am now taking courses at the Juilliard Foundation and really working at it. A few weeks ago Elizabeth Fuller, Angela Moore Place and Katherine Walker Bradford ('21) and I renewed our youth by going to a costume party clad in garments of about the vintage of '19."

1920

Class Editor: MARY PORRITT GREEN
(Mrs. Valentine J. Green)
433 E. 51st St., New York City

Katherine Cauldwell Scott sent us the following, which Helen Wortman Russell wrote to her: "You are very smart to keep up your strenuous athletics and raise two little girls to do likewise. My three are riding this winter and getting all the thrills out of it Allan and I used to get. Barb, age five, has won a blue and red ribbon in horse shows this winter, and we all feel proud of her. The boys ride in paper chases (our substitute for fox hunting), and Russ and I stay home and work on the dry rock wall, prune the fruit trees, spray the rose bushes and otherwise make ourselves useful. We are doing all our own gardening this

year, even to digging up the lawn, and the boys
are ambitiously starting on the vegetable garden. We have the starter of a tennis court,
and maybe by the time you get out to see us
my family will be able to challenge yours to
a set of doubles.

"I have rambled enough. I have no thrills to
relate as my days brim with happy doings
with and for my family. Gord is now thirteen,
weighs 135 stripped, towers over me and is an
ardent Boy Scout and Bruce is nearly ten."

1921

Class Editor: WINIFRED WORCESTER
  (Mrs. Harvey Stevenson)
  Croton-on-Hudson, N. Y.

Helen Hill (Mrs. Francis P. Miller) is living
near Washington, D. C. She has a boy about
three months old, and is writing a book which
will be out next fall.

Betsy Kales (Mrs. Francis Straus) has a
third child, who is now a year old. Betsy took
ten days off when he was born, but with that
exception has spent the last two years teaching
at Rush Medical, conducting an infant welfare
clinic two afternoons a week at Hull House,
and filling in odd moments with research.

Nancy Porter (Mrs. Michael Straus) has
moved to Washington, where she is, as she puts
it, living the life of a parent. All she has to
do is to adjust her hours to those of a husband
who works for a morning paper, which may be
any hours, and teach her children how to live
in a city.

Ellen Jay Garrison is thriving on university
life in Wisconsin. She says she loves the life
and the people, and her chief occupation is putting on white gloves and calling. She has made
sixty-five calls to date, and thinks she has only
sixty-seven more to go.

1922

Class Editor: SERENA HAND SAVAGE
  (Mrs. William L. Savage)
  106 E. 85th St., New York City

Catherine Rhett Woods and her husband are
living in Long Beach, Calif.

Marion Rawson has gone to Greece for a
few months of "digging."

Grace Rhoads is working toward her Ph.D.
She writes that Virginia Grace is at the American School of Classical Studies in Athens, and
that last summer she travelled through Italy,
France and England and then to Scandinavia.

Marnie Speer writes from Yenching, China:
"Life goes on here as it always does in China.
Excitements flare up and die down. When
things seem about to explode, nothing happens,
and when everything seems quiet something

blows up or collapses. Today's paper says all
Japanese women and children have received
orders to evacuate Peiping. That looks like
trouble. For the last six weeks we have talked
of nothing but the situation! No one thinks
the Japanese will try to take this part of China
to keep, but they may come in temporarily, and
even a few days of fighting would make a mess
of things. But there's no use prophesying, and
in the meantime college goes busily on."

1923

Class Editor: RUTH MCANENY LOUD
  325 E. 72nd St., New York City.

Elizabeth Philbrick was married to Donald
Frothingham on March 25th, with Mildred
Schwarz as maid of honor. After a wedding
trip to Bermuda, Betty started in immediately
on her duties as "house mother" at the Fenn
School in Concord, Mass., where her husband
teaches.

Margaret Hussey took a two-weeks vacation
from her Girl Scouts in February and went to
Porto Rico.

Emmeline Kellogg Adams is doing part-time
work in the administrative office of the Brearley School.

Frances Young Reinhoff is one of the 1500
"most important ladies in the United States of
America." She is so listed in *Principal Women
of America*, published at the Mitre Press, in
London, and quoted in an earlier number of
the BULLETIN. We haven't heard from Snip in
the last ten years, so we cannot elaborate on
this. Won't some one tell us what form of
activity has led to this honour?

1924

Class Editor: DOROTHY GARDNER BUTTERWORTH
  (Mrs. J. Ebert Butterworth)
  8024 Roanoke St., Chestnut Hill, Pa.

From the "Grand Hotel de Russie" in Rome
comes a letter from Lesta Ford Clay. Lesta
is on leave of absence from her job in the
library of the New York Academy of Medicine.
With her husband she is spending six months
in Europe studying modern architecture; so far
they have visited Stockholm, Amsterdam, the
Hague and Paris. Later on they expect to
spend a month travelling in Germany.

Sue Leewitz is back in New York this winter, living at home, doing charity work of various natures. Sue writes: "As far as travelling
is concerned, I went to Europe last March to
stay until July. I was mostly visting Pussy
(my sister), who is married and established in
Paris—and getting acquainted with her son,
my godchild, who has reached the ripe age of
twenty months. My last interesting bit of

travelling was in the winter of '30-'31, when I came back from Europe via the East, i.e., taking a round-the-world trip with my family."

News of Russ (Marion Russell Morris) was contained in Sue's letter; she has a daughter, Mary Ann, born last September 7th; the first child is a son, Frank Rockwell Morris, Jr., who was born in July, 1929.

1925

Class Editor: ELIZABETH MALLET CONGER
(Mrs. Frederic Conger)
325 East 72nd St., New York City.

Mathilde Hansen Smith writes: "My three daughters are flourishing in spite of hard times and a busy mother. I have a grand job right now, giving other girls a chance to start up a business career of their own. In other words, get distributors, especially in New England, to sell the Lauralei Lingerie on a 20% commission basis. The girls who are now selling it all over the country are not agents, but distributors, who are prominent in their own community, and mostly Junior League girls who would like to earn some money but who cannot take a regular job and be tied down to certain hours." Anyone interested can reach Mathilde at 12 Keene Street, Providence, R. I.

A letter from Clara Gehring brings very exciting news: "On Thursday, April 6th, I'm going to be married to George Percival Bickford, Harvard '21 and Harvard Law School '24· The past three and a half years I've had a part-time teaching job in the piano department of the Cleveland Institute of Music. I've also had a History and Appreciation Class for the Music Memory Contest of the Cleveland Orchestra. Our small Cleveland Bryn Mawr group has also struggled to keep alive our local scholarship fund and Bryn Mawr Summer School Fund."

Alys Boross Smith had a son, Peter Schermerhorn Smith, on March 20th.

And Hink (Etheline Hinkley Van Kleeck) also had a son in March, Baltus Van Kleeck, Jr. Hink's daughter, Elsey, is three and a half years old now.

Connie Miller Douglas seems to be a great traveler. She motored to Florida for February and in March went to Washington as a delegate to the Conference of the Women's Organization for National Prohibition Reform. Connie stayed with her husband's cousin, who is the Director of the Budget, and she had a delightful time hearing about Washington. Connie lives on Seventy-fourth Street in New York, and has a three-year-old son, Archibald Douglas, III.

On April 11th, Nana Bonnell Davenport had a fine son, the biggest of the three Davenport boys. He weighed 9 lbs. 9 oz.

1926

Class Editor pro tem: MARY C. PARKER
135 Charles St., Boston, Mass.

I have taken Happy's job during her absence in less bitter climes. I apologize now to all former secretaries for this column! I have ranted about our long silences, and small number of news items in the BULLETIN, but experience has taught me better! After all, though, even in these times one postcard is not an expensive luxury and can carry a lot of news. If you won't send news of yourself, why not send some about someone else?

A Christmas card from Anne Tierney, now Mrs. J. H. Anderson, indicates that she is very happily married and settled at Jullundur Cantonment, Punjab, India.

Rummy Muckenhoupt Smith has unfortunately been quite ill, but is now recovered and is living at 10 Adrian Drive, New York.

Edith Nichols Fitzell, her husband and small daughter, Jean, have migrated to San Francisco, where they are living at 342 Panorama Drive.

All the class will wish to express their sympathy to Miriam Lewis, whose father died in December. Miriam is still with the Curtis Publishing Company, and expects to have some of her poems published in the spring.

Can any one enlighten me, or the Alumnae Office, as to the whereabouts of Eleanor Stiltz? I have a letter for her from the Alumnae Office, and all my clues have failed.

1927

Class Editor: ELLENOR MORRIS
Berwyn, Pa.

Julia Lee McDill has a young son, John Lee McDill, born on January 30th. She is living at 255 Edwards Street, New Haven, Conn., and, although a wife and mother, is still prominent as a forester. She has been elected to the Society of American Foresters, a really great honor, as she is the only woman member. She writes that she expects to go on with her work again this summer in Vermont.

Julie also writes that Jane Sullivan Curtis with her husband and two sons is living in an eighteenth century chateau outside of Paris, while her husband does research work.

Liz Nelson Tate sends word of her second son, Thomas Nelson Tate, called Toby, born March 2nd. The Tates, as we may have mentioned before, live in Washington, D. C., and the first-born is now three and a half years old.

This department paid a visit the other day to Ginny Newbold Gibbon and her young son, Sam Gibbon, Jr., now over a year old and a most entrancing infant. He is hopefully called "Torchy," as there is a faint suspicion of red about his hair.

1928

Class Editor: CORNELIA B. ROSE, JR.
310 East 55th St., New York City.

Elinor Amram was married very quietly at Feasterville on April 3rd to Mr. Milton C. Nahm, Associate in Philosophy at Bryn Mawr. Mr. Nahm took his B.A. at the University of Pennsylvania in 1925 and his M.A. in 1926. He studied at Oxford for two years and was given the degree of B.Litt. there in 1929. He was an Instructor in Philosophy at the University of Pennsylvania, 1929-30, and came to Bryn Mawr in 1930. They will live in Haverford at the Old Buck Inn on Lancaster Avenue.

Our only other matrimonial news is the announcement of Ruth Creighton's engagement to William A. Webster, Jr., of Upper Montclair.

Jean Fenner writes from 922 Memorial Drive, Cambridge, Mass., that she has been studying there for the past two years, and that although she still calls her home New Orleans, she spends very little time there. Her aspirations, which at one time, she says, were musical, suddenly have become literary.

Gail Sampson, like a lamb, sends a report of her recent doings. Last year she resigned from her job in the Princeton University Library and went abroad for five months, three of which she spent in Rome. This year she has continued her interest in dramatic groups, such as the University League, the Women's College Club, and the newly created Princeton Community Players in the capacity of general utility man. Her other activities include having organized a most flourishing dancing club.

Brooksie seems to take after us, at least insofar as frequent changes of domicile are concerned. At present she is living at 61 East 66th Street, New York City. Ever since November of 1931, she has been working for the Commission on Administration of Justice of New York State. The commission was appointed by Governor Roosevelt to study the methods of administering justice and court procedure in the state.

1929

Class Editor: MARY L. WILLIAMS
210 East 68th St., New York City.

Billy Haley is staying, with her sister Peggy, at the Hotel Leonori in New York. They have both had a number of jobs, but are now (voluntarily) among the unemployed and devote their time to writing.

Marianne Barber spent the winter in Bryn Mawr after traveling abroad during the summer. She says that she has been writing "industriously, but not famously," and that when her novel does go across she will have all sorts of news.

Katharine Fleischmann Gaty has a son, Lewis R. Gaty, II, born December 18.

Winnie Trask Lee is going abroad the beginning of April, to remain in Switzerland for about six weeks.

The Editor spent the winter taking a secretarial course (all Class Notes typed by the touch system now), and is looking for a job at present.

1930

Class Editor: EDITH GRANT
Pembroke West, Bryn Mawr.

1931

Class Editor: EVELYN WAPLES BAYLESS
(Mrs. Robert N. Bayless)
301 W. Main St., New Britain, Conn.

The Class extends its sympathy to Peggy Nuckols Bell, who lost her brother recently in an automobile accident.

1932

Class Editor: JOSEPHINE GRATON
182 Brattle St., Cambridge, Mass.

News from Kay Franchot tells of several of our classmates. Kay herself is working at the Massachusetts General Clinic in Boston. Ann Willits is working at the Provident Trust Company in Philadelphia. Phyllis Simms is in Washington, doing social service work. Greta Swenson is also in Washington and hopes to spend another summer in the Mediterranean on the Odyssey cruise.

The Woods twins are, according to last report, planning to do graduate work at Radcliffe next year. They expect to specialize in Anthropology.

A. Lee Hardenbergh reports favorably on life in Vienna and Paris. In Vienna she managed to combine winter sports with attendance at a good many plays, operas and concerts. In Paris she lived under the wing of Winnie McCully and went to lectures at the Sorbonne now and then. Her plans now call for stays in Geneva, Rome, and Munich.

On April 1st, Clarissa Compton was married to Mr. A. Lincoln Dryden, Associate in Geology at Bryn Mawr. Mr. Dryden studied at Johns Hopkins, taking his A.B. in 1925 and his Ph.D. in 1930. Before coming to Bryn Mawr in 1930, Mr. Dryden worked with the Maryland Geological Survey, and with the Sinclair Exploration Company in Venezuela. Clarissa is sticking to her job in New York until the summer, but expects to settle down in Bryn Mawr next year and to do graduate work in Archaeology.

SCHOOL DIRECTORY

The Saint Timothy's School for Girls

CATONSVILLE, MARYLAND

Founded September 1882

COLLEGE PREPARATORY
AND
ELECTIVE COURSES

MISS LOUISA McENDREE FOWLER
Head of the School

WYKEHAM RISE

WASHINGTON, CONNECTICUT

A COUNTRY SCHOOL FOR GIRLS

FANNY E. DAVIES, LL.A., *Headmistress*
Prepares for Bryn Mawr and Other Colleges

MISS *Beard's*
SCHOOL

PREPARES girls for College Board examinations. General courses include Household, Fine and Applied Arts, and Music. Trained teachers, small classes. Ample grounds near Orange Mountain. Excellent health record; varied sports program. Established 1894. *Write for booklet.*

LUCIE C. BEARD
Headmistress
Berkeley Avenue
Orange   New Jersey

LOW-HEYWOOD
On the Sound ~ At Shippan Point

ESTABLISHED 1865

Preparatory to the Leading Colleges for Women.
Also General Course.
Art and Music.
Separate Junior School.
Outdoor Sports.

One hour from New York

Address

MARY ROGERS ROPER, *Headmistress*
Box Y, Stamford, Conn.

The Ethel Walker School

SIMSBURY, CONNECTICUT

Head of School
ETHEL WALKER SMITH, A.M.,
Bryn Mawr College

Head Mistress
JESSIE GERMAIN HEWITT, A.B.,
Bryn Mawr College

ROSEMARY HALL

Greenwich, Conn.

COLLEGE PREPARATORY

Caroline Ruutz-Rees, Ph.D. } Head
Mary E. Lowndes, M. A., Litt D. } Mistresses

Katherine P. Debevoise, Assistant to the Heads

THE
SHIPLEY SCHOOL

BRYN MAWR, PENNSYLVANIA

Preparatory to
Bryn Mawr College

ALICE G. HOWLAND   } Principals
ELEANOR O. BROWNELL }

The Kirk School

Bryn Mawr, Pennsylvania

Boarding and day school. Record for thorough preparation for the leading women's colleges. Four-year college preparatory course. One-year intensive course for high-school graduates. Resident enrollment limited to thirty girls. Advantage of small classes and of individual instruction when desirable. Informal home life. Outdoor sports.

MARY B. THOMPSON, *Principal*

SCHOOL DIRECTORY

Something to Say

_____—not just _saying_ something

A friend of CHESTERFIELD writes us of a salesman who had "something to say":

"I dropped into a little tobacco shop, and when I asked for a pack of Chesterfields the man smiled and told me I was the seventh customer without a break to ask for Chesterfields. 'Smoker after smoker,' he said, 'tells me that Chesterfields click...I sell five times as many Chesterfields as I did a while back.''

Yes, there's something to say about Chesterfields and i takes just six words to say i —"They're mild and yet the satisfy."

they Satisfy

BRYN MAWR
ALUMNAE
BULLETIN

CERTAIN ACADEMIC ANNOUNCEMENTS

June 1933

Vol. XIII   No. 6

Entered as second-class matter, January 15, 1921, at the Post Office, Phila., Pa., under Act of March 3, 1879
COPYRIGHT, 1933
ALUMNAE ASSOCIATION OF BRYN MAWR COLLEGE

Form of Bequest

I give and bequeath to the ALUMNAE ASSOCIATION

OF BRYN MAWR COLLEGE, Bryn Mawr, Pennsylvania,

the sum of...........................dollars.

BRYN MAWR ALUMNAE BULLETIN

OFFICIAL PUBLICATION OF
THE BRYN MAWR ALUMNÆ ASSOCIATION

MARJORIE L. THOMPSON, '12, *Editor*
ALICE M. HAWKINS, '07, *Business Manager*

EDITORIAL BOARD

MARY CRAWFORD DUDLEY, '96   ELLENOR MORRIS, '27
CAROLINE MORROW CHADWICK-COLLINS, '05   ELINOR B. AMRAM, '28
EMILY KIMBROUGH WRENCH, '21   PAMELA BURR, '28
ELIZABETH BENT CLARK, '95, *ex-officio*

Subscription Price, $1.50 a Year   *Single Copies, 25 Cents*
Checks should be drawn to the order of Bryn Mawr Alumnæ Bulletin
Published monthly, except August, September and October, at 1006 Arch St., Philadelphia, Pa.

VOL. XIII   JUNE, 1933   No. 6

In April the BULLETIN carried a statement of the experimental changes announced by the College for plans of admission, and President Park, on her page, explained the purpose of these experiments very definitely, i. e., to bring to Bryn Mawr students who have shown a high degree of ability but who are not able or at any rate likely to come to the College under the present requirements. This month there appears a brief statement under the academic announcements that shows that the experiment has begun to work, as yet how successfully, no one can tell. The thing that is significant is that there is an awakening interest on the part of both schools and students in districts where there has been no interest before because they have both felt that Bryn Mawr was ruled out for them. That this interest is genuine is shown by the fact that some of the students, who for one reason or another did not qualify under Plan D, have undertaken to go up for the regular College Board examinations. As yet they are too few in number to generalize about them in any way, but the significant fact of aroused interest remains. A more interesting group, perhaps, and one from whom in the end the College may derive the greater enrichment, is that group composed of students who decide late in school life that they wish to come to Bryn Mawr. Of course, at the present time economic reasons may turn the balance, but even when that is the case the implication is that the student knows what she wants and has a real purpose in coming to the College. She is no longer following the line of least resistance, going along paths that have already been mapped out for her. With the decision to change her plans and come to Bryn Mawr almost inevitably there is also a very definite desire to get a certain thing from the College, some specific training, that focuses all of her college life and makes her more interesting and significant both as a person and as a student. And after all, the taste for Bryn Mawr and the particular training that it can give is a rather mature taste, with all that that implies. No one can help being genuinely interested in the results of the experiments, or feeling that Freshman statistics are going to make exciting reading next fall, if the quality of the students is what these first windfalls indicate.

THE THERAPEUTIC VALUE OF DANCING

A Paper read at Mount Holyoke College, April 5th, at the Annual Meeting of the Eastern Society of the Directors of Physical Education in Women's Colleges

By JOSEPHINE PETTS, *Director of Physical Education at Bryn Mawr*

I shall begin this paper with the words of Havelock Ellis: "A man must make himself a work of art." Further: "To learn to dance is the most austere of disciplines, and even for those who have attained to the summit of its art often remains a discipline not to be experienced without heroism. . . . For dancing is the loftiest, the most moving, the most beautiful of the arts, because it is no mere translation or abstraction from life, it is life itself."

May I ask you as I read to think of dancing as "the most austere of disciplines," as a technique, strict and simple, but capable of awakening from the human being a power and energy which have slept for centuries? It is, indeed, the releasing of these smothered energies which will give us life again.

When we have in our schools the right kind of dancing rightly taught from the earliest years, then the person who will evolve under its delicate strength will be beautiful with vigor and force and intelligence such as we have not known in our time, with the ability to restrain and concentrate and direct this power to useful ends. This is much to ask of anything, but we are trying the experiment in a small school near Bryn Mawr and miracles are being performed before our eyes. I have seen them also happen in a school in Europe where dancing goes hand in hand with the development of the mind. For it seems to be undeniable, as John Dewey has said in his introduction to Mr. Alexander's latest book, "The Use of the Self," that there is "a great change in moral and mental attitude that takes place as proper coördinations are established."

Until this time, until dancing which is accurate is taught in the schools, those of us who teach in colleges are and will be faced with the following problem:

When a student enters college she moves badly. What is more, she has moved badly, that is to say, without precision, unrhythmically, for many years. Her movements are all down, heavy, she moves angularly, tensely "straining herself always to hold a balance between two points." The consequence is that her body has lost its equilibrium and lightness and strength. American girls are amazingly weak and stiff. You will disagree with me and bring to my attention the many athletic girls you know, but I ask you if one of them moves precisely, smoothly, or if she can. If you will watch a student as she walks, you will see how she approaches her goal, first one shoulder then the other, first one leg then the other, pulling herself there in a circuitous fashion instead of going with the simple directness which would save so much energy and take her there so much more beautifully.

A student who moves badly moves elaborately with many extra motions. It is for us to chip off all that she does not need, to give her simplicity and aliveness. This process is difficult. It takes patience and a most sensitive understanding on the part of the teacher, courage and tenacity on the part of the pupil, but it must be done.

Our problem, then, is to assist the college student to re-establish her equilibrium, to re-balance the weights of her body, to rediscover her lost rhythm, and in so doing to regain her calm. Our problem is to teach everyone in college to move well.

"To walk with the minimum fatigue being held more important than to run with the maximum speed."

For this, at this time, we need a medium which has therapeutic value. We find it in dancing. But, two things are demanded of dancing if it shall have therapeutic value. They are that it shall accurately conform to the physical laws of the body and that it shall express "strength, health, nobility, ease and serenity of living." The first, because, as you well know, function determines structure. The second, because "there are continual reactions between the body and spirit which the ancients did not neglect, but which we too often have misunderstood." These reactions we now realize must be taken into account in any work which would have a healing quality. Dancing, to be valuable from this point of view, must be done in groups so that it will be characteristically social and create in the individual a consciousness of the people with whom she is working which is at the same time impersonal and gracious.

From the mechanical viewpoint we may say that "that structure functions to the best advantage the weights of which are maintained and adjusted with the least expenditure of muscular energy."

In the body, the weights to be "maintained and adjusted" are the head, the chest and shoulder girdle with the arms, the pelvic girdle with the legs, all three of these weights being attached to the spine as an axis. The spine, then, we must consider as a flexible, weight-bearing rod which curves slightly, naturally, with four counterbalancing antero-posterior curves that give it flexibility and strength. Our entire mechanical problem in movement is to keep the three weights of the body in alignment over each other, both antero-posteriorly and laterally, as close to their axis as possible, and their axis as nearly as possible coincident with their common center of gravity. For this, the physiological curves of the spine must be kept shallow with the weights of the body held up to and concentrated at the lumbo-sacral junction, above the hips, to give them freedom of action. To accomplish this we cannot rely on the superficial muscles, whose function is something quite different, but upon the balance of the vertebrae on each other, this balance held by the ligaments and the deep-lying muscles of the spine. That is, the muscles which are close to the bones in question and not, as is the case with the superficial muscles, quite distant from them.

What we have in the average college student is exactly the opposite. How well we all know the exaggerated lumbar curve of the spine, the dorsal and cervical curves compensatorily distorted, all the weight of the body crashing down heavily through the hips, making them stiff, to the feet which are not meant for this purpose at all, and which immediately give way under the strain; and then the heroic but misguided effort to correct the difficulty by hauling in the abdominal muscles, thus making matters definitely worse.

What we must have if we will have correct movement, and therefore well-developed bodies, is movement which originates in the hips and which is guided, held high, exact and direct, by a central point close to the axis of the body, that is, the center of the chest. The hips are the power from which all movement proceeds, the arms and the legs and head following after and in sympathy with the movement of the torso. This movement is rare and extremely difficult because of the lack today of flexibility and strength through the hips, even in young people. The minute, however, that we reach out with arm or leg or head to start a movement, we have destroyed the unity and balance of the body. It is also true that when movement is initiated or carried on by the arms or legs or head, or all three, as is usually the case, it loses its spiritual quality. It becomes unconcentrated, uninteresting, weak and heavy.

It seems to me, the only thing which will satisfactorily correct poor posture of any sort is dancing that is based on the technique described above. And I say dancing, because exercise of any other kind is limited. It does not lead on through the spirit to the things which are eternal. Only dancing to great music does this. Great music recreates in the individual a sense of rhythm of the sort which induces a calm and tranquil state of mind. Therefore, fine music must be chosen for work which would have therapeutic value, and not that which "only makes the nerves dance." For self-possession is as much a part of beautiful movement as is the mechanical fact that the weights are well balanced.

If dancing, then, will transform the average college student into a living work of art, into a human being who has not only an educated mind, but an educated body as well, it must be in harmony with that movement which is peculiar to her nature, and it must be forever aware of the indomitable reaching upward of the human spirit.

May I end this paper with a word of thanks for its fundamental ideas to Isadora Duncan, the greatest dancer of them all, and to her sister Elizabeth, a great educator?

I should like also to mention several books which have been used for reference:

The Art of the Dance, by Isadora Duncan.
The Dance of Life, by Havelock Ellis.
The Use of the Self, by Mathias Alexander.
The Balancing of Forces in the Human Being, Its Application to Postural Patterns, by Mabel Elsworth Todd.
The Education of the Whole Man, by L. P. Jacks.

ANNOUNCEMENT OF A SPECIAL MEETING OF THE ASSOCIATION

As was announced in the April BULLETIN, Miss Thomas herself has solved the question of financing the Deanery as an Alumnae House. Since that time, Miss Thomas, in coöperation with the Executive Board and the Deanery Ways and Means Committee, has developed a plan which will make her gift not only available, but of the highest value both to the Alumnae Association and to the College. This plan in detail will be reported by Caroline McCormick Slade, 1896, Chairman of the Ways and Means Committee, at the Special Meeting of the Alumnae Association to be held on Sunday, June 11th, at 12.30 p. m., in Goodhart Hall.

THE EPSTEIN BUST OF LUCY MARTIN DONNELLY

Edith Finch, 1922, who owns the bust, has kindly consented, at the request of several Alumnae, to put it on view in the Library during Commencement week.

The portrait bust of Professor Lucy Martin Donnelly, done a year ago by Jacob Epstein and shown during last autumn's exhibition at the Museum of Modern Art in New York as one of the most important of contemporary works, has created a great sensation at the recent exhibition of Mr. Epstein's work at the Leicester Galleries in London. A few extracts from the reviews may be of interest to those who hope that some day this bust may be owned by the college. One reviewer who remarks on the extraordinary living quality of the bust says: ". . . it is the most remarkable exhibition of sculpture ever held in London. His portrait busts are sheer genius, brilliant beyond words. . . . The new Epstein show is the most significant of our time." Another remarks that "Epstein has done it again . . . when you see Mr. Epstein's work in bronze, you wonder why he bothers to carve stone. He is a modeller, and a modeller of genius. For Epstein's bronzes are unmistakably civilized. Where the carvings aim at crude strength, the bronzes achieve ultimate subtleties. They discover the inmost structure as well as every beauty of surface, so that when you go out into the street half the faces you meet 'look Epstein.' It is a sign of the essential, spiritual truth of Epstein's modelling." Speaking of the bust of Miss Donnelly, he says that it "is work quite beyond the reach of any other living sculptor, a miracle of sensitive modelling, uncannily alive."

All the reviews speak of this astonishing vitality. One more conservative critic is "bewildered" by it, for "it comes so near to an artistic effect, to that exact and sensitive appreciation of the model's individual irregularities which can make the artist's generalization really original and genuinely expressive, that one cannot understand why, in the last resort, these portraits should also seem over-expressive and with the same theatrical intensity. And the difficulty is most acute in Mr. Epstein's latest portraits, like that of Professor Lucy Martin Donnelly, and in the bronzes 'Oriel' and 'Isobel.' For in these the sculptor seems to have observed the characteristic and essential structure of his sitters with an astonishing certainty and brilliance. Moreover he has not been content with observation alone and his works are by no means purely descriptive. They obviously have a design."

The bust is one which inevitably must arouse controversy. There will always be those who, disliking Epstein's work, or modern sculpture in general, will dislike it, and those who, interested in such work, will passionately uphold its greatness and beauty. There will be very few who, caring for works of art at all, can remain indifferent. Particularly few will feel that, as a portrait, it does justice to Miss Donnelly: the profiles will please most; the full face will be considered a likeness by almost no one. For these more personal critics the question arises: should a portrait be a great work of art or a perfect likeness?—*can* it be a perfect likeness considering that the portrait is not the sitter herself but the sitter as seen through the eyes of someone else, someone who inevitably sees things with his own and no one else's vision?

THE NEW PLAN FOR THE GRANTING OF THE DEGREE OF DOCTOR OF PHILOSOPHY IN BRYN MAWR COLLEGE

Extracts from a Report Presented to the President of Bryn Mawr College by the Dean of the Graduate School, Eunice Morgan Schenck

I

THE PREPARATION OF THE NEW PLAN

The Work of the Committee of Students

The Students' Committee * of seven members was organized in the autumn of 1930. It proceeded by means of a questionnaire, sent to all graduate students, bearing upon such matters as 1) the relation of course requirements to the degree, 2) systems of examination, 3) publication of dissertation, etc., etc. Tabulating the fifty complete answers that were received, the Committee then conferred on debatable points with groups of students in different fields and with particularly interested and able students, and formulated a report which was forwarded to the Graduate Committee in the spring of 1931.

The seriousness and thoroughness of the students who worked on this report deserve the highest praise. They belong to the new generation of graduate students in America who have come up through Honours courses in their undergraduate years. Having been part of an educational experiment already, they have brought to their graduate work a new critical attitude and a new and very desirable self-consciousness. I believe that we can attribute largely to the grouping of our sixty resident students in Radnor Hall the opportunity that brought so quickly to the surface of discussion the ideas that were ultimately formulated in the students' report. Graduate students in this country have little chance, as a rule, to exchange ideas outside of the small band in each laboratory or seminary. So far as I have been able to learn, this is the first time that a group of graduate students has worked with a faculty group on questions of academic principle.

The Old Plan

The need for a change in the Ph.D. requirements was also being felt by an increasingly large number of members of the Bryn Mawr Faculty. The Old Plan provided a rigid system of preparation for the degree. The candidate, besides presenting a dissertation, offered a Major subject and two Minors. She was obliged to present a specified number of courses in each of these three fields and to pass written and oral examinations in the field of the Major and one Minor. In the

---

* This was a representative and, in my opinion, a very able Committee. Two of its members were graduates of Bryn Mawr College, one a graduate of the London School of Economics, one of George Washington University, one of Elmira College, one of Hunter College, one of Boston University. They represented all stages of graduate work: One had nearly completed her preparation for the Ph.D. degree (she received it at Bryn Mawr in 1932); one will probably take the degree in 1933; four others had already done some graduate work at Bryn Mawr, Columbia, Cornell, and George Washington University; one was in her first year of graduate work. Four of the seven had studied abroad. Their work was spread over the following fields: Chemistry, Geology, History of Art, Mathematics, Philosophy, Romance Languages, Social Sciences.

opinion of many members of the Faculty, the Old Plan tended to create an artificial programme to which students conformed to their detriment. It seemed much more desirable, in the case of the highest degree, that the student's programme should be established more flexibly, giving more place to independent work, and that the degree should be safeguarded not by the accumulation of courses to the candidate's credit, but by careful planning and supervision of her work and a greater insistence upon the most rigorous standards for examinations and dissertation. It was to be expected, therefore, that the report of the Students' Committee should find a highly sympathetic reception at the hands of the Graduate Committee of the Academic Council.

The Work of the Graduate Committee of the Academic Council

The work of this Committee began in the summer of 1931. A detailed study was made of the practices in granting the Ph.D. degree at the University of California, University of Chicago, Columbia University, Cornell University, Harvard University, Johns Hopkins University, Princeton University, and Yale University.

During the winter of 1931-32, the President of the College called two special groups together to meet with the Graduate Committee: 1) seven younger members of the Bryn Mawr Faculty who had recently taken their doctor's degree at the following institutions: Two from Radcliffe, two from Johns Hopkins, one from Princeton, one from Harvard, and one from the Massachusetts Institute of Technology; 2) five recent Doctors of Philosophy of Bryn Mawr College (one had received the A.B. degree from Bryn Mawr College and the four others had the first degree from Barnard, Goucher, and two from Oberlin) holding the following positions: Associate in Social Economy and Social Research, Bryn Mawr College; Associate in Biology, Bryn Mawr College; Lecturer in Latin, Bryn Mawr College; Associate in Mathematics, Bryn Mawr College; Assistant in Research Opthalmology on the staff of the Johns Hopkins Medical School at the Wilmer Institute.

These meetings furnished extraordinarily interesting educational discussion.

The Graduate Committee met often and at length and finally instructed a Sub-Committee to draft its plan. This plan was presented to a meeting of the Academic Council to which the President of the College invited *all members* of the Faculty and Staff concerned with graduate instruction. The suggestions arising from this meeting being incorporated, the plan was then presented for a vote of approval to the Council meeting of May twenty-fifth. The approval was granted. A final draft was made during the summer by the Sub-Committee and this draft became, by unanimous vote of the Council, on November seventeenth, 1932, the *New Plan*.

II
THE POINTS OF THE NEW PLAN

The New Plan proceeds along two lines:

1) To create individual and flexible programmes for the candidates so that they may work profitably and independently and reach the highest development of which they are capable during their period of preparation.

2) To safeguard the degree from any dangers that might result from this freedom granted to the student.

Supervision

What we believe to be one of the sources of strength of the New Plan comes from an element of the old system which has been taken over and developed. A Supervising Committee has already existed at Bryn Mawr for each candidate for the Doctor's degree. The Committee has come into action rather late in the candidate's career and has concerned itself with her examinations and the reading of her dissertation. Supervising Committees, because of their rather unwieldly size, often included members of the Faculty who had little interest in the student's field.

The new Supervising Committee, reduced in size, is made up of the professors most closely concerned with the student's interests under the chairmanship of a member of the Graduate Committee. It is appointed as soon as a student becomes a candidate for the degree, which may be as early as the spring of her first year of graduate work. An early meeting with the candidate is arranged, at which her plans are talked over, and this Committee must approve the general preparation proposed by the student and her department. At the end of the period of preparation this same Committee with one or two additional members serves as a Board of Examiners and reads the dissertation.

Preparation for the Degree

The existence of such a committee seems to safeguard both the candidate and the standards of the degree in what is the most radical change in the New Plan: the elimination of all formal course requirements after a student has been accepted as a candidate. The significance of this change is apparent when it is set against the old requirement of attendance at a fixed number of Graduate Seminaries, although it is to be kept in mind that a student under the New Plan is not accepted as a candidate until she has shown her mettle in at least two Graduate Units of work. (The Graduate Unit would correspond in general to the old Seminary.)

This freedom from course requirements corresponds to the spirit of the New Plan. It does not mean that the average candidate for the degree will not take courses. As a matter of fact, the New Plan recommends that, in most cases, at least five graduate seminaries be taken. It does mean, however, that in the opinion of the Bryn Mawr Academic Council the highest American degree should stand, as do the highest European degrees, on the final achievement of the candidates and should not be concerned with the gradual accumulation of academic "credits." The tendency to reduce course requirements is counterbalanced in the New Plan by the establishment of a new "independent unit of graduate work." This unit consists in work outlined and examined by an instructor but carried on by the student herself. The programme of most students in the future will probably include both formal seminaries and these new units. A Supervising Committee is, however, free under the New Plan to approve an entirely independent programme of preparation to be carried out on her own responsibility by the candidate, who would present herself for examinations without submitting any record of courses or "units" of work.*

---

* Three years remain the minimum of time allowed for preparation for the degree. Two of these must be spent in residence at Bryn Mawr under the New Plan as under the Old. In the case of Bryn Mawr graduates, however, and in the case of women who have held academic appointments at Bryn Mawr for at least two years (i. e. two groups whose work the Faculty has had a chance to weigh) the residence requirement may be reduced to one year.

Examinations and their Content

The examinations for the degree follow roughly the old system. They remain in two great divisions: a preliminary examination on the general field of the candidate's work and a final on the field of her special investigations. They must include both written and oral examinations.

Dissertation

The Bryn Mawr Graduate School can, I believe, be justly proud of the level maintained by its doctor's dissertations, and the passages of the old regulations concerned with the preparation and acceptance of the dissertation passed practically intact into the New Plan. Bryn Mawr, however, like every other institution in the country, has felt for its graduates the increasing difficulty of meeting the cost of the publication of Ph.D. dissertations. The New Plan maintains the principle of publication. It does not, however, insist on complete publication in all cases. Two reasons, in addition to the economic factor, contributed to this decision: 1) The Bryn Mawr Graduate School has gone through its pioneer period, has an established reputation and does not need, as in the first years, to prove the worth of its degree by the testimony of its printed dissertations. 2) By allowing the publication of significant parts of a dissertation in, for instance, a learned periodical which could not accept the whole piece of work, an important reading public is more surely reached than by a privately printed monograph. (This is especially true in the fields of Science.)

III

CONCLUSION

The validity of the New Plan remains for the future to prove. From the experience gained in the preparation, however, certain values have already emerged. The discussions between student and student, faculty member and faculty member, and between students and faculty brought to the surface many ideas not directly applicable to the requirements for the Ph.D. degree, but concerned with the whole question of graduate instruction. It was of inestimable value to the teaching members of the Committees to hear the ratings by our own students and former students of other institutions of the various forms of graduate instruction to be met in the classrooms of this country. For example, after working over a suggestion to introduce so-called "graduate courses" side by side with "seminaries" and segregate first-year graduate students in these more elementary courses, it was both interesting and useful to find that the experience of our groups was definitely against such a change. It was a satisfaction to find that the Bryn Mawr "seminary," at its best, appears to be a highly effective and flexible mode of graduate instruction, permitting great independence to the more advanced student and giving to the less advanced student the advantage of working with her more experienced fellows. The professor, by freeing advanced students from attendance on certain meetings, can give to younger students what they need without taking from the older students the time they can more profitably give to independent work on judiciously assigned problems. These are but some of the many points that came out in our consultations. The stimulating value of the consultations was unquestionable.

CAMPUS NOTES

By JANET MARSHALL, 1933

This month has seen two unusual performances from Varsity Dramatics and Varsity Players, any number of extremely interesting lectures and a new curriculum movement by the students. The plays were *Lady Windermére's Fan* and two old English miracle plays. The former was given in Goodhart, April 21st and 22nd, and was in some ways a very great success. The criticism that has been leveled constantly at Varsity Dramatics, on the score of producing nothing but "second-hand" Broadway plays in as close as possible an imitation of the Broadway manner, has at last aroused the organization to try something in a different line. While Oscar Wilde has been seen on Broadway in recent years, he is not generally considered a production of the Broadway school, and there is not much a college organization can do but revive old plays if it is to avoid current successes and has no original plays available. When the play was finally chosen and certain budding young actors from Princeton University had been signed for the male parts, it was decided that something new ought to be done with this time-honored vehicle, and it was decided to modernize it. Whether or not this was successful is a question that even the performance has not settled. The settings were extremely well done; nothing like them has been seen on the Goodhart stage in years. Gray curtains served for Lady Windermere's drawing-room; a classic portico against a deep blue cyclorama with black cypresses silhouetted against it, for the terrace and garden; and black oilcloth curtains, relieved by silver screens and ultra-modern furniture for Lord Darlington's rooms. The costuming in the ball-scene was most unusual, for all of the guests wore different combinations of black and white except Mrs. Erlynne, who dominated the scene in brilliant magenta. The script was cut and changed with surprising liberty—the terrace of the house was used as the setting for the ball, and all of the offendingly dated soliloquies were cut or pantomimed. Whatever the faults or merits of the performance, and there were many of both, the producers did not err this time on the side of the beaten paths. The mistakes that were made were to a large degree those of experimenters, and experimentation is, in the minds of most of the interested students in college now, the main function of a college stage.

The other plays showed still another possible function of a college group: that is, producing old plays not generally known, in an authentic manner. The two Easter Miracle plays, *The Deluge*, which was performed on Merion Green, and the *Sepulchrum*, which was chanted in the cloisters, were both as close as possible to the originals. The English and Latin faculties and the Music Department assisted, and the directors did some nice pieces of research before they began their work. Costumes and scenery and language were very carefully worked out, and the music of the chants in the *Sepulchrum* learned from the original. Then, and this to their great credit, the directors of the *Deluge*, and to a less but sufficient degree of the *Sepulchrum*, allowed their actors the freedom that they needed really to instill life into these old, old forms. The result was charming and probably more worth while than anything Dramat has done in the last three years. The same spirit that characterizes May Day was in the play on the Green, with its folk-dancers and its informal gaiety; and the play in the Cloisters, while it had a tone all its own, was faintly reminiscent of the solemnity of Lantern Night. In short, all of the best of Bryn Mawr's individual traditions plus a great deal of very original work went into these short Easter plays, and the result cannot be too highly praised. This is a kind of work that only a college group can do, and the kind of work they certainly should do more often.

Before passing to the subject of the Honors Questionnaire and its results, some mention should be made of some of the lecturers that have appeared at College recently, for it has been a stellar array. Mrs. Pearl Buck spoke on the Chinese Sense of Humor in the same week that the famous Professor Robert Millikan spoke on his work, "Probing the Nucleus of the Atom." Two other lecturers in the next week were Dr. William Pepperell Montague, of Columbia, who spoke on "The Materialistic Theory of the Mind," and Mr. Lincoln Kirstein, who spoke in two lectures on the Russian ballet, concerning which he is the world's foremost authority. Then as a climax came T. S. Eliot's lecture on Modern Poetry in the last week of the month, and on this lecture I should like to comment briefly. It was, of all these unusual and interesting figures in widely divergent fields, a modern poet who drew the greatest crowd from the College. It was a man reading his own and contemporary works who, as I see it, has provoked the greatest amount of criticism on the campus. Part of this is no doubt due to the fact that Mr. Eliot is a widely publicized poet, that he has been studied to some degree by everyone who has taken the Freshman English course, and that his lecture, as some of the others were not, was open free to students. But it seems to me to show a very vital kind of interest in the student mind, which shows again even more clearly in the questionnaire I am going to report below. Modern literature and modern art are of unusual interest to the Bryn Mawr student body. They outrank any other group of subjects, either because the average student feels them more important to her enjoyment of life, or because the many students in College who cherish some type of creative ambition find in such lectures and courses the greatest spur and inspiration.

The questionnaire to which I have alluded was really circulated with an idea of finding out how much and why, or the reverse, the average student was interested in taking honors work in her major subject. The results showed that the great majority of upperclassmen, for it was only upperclassmen that answered the questionnaire, were definitely interested in taking honors, and the reason given by most of them for this desire was the opportunity to do wide reading in a chosen field. The questionnaire also brought out other interesting bits of information which are perhaps even more important. In the first place, the students have no radical criticism to make of the curriculum as it stands; if it be amended, they would amend it on the side of more freedom in choice of subjects, and one of the most interesting votes in the whole affair was that which showed that an overwhelming majority of students desired more than any one thing in College a general flexibility of mind and a more comprehensive knowledge. The complaint registered as an answer to the question, "What do you most want from college that you feel you have no opportunity to get?" was that the curriculum is unreasonably barren of courses on modern trends in art and literature. Other modern trends are also felt to be neglected, but it is the fields of art and literature where the neglect is most greatly felt by the students. This complaint was made not "as an appeal for reform" in the curriculum but rather "as a suggestion for improvement," for as I have said, the student body feels that on the whole the curriculum is unusually adequate to their needs and desires. But it seems to me, in view of what I have noted above, an important suggestion. Of the possible interpretations of this interest, I incline toward the one that College is unusually full of people who wish to create and who are searching about for a medium. The popularity of the experimental writing course, of the rhetoric and short-story courses, and of the playwriting class give ample testimony to this theory; and as many of us are still groping for our proper medium, it seems only logical that as prospective members of the world of modern art and literature we should desire to know, and to know as only a well-organized and conducted course can teach one, what is going on in that world.

ANNOUNCEMENTS OF FELLOWSHIPS AND SCHOLARSHIPS

Little May Day was celebrated on May 5th on one of the few sunny days of this spring, with the campus looking its most beautiful, decorated by the flowering shrubs in full bloom. Miss Park alluded to the hodge-podge of tradition which has grown up in connection with this occasion—strawberries and sausages for breakfast; May baskets, May pole dancing and hoop rolling; singing of Latin hymns and announcing of academic awards. The depression has not done away with any of these elements, which somehow make a festival full of meaning.

Among the long list of honours, a certain number will be of especial interest to readers of the BULLETIN. Of the twenty resident Fellows for next year five are holders of degrees from Bryn Mawr: Virginia Grace, A.B. 1922; M.A. 1929; Fellow in Archaeology; Marianna Jenkins, A.B. 1931, Fellow in History of Art; Agnes Lake, A.B. 1930; M.A. 1931, Fellow in Latin; Hope Broome, M.A. 1932, Fellow in Biblical Literature; Faith Baldwin, M.A. 1931, Fellow in Greek. Five members of the Class of 1933 have been granted Graduate Scholarships: Jeannette Le Saulnier (Regional Scholar from District IV.), in Archaeology; Emily Grace in Greek; Joyce Ilott in Mathematics; Charlotte Balough in Psychology; Mabel Meehan, to be studying in Latin as Scholar of the Society of Pennsylvania Women in New York; Elizabeth Ufford, A.B. 1929, and Laura Hunter, A.B. 1932 (daughter of Helen North, 1908), to be Scholars in Biology. Three former Fellows are to return as Graduate Scholars: Olivia Futch in Education; Esther Metzenthin in German; Elizabeth Fehrer in Psychology.

In this connection might be mentioned the holders of the three European Fellowships for next year, which were announced earlier in the year. The Mary E. Garrett European Fellowship is to be held by Margaret Hastings, A.B. Mount Holyoke, 1931, and M.A. 1932, Fellow in History at Bryn Mawr, 1932-33. The Anna Ottendorfer Fellow is to be Irmgard W. Taylor, M.A. University of

Pennsylvania; Instructor in German at Bryn Mawr, 1931-33. The Fanny Bullock Workman Fellowship was awarded to Ann Hoskin, A.B. Oberlin College, 1929; M.A. Bryn Mawr, 1930; Fellow in Archaeology at Bryn Mawr, 1932-33.

On the long list of undergraduate awards and scholarships the names of the Regional Scholars appear frequently. To Elizabeth Mackenzie, Regional Scholar from Western Pennsylvania, with an average of 89.58, have been awarded both the Maria L. Eastman Brooke Hall Memorial Scholarship, given annually to the member of the Junior Class with the highest record; and also the Charles S. Hinchman Memorial Scholarship, awarded to the student whose record shows the greatest ability in her major subject. Marianne Gateson, Catherine Bredt, and Mary Pauline Jones, Regional Scholars from Eastern Pennsylvania, have been given respectively the first Sheelah Kilroy Memorial Scholarship in English, the Anna Powers Scholarship, and the Evelyn Hunt Scholarship. Catherine Bill, Scholar from District IV., has been awarded the Mary E. Stevens; Mary Askins, special Regional Scholar from Baltimore, is to hold the first Maria Hopper Scholarship, and Frances Porcher, Scholar from District III., the Mary Anna Longstreth Scholarship. Sophie Hunt (daughter of Hope Woods, 1904), Regional Scholar from New England, was awarded the Constance Lewis Memorial Scholarship. Frances Pleasonton, also from New England, is to hold the Abby Brayton Durfee Scholarship. Alice Raynor, New Jersey Scholar, has been chosen for the Alice Ferree Hayt Memorial Scholarship. Suzanne Halstead, formerly Scholar from New England, was awarded the Amelia Richards Scholarship; and Eva Levin (daughter of Bertha Szold, 1895), former Baltimore Scholar, has been awarded for excellence of work the first Elizabeth S. Shippen Scholarship in Science.

The James E. Rhoads Scholarships for the junior year will be held by Diana Tate-Smith, formerly Regional Scholar from New York; and that for the sophomore year by Elizabeth Wyckoff, who held this year the Anne Dunn Memorial Scholarship given by the Brearley School of New York. Alumnae will be interested to know that the Chinese Scholar, Vung-Yuin Ting, leads the junior class with an average of 91.8. The Japanese Scholar, Shizu Nakamura, has also made an excellent record.

Announcements were made of a number of awards given to Bryn Mawr graduates by other institutions. Among these may be mentioned the appointments of Dorothy Burr, A.B. 1923, as an Agora Fellow excavating at Athens, and of Mary Zelia Pease, 1927, as Research Fellow of the American School cataloguing the new museum in Corinth. Aline Abaecherli, Ph.D., 1932, has been awarded a two-year Fellowship at the American Academy in Rome. Beth Busser, 1933, has been given a scholarship by the Institute of International Education to be held at Munich next year.

NEXT COUNCIL MEETING

The next meeting of the Alumnae Council will be held in Boston on November 16th, 17th, and 18th. Marguerite Mellen Dewey, 1913, Councillor for District I., and Mary Richardson Walcott, 1906, President of the Boston Bryn Mawr Club, will be in charge of arrangements.

ACADEMIC ANNOUNCEMENTS

NEW COURSES FOR NEXT YEAR

The course, *Modern Poetry,* which will be given by Hortense Flexner King, is no longer to be a course exclusively for poets, but rather a course for those interested in recent developments in poetry. The poets will be allowed to put their ideas into verse, but the rest of the class will be expected to criticize the poetry they read and discuss it in class.

The Modern Novel, given by Clara Marburg Kirk, who is this year assistant professor of English at Vassar College, will replace a part of Miss Crandall's work next year. This course will be a critical study of the novel, to complement the new course given by Cornelia Meigs, which will be the actual writing of fiction. Mrs. Kirk will also give a course in Criticism, which will replace the course of the same name given for many years by Miss Crandall.

The course in Astronomy, which is an introductory descriptive course in the subject given a few years back by Professor Huff, will be revived next year by Professor Michels and will fill a real need in the science curriculum.

Another course, new to the curriculum, will be Professor Ernst Diez's advanced course in the History of Art, which has been given the title in the calendar of the *Philosophy of Art.* This will be a treatment of the historical development of artistic methods and will include a study of the evolution of the terminology of modern art.

The Social Economy department will offer a course, *Social Investigation,* to be given by Professor Kingsbury. Miss Kingsbury has found an increasing demand on the part of the students for more undergraduate work in preparation for social work and social research, and she hopes that this course can be made to fit the needs of many undergraduates who are taking their first step in this direction.

It will be of interest to the alumnae to know that the course in Play Writing, given by Miss Latham from Barnard, which has been such a success during the current year, is to be continued next year.

Professor Rhys Carpenter is to give a part of the major work in Greek, replacing that given for so many years by Mrs. Wright. The second-year Greek course next year will include work on Plato and Aristophanes, replacing Mrs. Wright's course in Greek Literature.

REGISTRATION SHOWS RESULTS OF EXPERIMENTAL CHANGES IN METHODS OF ADMISSION

There has been a marked increase in the number of students applying for entrance to Bryn Mawr since the new plans of admission were announced in March. One is conscious of a stir and interest all over the country, both on the part of the schools and the students themselves. Schools everywhere seem to be particularly interested in Plan C (the two-year plan, with two examinations at the end of the Junior year, and two at the end of the Senior year), and already those which before have hesitated to prepare students for Bryn Mawr because of the inflexibility of the examination schedule, are proposing students for entrance in 1934 under this plan. Even if schools have no prospective candidate for the immediate future, they have written letters of inquiry or approval. The students who so far have requested to enter by this plan seem to be exceptionally good; often standing at the head of their classes, and with admirable general records.

The plan which has aroused most interest in the students themselves is Plan D (known as the Harvard Plan), although it is available only for schools geographically remote from the college. For that reason it has not affected registration to any great extent—only four or five students are applying for admission under it next year—but has brought letters from the students themselves who apparently are having their attention focused for the first time on an Eastern college, and the possibility of going to one as a result of standing at the head of their classes. Even if they have been, for one reason or another, refused admission under Plan D, this awakened consciousness of their own abilities is leading certain of the students to try for admission under the College Board Examinations.

The experimental change which has probably caused the most definite increase in registration, is the announcement made by the Committee on Entrance Examinations, and reported in the May BULLETIN, that it is willing to consider the applications of particularly able students who have not had exactly the entrance units that are usually required. The variations are often interesting, and the students whom the schools have suggested as meriting this special consideration seem to be most promising. It is now possible, for the first time, for the Entrance Committee to consider the applications of very able students who have decided late in their school courses that they wish to come to Bryn Mawr.

SPECIAL AWARDS TO MEMBERS OF THE FACULTY

Dr. Gustav A. Hedlund, Associate in Mathematics, has recently been granted a National Research Fellowship for mathematics by the National Research Council. He will have leave of absence next year to study in Princeton.

Mr. Jean M. F. Canu, Associate Professor of French, has just won a prize of $1,000, given by the Strassburger Foundation. *The New York Times* of May 6th says: "The Strassburger Foundation's annual $1,000 prize for an article or articles appearing in the French press calculated best to serve Franco-American friendship was awarded to Jean Canu for his article entitled 'The United States by Automobile,' which appeared in *Je Suis Partout.*"

Dr. T. Robert S. Broughton, Associate Professor of Latin, has been given a special grant from the Johns Hopkins Fund for Research in the Humanities, which will enable him to take a trip this summer to Asia Minor, to further his work in connection with an economic study of the ancient Roman provinces.

DOINGS OF ALUMNAE

MARIAN MACINTOSH AND HER PAINTING

By Grace Latimer Jones McClure, 1900

Miss MacIntosh has a particular claim on the readers of the Bulletin *because she was its first editor when it started as the Quarterly in 1907*

"It was always rather taken for granted that Miss Marian MacIntosh would follow a career in private school work here in Philadelphia. She had character and position and culture and individuality and more scholarship of a broad kind than any one else in sight."

Thus wrote Sarah D. Lowrie in the *Public Ledger* when in 1923 Marian MacIntosh was having her first one-man show in Philadelphia. Miss Lowrie expressed the feeling of many of Marian MacIntosh's friends when we learned that she had given up teaching, in which she had had marked influence, to follow what seemed the baleful whisperings of her Irish fairies. It was in 1919, in Keene Valley, that I first heard talk about an artist in the neighborhood named MacIntosh, a woman of great promise, who had studied in Munich under Heinrich Knirr, and had then, after some time spent in Vienna, come back to America for several summers of work and criticism with Henry B. Snell in Gloucester. Like every one else, I wanted to meet her, and my breath was taken away when I came face to face with an old friend. Marian MacIntosh's charm, her bright eyes and cheeks and her unfailing Irish wit and good humor, will always be remembered by the Bryn Mawr undergraduates who in the late nineties frequently met her at tea in Martha Thomas's infinitesimal sitting room under the stairs of Pembroke East. The success that came as soon as she began to exhibit, showed that in giving up what Miss Lowrie called the "sure and obvious of teaching," Marian MacIntosh had indeed listened to voices —but that they had been the clear call to forget prudence and follow her talent and long-cherished ambition into the world of inspirational and interpretative art.

In 1919 came her first real recognition, when *Evening in the Harbor* was accepted for hanging in the annual exhibition of the Chicago Art Institute—and was immediately sold! Between 1920 and 1923 her pictures were passed by the juries of the Chicago Art Institute, the New York Academy of Design, the Cincinnati Museum, the Pennsylvania Academy, and many lesser galleries. It was obvious that here was an artist of unusual power.

In 1922, the Gold Medal of the Philadelphia Plastic Club was awarded to Marian MacIntosh for the best work shown in any medium, and the picture, *Grey of Dusk,* which had been painted at Boothbay Harbor, was purchased by a Chicago collector. That same summer she showed twenty-five canvases at Jordan Pond, Mount Desert; and among the criticisms of this show was the following (*abbreviated*) from the *Bar Harbor Times:* "The exhibition is varied in character; there is a wide choice of treatment and subject, yet all the pictures are unmistakably 'somewhere in Maine.' One of the paintings was reproduced in the *Christian Science Monitor* of August 17th. Miss MacIntosh painted a gold medal picture of the *Weir* at West Harbor last year, and is exhibiting a number of pictures in which mood and mystery are outstanding features. This is particularly evident in her picture, *Gulls' Weather,* which, if it does not take a gold medal at Boothbay Harbor, will receive that recognition at some other gallery before the coming winter closes."

In 1923 two MacIntosh canvases were accepted at the annual exhibition of the Pennsylvania Academy, four or five pictures were shown at a ten-men exhibit at the Philadelphia Art Club, and there was a one-man show at the McClees Gallery in Philadelphia. The critics were exceedingly favorable. Admitting in the work of the new artist some still unsolved problems of technique, Dorothy Grafly wrote in the *North American* (abbreviated): "Miss MacIntosh has something to say. She appreciates all of the out-of-the-beaten-track places and she knows the atmosphere of New England inlets and promontories. Seaweed tangles intrigue her fancy, and that mist of gray and green with which all coast dwellers become familiar. One feels it stealing over the land in *Wind and Sea and Sailor.* The thought that stirred the artist's conception is at once communicated to her audience. A title is unnecessary.

"Miss MacIntosh paints with feeling. Her work possesses atmosphere, at times curiously mystical, due, perhaps, to a remote Irish background. . . . It is the mood that appeals to her—a poetic quality of impression. It is a genuine relief to find idealism rather than materialism in the work of a contemporary artist. . . . She holds the key to emotional appeal through the creation of moods, not objects."

It was after the McClees exhibition that Henry Voison and Comte Chabier wrote the following unsolicited criticism in the Paris *Revue du Vrai et du Beau:* "J'ai beaucoup goûté les envoi de miss Marian MacIntosh, *Gulls' Weather* et *An Island Farmstead,* peintures d'un tout-à-fait personnel, hardi et savoureux, d'une technique en même temps savante et libre. La première de ces oeuvres, surtout, est très évocatrice; ce vol de mouettes est un vision d'une éloquence sobre, vraie, et pittoresque. . . . Cette artiste possède un très beau sentiment de la lumière et de l'atmosphère, une vision fraîche, subtile et sensible, d'une saveur colorée vraiment rare."

In September, 1924, the *Trenton Times,* commenting on her large painting exhibited and sold in the Exhibition of Contemporary Art at the New Jersey State Fair, named Marian MacIntosh already one of the best-known women painters in the United States. And regarding a one-man show which by invitation she held that autumn in the Washington Arts Club, the art critic of the *Washington Post* said:

"Marian MacIntosh paints with her soul rather than her brush, and her soul sees and says strangely interesting things. There is great variety in these paintings . . . which are of no special locale. . . . There is a broad quality common to human beings in general in these sea and harbor views that lifts and carries one out to the great universal. There is vivid color and movement in *A Sunny, Windy Day.* The tenderness and softness of *Birches in the Sun* is a delight. *Gloucester Guinea Boat* is original and interesting as a decoration. *The Homing Tide* and *Evening in the Harbor* are especially poetical. In *Gathering Peat* there is the pathos of Synge's *Riders to the Sea.*

"It must be the Celtic nature of the artist that is largely responsible for the spiritual quality that is so noticeable. . There is more than painter's technique to take cognizance of in these scenes—things of emotional content, and of how the mind of the onlooker reacts to the artist's moods."

Of the Washington show, Leila Machlin, of the *Washington Sunday Star,* wrote: "Miss MacIntosh's paintings make a very impressive showing. They are fair-sized canvases, painted with so much vigor and strength that they seem to need more space for display. It is as if one attempted to bring indoors the bigness of the universe. . . . Her Irish themes have a melancholy pathos of Irish folklore. She has a message."

The acceptance in exhibitions, and the sales of Marian MacIntosh's pictures continued to keep up a good average. The summer of 1926 she spent at Connemara, in the west of Ireland, and in the Basque country; and the following winter she had a first showing of this work in Princeton. At this time, Alfred Young Fisher wrote: "The indefinable mystery of the Celtic atmosphere and the sublimity of the Celtic mind are qualities found in the work of Miss Marian MacIntosh. . . . Her paintings are artistically sincere; they present us with the mystical, the non-rationalizable—which is *truth.*"

In the summer this same one-man show was repeated in Gloucester, where twelve of the pictures sold at once. In December, 1927, the Irish, the Basque, and other canvases, were shown in a one-man exhibition in the Ainslee Galleries in New York, and the *New York Times* critic wrote: "The best of these paintings have a quality of surface that artists consider the primary aim of a painter. . . . *Birches by the Sea,* in the Maine series, is a beautifully luminous canvas; the painting is not mere surface, however, for the azure of sea and sky seen through the branches import a feeling of great depth." The *New York American,* the *New York Evening Post,* and other papers carried reproductions and favorable criticism of the Ainslee show.

Tinkers Hollow was later that winter awarded the Landscape Prize of $100 at the Thirty-seventh Annual Exhibition of the National Association of Women Painters and Sculptors, of which Marian MacIntosh had long been a member. This picture was later exhibited at the Corcoran Gallery in Washington, where it received exceptional notices.

As the seasons pass, the work of Marian MacIntosh continues to be shown in Gloucester, in Princeton (where she has lived since 1916), in New York, Philadelphia, Boston, and Washington; and everywhere comment is favorable and increases in volume. The *Christian Science Monitor* has reproduced three pictures and carried flattering articles. In its Sunday Pictorial Section the *Boston Herald* of July 28, 1929, reproduced *On Cape Ann.* In December, 1932, the *Philadelphia Inquirer* had in its *Gallery and Studio* column a boxed announcement that ran as follows:

THE MOST BEAUTIFUL CREATION SEEN LAST WEEK

The Lute Player, by Marian MacIntosh

In the thirty-ninth annual exhibition by members of the Art Club.

Three years ago, Perry Cott, recently appointed Assistant Curator of the Worcester (Mass.) Museum of Art, commented as follows on Marian MacIntosh's paintings: "To the romantic appeal inherent in her subjects, the artist adds interpretation that is always vigorous and personal."

For their admirable technique—especially for their unusual, fine handling of color—Marion MacIntosh's paintings have, as we have seen, been widely approved by professional critics and judges; but they have also had strange power of appeal to that large group of museum visitors who complacently confess that "though they know nothing about art, they do know what they like."

Something in that first picture exhibited in Chicago spoke direct to the heart of a man who in five minutes had what was for him a unique experience—he fell in love! He said to himself, "I must possess that picture or die trying." The next autumn, in much the same way, another picture, *Stepping the Mast*, spoke to the Nautilus Club of Oklahoma City, which bought the picture and presented it to the gallery of the high school. "Every one is delighted," a teacher wrote. "We cannot keep the children away from it—they want to stand and look. One boy looked at it a few minutes, then remarked, 'Why, you can smell the salt air!' You have done a very lovely thing for our high school here in giving us such a glimpse of another kind of life in such a vivid and beautiful way."

The following letter, written in 1922, tells its own touching story: "Your picture, *Looking Westward*, at the women artists' exhibition in New York is undoubtedly the best and most beautiful one there. I am an artist myself and a writer and speaker on art, and I am in love with your wild rocks and your great color strokes and wonderful contrasts. But I am unable to buy it. I wish to recommend it to some one at whose house I may have the privilege of seeing it frequently; but although the price is very cheap indeed, my friend cannot consider it at even that sum. Therefore I suggest that in case nobody buys the picture, you reduce its price as much as you can. I know how audacious and impertinent my request is, but I hope to be pardoned."

Yet another man, from Helena, Montana, fell in love with Marian MacIntosh's work, and carried home from the Ainslee Gallery four canvases, lamenting that he had not room to hang a fifth, *Birches by the Sea*, which was too large for his rooms.

So the warm, inspiring personality of Marian MacIntosh speaks out from her canvases, winning understanding and admiration for the artist, just as the wholesome, kindly, engaging presence of the woman brings her friends and admirers wherever she appears. Among the Bryn Mawr alumnae, an increasing number are making notable contributions to art; but future students on the campus, finding inspiration and delight in the paintings of Marian MacIntosh, will always know her as the first Bryn Mawr artist to gain national recognition.

COLLEGE VERSE RADIO BROADCAST

As part of the Seven Colleges Radio Program, the poems of Hortense Flexner King, 1907, will be broadcast over W. O. R. on Thursday, June 1st, at 5.15 p. m. (New York Daylight Time). On Saturday, June 3rd, at the same hour, poems written by Bryn Mawr Undergraduates in Mrs. King's poetry course will be broadcast. Poems of Margaret Bailey, 1907, will also be read on June 1st.

AN INVITATION FROM THE COLLEGE WOMAN'S BOARD AT THE CHICAGO FAIR

Bryn Mawr graduates as well as undergraduates who attend "A Century of Progress," Chicago's 1933 modernized World's Fair, will benefit by the special central meeting place on the grounds arranged by the College Woman's Board for A Century of Progress.

Through the courtesy of the publishers of *Time* and of *Fortune*, space has been given to the College Woman's Board in the Attractive *Time-Fortune* Building for the five months of the Century of Progress, from June 1st to November 1st.

The member colleges are, as of April 1st, Barnard, Bryn Mawr, Connecticut College, Elmira, Goucher, Lake Erie, Mills, Milwaukee-Downer, Mount Holyoke, Radcliffe, Randolph-Macon, Rockford College, Smith, Sweet Brier, Trinity, Vassar, Wellesley, Wells.

The board will sponsor, for those visiting Chicago alone, the superb new Harriet McCormick Memorial Y. W. C. A., at Dearborn Street and Chicago Avenue, which is close to the entrance to "A Century of Progress," as well as the Chicago College Club at 180 East Delaware Place. Reservations should be made in advance direct to the above addresses.

Please tell all of your friends of our existence. There is no charge for the services of our central meeting place. It is simply our way of saying welcome to our city and the "Century of Progress." We want to help you enjoy it. For any other information you may address Mrs. Edwin P. Dewes, 2314 Lincoln Park West, Chicago.

PLANS FOR COMMENCEMENT WEEK

The Class Suppers or Class Picnics will be held Saturday evening, June 10th. At 12.30 on Sunday there will be a special meeting of the Alumnae Association. This will be followed by the Alumnae Luncheon at 1.15 p. m. in Pembroke, at which President Park and representatives of the reuning classes will speak. Sunday afternoon the Association will have a tea for the graduating class. The Baccalaureate Sermon will be preached that evening by Rabbi Wise. On Monday two picnic luncheons have been planned, one for the classes 1894-97, and one for 1913-16. The Alumnae-Varsity Tennis Tournament will take place that morning, and the Senior Garden Party will be held on the campus that afternoon. Commencement will be held in the Auditorium of Goodhart Hall at 11 o'clock on Tuesday, June 13th. President Wooley, of Mount Holyoke, will deliver the address.

MEETING OF THE BOARD OF DIRECTORS

The Board of Directors of the College met at the office of the Provident Trust Company, Philadelphia, on Thursday, May 18, 1933. All five Alumnae Directors and the three Alumnae Directors-at-large were present.

CLASS NOTES

Ph.D. and Graduate Notes
Editor: MARY ALICE HANNA PARRISH
(Mrs. J. C. Parrish)
Vandalia, Missouri.

1889

No Editor appointed.

1890

No Editor appointed.

1891

No Editor appointed.

1892

Class Editor: EDITH WETHERILL IVES
(Mrs. F. M. Ives)
145 E. 35th St., New York City.

1893

Class Editor: SUSAN WALKER FITZGERALD
(Mrs. Richard Y. FitzGerald)
7 Greenough Ave., Jamaica Plain, Mass.

I trust that '93 will be patient and forgiving with me in this, my new undertaking—and will help by sending me a line from time to time, even if there is no epoch-making event to chronicle.

Lida Adams Lewis rented her Indianapolis house for the winter and has been staying at Southwest Harbor, Maine, in "a dear little white farmhouse" built for winter use. She complains of a very mild winter, with less snow than they hoped for: a "guest membership" in the Woman's Club, a radio loaned by a summer resident, and a wood-consuming Franklin stove have made the winter a happy one.

Mary Atkinson Watson writes that the great event of the year was the marriage of her daughter, Elizabeth. The wedding was by the Friends' ceremony, and the young people will live with Mary for the present.

Jane Brownell has been caring, with the aid of a nurse, for her sister Harriet, who has been seriously ill with pneumonia. May the summer bring rest and refreshment from this long strain!

Helen Hopkins Thom seems to have become a professional grandmother and to revel in it. Her six grandchildren all live near her, and all visit her during the summer when she moves to her farm on Chesapeake Bay, which she calls her "real home." Two summers ago she made a delightful motor trip through the south of England. The latchstring is always out at her Baltimore home for members of '93 who may be passing through!

Julia Landers is the real politician of the class. The last time I saw her was when she and I were both delegates to the New York Democratic Convention of '24. Now her letterhead reads:

Marion County Accident Prevention Bureau
Charles L. Sumner, Sheriff
Julia E. Landers
School Safety Director

She writes: "I have charge of the Boy Patrols in the 48 schools in Marion County outside of the city limits, and I keep my little army of Police Boys—over a thousand—up on their toes. I have charge of the safety regulations for the 97 bus drivers in this county and run a traffic class for motorists who dare to pass a school bus when it is loading—unlawful in Indiana. The job is an administrative one, and I set my own hours. My car is driven by a Trusty from the jail, and for one who grew up in a very conventional social atmosphere it is great. I have decided that I ought to be a traffic expert—it fascinates me so much."

Lillian Moser says she is living quietly in her old home with a friend. She is active in the work of her church (Episcopal), is an associate member of the Morning Musicals, and on the Board of Managers of the Old Ladies' Home! She spends her summers in Portland, Maine, driving herself and a friend back and forth.

Elizabeth Nichols Moores, after living 37 years in Indianapolis and Dayton, has come back to live with her sisters, who have built a Dutch Colonial house just across Roberts Road from the campus. Her daughter remains in Dayton as a psychiatric social worker, and her son is in business in Indianapolis. She has been taking beginning Italian at the College.

Nellie Neilson is teaching at Mount Holyoke and writing. In the summer she works at the Record Office in London and visits her sisters in England and France. She is writing a book on *The English Forest Administration between 1327 and 1336* for a Mediaeval Academy undertaking, and is tied up with one or two other prospective volumes of mediaeval studies. She may delve in mediaevalism, but when I saw Nellie last there was nothing of middle age about her—the same old spirit and charm are there.

Bertha Putnam has leave of absence from Mount Holyoke for next year and plans to make London her headquarters and to devote most of her time to finishing a volume on which she has been working for about 25 years. It is entitled *Early Proceedings Before Justices of the Peace,* and will be published in the Ames Foundation Series of the Harvard Law School.

She is also seeing through the press a volume for the Kent Archeological Society called *Kent Keepers of the Peace, 1316-1317*, and hopes to finish a section on the Keepers of the Peace for a coöperative study on *The English Government at work, 1327-1336*, this whole "peaceful" study being under the direction of the Mediaeval Academy.

Harriet Seal is living quietly *alone* in an apartment hotel in Germantown. She writes that social problems interest her greatly and she has been helping with the "United Campaigns" for several years and following up some special cases, some colored people and some foreigners. She is also much interested in her Sunday School class, which helps keep her young in thought and feeling.

Helen Thomas Flexner writes that she has no particular news to send, but perhaps not all our members know that her son William is Associate in Mathematics at Bryn Mawr and last June married a member of the Class of '28, so Helen keeps in close touch with the College.

Louise Brownell Saunders is another that sends no news, a dangerous thing, for then it has to be supplied by me. Her second daughter, Olivia, was married in January and is living in New York.

Frances VanKirk is busy with household tasks and is on a few committees that lift her "sufficiently out of the home-keeping rut." She ought to be puffed up with pride, and would be, if she knew all the affectionate and appreciative words that have come to me along with that unanimous vote of thanks for her long service as Collector and Editor.

1894

Class Editor: ABBY BRAYTON DURFEE
(Mrs. Randall Durfee)
19 Highland Ave., Fall River, Mass.

1895

Class Editor: ELIZABETH BENT CLARK
(Mrs. Herbert Lincoln Clark)
Bryn Mawr, Pa.

1896

Class Editor: ABIGAIL CAMP DIMON
School of Horticulture, Ambler, Pa.

Ruth Furness Porter attended the inauguration and paid a short visit to her daughter Nancy, who moved with her family to Washington in February.

Hilda Justice spent three weeks in March and April at Winter Park, Florida, visiting her cousin, Mrs. Chase.

Two members of '96 were honored at the International Flower Show in New York this year. Emma Linburg Tobin was a member of the committee of the Trenton Garden Club that received special mention for their demonstration of an aquatic garden, in the section of the Garden Club of America. These gardens were not in competition, but were designed to show what could be done with a small outlay. In the Trenton garden were two pools, one round and one rectangular, surrounded by cedars, junipers and shrubs. In the pools grew aquatic plants of various kinds, and around them, among rocks, were ivy, andromeda, epimedium and other suitable plants.

Pauline Goldmark received a silver medal for a photograph of a pergola with freesia at Ravallo, in the class of European gardens in the section of the Federated Garden Clubs of New York State.

The class will be sorry to learn that early in April Dora Keen Handy was hit by the propeller of an airplane from which she had just alighted at Oakland, California. She was taken to the Merritt Hospital, Oakland, and a collarbone, shoulder-blade and six ribs were found to be broken. At the time this note was sent to the BULLETIN she was still in the hospital, making a good recovery.

1897

Class Editor: FRIEDRIKA HEYL
104 Lake Shore Drive, East, Dunkirk, N. Y.

The class extends loving sympathy to Mabel Searle and her sister. Their mother, who had been ill for over a year, died shortly before Easter at their home in Haverford.

Alice Cilley Weist writes with enthusiasm that she came back to Bryn Mawr early in March to be assistant to the Principals of the Shipley School until October.

Those of us who are present on Commencement day will have a special interest in watching two of the graduating class march up and take their degrees—Louise Esterly and Elizabeth Bethune Jackson.

The class supper will be held on June the 10th. There will be some, unfortunately, who cannot be present. We hope that each one who cannot come will send some sort of message to be read at the supper.

1898

Class Editor: EDITH SCHOFF BOERICKE
(Mrs. John J. Boericke)
328 Brookway, Merion Station, Pa.

Betty Bancroft, as Acting Secretary, sends in the following:

The class extends its sincere sympathy to Edith Boericke, whose husband, John J. Boericke, died April 19th. Edith is bravely going on with her daughter's wedding plans. She and young Edith will go to Round

Mountain, Nevada, in June, where young Edith's marriage to Alexander F. McCandless will take place. After that Edith will visit in the West for several months.

Catherine Bunnell Mitchell writes that Alice Hammond will spend the summer with her in Los Angeles.

1899

Editor: CAROLYN TROWBRIDGE BROWN LEWIS
(Mrs. H. Radnor Lewis)
451 Milton Road, Rye, N. Y.

Dorothy Meredith Fronheiser has been demonstrating that mother-in-laws today are a far cry from the caricatures of yesterday. She has been visiting her Katherine, who in February married John Mason Brown, the Dramatic Critic of the *New York Evening Post,* in their lovely studio apartment.

Dot spent the May Day week-end with Katherine Middendorf Blackwell at her wonderful 200-year-old home in Yardley, Pa. To us who know Katie all I need to say is that it is the ideal setting for her, and it wasn't surprising to hear her say, "Every day is wonderful to me here."

So that several Bryn Mawrites who live in the vicinity might see Dorothy and enjoy sort of an unofficial reunion, Katie gathered around her luncheon table Emma Linburg Tobin, '96; Aimee Leffingwell McKenzie, '97; Grace Jones McClure, and Cornelia Halsey Kellogg, both 1900; Laura Peckham Waring, and your Editor —and did we pow-wow? I'll say we did. Unfortunately Mae Blakey Ross had been in an automobile accident about two weeks before, and while she mercifully was not seriously injured, she couldn't be with us.

Another honor is coming to '99 in the fall, when Houghton Mifflin publish a novel destined to be the book of the season by our Cora Hardy Jarrett. Cora has been hiding her talents under the "bushel" of a *nom de plume,* Faraday Keene, but her publisher insisted on the world knowing the authoress by her own name.

Imagine what our feelings would have been had we been invited by the President to a reception for the undergraduate daughters and nieces of Bryn Mawr graduates! Anita Fouilhoux (Jean Clark's daughter) and Honora Dickerman (Alice Carter's daughter) represented '99 at the reception recently given by President Park in honor of President-Emeritus Thomas.

1900

Class Editor: LOUISE CONGDON FRANCIS
(Mrs. Richard Francis)
414 Old Lancaster Rd., Haverford, Pa.

1901

Class Editor: HELEN CONVERSE THORPE
(Mrs. Warren Thorpe)
15 East 64th St., New York City.

Lucia Holliday Macbeth writes: "Your letter went to California and then came east again, for I am having a vacation from my regular life. Eighteen months ago I bought an old farm house in Vermont, where I expect to spend my summers and where I shall welcome any traveling Bryn Mawr friends. My post office and telephone are Springfield, Vermont, but our rail center is Bellows Falls, 9 miles distant. When I left there last October I settled in Cambridge, where my only child is in Harvard Law School, and I have passed a very pleasant winter here."

1902

Class Editor: ANN ROTAN HOWE
(Mrs. Thorndike Howe)
77 Revere St., Boston, Mass.

1903

Class Editor: GERTRUDE DIETRICH SMITH
(Mrs. Herbert Knox Smith)
Farmington, Conn.

Word has just been received of the death of Elizabeth Baggaley Carroll last August. The class extends warm sympathy to her family.

Margaretta Stewart Dietrich took a most interesting and adventurous automobile trip from Santa Fé, New Mexico, to Mexico City, motoring down the west coast of Mexico. She took a cat with her. Coming back, she and the cat flew from Mexico City to El Paso—to which point the automobile had been shipped.

1904

Class Editor: EMMA O. THOMPSON
320 S. 42nd St., Philadelphia, Pa.

1905

Class Editor: ELEANOR LITTLE ALDRICH
(Mrs. Talbot Aldrich)
59 Mount Vernon St., Boston, Mass.

Alberta Warner Aiken, the notice of whose death appeared in the May BULLETIN, was such an integral part of her class that we were accustomed to count on her loyal and interested presence at all college gatherings. Our minds go back to undergraduate days when she and Jane Shoemaker, the Jallies, took their very individual place in Rotten Row. Alberta's willing readiness then to do more than her share of any work that needed doing remained characteristic of her always. Her life was lived in unspectacular generosity and kindliness. She carried with competent and practical common sense the responsibilities of her immediate community. That she was valued and loved was evident by the large number of people who came to her funeral. The sympathy of the class goes out to her husband and to her daughter and son.

The class extends its sympathy also to Edith Longstreth Wood, whose mother died early in May.

Gertrude Hartman came to Boston in April to speak under the auspices of the Book Shop for Boys and Girls on a subject connected with Progressive Education.

For many months we have been trying vainly to get into communication with Frances Hubbard Flaherty. The rumor reached us that her husband was making a moving picture on the Irish coast. Now, at last, a letter written to a classmate in October, 1932, has come into the hands of the Editor and is herewith quoted. We shall hope for later news before long. The address at the letterhead is Crookawn Glos, Kilmurvey, Aran Islands, County Galway, Ireland.

And here are the contents: "Aran is an archaeological mecca, as you know. Monica and I are for the time alone with our pigs and ponies, donkeys and dogs, cats and chickens, turkeys, sheep and rabbits—and our 'primitives.' While Bob is in London we are putting in days of sunshine building a garden out of the virgin rock, and adding our quota to the 2,000 miles of stone wall on our little 9x3 island! The wall is to enclose two little cottages leased to the Flaherty family and heirs for 99 years! Imagine us having a "home" at last. You see, we haven't too much faith in Geneva, so we are preferring bare rock and potatoes on the fringe of the world to air raids and such at its heart. The children laugh at the excuses I concoct against every suggestion for me to make a trip away from my 'Island of the Saints.' Come and see us, but send word before you start. In spite of everything, we might be somewhere else."

Katrin Southwick Vietor writes the following news about herself and family: "In the midst of the devilish task of Lists, I'm going to relax by telling you that all of a sudden it's been decided. Tinkle is to be married May 26th (my 50th birthday) and Southwick 5 days later, and then Ernest, Joy and I will sail that night for Marienbad!

"Tinkle is having a big wedding up at 'Little Brook,' our place in Greenwich, in the house—then live in The Play House—on the place—doing her own work with a bit of help now and again from Bill. Southwick and Barbara plan to be married very quietly in her apartment in town and then go out West, as they think they'd like to start there.

1906

Class Editor: LOUISE CRUICE STURDEVANT
　　(Mrs. Edward W. Sturdevant)
　c/o 4th Regiment, U. S. Marines, Shanghai.

The heading to this column is hardly accurate, as Louise Cruice Sturdevant ceases herewith to be Class Editor. A Class Editor two months distant by mail is hardly practical. Mary, please take notice. It is just an efficient way of giving her new address to all her Bryn Mawr friends. She sails from New York on the Army Transport *Grant* May 9th. She spends a day in Panama, a week in San Francisco, a day in Honolulu, and a week in Manila. There they leave the transport, and after a week's wait take a Dollar Liner, stopping two days in Hong-Kong, and arriving in Shanghai, if all goes well, July 7th. Unfortunately army transports do not stop at San Diego, so she misses seeing Dotty Congdon. Mail at the above address will be appreciated.

NOTE P. S.—Dorothy Congdon Towner is still running her Little Shop in spite of the depression. Her son is a Sophomore at Leland Stanford.

Marjorie Rawson visited Elsie Barber Biglow in March and had various informal reunions with Margaret Scribner Grant, Scribby and Cruice. Elsie, Scribby, and Marge attended a lecture on surface chemistry at which Scribby, your Editor must record, fell asleep. Grace Wade Levering had them all for luncheon one day when Jessie Thomas Bennett happened to be in Baltimore. Their admiration was divided between Grace's beautiful jonquils and her champion Irish setters. Marjorie has been doing fine work in collecting funds for the Louise Hyman Pollak Scholarship.

Laura Boyer has a new address: 395 Washington Avenue, Pelham, N. Y. She is still in the same office of the Episcopal Church Diocese of New York, busily engaged in organizing adult study groups and training leaders for them. They are making a special study of the American Indian. They have some 150 groups, and have had many experts speaking to them.

Louise Fleischmann Maclay's daughter, aged 10, at the Brearley School, having seen May Day, has determined to go to Bryn Mawr. Louise wants her classmates to remember that their farm at Millbrook, where they spend their summers, is on the direct motor road to the Berkshires via the Hudson River. There they raise horses, flowers, and welcome their friends. Her telephone number is 72. As Alumnae Director she has attended various meetings at Bryn Mawr and is on the Buildings and Grounds Committee.

Lucia Ford Rutter has only one child left at home, the others being all away at school or college. Her older girl is at Vassar. She is continuing ten years' membership on the local school board.

K. V. Gano is also keeping shop. She is selling children's clothes and is getting a little shattered over it.

Catharine Anderson is selling women's garments. 1906 has certainly rushed into trade.

Ida Garrett Murphy writes that they plan to spend the summer at home, "third class." Her boy, Campbell, is a Freshman at Swarthmore. She is still busy with the League of Women Voters, and finds the local Solons stupidly unresponsive to welfare legislation.

Helen Haughwout Putnam has a new address, 126 Adams Street, Milton.

Josephine Katzenstein Blancké is still teaching at the West Philadelphia High School. She is as keen about tennis as ever, and I'll bet as good. She is also much interested in the theatre. This year, through a group organized by her sisters, she has been able to help many children with food and clothing so that they could continue at school.

Jessie Thomas Bennett has just bought a lovely site overlooking miles of rolling Pennsylvania hills, where she is planning to build a new house. It is near her present farm, but being on top of the ridge has a far more beautiful view. Her bull terriers continue to capture blue ribbons at all the dog shows.

1907

Class Editor: ALICE HAWKINS
Taylor Hall, Bryn Mawr, Pa.

The past month has seen a rush of 1907 to the campus. Ellen Thayer accompanied Julie Benjamin Howson and her daughter Joan to see the Varsity play, *Lady Windermere's Fan.* By a special dispensation all three were allowed to stay in the Alumnae Room in Pembroke, and thus were able to hang around until midnight after the play, picking up stray crumbs of gossip from Bunny Brownell Daniels' daughter, Susan. The jaws of the elders kept dropping in astonishment at the number of young men who were dashing in and out of Pembroke all afternoon and evening.

The next visitor was Tony Cannon, who came to speak to the students about training in social work. She kept a large group so much interested that they almost forgot to go to dinner.

Hard on Tony's heels came Peggy Ayer Barnes. She seemed to enjoy disrupting the earnest lives of her classmates, M. O'Sullivan at Rosemont College, E. Schenck, Tink Meigs and A. Hawkins, as well as a number of other denizens of the Bryn Mawr campus, including the President, the Director of Publications, and several Full Professors. However, all concerned

considered the time well spent. Dr. Leuba talked to her for *two hours,* and a few days later remarked to A. Hawkins that he thought of all the major classes he had ever taught he remembered most clearly that in which the rollcall included the names of Ayer, Benjamin, Brownell, Cannon, Dorsey, Fabian, Harley, Hutchins, Hawkins, Pope, Seaver, Williams, Woerishoffer. (List supplied by your Editor.)

Also present in one year or the other were such highlights as L. Cruice, J. Hewitt, A. MacClanahan, E. White of 1906, and M. Copeland, L. Foley, T. Helburn, L. Milligan, M. Plaisted of 1908. No wonder he remembers those classes, and no member of them will ever forget those thrilling hours in the Library classroom.

1908

Class Editor: HELEN CADBURY BUSH
Haverford, Pa.

Ethel Vick Wallace was married last September to Elbert J. Townsend, a widower with two children, Elinor 13 and Ted 11. "Stepping into a ready-made family is quite a lively proposition, but the children have been so coöperative and responsive that our winter together has been a very happy one. Elbert and I had worked together for years on the Children's Home Board, and I succeeded him as President of the Board. We live in Le Roy, New York, an attractive town not far from Rochester, so we get really fine concerts at the Eastman Theatre." All the happiness in the world to you, Ethel, from your classmates!

Nellie Seeds, not to be daunted, has bought a 200-acre farm in the rolling hills of Northern Dutchess County, N. Y. She is starting a farm school and camp in July. "I suppose only an intrepid 1908er would be rash enough to begin a new venture in these days. But, at any rate, I am going to try it. We shall follow Dr. Kilpatrick's principle of 'Learning through Doing,' and make the whole life of the school an educative process."

Linda Castle, who commutes from Honolulu to New York each year, came on during the very early spring. She cast a maternal glance at Gwen (Vassar) and spent most of her time visiting her classmates. Terry Helburn, Martha Saxton, Virginia Claiborne, Margaret Franklin were among the lucky ones. Emily Cheston, true to form, sped to New York just to ride with Linda from New York to Philadelphia on the train, which brings me to Emily Cheston. She is giving a series of Garden Lectures. She offers an amazing choice of subjects, such as "Gardening for the Amateur," "A Garden for Fragrance," "John Bartram (1699-1776), Colonial Botanist," and so forth. Her lectures are as lively and gay and entertaining as serious, instructive talks can possibly be.

Louise Carey Rosett claims to have become so sedate that she despairs of the three husbands promised her in the class prophecy.

Josephine Montgomery's eldest daughter, Mary Dudley, transferred from the University of Wisconsin to the University of Arizona for the spring semester. State universities have that pleasant system of reciprocity, and Mary Dudley has immensely enjoyed her experience.

Terry Helburn wrote me a long letter, repented her good act, cut the letter in two, and here it is. "But the great Bryn Mawr event of the season for me was the dinner tendered by Margaret Franklin to Marjorie Young Gifford on her annual visit to New York. Dorothy Forster Miller, 1907, who may not for that reason be eligible to mention in your column, was also there with her husband, and Marty Saxton and I without ours, and a good time was had by all—whether or not, if you get what I mean.

"On another red-letter day Linda Schaeffer Castle came to tea and Margaret Franklin regaled us with such exciting stories of her lodgers who turned out to be burglars that I could not get a word in about my trivial adventures. The private lives of my classmates seem to be much more exciting than mine!

"I have stayed at work in town most of the winter, though I have paid two visits to Pittsburgh, one to Baltimore, and am planning one in the near future to Boston—all with new plays. I never see any of my Bryn Mawr classmates in these towns for the simple reason that I can never remember their married names, and no matter how wistfully I study the phone book, it conditions no Bryn Mawr reflex. The only Bryn Mawrtyrs I've seen of late are Barbara Spofford Morgan and Miss Ely on the stage of the Metropolitan, where we sat in state listening to G. B. S."

1909

Class Editor: HELEN BOND CRANE
70 Willett St., Albany, N. Y.

1910

Class Editor: KATHERINE ROTAN DRINKER
(Mrs. Cecil K. Drinker)
71 Rawson Road, Brookline, Mass.

1911

Class Editor: ELIZABETH TAYLOR RUSSELL
(Mrs. John F. Russell, Jr.)
333 East 68th St., New York City

Isobel Rogers Kruesi's children are William, 12 years; Frank, 11; Oscar, 9, and Paul, 5. They have all enjoyed a recent preliminary view of the "Century of Progress" and recommend it heartily.

Margery Hoffman Smith closed her eastern trip with a few days in Bermuda, "dear to

memory and to the pocketbook," and has returned to Portland.

Anna Stearns' appeals for the Alumnae Fund are out and she hopes to lure a few dollars to the cause.

Helen Emerson Chase has not only been to Nassau to bask in the sun, but also to Peterboro for winter sports, since Christmas.

We are very glad to hear that Mary Minor Taylor has recovered from the trouble she had with her eyes, which necessitated a prolonged stay in Johns Hopkins Hospital, and has returned home.

Catherine Pevear, Mary Case Pevear's elder daughter, will complete her course in physical education at N. Y. University this June. Catherine's engagement to Allen Whittemore has been announced recently.

After June 15th please address your editor at Watch Hill, Rhode Island.

1912

Class Editor: GLADYS SPRY AUGUR
(Mrs. Wheaton Augur)
820 Camino Atalaya, Santa Fé, N. M.

Just as the BULLETIN was going to press word came of the death of Clinton Gilbert, Pauline Clarke's very distinguished husband. The class send her their love and sympathy.

1913

Class Editor: HELEN EVANS LEWIS
(Mrs. Robert M. Lewis)
52 Trumbull St., New Haven, Conn.

1914

Class Editor: ELIZABETH AYER INCHES
(Mrs. Henderson Inches)
41 Middlesex Road, Chestnut Hill, Mass.

Dorothy Godfrey Wayman is still living in Falmouth and writing. Her latest is a serial that came out in *Liberty* this winter called "Dark o' the Moon."

Harriet Sheldon and her mother are living with her sister at 74 Auburn Ave., Columbus, O.

Mary Woodin Miner's father is the new Secretary of the Treasury.

Ida Pritchett is doing photographs madly for some of the garden clubs of Philadelphia and the neighborhood. One of her pictures is hung at the International Salon of Photography at the Pennsylvania Museum.

1915

Class Editor: MARGARET FREE STONE
(Mrs. James Austin Stone)
3039 44th St., N. W., Washington, D. C.

Mary Gertrude Brownell Wilson writes from Croton-on-Hudson:

"The Hessian Hills School, very modern and very progressive, is the center of the community in which we live. My husband teaches there, and my son, Winthrop, now nearly six, is a student.

"Aside from taking my family to school and back, I am working to raise sufficient money to enable the school to function efficiently next year. Like all progressive schools, we were hit pretty hard by the depression.

"On January 25th, with Emily Noyes Knight, who was on from Providence, I went to New York to the dinner given for President Park by the New York Bryn Mawr Club. That institution has moved downtown to the Park Lane Hotel, into some attractive and convenient rooms. At our table the red and the green seemed to predominate—for 1913 was represented by Gordon Hamilton, Maud Dessau (just back from Paris), and Mary Tongue Eberstadt. Susan Brandeis and Dorothea May Moore sat with us on the 1915 side of the table.

"Miss Park spoke in her usual entertaining manner on the finances of the college, and she can be amusing even on so painful a subject . . .

"I see that there is to be a reunion, and I fear I won't be able to be there, as we shall be moving to Rhode Island about that time—that is, if some affluent people come along and kindly rent our house so that we can get away for the summer as we did last year. We went to Matunuck, where we all acquired lovely coats of tan, and my husband wrote a book that was accepted by the first publisher who saw it. Let's hope he brings it out before bankruptcy overtakes him, as seems to be the fate of most publishers at present."

Isabel Smith, as Dean of Scripps College, is to take part in a Conference on the Housing of College Women, under the auspices of the American Association of University Women, in Minneapolis on May 17th. Peggy Stone was invited to sit in on the Conference, but is unable to leave her four children for such a long trip. However, she hopes to leave them in June for a short time to attend reunion.

And speaking of reunion, you have all had those inspiring appeals from Adrienne Kenyon Franklin and Mildred Jacobs Coward, to which nothing needs to be added. This is just to *remind* you: if you haven't already sent in your acceptance, DO IT NOW.

1916

Class Editor: LARIE KLEIN BOAS
(Mrs. Benjamin Boas)
2100 Pacific Ave., San Francisco, Calif.

1917

Class Editor: BERTHA CLARK GREENOUGH
203 Blackstone Blvd., Providence, R. I.

Helen Harris writes that "running a New York Settlement in these depression times keeps me so close to poverty, undernourishment and general unhappiness that I wonder if there are anywhere in the world people with jobs who can pay their rents and who don't acquire food through 'Home Relief.' I don't think most of the more fortunate have the slightest idea how bad it really is for the 12,000,000 unemployed. If any '17ers are curious, though, I'd love to show them—in between cups of tea! Union Settlement is easy to get to."

Although your Editor was not fortunate enough to see her, she understands that Countess Alef de Ghize, Eleanor May Jencks, was in the vicinity of Providence the end of April and was at a dinner given for the Governor of Rhode Island and the Governor of Massachusetts.

1918

Class Editor: MARGARET BACON CAREY
(Mrs. H. R. Carey)
3115 Queen Lane, East Falls P. O., Phila.

1919

Class Editor: MARJORIE REMINGTON TWITCHELL
(Mrs. Pierrepont Twitchell)
Setauket, L. I., N. Y.

Spring is bringing up a crop of gardeners in 1919. Here's Jane Hall Hunter with a newly painted house and an endless number of seeds brought home by a husband who has a weakness for Henderson's and Stumpp and Walter's, and just can't pass by their doors without a stop. The Hunters and Win Kaufmann Whitehead and her husband are tripping the light fantastic often these days—"the depression dwindles almost into insignificance under the influence of the latest fox trot and tango." Peter Hayman Dam also digs in a garden. She says "Fran Allison was here for a weekend before Christmas—hasn't changed a bit—and we had an evening with Peg Bettman and managed to get in a good deal of chatter."

A delightful letter from Jinkie Holmes Alexander: "The news of myself is mostly the sort of thing that time drops in its wake—you know, houses and gardens, bobbed hair, an increased tolerance for cocktails and highballs, the great game of making ends meet, and the patter of little feet slithering down the stairs. Janet Marjorie is officially the child's name, but she is called Tonnage because of the fatness that was present at birth, and is still visible at 17 months. The rather more than plump legs move with unbelievable speed, supporting a spirit gleefully bent on destruction. A West Highland terrier with a passion for little children and rubber toys that squeak, lends his bit of quiet to the house. Before the depression hit us (and Janet Marjorie? Query by Ed.) we did a fair amount of pleasant traveling here and in Europe, but now we stay put more. Hence the house. Last summer we went camping on Georgian Bay with a lawyer, a biologist, a neurologist, a Hungarian opera singer, an Austrian architect, and wives of assorted ages, nationalities and tempers. A lot of fun and some distress was had by all. I wrote a novel last year, but so far no one has published it. I'm starting another one. After all, it's a very cheap amusement. Beany Dubach was here for a bit last spring. She's now in Denver doing pre-medical work. Fran Allison Porter and husband and two children are probably coming back here to live next fall. And that's all the news I know." Jinkie's address is 7027 Maryland Avenue, St. Louis.

1920

Class Editor: MARY PORRITT GREEN
(Mrs. Valentine J. Green)
433 East 51st St., New York City

Very indirectly we hear that Margaret Littell Platt is illustrating a children's book soon to be published.

In the *New York Tribune* of May 3rd the League of Women Voters of New York City submit a list of eleven outstanding women educators for consideration as President of Hunter College. Among these is Millicent Carey MacIntosh. The report goes on to say that these are women "whose fine administration and scholastic experience in well-known institutions of higher learning especially qualify them for consideration as head of a women's college."

From Teresa James Morris we have received a letter of bitter criticism because she found on page 11 of the April BULLETIN the statement: "I am glad to report that water polo is dead at Bryn Mawr."

"I am not in sympathy with that! Second-team athlete that I was (and am), I now turn my attention to tennis (Chevy Chase Club team), and throw in a little golf, swimming, and riding. To my surprise, I even appeared in the newspaper as No. 12 in District of Columbia ratings in tennis for 1932. They have a curious system of rating, as I doubt my really being No. 300, or even No. 3000."

"My husband is coaching the baseball team at George Washington University here. They've never had a baseball team before. The games are to be played at night in the American ball park."

1921

Class Editor: WINIFRED WORCESTER STEVENSON
(Mrs. Harvey Stevenson)
Croton-on-Hudson, N. Y.

The class extends its deepest sympathy to Margaret Morton Creese, whose oldest child, Jimmy, died suddenly in April.

Eleanor Boswell is now Mrs. W. Stuart Murrio, of 24 Fellows Road, London, N. W. 3.

Becky Marshall and Eleanor Bliss are still at Johns Hopkins. Becky does clerical work for the Heart Station, whatever that may mean, and Eleanor is completing three years of devotion to the common cold. She says she knows almost everything about the cold except how to prevent or cure it.

Silvine Marbury Harrold has been visiting in Baltimore. When at home in Macon she gives all the time that her children leave her to working at a milk station and baby clinic.

1922

Class Editor: SERENA· HAND SAVAGE
(Mrs. William L. Savage)
106 E. 85th St., New York City

Virginia Grace has an article in the Journal of Hellenic Studies, Vol. LII. (1932), entitled *Scopas in Chryse.*

1923

Class Editor: RUTH McANENY LOUD
325 East 72nd St., New York City

Katherine Shumway Freas has now lived for three years in the Belgian Congo, and has come to feel entirely at home ·"in a land where, little over fifty years ago, men were savages, carried on tribal warfare, sold each other into slavery, and practised all the hideous arts of witchcraft, including trial by poison." She goes on to picture her own work: "What amazes me most is the skill and intelligence with which those who have been trained go about their work, whether it be a clerk in one of the commercial centers, an engineer on the railroad, a teacher or a carpenter here at the station, or a medical assistant at the hospital, of which my husband is in charge. In the last-named capacity they make all the preparations for an operation, give the anaesthetic, assist at the operation, take care of all the dressings, attend to all the routine dispensing of medicines and giving of injections, microscopic examinations, and diagnosing of all but the most difficult cases, checked often, of course, by the doctor. And fifty years ago. . . . Truly, it is amazing! They prove often most apt pupils, as I have reason to know from my school work in the teacher-training course of which I have, for the past two years, had charge. You should see me trying to ·teach methods and a bit of Child Psychology in Kikongo, sometimes in French, which is the official language of the colony. And my pet hobby has been our demonstration classes and practice school, where one of our most able teachers, under my direction, has done the supervising. Last year, with his help,

I managed to evolve a very simple program for our village schools and get into shape two little booklets in the native language of teaching helps and daily lesson outlines, which have been put into all the schools where we have teachers —nearly 200. We had great fun doing it and I learned a lot of the language in the process."

Marion Lawrence writes: "At long last my article is out, 'Columnar Sarcophagi in the Latin West,' published in the *Art Bulletin* for June, 1932. This is my fifth article, the fourth on Early Christian Sarcophagi, and incorporates all my work on them to date. There will be other sections, however, to come, as it is a big subject. This is also my fourth year of teaching History of Art at Barnard, where I am beginning to feel like one of the old guard."

Marion got her Ph.D. from Radcliffe last June, and spent the summer traveling in Europe and studying sarcophagi and mediaeval manuscripts.

Laura Crease Bunch has gone to Washington, D. C., hoping to find a greater demand for bridge teachers than New York has evidenced, though, as a matter of fact, she has been very busy here all winter. She is staying at the Holton Arms School.

1924

Class Editor: DOROTHY GARDNER BUTTERWORTH
(Mrs. J. Ebert Butterworth)
8024 Roanoke St., Chestnut Hill, Pa.

Beth Tuttle Wilbur, who is living in Bryn Mawr again, has the record for moving. Just after her son, Donald Elliot, Jr., was born— the daughter Betsy is now five and a half, Ellio is over three—the Wilburs moved to Chicago for a short time, then to Minneapolis, and ended up two years ago in Cambridge, where Don attended the Harvard School of Business Administration. "That," says Beth, "was just the place to be to watch the wheels of depression go round." While in Cambridge, Beth studied piano at the New England Conservatory, took fancy skating lessons, played hockey and had her appendix removed. They spent practically all winter nearby on a big sailing vessel where the children slept in blanket lockers and rope bins. Last summer was passed in Maine, and now the four Wilburs are occupying a two hundred-year-old farmhouse and find there is no place like home.

Two trips to Arizona in the past two years, and one to Germany—with her husband—when he went to work in a laboratory in Munich— may seem like no traveling at all to Betty Hale Laidlaw. Betty, who is living in New York, writes that she isn't doing anything at present, besides housework. Her profession is really

medicine, in its early stages, but since her marriage in 1930 she has done nothing in that field.

The Junior League National Conference is about to burst upon Philadelphia. Blanche McRae Baker is to be billeted with your editor. Jean Palmer decided to forego our company as she always types all night and thinks it kinder to stay elsewhere. As we have only three spare beds we can't accommodate more Bryn Mawrtyrs this time. Having lived South, East and West, some eight girls asked to stay with us. Carrie Remak, Jane Yeatman Savage, Lucylle Austin and Bess Pearson, who is being married June 16th, are also billeting delegates in Chestnut Hill. So it promises to be a very exciting week, with much gossip.

1925

Class Editor: ELIZABETH MALLETT CONGER
(Mrs. Frederic Conger)
325 East 72nd St., New York City

It is June, and again life is looking like a broad highway with cross-roads to all the people who make commencement speeches. We have decided definitely that the figure is a poor one. Somehow, a kaleidoscope would be closer; at any rate, the picture should be laid in the element of time rather than that of space. We wish we were important enough to make commencement speeches.

In a Madison Avenue street car last week we met Jean Gregory seeing New York and looking very well indeed. She *is* getting her M.A. in History in Montreal, so we guessed right last month. She told us also that Virginia Lomas has just had a part in the Comedy Club play, *The Perfect Alibi*, and she gave us news of Sylvia Saunders.

In January or thereabouts Via was married to Mr. James Agee, one of the Editors of *Fortune*. They are living downtown in Perry Street in great secrecy—no telephone and a semi-private address.

In February at a cat show at the Ferargil Gallery we fell upon a charming etching by Jane Belo.

More details of Clara Gehring's wedding have come through Libby Wilson Jackson. The Bickfords went to the West Indies on their wedding trip and are living now at Ambleside Apartments, Ambleside Drive, Cleveland.

For herself, Libby writes that life is very hectic. She is really keeping house in two places at once—living in Memphis, but helping to run her father's house in Trenton. Her baby is now a big girl, and "so crazy about Sunday School that she wants to go every day."

Libby Wilson lost her mother in August. The class sends her deepest sympathy.

1926

Class Editor pro tem: MARY C. PARKER
135 Charles St., Boston, Mass.

1927

Class Editor: ELLENOR MORRIS
Berwyn, Pa.

One more baby to chronicle! And this time a girl, after all that long list of boys last month. The fond parent has not got around to informing us herself as yet, but it is reported that little Mary Elizabeth Kyster arrived in the Philippines this winter, and if Mary Cruikshank Kyster ever sees fit to write us we will tell you more about her.

According to Mrs. de Laguna, Freddie has departed to Alaska with her Dane to dig. The name of her escort was not supplied, nor any further details, but we wish her great success with excavations!

No other news being forthcoming, we shall fall back on our own antics, and tell you that we broke a collarbone a few weeks ago when our horse fell in a paper chase. It is quite well now, thank you, and we are terribly busy being Assistant Secretary on the Philadelphia Conference Committee. The Association of Junior Leagues of America are having a big pow-wow here in May, and we have had a big time getting ready for them.

1928

Class Editor: CORNELIA B. ROSE, JR.
310 East 55th St., New York City

Elizabeth Bethel writes from Paris of her winter abroad: a visit to Frances Bethel Rowan in Berlin, where her college German proved inadequate for conversation with her young niece, who speaks only that language; then five months in Paris, and, just before she wrote, a short trip to Italy. She is coming back to a new job at Yale next year, where she will be secretary to Professor Whitbridge, one of the House Masters under the new scheme which will divide the university up into a number of separate colleges along the lines of the Oxford system.

Ruth Creighton was married on April 29 to William A. Webster, Jr., of Upper Montclair. Mr. Webster is with J. P. Morgan & Co., and Ruth expects to keep her job at the Chase. They will live at 257 North Mountain Avenue, Upper Montclair, N. J.

From Ruth we learn that Doris Ames Clivis, '27, has recently heard from Mrs. Wray of the birth of Louise Wray Moro's second son. In such devious ways do we glean tib-bits!

Skee McKee is industriously interning at the Tampa Municipal Hospital in Tampa, Fla. She says that she is learning lots, working hard, and has been swimming all winter. In July she returns to New York and expects to interne another year or so before she blossoms out as a baby specialist. Skee says that Emma Gillinder still is working on her elegant job with the Texaco Company, where she is in charge of the research library, among other things.

Magdalen Hupfel Flexner has been putting her dramatic ability to work for the benefit of Varsity Dramatics and has this spring directed *Lady Windermere's Fan* and that great campus innovation, the Faculty Show.

1929

Class Editor: MARY L. WILLIAMS
210 East 68th St., New York City

Vicky Buel has announced her engagement to Dr. Hugh Currie Thompson, Jr., of New York. He is a graduate of Yale and of the College of Physicians and Surgeons of Columbia University. They expect to be married next autumn.

Nancy (Carr) Friendly has a daughter, Margaret, born in March.

Another engagement is that of Lysbet Lefferts, who will marry Philip Golden Bartlett early this summer.

1930

Class Editor: EDITH GRANT
Pembroke West, Bryn Mawr, Pa.

Phyllis Wiegand Tilson has a daughter, named after herself, born the 16th of March. We seem to have several candidates for some future class at Bryn Mawr, that of '54, according to the closest estimate of which our arithmetic is capable.

Violet Whelan writes that she is engaged to Mr. William Glasgow Bowling, of St. Louis. He is an instructor in English and Assistant Dean of Washington University there.

Olivia Stokes has returned from her African travels, which were most successful and interesting. We cordially invite her to resume her old job as Class Editor.

We wish to announce the marriage of Elizabeth Stix to Mr. Merle Fainsod, which took place on April 27th in Leningrad. Mr. Fainsod returns to Harvard next year as Instructor in History.

1931

Class Editor: EVELYN WAPLES BAYLESS
(Mrs. Robert N. Bayless)
301 W. Main St., New Britain, Conn.

Ruth Levy has a position in the University of Pennsylvania Museum.

Ethel Sussman was married, apparently some time ago, to Mr. Richard Barmon. I am sorry there was no mention of it before.

Dorothy Asher has had a position as biochemist at Children's Hospital in Philadelphia

since July. This February she received her
M.S. in Physiological Chemistry from the
University of Pennsylvania. She published a
paper with Dr. James Jones in the *Journal of
Biological Chemistry* for March.

1932

Class Editor: JOSEPHINE GRATON
182 Brattle St., Cambridge, Mass.

Alice Bemis has announced her engagement
to Charles Goodrich Thompson, a young lawyer
from Boston, who is practicing in New York.
They will be married in June at Alice's summer home in New Hampshire, and will live in
New York.

The following letter has just arrived from
Libby Gutmann in Athens: "I spent last summer in Paris, absorbing a certain amount of
French and trying to learn a little archaeology
in preparation for my trip. Knowing my aunt,
Hetty Goldman, 1903, you can imagine my
disappointment when she was obliged to return
to America, but it seemed most sensible for
me to come on to Greece, which I accordingly
did, spending three days in Venice on the
way. Having heard about said city all my life,
I still found it hard to believe what I saw.
There is something distinctly unreal about getting off a train—very modern and smelly—and
being handed into a gondola for transportation
to your hotel.

"The approach to Greece by boat through
the Gulf of Corinth was tremendous—I was especially lucky in finding a passenger who knew
the Corinth region and could point out the
landmarks.

"I spent an aggregate of about three weeks
in Athens and four weeks on the road, taking
the regular Northern and Southern trips with
the School. It's a wonderful system. We
traveled by car, stopping at all the chief sites
for a detailed account of their archaeology.
I was quite appalled at the way in which the
Director would look at a stylobate and a few
loose architectural blocks and proceed to re-
construct the whole building.

"The Northern trip covered the territory between Athens, Eretria, Lamia, and Delphi; and
the Southern one 'did' the Peloponnesus with
the great exception of Olympia for which they
later had a special trip. Greece was pretty
thoroughly dried out, by that time, so that
the coloring was mostly in tawny shades of
parched earth and grass. Consequently the few
patches of cottons and cypresses stood out in
especially marked relief. The mountains—I'd
never before realized how completely Greece
consists of a mass of mountains—practically
devoid of trees, showed the shades of modeling beautifully.

"It's a country of contrasts, and in a single
village one can easily find a radio and a woman
spinning wool by hand, while in the country
we saw little boys treading grapes with bare
feet! I could go on forever, but I shan't.

"When I left Greece about the middle of
November and went to Berlin with the idea of
learning the blessed 'Dutch,' I took up lodg-
ings in a 'Studienhaus,' a sort of glorified dormitory under private auspices, for the housing
of 'high class' German girls. There, too, to my
great surprise and delight, I found Lu Evers.
She was studying German at the university
and spent much time with her dozens of relatives. When she did on occasion condescend to
be home, we had some awfully good times together. When last heard of she was on a
bicycle tour, about three days out, in Halle.
She was feeling, it would appear from her
allusions, very much stretched as to muscles.

"I spent three months in Berlin studying
archaeology—unfortunately as a hearer only—
at the university, and incidentally acquiring a
fairly presentable working knowledge of the
German language. The political situation was
interesting but, contrary to reports, the city
was in general quiet and even when the
Reichstag was being burned we passed close
by without scenting excitement.

"On March first I left Berlin and returned
directly here. I studied for about a month and
then had a chance to earn board and lodging
by painting the plaster restorations on the pottery in the Corinth Museum. It's great fun.
I get a chance to handle almost every piece in
the cases—mostly pre-historic, so far—and
there's some lovely stuff among it. Also it
gives me a chance to share in the life of an
excavation, which is grand experience. Corinth
is beautifully situated, with an ever-changing
view across the Gulf to the Attic mountains.
There are a couple of guitars and good voices
among the 'dig' hands and the result is many
a jolly evening, in nearly every known language. I was down there about ten days before
Easter and expect to return after the holidays.

"Today I went on a tour to the temple of
Athena at Ægina. The remains are beautiful
and in a stunning situation. Also the masses
of scattered architectural blocks made excellent exercises in identification. I felt a little
like Alice in Wonderland, always guessing but
having no one to tell me whether I was right.

"Priscilla Rawson has been spending most
of the winter studying music in New York,
according to an aunt of hers whom I met here.
Otherwise I've heard from or about no one in
our class."

We wish to extend our deepest sympathy to
Dodo Brown who has recently lost her mother.

SCHOOL DIRECTORY

Well, that's something about
cigarettes I never knew before

I'd never thought much about what's inside a Chesterfield cigarette. But I have just been reading something that made me think about it.

Just think of this, some of the tobacco in Chesterfield — the Turkish — comes from 4000 miles away! And before it is shipped every single leaf is packed by hand.

Of course I don't know much about making cigarettes, but I do know this—that Chesterfields are milder and have a very pleasing aroma and taste. They satisfy—and that's what counts!

the cigarette that's MILDER
the cigarette that TASTES BETTER

BRYN MAWR
ALUMNAE
BULLETIN

COMMENCEMENT

July 1933

Vol. XIII   No. 7

Entered as second-class matter, January 15, 1921, at the Post Office, Phila., Pa., under Act of March 3, 1879
COPYRIGHT, 1933
ALUMNAE ASSOCIATION OF BRYN MAWR COLLEGE

Form of Bequest

I give and bequeath to the ALUMNAE ASSOCIATION

OF BRYN MAWR COLLEGE, Bryn Mawr, Pennsylvania,

the sum of.............................dollars.

BRYN MAWR ALUMNAE BULLETIN

OFFICIAL PUBLICATION OF
THE BRYN MAWR ALUMNÆ ASSOCIATION

Marjorie L. Thompson, '12, *Editor*
Alice M. Hawkins, '07, *Business Manager*

EDITORIAL BOARD

Mary Crawford Dudley, '96
Caroline Morrow Chadwick-Collins, '05
Emily Kimbrough Wrench, '21
Ellenor Morris, '27
Elinor B. Amram, '28
Pamela Burr, '28
Elizabeth Bent Clark, '95, *ex-officio*

Subscription Price, $1.50 a Year   *Single Copies, 25 Cents*
Checks should be drawn to the order of Bryn Mawr Alumnæ Bulletin
Published monthly, except August, September and October, at 1006 Arch St., Philadelphia, Pa.

Vol. XIII   JULY, 1933   No. 7

LAUDEMUS ALUMNAS
Reprinted from the College News of June 13th

If during the week-end that the reuniting alumnae spend at Bryn Mawr, a closer rapport could be established between them and the undergraduates, we feel that the undergraduates would be immensely benefited. The alumnae embody the traditions of Bryn Mawr, and since we are firmly convinced that we and our contemporaries have ceased to feel that we must be the Wild Younger Generation and despise the past merely because it is the past, we can therefore ill afford to disregard tradition. Nothing could have been more stupid than the recent style of overthrowing traditional ideals without considering the possibility that they might be intrinsically valuable.

The attitude of the alumnae as a whole toward Bryn Mawr and the achievements of her graduates is a part of the tradition most significant for us. Their tolerance of the present undergraduates, and their interest in recent developments in college education show a complete freedom from the idea, popularly expected of alumnae everywhere, that their college has been going rapidly down hill ever since their particular class graduated. It will not be easy for the present students to maintain the open-mindedness toward innovations that the alumnae have postulated for us. Furthermore, although most of the alumnae are working, they have not confined their interests to their work alone, but are in touch with recent trends in economic theory, education, literature, and international problems. They have made Bryn Mawr women recognized and responsible workers and authorities in all fields open to women, and have even broken into some fields, such as banking, that had until recently been occupied by men alone.

We feel that their open-mindedness, their belief in the power and influence of Bryn Mawr women, their pride in Bryn Mawr achievements, and their unwavering confidence that we, in full consciousness of our position as young Bryn Mawr graduates, will try, as they have done, to make ourselves influential, bring to the undergraduate a new idea of what it has always meant to be a Bryn Mawr alumna, and of what they trust it will continue to mean.

SPECIAL MEETING OF THE ALUMNAE ASSOCIATION, JUNE 11, 1933

THE REPORT OF THE WAYS AND MEANS COMMITTEE ON THE QUESTION OF USING THE DEANERY AS AN ALUMNAE HOUSE

Mrs. Clark, after calling the meeting to order, read, to bring it back to the mind of everyone present, the Resolution which was offered at the time of the Annual Meeting:

Resolved: that though Miss Thomas' decision to discontinue making the Deanery her home is news we deeply deplore, her generous offer to the Alumnae Association of a completely equipped Alumnae House is a mark of confidence and affection for which our appreciation can never find adequate expression. In order that all alumnae may share in accepting this gift, I move: that a Ways and Means Committee be appointed by the Chair to present a plan to the alumnae in June at a meeting especially called to pass upon this delightful and unusual project.

She then explained: "This is the special meeting that the Chair has called in accordance with the instructions presented in that Resolution. The Ways and Means Committee which was appointed consisted of: Caroline McCormick Slade, Chairman; Elizabeth Bent Clark, ex-officio; Martha G. Thomas, Frances Fincke Hand, Caroline Chadwick-Collins, Louise Fleischmann Maclay, Millicent Carey McIntosh, Lois Kellogg Jessup, and I should like to say, before asking the Chairman of the Committee to present the details of the working out the ways and means of using this remarkable gift, that this committee has met as a committee and as individuals with a great many members of the Alumnae Association and has worked out with great thought and care all the phases of the proposition. I shall now ask Mrs. Slade to present to you the plan."

Mrs. Slade spoke without notes and with the most delightful informality and warmth of feeling. The following is the written report which she presented to Mrs. Clark, as President of the Alumnae Association, and which gives in a condensed form the various points that she made:

"The Ways and Means Committee appointed at the annual meeting of the Alumnae Association has carefully considered Miss Thomas' gift and has gone over in great detail the question of the use of the Deanery as an Alumnae House, and the methods by which it can be operated.

"As a result they beg to submit the following report:

"The Deanery building, consisting of two small cottages on the property originally purchased as the site of the College, was remodeled and greatly increased in size and put into its present form by Miss Garrett as a home for Miss Thomas and herself, and as a center to which to bring distinguished guests to the new College at Bryn Mawr. At that time it was agreed by the Trustees of Bryn Mawr College that Miss Garrett and Miss Thomas, either or both, had the privilege of using it for life, but could at any time turn it back to the College.

"When last January Miss Thomas decided not to continue to make her home at Bryn Mawr she consulted President Park as to possible uses to which the Deanery might be put. President Park said that the Deanery was not adapted for dormitory or lecture room use or for other immediate needs of the College, and that if it were returned to the College it would have to be closed. Miss Thomas has long hoped that the Deanery might in the future become an alumnae center and has often spoken of her wish ultimately to make this possible. Therefore, with President Park's coöperation and approval, she asked the Board of the College to turn over her rights in the Deanery for the use of the alumnae. With this request granted, Miss Thomas offered to the alumnae her furniture and furnishings, including her pictures, her rugs, and all of the equipment which has made the beauty of the Deanery.

"This gift was announced to the Alumnae Association and this committee was appointed. We understood our first duty to be the working out of a plan by which the necessary expense of maintaining the Deanery could be met. It seemed that a fund of $5,000 a year would be necessary to do this, and the committee suggested that an attempt be made to raise $20,000 in order to have a four-year period guaranteed before the house should be opened. Miss Thomas was unwilling to have this burden laid upon the alumnae, even in the form of loans to be repaid by her at a later date, and she offered to provide $5,000 a year for the four-year period suggested, which completely solved the initial problem.

"After serious consideration as to how best to carry out the plan, the committee, in consultation with the Board of the Alumnae Association, reached the unanimous conclusion that it would be better to request Miss Thomas to make her gift to Bryn Mawr College direct, rather than to the Alumnae Association itself. As the house is the property of the College, it greatly simplifies the situation to make the furniture, furnishings, and so on the property of the College, the whole building, furnishings, and equipment to be set aside for use as an alumnae center, with the further understanding that a Deanery Committee be created, to consist of the alumnae members of the Board of Directors and the President of the Alumnae Association.

"As the majority of the alumnae members of the Board are elected by the Alumnae Association, this would place the management in the hands of alumnae chosen by the Alumnae Association and would give the rotation in office made possible by the annual change of one Alumna Director. To this Miss Thomas agreed, and, as it had the unanimous endorsement of the Board of the Alumnae Association, it was placed before the Board of the College, who have also given it their approval. Under this plan the Deanery Committee would at present consist of one Alumna Trustee, three Directors-at-large, five Alumnae Directors, and the President of the Alumnae Association, making ten in all. It is suggested that this Deanery Committee elect four officers, a Chairman, Vice-Chairman, Secretary, and Treasurer, and that these officers, with two essential sub-committee Chairmen, namely, the Chairman of a House Committee and the Chairman of a Committee on Entertainment, constitute an Executive Committee. The Deanery will be turned over to the Deanery Committee some time in September.

"Miss Thomas consents to receive the alumnae on the 7th of October, which will mark the formal opening of the Deanery as an Alumnae Center."

*　　*　　*

In commenting on this solution of the various problems, Mrs. Slade stressed the fact that plans are still in the making and that there are a thousand details still to be worked out, but the aim of the committee will be to make the Deanery a centre to which all the alumnae will want to come back, and also to devise ways in which it will best serve to enrich the life of the College. Miss Thomas herself is superintending all the arrangements, and is seeing that every rug and picture and book is in its right place before the Deanery is turned over, swept and garnished on September 1st. That she has postponed her sailing in the fall, to receive the alumnae in the Deanery when it is formally opened, is the final touch of generosity and graciousness.

Motion moved, seconded and carried that the Report of the Ways and Means Committee be accepted as presented by Mrs. Slade.

After various interested questions from the floor, a standing vote of thanks was called for to express appreciation of the work of Mrs. Slade's committee, and of Miss Thomas' generosity.

Mrs. Clark then announced that a rising vote of thanks to express the appreciation of the Association would be in order, to be carried to Miss Thomas in a letter written by the Secretary. Various alumnae who had seen Miss Thomas spoke of the warm personal interest and pleasure that she herself feels in the whole undertaking.

The meeting closed with the following Resolution to the retiring members of the Faculty:

Whereas, With the end of this college year, Dr. Wilmer Cave Wright, Professor of Greek, and Dr. Regina K. Crandall, Professor of English Composition, and Dr. James H. Leuba, Professor of Psychology, retire from the faculty of Bryn Mawr College, and

Whereas, To many of us gathered here today, their teaching of long years ago has continued to be an ever-freshening inspiration, and

Whereas, The stimulus of their presence on the campus has been of untold benefit, in all these changing times, therefore

Be It Resolved, That the Alumnae Association of Bryn Mawr College records its keen appreciation of their high standard of work, of their brilliant achievements, and its keen regret at their retirement.

ANNOUNCEMENTS

The University of Pennsylvania conferred on President Park at its Commencement this June the honorary degree of LL.D.

The Bryn Mawr Club of Cincinnati is much gratified that the response to its appeal for the Louise Hyman Pollak Memorial has been so very generous. To date there have been 78 contributors to the fund. The sum of $1,500 has been presented to the Bryn Mawr College Library. Promises of future contributions give augury of further increase. The books purchased are marked with a special plate.

The House Committee hopes to have the Deanery ready for occupancy by October 2nd. Requests for reservations cannot be received until after September 1st, and should be made directly to the Deanery.

TRIBUTES TO THE THREE RETIRING PROFESSORS

WILMER CAVE WRIGHT

Remembering mornings in Room A, I see the red book called Greek Literature—*A Short History of Greek Literature,* by Wilmer Cave Wright. From that solid base sprang up, under the skillful hands of its author and our teacher, an edifice for our delight. We knew the facts, the names, the dates, the book contained; we had to. We knew the picture of Greek literature which it presented with extraordinary scope and clarity for so brief a work. By its full, beautiful, and apt quotations we knew, from the book alone, something of the literature itself. Those pages did not set us apart to look at this art from afar; they took us into the midst of it, so that, most difficult of all tasks for a text-book to accomplish, we felt the impact of a genius two thousand years dead. This was the beginning only. In the classroom the book flowered. The margins of my own copy are lined with notes; I hold it very dear, for it is an "author's copy" in the sense that it contains far more of the author herself than the limitations of a printed book allow. References, more quotations, explanations, phrases that suddenly, in a word, illuminated the meaning of a play or a period. I am sorry for the numberless students who, assured of a memorable course in Greek literature with this book in their hands, yet lack its inspiring development which was our invaluable privilege.

To read Greek with Mrs. Wright was an instruction in all literature. The beauty and interest of play, and poem, the indefinable and unforgettable charm of a language which has never been equaled as a vehicle for the finest thoughts of the human mind, were sufficient in themselves to make a course of lasting value. To this our professor added a knowledge of other literatures that provided a breadth of interest few courses can supply. In particular that bond, most fascinating in its own right and of special interest to us, between the Greek and the English was illuminated for us by Mrs. Wright's knowledge. Not only knowledge; a feeling for the word, for that combination of words, which, strange and unreasonable perhaps, strikes with a flash, crystallizing emotion into poetry; a feeling for the genius, common alike to the English and the Greek, which achieves magnificence in simplicity and beauty without elaboration; a sense of the spirit, as well as understanding of the fact, behind the art of all peoples and especially of these two—for these, beyond and above the field of knowledge and the requirements of instruction, we are grateful to Mrs. Wright. "Beauty itself, brightly shining, it was given them to behold."

JOSEPHINE YOUNG CASE, 1928.

JAMES H. LEUBA—AN APPRECIATION

Fear, awe and a sense of the sublime. To generations of Bryn Mawr students those abstractions must be forever associated with an erect figure, a flashing eye, an incisive diction that over-rode with little compromise the difficulty of a foreign tongue. How many midnight discussions had their origin in Dr. Leuba's General

Psychology Class? How many convictions and standards owe their stability now to foundations laid and tested by him?

Most undergraduates coming from schoolrooms where the teacher, animated by kindness and enthusiasm, tried her best to teach her pupils the *right* answer, found Dr. Leuba's classroom tactics a terrifying experience. The fear that he loved to analyze, with its paralyzing physical manifestations, was an emotion well known there. In my own time we were unable to decide whether it was better to profess ignorance immediately, or whether to risk the ruthless barrage of questions which followed, in staccato phrases, the correct answer to the first inquiry. It was a real baptism of fire, an initiation into the adult world. The way to knowledge was not to be found by looking up answers in the back of the book—even in James' Psychology, which somehow, in this iconoclastic atmosphere, took on the nature of a Book of Revelation—nor by any pleading for help.

Yet guidance was always there. There was never any one more eager and willing to lead on to the heights where wisdom might be found, but it must be clearly understood that little would be done to mitigate the hardships on the journey thither. Perhaps to some readers the analogy of Pilgrim's Progess may seem far-fetched and inapt, but the elements of likeness were there. The hatred of sham and superficiality, the impatience with smugness and self-satisfaction, the contempt for cherished sentimentalities which had no real justification; all these constituted strong meat for many of the babes who were obliged, willy-nilly, to include psychology in their mental diet. To a few it proved indigestible, but to the vast majority it gave nourishment which made for lasting power. The relentless sifting of evidence and the dissecting of motive, which were an invariable part of all discussion, created as great a respect for truth as any laboratory method. By casting away prejudices and passions, one might see more clearly the thrilling possibilities of the human mind. Adventurous, romantic, awe-inspiring—all of these it was made to seem when presented at white heat by a teacher whose mind could never fail to strike sparks for those whose lamps were trimmed and ready.

All of those who had the privilege of studying with Dr. Leuba must feel that his leaving Bryn Mawr ends an era that to many of us seems in retrospect a Golden Age, and all will unite in wishing for him many years of fruitful leisure.

ALICE M. HAWKINS, 1907.

REGINA K. CRANDALL

Those who had the good fortune to come as freshmen into Miss Crandall's division in English Composition had somewhat the experience of raw recruits in an old regiment. It was a formidable experience—to at least one immature, muddle-headed freshman of my acquaintance an interview with Miss Crandall was an ordeal! No unsound construction escaped notice, no paltry repetitiousness, or faulty metaphor, or awkward turn of phrase could survive her crisp, searching criticism. But the challenge was stronger than the discouragement. It was Miss Crandall's special gift that she could enlist the efforts not only of the exceptional student, but also of the plodder, who must labor mightily for all she gained.

English Composition was merely the medium in which she worked. With it she taught us craftsmanship, a feeling for clear thinking and the adroit use of words to express thought. She insisted that we develop, each for herself, a critical faculty, that we establish our standards and live up to them, that we be satisfied with nothing less than our best. It was a whole philosophy in miniature. She abhorred all sham, while a piece of writing showing the authentic light touch, or a serious effort honestly and thoughtfully worked out, never failed to win her praise. Even her praise bore the characteristic stamp of her dry humor. There was a flick in the tail of it that quelled complacency and made one work the harder.

Although one remembers with the utmost gratitude and pleasure the quality of her teaching, and the flash of critical humor that enlivened and made vivid all her class work, it is the warm and genuine interest that she felt in her students as individuals, and the gift for friendship—a rare and discriminating gift which she nevertheless bestowed generously—that makes each one of us who was in any way associated with her have a sense of personal loss at the thought of her retirement.

IDA W. PRITCHETT, 1914.

AN OPEN LETTER

To the Editor of the BULLETIN:

The article in the April Bulletin, "Bryn Mawr Science—In the Field," interested me very much.

May I, however, call your attention to a paragraph which seems to me misleading? The paragraph referred to reads:

"On the other hand, nine former Bryn Mawr students are now on the faculties of women's medical schools." . . .

There is only one woman's medical school in the United States, the Woman's Medical College of Pennsylvania.

This institution ranks with the other acceptable medical schools of the United States before State Boards of Licensure, the National Board of Medical Examiners, the Association of American Medical Colleges, and other rating bodies. It outranks in age the majority of the medical schools in this country, having been founded in 1850.

It seems fair, therefore, in such an analysis as was made of the teaching positions held by Bryn Mawr graduates in medical schools, that the Woman's Medical College of Pennsylvania should be mentioned by name, as are Johns Hopkins, Columbia, Cornell, etc.

It is perhaps worthwhile to note that a number of the Bryn Mawr graduates holding the teaching positions in the co-educational schools referred to received their medical training and their first medical teaching appointments at the Woman's Medical College of Pennsylvania.

MARTHA TRACY, M.D., Bryn Mawr 1898,
Dean of the Woman's Medical College of Pennsylvania.

ADDRESS BY PRESIDENT-EMERITUS M. CAREY THOMAS AT THE OPENING OF THE BRYN MAWR SUMMER SCHOOL FOR WOMEN WORKERS IN INDUSTRY

After being abroad for so many years during the sessions of the Summer School I am very happy to be here today.

This is the fourth summer that our students have come to the school in the midst of great financial anxiety, which has never been so great as this summer. Although the industrial and white collar workers are suffering more than any others and the suffering everywhere is appalling, millions of people of small means, belonging to what is called abroad the middle classes, have lost not only their jobs, but the savings of a lifetime through the failure of banks, building and loan associations and insurance companies. Doctors, nurses, lawyers, architects, artists, musicians, actors, singers, small merchants of every kind, and above all, school teachers, have no work. The impoverishment of these middle classes means the unemployment of thousands of domestic servants, janitors, chauffeurs, laundresses and many independent little mechanics and men in small business, and as a total result a terrific drop in the purchasing of everything manufactured or grown. This is true not only in the United States but in Great Britain, France, Germany, Italy and elsewhere. Misery is world wide. Unemployment is world wide. Millions of workers the world over are eager for jobs and can get none, and their savings are now after three years exhausted. Many of them are living on doles so small that they are falling gradually to the level below which they will die of starvation. Let me say here that if you are unemployed you need have no hesitation in applying for unemployment relief. It is your due. You are unemployed because of the failure of your government to prevent unemployment. It is not your fault. You are entitled to be fed and clothed until you are provided with work. I believe—and this is what I have come here to say—I believe that there are signs that the present darkness is the profound darkness that comes before dawn, that we are now at last beginning to see the light of a new day breaking. Many things are becoming clear to us which before this we have been too blinded to understand. First, our great capitalistic system has failed the world over and must be made over from the bottom up or done away with. Second, Democracy is failing. It must be reconstructed anew and made to work for the good of us all or it too must perish and we shall have here in the United States and in the republics of Great Britain and France dictators, which is a polite name for tyrants such as are ruling in Russia, Italy and Germany. Bad as democracy is, it has within itself the possibilities of reform. Beneficent as tyrants may be at first, as I believe Lenin and Stalin have been, tyrants have within themselves impulses that cannot fail to become tyrannical. Free speech, free-thought reform, growth, new ideas, become more and more intolerable to tyrants and so must inevitably be stamped out by banishment, killings and machine guns. Our great western democracies are now being menaced by our ignorant vote-seeking political leaders and legislators. As we were betrayed in the great war by our politicians, diplomats, religious teachers, economists and governments, so now we are being betrayed by our great bankers, railway presidents, great industrialists and again by our economists and our governments. We are today in the grip of the sinister tentacles of the great octopus of Capitalism which has brought us to our present miserable estate. If Democracy is to survive, it must build anew an ordered world for us to live in on a scientific basis without silly mediaeval inhibitions. If even one-half of the human ability that has been devoted to scientific research of the heavens above and the earth beneath, fighting of disease, inventions, industrial machines, automobiles, gases, could now be devoted to our nothing-like-so-difficult social problems, Democracy can be saved.

- Some elementary steps to be taken at once are even now clear. In spite of our short-sighted politicians and governments we must have world peace or we shall all be destroyed in the next war. The population of every civilized country now exceeds its available jobs and other resources and must be scientifically regulated by birth-control clinics. As Democracy depends for its existence on intelligent votes, the ever-increasing production of morons must be scientifically checked and insane and weak-minded people must be prevented from having children.

Child labor below the age of 16 must be done away with, and up to this age every child must be given the best possible compulsory education. Cut-throat and predatory competition must be forbidden by laws strictly enforced. Profits on capital must be reduced by law to a fair percentage, probably 6 or 7 per cent. on overhead costs and wages. Wages must form a much larger percentage of the overhead, probably 50 per cent. instead of 17 per cent., as it is at present, for shorter hours, probably eight hours daily for a five-day week. There must be no seasonal employment. Intelligent planning can easily space work so that the same wages are paid all the year round. There must be old-age pensions, free contributory medical insurance as in England, and unemployment insurance maintained by the employer and taken out of overhead expenses before profits are estimated. The same short hours and the same fair wages must prevail in agriculture as in manufactures, and food prices will rise a little in consequence, but not too much when transportation and the present extortionate profits of the middle distributors of food are regulated. Cheap machine production must work full speed all the time in order to put the comforts and amenities of life within reach of all industrious workers. Government must own and operate all public utilities, all railways and other transportations, all ammunition and armament factories. We must have a government of experts appointed by the President and his cabinet who must be held responsible for their uprightness and for the ability of the experts they appoint.

These are a few of the things that, it seems to me, must be done immediately to save us, and there are many others. It seems to me self-evident that if working men and women who form the vast majority in every country are to put through even such obvious reforms as these which affect them vitally *they must form a Labor Party* to enact them into law and to see that they are honestly enforced. I recommend this to you for your consideration and discussion. The United States has no Labor Party and we are behind all other civilized countries, all of which have labor parties in their respective legislatures. In our social, and above all, our labor legislation, laws such as they are, are far worse enforced than theirs.

THE COMMENCEMENT WEEK-END

The late date of Commencement this year meant that for the first day or so the heat was almost unbearable, but the shade of the campus and the cool magic of the Deanery garden, the green slopes of Wyndham, and the sound of water in the cloister, had a power and charm that aroused even the most detached alumna, and on every side one heard, "It is the nicest Reunion we ever had." Then, on Commencement Day itself, there came the change. The wind blew fresh, the May Day banners on Rock Tower stood out straight from their poles, and everyone moved out to sit in the sun and said, as if it were a new discovery: "Isn't the campus lovely?" Altogether the weather played a potent part.

The classes were evenly divided on Saturday night: four had picnics and four had suppers in state. The picnickers later adjourned to the Deanery garden, never more lovely, somehow, than this year. The wet spring had made it more fresh and beautiful than ever. Everyone was very conscious of Miss Thomas' generosity in giving us the freedom of it, and again and again the groups that sat there wondered curiously about the Special Meeting called for the next day and what the Ways and Means Committee would report that Miss Thomas had worked out with them, so that the alumnae might always enjoy not only the great house itself, but the beauty of the garden. How happy the solution was, not only for the alumnae, but for the College, is reported elsewhere in the BULLETIN.

The fact that more people wanted to come to the luncheon on Sunday than could be crowded into Pembroke dining room, although it was the hottest day of the year, again indicates the interest and enthusiasm that everyone felt. Mary Tongue Eberstadt, 1913, and Harriet Moore, last year's European Fellow, both spoke briefly, and then President Park passed the year in review, and found the college world on the whole a good world. She said that she felt that the College had never been more alive intellectually; that the whole quality of the teaching had never been more stimulating or the students more alert. Although there were only nine fewer students in College this year than last, there was a larger proportion of non-residents, so that Wyndham was not needed. This year there is an increase in registration over this time last year, and Wyndham may again be opened next fall. However, the proportion of students needing scholarship aid has increased. Instead of its being one in seven, it is one in three, figures identical with those that Harvard has published. This increasing need creates a problem that is far from being solved, although the College has, by drastic cuts, again balanced its budget. President Park touched lightly, by way of review, on various points that she had brought up at different times in the BULLETIN, and then paid a warm tribute to the three retiring professors who for many of us are an integral part of our four years at Bryn Mawr:

"Three professors of the College retire this year after long and valuable service at Bryn Mawr.

"Professor Wright came as one of the first Fellows in Greek in 1892, followed Professor Shorey to Chicago, and later returned to Bryn Mawr as reader in 1897. Since 1921 she has been full professor. Her History of Greek Literature and her translations in the Loeb Classical Library and elsewhere have made her widely

(10)

known. She has kept the wide range of reading and the clarity of writing which she brought with her from Girton, and has trained her classes to attempt her own standards.

"Professor James Leuba has taught Psychology at Bryn Mawr since 1897 and has been Professor of Psychology since 1906. His European training, which demands industry in addition to the scholar's gifts, his stern standards both in his own field and in general college matters of admission, of curriculum—all these have not prevented his throwing his influence in college policy constantly toward the liberal side. His outward strictness with his classes, his inner kindliness and sympathy, many generations of his students know. Outside Bryn Mawr his reputation is international. In his retirement Bryn Mawr loses an eminent man as well as an old and trusted friend.

"Miss Crandall came to Bryn Mawr in 1902, and since 1918 she has been been Margaret Kingsland Haskell Professor of English Composition. Her contribution to her own department and to the College has been a distinguished and delightful one. To no member of the faculty, I believe, do students more frankly and more warmly pay their debts of gratitude. Her power to stir the mind, her keen and kind criticism, her generous interest in her students, persist in the memory of the older graduates of the College whom she taught, as vividly as in the memory of last year's classes. The same interest and judgment she has given to College matters—always to their advantage."

In closing, Miss Park again sounded a very optimistic note, speaking in general of the really extraordinary gifts that have come to the College since she addressed the alumnae last June. The total includes gifts for scholarships, both regional and special, the fulfillment of pledges, gifts toward memorial endowments, books for the Library, and special gifts for the various departments and for the infirmary, and the President's gift and the special fund pledged by the Alumnae Association, but that, in a year like this, that the sum of them should amount to almost $95,000 is a very genuine tribute to the College.

The usual things took place the rest of Sunday and Monday. After the luncheon there was the tea by the Alumnae Association to the Seniors. The Undergraduates are just discovering the alumnae, as one can see from the *News* editorial that is reprinted in this BULLETIN, instead of an editorial by the editor. Like all converts, they are zealous, and the experience is pleasant for both groups. Certainly it makes a party a success. At night Rabbi Wise preached the Baccalaureate sermon to a large audience. On Monday, Alumnae vs. Varsity tennis, picnic lunches, Garden Party, gay and colorful the length of Senior Row, and finally, Senior singing in the warm dusk, all followed in a pleasant ordered round.

Commencement Day was a miracle, cool and invigorating, after the muggy heat that had preceded it. Following the precedent that she has established, President Park spoke very briefly, mentioning the special undergraduate and graduate scholarships and fellowships, and citing the special distinctions won abroad and at other colleges and universities by members of the graduate school, as she led up to the dramatic announcement of Bryn Mawr's own European Fellow from the senior class, Josephine Justice Williams, of Jenkintown, prepared by the Irwin School. "By the vote of the Faculty this year, the committee on the choice of the European Fellow was directed to bring in the name of an alternate who will succeed to the honours, rights and dignities of the European Fellow if for any reason she cannot carry out her plan for the use of the Fellowship within four years of her graduation." Rebekah Lockwood Taft, of Andover, Mass., prepared by Wykeham Rise, was chosen as the alternate. The action was made retroactive, and consequently Lucy Sanborn, also of Andover, Mass., was named as alternate for the European Fellowship of last year. Of the ninety individuals who received the B.A. degree, eight took their degree *magna cum laude*, and twenty-one *cum laude*. In addition (the figures in some instances overlap), it might be noted that twenty-two received their degrees with distinction in their major subjects.

President Park took this opportunity again to pay her tribute to the three retiring professors before she introduced President Woolley, of Mount Holyoke College, the Commencement speaker, who discussed *An Age of Power,* "an Age of Power indeed from the mechanical point of view . . . and yet painfully deficient in the kind of power that it most needs." The power that is needed, Miss Woolley felt, to make possible the "substitution of good will for ill will, of trust for distrust, of concord for discord, of friendliness for hatred" in a war-scarred world, is three-fold: the power of thought, the power of beauty, and the power of a new spirit in world relationships. Many of her illustrations were drawn from her own experiences at Geneva.

ALUMNAE ATHLETICS

In spite of the heat, the alumnae-varsity tennis matches took place according to schedule. Eugenia Baker Jessup, 1914, acted as captain of the alumnae team, which included Elizabeth Maguire, 1913; Helen Kirk Welsh, 1914; Mary Hopkinson Gibbon, 1928; Elizabeth Baer, Molly Frothingham and Elinor Totten Turney, all of 1931. Miss Maguire and Miss Frothingham in doubles achieved the only victory for the alumnae, although several of the other matches, notably that in which Miss Baer and Mrs. Turney displayed their old team-work, were well worth watching.

NEXT COUNCIL MEETING

The Alumnae Council will meet next in Boston on November 16th, 17th and 18th. The committee in charge will include Marguerite Mellen Dewey, 1913, Councillor for District I.; Mary Richardson Walcott, 1906, President of the Boston Bryn Mawr Club; Elizabeth Harrington Brooks, 1906, Chairman of Hospitality; Alice Ames Crothers, 1913, Chairman of Dinner; Kathleen Johnston Morrison, 1921, Chairman of Program; and Susan Walker FitzGerald, 1893, Chairman of Publicity.

We have received from the Wedgwood Company assurance that they will ship the Bryn Mawr plates from England on August 4th. We should be glad to receive any special instructions about shipping any of those already ordered, since it is quite possible that the addresses given when the order was placed may not be correct now.

COMMENCEMENT HONOURS

Throughout their college careers, two groups, Alumnae Daughters and Regional Scholars, are followed with special scrutiny by BULLETIN readers. Of the sixteen who entered as Regional Scholars, one, Eleanor Chalfant, from Pittsburgh (daughter of Minnie List, 1907), graduated *magna cum laude,* and nine *cum laude.* These are Alice Brues and Tirzah Clark, from New England; Ellen Nichols (daughter of Marjorie Wallace, 1908), from New York; Jeane Darlington, from New Jersey, and Eleanor Yeakel, from Pittsburgh; Jeannette Le Saulnier, from Indianapolis; Cecelia Candee, from Chicago, and Caroline Lloyd-Jones (daughter of Caroline Schock, 1908), from Madison, Wisconsin; Anne Burnett, from St. Louis. Miss Brues, Miss Clark, Miss Darlington, Miss Le Saulnier, Miss Lloyd-Jones and Miss Burnett all took their degrees with distinction in their special subjects. Three other Regional Scholars were in the upper half of the class, and one, Elizabeth Sixt, of Cleveland, has been spending her senior year in Germany and has yet to take her final examinations.

Of the sixteen Alumnae Daughters who entered with this class, one has transferred to another college and two have stayed out a year and will graduate in 1934. In addition to those who have been mentioned above, Grace Dewes (daughter of Grace Wooldridge, 1909), of Chicago, and Elizabeth Jackson (daughter of Elizabeth Higginson, 1897), of Boston, took their degrees *cum laude.* Miss Jackson and Evelyn Remington (daughter of Mabry Parks, 1905), of Philadelphia, received distinction in their major subjects. Miss Remington and Louise Balmer (daughter of Louise Congdon, 1908), of California, both graduated in the upper half of their class.

While we cannot attempt to analyze the records of the sisters, nieces and cousins of alumnae, we feel that we may make an exception in the case of the Bryn Mawr European Fellow of 1933, who is Josephine Williams, of Jenkintown, Pa., niece of Helen Williams Woodall, 1898. Miss Williams was the holder for 1932-33 of the Charles S. Hinchman Memorial Scholarship, awarded for special ability in the major subject, and received her degree *magna cum laude* with distinction in Mathematics.

Of the twenty Masters of Arts, five are Bryn Mawr A.B.'s: Margaret Dent Daudon, 1920; Emily Jane Low, 1931; Pauline Engle, Virginia Butterworth, and Ann Weygandt, all of 1932. Of the eight Doctors of Philosophy, four hold both B.A.'s and M.A.'s from Bryn Mawr: Jean Wright, 1919; Grace Rhoads, 1922; Mary Woodworth, 1924, and Mary Zelia Pease, 1927; and three others hold M.A.'s: Edna Fredrick, Margaret Jeffrey and Irene Rosenzweig. The eighth, Edith Fishtine, held the Rubel European Fellowship in 1930-31.

ERRATUM

Through a regrettable oversight the name of Janet Barber was omitted from the list of scholarship holders published in the June issue of the BULLETIN. Miss Barber, who is the daughter of Lucy Lombardi, 1904, was awarded a second Charles S. Hinchman Memorial Scholarship for special ability in her major subject, History of Art.

ON THE CAMPUS

THE UNDERGRADUATE POINT OF VIEW

By Janet Marshall, 1933

In this last article I wish to give the hard-won conclusions, most of which I am afraid I have already hinted at very broadly during the course of the year. First of all, it is evident that the class which graduates this June is perhaps the best class by which to judge what the economic depression can do to a group of students. The Class of 1933 came in in September of 1929, which was the balmiest day of the boom, and their four years of college have been four years of steadily sinking stock-markets and world markets. They are a better cross-section than classes either before or after them, because they reach from one extreme to another in those critical four years. First of all, many of their number have dropped out, an unusual proportion, but one which in itself does not alter the general tone of the class, for poverty, like the gentle dew from heaven, falls on the brilliant and the dull alike. But it is noticeable that the number who have survived have been changed by the implication of this thinning in the ranks. The feeling seems to be that if we have stayed in when so many others have been forced to leave, there is a responsibility, not only to the parents who may or may not be making sacrifices to keep us in, but to the community as a whole. If every one cannot afford a college education, then those of us who can, have a duty to that opportunity; we have to make it count for something. We must carry the "college student's burden"; we must be really educated and usefully educated. This may sound like idle moralizing, and I do not mean to infer that the whole student body has taken to its books like rabbits to their holes, but there has been a definite change of tone scholastically. Students are more interested in general information and practical knowledge than they were. Dr. Fenwick's current event lectures are packed with listeners. Mrs. Smith's lectures in chapel on the economic situation are well attended. History and politics and economics and finance are gaining over the more liberal arts as favorite subjects. There is a definiteness of purpose and a seriousness that were sadly lacking at times in 1929. As to the general level of work, it is no wonder that with about one-third of the College receiving help of one sort or another in the financing of their education, from the loans and scholarship funds, there should be a lift in the level of work. It shows most of all in the senior class, for, as I have said, they were, when they came in, a perfectly normal boom-era class. The student body is really learning how to learn and trying to make a serious choice of what to learn. If the depression has taught them this, then we should have depressions regularly and with all possible acuteness.

The other conclusion I wish to draw seems at first to be in direct contradiction to the one above: the students, while they have learned how to work, seem to me to have learned how to play as well. Probably they knew before, but when there were greater funds at everyone's disposal, most of the playing was done away from College. Cut allowances and budgets threw many people back on the campus for their recreations, and the result has been the rejuvenation of one campus activity after another, as I have tried to point out all year. Athletics have been reorganized, and at least one new varsity team, the fencing team, has been added. Dramatics have been reorganized under the dual leadership of Varsity Dramat and Varsity Players, and the number and variety of plays has increased noticeably. I have already noted what a tremendous amount of excellent work the musical organizations have done, but in confirmation of my own conclusions about their work there is the great compliment Mr. Stokowski paid the choir after the performance of *Parsifal* when he told Miss Park that it was one of the best choirs with which he had ever worked. The Bryn Mawr League, too, has taken a new lease on life, and due to the work of approximately one-half of the student body who participate in the activities, Blind School, the Americanization work, and Bates House and the Summer School have been attended to in a very splendid way. Despite the growing difficulty of raising money for the latter two organizations, they will continue this summer as planned, and the League has a very great deal of which to be proud.

An account of the new spirit in activities could be interminable, and what I have said above is enough to illustrate the point I wish to make. We have learned to spend our leisure time at College and to spend it to some advantage. It is not that we play more, but that we have extended the idea of getting as much as possible out of the scholastic side of College to the extra-curricular activities. Here, too, it is felt there is much to be gained, and people have consequently picked the activity in which they have the greatest interest and tried to make it count for something. Again, if this can be laid to the door of the depression, we can say that the depression has made College a more interesting place in which to live.

CAMPUS NOTES

By Elizabeth Hannan, 1934

Little May Day festivities this spring paled before the great event of the season, the Faculty Show. The amount of interest shown by the student body in the casting and repertoire of *Restraint Necessary* was phenomenal for a group which takes campus amusements as a matter of course. Never before has so much curiosity been manifested, not even in the days when the Freshman Show divided the campus into two groups, the hunters and the hunted. "Authentic news" beforehand ranged from the startling report that Miss Park and Dean Manning were slated to sing *Edie Was a Lady*, to the pessimistic pronouncement that the show would be a glorified lecture. That the faculty preserved the secrets so well is a tribute to their organizing ability; only one student scouting party found its way in, and the spies lost their shoes and coats when discovered and forced to beat a retreat.

Fortunately for the self-control of the rest of the student body, the great day finally arrived. *Restraint Necessary*, primarily intended to raise money for a scholarship in honour of Dr. Leuba, who is retiring this year, performed another function and, in the words of the *News* review, "made the student body toss the cap of its admirable reserve over the mill completely." Mr. E. M. M. Warburg, Lecturer in Modern Art, as an Ed Wynnian master of ceremonies, introduced to his howling audience prominent members of the administration and faculty, all of whom vindicated their positions by being conspicuous hits. During the intermission, posters used to advertise the show were auctioned off by Dr. Fenwick. The six caricatures done by Mr. Wyncie King were bid highest: those of Miss Park, Dr. Gray, Dr. Herben, and Mr. Warburg were bought by Pem East, Rockefeller, Pem West and Merion, respectively, while those of Dr. Leuba and Dr. Fenwick passed into private hands. The proceeds of the posters, combined with the box-office receipts, added nearly $800 to the fund. It is to be hoped that the faculty will discover some worthy object once every year for which to raise money, and make the Faculty Show an annual tradition.

The Gilbert and Sullivan operetta, fortunately long a tradition, was *Patience* this year. The lapse of one year because of Big May Day has not diminished the Glee Club's genius for producing Gilbert and Sullivan. Undoubtedly a large share of the credit is due to Mr. Willoughby, who directed the acting and conducted the music to perfection. For those who have seen the Heavy Dragoons in other productions drill in helter-skelter fashion, the faultless line maintained was amazing. Not only was the detail well done, but the acting was above the common level.

The dance afterward, sponsored by Undergrad and given in the gymnasium, was even more crowded than usual. Its success was certainly not due to the orchestra, since only three pieces out of seven found their way through the woods and fields to Bryn Mawr. In spite of this disaster, the dance went off in a way that showed Bryn Mawr to have mastered the technique of playing hostess collectively. The presence of six or more couples from the younger faculty gave a certain air to the dance which is lacking in a purely undergraduate assemblage. To the alumnae who were in College in the days of faculty-student segregation, it must seem strange to hear of such rapport between the two. We can only say that both professors and undergraduates seem to amuse each other and to enjoy their frequent contacts under the present regime. An editorial in the *News* on May 17th deplored the "attitude of hostility" between faculty and students, and declared that "Undergraduates who do not assume a formal personality when brought into contact with members of the faculty exist, but as a class which stands in brilliant distinction to the masses." We hesitate to quarrel with the *News*, but it seems obvious enough that there is a good deal of friendliness manifested on either side, enough to convince one that professors and students form a congenial group.

To return to the sphere of purely undergraduate activities, it is interesting to observe the present revival of interest in fencing. Under the instruction of M. Fiems, the fencing team has worked up to a high degree of excellence. Although it was defeated by the New York Fencers' Club in the meet on May 16th, the cause may be attributed to lack of experience rather than weak fencing. M. Fiems said that he was "pleased with the way the Bryn Mawr fencers had been working, especially as to form, combativity, vigor, and readiness to touch and defeat their opponents as much as they could. There seems a chance at this point that fencing may become as suddenly popular next year as Duncan Dancing has been for the last several years. Probably the only obstacle to more complete popularity is the fee which it is necessary to charge. However, next year promises to be one of success for the team, as all but two of the varsity fencers are returning to College.

PARAGRAPHS ON VENEZUELA

By L. M. HALEY, 1928

Aroa, a little town buried in jungle in the Andean foothills, was our goal; or more specifically, the old Spanish copper mine in the mountains just back of it. The town is not many miles inland, but nevertheless is exceedingly difficult to reach. There is a splendid paved road from Puerto Cabello to Barquisimieto, and you can travel by automobile part way on this. It leads through the narrow cobbled streets of Puerto Cabello, past the ruined tangerine walls of a Spanish fort dominating the *cordillera* which faces the sea, and straight into miles of cocoanut groves. It is only when you leave the main road and take the dusty one to Marín that the jungle begins to close in on you. You cross muddy rivers and chill under infinite layers of fronds and leaves. Now and then you pass an Indian, very dark and clad only in ragged trousers and faded sweater. He will always be carrying a *machete*. It began to rain at this stage of our journey. There was a dull singing among the million leaves, a rain-crater or two in the streams. The leaves were so thick that the rain sounded as though it were dropping on a wooden roof over our heads.

But after four hours of jolting even our orchid-hung green tunnel began to seem monotonous. We sighed with relief and exhaustion when finally we shot out of its gloom into a bowl in the hills. There was a dirty board station at the edge of the jungle. The dusk was already gathering, the sun having just sunk behind the western ridges. The car did not stop at the station, but rattled on through the edge of Aroa, and on up again into the mountains. We sped past houses painted in jewel-colors, and glowing with startling intensity in this particular twilit atmosphere. A few women in gaudy Mother Hubbards stood with folded arms under the acacias at their doors. Naked babies hid behind their parents' skirts.

Our house was hung on the mountainside, just above the *quebrada,* or stream. A high wall and a terraced garden shut it away from the trail which skirted the stream below it. At the foot of this wall the Indians from the *monte,* which converged behind the house, always stopped to wash their feet and don sandals and coats (required by law in the villages) before proceeding to Aroa.

The house was very old, perhaps a hundred years or more. Its walls were two feet thick and its beams and floorboards hand-hewn. The principal room was paneled with dark clapboards, but the dining and bedrooms had whitewashed walls against which the primitive black furniture and calico hangings contrasted effectively. A verandah, with a bamboo roof, ran the length of the house and overlooked the terraced garden. Every kind of tropic bird frequented this garden; everything grew in it: jessamine, fruit trees, gardenia and hibiscus, the cloudy bougainvillea, the spotted caster-oil tree, the bamboo, that ambush for snakes, and the innocent rose tree.

The native servants, part Indian, part Spanish, were not too efficient. But they were picturesque. The female servants wore the most brilliant lawns and calicoes the village afforded, over a half dozen eyeletted petticoats. The house boy got into starched whites to serve the meals, but when he was killing turkeys or scrubbing the verandah he put on denim. When he scrubbed, he knelt in the wet part to wash the dry. Months of telling him to keep working back in the dry as he scrubbed made no impression. He was about fifteen years old, a sturdy boy with a shy smile and enormous hands and feet. His hair was always tossed into dull elf-locks. I never got to the point of understanding his Spanish. I remember one night when I took him into the small firelit kitchen to ask the cook to translate for me. Her I could understand without difficulty. We found her squatting before the stove, into which she was poking wood. Her straight black hair was bound up with scarlet and turquoise ribbons and glistened in the red stove-light. I particularly remember her green lawn dress with white dots in it, and the black velvet bands with which the skirt was trimmed. She was a languid spinster of advancing age, with sad, grey eyes and sunken cheeks. She was respected to an unusual degree in the village. We had a very satisfactory conversation while she knelt thrusting wood into the roaring stove and I sat on the heavy kitchen chair, and Francico, the house boy, put on his big black felt and prepared to walk to his mother's house near Aroa. María and Francico told me all about their feud with the village witch, Isabela, who they feared would ambush them some night with a *machete*. We became so friendly that María told me about her health, whipping out her false teeth with a conjurer's gesture as an ultimate favor. The teeth grinned in the light from the stove door for a moment before she put them into her mouth again. At that I wished her *buenos noches* and left.

One morning a vegetable woman from the *monte* came early with a bag of cabbages. María squatted on the kitchen porch, poked and punched the heads to test their hardness. She had selected two and was inspecting a third when a black scorpion dropped out of the frilled leaves almost at her feet. She sprang up, screaming, for the black scorpion is deadly. But the woman from the *monte* burst into peals of laughter; she kicked the intervening cabbages out of her way and set her thin sandal on the creature. The insect is like rubber—a difficult thing to crush. She managed it, however, and still laughing at the effeteness of María, tied her money in her handkerchief with her teeth, shouldered her sack of cabbages and went her way.

The mine itself is hundreds of years old, but recently immense new bodies of copper ore have been found in it. Whole mountains are honeycombed with tunnels, all sweltering hot and permeated with an overpowering odor of ammonia from the droppings of a million or so of bats. The Indian miners work naked, and for very short shifts. The heart cannot stand the strain of such an atmosphere for more than a few hours together. The miner puts on his coat and trousers at the mouth of the tunnel, whistles to his dog who, with a crowd of starveling, mangy, good-humored companions has been waiting for him, and eats his banana and rice under the nearest shade tree. On pay day the flute players and sweet-sellers gather about him on the hill in front of the office. He buys candy and cakes from children who carry them in the great flat wooden trays their mothers use for washing-boards at the stream. Our *minero* then goes down the valley to the hot cobbled streets of Aroa, bound for a cockfight in the *teatro*, the walls of which looking as though they had been painted with sour cream, rise above the trees of the *plaza*, just ahead.

THE ALUMNAE BOOKSHELF

INVINCIBLE LOUISA: The Story of the Author of "Little Women," *by Cornelia Meigs*. Little, Brown, and Company, 1933.

"Written primarily for younger readers," the publishers say, but readers of all ages can hardly fail to be charmed by Miss Meigs' vigorous and sympathetic portrait. With her first presentation of the "small, red, but extremely vigorous and sound baby, who, so it was settled even then, was to be called Louisa May Alcott," Miss Meigs suggests what the future was to bring to Louisa and the rest of the Alcott family. "It was a time of great happiness, peace and security, those first two years of the Alcotts' married life. Happiness was to continue, sometimes interrupted in strange ways; but peace and security were not to come again for a very long time. When they were achieved, they were to be won for them by Louisa; by Louisa battling against overwhelming odds for half her life, bound never to be conquered, even though every circumstance seemed to be against them all." Miss Meigs goes on, with a wealth of picturesque detail and life-like portraiture, to tell the story; the childhood enviable in spite of its vicissitudes, the transformation of the long-legged tomboy into the shy and sensitive girl, the long struggles and the final unexpected fame. It is a moving story, told with a sympathy too sure and swift ever to fringe on sentimentality. Miss Meigs is wise enough never to over-point the moral, but her quiet emphasis on the heroic quality in Louisa, her gentle but incisive comments, as well as the story itself, will stir many a young reader to admiration for Louisa's high courage and gallantry.

Older readers will perhaps find their chief interest in the picture the book gives of a conception of life, and a way of living, that within their own memories has come to belong to a detached and remote past, rather than to a continuous and living tradition. The book is the history of a family, no less than the biography of an individual. It is the story of a family held together by no material security nor stability (Miss Meigs notes the fact that in the first twenty-eight years of Louisa's life the family achieved the record of twenty-nine moves), but by bonds of affection and loyalty which for its members were stronger than anything else in the world. One of the most moving pages in the book is that which tells how, at the end of the unhappy Fruitlands experiment, that early communistic wave broke against the strong rock of the Alcott family, and receded, leaving a dark memory, but an undivided family. They went their way together, "poor as poverty, but serene as heaven," as their saying was. Miss Meigs tells a characteristic story of Bronson Alcott returning from a lecture tour and producing as the fruit of his enterprise a single dollar. "Another year, I shall do better," he observed cheerfully. After a minute of choking silence, "I call that doing *very well*," said Abba Alcott, as she threw her arms around his neck. It was to the maintenance and care of the family that Louisa's whole energy and whole life were devoted; as Miss Meigs says in her concluding sentence, "that was the whole of what she had wanted from life,— just to take care of them all."

And so, while eager young readers turn the pages swiftly to see what happened to Louisa next, older readers will tend rather to linger over the book, reflecting with Miss Meigs on life as the Alcotts lived it and as we live it.

MARGARET GILMAN, 1919.

THE ROMAN WAY, by *Edith Hamilton*. W. W. Norton & Co., Inc., New York, 1932. pp. 281. $3.00.

This book, written with the ease and charm which have won favor for *The Greek Way*, bears witness on every page to Miss Hamilton's statement that she has long read Latin for her own pleasure. Her illustrations and her quotations, often in felicitous translations, are not the hackneyed ones that are to be found in the ordinary handbooks; they are such as could only be secured by the thoughtful reader who has ranged widely and independently. She has been successful in her attempt to give us her picture of what the Romans were as they appear in their great authors, and the picture is a very attractive one. The tumultuous audiences who witnessed Plautus' plays, the cultivated group for whom Terence really wrote, the political turmoil of the age of Cicero, the peaceful life of Horace's Rome, the vice and decadence of the age of Juvenal, are all described in a manner which shows that Miss Hamilton has lived in her subject. The picture of Juvenal's Rome, illustrated, of course, from Tacitus, too, and contrasted with the asceticism of the Stoic teachers of the day, is especially successful. The estimates of Catullus the love poet, of Horace the artist, of Virgil and Livy the Romantics, are sure in their appreciation and their understanding. Curiously enough, there is not a word about the most original genius of the Romans, Lucretius. Yet the pages of the *De rerum natura* could have made their contribution to *The Roman Way*.

On historical and political matters Miss Hamilton is less sure. She is particularly unfortunate in her statements about Cicero's governorship of Cilicia. He did not expect the governorship when he came forward as a candidate for the consulship. He made a deal with one of his opponents to avoid the possibility. When—contrary to his expectation, as he himself says—he was forced to go out to a province, he did not accept the task in the uncomplaining manner which Miss Hamilton indicates. "Do everything you can to keep my governorship from being prolonged," he writes to Atticus. "I can't tell you how I long for the city and how hard it is to stand the insipidity of all this." Cicero did not while in Cilicia "live for months as a fighting general." About Caesar it is hardly accurate to say that he "conquered the west and made northern Africa a province of the Roman Empire."

But in spite of some misstatements and some historical judgments which seem to be open to question, the book is written with a genuine feeling for the life and the literature of the Romans.

LILY ROSS TAYLOR,
Professor of Latin, Bryn Mawr College.

The college library has received two unusual gifts from alumnae this spring. One is a copy of the earliest printed Albertus Magnus, the gift of Eleanor Wood Whitehead, of the Class of 1902. This book was printed in the fifteenth century (about 1470), "probably from the first type ever made."

The other is a copy of Violet Oakley's *Law Triumphant*, given by Gertrude Houston Woodward, of the Class of 1932. The portfolio contains reproductions of some of Miss Oakley's best-known murals and portrait drawings made at Geneva during the 1927, 1928, and 1929 sessions of the League.

CLASS NOTES

Ph.D. and Graduate Notes

Editor: MARY ALICE HANNA PARRISH
(Mrs. J. C. Parrish)
Vandalia, Missouri.

1889

No Editor Appointed.

1890

No Editor Appointed.

1891

No Editor Appointed.

1892

Class Editor: EDITH WETHERILL IVES
(Mrs. F. M. Ives)
145 E. 35th St., New York City.

1893

Class Editor: SUSAN WALKER FITZGERALD
(Mrs. Richard Y. FitzGerald)
7 Greenough Ave., Jamaica Plain, Mass.

Very little grist has come to my mill this month. I think it is because we have all been silent so long that it seems as if we ought to have something very important with which to appear upon the scene. But as a matter of fact the little items of current news are of real interest and are what make us feel that we are in friendly touch with one another. Please write me during the summer or in the fall something of your summer doings.

Lucy Donnelly writes: "My personal life is merged in official business. . . . I was in England at work last summer, but am staying in America this year for the Admissions Committee that meets late in July."

Lucy Lewis says she is feeling the depression —but Lucy was always original. She says she is like the man who, when asked what he thought about going off the gold standard, replied, "I have been living on the copper standard so long that I think it will make no difference to me." Let's hope for Lucy's sake that copper will go up!

Susan Walker FitzGerald reports much activity at the moment. At this time of year her work as Treasurer of the New England Regional Scholarships Committee is very heavy, for money does not come easily these days, while candidates do. Also as President of the Women's Alliance of her Church, she has to plan now for the Program for next winter's meetings and the Annual Fair that is the great money-raising activity.

Her daughter Rebecca (B. M. 1926) was married on June 22nd to Walter Beckman Pederson. Nancy (B. M. 1923) works in the Brookline Public Library. Susan (B. M. 1929) teaches in Public Junior High in Jamaica Plain, and her son Leigh is just completing his sophomore year at Princeton.

1894

Class Editor: ABBY BRAYTON DURFEE
(Mrs. Randall N. Durfee)
19 Highland Ave., Fall River, Mass.

It is a great disappointment that I cannot be at the picnic of 1894-1897. My two lovely granddaughters are with me this summer and I felt I must be at home. In all my class letters, I have remarked that I have served for 25 years as Secretary and Collector combined, and suggesting that somebody take my job, but I have heard no reply. In fact, I hear from very few.

Elizabeth Clark writes from Brooklyn, that her father died last May, and of her mother she says: "Mother has been hovering between life and death ever since, a marvelous spirit in a very fragile body. As for me, I am trying not to degenerate into a housekeeping 'automaton.'"

Emilie Martin writes from Mount Holyoke of her disappointment at not coming this June. She is a member of the Board of Admissions and will be at the college through July.

Elizabeth Hench is living in Carlisle, Pa. Her address is 19 Pomfret Apartments.

Edith Hamilton's address is 24 Gramercy Park, New York. She has published a delightful book, "The Roman Way," a companion to her former book, "The Greek Way."

Sarah Darlington Hamilton writes from Yuma, Arizona: "What a pleasure it would be to attend the Reunion, but distance makes that impossible. Our older boy, Joseph, has his job in the Government Civil Service in Brownwood, Texas, though his salary is cut to the bone. Our younger boy, Louis, has graduated with honors from the University of Arizona, at Tucson. My husband had the greatest per cent of first-class grapefruit that went through the packing house, but even that did not yield sufficient return to pay for all the expense. Do give my kindest regards to every member of '94."

Those who came for Reunion were: Marie Minor, Martha La Porte, Mary Harris, Fay MacCracken Stockwell, Margaret Shearman and Anna West.

1895

Class Editor: SUSAN FOWLER
The Brearley School
610 East 83rd St., New York City.

The Class of 1895 mustered nine members for the buffet luncheon at Wyndham on Monday, June 12th. We enjoyed meeting again not only ourselves but three other contemporary classes. '95's representatives were Lucy Baird, Louise Davis Brooks, Sue Fowler, Madeline Harris Brown, Julia Langdon Loomis, Edith Pettit Borie, Esther Steele, Frances Swift Tatnall, and our contribution to the whole Alumnae Association, Elizabeth Bent Clark, its President, who much enhances our class pride. The younger Alumnae may not as yet join with us in our pleasure at our survival powers. We looked to one another grandly alert, and, socially speaking, productive!

1896

Class Editor: ABIGAIL CAMP DIMON
1411 Genesee St., Utica, N. Y.

The announcement of the Spring Inspection of the Brooklyn Botanic Garden held on Tuesday, May 9th, contains the following: "3. Photographs of Illustrations in the *Codex Juliae Aniciae*, of Dioscorides, 512 A. D. The original plant paintings date from the first century A. D. They were drawn by Dioscorides, a physician of the Roman Army at the time of the Emperor Nero. He traveled widely over the Roman Empire collecting and drawing pictures of medicinal plants. The *Codex* of 512 A. D., in the Vienna National Library, is a copy of the original manuscript of Dioscorides, made as a wedding present for a princess of the Eastern Empire, Julia Anicia. It is the oldest existing Ms. herbal. These photographs were lent for this exhibit by Miss Pauline Goldmark, of the Hartsdale (N. Y.) Garden Club." The photographs were made for Pauline on one of her recent visits to Vienna by permission of the Vienna National Library.

Effie Whittredge writes from "Planterrose," Moumour, par Oloron Ste. Marie, Basses-Pyrénées: "I have been over here in France ever since the eighth of February, visiting a friend of mine who has a chateau in this marvelous country. We intended to go to Rome for April, motoring from here in my friend's Ford (I did not bring my car with me this time), but the financial upsets at home have made us stick right here. I have had two short, very interesting trips into Northern Spain, the old Kingdom of Aragon. I am sailing home on May 14th, and hope to take in the reunion."

Those of '96 who enjoyed Mary Boude Woolman's hospitality at her Valley Forge Camp during the 1929 reunion and are anticipating the class supper there this spring will be in-

terested to hear that on Saturday, May 13th, Louis Edouard de la Boulaye, French Ambassador to the United States, spoke at the dedication of a tablet in Valley Forge to General Louis Lebegue Duportail, an engineer in Washington's Army. The tablet was erected as a tribute to the work of General Duportail, who was the designer of the forts at Valley Forge. The plans drawn by the General were found in the rafters of the house now occupied by Mr. Henry N. Woolman, Jr., (Mary's husband), President of the Valley Forge Board of the University of Pennsylvania, and the tablet is on the wall of this structure.

Edward Porter, son of Ruth Furness Porter, volunteers some criticisms of '96 notes and information about class members as follows: "As a member of the American Society of Bryn Mawr Husbands, I would like to register a protest. The class of '96 has been getting very lax lately. It seems only fair that husbands should have their class notes to read. I am sure if Frances Perkins had statistics on the readers of the Alumnae Bulletin they would be found to be mainly husbands. Your class is so lax that the only way to find out about them is through other classes. Thus Pauline Goldmark should be put to shame that one has to read about a whoopee party held by '97 to find out about her.

"E. B. K. stayed with Ruth W. Porter, whom you all remember as Ruth W. Furness, the shy little girl from Chicago. E. B. K., by the way, is attending a meeting of the Society of University Women in Minneapolis. The great event occured May 13th and 14th. Edith F. Wyatt was invited to lunch Saturday along with Mrs. Harold Ickes. When I and my wife, Audrey F. Porter of the class of 1922 arrived, there was a discussion going on about the Illinois Legislature, Negroes, Indians, and I believe Mary Hopkins, who cries when arrested.

"Sunday arrived and nothing much happened, but in the afternoon Miss Mary Herr of the Class of 1909 and Mrs. Nat Blatchford of 1908 arrived to call.

"E. B. K. is stopping in Madison on her way back to see Mrs. Johnson (Elizabeth Hopkins).

"Edith Wyatt is anxious to go to a beer garden."

REUNION NOTES

With all its old zest for being together and all its old expectations of finding "durable satisfactions" in its reunion, '96 met this year for the first time since 1929. The Committee, having been duly warned by Ruth Furness Porter that there should be a minimum of stunts, and plenty of time for discussion, and believing that the essence of a happy reunion is freedom within a simple schedule, began the program by a picnic supper at Valley Forge.

Lucky '96 to have Mary Boude Woolman's camp to go to and her hospitality to enjoy! On the porch of the cabin in the woods overlooking the Valley Creek, twenty-three of us gathered around a long table, set with bowls of coreopsis and white iris. Here, after a delicious meal, our president, Elizabeth Kirkbride, called on each in turn for her history, and we sat from six until nearly eleven, till the stars came out above the woods and the valley stream could be heard, but no longer seen, below us. Our president is in her second term as director of the North Atlantic Section of the American Association of University Women.

Lydia Boring told of her own and her sister's experiences in China. Mary Mendinhall Mullin of a trip to see the eclipse; Anna Green Annan showed photographs of two beautiful grandchildren, and Clara Colton Worthington described her perfect daughter-in-law. Clara is soon to fly to Salt Lake for a visit. Anna Scattergood Hoag told of her three married sons and of our class baby's newly-adopted little boy. Lucy Baird told of her hand weaving; Mary Hill Swope gave news of her family, especially of a new granddaughter, her namesake, and told of her daughter Henrietta, whose job it is, at the Harvard Observatory, to shepherd the variable stars. Georgiana King reported the success of her graduates and the recognition of the Bryn Mawr Art Department by other colleges. Ida Olgivie, Director of Geology at Barnard and second in command in the Department of Geology at Columbia, gave an account of her two farms. Hilda Justice's latest trip was to Syria, Persia and Russia and she hopes to go on a pack trip in Canada this summer. Emma Linburg Tobin is a National Director of the Farm and Garden Association and the proud mother of a junior, Peggy Tobin. Clara Farr is Registrar of the Pennsylvania School of Social Work in addition to her many other positions.

In answer to a question as to news from Masa Dogura Uchida, Caroline McCormick Slade described her visit to Masa and her experiences in Mukden in September, 1931, at the time of the first bombardment. It was a bit of history in the making told with great vividness, and for the rest of the evening Carrie held us spellbound with her graphic tale.

On Sunday we followed the crowd to the Alumnae Meeting with its announcement of the final details of Miss Thomas' gift of the Deanery; to the Alumnae lunch, and the tea to the Seniors. At Tirzah Nichols' tea party on Sunday afternoon, in her lovely new house, '96 continued its reminiscences with a sonnet written for the reunion by Charlotte McLean and read by our President.

A Revival of the Sonnet
FORTY YEARS AFTER
By a Paleolithic of the
Freshman English Class of '92-'93

It runs a b b a, a b b a,
The octette I for '96 would frame
"Who lisped in sonnets for the sonnets came."
Precocious class! it billowed on its way.
My octette lifts its crest in radiant spray
And thunders on to sound our classmates' fame
Who mountains climb or woman's suffrage claim
Or shine in letters, art or pedagogic sway.
My sextette runs c c, d d, e e,
But proper sextette it will never be,
It ought, but will not, fall and ebb
Our class of grannies always will be "deb."
Let each and all our arbor vitae preen,
And keep perennial our living green.

Pauline Goldmark told of making photostat copies of an old codex of Botany (now in Vienna) made by Nero's physician; Katherine Cook told of her niece Katherine Jones' approaching wedding, and her own plans for Norway this summer. There were many messages from the absentees: May Jewett was unable to come for the cheerful reason that business is picking up; Rebecca Mattson Darlington has sailed for Italy where she will attend a summer institute at Perugia, and will see Mrs. Giles; Mary Crawford Dudley is already at Les Eboulements; Polly McKeehan Core has been in Cambridge while her daughter was at Boston University. Josephine Holman Boross has spent the winter in New York near her two new grandchildren; Eleanor Lattimore is Associate Director, Curriculum of Social Work of the University of Buffalo, a "fascinating and utterly absorbing job;" Cora Baird Jeanes is taking a house in England for the summer; Mary Brown Waite's husband has just completed the marvelous new terminal in Cincinnati; Edith Wyatt wrote of recent journeys in the West; Clarissa Smith Dey is already in Maine.

At the joint picnic at Wyndham for '94, '95, '96 and '97, on Monday, Florence King, Abba Dimon, and Dora Keen Handy made their appearance. Dora arrived by aeroplane from California, where she has been recovering from a serious accident. Abba is Assistant to the Director at the School of Horticulture, of which Hilda is a member of the Board, and Florence is active in city Garden Club work in New York, and is going abroad for the summer.

On Monday afternoon, '96 carried out a plan of long standing to visit Hannah Cadbury Pyle's Rose Gardens at West Grove and enjoyed tea in the quaint gardens of the old Red Rose Inn. There the motto on the old sun-dial, "Time takes all but Memories," seemed to speak for us of our renewed joy in being together.

1897

Class Editor: FRIEDRIKA HEYL
104 Lake Shore Drive, East, Dunkirk, N. Y.

On Friday, June 10th, having been duly authorized by our perennial President, M. Campbell, to assign rooms to our classmates, decorate tables, etc., Sue Blake and F. Heyl, who happened to be on the campus because she had been visiting at Marion Park's for several weeks, opened the Class Headquarters in Pembroke West. Everyone was delighted to find that our rooms were all together on the second floor. During the day, twelve turned up —Cornelia Greene King; Anna Lawther, about to sail for Europe to meet her nephew and niece who are returning from a trip around the world; Elizabeth Esterly from Portland, Oregon, who had not been East for years; Rebecca Chickering, Elizabeth Caldwell Fountain, Euphemia Mann, Elizabeth Higginson Jackson, Marion Taber, Clara Vail Brooks, Mary Peckham Tubby, Elizabeth Sedgwick Shaw, Mary Campbell. We regretted cancellations from Ida Gifford and Elizabeth Seymour Angel.

Late in the afternoon three '97 cars took us out to the Shipley School Farm where, due to the gracious hospitality of Eleanor Brownell, Alice Howland and Alice Weist, we had a delightful hour at a garden-party tea where youth and old age wandered together among the delphinium and roses—a really charming setting and a peppy school band. We all enjoyed visiting with Delia Smith Johnston, '26, who is a teacher at the school.

We had our Class Supper that evening in the Common Room. Our main line classmates, Grace Albert, C. Stubbs, A. Thomas, the two Pennypackers, E. Brownell, M. Converse, Mary Fay, B. Towle, A. Weist, and Helen Biddle, brought the number up to twenty-four and we all sat down at one long narrow table decorated with small branches of blooming linden from Sue Blake's trees.

Our President was never in better form. Everything went off most happily during the meal (a delicious supper, by the way, served by the college), and later when she presided at a most informal business meeting and read messages from absent classmates. I regret that it is not possible to speak of all these messages which were enjoyed so thoroughly—but a letter from Florence Butler, whom we thought we had lost, brought a very welcome *Aloha* from Hawaii.

We learned from M. Campbell that there had been a unanimous response to the suggestion of a gift to the college in honor of Margaret Nichols Smith. The gift of books (on Child Psychology, Education and Philosophy to be chosen by the Library and the departments interested), together with the amount of the contributions to the Alumnae Fund already made, and the larger amount that the class hopes to collect for this year, will constitute our reunion gift to the college. The class gave gifts of books to Louise Esterly and Betsy Jackson.

Between the Garden Party on Monday, where we were all guests of Betsy Jackson, and the Senior singing, we went to Mary Converse's lovely house for supper and had a happy repetition of that delightful event which has been such a big part of our reunion fun for so many years.

Elizabeth Esterley's husband and son and Bessie Shaw's husband added a very pleasant note to the occasion.

We must leave it to the imagination to fill in the gaps between the outstanding events with informal breakfasts and luncheons or tea at the College Inn and at G. Ely's; the evenings in Miss Thomas' beautiful garden—not the least part of her wonderful gift to the college; the drives to Valley Forge along roadsides lovely with roses and fragrant with honeysuckle; the hour spent in the music room on Monday morning, a cool breeze blowing in from the Music Walk, where Mr. Willoughby played the organ given by Clara Vail Brooks.

The '97 banner which hung outside of Pembroke West has been hauled in and returned to the Alumnae Office. May we meet again before the silk flag which hung on our door is entirely disintegrated! And meanwhile our sincere thanks for the hospitality extended to us by everyone connected with the college.

1898

Class Editor: EDITH SCHOFF BOERICKE
(Mrs. John J. Boericke)
328 Brookway, Merion Station, Pa.

1899

Editor: CAROLYN TROWBRIDGE BROWN LEWIS
(Mrs. H. Radnor Lewis)
451 Milton Road, Rye, N. Y.

Something new in book publicity is an event hailed with enthusiasm by everyone in the publishing and advertising fields. And the latest, ingenious novelty is the origination of a '99er, Laura Peckham Waring. It depicts in plasticine, in a most realistic and wonderfully clever fashion, the setting of the imaginary town of Deptford, Connecticut, the characteristic New England village selected by Cornelia Penfield as the scene of her thrilling mystery tale, *After the Deacon was Murdered.* These miniature landscapes, as Laura calls them (we hope she has them patented), have been exhibited in Putnam's in New York, Bridgeport, Stamford, New Haven, Plainfield, Montclair and Bamberger's in Newark.

We just have the announcement, no details, that Molly Thurber Dennison's daughter, Mary, was married to David Walter Stickney, on Saturday, May 27th, at Framingham, where Molly has a lovely old house.

Emma Guffey Miller writes: "My article (May BULLETIN) has just been republished in a Pittsburgh paper and I am receiving requests from college professors to use it in their studies. All of this, of course, would turn my head, if it were not for the fact that Mr. Miller now outranks me by being just appointed a member of the Interstate Commerce Commission."

Dear Classmates:

You will recall that at our last reunion after all expenses were paid we had a tidy sum left over. Some of the class spendthrifts wanted to "blow it in" at once on further enjoyment but the thrifty members voted to keep it as a flower fund for '99 obsequies. It was given into my hands and deposited in a trust company in Pittsburgh where it drew interest until the late unpleasantness when the bank went into the hands of a receiver.

When this fund was under discussion some of the class requested elaborate floral emblems; Eve Walker asked for a blanket of violets; Katie Mid, true to class colors, requested a wreath of green orchids, while Callie insisted on a vase of Madonna lilies. Now they may have to be satisfied with much less and rest "with a little Bryn Mawr Daisy nodding gently overhead."

May this be a lesson both to the extravagant and the thrifty and let us hope that under the new banking laws the sarcophagi of '99 may yet be adorned with worthy floral offerings.

Yours still hoping, GUFFEY.

1900

Class Editor: LOUISE CONGDON FRANCIS
(Mrs. Richard S. Francis)
414 Old Lancaster Road, Haverford, Pa.

Fourteen members of the Class came to an informal supper on the veranda of the College Inn on Saturday evening before Commencement. Amusing toasts were made by Grace Jones McClure on the Advantages of Middle Age; by Cornelia Halsey Kellogg on the Delinquencies of Middle Age; and by Emily Palmer on the Disadvantages of Being Young. Louise Congdon Francis was toastmistress. The other ten present were: Edna Floersheim Bamberger, Helen MacCoy, Helen McKeen, Alletta van Reypen Korff, Renée Mitchell Righter, Lois Farnham Horn, Marion Hickman Quattrone, Susan Dewees, Elsie Dean Findley and Ellen Baltz Fultz. Helen MacCoy was master of ceremonies, chief cook and bottle washer and good fairy to the Class. The success of the "reunionette" is due to her.

On April 22, 1933, there was presented at the Shakespeare Theatre in New York a ballet pantomime entitled *Namba or the Third Statue*. The Aleta Dore Ballet performed the pantomime, but the scenario was written by our own gifted and versatile Grace Latimer Jones McClure.

The Class will all sympathize with Johanna Kroeber Mosenthal in the death of her mother.

The Class will all sympathize most deeply with Frances Rush Crawford, whose son has recently been killed in an automobile accident.

1901

Class Editor: HELEN CONVERSE THORPE
(Mrs. Warren Thorpe)
15 East 64th St., New York City.

Ella Sealy Newell writes that all winter she has been personally bossing a gang of unemployed men from eight A. M., to five P. M., landscaping public parks and boulevards in Galveston. She is also on the Board of Red Cross Nursing and the Christian League.

1902

Class Editor: ANNE ROTAN HOWE
(Mrs. Thorndike Howe)
77 Revere St., Boston, Mass.

1903

Class Editor: GERTRUDE DIETRICH SMITH
(Mrs. Herbert Knox Smith)
Farmington, Conn.

1904

Class Editor: EMMA O. THOMPSON
320 S. 42nd St., Philadelphia, Pa.

A letter from Sue Swindell Nuckols brings good news. "How many grandmothers have we in 1904? You may now add me to the list. Douglas Montaigne Bell, 3rd, arrived safely of the morning of May 1st, so Bryn Mawr acquired a mother and a grandmother at the same time. Margaret and the baby are both fine. We have had them with us since May 12th, and it has been a godsend to both my husband and me to have that precious baby in the house right now—it has given us a new interest in life when we most needed it.

"My eldest son Carlyle will be at home for a couple of weeks this month before starting in as interne at Union Memorial Hospital in Baltimore for a year. He receives his Doctor's degree from Johns Hopkins this June. He is a member of Alpha Omega Alpha, the honorary medical fraternity." Doubtless you recall that Margaret, the mother of Sue's grandson, was Queen of the May in the Fete of 1928.

The Constance Lewis Memorial Scholarship has been awarded for the year 1933-1934 to Sophie Hunt the daughter of Hope Woods Hunt.

Agnes Gillinder Carson's daughter, Emmeline Margaret, graduated this June at Bryn Mawr.

Mary James writes to me from Wuchang, China, that the hospital work is as strenuous as ever and the demands for aid very great.

Lydia Boring sends me this fascinating bit of news: Radiogram received from Alice Boring, sent May 18th by the amateur radio station of the Physics Department of Yenching University, Peiping, where she teaches—picked up by an amateur station at Carmel, California, and mailed to Philadelphia, reaching here May 23rd. It said that "Yenching University expected to complete its spring semester, that the spirit of faculty and students was splendid and that Peiping was still peaceful."

During the hurricane of May 24th, 1933, many campus trees were uprooted—one of the large maple trees of Senior Row was blown down and its branches, falling against our class tree, broke off about two thirds.

Ethel Peck Lombardi's daughter Carolyn, (B. M. 1932) was married on May 8th, to Charles Renton McCormick, Jr., on her arrival in New York after a year abroad.

1905

Class Editor: ELEANOR LITTLE ALDRICH
(Mrs. Talbot Aldrich)
59 Mount Vernon St., Boston, Mass.

Helen Sturgis was scheduled to lecture on May 23rd, at the New York Psychology Center. She is characterized as "Lecturer, Teacher and Student" and her subject, "What is the Bright Side of the Present Crisis?" She writes: "You ask for news of me. I am more deeply than ever entrenched in Freemasonry—or rather, Co-Masonry as the pioneer Order for men and women is called—and I suppose because it is so near and dear to my heart, and to me spells one of the most progressive and vital institutions of the coming era, I seem able to expatiate upon its age-old principles. So I have been lecturing quite a bit this winter on this and kindred subjects. (Would any 1905er in her wildest moments have ever prophesied such a stunt for me!) I have also just 'put on' a small entertainment, not exactly in Freddy's magnificent style, but nevertheless a surprise to my family, for I certainly had never before attempted to write and stage a farce, or write a song. Great fun, though a heap of work."

The class extends its warmest sympathy to Alice Meigs Orr, whose husband died suddenly on June 5th. Her eldest son, Montgomery Meigs Orr, graduated this year from Princeton, with highest honors in Architecture. He and Po plan to carry on his father's business, at least until architectural prospects are brighter. Her second daughter is to spend next winter with Tink, and go to school in Bryn Mawr.

Our sympathy goes also to Marcia Bready Jacobs whose mother died during the winter. Marcia and her husband plan to go to France again this summer to visit her brother.

1906

Class Editor: LOUISE CRUICE STURDEVANT
(Mrs. Edward W. Sturdevant)
c/o 4th Regiment, U. S. Marines, Shanghai.

1907

Class Editor: ALICE HAWKINS
Taylor Hall, Bryn Mawr, Pa.

Anna Buxton Beck came to Commencement to see her niece, Elizabeth Edwards, graduate. She was in fine form and displayed her handsome husky blonde elder son, who bashfully admitted, when questioned, that his mother still sang the old favorites. Bux accosted Mr. Samuel Arthur King on the campus, and challenged him to remember her. Without an instant's hesitation, he began to quote, giving a perfect imitation of Bux as Silenus.

Minnie List Chalfant had good reason to feel proud of her daughter who graduated *magna cum laude*, ranking eighth in her class.

Bobby Ristine and Bunny Brownell Daniels also attended some of the Commencement Week festivities, so that, with the regular campus dwellers, 1907 had a very respectable gathering. Eunice Schenck, we are glad to report, is feeling herself again after several months' illness. Tink Meigs has pretty well committed herself to Bryn Mawr by buying a house not far from the Church of the Redeemer. Hortense Flexner King has about decided to abandon her attic, where so many of her students love to visit her and her husband, but will move only a few yards away into one of the new housekeeping apartments of the College Inn. By the way, don't miss her poems in the *New Yorker* and other magazines.

Helen Roche Tobin arrived the day after Commencement to see her daughter graduate from the Baldwin School, where she has made a name for herself in all sorts of activities. She hopes to enter Bryn Mawr in the fall.

Dorothy Howland Leatherbee's son, John, graduated this year from Harvard. He had the leading part in the Hasty Pudding show this spring. Her elder daughter, Virginia, is a Freshman at Vassar, and is Treasurer of her class. The younger girl, Anne, will be a Senior at High School next year, and wants to take a business course after that.

Janet Russell now lives in Greenfield, Mass., all year 'round, and finds "country life more satisfactory than city life." She is the Vice-President of the Deerfield Valley Art Association, which put on a three weeks show of local art. She says that her title is just another name for janitor and general hostess. She is also President of the Girls Club and an active member of the Board of Organized Work of the hospital.

Dorothy Wight is Secretary for Membership and Art Classes at the Art Museum in Montclair. It is really remarkable to find 1907 so active in this line. Bess Wilson took to painting landscapes a few years ago, and they weren't bad either, but she has decided to put her spare time into music, studying piano with Julius Leefson of Philadelphia.

Tony Cannon recently flew from New York to Detroit to address a convention of social workers.

1908

Class Editor: HELEN CADBURY BUSH
Haverford, Pa.

1909

Class Editor: HELEN B. CRANE
70 Willett St., Albany, N. Y.

Frances Browne writes: "Life at Milton becomes always more active and absorbing. I have this year taken under my 'directing' wing a primary school called the Milton Preparatory School, which is a delightful addition of some 45 youngsters from kindergarten age on up. I find companionship with many energetic people in many interesting neighboring schools; and various opportunities to compare notes and confer on common enterprises and problems. This being a time of necessity when we must think things through and recognize real values everywhere, one might hope to unearth a few stout virtues in one's soul; but I find nothing but the same old delinquencies. . . . Here's hoping we may all be able, like our phoenix, to rise from the flames of our present daily living with wings flapping in triumphant greeting to our 25th reunion in 1934."

It is always cheering to the editor to find any of our reticent selves appearing in print. Some weeks ago the humorous page of the *Saturday Evening Post* carried a parody on "If" (with apologies to no one, since it isn't in verse), on the noble art of sales resistance. It was signed Margaret Ames Wright; and if she is going in for wit we think she should contribute some of it to our columns.

Gene Miltenberger Ustick sends in this startling bit of news out of a clear sky: "Lee has got a research fellowship at the Huntington Library in Pasadena. We have rented our house (in Cambridge) from July 1st for a year and are going to California almost immediately, taking in Dorothy North, the Fair, St. Louis and all points and relatives west, until they will have no more of us nor we of them— and then across the desert."

Mary Nearing Spring: "Sorry not to write you sooner, but the Springs hadn't any plans

till a week ago. We are sailing for England, June 24th (my first look at it), to be gone till September, we hope."

1910

Class Editor: KATHERINE ROTAN DRINKER
(Mrs. Cecil K. Drinker)
71 Rawson Road, Brookline, Mass.

1911

Class Editor: ELIZABETH TAYLOR RUSSELL
(Mrs. John F. Russell, Jr.)
Watch Hill, Rhode Island.

Margaret Dulles Edwards has been taking a course in Religious Education in New York.

Ruth Wells writes that she is more radical than ever and has her face set firmly toward the Left.

Helen Emerson Chase ran the Providence Flower Show in May.

Ruth Vickery Holmes' two daughters have been spending the spring in Bermuda.

Catherine Delano Grant plans to sail on the "Minnetonka" on June 23rd, with all her children to spend the summer with "Scottie" in Dinard. The two oldest boys will return in the fall for school and college. Catherine will probably settle down somewhere in Europe for the winter.

Norvelle Brown will spend the summer in New Canaan.

Louise Russell will be in Cooperstown with her sister.

1912

Class Editor: GLADYS SPRY AUGUR
(Mrs. Wheaton Augur)
820 Camino Atalaya, Santa Fé, N. M.

Carlotta Welles Briggs has a second son, born in New York about the middle of May. She, her husband and the two children have returned to France.

Dickson Hunt, Pinney's oldest son, graduated from Solebury School this June. He was the only Senior to receive his diploma with honor. In addition he won the prize for the highest record in scholarship, character and spirit for four years. Dickson will enter Haverford College in the fall. Later he expects to study medicine.

Ruth Akers Dixon has written from Long Beach, Cal., "However, you wanted to know about the earthquake. Its strength was 4.6 as compared to San Francisco's 2.9. But theirs lasted nearly two minutes and ours lasted eleven seconds. Their water mains broke so they were helpless in fighting the fires that naturally broke out. Here ours stayed whole so all fires were under control within a few hours. But all of our fire stations but one fell, two fireman were killed, and nearly every school went down, at least was damaged too much to use again. So after four weeks of vacation the schools reopened in bungalows hastily constructed, and as there are not enough of these, all pupils have a half day session. But if the quake had not come when it did —at 5.55 p. m.—the death list would have numbered many thousands. As it was, even the business section was nearly empty, all the schools, theaters, etc. And it was the brick buildings that went down though more than two thousand bungalows went off their foundations. Our house was undamaged except the chimney fell breaking holes in the roof. Inside a great deal was broken—mirrors, dishes, etc., but none of our plaster fell. It did in many places. My two boys were in bed with measles, so we stayed in with them all night. Most everyone camped in vacant lots. The serious loss we felt was my sister's husband's ice plant—three large brick buildings fell in ruins, with no earthquake insurance. He was there but escaped injury by crawling under a table."

Frances Hunter Elwyn is on the staff of the National Committee on Maternal Health. She is still very actively interested in the school at Croton-on-Hudson. Her son David "is in England for a year, working on a farm in Beaconsfield, Bucks, taking French, music and riding lessons afternoons and enjoying it tremendously."

Governor Pinchot of Pennsylvania has appointed Margaret Garrigues Lester one of the Trustees of the Montgomery County Mothers' Assistance Fund.

Pokey Fabian Webster writes: In January, Billy and I went to Evanston where we spent five wonderful weeks at mother's. While there we acquired little sister Frances Margaret (then six weeks old) from "The Cradle." She is a dear little thing, weighing only nine pounds now, at three months; with lots of dark hair which I think will be curly. Her eyes are gray and people say she looks enough like me to be my very own.

Rebecca Lewis has a lovely new apartment, at 256 Bradley Street, New Haven, Conn.

1913

Class Editor: HELEN EVANS LEWIS
(Mrs. Robert M. Lewis)
52 Trumbull St., New Haven, Conn.

TWENTIETH REUNION

Thirty nine members of the Class and Alice Page Loring were here for the class meeting (in the shade, thermometer at 90°) and for the Class Supper in Wyndham on Saturday night, June 10th. Each member present arose and told her life history in a minute and a half during dinner (more of this later) and the more serious speeches followed the coffee. Yvonne, as toastmistress, advanced the theory that we should know by now, what use, if any,

a college education was, and called on Maud, Helen Richter Elser and Louisa Henderson Pierce to speak in turn on "The Use of a College Education in Business"; "In the Creative Arts," and "In the Use of Leisure." As I write the last, I remember that I used the word "serious" in connection with these speeches and lest any of you should think that Louisa had suffered a complete change, I hasten to add that it is my choice of words which is inaccurate. Various communications were read from various absent members. From Puddle a telegram came—"Am desolated not to be present. Whooping cough in two sons, teething in two puppies, extreme emptiness in two family purses prevent." From Louise Matlack a letter: "As Schmidt and Matlack can't come together the reunion seems to be off for both of us. Schmidt had to move from an early American house to an old English one, thus changing her point of view and her accent. I was going to make a speech this year to tell you how my college career helped me to bring up my three sons, 9, 11, and 12. How easy it has made it to explain to them technocracy, going off the gold standard, and the advantage of Sims' system over the dear old forcing two bid and all those little things that without a college education a mother has such trouble in making clear."

Sunday we breakfasted in Denbigh—Denbigh unchanged, breakfast improved after 20 years. Most of us sweltered at the Alumnae luncheon where Mary Tongue Eberstadt made, for the reuning classes of our group, a speech which was an admirable mixture of thought, humor and brevity.

Monday we picnicked (temperature still 90 degrees) in the shade of Wyndham with the other reuning classes.

For the benefit of those of you who could not come I append the following news, collected at the class supper:

Teaching

Alice Patterson Bensinger—Head of the Mathematical Department, Agnes Irwin School, Philadelphia.

Grace Bartholomew Clayton—Music, Friends' Select School, Philadelphia. Has two sons.

Laura Kennedy Gidley—Spanish, Stuyvesant High School, New York.

Marguerite Bartlett Hamer—History, University of Tennessee.

Florence Irish, History, Agnes Irwin School, Philadelphia.

Beatrice R. Miller—Physics, Overbrook High School.

Margaret Munroe, French and Latin, Friends' Central School, Philadelphia.

Adelaide Simpson, Latin, Hunter College.

Other Paid Occupations

Maud Dessau—Returned this winter from almost ten years of banking in Paris; now in exporting business with her brother in New York.

Apphia Thwing Hack went with the archaeologists of the University of Cincinnati to Troy and spent two months of most interesting digging.

Clara Belle Thompson Powell—In charge of radio advertising.

Elizabeth Shipley—Social worker at Sleighton Farms, a school for delinquent girls (near West Chester).

Parents and Other Unpaid Occupations

Lucile Shadburne Yow's oldest daughter, Katherine, aged 21, graduates from Smith this year with honors in music.

Sylvia Hathaway Evans' oldest daughter, Sylvia, aged 17, graduates at the head of her class at the Germantown Friends School and enters Bryn Mawr in the autumn.

Natalie Swift and Dorothy Blake spent the winter in Spain and Majorca.

Helen Richter Elser has been writing plays and does a lot with her music.

Mary Shenstone Fraser's husband is Professor of Preventive Medicine in the University of Toronto.

As a record of what can be accomplished after 20 years I submit the following letter from Dorothea Clinton Woodworth:

"I came to the University of California at Los Angeles in September, 1926, and have been for the past five years Assistant Professor of Latin and Greek. My work is thoroughly delightful to me, especially since the university has been occupying its new campus. Aside from my regular teaching schedule of ten to twelve hours a week, I do most of the advising of students majoring in Latin or in Greek, and am also one of the general advisers of the University. As to my own work, though naturally my time for it is limited, I published two articles in Classical Philology last year, and am now working on a text book (which I expect to finish during the coming summer), and also on an article, or perhaps several articles, which will be part of a study of the 'class struggle' in the Roman Empire.

"My husband is teaching French in the Cumnock (Junior) College of this city.

"My children—still four in number—are making due progress, which has been only trivially interrupted by four light cases of measles in the past three weeks. (I mention the measles because it is the first illness that any of them have had since the chicken-pox four years ago. They are as nearly perfect in health as any children I know.) Howard will be 10 in July. He attends the University Elementary School, which is the experimental school attached to the Teachers' College of this university; he is in the Opportunity Room, and is one of those embarrassingly 'superior' children who excel in their own chosen lines and have to be urged to coöperate in the handwork and other 'modern' devices of these progressive schools. Beatrice, who was 8 in December, lacks the phenomenal I. Q., but has enough energy for ten children; she organizes the games, dramatic entertainments, and buying expeditions for the whole family, and sometimes for the neighborhood—not to mention being an expert leader in mischief. Lewis, nearly 7, in the second grade, is temperamental, artistic, fond of music, an insatiable reader, and in behavior either quite angelic or quite diabolic, as the mood strikes him. Douglas, 5 last month, is so far distinguished chiefly for size, as he weighs 61 pounds and measures four feet and one inch; he is the only California native son, and certainly lives up to the advertisements, for he is perfectly healthy, perfectly happy, highly intelligent (I. Q. 160), and is unanimously rated by housekeeper, neighbors, and kindergarten teacher as the best-behaved child in the neighborhood. I really can't think of anything derogatory to say about him myself!"

Those present at Reunion were: Alice Patterson Bensinger, Grace Bartholomew Clayton, Helen Wilson Cresson, Maud Dessau, Mary Tongue Eberstadt, Helen Richter Elser, Lillie Walton Fox, Mary Shenstone Fraser Laura Kennedy Gidley, Helen Lee Gilbert, Apphia Thwing Hack, Louisa Haydock Hackett, Sara Halpen, Marguerite Bartlett Hamer, Alice Selig Harris, Yvonne Stoddard Hayes, Katherine Williams Hodgdon, Florence Irish, Olga Kelly, Gertrude Hinrichs King, Helen Evans Lewis, Frances Livingston, Katherine Page Loring, Katharine Page Loring's child, Beatrice Miller, Margaret Munroe, Clara Owen, Ethel Vernon Patterson, Louisa Henderson Pierce, Clara Belle Thompson Powell, Lucinda Menendez Rambo, Gwendolyn Rawson, Elizabeth Shipley, Adelaide Simpson, Cecile Goldsmith Simsohn, Helen Barrett Speers, Natalie Swift, Lucile Shadburne Yow, Elizabeth Y. Maguire.

1914

Class Editor: ELIZABETH AYER INCHES
(Mrs. Henderson Inches)
41 Middlesex Road, Chestnut Hill, Mass.

1914 came back to its Twentieth Reunion, 40 strong. They came at intervals during the day in Fords, Franklins, Nashes and Packards, and on the good old Pennsylvania Railroad, until at 5 o'clock, with practically everyone present in the Pembroke East sitting room, Lill Cox called a class meeting to order.

At 6 o'clock, having discussed finances, the form of Reunion Gift, and the possibility of future wedding presents, the class adjourned to Wyndham lawn for a picnic supper. Sitting on the grass in cotton prints or white tennis dresses, 1914 watched 1913 in full dress sweeping into Wyndham for their Reunion dinner. The conversations among the 1914ers, it was noted, had swung from one topic of feeding babies to the choice of preparatory schools, college entrance requirements, and how to get one's daughter into Bryn Mawr.

This subject was continued late into the night, and again at Ida Pritchett's tea in her delightful garden at Haverford on Sunday afternoon.

Monday morning, Eugenia Baker and Helen Kirk fought hard and nobly in tennis for the glory of the Alumnae against the varsity players, but in spite of their valiant efforts they were defeated.

At noon on Monday, 1914 joined 1913, 1915, and 1916 in a picnic at Wyndham and enjoyed seeing again the members of these classes.

One hour after the picnic was over most of 1914 had gone, but each and every member had declared that they had enjoyed this Reunion more than any other, and would never miss another, especially the 25th in 1938! Those present at Reunion were Rena Bixler, Eugenia Baker, Elizabeth Ayer, Mary Coolidge, Jessie Boyd, Mary Sears, Lillien Cox, Lucile Thompson, Elizabeth Braley, Wynanda Boardman, Eugenia Jackson, Dorothy Weston, Isabel Benedict, Janet Baird, Mildred Baird, Josephine Niles, Anita Tinges, Mary Schmidt, Montgomery Arthurs, Mary C. Smith, Edwina Warren, Helen Kirk, Elizabeth Bryant, Mary Haines, Caroline Allport, Katherine Shippen, Christine Brown, Elizabeth Atherton, Ida Pritchett, Elizabeth Colt, Ethel Dunham, Harriet Sheldon, Rose Brandon, Miriam Ward, Dorothea Bechtel, Mary Shipley, Jean Batchelor, Jean Barstow, Mary Buchanan.

EUGENIA JACKSON SHARPLES.

* * * *

Elizabeth Reynolds Hapgood is again in New York after spending two years in Europe educating her children. She finds it hard to adapt herself to life in a hectic city, but considers that the Lincoln School makes her return distinctly worth while.

Helen Hinde King has a beautiful place in Lake Forest. She has two charming children. She is very much interested in gardens and riding, and was President of the Garden Club of Lake Forest two years ago.

Helen Porter Simpson has gone abroad alone for six weeks. Her husband is now head of the 15th assembly district in New York City.

All winter Jean Davis has given a regular course in Sociology in Auburn Prison. This summer she plans to study several American prisons as she studied English prisons last summer. For three weeks in July she is to lecture on criminology in the New York Training School for Girls at Hudson. This is the first course for college girls ever held on the spot in the reformatory and lasts six weeks in all. Jean is interested in training college women as volunteers to help parole workers. In August she will be in the new Federal Prison for Women at Alderson, W. Va. She apologizes for not finding time to return for Reunion.

Cleos Rockwell Fenn has a daughter, Janet, born in Baltimore April 11th. Her husband is a minister.

1915

Class Editor: MARGARET FREE STONE
        (Mrs. J. Austin Stone)
        3039 44th St., N. W., Washington, D. C.

Reunion has come and gone, but the memory of it will be with us for many a day. It seemed to the Editor that, *granted* that we are older, we are really much handsomer than when we were in college. And as our theme song throughout was "Life Begins at Forty," we came away feeling that, after all, it will be several years before we are found mumbling in a corner.

Our class meeting in Rock at 7 o'clock on Saturday evening, June 10th, took us back to the class meetings of college days. We good-naturedly disagreed about everything and reached decisions with great difficulty! However, we were steered safely through discussions of dues, Reunion Gift and a Nominating Committee by our patient and tactful Chairman, Adrienne Kenyon Franklin. (The results of our discussions will be sent you in a circular letter soon.)

It was with sincere regret that we deferred to Hat's wishes, expressed in a letter to the class, and accepted her resignation as our President. Thereupon a motion was made and enthusiastically passed making Hat the Honorary President of 1915 for life.

At the class supper Isabel Foster was our very able Toastmistress. She first introduced Bertha Ehlers, who spoke about the Alumnae Fund, urging more and more of us to send our contributions to the undesignated fund, so that the money may be used where it is most needed.

Helen Taft Manning, in a most illuminating talk, told how the College has weathered the depression during the past year. Room rents have had to be adjusted, and unexpected loans to students have had to be made in some cases, but these have been offset by economies effected along various lines: salaries, upkeep of buildings and grounds, etc. Helen also spoke about the fact that two new plans for admission to the College have been worked out in the hope of widening the field from which students are gathered.

The one thing lacking in our whole Reunion was that, in the excitement of moving from the dining room to the sitting room to see pictures of husbands and children on a screen, we forgot to have Helen sing "That is Love." This really must be put in the regular agenda of the next Reunion, for no Reunion is complete without it.

The pictures of families were much enjoyed, and the only regret was that some of us had forgotten to bring any.

Isabel, taking upon herself the rôle of newspaper reporter, interviewed the various members present as to affairs of the day as well as to their jobs, and an astounding amount and variety of activity were reported. Isabel herself is an editor of the Hartford, Conn., *Courant*, and is the first woman to have that job. She has been having a grand time exposing graft in certain quarters. At midnight, when the interviews were over, some of us adjourned to the flowering crab-apple tree and sang, a bit weakly, it must be admitted.

After an interesting Sunday spent at the general Alumnae Meeting and Alumnae Luncheon and in visiting old haunts, 1915 gathered for supper at the home of Anna Brown in Overbrook. In addition to the fact that the supper was delicious, this was a most enjoyable occasion, for we all told any bits of news we could about those not able to be present at Reunion. Also, the Editor read aloud letters that had come to Adrienne from Lucile Davidson Allsopp, Rachel Ash, Hezzie Irvin Bordman, Atala Scudder Davison, Susan Brandeis Gilbert, Ethel Robinson Hyde, Myra Richards Jessen, Eleanor Freer Karcher, Emily Noyes Knight, Laura Branson Linville, Gladys Pray Michaels, Ruth Tinker Morse, Mary Marjory Thomson and Mary Gertrude Brownell Wilson.

Reunion was a grand and glorious occasion, and the Editor would advise everyone to buy a pair of roller skates or a bicycle right now, so that if the depression is still with us when the next Reunion rolls around we'll have some means of getting there! Besides, it's much safer to be one of those present when the gossiping is going on in the wee sma' hours!

1916

Class Editor: LARIE KLEIN BOAS
(Mrs. Benjamin Boas)
2736 Broderick St., San Francisco, Calif.

We have met and talked and listened and walked through miles of corridors, sat through a banquet, a luncheon and several meetings, and have marveled at the new ways of undergraduates who industriously press their clothes. At the Class Supper in Denbigh Hall were Helen Robertson, Reunion Manager; Virginia De Macedo Raacke, Pokie Smith, Ad Werner Vorys, Eleanor Hill Carpenter, Doddy Sangree, Jute Chase Locke, Nannie Gale Wolfe, Florence Hitchcock, Annis Thompson, Frances Thompson Mudd, Constance Dowd. Emily Wagner came on Sunday.

The only competitive sports in which we indulged were long-distance talking and sitting up late. Ad Vorys, Florence Hitchcock and Anna Lee tied for first place (what it is to be young!). Our intellectual discussions centered about a little volume entitled "Life Begins at Forty."

Mrs. Branson invited all 1916 to supper Sunday and we greatly enjoyed talking with her in her delightfully cool home.

It was really surprising that so many of us still had the price of a ticket to Bryn Mawr, and next Reunion, in 1938, we hope that many of those who missed the party this year can come.

As Ad said, it's really fun to be at Bryn Mawr, even if you are all alone. Ad said that she would have had just as good a time even if none of us had come.

Everything went off smoothly, thanks to Bobby's efficient management, and we even had clean towels for those who came only for the day.

1917

Class Editor: BERTHA CLARK GREENOUGH
203 Blackstone Ave., Providence, R. I.

Our deepest sympathy is extended to Lovira Brown Lamarche, whose only child, a boy about 4, died in February. "Lovey" has been in Lowell, Mass., this winter, as her husband's business is now there.

Elizabeth Emerson Gardner is planning to move up to Mantunuck, R. I., about the middle of June with her three children. Her husband has gone to the Economic Conference in London as an expert.

1918

Class Editor: MARGARET BACON CAREY
(Mrs. H. R. Carey)
3115 Queen Lane, East Falls P. O., Phila.

1919

Class Editor: MARJORIE REMINGTON TWITCHELL
(Mrs. Pierrepont Twitchell)
Setauket, L. I., N. Y.

Louise Wood's "Study Year in Europe" for young girls this coming year will be mostly in

Rome, October 15th to April 15th, with an optional trip to Paris, April 15th to June 1st. Louise's address is the Travellers' Bank, 18 rue de la Paix, Paris, France.

Edith Rondinella Rudolphy spends much time visiting in her Home for blind women. Her doctor husband was recently made their ophthalmologist. They spent a week-end last fall with Elizabeth Hurlock Beekman and her husband in Harrisburg. Edith just finished another year at the Irwin School, teaching music appreciation for the Senior Class twice a week. She has also been Chairman of the Parish House Committee of Holy Trinity Church: "Quite a job to keep track of all the supplies and do all the purchasing from furniture to can openers." .

Who else is going to the World's Fair? The Editor hopes to get there in July. If girls who are going from 1919 will write to her, she'll try to get them in touch with other classmates who are going.

The Editor took a little 8-year-old girl from a destitute family for two months this spring, and had a grand time buying girl's dresses and tying hair ribbons—a new experience for one with only a 12-year-old boy!

1920

Class Editor: MARY PORRITT GREEN
(Mrs. Valentine J. Green)
433 East 51st St., New York City.

From Mary Hoag Lawrence: "As I remember it, I appear but about three times in ten years in the alumnae news, but this is one of the times. Kindly publish to all that Mary, now two and a half, has recently acquired a brother, Billy, just two years her junior and just as good as gold. Between these far-between excitements in our family we live the most everyday kind of life, but seem to be busy, and reasonably happy, in spite of its apparent humdrumness.

"I took a trip the end of April to see Marguerite and her son, and my family, in Haverford; incidentally, saw Marge Canby Taylor and three lovely looking daughters; and Peggy Dent Daudon, who lives two doors from my parents and has two stunning children. Went to Mrs. Buck's lecture in Goodhart. I have never seen anything more sophisticated than the ushers. We were never half so young actually or so old looking in our college days.

"My Billy had quite a dramatic entrance into the life of 1920. On my return from Philadelphia I had him (just acquired that p. m.) and Mary, and so took a drawing room on the Federal. Marge Canby used the other ticket and nearly lost her balance, if not her reason, at seeing two children where but one had been before. I immediately had' the club

here to lunch, and I think gave each one a good surprise, as she passed a sleeping infant on the porch—totally unexpected.

"I have seen something of Miriam O'Brien Underhill lately, as she has made me a tailored suit. Did you know we had an accomplished tailoress in our midst? ˙ It is really tailored, too, and I for one am overcome at her ability."

1921

Class Editor: WINIFRED WORCESTER STEVENSON
(Mrs. Harvey Stevenson)
Croton-on-Hudson, N. Y.

˙Margaretta Archbald was recently married to Frederick Kroll. He is the son of the Bishop of Haiti, and they expect to live there.

1922

Class Editor: SERENA HAND SAVAGE
(Mrs. William L. Savage)
106 E. 85th St., New York City.

The Editor has a third child, a second daughter, born on June 1st, entered on the birth certificate as "A Female Savage."

1923

Class Editor: RUTH McANENY LOUD
325 East 72nd St., New York City.

1924

Class Editor: DOROTHY GARDNER BUTTERWORTH
(Mrs. J. Evert Butterworth)
8102 Ardmore Ave., Chestnut Hill, Pa.

Mitzi Faries gives the following account of her activities since graduation. She writes: "After college I taught four years at Holton Arms School in Washington, Social Science, Psychology and Physical Education. I got my M.A. at Columbia, and now this is my fourth year as Associate Professor in Physical Education here in college. I travel practically none, though last summer I drove to Colorado, gaped at Pike's Peak and the Rodeo in Cheyenne, spent six weeks studying dancing at the Perry-Mansfield Camp in Colorado. During the winter Mitzi's address is 574 South Main Street, Harrisonburg, Virginia.

From Fort Wm. McKinley, Philippine Islands, Connie Lewis Gibson writes: "We have no children; my occupation outside the home is really, I suppose, 'Social Welfare.' I belong to an organization known as the 'American Guardian Association,' whose purpose is 'to guard and care for children wholly or partly of American blood who are without proper protection.' This is very absorbing work, and as long as there are soldiers and sailors, I suppose there will be plenty of it. We travel whenever possible. So far we have made one very interesting excursion into the head-hunting country, which is in Northern Luzon (the northern part is our island) and several lesser trips among the non-Christian tribes. Next month we go to the Southern (Philippine) Islands to visit the Moros, and on to Borneo and Sumatra. I hope to get up to China and Japan in the fall on a combined shopping and sight-seeing tour. We have one Bryn Mawr girl on the post, Mary Sherman Harper, '27, and another one on a fortified island nearby, Mary Cruikshank Kyster, also '27. Life here is really delightful, and while we experience nothing of the lotos eater's sensations of forgetfulness, it is so calming and soothing that one hates to pull up roots and depart. Please remember me to any '24's you see, and tell them that Manila is a lovely place to visit, and until June, 1934 (as far as I know), I shall have lots of space to accommodate them."

There, aren't those two glorious letters? Take note, all you slackers, and write me life histories before September.

The Junior League National Conference was a great success; at least, we in Philadelphia think so. Bryn Mawr graduates seem to make excellent League material, as College was well represented. Blanche McRae Baker looked exactly the same, and proved the most charming of house guests.

The class extends its deepest sympathy to Louise Howitz, whose mother died very suddenly on May 8th.

1925

Class Editor: ELIZABETH MALLET CONGER
(Mrs. Frederic Conger)
325 East 72nd Street, New York City.

Cheers! An unsolicited note from Nichols Road, Lexington, Mass. "Olive Sears Taliaferro is now the proud mother of twin sons, Richard Nelson, Junior, and Henry Sears, born May 12th. Sister Betsey is now almost 3 years old." These are our first twins, and we hope they will come to Reunion to play with Madeleine Pierce Lemon's twin daughters on the Denbigh Green.

Kay Starr Oliver had a second little daughter on May 23rd.

Nana Bonnell Davenport is spending the summer at Compo Road, Westport, Connecticut, with her husband and three sons—Henry, Stephen (Henry, then Richard and John!), and Samuel Chase Davenport.

Helen Herrmann is teaching Economics at the Bryn Mawr Summer School.

1926

Class Editor: HARRIOT HOPKINSON
Manchester, Mass.

Well, well, I am sure it is of absorbing interest to you all to know that your Editor is at home again after some months in Egypt. And

if you were only all around here this minute, how she would love to tell you about sunsets on the Nile, the Southern Cross in the Sudan, how a gargling camel rises to his feet right under you in three installments, how to count to ten in purest Arabic, what Rameses II's wife's muslin ball dress was like, how to fall comfortably off a donkey, and the present position of the Nationalist Party. Thanks to Molly Parker, we are able to report the following:

Katharine Slade was married April 22nd to Robert Newbegin, of Cambridge, Mass. He is in the consular service, and they have gone to live in Mexico City.

Pegome Huber Chesser is reported to be living in Greenwich Village, with a job in an art shop.

Eleanor Stilz's whereabouts have at last been ascertained, after unearthly mystery. She does hospital work, and is living at 228 Harvey Street, Germantown.

Margin Wylie Sawbridge is reported to have returned to her native shores from England in May, accompanied by her young son, to spend the summer in Ipswich, Mass.

Alice Wilt Askew has been taking a most active interest in the Forest Hills Women's Club; she played the hero's part, in fact, in one of the dramatic productions there.

Pussy Leewitz Iselin is another foreigner, like Margin, who has been in this country recently. She accompanied her husband, who is a surgeon, to the medical conference at Johns Hopkins recently, and with them came their sons, François, age about two and a half, with a mop of curls like his mother's, and Jerome, age three months.

Another Parisian is Betty Cushman, who, we hear, lives in a delightful pension with a garden at 53 rue Claude-Bernard, and very much enjoys her work at the American High School. Her time sounds well filled, for apparently she teaches English, Latin, History, and perhaps a little more.

Elinor McKee Brooks works with her husband at a highly successful soap shop in Toronto.

What a quantity of little boys, to be sure, seem to belong to our class! Word has reached us that Dot Lefferts Moore's Peter is, at three and a half, particularly charming. Dot and her family have moved for the summer out to their house at Wilton, Conn.

Franny Jay, after an independent winter with an apartment of her own on East End Avenue, and playing a lot of squash with the Cosmopolitan Club team, has joined her family at Mt. Kisco for the summer. Here we expect she will reap what she sowed (or vice versa, if you can excuse this) at the Columbia course in Horticulture last winter.

Tommy Tomkins Villard and her husband are sailing August 18th for Europe—a six weeks' trip in Paris and the French countryside.

The class extends its deepest sympathy to Deirdre O'Shea Carr on the death of her baby son early this spring.

Molly Parker wants her appreciative thanks to go to those of you who answered the Agony Column plea not long ago with most helpful letters of news. Won't you do the same for me?

1927

Class Editor: ELLENOR MORRIS
Berwyn, Pa.

1928

Class Editor: CORNELIA B. ROSE, JR.
40 Fifth Ave., New York City.

Mattie Fowler Van Doren's second son, Charles Fowler Van Doren, was born in New York on May 16th.

Peggy Hess De Graaf's son was born in Portland, Oregon, on May 21st. We have been unable to learn his name.

Mary Johnston Colfelt has moved to Bryn Mawr from Wynnewood to be nearer the fox-hunting country. Her new home permits her to keep her five horses on her own place instead of boarding them, and she also has room for a large number of dogs.

Dot Miller, who was resident fellow at College in Biology this year, only has one more year's work to do for her Ph.D.

Please note that your Editor has moved once again, this time to stay put for just three months.

1929

Class Editor: MARY L. WILLIAMS
210 East 68th St., New York City.

1930

Class Editor: EDITH GRANT
2117 Le Roy Place, Washington, D. C.

Mary Brayton Durfee's engagement has been announced to Charles Dennet Brown, of Flushing, Long Island. Mr. Brown is in business with his father. Mary was here in May for the Junior League Conference in Philadelphia. She came out to Glee Club and spent the night. Glee Club brought back several more members of the class. Dot Cross, Mary Hulse, and Katie Howe were among those present.

Tootie Johnston Olmstead has a son, our first boy in a long time. Two more daughters have also appeared during May. Ruth Lawrence Wittmer has one, Anne Davies, born the 4th, and Joy Dickerman St. John has one, Cora Alice, born the 18th of May.

Margaret Lee Burgess was married recently in New York to Mr. Sheldon Dick, with Margaret Barker as her only attendant.

Lois Davis Stevenson is returning to this country, as her husband is going to study at the Harvard School of Forestry.

Annie Leigh Broughton and her daughter are spending the summer at the Hobsons' in Richmond, while her husband pursues Roman inscriptions through Asia Minor.

1931

Class Editor: EVELYN WAPLES BAYLESS
(Mrs. Robert N. Bayless)
301 W. Main St., New Britain, Conn.

Although while we were in College no one could have possibly persuaded us that any good could come out of a reunion, the thirteen of us who vied with the insects in a vigorous attack upon the chicken salad at the picnic on Saturday night and the eighteen of us who gathered at Miss Park's for breakfast on Sunday morning must by this time be convinced that there is nothing, after all, to be compared with a reunion when it comes down to the problem of a ways and means of gleaning *news* about most of the class.

First of all, of course, with "bird-in-hand" tactics, each one of us who was present pounced upon the others with horrible avidity, demanding information as to what "they were doing," spurred on by the hope that she in her turn would be asked to divulge the intricacies of her life during the past two years. The results of our findings are somewhat to this effect—we use "somewhat" advisedly, since the heat and our lack of a public stenographer make our accuracy in some cases slightly questionable.

Libby Baer has a position in the History Department of the Enoch Pratt Free Library in Baltimore. Ginny Burdick persists in her original field of Education (or so she herself interprets it) and will be Executive Secretary at Mrs. Day's School in New Haven this fall. Peg Findley and Patsey Taylor (we *meant* to do this thing alphabetically) are still discovering new mysteries in the life cycle of mice at the genetics laboratory of the Carnegie Institution in Cold Springs Harbor—a scientific pursuit which can be agreeably combined with all the advantages of social life on Long Island. Molly Frothingham is chaperoning four sophomores from Smith on a trip to Europe this summer. Betty Doak seems to be carried away by the teaching profession to the extent of doing some this summer at Vassar and then beginning in real earnest at Rosemary in the fall. Libby Howson is working with the Federation of Churches in Bryn Mawr (does that make sense?). Betty Mongan is still in the New London Museum and would like any of '31 who happen to be in her neighborhood to stop in and visit her. Dorothy Pizor has been taking a business course. Ginny Shryock and Esther Thomas will be in Chicago until the 1st of August this summer; Esther expects to take more education courses at the university to add to her dexterity (and it is that) in handling some twenty-odd little boys in the second grade of Episcopal Academy in the winter. Katherine Sixt was married June 24th to Frederick Cooper, of Wayne, Pa. He's a metallurgist and they are going to live at Burlington, New Jersey. Tatnall also has the teaching urge and will be at St. Timothy's, in Baltimore, next year, teaching history. Bobsey (Totten) Turney made a special point of insisting that her husband's name was *Clayton;* the Turneys are planning a wonderful trip to Wisconsin for vacation in August. Caccine Thurber is living in New York and has a very good job as secretary to the President of American Factory Made Houses, Inc. Marion Turner has returned from a thrilling trip to Europe, where she acted as chaperone for a 17-year-old girl, and now she has a secretarial position in Baltimore. Ruth Unangst is studying for a Ph.D. at the University of Pennsylvania. Evy (Waples) Bayless cannot extol too highly the delights of housekeeping in New Britain, Connecticut. Janie Low is taking her M.A. at College this year and is spending the summer in Bryn Mawr.

So much for those of us who were there. And when we had exhausted all the possibilities of conversation among ourselves about ourselves various and sundry bits of information about those who had not been able to get back began to trickle through. We decline to vouch for the authenticity of it all, proceeding on the theory that some news is better than no news; if we have shot too wide of the mark, the Class Editor would be delighted to make amends in subsequent issues of the BULLETIN. Babe Adams is working as assistant to a doctor in New York City. Jimmy Bunn is running a bookshop in Rocky Mount, North Carolina. Angie Burrows has started work on her Ph.D., having gotten an M.A. at Columbia during the past winter; this summer she is spending abroad. Elizabeth Cook is also working for a Ph.D. at Hopkins, where she is a part-time instructor. Toots Dyer is studying at a dramatics school in London. Bev George is taking up law at the University of Richmond. Jane Moore has been studying economics in Boston, and rumor has it that she and Mary Oakford are living together there; Mary is studying architecture at M. I. T. and reports that she is having a wonderful time. Peggy (Nuckols) Bell sent her regrets that she was unable to come to the Reunion, adding that her small son was definitely worth the sacrifice. Peggy Scott is studying in Boston. Peggy Shaughnessy is planning to make use of her fellowship next year, doing work at the University of London. Syd Sullivan was married on June 8th to Jameison Parker; Syd lately has been adding to her literary laurels by an article published in *Vogue,* and now it appears that she is "ghost-writing" a book. Helen Snyder has finished her second year in medicine at Johns Hopkins and is said to be having a very gay time in Baltimore. Hilda Thomas has completed a year of teaching at Wykeham Rise and has not yet decided what she is going to do next fall.

Ami Kennedy Hauck writes: "Bobby McKinney McIntosh had a second daughter, May 11th. The elder daughter is Marion but I don't know the baby's name.

"Virginia Smith Lydgate had a daughter, Sally Jean, in March, and I had my second daughter, Jean, in February. My first little girl's name is Carolyn. My husband is being sent to London on business, so we are taking the children and are going to spend the summer somewhere within commuting distance of the city.

"Louise Howland has been working for the Health Department of Yale University, and Kay Winship has been out in California for the last year."

Dot Jenkins was married to Edwin Macdougall Rhea, on Monday, June 26th, at half after five o'clock in the afternoon, at the Church of the Ascension, Pittsburgh, Pa.

The engagement of Mignon Sherley to R. B. Acker, son of Mrs. Charles E. Acker, of Washington, D. C., was announced at Olive Sherley's wedding on April 22nd. Mr. Acker graduated from Harvard in the Class of '29 and later studied at Columbia and at the University of Leyden for three years. He is connected with the Freer Gallery of Art in Washington and is at present in Kyoto, Japan, studying. He will return to America in August, and he and Min expect to be married in Canada at the Sherley's summer place, "The Torn." They will then leave immediately for Japan for two years.

Barbara Kirk was married on the 10th of June to Andrew Foster, oldest son of Frank Brisben Foster, of Haverford, Pa. Andrew is a graduate of Dartmouth and then of Cambridge, where he majored in history. Last June he was one of eight candidates who passed the United States Foreign Service Examinations so well that a diplomatic post even in 1933 has been reasonably assured. The wedding took place at 3 o'clock at Bab's home in Merion. It was a very quiet wedding.

Dr. Kirk gave Barbara away, and Mr. Foster, Andrew's father, was his best man.

Rhys Caparn, who has during the past three years been studying sculpture under Navellier in Paris and under Archipenko in New York, has designed the signs of the zodiac on the band of the new bronze armillary sphere in the Brooklyn Botanic Garden. The Brooklyn Museum has placed on view the "pink torso" she did.

1932

Class Editor: JOSEPHINE GRATON
182 Brattle St., Cambridge, Mass.

On Saturday, June 10th, there was a great influx into Bryn Mawr of members of 1932 who have been scattered in many places during the last year. A picnic supper was held by the brook down in the hollow behind the Library, and was enjoyed by Molly Atmore, Kate Mitchell, "Tommy" Thomas, Nancy West, Laura Hunter, Sally Black, Ellen Shaw, Anne Willits, "Tag" Taggart, Clarissa Brown, "Wiggie" Weygandt, the Woods twins, Hat Moore, Betty Converse and Jo Graton.

Sunday morning Miss Park gave a breakfast party for the reuners of 1931 and 1932, where "Gilly" Gill, Denny Gallaudet and Dolly Davis joined us. The Alumnae Luncheon at noon in Pembroke dining hall was a pleasant event, followed by speeches, including one by Miss Park telling all that has gone on at College since we left, and one by Hat Moore on "The Practical Value of a Bryn Mawr Education." In the course of these festivities, a great deal of class news has been unloosed. Betty Barker has been studying at the University of Pennsylvania during the past year, and has received a scholarship there for the coming year. Sue Hardin has left Miss Miller, for whom she was acting as social secretary, and has a governess' position on the Main Line. Laura Hunter has received a scholarship in the Biology Department at Bryn Mawr for next year; she is spending the summer at the Woods Hole Laboratory. Ruth Milliken is planning to spend next winter at Oxford studying philosophy. Edith Watts has taken a business course in Philadelphia and is now in Boston cataloguing a library.

Greta Swenson is going on the Odyssey Cruise again this summer. "Footie" Foote has been taking a business course in New Haven. "Tommy" Thomas has an advertising job in Pittsburgh after July 1st. Dolly Tyler is returning from England at the end of June, and will work for the Institute of Pacific Relations. During August she and Hat Moore will attend a Pacific Relations conference in Banff. Hat is planning to take her fellowship next year, just where she will study she has not yet decided. Betty Converse is going to Salzburg this summer to dance.

Dorothea Perkins will spend the summer at Bryn Mawr Summer School. Emma Paxson had a nervous breakdown during the winter and was taken on a round-the-world cruise, stopping in on Connie Ralston in Honolulu on the way. Kit Coleman received her Bachelor's degree from Goucher this year; she is now doing library work.

Eleanor Renner has announced her engagement to Wallace de Laguna. They are to be married on September 23rd and will live in Cambridge, where "Wally" will continue his studying.

Molly Atmore has announced her engagement to Edward Ten Broeck, a chemical engineer, who is working for the Atlantic Refining Company.

Elizabeth Gill is to be married to William Lathrop on August 1st in Milwaukee. They will live in Devon, Pa.

Mary Burman has announced her engagement to Dr. Howard Smith, of Baltimore.

Dot McClatchy has announced her engagement to a young Austrian whom she met while studying in Vienna last summer. She is at present with her family in Philadelphia.

Alice Bemis was married to Charles Goodrich Thompson on June 17th in South Tamworth, N. H. They will live in New York, where "Charlie" is practicing law.

Carolyn Lombardi was married in New York on May 8th, to Charles Renton McCormick, Jr.

We wish to congratulate Margaret Peter Fritz and her husband (very heartily, though we are somewhat late) on the birth of their daughter "Peggy," who is now eight months old and has one tooth.

The following girls received Bachelor's degrees from Bryn Mawr this year: Marjorie Trent, Ella Rutledge, Ann Burnett, Gene Harman, Margo Reinhardt Pyle, Sally Black, Grace Dewes, Elizabeth Gill, Connie Gill, "Pinkie" Pinkerton, Migs Waring Evans, and Priscilla Rawson. "Hon" Engle, "Wiggie" Weygandt, and "Butler" Butterworth received Master's degrees at Bryn Mawr.

1933

Class Editor: JANET MARSHALL
112 Green Bay Road, Hubbard Woods, Ill.

At the last class meeting held on June 12th, the following officers were elected to serve until the first reunion: President: Ellinor Collins; Vice-President: Elizabeth Edwards; Secretary: Ella Berkeley; Class Collector: Betsy Jackson; Class Editor: Janet Marshall. Margaret Collier was chosen to be Reunion Manager and Ellinor Collins to represent 1933 at the Alumnae Council which will meet in Boston in November.

Fit as a Fiddle

Ready for most anything

just having a good time
swinging and smoking.
Well yes, Chesterfield—

They Satisfy

... all you could ask for

THE CIGARETTE THAT'S MILDER
THE CIGARETTE THAT TASTES BETTER

BRYN MAWR
ALUMNAE
BULLETIN

THE OPENING OF COLLEGE

November, 1933

Vol. XIII   No. 8

Entered as second-class matter, January 15, 1921, at the Post Office, Phila., Pa., under Act of March 3, 1879
COPYRIGHT, 1933
ALUMNAE ASSOCIATION OF BRYN MAWR COLLEGE

Form of Bequest

I give and bequeath to the ALUMNAE ASSOCIATION OF BRYN MAWR COLLEGE, Bryn Mawr, Pennsylvania, the sum of........................dollars.

BRYN MAWR ALUMNAE BULLETIN

OFFICIAL PUBLICATION OF
THE BRYN MAWR ALUMNÆ ASSOCIATION

MARJORIE L. THOMPSON, '12, *Editor*
ALICE M. HAWKINS, '07, *Business Manager*

EDITORIAL BOARD

MARY CRAWFORD DUDLEY, '96　　　　　ELLENOR MORRIS, '27
CAROLINE MORROW CHADWICK-COLLINS, '05　　ELINOR AMRAM NAHM, '28
EMILY KIMBROUGH WRENCH, '21　　　　PAMELA BURR, '28
ELIZABETH BENT CLARK, '95, *ex-officio*

Subscription Price, $1.50 a Year　　　　　　*Single Copies, 25 Cents*
Checks should be drawn to the order of Bryn Mawr Alumnae Bulletin
Published monthly, except August, September and October, at 1006 Arch St., Philadelphia, Pa.

VOL. XIII　　　　　　NOVEMBER, 1933　　　　　　No. 8

Out of the mass of discussion about education, in these years of the locust, certain points of view gradually crystallize. The cultural college is not a luxury, but a necessity, a way of finding in a changing world certain unchanging values among the things of the spirit and the intellect. It was interesting and significant that that note was struck in all the speeches at the Haverford Centenary, which was celebrated this October. It is, perhaps curiously, as one looks back, the note that each of us remembers from Chapel speeches fifteen, twenty, or even thirty years ago. Was there one among us, even then, who did not feel that she was living in a changing world? The change is a matter of degree. One had the sense of new things coming rather than of old things being swept away. Foundations were there to be built upon; now the building must be done from the ground up. That is the reason that what President Park had to say to the Freshmen, and not only to the Freshmen but to the College as a whole, both graduate students and undergraduates, was so pertinent. It was an effort to arouse in them those qualities of mind and spirit, that will enable them to make adjustments to whatever conditions they may meet, like adult human beings and not, to quote *1933*, with part of which President Park ended her speech, like

> "adolescents
> Screaming from well lined nests."

Many visitors to the Campus who have been struck by the too great contrast between, say, the dignity and beauty of the library and the extreme informality of the clothes and manners of the students in it, will be glad that the students were reminded that "The College is not after all an informal place, nor a place where you alone live, move, and have your being. Many other people come and go on the Campus daily, and the pleasure or pain in its look and its upkeep belong to us as much as to you." It certainly is true, again to quote, that only old ladies "hope to return to the lotuses," but beauty and order are not, surely, things of the past, but also must be things of the future, in whatever political or economic or intellectual terms that future may express itself.

EDUCATION FOR A CHANGING WORLD

PRESIDENT PARK'S ADDRESS TO THE FRESHMEN

In our college world, relative peace and rising courage seem at the moment possible; we may cautiously, eye on barometer, unreef our sails again and hope to make some headway. That is true and heartening and unexpected. But around and before us lie the anxious problems and uncertainties of the economic, political, financial world to which we are each of us connected by so many personal threads. Your father's business ties you to them, your mother's purchases, the hole that the bill for your tuition makes in the common purse. I am out of the college office and in Washington or New York every hour—the ups and downs of college investments, the discussion of N. R. A. policy as applied to college employees, my weekly afternoon at the county-seat listening to discussion of this winter's relief problem—all these take me there. In the end, and a not remote end, as the world careens and rights itself or sinks, so Bryn Mawr College will career, right itself, or sink.

It is not then a time when we can think of ourselves as a compact, smug little crowd gathering in this brisk, blue morning, carried on the momentum of a social class or a family or a distinguished academic past, pretty sure to be on the winning side in the future. No such pretty picture. We don't even know what the alternative is: only that a current not on the surface but strong, from deep below, a force neither entirely understandable or controllable, is taking us from a past in which you, like your mothers and grandmothers, have lived into a future in which you must live, make your friends or enemies, earn your livings, marry, plan the lives of children, grow old, but whose economic or political conditions, whose government, religion, philosophy, are now behind a bank of fog which doesn't yet lift—out of your sight but also out of the sight of all experts or prophets.

This is the shift in our problem. For many years Bryn Mawr College has set out to prepare its students to live in an America whose ways we knew, whose slow progress toward liberalism we could calculate. Bryn Mawr College must now prepare you, or rather you must prepare yourselves, from the teachers, the books, the laboratory apparatus which we can put at your disposal, to meet something as yet not developed, something about which we know only that it will be different from anything of which up to now we have had experience. We can no longer educate directly, that is, turn out a definite kind of young woman for an exactly defined place.

How does one educate another person, how does one educate oneself for change, for unknown demands, for indefinite responsibilities? And we have, I think, all come to believe that this change you are to meet will be abrupt and final; it will not be a turn or twist to find our way back to old habits of life, old comfortable ruts of thought and theory. If, for instance, democratic government in America is to continue, its machinery must not be revised and revamped, but largely scrapped and a new apparatus adapted to this period worked out. Without charts or prophets we are dependent on seamanship; to drop figures and come to prose, on the careful and accurate use of an intellectual training.

(2)

You must get the largest possible amount of that training during the next one, two, three or four years that remain of your formal education. Throw away the old charts and close your ears to the medicine man.

What is education for a change? I think I know some things which must be included in it.

First of all, I have often said before that education *must* include, and I hoped at Bryn Mawr *did* include, information, definite and presented in such a form that it could be got at quickly—finger-end facts. In the face of what is before you, a method of testing facts is as necessary as the facts themselves. Much of what is now in the store-houses of so-called educated people is out of date or partisan, collected to defend emotional convictions. It all needs a sieve, and much of it can't be used again. The students of this year need training in the establishing of proof, in the estimating and measuring of probabilities, in the desire and ability to correct themselves as quickly as they correct others. The teachers of this year must make sure the students know methods of using and testing facts. In general, that should mean more discussion and less monologue in the classroom and out of the classroom. You have two handicaps: neither women nor Americans like discussion, but I beg you to be less ready to be idle or docile listeners. I wish that outside the class room a debating club might crystallize the discussion habit, but no debating club will succeed except in an atmosphere of continual private discussion.

A second necessity is ready personal adjustment to other people, so that you can effectively work with them though they may be totally different from yourselves. Whatever final cosmos comes out of this chaos will come, I believe, from the creative power not of the individual, but of the group. Unless one can work as a member of a group, then he is likely to be negligible. To be a member of a group means on the intellectual side an understanding of one's own psychology and that of others; it means a power to criticize objectively and to subject one's ideas to criticism, to follow intelligently where one can not lead—and few can. The individual must be independent and tolerant; those two virtues I have often begged you to strive for. As a member of a group you must add to independence and tolerance, willingness to sacrifice in non-essentials. And this generation must relearn loyalty to an idea, for what is made out of many minds is a new thing and it will demand a new loyalty of its own.

Now this small community should and does offer good rehearsals for this. I wish our groups might be more varied, that we might devise projects large and small in which faculty, alumnae, employees, worked with graduates and undergraduates to some common end. Miss Addams who comes this month to the College has, I believe, an experience unequaled in America in the ways of working with large and small groups made up of totally unlike individuals. I hope that as you listen and talk with her you will come to see how that has been possible.

If elasticity is the correct opposite of rigidity, then elasticity is the third quality in which Bryn Mawr should at this moment train its students. Long ago a wise young cousin said to me, "If you think a thing can be done in only one way, that is a sign you ought never to do it that way again." In my old Swiss *Baedeker* there are eleven numbered ways set down to walk from Zermatt into Italy, although the eleventh is up the Matterhorn on the Swiss side and down on the Italian! There are eleven ways probably to reach each political, economic or religious objective in the value of which we shall find ourselves believing. If one fails, an unprejudiced and quick-moving mind can turn to a second, can combine, readjust and move on. Now the College, I believe, has gained greatly in doing away with its own rigidity in these recent years. The changes in entrance requirements, in the curriculum, the variety of forms in which work is presented, the easier relation with schools, show we can with good grace urge elasticity on you. You, on your side, should first accept variety, not as an unpleasant surprise, but as part of a lesson which you will at once put to practice. You can even demand it and be listened to! Fixed ideas, narrow sectional, national, racial prejudices, crystallized likes and dislikes, will make you fumble in meeting this new world. No dull mistakes can be made, everything must be seen with fresh eyes. No opinions must be impervious to reasoning; any habit must be subject to change.

And lastly, fearlessness and persistence are the matrix in which such adaptability, such power to work with other people, such ability to test the truth, are imbedded. For them, too, there can be a kind of training, self administered largely. They can develop where they are not inborn. And they are so clearly demanded that they need no more words.

In some such way as this you can begin today education for a quick change, not education for a slowly changing or an established order. And if you are farseeing and wise, you may have a hand in it for more than yourself.

Not charts or prophets, but seamanship. I am quoting inexactly from Archibald MacLeish's poem, *1933*. I shall end with an exact quotation:

"Elpenor, Odysseus's dead pilot is speaking to him in Hades where Odysseus has come to ask the way *back to Ithaca*."

> "For myself—if you ask me—
> There's no way back over sea water
>
>   *   *   *   *   *
>
> You had best—trusting neither to
> Charts nor to prophets but seamanship—
>
> You had best—if you ask me—
> Sail on by the sun to the seaward
>   *   *   *   *   *
>
> Bring yourselves to a home:
> To a new land: to an ocean
>
> Never sailed: not to Ithaca:
> Not to your beds—but the withering
>
> Seaweed under the thorn and the
> Gulls and another morning. . . ."

At Haverford's Centenary celebration on October 7th, President Park represented Bryn Mawr and was one of the five women in the procession.

PROGRAM FOR THE THIRTEENTH ANNUAL MEETING
OF THE ALUMNAE COUNCIL

November 16th, 17th and 18th, 1933

THURSDAY, NOVEMBER 16th

Arrive in Boston during course of morning.

12.30 P. M.   Luncheon at home of Mrs. James Torbert (Elizabeth Townsend, 1906) for members of the Council and their hostesses.

1.30 P. M.   First Business Session of the Council at Mrs. Torbert's.
Discussion of Financial Problems of the Association.

3.30 P. M.   Parent-School Meeting at The Winsor School.
Address by President Park on
"Colleges Today."
Tea will be served after the meeting.

7.30 P. M.   Dinners at homes of Alumnae, followed by *Scholarships Conference at home of Mrs. Robert Walcott (Mary Richardson, 1906) for District Councillors and other members of Council especially concerned with Scholarships.*

FRIDAY, NOVEMBER 17th

10.00 A. M.   All-day meeting and luncheon at home of Mrs. Talbot Aldrich (Eleanor Little, 1905).
Reports from District Councillors.
Questions for Discussion, led by Chairmen of Standing Committees.

7.30 P. M.   Dinner at the Women's Republican Club for members of the Council and Alumnae of District I.
Address by President Park on
"Prevailing Winds at Bryn Mawr."

SATURDAY, NOVEMBER 18th

9.30 A. M.   Meeting at home of Mrs. Aldrich.
Phases of the College:
The Undergraduate Point of View.
Josephine Williams, 1933.
Mary Nichols, 1934.
The Graduate School.
Margaret Morriss, Ph.D. 1911, Dean of Pembroke College, Brown University.
Eunice M. Schenck, 1907, Professor of French and Dean of the Graduate School, Bryn Mawr College.
The Board of Directors.
Virginia McKenney Claiborne, 1908, Alumnae Director.

12.30 P. M.   Close of Council.

SIDELIGHTS ON EUROPEAN OPINIONS, 1933

By ELEANOR LANSING DULLES, 1917

It was disconcerting to have my six weeks' vacation disturbed by international crises. My husband and I had rationed our time between June 24th and August 7th with considerable care, hoping to see a number of friends scattered widely over Europe, and planning to insert some short trips to the country. In Basle we were told that the London Economic Conference would last long enough to suit our itinerary. In Geneva two days later it was rumored that the meeting might end any day. In fact, as I found out later, there was at this moment an almost unanimous agreement for immediate adjournment. Then, when we hurried on to Paris, the news was fairly definite that the Conference would continue until the 27th of July, and that gave us time for a short trip to Brittany.

As the result of our stimulating and diverting travels in France and Switzerland, we reached London on July 22nd in a vigorous state of health and with a keen curiosity to know how a conference, which seemed to be doing nothing, was going through the motions of international negotiation in the traditional manner. The first rumors and comments that greeted us were a distinct surprise. The Conference, though totally powerless to go counter the strong disturbing influences from America and elsewhere, and unable to break the tariff deadlock, was accomplishing a few inconspicuous but really worthwhile things. Moreover, the Americans, who had come in for round abuse during the early part of July, were now spoken of with either sympathy or toleration, according to the views of the various critics.

It was none too easy to attend more important sessions of the Conference, since the space allotted to the public was small, but it was possible to get tickets through the secretariat. In this group I found several friends from Basle and Geneva, and armed with a few admission tickets, I found entrance to the various lounging rooms fairly easy. It was usually assumed by the guards that I was a newspaper reporter, since no women economists were in evidence at such gatherings. I hung around the very comfortable refreshment room, and listened also to some rather perfunctory speeches in the assembly hall.

World-famous men could be seen in animated conversation here. Familiar figures were seen conferring together, the sound money men sighing over a lost world, the managed-money experts gloating over apparent gains for their theories. Keynes was much in evidence, it was said, but he had gone to the country by the time I arrived. Schacht, in all probability much the tallest man at the Conference, towered over his colleagues. He was seen infrequently, but his statements from the Nazi Germany on finance were listened to with great interest and concern. There was a mixed group of statesmen and economists gathered in heated discussion, or expressing a typical conference boredom. I saw many familiar faces and some old friends. Among the experts I found Walter Gardner (husband of Elizabeth Emerson, 1917), who had early made a good name for himself for his thorough knowledge of monetary affairs.

This gathering reminded me of my struggles to untangle international relations when I was researching in France and Switzerland. Indeed, when one entered the conference rooms of the Geological Museum in London, especially arranged for the Conference, one could easily imagine oneself in Geneva. There was about the building, the organization of the meetings, and the outstanding figures who dominated the conversations, the atmosphere of internationalism which was striking to all those who have followed recent conferences. In fact, a number of observers commented on the fact that there had been already developed a body of international functionaries, of men with a world viewpoint, and that there was a well-ordered technique for international discussion. This was evident in the careful arrangement of meetings, the quick preparation of reports and the activity of a competent secretariat made up of men adept in bringing together those with different ideas and conflicting lines of policy and interests. It was the result of more than ten years of practical experience in internationalism. This accomplishment is a first step, and certainly an important step in the developing of international government.

In spite of this reassuring impression, one has to admit that the Conference was poor in results and tragically futile in its inability to make the much needed world adjustments. Certainly it is not surprising that the few valuable accomplishments were concealed by one major disturbance which had prevented official agreement on any important point.

The disturbing episodes at the beginning of July had brought profound discouragement. It had been a shock to financial opinion to know that there was no hope of early currency stabilization anywhere. This was the more upsetting to the Conference since it was widely known that the negotiations for a temporary arrangement to steady exchange rates of the three major currencies had been carried to a point of tentative agreement, and had been thought to have the full sanction of the President. His message announcing the firm intention to keep a free hand in money matters and to avoid agreements which might restrict his liberty of action, was considered by many to be a partial repudiation of the Americans in London. Since it was followed by the uncertainty occasioned by Mr. Moley's short visit, and a lack of full information of the intentions of the Administration in these matters, it led to considerable confusion and bitterness. The public, for the most part, lost interest at this stage, and the further proceedings of the Conference were ignored or barely mentioned in the press. There was, in fact, little of a concrete nature to discuss.

Actually, some have claimed that the work of the Conference after July 3rd was in many ways more important than what had been accomplished in the more hopeful early weeks. It was possible, because of the patient forbearance and painstaking efforts of many of the delegates, to bring about a considerable measure of friendly understanding as to the nature of the difficulties and the importance of continuing to work for international adjustment. Coming to the Conference after the difficult days in early July, I did not at first believe that this better spirit was prevailing. It was only after talking to the representatives of a number of countries with widely divergent views that I realized that the American efforts in industry and finance were being looked upon with a considerable degree of understanding, and that there was a readiness to admit that a national emergency called for exceptional measures, even though the particular measures adopted were condemned by a great many of the economists at the Conference.

In any case, one real accomplishment seems to have developed from the long discussions of monetary problems. There emerged an almost unanimous agreement as to the general form of gold standard which would be adopted as a basis for the currencies of the world.

I found no evidence of serious opposition to the plans outlined in London to restore some form of gold standard as soon as American conditions would permit their participation in this part of reconstruction. The idea of the manner in which this standard was to work in future was influenced by a knowledge of the weaknesses in the past fifteen years. For instance, to prevent hoarding, it was generally thought that gold should never again enter into hand-to-hand circulation. Many agreed that only those engaged in international trade, or requiring gold for large transactions to stabilize international values, should be given the metal freely. In other words, a gold bullion standard, with economies in the use of the metal and a good deal of supervision, was an important feature of these plans for the future. In addition to this modification, some account was taken of the growing desire to stabilize national prices, even at some expense in the way of fluctuating exchange rates. These ideas were incorporated in various memoranda which were not in most cases official or definitive. Many of them were little more than expressions of a consensus of opinion, but they indicated a core of common principles and a real measure of agreement as to future monetary arrangement.

Even though this agreement was not publicly admitted, it is significant that there were clear signs of substantial progress in the outline of plans to use gold bullion as a foundation for money. Never before in the history of the world has there been a general understanding on this point. Never have the technical problems for regulating the currency been carried so far in conferences of more than sixty countries. To a considerable extent the way was thus prepared for a gradual restoration of monetary stability once the conditions in the United States shall have been clarified.

Credit for this real achievement should be given in a very large degree to Leon Fraser (American), newly elected President of the Bank for International Settlements. Observers from many countries admitted that he came to the Conference fully prepared with ideas of what might be accomplished, that he had a keen sense of practical responsibilities, and that his forceful personality led the commission of which he was a member in a logical way from point to point, until a fairly definite outline of monetary principles had been laid down.

There was almost equal unanimity as to the dignity and force of Secretary Hull under difficult conditions. It was frequently said that his personal integrity was in considerable measure responsible for the note of friendliness which characterized the closing days of the Conference.

The last meeting of the Conference was particularly interesting because of the succession of eminent speakers who expressed their frank opinions on the economic situation. There were a few who glossed over the failure to accomplish any immediate practical results, but on the whole the discussion was illuminating because of the outspoken expression of differences. Colijn (Holland) gave a forceful but somewhat inflexible expression of the free-trade classical economist approach to world problems; he recalled the succession of warnings he had given that the constant increase of restriction and interference would lead to inevitable disaster and pointed to recent events as the justification of this point of view. At the other extreme, and yet striking somewhat the same note at times, Maisky, representative of the Soviet Republic, indicated the successive mistakes of capitalist governments. He insisted that they had failed to make use of the alleged advantages of capitalism in that there was a paralyzing inability to act together in an emergency. He concluded that the individualistic regime could not long survive the complete incompetence and lack of plan which he found in every international conference.

In the final meeting there was an atmosphere of friendly understanding which was induced partly by a feeling of relief that the difficult session had adjourned without having caused any serious intensification of rivalries. Some, equipped with long experience in international deliberations, realized that this might mark a turning point in the manner of conducting international negotiations. There was a growing cynicism as to the possibility of success of large gatherings, such as those which had been held in recent years to settle questions of Reparations, of Disarmament, and other problems of the first importance. There was a thought in the minds of some that the international organizations should be given the function of preparing technical matter and arranging detail, but that larger decisions regarding principle and aims must be handled by smaller groups. At the very moment, then, when accomplishments seemed negligible, there was a notable growth in clear-sighted opinion.

Meanwhile I tried to get some idea of economic opinions and found that the English were watching the American experiment with the keenest interest. The economists whom I met generally expressed a tolerant skepticism. This was tempered in certain cases by a willingness to have another country try a bold experiment which probably would not cost their own nation much direct sacrifice. Professor Maynard Keynes and Ralph G. Hawtrey were, of course, eager to see the American attempts at national self-sufficiency and controlled inflation carried far. Others, in the Bank of England, the London School of Economics, in banks and universities elsewhere, were dubious as to the probable success of the venture. Inflation was always suspect to them. Government interference in industry could not develop balanced adjustment in a few short months, most of them asserted. The threat to the bond market, industrial reserves and international trade was, in their opinion, very serious. England had definitely turned away from public works and doubted the advisability of using them as a recovery instrument. The high costs involved, the scarcity of suitable projects, and the delay in getting them under way had led to their abandonment. Only in the case of agriculture did I find any general inclination to employ government funds as stimulants. These observers had placed the turning point of the world depression in the summer of 1932, and claimed a fairly steady improvement for many countries, including England, since that time.

In both England and on the continent, however, the hopes for economic revival were seriously disturbed by the Nazi regime and the threatening nature of the political changes in Germany, Austria and other strategic points. The discussions of disarmament and peace machinery were interrupted by forecasts of when the next war would break out. There seemed to be little hope of the restoration of democratic governments in Central Europe; and many signs of terror and violence on every hand.

Both Geneva and Basle seemed to be marking time. The Bank for International Settlements had made some minor adjustments in its method of doing business which were described to me. It had taken on new functions in connection with international gold holdings, and was devoting its major attention to developing carefully elaborated plans for the future of international finance. At the League there was a consciousness of the deflation of many extravagent hopes, but the momentum of the large organization which had responsibility in handling many critical problems affecting all countries of the world was not halted by the depression of spirit or the economies necessitated by world economic conditions. There was a sense of temporary inactivity, but no idea of a permanent shrinkage in the importance of the League. The private educational and propaganda committees were still in evidence. Many of the regular visitors to Geneva gathered on the new swimming beach at the Quai Mont Blanc, and a lightness of spirit stimulated by the mountain air, seemed to survive the more gloomy atmosphere of the conference rooms.

In view of the prevalence of crises and depression I was glad that my more serious interviews were balanced by days of bicycling in Britanny and a short walking trip. The Vosges Mountains are surprisingly unspoiled by tourists and automobiles, and constitute a perfect region for such an undertaking. Even here, however, we found signs to remind us of the war heritage and the menace of the future. The mountains, which form a massive wall of abrupt wooden slopes and dramatic cliffs, are scarred with the signs of battle. On some of the more impressive heights thousands of soldiers are buried, and the peasants still bend over their wine with murmured gossip of spies and treachery. It was something of a surprise to realize that many of the mountain dwellers spoke German as willingly as French, and that inevitably, should war break out, this impressive strip of mountain territory would again be blasted by destructive artillery fire.

It seemed to us that Europe, here as elsewhere, was restless and uneasy. The hope of a sound economic recovery, or the less reasonable expectation of a political miracle, were clung to by those who refused to accept the serious menace of the moment. Desperately, and yet with unceasing patience, high-minded men in Geneva and Basle, London and other centers of diplomacy and financial adjustment, continued their work for peace. It is impossible to see exactly what fruit these efforts will bear. There are times when the difficulties seem insuperable. There are people who argue with a cynicism which is hard to accept that the postponement of conflict may make the troubles in Europe worse rather than better. Such a view is not held, however, by those close to the negotiations and thoroughly versed in the practical details. These men still hope for adjustment. The observer who is completely convinced of the futility of war finds it reassuring that despite the distressing events of recent years both the spirit and the machinery of international coöperation survive.

After the BULLETIN had gone to press, word came that because of illness, Miss Addams would have to change the dates for her lectures to November 27th and December 4th. The other lectures will take place on the dates scheduled on page 18.

REGIONAL SCHOLARS

A large and brilliant blue eagle should unquestionably be affixed to the head-quarters of the various Regional Scholarships Committees. These gallant ones continue to do their part in any deal, new or old, and N. R. A. for them might seem to have the additional significance of New Regional Awards. Although, as is only natural, the total number of scholars sent and the total amount of money raised both fall somewhat behind the record of the last two years, the result still remains amazing. Thanks to the efforts of twelve of the committees, more than $12,000 is available for the use of thirty-six students during the year 1933-1934.

District I., New England, is responsible for eleven Scholars (three Seniors, one Junior, three Sophomores, four Freshmen); District II., with its four commit-tees in New York, New Jersey, Eastern Pennsylvania and Delaware, and Western Pennsylvania, is interested in fifteen (five Seniors, three Juniors, four Sophomores, three Freshmen); District III. sends five (one Sophomore and two Freshmen from Baltimore; one Junior from Washington; one Freshman from the South); Districts IV. and V. each have two (one Junior from Ohio and one Freshman from West Virginia; one Sophomore from Illinois and one Freshman from Iowa); the Northern California committee of District VII. continues its Scholar, now a Senior. For the first time in years there is no Scholar either from Southern California or from St. Louis, of District VI.

As usual, the Freshmen Scholars are a promising lot. Under the present more flexible plan of entrance requirements, it is impossible to give the old style numerical rankings when all candidates took the same kind and number of examina-tions, but it is perhaps understating the case to say that everyone of the twelve enters with a credit average in at least half the subjects in which she offered exami-nations, and that three of them might be counted in the first ten of the class and four more in the second ten.

A few statistics may be of interest. All but two of the Freshmen Scholars entered on Plan B; the others on Plan A. Four were prepared entirely by private schools, three entirely by public schools, and five by both private and public schools. Ten of them are below the median age of eighteen years (the average age is 17 years 11.1 months), and two are eighteen and a few months. We have this year only one who is an alumnae daughter, Louise Dickey, whose mother is Louise Atherton, 1903.

ARTICLES SPONSORED BY THE COMMITTEE OF SEVEN COLLEGES

In the September number of the *Ladies' Home Journal* is an editorial on scholarships, and in the September number of *College Humor and Sense* an article by Henrietta Sperry Ripperger, entitled "Four Ways of Financing An Education." Both are of great interest to alumnae at the present time.

In the August number of *Good Housekeeping* was another article by Mrs. Ripperger called "When You Choose Your Daughter's College."

BALLOT

[The Nominating Committee presents the following ballot for the consideration of the Association. According to the By-laws, additional nominations for any of these offices may be filed with the Alumnae Secretary before December 1st.]

Officers and Directors of the Association for Term of Office 1934-36

PRESIDENT

ELIZABETH BENT CLARK, 1895
(Mrs. Herbert Lincoln Clark)
Haverford, Pennsylvania

VICE-PRESIDENT

SERENA HAND SAVAGE, 1922
(Mrs. William L. Savage)
New York City

SECRETARY

JOSEPHINE YOUNG CASE, 1928
(Mrs. Everett Needham Case)
Cambridge, Massachusetts

TREASURER

BERTHA S. EHLERS, 1909
Upper Darby, Pennsylvania

CHAIRMAN OF FINANCE COMMITTEE

VIRGINIA ATMORE, 1928
Wayne, Pennsylvania

(Class Collector, 1928; Assistant Secretary Atmore & Co., Inc., Philadelphia, 1929-33; Former Secretary Soroptimist Club, Philadelphia)

DIRECTORS-AT-LARGE OF ALUMNAE ASSOCIATION

CAROLINE MORROW CHADWICK-COLLINS, 1905
(Mrs. James Chadwick-Collins)
Bryn Mawr, Pennsylvania
and
ALICE SACHS PLAUT, 1908
(Mrs. Jacob M. Plaut)
Cincinnati, Ohio

(12)

District Councillors for Term of Office 1934-37

COUNCILLOR FOR DISTRICT I.

(Maine, New Hampshire, Vermont, Massachusetts, Rhode Island, Connecticut)

MARY C. PARKER, 1926

Boston, Massachusetts

(Assistant to the Director of the Museum of Fine Arts, Boston; Representative to the Alumnae Council in Cincinnati in 1926)

COUNCILLOR FOR DISTRICT IV.

(Ohio, West Virginia, Kentucky, Michigan, Indiana)

ELIZABETH SMITH WILSON, 1915

(Mrs. Russell Wilson)

Cincinnati, Ohio

(Social Case worker for Associated Charities and for Red Cross of Cincinnati, 1917-19; Graduate Student Stanford University, 1919-20; teacher of English and Civics at Hughes High School, Cincinnati, 1920-23; some time member of the Board of the Cincinnati Community Chest, of the Maternity Society, of the Cincinnati Chapter of the Red Cross; former President of the Bryn Mawr Club of Cincinnati; former Regional Scholarships Chairman for District IV.; at present Regional Scholarships Chairman for Cincinnati.)

COUNCILLOR FOR DISTRICT VII.

(Arizona, Utah, Nevada, Idaho, Washington, Oregon, California)

LESLIE FARWELL HILL, 1905

(Mrs. Edward Buffum Hill)

Ross, California

(Director of local chapter of Red Cross in charge of Community Chest; Vice-President of Women's Auxiliary of St. John's Church; Regional Scholarships Chairman for Bryn Mawr Club of Northern California.)

Nominated by the Nominating Committee.

ELIZABETH NIELDS BANCROFT, 1898, *Chairman.*
NATHALIE SWIFT, 1913.
EVELYN HOLT LOWRY, 1909.
KATHARINE WALKER BRADFORD, 1921.
JULIA LEE McDILL, 1927.

NOTE

According to the amendment to the By-Laws passed at the Annual Meeting, February 11, 1933, nominations for Alumnae Director will be published in the April issue of the ALUMNAE BULLETIN. Suggestions for these should be sent either to the District Councillors or to the Alumnae Secretary before January 1st.

THE PRESIDENT'S PAGE

SOME OF THE ANNOUNCEMENTS MADE BY
PRESIDENT PARK TO THE STUDENTS

The College opens with 401 students, Graduate and Undergraduate. Wyndham is in use again, to help accommodate the entering class of 124 students, one of the largest in the history of the College.

* * * *

A most distinguished foreign visitor comes to the Faculty this year, Dr. Emmy Noether, a member of the mathematical faculty of the University of Göttingen. Dr. Noether is the most eminent woman in mathematics in Europe and has had more students at Göttingen than anyone else in the department. With other members of the faculty, Dr. Noether was asked to resign from the University in the spring. To our great satisfaction the Institute of International Education and the Rockefeller Foundation have united in giving to the College a generous grant which makes it possible for the Department of Mathematics to invite her here for two years. Her general field is Algebra and the Theory of Numbers. Dr. Noether does not, I understand, speak English well enough to conduct a seminary at once, but she will be available for consultation by the graduate students and later, I trust, can herself give a course. I need not say that I am delighted Bryn Mawr College is one of many American institutions to welcome the scholars whom Germany has rejected. For the time only we must believe Germany has set aside a great tradition of reverence for the scholar and for learning. I am glad also that the College can entertain so distinguished a woman and that the students in mathematics can profit by her brilliant teaching.

* * * *

The Mary Flexner lectureship is to be omitted this year in favor of the Anna Howard Shaw Foundation series for students in the social sciences. It resumes its distinguished course next year with a lecturer to be chosen by the Department of English. And in future I think there will ordinarily be two years when the Mary Flexner lectureship in the humanities is given, followed by a year in which the Shaw lectureship in the Social Sciences takes its place. Those of you who read Mr. Whitehead's new book, *The Adventures of Ideas*, this summer will have noted that five chapters in that book are designated as lectures on the Mary Flexner lectureship at Bryn Mawr College.

* * * *

Of our own faculty, Professor Henry Cadbury returns from a sabbatical year divided between England and Palestine to his work at Bryn Mawr. As I announced last year, Professor Cadbury accepted a call to become Hollins Professor of Divinity at Harvard, to take effect a year from now. I am proud that for eight years his name and fame have shed lustre on us and grateful to him for proposing to return for a year before he goes to his Cambridge work. Professor Agnes Rogers, who has been in England and Scotland on sabbatical leave, is unfortunately unwell and unable to return to Bryn Mawr for the first semester. Dr. Lelah Crabbs, who was lecturer in education last year, has—at, I fear, a good deal of inconvenience to herself—consented to return and to carry Miss Rogers' courses for a semester longer, so that the continuity of work in the department may be unbroken. I hope that Miss Rogers herself may be able to resume her courses, undergraduate and graduate, in February. I spoke last year to the students of the new appointments for this winter—Dr. Ernst Diez, a returned wanderer, Associate Professor of History of Art; Dr. Clara Marburg Kirk as Associate Professor of English Composition; Dr. Donald MacKinnon as Associate in Psychology; Dr. Herbert A. Miller as Lecturer in Social Economy; Dr. Richard Bernheimer as Lecturer in History of Art, and Dr. Florence Whyte as Instructor in Spanish. Mrs. Hortense Flexner King will teach this year, in addition to her course in modern poetry, a division of freshman English.

* * * *

With the opening of the college year two enterprises interesting to all are launched under new flags. The College Inn, since its beginning managed by a small and special Inn Association, has now come under the control of the Trustees of the College. The Inn itself has been made into small apartments and will in the end, though perhaps not this year, be entirely occupied by permanent residents. The Tea Room, however, has not only been kept, but enlarged and beautified. Miss Sara Davis, an experienced manager of similar tea rooms, has taken it in charge, and her assistant manager is Miss Marion Black, whom all the College of two years ago knew as the efficient and delightful deviser of May Day costumes. Miss Davis and Miss Black and the tea room committee as well are anxious to make the tea room the most comfortable and the most pleasant of the neighborhood. It is for the students first of all, to give them what they want at the time and in the time they want it. I shall ask the undergraduate members of the College Council to act as a consulting committee for Miss Davis. One request, however, I make myself. I ask that the students do not go over to the tea room in clothes which are so informal as to surprise the visitor. The College is, after all, not an informal place, nor a place where you alone live, move and have your being.

COLLEGE FINANCES

It will be remembered that at this time last year Mr. J. Henry Scattergood, Treasurer of the Board of Trustees of Bryn Mawr College, authorized the Comptroller to give to the BULLETIN for publication some comparative figures in regard to the College income, showing the remarkably healthy state of the College finances. The alumnae will be glad to know that Mr. Scattergood is again able to issue a satisfactory statement. At the close of the fiscal year of the College, June 30th, 1933—a year in which almost all individuals and institutions throughout the country experienced a severe diminution of both capital and income—the receipts on invested funds held by the College had decreased only about 6% from those of the previous year, a falling off of about $20,000. The following figures speak for themselves:

Cost or Book Value	Fiscal Year	Actual Income	Net Interest
$6,340,668.58	1931-32	$315,877.14	4.982
6,383,787.67	1932-33	295,859.97	4.634

ON THE CAMPUS

By J. ELIZABETH HANNAN, 1934

The first week of the college year would be an excellent time for alumnae to revisit Bryn Mawr. Then it is that one sees the undergraduate body in fine fettle, attacking its problems with vigor—seniors boning for the German oral, freshmen listening with rapt attention to assorted advice, and everyone airing her pet theories concerning the world in general and Bryn Mawr in particular. It is the healthiest and most unacademic week from October 1st to Commencement Day, a reprieve before certain self-imposed habits, such as studying, eating too much, and planning erratic week-ends, are revived. The cool and homogeneous mass that greets the outsider's eye after the first glow of returning has worn off is not half so attractive as this crowd of newcomers. The discovery of the College by freshmen and its rediscovery by upper classmen lends a charm to every person and a freshness to everything which soon disappears. In short, a change does wonders. The trouble has always been, however, that boredom succeeds effervescence and the first flourish remains a lonely flourish, with little relation to campus spirit for the rest of the year.

That has been our impression of late years. Whether a change in attitude is imminent this year remains to be seen. It has been said, and alumnae have probably noticed the phenomenon, that Bryn Mawr moves in cycles, from collegiate to sophisticate and back, experiencing varying shades of each by the way. According to sound observers, we are now having a collegiate revival, aided by renewed interest in athletics, by the enthusiasm of a new and powerful freshman class (124 in number), and by an unabashed desire on the part of the undergraduates to learn.

The swing to athletics which got under way last year with the determined efforts of the athletic element to make Bryn Mawr "sport-minded" will be actively encouraged again this year. Freshman hockey material, which roams the campus in force, will be canvassed by the *News* sports-writer; swimming tests disclose that there will be plenty of freshmen to fill up the ranks when the champions of '34 have graduated; and the dance will be publicized through a series of articles written by Janet Barber for the *News*. Most of the competitive sport will be intramural, so the consequence will probably be a rebirth of defunct class spirit. Such mock struggles as occur at Parade Night are simply an excuse for a riotous torchlight parade, which in itself is such a rousing spectacle that we could wish for one every week. This year the sophomores won the game of "Hunt the Tune," but they may well be shy of anything like hand-to-hand battle with the freshmen, and we should advise them to fight it out on the playing fields, where the teams are equal by rule. There are dangers in this collegiate renaissance, the most obvious being that the freshman class might suddenly become conscious of its youth and strength, and set up a dictatorship over the rest of the College.

As this year's class seems much more at ease than last year's, one is forced to the conclusion that Freshman Week, though frequently abused as being too long, is a good institution, both for freshmen and administration. Apparently there is a definite need for freshmen to get acquainted with the Dean, as disclosed when a freshman glorified the Junior Class President with the title of "Dean." Such untoward mistakes should be guarded against. In an early issue of the *News*, a survey of the question of whether Freshman Week is valuable or not will be made. Although discussion of the question has been frequent and has become hackneyed, a comparison based on the results last year, when the week of grace was omitted, and this year, when the custom was resumed, will be interesting. One might conclude that the enforced delay in starting classes stimulates freshman interest in what is to come. At least, last year's freshmen did not inquire of one at breakfast just what the Philosophy course covers.

That, however, may only be part of that frank wish to get knowledge, which existed in more sophisticated periods, but was kept under cover as a concession to good taste. A striking instance of the trend to a serious attitude was furnished at Miss Park's opening address; there was plenty of laughing and clapping of hands when the improvement of the Tea Room service (that thorn in the side of so many Bryn Mawr generations) was announced, but when President Park turned to the subject of the present economic situation and emphasized the uncertainty of the future, the whole atmosphere changed, and her audience became a sober, grimly attentive group.

For several years we have been reading happy articles written by prominent educators concerning the change that has come over undergraduates during the depression. Dr. Christian Gauss, Dean of Princeton, said a few weeks ago in the *Times*, "Nowhere in the world is Shakespeare's 'Sweet are the uses of adversity,' so true as upon college campuses. That is because complacency, cock-sureness, and the closed mind which they beget are the deadliest enemies of true education. Before a student can be initiated into any sort of intellectual discipline, this barrier must be broken down, and in most cases this task, the most difficult for the teacher, has been accomplished by events and personal experience"—meaning that unprecedented purge, the depression. We do believe that it has made the post-1929 undergraduate more serious, but that alone seems a pretty doubtful gain. A death in the family is sobering, too. It may be that we are still in the grips of the "complacency, cock-sureness, and closed mind" of yesterday, but we do not believe that Bryn Mawr needed such a large scale chastening or that there ever were more than a few clam-like minds on the campus. However, as Miss Park pointed out, it is now necessary to change our approach to our studies and learn methods, not only facts, training the mind to a new kind of openness, not that implied in the above quotation (a mere willingness to be taught), but the sort that fortifies one for sudden and drastic change.

A minor test of the College's capacity for change, as well as its reaction to the "Buy Now" campaign, will be made this week when the question of having college-wide subscription to the *News* is reopened. Last year the vote in favor of compulsory subscription was won by such a slim margin that the *News* board decided not to press the matter. Objection will undoubtedly be renewed on the ground that all compulsory dues are bad, but the *News* can this year plead that an impecunious campus publication has the same right to be college-supported as the farmers have to be subsidized by our government. A precedent like that can scarcely be ignored.

ANNA HOWARD SHAW MEMORIAL FOUNDATION

INTERNATIONAL RELATIONS AND INTERNATIONAL PEACE

I.

MONDAY, OCTOBER 16TH

MISS JANE ADDAMS
Subject: THE HOPES WE INHERIT

II.

MONDAY, OCTOBER 23RD

MISS JANE ADDAMS
Subject: OPPORTUNITIES OF THE NEW DAY

III.

MONDAY, OCTOBER 30TH

MRS. VERA MICHELES DEAN
Subject: FASCISM OR DEMOCRACY IN EUROPE?

IV.

MONDAY, NOVEMBER 6TH

MRS. VERA MICHELES DEAN
Subject: THE NEW EUROPEAN BALANCE OF POWER

V.

MONDAY, NOVEMBER 13TH

MRS. DEAN AND DR. MILDRED FAIRCHILD
Subject: THE SOVIET UNION AT THE END OF THE FIRST FIVE-YEAR PLAN

VI.

MONDAY, NOVEMBER 20TH

MRS. F. LOUIS SLADE
Subject: THE FAR EAST

This year for the first time a series of lectures under the Anna Howard Shaw Foundation, established in 1928, will be held. The purpose of the lectureship is to establish a memorial to Dr. Shaw at Bryn Mawr College to take the form of a course of lectures to be given by persons, preferably women, eminent in politics, social science or in any other field of scholarship, who should, whenever possible, take up residence at the college for varying periods of time for conference and consultation with the faculty and students of the College.

Conferences in connection with Miss Addams' lectures will be held under the direction of Miss Emily Greene Balch, 1889, National President of the Women's International League for Peace and Freedom.

THE ALUMNAE BOOK SHELF

Reprinted from New York Herald-Tribune Books, October 1, 1933

JUNKET IS NICE, *by Dorothy Meserve Kunhardt.* Harcourt, Brace and Company, New York. $1.

Once there was a new, new book with a red jacket and a red cover, and a man who had on a blue shirt and a yellow tie saw the book with the red jacket and the red cover in a book store, so he went into the store and bought the book and took it to his white home that had three boys and one girl in it and two dogs and two cats. So when the man got to his white home he said, if you guess what this red book with the red jacket is about I will give it to you for your very own, but before you start guessing I will give you a little help and tell you what the book is NOT about and it is NOT about a zebra in the Bronx Zoo that went there in a Checker taxicab and it is NOT about seven boys shining wet fire engines with a wet gray rag.

Then the two dogs and the two cats and the littlest boy who was not one year old and the girl who was two years old didn't guess anything because they didn't know what guessing was or even what a book was. So one of the boys who was five years old and had on brown overalls guessed it was a book about yellow carrots with green tops. WRONG, said the man, and went on reading. And the boy who was six and a half and a little more than a half so it was really seven who had on blue overalls guessed it was about a boy who was eating chocolate ice cream with a shiny black and white spoon. WRONG, said the man, and went on reading. Then the five-year-old boy and the nearly seven-year-old boy said, I guess it is about JUNKET IS NICE! RIGHT, said the man, so here is the book with the red cover and the red jacket for your very own. And the boys said it was the best book that anybody ever wrote in the whole world and the country. RIGHT, said the man, who had read a million and a hundred books. I think that it is a book with the greatest sympathetic simplicity and the most poetic and affectionate imagination I ever saw, and I don't except Little Black Sambo or Alice's Adventures in Wonderland. RIGHT, said the boy in the brown overalls and the boy with the blue overalls so you would think there was only one boy talking, they did it so together. And they said, can we have two hundred and a hundred bowls of junket for supper. And the man said, Yes, but why do you want junket, and they said together, because JUNKET IS NICE! Read it every day before supper. So every day before supper the man read the book, and if you guess that the boys or the man ever got tired of it you are WRONG. FRANKLIN P. ADAMS

THE COLLEGE BOOK SHOP REORGANIZED

The old Bryn Mawr Coöperative Society in the basement of Taylor has been reorganized and will now be called the Bryn Mawr Book Shop. The entire profits of the shop, except for salaries, will go to scholarships. To alumnae ordering any standard book, delivery can be guaranteed within four days. In addition to this service, there is also a lending library. Magdalen Hupfel Flexner, '28, is in charge.

ALUMNAE RESPONSIBILITY TO THE COMMUNITY

The following letter was sent to each Vassar Alumna by the President of the Vassar Alumnae Association. The Secretary of the National Education Association of the United States forwarded copies of it, and in his letter enclosed with it urged that every college in the country send a similar appeal to its graduates.

June 6, 1933.

To the Alumnae of Vassar College:

At a time when the children of our country need all the mental and moral training possible, thousands of schools have been closed, and in thousands of others the classrooms are hopelessly over-crowded and valuable opportunities are being curtailed. Also, women and children in many places are working long hours for less than starvation wages.

Obviously the public school systems are the first to suffer at the hands of politically-minded councils that are trying to reduce budgets, and obviously, too, the present situation offers a chance to those employers who are unscrupulous enough to take advantage of all classes of workers.

With the approval of the Board of Directors and the Council of Representatives, I am writing to beg that each one of you become *aware* of the situation in your community as it relates to the welfare of the public schools and libraries, and to the exploitation of workers. If you find that the public school budget or the number of teachers is being decreased beyond the point where it is absolutely necessary or in every way justified, or that employers are breaking down hard-won labor laws that it may take years to rebuild, will you ally yourself with any existing non-political group that is taking steps to combat such conditions, or, if necessary, help to create such a group? Will you also write the Executive Secretary of the Association, giving a picture of conditions in your city and of the attitude of the citizens towards unjustified encroachments, if any, on the educational system or the labor laws?

It is not our purpose to suggest affiliations with any political organizations. You may find already at work in your vicinity a branch of the League of Women Voters, or some other body, such as the citizens' group in Baltimore, which you can join.

ALUMNAE DAUGHTERS IN THE CLASS OF 1937

Daughters	Mothers	Class
Agnes. Allinson	Mary Shipley	1914
Louise Atherton Dickey	Louise Atherton	1903
Sylvia Hathaway Evans, Jr.	Sylvia Hathaway	1913
Sarah Ann Fultz	Ellen Baltz	1900
Esther Hardenbergh	Margaret Nichols	1905
Margaret Gracie Jackson	Elizabeth Higginson	1897
Kathryn Moss Jacoby	Helen Lowengrund	1906
Jeanne Macomber	Harriet Seaver	1907
Louise Emily Steinhardt	Amy Sussman	1902
Jill Lit Stern	Juliet Lit	1910
Eleanore Flora Tobin	Helen Roche	1907
Granddaughter	*Grandmother*	*Class*
Laura Gamble Thomson	Ann Taylor Simpson	1889

CLASS NOTES

Ph.D. and Graduate Notes

Editor: MARY ALICE HANNA PARRISH
(Mrs. J. C. Parrish)
Vandalia, Missouri.

Ellen Ewing Long and her husband, the Reverend Harold B. Long, who moved last winter to Tacoma, Washington, announce the birth of a daughter in August.

Martha Bunting, Ph.D. 1895, has been in poor health lately, but she is still engaged in research in American History, especially in regard to members of the Society of Friends in the Colonial period. In September, 1933, she was notified of her election as a Fellow of the American Association for the Advancement of Science.

1889

(The following news of the Class of 1889 was sent to the Alumnae Office.)

Emily Greene Balch will have charge of the conferences in connection with Miss Jane Addams' lectures to be given at the College under the Anna Howard Shaw Foundation.

Anne Taylor Simpson's granddaughter, Laura Gamble Thomson, '37, has the distinction of being the first granddaughter to enter Bryn Mawr College.

Anna Rhoads Ladd spent the month of September at Southwest Harbor with Lida Adams Lewis. Her daughter Margaret, Bryn Mawr '21, took her Ph.D. at Columbia in June. The title of her thesis, which has not yet been published, is entitled: "The Relation of Social, Economic and Personal Characteristics to Reading Ability." She is "afraid" that she will spend the winter with her family.

Julia Cope Collins spent two weeks at her camp at Littleton, New Hampshire. Her husband took part in the activities of the Haverford College Centenary, held in early October.

Leah Goff Johnson and her husband went, as usual, to their farm at Woodstock, Vermont. She is now engrossed in activities connected with Jefferson Hospital, Philadelphia.

Alice Anthony writes from Pasadena, where she is living near her sister, Emily: "I think of my friends in the East very often and would enjoy seeing them."

Mary Garrett Williams travelled to the Near East in the early spring of 1933, her objective being the Friends Mission, near Jerusalem. On account of an accident to her knee on the steamer she was kept a prisoner for some weeks in a hospital in Alexandria, but reached Ramallah in time to paint many of the wild flowers that grow on the surrounding hills. On her return trip she spent three weeks with her daughter, Mary, near Grasse, in Southern France. In July she went to her summer home in Ogunquit, Maine. Her water colors (250) of Maine flora were exhibited by the York Garden Club in connection with a "Save the Wild Flowers" meeting.

Lina Lawrence is living in New York City with her niece Marian (Bryn Mawr 1923), who is teaching art at Barnard College.

Martha G. Thomas reports that "Whitford Farm" (for the second time) won the first prize for raw milk at the State Farm Products Show, January, 1933. She is a Trustee of West Chester State Teachers College, one of the Board of Corporation of the Woman's Medical College of Pennsylvania, a manager of the Chester County Hospital and especially interested in its School of Nursing, and Director of the State Council of Republican Women.

Ella Riegel plans to attend the Pan-American Congress to be held in Montevideo in November.

Other members of '89 are doing interesting things and will be heard from in a later BULLETIN. The Class of '89 was among the first to show its appreciation of Miss Thomas' generous plan for the Alumnae House by having a Class Tea in the Deanery Garden.

1890

No Editor Appointed.

1891

No Editor Appointed.

1892

Class Editor: EDITH WETHERILL IVES
(Mrs. F. M. Ives)
Dingle Ridge Farm, Brewster, N. Y.

The class offers its sincerest sympathy to Helen Clements Kirk on the death of her husband, Dr. Kirk, who died July 20th, six weeks after the wedding of their youngest daughter, Barbara (Bryn Mawr '31), to Andrew Brisbin Foster, of Haverford.

Your editor is proudly announcing the birth of a second grandchild, Paul Ives Bartholet, on August 17th. This is the son of her daughter Elizabeth (Bryn Mawr '24). The first grandson, now two years old, lives in Seattle and his grandparents have never seen him, so they are congratulating themselves on having a grandchild that comes within their range of vision. They are planning to remain late in the country this year, as the above address indicates, and return early in the spring.

1893

Class Editor: SUSAN WALKER FITZGERALD
(Mrs. Richard Y. FitzGerald)
7 Greenough Ave., Jamaica Plain, Mass.

1894

Class Editor: ABBY BRAYTON DURFEE
(Mrs. Randall Durfee)
19 Highland Ave., Fall River, Mass.

The class extends its sincere sympathy to Fay MacCracken Stockwell, whose husband, the Reverend Doctor Frederick E. Stockwell, died in Philadelphia, June 27th. Dr. Stockwell was College Secretary of the Board of Christian Education of the Presbyterian Church.

1895

Class Editor: SUSAN FOWLER
c/o The Brearley School
610 East 83rd St., New York City.

Readers of the news of '95 are hereby notified that they are not to expect a repetition in this place of the delightful qualities of style that marked the note which was printed under my name in the July BULLETIN; that pleasant little piece was kindly supplied by a ghost writer in the Alumnae Office in order that a report of the reunion might appear promptly.

Frances Swift Tatnall is principal of Mrs. Tatnall's School of Girls, in Wilmington. She started the school in 1930 to meet the need for a non-coeducational school. Her daughter, Frances (Bryn Mawr '31), is to be a teacher of history this year at St. Timothy's School, Catonsville, an arrangement which I find very interesting since my sister is head of that school.

Mary Ellis is a vigorous and skilful gardener as well as the very busy head of a school, Springside, in Chestnut Hill, Pa.

Madeline Harris Brown spent July and August at Montrose, Pa., as usual; among her summer visitors was her very own granddaughter.

Rosalie Furman Collins was with me for a week in September, at South Hadley, Mass. Rosalie is president of a women's club in Cranford, N. J., and chairman of the Chapter of the Junior Red Cross there; and she is an active performing member of the Cranford Dramatic Club. Her son, John Dillard Collins, took his degree in June at the Massachusetts Institute of Technology, in the First Honors group. Rosalie was at College at reunion time, though not on the day of the Wyndham luncheon.

Bertha Szold Levin travelled last winter in Egypt, Palestine, and Syria. She visited her sister, Henrietta Szold, who lives in Jerusalem, and is a member of the Jewish National Council and Chairman of the Committee for German Refugees. Bertha's daughter, Eva Levin, is now at Bryn Mawr in the Class of 1934.

In answer to my September class letter, Edith Pettit Borie sent me an account of her Mexican impressions:

"We spent July and half of August last summer in Mexico. My imagination about our neighbor having never been excited, I was so unwritten a sheet that I had not read Prescott's Conquest till I was about to start! So I had that prized equipment, a blank mind, and I had an extraordinarily good time getting it scribbled over. Mexico gave me the illusion I was all young again.

"Indians and the Indian problem became at once interesting. The State is busy studding the country with admirable schools, just as the Spaniards had studded it with churches, great golden baroque churches, one or more to every tiny village. The State is trying to arouse the Indian to be politically-minded, or at least to want money. But he still seems preoccupied with his own inheritances, and to want nothing but land enough to feed his village. Spanish Catholicism he has made his own, and no one quite knows how much of his own idols are behind the altars.

"We saw something of the young artists and architects down there who are allowed to design and paint all the new school buildings, often just open-air, adobe-walled affairs, full of color. The subjects of the frescoes are social propaganda, but they become as familiar as were the Days of Judgment in the mediaeval churches.

"My son, Peter, joined the Seminar, arranged each year by the New York Committee on Cultural Relations with Latin America, and heard very good lectures on Mexican history, economics, and home industries. The government encourages its members to talk to the Seminar and opens ways of approaching the country. My husband and I were often guests at these talks, and heard first-hand accounts of the government's problems.

"The summer climate is almost perfection, once you are on the great plateau. One basks in the sun at noon, and needs a blanket at night. The rains rarely begin till late afternoon, and the mornings are always radiant.

Landing at Vera Cruz is a tropical experience! But having reached a healthy maturity in Philadelphia, I saw no reason to get uppish. And in five or six hours the railroad crosses a pass ten thousand feet high, before it goes down three thousand feet to the Mexican plain. The country is excitingly formed, romantically violent, with its jungles and deserts and mountains, and the three snow-capped volcanoes. And its flowers!

"Do go as quickly as you can to where you can feel alternatively that you are in a world of pastoral poetry, or in a mild Soviet Russia."

1896

Class Editor: ABIGAIL CAMP DIMON
1411 Genesee St., Utica, N. Y.

1897

Class Editor: FRIEDRIKA HEYL
104 Lake Shore Drive, East, Dunkirk, N. Y.

1898

Class Editor: ELIZABETH NIELDS BANCROFT
Acting Secretary
(Mrs. Wilfred Bancroft)
615 Old Railroad Ave., Haverford, Pa.

1899

Editor: CAROLYN TROWBRIDGE BROWN LEWIS
(Mrs. H. Radnor Lewis)
451 Milton Road, Rye, N. Y.

1900

Class Editor: LOUISE CONGDON FRANCIS
(Mrs. Richard Francis)
414 Old Lancaster Road, Haverford, Pa.

On September 27th Edith Crane Lanham died after a long illness. Her death is a great sorrow to 1900.

The class will like to read part of a letter which she sent on July 29th to Helen Mac Coy, thanking her for her part in a series of letters which she had received from various members of 1900:

"I've had a wild dream of writing each classmate myself, and actually began the undertaking, but found it impossible of accomplishment. How I long to answer every writer! No matter; each of them belongs to me in some real sense, for the thirty-three years of our more or less vital touch have brought me, at least, enrichment. Thank you for these latest happy contacts.

"Will you be so kind as to express my grateful appreciation in the ALUMNAE BULLETIN? And the dear people who took the trouble to write me ought to have a cordial word in reply, if you can manage to send them a copy of this useless but well-meaning screed. I thank everyone of you!"

Edna Fischel Gellhorn spent two days in Washington in September, representing consumer interests in drawing up the milk code for the N. R. A.

Cornelia Halsey Kellogg has been made Honorary President of the National Council of State Garden Clubs Federations, which has about 75,000 members. She is one of the County Directors of Emergency Relief in New Jersey. She also is on the Compliance Board for the N. R. A. in Morristown. When last heard from she was passing on hours and wages for laundry workers. A note about the wedding of Cornelia's daughter appears under the 1927 notes.

If any proof were needed of the perennial youth of 1900, Jessie Tatlock's latest achievement would be proof positive. In June she secured her Ph.D. from Harvard in history. We all congratulate her on her degree and on her well-earned delightful summer in her cottage at Southwest Harbor.

Grace Campbell Babson is always an inspiration to us. She writes: "I'm head of the county health work; so am always busy."

Hilda Loines is still hard at work over the Brooklyn Botanic Gardens. She is the only woman Chairman of a Botanic Garden in the country. Hilda spent last winter in Florida.

Mira Culin Sanders is Chairman of Conservation in the Pasadena Garden Club. Her husband has just written a book on California wild flowers. Mira is also active in International coöperation affairs.

Caroline Sloane Lombardi is living in Palo Alto with her daughter, who is a laboratory technician in the Palo Alto Hospital.

Elizabeth White Edwards' daughter graduated in June at Wheaton College. Johanna Kroeber Mosenthal's daughter graduated from Vassar.

Lotta Emery Dudley is still living in England. She writes that she is doing "far-reaching and humanistic research work which brings her into touch with embassies, ministries, and savants."

1901

Class Editor: HELEN CONVERSE THORPE
(Mrs. Warren Thorpe)
15 East 64th St., New York City.

Ellen Ellis has been to Russia this vacation, as part of a tour which included also Copenhagen, Helsingfor and other Baltic ports.

1902

Class Editor: ANNE ROTAN HOWE
(Mrs. Thorndike Howe)
77 Revere St., Boston, Mass.

1903

Class Editor: GERTRUDE DIETRICH SMITH
(Mrs. Herbert Knox Smith)
Farmington, Conn.

Charlotte Morton Lanagan writes: "After the way we moved about in Schenectady those four years, I am surprised to find myself in the same house—our own—after a year! We have our camp in the Helderbergs, and I picked up an ossified sponge out there last week, showing that something was there a few million of years before us!"

Agatha Laughlin writes: "I have come East for the summer to see my family and friends and will not return to California until October. After November 1st, my latch string is out for any of 1903, and I hope anyone who comes to San Diego or nearby will look me up. I am only twenty miles from San Diego, in a quiet and pleasant valley in the hills."

Elizabeth Eastman writes: "Any tendency to a fatuous and expansive autobiography is curbed by the wise limit of a postal card! I am still living in Washington with my brother, who was recently appointed Federal Coördinator of the Railroads. My own work seems to be largely serving on various boards, and I am still Chairman of the Women's Joint Congressional Committee and deeply interested in political questions. Warmest greetings to all 1903."

Betty Breed writes: "Our youngest child, Henry, has just graduated from Princeton. Carrie Wagner came to the Blair commencement to see her nephew, Richard Parish, graduate with honors. Charlie and I are leaving next week for a canoe and fishing trip in northwestern Ontario, where we shall cover about 150 miles in canoes and on foot. This is a sequel to a trip we took last summer. We had a nice visit from Agnes and Howell Vincent in April. Best wishes."

Eva White Kab writes: "The only Bryn Mawrter whom I have seen in several years is Grace Latimer Jones McClure, who made an address before our Federation. I enjoyed the address and seeing her."

A delightful card from Ida Langdon reads as follows: "If I had any news a plea phrased as yours is would instantly draw it from me. I am, in fact, almost moved to invent some. But honesty prevailing, I can only say that the winter behind me was, happily, full of work, but empty of event, and the summer ahead promises to be altogether quiet. I have no radio and I do not play bridge. I mean to fill my vacation with old stories, old plays, and old poetry. And having thus spoken, I have given you my news."

Edith Clothier Sanderson is still working at the Grenfell Labrador Industries Shop in Philadelphia, and living, in Haverford. She expects to have a look at the World's Fair in Chicago later in the summer.

Martha White in future will spend most of her time in the West and in Florida, with New York a detour. Things have worked out that way. She has bought half interest in a horse and hog ranch in Arizona, which raises thoroughbred horses, Percheron drafts, and Hampshire hogs. The hogs were supposed to pay the overhead for the horses, but if the horse market continues to rise, it may be the other way round.

Eunice Follansbee Hale writes: "Busy with a connection at the World's Fair, i.e., The Children's International Library on the Enchanted Island. One classmate, Rosamund Allen Evans, has just left me and I expect Anne Sherwin soon. Please, all classmates who come to the Fair, look me up. Home practically all summer."

Lillian Mooers Smith writes: "My daughter graduated this year from Abbott Academy, and my son from Methuen High School. Everett is planning to go to Yale, but Clara will keep me company at home next year."

Florence Wattson Hay writes: "We are still clinging to our cliff dwelling in spite of the efforts of man and nature to dislodge us. Last summer a man on a loaded 5-ton truck crashed into our car as we were backing from the garage and hurtled us, car, end of garage, etc., 45 feet into our garden, almost over the 60-foot bluff. Then on March 10th along came the earthquake, shaking our house almost off its pins and into the ocean. Rumor has it that we may be moved to Cleveland, Ohio, in the spring of 1934."

Flora Gifford writes: "I have my headquarters at this charming seaside village. The climate is the most equable I know, the scenery lovely. In the last two years I have seen quite a bit of California, Pasadena, Ojai, Carmel, Berkeley, Palo Alto. I have escaped the earthquakes."

Dothie (D. Day Watkins) has built a brand new house for a new family which she hopes to find. In other words, she is starting a small school for small children between the ages of 6-12, at Hampden, Sidney.

Marjory Cheney writes: "Having been licked in the primaries last autumn I did not return to the Legislature last winter but had the satisfaction of seeing Gertrude Smith winning respect on all sides as a member. I worked as a lobbyist for the Child Welfare Commission all winter and found trying to insert ideas into the heads of the General Assembly was almost harder work than being a member and letting other people's ideas roll off. Most of the Commission's program perished, but one important bill was passed which will improve the chances of neglected babies in Connecticut.

I am soon going up to Ogunquit, to Mr. Woodbury's summer art school, which is great fun and calculated to keep one's mind off everything but painting. I recommend it to the middle-aged who want a change of preoccupations. Anyone can learn to paint enough to enjoy it if she puts her mind on it. That is not to say that others will enjoy her paintings, however. Since art seems to have ceased any attempt at communication, what's the odds?"

Elizabeth Snyder Lewis' mother very kindly sent the following news of Elizabeth's children, Mary ten years old and Ray nine: "Ray is writing a comic strip, started it at eight years —shows some ability."

Maidie Williamson is on her way to the White Mountains, having no car, which she says is news in these days, and New England having no train she is cudgeling her brain just as to how she is going to get to her hostelry, which is called the Crawford House.

Emma Crawford Bechtel writes that she has a new address, 6608 Wayne Avenue, Mount Airy, Philadelphia. She says also that her son, Richard C. Bechtel, is a Sophomore at Bowdoin College, and her daughter Thalia has been awarded the Philadelphia Branch Scholarship for Vassar. She was graduated in June from the Germantown Friends School.

Amanda Hendrickson Molinari writes from Finland, in July: "You often ask me for news, but since I do not often seem to be doing anything original it never seems worth telling. At present we feel we are quite original, for we have brought our own car with us via Norwegian coast by steamer, landed at Kirkenis, in the Arctic Ocean, and drove down on the only road in the Arctic Circle, through Lapland. The country is all lakes and forests, the roads all sand and curves, the houses all log cabins. This, with the great honesty of the people, is all a delightful change from the rest of Europe. My greetings to you and 1903."

Maude Spencer Corbett, who lives in Styning, England, sends the following news: "We are just back from a holiday in Italy which we took in our little 8 H. P. open, single car. We went all the way out (900 miles) on 20 gallons of petrol! My oldest son has an aeroplane on one of the big navy carriers, the Courageous. The other one is at the London School of Architecture. I haven't seen anyone from Bryn Mawr for years, and would be more than delighted if any or all of you would turn up here at any time! We are only 50 miles from London."

Eleanor Burrell Hornby writes: "My eldest son, Raymond, Jr., is a Sophomore at Stanford. For myself, I had a very quiet year; the doctor ordered a halt, so I'm off everything but Assistance League and Hospital boards."

From Alice Lovell Kellogg: "Nothing exciting happens. My youngest children, the twin daughters, graduated from high school this June and will go, one to Scripps College and one to Pomona (both in Claremont, California), next year. The boy will take his second year in San José State College and transfer the year after to Stanford.

"We have spent the last four summers camping in the various western National Parks. This summer we are late getting off, but expect eventually to have about six weeks in Sequoia and General Grant Parks.

"I keep busy winters in the A. A. U. W. and am at present Corresponding Secretary. I do wish some 1903-er would come out this way. I haven't seen anybody for a long time. My best wishes to the class."

Gertrude Dietrich Smith flew to Santa Fé the latter part of July to be with Margretta Stewart Dietrich for the Domingo Corn Dance.

1904

Class Editor: EMMA O. THOMPSON
320 S. 42nd St., Philadelphia. Pa.

Helen Arny Macan sends the following: "The Board of Trustees of St. Agnes' School announces a change in the headship of the school. The new head is Helen Arny Macan, who comes to St. Agnes from the College Hill School, of Easton, Pa., where she was headmistress for four years. After leaving Bryn Mawr College, Mrs. Macan went abroad for special work in French, and then returned and taught history in St. Timothy's, at Catonsville, Maryland.

"Under the direction of Mrs. Macan, St. Agnes' School has added a college preparatory course in chemistry to the course in general science now given, so that the school may be accredited by the Department of Education of the State of Virginia." St. Agnes' School is at Jefferson Park, near Washington, D. C.

Dr. Alice Boring visited Dr. Mary James, at Wuchang, China, this summer. Alice had a splendid vacation tramping in the mountains. During the summer we saw Daisy Ullman. She is looking forward to our next reunion and sends her best wishes to all the class. We motored out to Lake Forest and saw the splendid new buildings of Ferry Hall, the school where Eloise Tremain is headmistress.

Eleanor Silkman Gilman's daughter, Elizabeth Drinker, was married to Kent Smith on September 6th.

A letter from Lucy Lombardi Barber reads as follows: "I know you will all be interested to know that a selection of more than thirty poems from the many written by Marjorie Canan Fry, has been privately published, and that a copy is to be presented to the Bryn

Mawr College library for the alumnae shelf. The poems reflect such a lovely spirit, such sincere faith, and such intense joy in the simple things of life that I feel they make a beautiful memorial to Marjorie."

The Class Editor explored the Deanery with interest and pleasure before the formal opening.

1905

Class Editor: ELEANOR LITTLE ALDRICH
(Mrs. Talbot Aldrich)
50 Mount Vernon St., Boston, Mass.

Florence Craig Whitney's son, Craig Whitney, is engaged to Ann Van Duzer Ward, of New York City.

Clara Porter Yarnelle has entered the grandmother class and finds "him" an absorbing and happy interest amidst the many problems of present-day life. She has had really tragic ones in the past year—the deaths of her mother and brother-in-law and serious illness of her husband and her father.

Portions of another letter from Frances Hubbard Flaherty are shared with us by the recipient. She writes from the Aran Islands still: "Summer is here at last and I sit here like a goggle-eyed hen waiting to gather her brood under her wing again. Barbara is home from London and a try at art school, four paintings under her arm and a sheaf of drawings—the usual thing, and Matilda is here—Jaynesie's Matilda—great, tall, lanky child, as sweet as she can be, the spitten image of Alice—humourous like Len. Next to come will be Frannie, barging in, as Barbara says, like a full-rigged ship—176 pounds of her, hearty and hale. With herself and the three schoolmates she's invited (a gift for spontaneous hospitality like Bob's) she'll over-run us all. And with her comes Monnie, a different Monnie everytime she comes—growing so fast and so tall like David. No baby left any more for the poor old hen!

"Bob and the film are just about ready to beat a retreat to London. Meaning that the film is almost done. *Gott sei dank!* It has been, as it always is, a fearful, nerve-wracking job. Only my nervous resistance has become remarkably tough. You wouldn't know me in my resilient middle age. It comes from working in the garden, digging in the dirt. The Aran dirt is gorgeous—prodigious. You never saw, never ate, such vegetables as mine!

"When we leave here in September, address c/o Brown Shipley & Company, 123 Pall Mall. We shall stick in London till we know our fate—a hit or a flop. If it's a hit—won't we be the roaring lions! If it's a flop——! Interesting contrast in alternatives."

Frances Hubbard Flaherty has left her island temporarily. Her husband has finished his film and the children are in English schools.

Frances is spending a few months in London so that the family may be as near together as possible.

1906

Class Editor: LOUISE CRUICE STURDEVANT
(Mrs. Edward W. Sturdevant)
c/o 4th Regiment, U. S. Marines, Shanghai.

1907

Class Editor: ALICE HAWKINS
Taylor Hall, Bryn Mawr, Pa.

The class will be grieved to hear of the death of Alice Baird Roesler, on August 2nd. Everyone will wish to extend the deepest sympathy to her husband, her daughter, and her three sons.

During the summer Alice Sussman Arnstein broke her silence of many years. "In this last year I lost my dear sister, Amy Sussman Steinhardt, 1902, and my husband. I run a gift shop in San Francisco, 'The Alice Arnstein Shop.' I am now in New York with my daughter, Katherine, and son, Peter, on my way to England and France, partly to recuperate, partly to buy. My oldest son, Eugene, is married and is living in New York. . . . My second son, Richard, is also working, and both boys are a credit to their grand alma mater, Bryn Mawr College. This does not mean that the two younger ones will not some day follow in their footsteps. . . . My best and fondest of good wishes to Bryn Mawr and all the Mawrters, of whom I hold the tenderest memories."

Another stranger and sojourner on the Pacific coast, Emma Sweet Tondel, writes from Seattle: "You are right in feeling that I am still interested. I always shall be. Adherence to the scholarship standards of Bryn Mawr has been the principle which has inspired and sustained me in guiding the education of my lone child. Perhaps when he goes out in the world, he will be able to repay in some measure all that I owe to my association with the College and with 1907. I have followed the careers of all of you with intense interest and glory in the honours which have come to Eunice, Peggy, Tink, Margaret Bailey, and all the rest. I would sacrifice much before I lose touch with you."

In the Class of 1937 are Eleanore Tobin, daughter of Helen Roche, and Jeanne Macomber, stepdaughter of Harriet Seaver. That makes six 1907 children now in college, as Helen Smitheman Baldwin, Grace Brownell Daniels, Brooke Peters Church and Margaret Reeve Carey each have a daughter there. Eleanore Tobin covered herself with glory by winning the newly-established Scholarship offered by the Directors of the College.

Peggy Barnes' new novel, "Within This Present," will be published by Houghton Mifflin in November.

Dorothy Forster Miller now has a real estate salesman's license, and is renting agent and manager of an apartment house in New York which has forty apartments and a restaurant.

Grace Brownell Daniels is Finance Chairman of the Queens County League of Women Voters and is "helping" on the Consumers' Advisory Board of the N. R. A. Her second daughter, Josephine, has entered Radcliffe.

Marion Bryant Johnson has been doing full-time work on the Illinois Emergency Relief Commission.

Katharine Harley has moved to Chelten Arms, 500 West Chelten Avenue, Germantown.

Edith Rice is head of the Foreign Language Department of the Kensington High School, Philadelphia.

Grace Hutchins is doing research for the Labor Research Association in New York. She has recently published a pamphlet entitled "Child Labor Under Capitalism."

Nancy Schneider is still secretary to her uncle, the President of the University of Cincinnati.

Ruth Hammitt Kauffman had a novel published this spring, "Tourist Third." She writes that she is now in the process of writing a text-book on narcotics and that her next novel will be entitled "Spun Gold."

1908

Class Editor: HELEN CADBURY BUSH
Haverford, Pa.

Margaret Lewis' husband, Lincoln MacVeagh, has been appointed American minister to Greece.

Linda Schaeffer Castle and her son, Alfred, atended the School of Pacific and Oriental Affairs of the University of Hawaii summer session in Honolulu.

1909

Class Editor: HELEN B. CRANE
70 Willett St., Albany, N. Y.

One of the nicest features of our brief summer vacation in Maine was part of a day spent with Shirley Putnam O'Hara at Goose Rocks Beach, near Kennebunkport. Behind the O'Hara cottage is a gallery which houses Eliot O'Hara's water colors, as well as loan exhibitions from other well-known painters; Mr. O'Hara's idea being to give his students an opportunity to study other styles and techniques as well as his own. We were particularly enthusiastic over his Maine beach studies and the few South American pictures that were on exhibit at the time. In the same building, Shirley has her "Out-of-the-Way Shop," full of delightful and unusual gifts from many parts of the world. Incidentally, she manages both gallery and shop with ease and grace, and brings up Desmond and June, all, apparently, with a turn of the wrist. Part of a day in Portland was all we had with Sally Webb, summering near Boothbay Harbor.

Frances Ferris, after having motored through most of Maine, Vermont, New Hampshire and Massachusetts, came back through Albany, and we had a rainy Labor Day week-end in the Catskills—seeing more of each other than the surrounding country, heavily veiled in mists.

A mutual friend and later a skimpy post-card informed us that Mary Allen was in Germany from March till the end of August. She added that she had "no news"—probably meaning none that would pass the censor on a post-card. She *says* she expects to be in Worcester for a long time to come, but we doubt it.

Gene Mittenberger Ustick reached California at some unknown date and spent a month at La Jolla. She will be in Pasadena until next summer, where her husband is doing research in the Huntington Library. Her address is 932 South Madison Avenue, Pasadena, Calif.

Nellie Shippen (the solitary individual out of ten to send back her return post-card) is still with the editorial department at Macmillan's; but she has a new address, 14 East 8th Street, New York City. "Early in the summer Frances Ferris and the Shippens went swimming at Pocono Lake Preserve. Later my two sisters and I went by Ford to Quebec and visited Dorothy Smith Chamberlain and her three little daughters at Squam Lake on the way."

These items are "lifted" from a recent letter of Caroline Kamm McKinnon's to Sally Webb:

"Early this year I accepted a place on the Board of Directors of our Portland Y. W. C. A. It is my first experience of anything of this kind, and I am finding it most interesting as well as educational. . . . These are interesting and difficult times from any point of view. I think perhaps it is specially interesting to begin work in an organization like this when there is a revaluing and restating of purposes. . . . I wish you were here to spend lazy days with me in my garden. It is nicer this year than ever before. I can at last begin to see my ideal coming nearer. Of course, there will always be details to work out and changes to make, that is what keeps a garden interesting, but the general outlines are right at last. My made-over living room is a constant joy, for the views of the garden from the south and west windows are just as lovely as I had hoped they would be."

1910

Class Editor: KATHERINE ROTAN DRINKER
(Mrs. Cecil K. Drinker)
71 Rawson Road, Brookline, Mass.

1911

Class Editor: ELIZABETH TAYLOR RUSSELL
(Mrs. John F. Russell, Jr.)
1085 Park Ave., New York City.

The Class sends its deepest sympathy to Ruth Vickery Holmes, whose youngest child, Constance, died in July, and to Emma Forster upon the death of her mother after a long illness.

Ellen Pottberg Hempstead's new address is Livermore Falls, Androscoggin Co., Maine.

Hannah Dodd Thompson's oldest daughter, Sarah, is a Sophomore at Wilson College.

Constance Wilbur McKeehan's oldest son, Wilbur, won the poetry prize in Junior High School among several hundred contestants.

Emily Caskey was obliged to take a rest cure for several months' duration last winter, but has resumed her duties as a district missionary treasurer of some forty organizations near Glenside, Pa.

Ruth Wells spent her vacation in Wisconsin. She is Vice-President of the Quota Club in New Bedford and Secretary of the Foreign Relations Association.

Anita Stearns Stevens' oldest daughter, Alice Anita, was married to Mr. John Handy Henshaw in Greenwich, Conn., on July 29th.

Amy Walker Field's son James, graduated from Milton Academy last June with high honors.

Please all take notice of your editor's new address and send word of your winter plans.

1912

Class Editor: GLADYS SPRY AUGUR
(Mrs. Wheaton Augur)
820 Camino Atalaya, Santa Fé, N. M.

During the summer Mary Alden Lane and her husband and three daughters stopped to see the Class Editor on their way through Santa Fé. They just had had a terrible experience with a Kansas flood.

Lorle Stecher and her husband spent the summer as usual at Hawaii National Park, of which she sent the most exciting and beautiful picture.

The Editor herself went to the Hopi Snake Dance, and on the way home stopped at Mesa Verde and the Indian Ceremonial at Gallop. Most of her summer she has spent touring the state for Prohibition Repeal.

Cynthia Stevens, the Class will be amused to know, came dashing up from Baltimore the moment the Deanery was informally opened, to stay very firmly in Miss Thomas's own room. According to her own report, she spent most of her time hanging out of the window and admiring the garden.

The Class will unite in sending warmest love and sympathy to Carmelita Chase Hinton, whose brother Clement, an eminent civil engineer, was killed on September 18th, when he was blown from the Delaware River Bridge, which he had helped to build. He was making an inspection trip, preliminary to the start of new construction. Carmelita herself had been abroad all summer with her own and Clement's children at an International Camp.

1913

Class Editor: HELEN EVANS LEWIS
(Mrs. Robert M. Lewis)
52 Trumbull St., New Haven, Conn.

1914

Class Editor: ELIZABETH AYER INCHES
(Mrs. Henderson Inches)
41 Middlesex Road, Chestnut Hill, Mass.

1915

Class Editor: MARGARET FREE STONE
(Mrs. James Austin Stone)
3039 44th St., N. W., Washington, D. C.

For some unaccountable reason the Editor forgot to send in the names of those present at the class supper in June. Here they are now, with apologies for the delay: Kitty McCollin Arnett, Anna Roberts Balderston, Frances Boyer, Anna Brown, Mildred Jacobs Coward, Isabel Foster, Adrienne Kenyon Franklin, Edna Kraus Greenfield, Ruth Hubbard, Mildred Justice, Florence Hatton Kelton, Zena Blanc Loewenberg, Helen Taft Manning, Dorothea May Moore, Anne Hardon Pearce, Ruth Glenn Pennell, Florence Abernethy Pinch, Cecilia Sargent, Katherine Sheafer, Elsie Steltzer, Peggy Free Stone, Cleora Sutch and Helen McFarland Woodbridge. Anna Brown tells me that Elsa Scripture Kidd blew in for the picnic on Monday.

The following excerpts are from letters written to Adrienne in response to her reunion appeal:

Lucile Davidson Alsop: "I am so disappointed—so really deprived, I feel—to miss reunion this year. When I tell you I am writing this note from a hospital bed you will understand. . . . It has been a slight diagnostic operation, with a happy ending, but enough to keep me quietly at home these coming ten days. . . . If our world hasn't utterly collapsed about us, can't 1915 have a reunion again in 1935?"

Atala Scudder Davison: "Much as I should like to, I can't come to reunion this year. I am sailing on June 17th to see my oldest boy, who is at school in Switzerland, and between now and then I must get the house ready for summer tenants and take the other two children north and settle them with my father. This schedule simply won't include reunion, much though I regret it. . . . I shall have to put off seeing you all till next time. I shall, however, be seeing Mary Goodhue Cary in the Tyrol this summer—we are planning to join forces and share expenses there!"

Ruth Tinker Morse: "Very sad indeed not to accept the cordial invitation to join 1915 this week, for this reunion is the first I have missed. Nothing exciting to relate, as my interests are mostly domestic. We came here to Massachusetts two years ago and like it a lot. Also added another daughter to the family. See quite a lot of Gertrude Emery and Vashti—the latter having just gone home on a vacation, taking my boy with her (via Hops in Cleveland and the Fair in Chicago). Now you know what a nice aunt she has turned out to be."

Mary Gertrude Brownell Wilson: "It looks now as though June 10th would find me busily packing to go to Rhode Island for the summer, though I shall certainly miss being at the reunion. . . . Now that I live right outside New York, I see many traveling friends—among them Goodhue, who passed through last month on her way to sail for Germany. She is exactly as ever, though thinner and handsomer. She seems to lead an interesting life, representing America for the Quakers in Berlin, where she and Dick and their two children plan to be for another year. . . . Good luck to all, and I hope to be at the next reunion."

Susan Brandeis: "I have to say, like Mary Gertrude, that I must move my family to the country before the day of the reunion, and can only send letters and snaps. Louis is just finishing the first grade at Horace Mann, Alice has finished kindergarten and received the prize, and the baby, Frank, copies everything at the advanced age of two and a half. We have moved our office to 745 Fifth Avenue, where I still practice law with my husband. We are going up to Chatham, Mass., for the summer and hope that some of you will be in the neighborhood and will come in to see us."

Hezzie Irvin Bordman: "Unfortunately, I feel that I cannot leave home this spring, since my husband is back in the Philippines and I have the responsibilities of my complicated family—my mother and aunt, who are above 70, and my daughter, Mary Constance, and son, John Bordman, Jr., who are 4 and 2 respectively! If only Concord were not so far from Rockefeller! . . . I hope the weather does not fail you as it did on the day of the Garden Party. I think the program sounds very interesting, and we are certainly indebted to you and Mildred—to all of you who have worked so hard for our scattered members."

Mary Marjory Thomson: "I sincerely regret not being able to be with you this reunion. Do let me recommend a splendidly satisfactory profession for 1915's daughters, in case they ever begin looking for one—that of psychoanalyst for children. The many years of acute anguish that can be saved an individual by a few months' skilled work during his childhood are worth a vast deal more than the doctor's years of preparation. I will always be glad to discuss this with any of our Class at home or in my office in New York City. Much love to you all."

Gladys Pray Michaels: "My oldest boy, Parker, is graduating from grammar school. . . . Parker is a Boy Scout and marched in the Memorial Day parade here yesterday. My youngest son, Bobby (age 8), is going to camp for the first time this year—if he does not get the measles before July! . . . We all love New Rochelle, which is right on Long Island Sound, and enjoy the sailing and swimming all summer. . . . I am active in the New Rochelle Woman's Club in the International Co-operative and Music Sections. I also belong to the Woman's Forum in New York and the American Criterion Society and the D. A. R. Please extend a cordial invitation to any 1915 in this vicinity or passing through New Rochelle to come to see me."

Emily Noyes Knight: "When you are all seated at Class Dinner on June 10th, singing the songs the words of which I disremember or the tunes, I will be finishing the Jacob's Hill Horse Show in Providence and about to migrate to that shore of Atlantis known as Matunuck, not solitarily, but accompanied by husband, child, mother, household, horses, dog, cats, bird, fish, turtles and what was once a lamb but is now distinctly mutton. I will think of you all and hope to hear of your varied and useful lives. If I were with you I might say let us not try to recapture the past or many more things, but I am certain I would say—will Helen Taft Manning sing *That Is Love*—keeping her more recent successes for encores."

Rachel Ash: "I shall be on my way to Milwaukee Saturday to attend the meeting of the American Heart Association. The subject of discussion this year—rheumatic infection—is one in which I am especially interested, and I do not feel that I can afford to miss it."

Laura Branson Linville: "My husband has gone to the University of Kansas for his class reunion, and this summer he and I are going to Harvard, he to renew his memory of his graduate days there and I to study. My new family includes Byron and Henry, Jr., who are in the high school at the Lincoln School, and Rhoda, who is a graduate of Cornell and has been studying this year at Northwestern. They are all blondes, taller than I, vigorous and self-reliant. It is fine to have a family all grown up. My love and good wishes to everyone at 1915's reunion."

Myra Richards Jessen: "I have been in bed several days with a new phase of my pet ailment—indigestion—and the doctor has told me today that I have to rest in the same way for another two weeks. This cuts out all the reunion and my academic obligation to appear at Baccalaureate Sermon and Commencement. . . . It is a great disappointment not to see the Class in toto and to trail along in the procession with a new gown and hood, an investment which swallowed up all the summer wardrobe budget!"

Eleanor Freer Karcher: "Sorry I can't come East this year, but again I have to put it off until next reunion. Shortage of help and finances, three rapidly growing older ones and a small Karcher in the offing in September are keeping me right here."

Ethel Robinson Hyde: "Sorry not to be with you, but I consider one should be rather young to undertake hitch-hiking! . . . In 1931 I was quite an ardent committee woman. Every day in the week except Saturday (my children's day) I kept appointments so meticulously I might almost as well have had a paid job. At the Women's City Club of Detroit I was on the Finance Committee (never having been much at math. in school I have turned out to be rather good on finance committees), and also Vice-Chairman of the House Committee. At Neighborhood House (a settlement house) I was President of the Board of Directors. Here, too, I am a pillar of the Finance Committee, now that my two years' presidency is past. And we really are in "big business," because we own property worth, according to 1929 estimates, $900,000, and run the settlement entirely on our income from these holdings. And there were many other committees—hardly a week passed me by without a call to be on another one. Well, I became restless, the women I met were capable, interesting, life was alert and alive, and yet I felt rather unproductive considering the energy expended. Gradually I slid out from under these responsibilities, became intensely domestic, rearranged my house, did the friendly cup of tea sort of thing. Life was leisurely, delightful—when dawned February 11th. All Detroit banks closed—and stayed closed for 70 days. We were all limited by the cash we happened to have on hand that Saturday—there was no source from which to secure more, and no knowing how long our pennies must last. The two largest banks never have and never will open. . . . The garden season is here and Lou loves it. At 5.30 this morning he was out there setting out some choice specimens he

secured last night. Our three girls reflect all the excellent points on the paternal side. Betty, aged 13 now, brought home a silver loving cup from camp last summer, for being the best all-around camper. Barbara, aged 11, has just taken herself up to the finals in the annual Michigan school spelling bee. . . . Jean, aged 7, will take all loving cups, and all medals, given time. Enough of the Hydes. Let me pass on news of Marie Keller Heyl. She took a party of five girls (two of them her own Chickie and Dorothea) abroad in January and will bring them back in July. After a month of study in Paris they went to Germany. Though study is the primary purpose, they seem to be enjoying a jolly winter. Each of Marie's girls had previously studied abroad for one year. Their command of German, according to Marie, and she should know, is excellent. Dear me, and I mention spelling bees!"

1916

Class Editor: LARIE K. BOAS
2100 Pacific Ave., San Francisco, Calif.

With this issue I sing my swan song and turn over all and sundry, including the news items that do not come in, to that noble woman, honest scribe and fine scholar, Miss Catherine Godley, 768 Ridgeway Ave., Cincinnati.

I have thought of writing my experiences as Class Editress—a manual for the young, in what not to be, and how not to write. The only voluntary contribution I received last year was one splendid effort from the pen of Juliet Branham, soundly and fairly berating me for my loose ways. I hasten to quote verbatim. "When I saw that you were to manage the column in the BULLETIN, I thought now there will be news, and such 'news!' Well, my dear, how you have disappointed me. As a temporary member of the Class, and one not loved with the abandon I could desire, it would interest you or nobody for me to answer that post-card of yours a year ago. But I would so enjoy occasional news of the people in the Class. Don't you see how all of us would sit up to hear the tales of others, especially a little scandal and a little misfortune?

"I live in the suburbs. Probably most of us live in the suburbs, and only you can tell us who has the dreariest life. And what has become of you? Instead of that bleak and solitary address of yours each month, couldn't you essay a complete, subtle and explicit account, at least, of your own life and ambitions? For example, do you possess three children, and have you a membership in the Teacher-Parent Association? Or, on the other hand, are you a mother of six or a woman of fashion?

"The magazine comes monthly, and though for the first two or three numbers I enjoyed knowing that you lived in California and in San Francisco, that romantic city, I am losing my first relish of the fact. What has become of the girls I used to know—the thin ones and the fat ones? You as a lover of musical comedy may be able to finish that quotation—I can't."

Dear sweet Juliet, you finished me, if not the quotation. But it is obvious that if Kith wishes again to take a sabbatical year, that you, and you only, have all the qualifications for a successful Class Editress. My heartiest!

And now for a little summing up. Here are some notes on 1916 members, taken at the class supper at our most recent reunion.

Adams, Jessie—Seen in Atlanta about four years ago by Chase.

Alden, Ruth—Seen by C. Dowd in Saratoga Springs lately. Is moving to Buffalo to live. Has one little girl.

Baker, Virginia—A. Smith sees her every June, when they are marking College Entrance Boards; Virginia, Latin, and Agnes, Algebra. Virginia teaches in Miss Madeira's School in Washington.

Belville, Dorothy—Married; lives in California and keeps an apiary.

Bensberg, Bright—Raises English bulldogs.

Brakeley, Elizabeth—Very thin, very charming, very beautiful; E. Hill and A. Lee saw her recently in B. M., where she was resting after an illness. She is a successful Pediatrician in Montclair, N. J.

Branham, Juliet—Has four children in New York. (Editor's query: How many has she in New Mexico?) Went to World's Fair instead of reunion.

Branson, Polly—Carmelite Convent in Oak Lane. Several reports that she is well and happy.

Bridge, Isabelle—Seen in Greece by E. Hill, who reports her thin, beautiful and possessed of an English husband. She and her husband were writing and speaking of some land that should have gone to Greece instead of Italy, and so they won Mussolini's displeasure and are forbidden to enter Italy.

Bryne, Eva—Reports her only notable achievement lately, singing over radio in a quartet with C. Westling, 1917.

Burt, Alene—Seen on B. M. campus last May Day, wearing orchids. Did not show up for reunion, although expected.

Chase, Helen—Has five or six daughters.

Chase, Margaret—Has two daughters and lives in Middletown, Pa.

Crowell, Caroline—College Physician at Austin, Texas, and working in hospital at night on emergency cases. Busy and therefore happy.

De Macedo, Virginia—Still married to the same husband, still teaching French and German at the Germantown High School in the winter, and going to a camp in Vermont in the summer.

Dillingham, Louise—Went to Mexico City with the Crenshaws this last summer. She is now head of the Westover School, one of the few successful private schools today. She is very popular with teachers, parents and pupils.

Dodd, Margaret—Living in Nashville, with sister. Doddie has four daughters. They are all going to New England for the summer and then back to Nashville.

Donchian, Eugenie—Living in Glendale, California. Has two sons and one daughter. They are, from reports, prosperous and happy.

Dowd, Constance—In addition to her summer camp, she is the sole psychologist at a New York hospital, in a department formerly having over forty members. Low funds forced much curtailment of activities in general, but C. D. manages to be more than busy. Since these notes were completed, C. D. has truly managed that—as, in addition to all else, she has now acquired a husband, of whose name I am still uninformed. They will live in Cincinnati. Is he a lucky fellow and to be congratulated? 1916 thinks so.

We have many more notes, but as space prevents using them in this issue, we will forward same to Kith, who will begin where we left off in the "D's." Watch for Engelhard, Margaret, in our next issue.

And speaking of Margarets, our other one, to wit: Margaret Kingsland Haskell, of Evanston, Ill., has qualified by examination to practice as an English barrister. She was "called to the bar," meaning that she was officially granted a lawyer's rights.

1917

Class Editor: BERTHA CLARK GREENOUGH
203 Blackstone Blvd., Providence, R. I.

1918

Class Editor: MARGARET BACON CAREY
(Mrs. H. R. Carey)
3115 Queen Lane, East Falls P. O., Phila.

Having heard that Jeanette Ridlon Piccard was to participate in stratosphere experiments at Chicago this summer, the Editor wrote her for particulars. Part of her answer follows: "The newspapers carried all the news 'that's fit to print.' The truth, you know, is never suitable for publication. Suffice it to say that it was a great joy to us to have the visit of our brother, Auguste, last winter. That is a truth which bears the light. Furthermore, we were completely wrapped up for many months this summer in the preparations for the flight which grew out of that visit. Jean spent many weeks in Midland working on the construction of the gondola. Commander Settle had entire charge of the construction of the balloon. He used the general design given him by Auguste when he was here in March. He depended on his own ideas for the detailed development. In view of this fact, with the subsequent unfortunate outcome, I cannot but be glad that Jean did not go up with Commander Settle for pilot, as had been originally planned. For the future we have many hopes and plans, but nothing of a sufficiently definite nature to bear talking about."

Kate Dufourcq Kelley came across with such a voluminous letter that a certain amount of editing will have to be done to get it within the compass of the BULLETIN. "My activities during the last few years sound very formidable, but they really were very enjoyable. I have been Secretary, Treasurer and Bible Class teacher in our local Episcopal Sunday School since 1929 and am still going strong. We have an enrollment of about 150. Finance Chairman, Hastings Woman's Club, 1930-31. Committee member of the Westchester County Children's Association, 1930-31. Employment Chairman Mayor's Relief Committee, 1931-32. My job was to find jobs for the unemployed, and to coöperate with the Wicks Administration in County Relief Work. It meant being in the office daily from 9 until 12, and on call at home all the rest of the twenty-four hours. We had all sorts of excitement, problems and scandals. I resigned from this fascinating work after a year, because by that time the depression had caught up with me, and I felt that I must use my leisure for something remunerative. 1931-32, substitute teacher in Latin and French at the Hastings High School. 1931-32, member Program Committee, Hastings Literary Club. Partner in The Swap Shop, a venture undertaken last spring by three other women and myself. We were a combination Woman's Exchange, Lending Library, Gift Shop, Tea Shop, and what-have-you." And as an after-thought she adds, "P. S.—My small son (8½) is fine."

The Editor suggests that others of the Class who have been requested for news might profitably (for others, if not for themselves) follow the example of these two. And remember, it is not necessary to withhold news until specifically asked to send it!

After a very strenuous spring with children's illnesses and the death of my mother, we had a long, pleasant summer at Portsmouth, N. H., at the Carey summer home, which my children inherited a year ago. The house is on a salt creek, half a mile from the sea—a delightful combination of country and ocean, and a house large enough to hold many guests. We had a household of anywhere up to nineteen a good deal of the time, among those present being Helen Hammer Link and family. Her daughter is as tall as Helen and goes to boarding school this fall. They had just closed a successful season at their camp for girls, where Elsbeth Merck Henry's oldest was for the summer, and were planning to go home to Pittsburgh by way of Chicago. My children are all in school this year—Henry (11½) and John (9) at Penn Charter, Bill (6½) and Alida (5) at the Germantown Friends', where Ruth Garrigues teaches.

Katharine Holliday Daniels is President of the Indianapolis League of Women Voters and has been appointed a member of the Consumers' Advisory Board, to represent the buying public in the administration of the National Recovery Act. She has been to Washington three times since June and has spoken for her committee before the International Congress of Women in Chicago.

"Dear Old Peg:

"Will you please put a few lines among our Class Notes to remind 1918 that we are having a reunion next spring? I will spare our blushes by not specifying *which* reunion it is, but I hope everyone will begin saving up now, so that she will be able to come for their fun next June. The railroads heard about our plan and cut their fares to 2c a mile, and that ought to help. Our headquarters will be in Denbigh and the Class Dinner will be on Saturday night, June 2nd. Watch these columns for the latest dope.

"When Helen Walker sent in her resignation as Secretary last spring, I'm sure she didn't imagine how her bad example would spread. But since then Charlotte has written me, asking to be relieved of her job as Vice-President and Treasurer, and Louise finds that the charms of Class Collector are palling on her. Something tells me they remembered about this reunion business! If I'd thought quickly enough, I might have done the same, but now there is nobody left for me to resign to. Well, at least I no longer have 30,000 children to look after, so 100 classmates seem rather simple and pleasant. I hope some of them will surely help me with the regular jobs and the special preparations for reunion.

"My family and I had a gorgeous summer at a little place on the coast of Maine called Blue Hill. There we learned to sail—after a fashion. Don't tell me one can't get a new idea after 30; I've proved the contrary, even if some of my ideas seemed peculiar to real sailors. My old roommate, Posey Fiske, and her family were not far away, so we saw each other several times. Now we are back in Morristown, settling down to schools and winter jobs.

"Lots of love to you and all the Class from "RUTH CHENEY STREETER."

1919

Class Editor: MARJORIE REMINGTON TWITCHELL
(Mrs. Pierrepont Twitchell)
Setauket, L. I., N. Y.

In the July 15th number of the *Saturday Evening Post* appeared a most thrilling article by Helen Karns Champlin describing her experience during the hurricane in Puerto Rico. Catherine Taussig Opie has a daughter, Helen, born May 28th. They live in Oxford, where her husband teaches at Magdalen College.

Peggy Rhoads and Jane Hall Hunter spent most of the summer in the hospital. Peggy recuperated in lovely Bynden Wood, Wernersville, Pa., while Jinnie celebrated her recovery by moving from Glen Ridge, N. J., to 7904 Lincoln Drive, Chestnut Hill, Pa. Her 12-year-old son, De Forest, spent a week with Remington Twitchell. De Forest had been on a horse for just one-half hour lesson before he came, and the boys rode five miles the first day!

Feeny Peabody Cannon writes: "I haven't much news except the arrival of my fourth child, second daughter, born April 28th, 1933, at 3 p.m. Name, Margaret Peabody Cannon, called Peggy: not original, but nice. I have just gotten through two years as President of the New Haven Junior League and am quite looking forward to being domestic again, with a visiting Nurse Board Meeting and Connecticut Birth Control League Meeting thrown in for variety."

The Editor and her husband and son rented their house for over a month this summer, and gallivanted to the World's Fair. We spent ten days of ten hours each right at the Fair. We also called on Emily Matz Boyd and saw her three lovely children, met her lawyer husband and renewed auld acquaintance. She says that Lib Fauvre (Mrs. Wynn Owen) is living at 1459 N.' Delaware Street, Indianapolis. We also had a most delightful luncheon with Clara Hollis Kirk at the unusual Saddle and Cycle Club, a country club right in the city. Clara looks not a day older than in 1919. She is writing skits for the radio. She says Elisabeth Carus has been working in Chicago, but I was unable to get in touch with her. After lunching with Clara, we drove two hours out into the country to Milly Peacock Haerther's beautiful home. There was the same old Milly, efficient as ever, managing golf tournaments as well as a large estate. Her two boys and Rem had a wild Indian time swimming in their pool. Milly's array of silver cups won at golf were quite overwhelming. After leaving Chicago we visited Hazel Collins Hainsworth in Wyandotte, Mich., spending a day going through the Ford factory and Greenfield Village with her. From there my husband flew back to New York for

business, and Rem and I drove home alone, taking nearly two weeks, visiting along the route. Shortly after we left, Hazel and her husband and 8-year-old Joletta took a trip back to Cleveland in order to move their things definitely to Wyandotte, where they have been living temporarily for the past year. Since returning in August, we have taken two children to keep permanently, we hope, although the permanency is not entirely settled yet: a brown-eyed boy of 5, Charles, and a 2-year-old, blue-eyed, blonde, curly headed girl, Doris. I am having a wonderful (and busy) time being the mother of three in such a sudden swoop. I do not agree with those people who say three are equal to only two!

1920

Class Editor: MARY PORRITT GREEN
(Mrs. Valentine J. Green)
430 E. 57th St., New York City.

We have a new complaint: so much news of 1920 that we will just draw lots to see what we will put in each month. Coming back from the country with a 2-months' baby (Lucy Porritt Green, born at the N. Y.-Cornell Hospital on July 9th) and temporarily being without a maid or nurse, we were so inspired to work that we sent out return post-cards to all those whose addresses we had on hand (ninety-seven). The results were wonderful. Many thanks for the prompt responses. We would greatly appreciate the addresses of Mary Louise Mall Pearse, Margaret S. Cary Smith, Helen Strayer, Margaret Train Samsonoff—if anyone knows them.

From Millicent Carey McIntosh—"The McIntoshes spent three weeks this summer climbing in the Tyrol and Dolomites, and ten days in September salmon fishing in Cape Breton. Louise Sloan bought a sailboat and took various perilous trips this summer. Lois Jessup took her son and nephew to the Chicago Fair. Philip Jessup went as a delegate to the Pan-American Conference at Banff. Margaret Ballou Hitchcock was at Sunapee Lake this summer. She is teaching English again at Miss Foote's School in New Haven. Both her children are in the school. She is Chairman of the B. M. Summer School Committee."

From Margaret Hawkins—"Sorry—nothing new in my life to recount. Still slaving along, grinding out scenarios for a living—under contract at present to Paramount. Address, 6626 Franklin Avenue, Hollywood."

From Miriam Ormsby Mark—"Have the same one boy—Ormsby—that I've had for nine and a half years! We bought a house in the spring, so hope my address is changed for the last time—248 Linden Avenue—same street

Nat Gookin lives on. We love the house and garden, remodeled quite a bit, including oil burner, electric icebox and what not, so our travels about which you inquire will be non-existent for many months!"

From Agnes Johnston Pennington—"I have two children, a boy and a girl, and we all are going to school together, they as pupils in the Child Institute, Department of Psychology, Johns Hopkins University, and I as a teacher there. In my spare moments I am studying at the University, trying to get my B. S."

From Martha Prewitt Breckinridge—"To date: one 4-year-old daughter, Kate—as beautiful, brilliant, beatific, as all one-only children are—my total output in that direction; thousands and thousands of as yet unprinted witty words, all according to Savage's Short Story Course, constitute my literary effort. And next month I open here *Au Pays Basque* (scenic effects suggested by Eleanor Mercein, kind lady) to feed the public, and indirectly to eke out what people aren't spending on yachts these lean years (my husband's racket). So drop in this winter—it's within fifty feet of the Federal Highway on the straight route to Miami—and I'll give you lunch—'on the house' at Fort Lauderdale."

From Dorothy Smith McAllister—"No travels and no new children. Mary is 8 and Claire nearly 4. My outside activities include being a member of the Michigan State Liquor Control Commission, a member of the committee to draft a liquor control law for our state after Repeal, State Legislative Chairman for the Association of University Women, President of the Alliance Francaise."

From Natalie Gookin—"When your card came I was away, for my father and I had gone out to Estes Park, Colorado, for just a three weeks' stay. I drove the Buick as usual and we had a very happy vacation seeing all our friends in the place we love best. Otherwise I have no news about myself, as I lead a very uneventful life. I am keeping house for my father and doing my own work, and as my aunt, who lives with us, is rather an invalid now, I am very much tied down and seldom get into town or away from my duties much. I do see Alice Rood Van Deusen quite often, for she and her husband moved last spring into a new house they built (at 2011 Beechwood Avenue, Wilmette, Ill.), which is only about two minutes' drive from here. Belinda has a second daughter, born July 3rd. Laura Hales was in England the first part of the summer. I saw Marge Canby Taylor and Edith in July, when they came to the Fair."

From Marian Gregg King—"My address is now 26 Arundel Place, Saint Louis. I am in the real estate business. I have three children, Gregg, Lucia, and small Clarence. Lucia has

been entered at Bryn Mawr since May 18th, 1924, the day she was born."

From Agnes Rose—"My job is about the same. I am still teaching math. in Linden High School, Linden, N. J. This past June I received an M. A. from N. Y. U."

From Margaret Littell Platt—"The two girls will be at the Brearley, where also will be their mother teaching hand work with and under Pic Loud, '23. The book illustrated is *Tabitha Mary*, by Ethel Parton, Viking Press."

From Jerry Hess Peters—"My news is so prosaic I hesitate to send it. Three small sons, from 10 to 3, keep me so busy—with Junior League on the outside—that I am housewife in capital letters. We are all well and happy, which is what counts."

1921

Class Editor: WINIFRED WORCESTER STEVENSON
(Mrs. Harvey Stevenson)
Croton-on-Hudson, N. Y.

1922

Class Editor: SERENA HAND SAVAGE
(Mrs. William L. Savage)
106 E. 85th St., New York City.

1923

Class Editor: HARRIET SCRIBNER ABBOTT
(Mrs. John Abbott)
70 W. 11th St., New York City.

If you think that you are doing nothing of any importance, let us know. Send us word of yourself without the preface, "There is so little to say about myself that I hesitate to bother you with it at all." We are convinced that no one need go to such lengths as getting a Ph.D., practicing medicine or having a baby to make news. The purpose of this column is to keep members of the Class in touch with one another, in the light of which your doings, worthy or feckless, are of interest. Just write us something and see if we don't print it.

Ruth MacAneny Loud played in four tennis tournaments this summer, with very happy results in one singles and three mixed doubles. This winter she is to be assistant in Dramatics and Handwork at the Brearley School. "Bitter and Loud, Antiques," will continue as usual.

Dorothy Stewart Pierson is living in a charming house she and her husband built in Cold Spring Harbor, with their three children. She has been an assiduous gardener all summer, raising spinach that melts in your mouth. Is that last news?

Star MacDaniel Heimsath may go to the head of the class for voluntarily sending a resumé of her life since last January, when she made a flying trip to Texas and Mexico. In July she motored with her husband and sons to San Antonio. August finds her in the north woods of Wisconsin. "In winter life is very crowded in Evanston," she writes; "my husband's church is full of interest. I have a carrel in the library at Northwestern University, where I'm doing a bit of research. I'm on the Advisory Council there too, which keeps me in touch with the students. And always there are two most imperious little boys to run after and obey!"

Dorothy Meserve Kunhardt's book for 4-year-olds was published in September by Harcourt, Brace and Company. It is called *Junket Is Nice*, is very clever and has no moral despite the title. Personally, we've always had a sneaking liking for junket, anyway.

Nebulous bits of information have come to us about Helen Rice, who took a motor (?) trip out West (destination unknown). We do know, however, that she won a mixed doubles tournament before leaving.

Mildred Schwarz went to Chicago last summer, where she visited the Fair and Marion Holt Spalding. She has now returned to *Fortune,* for which she is doing a story on Woolworth's.

Katherine Strauss Mali spent the summer in Oyster Bay, but she and her husband took "a couple of three-day week-ends doing strenuous things in the Adirondacks and White Mountains, and returning exalted with that peculiar exhilaration that comes to the climber of a mountain that can be seen just as well from below." She adds also, "Harriet Price Phipps' perigrinations would fill a book. She sent us a magnificent 31-pound salmon from her fishing preserve in the Gaspé Peninsula last spring. She is now just back from Murray Bay."

1924

Class Editor: DOROTHY GARDNER BUTTERWORTH
(Mrs. J. Ebert Butterworth)
8102 Ardmore Ave., Chestnut Hill, Pa.

It is with deep sympathy for her family that we announce the death of Anna Pratt Abbott, in August, at her home in Boulder, Colorado, after an illness of a month. Her father, Dr. Pratt, Professor Emeritus of Biology at Haverford College, and Mrs. Pratt were with her at the time. Besides her husband, Anna is survived by two children, David and Agnes.

Elizabeth Ives Bartholet has a son, Paul Ives, born August 17th.

The marriage of Elizabeth Briggs to Richard E. Harrison took place on August 22nd.

Sarah Wood's wedding date was September 5th. She was married to George Eugene Buchanan, of Bronxville, New York, with Elsa Molitor Vanderbilt as her matron of honor.

Some information on where these brides are now residing would be a great boon to the Editor.

The only kind-hearted member of '24 is Mary Rodney Brinser. As I was literally biting my fingernails and taking it out on the children, along came a letter from Mary, enclosing clippings and much news. She is still being "Ann Stevens," daily at 11.30 over WOR, answering such questions as "How can I lengthen a boy's knickers several inches, so it won't show?" "What shall I wear to the inaugural ball?" "How can I give some financial aid to one of my neighbors without hurting her feelings?" No doubt Mary has an answer for any question. I wish she could spend a few days with my boys.

So many have requested a resumé of my activities that, at the risk of being personal, I set forth the following facts for their especial benefit:

I am still happily married, very much a housewife, have two boys, Jimmy and John, ages 8 and 6, both attending Penn Charter. For the first time in nine years I have some leisure time, so am concentrating on music again, play at golf, teach a Sunday School class, garden, work on a hospital committee, and am anticipating painting scenery and making costumes for some Junior League children's plays this winter. For pleasure I read, play contract and do a slight amount of bumming and gadding.

This summer I took an extended motor tour, South, West and North, with my husband, who still enjoys my company, strange as that may seem. Just now I am grubbing with house cleaning and bursting with excitement over the prospective visit of Martha Cooke Steadman, who hasn't been East for five years.

1925

Class Editor: ELIZABETH MALLETT CONGER
(Mrs. Frederic Conger)
Dongan Hills, Staten Island, N. Y.

1926

Class Editor: HARRIOT HOPKINSON
Manchester, Mass.

1927

Class Editor: ELLENOR MORRIS
Berwyn, Pa.

Only two weddings this summer, and one birth, or, at least, that is all that has reached these ever-open ears. We feel that our classmates must be holding out on us.

On August 8th Kitty Harris was married to Mr. Henry Phillips, Jr., in Germantown. We are sorry that we weren't able to get to the wedding, and we have heard no account of it.

It was with deep disappointment that we also missed the wedding of Darcy Kellogg and Mr. Landon Thomas, of Augusta, Georgia. This took place in the garden of the Kelloggs' place at Dark Harbor, Maine, on August 19th. The bride and groom left the island by airplane for a trip through the Canadian Rockies, and we understand that they are going to live at Hickman Avenue, Augusta.

Minna Lee Jones Clarke has a baby boy, exact age and name unknown.

Connie Jones is back at the Baldwin School, and Natalie Longfellow has arrived to teach science at the Shipley School.

Freddie deLaguna is back from Alaska with all sorts of prehistoric bits, and has a job at the University of Pennsylvania, cataloguing and writing them up.

Gladys Jenkins Stevens has gone abroad with her husband. Two little girls are left at home on Long Island.

The Kysters are still at Fort Mills, Corregidor, Philippine Islands, and Crooky writes that little Mary Elizabeth is doing splendidly. From her picture she looks like a very entrancing, but serious-minded young lady. We suppose Lt. Kyster is serious minded.

1928

Class Editor: CORNELIA B. ROSE, JR.
57 Christopher St., New York City.

The class wishes to extend its sympathy to Marjorie Young Otto whose husband was killed in an autogiro accident this summer.

Just too late for our last Notes, Martha Ferguson was married on June 28th to Charles Breasted, executive secretary of the Oriental Institute of the University of Chicago. They were married in Tyrone, N. M., and Martha wore a gingham dress and a sunbonnet, according to newspaper accounts.

Nina Perera's engagement to Charles Wood Collier has been announced. Mr. Collier studied at Stanford and Columbia, and took his degree in architecture at M. I. T. At present he is assistant to the Commissioner of Indian Affairs. By the time these notes appear, the wedding will have taken place.

Lucile Meyer Durschinger writes that her son, John Albert, was born in Pittsburgh on March 27th. If you only knew how unsolicited news warms the cockles of your Editor's heart, we are sure that more of it would be forthcoming. Lucile is living at 9316 Frankstown Road, Wilkinsburg, Pa.

Alice Palache has been with the Fiduciary Trust Co., of New York, since May in a very nice job in the investment department. From

Palach we heard that Mary Adams has gone to Ireland this summer with K. Balch, '29, to study the political situation. Also, that Lib Rhett has moved from Short Hills back to Garden City.

It is a little hard to keep up with the activities of our most widely known classmate, for all the publicity she receives. After "Christopher Strong" and "Morning Glory," Katharine Hepburn is about to appear as Jo in "Little Women." The schedule thereafter seems to be one more picture, either one by G. B. Stern or "The Age of Innocence," of Edith Wharton's, and then "The Lake," to be produced by Jed Harris in New York. It is now running in London and seems to be a hit.

1929

Class Editor: MARY L. WILLIAMS
210 East 68th St., New York City.

The few items which we have been able to garner this summer are mostly in the nature of vital statistics, with two births and three marriages:

Barbara Channing was married to Francis Birch on Saturday, July 15th, at Kensington, New Hampshire. They will live at Kensington, New Hampshire.

Clover Henry was married on September 13th at the Belgravia, London, to David Graham, son of Mrs. William Graham, of Newpark, Antrim, Ireland, and the late Mr. Graham. He was graduated from Queen's College, Belfast, and later attended the Massachusetts Institute of Technology and the Harvard School of Business Administration as a Commonwealth Fellow. He was formerly with J. P. Morgan & Co. in New York, and is now in the London branch of the J. Walter Thompson Company. They will live at Swan Court, Manor Road, Chelsea, London.

We are certainly going in for Englishmen, for on August 2nd Lenette Jeanes was married in Radnor, Pa., to Captain Walter Henry Bromley-Davenport, of The Kennels, Capethorne, Chilford, Cheshire, England. He was welterweight boxing champion of the British Army in 1926. They will live at Bye Ways, Binfield, Berkshire, England.

Elizabeth Linn Allen has a daughter, Constance, and Jane Barth Sloss has a second daughter, Janet. We have no further information about these infants, but any details will be welcome.

Becky Wills Hetzel, with her husband and two children, Fritzie and Helen, were supposed to have returned during the summer for a two years' residence in Munich; we are now in the dark, however, as to their actual arrival or future plans.

1930

Class Editor: EDITH GRANT
Rockefeller Hall, Bryn Mawr, Pa.

1931

Class Editor: JANET WAPLES BAYLESS
(Mrs. Robert N. Bayless)
301 W. Main St., New Britain, Conn.

Lucy Sanborn has been elected teacher of English at the high school at Haverhill, Mass. For the past two years Lucy has been assistant psychologist at the State Clinic at Hathorne, Mass.

1932

Class Editor: JOSEPHINE GRATON
182 Brattle St., Cambridge, Mass.

Margaret Peter Fritz and her family have moved from Bryn Mawr Gables to a house on Radnor Road, Bryn Mawr.

On July 8th, the Class Baby of 1932 was born to Mr. and Mrs. H. George Wilde (Marjorie Field), in Lenox, Mass., at the Field's summer home. The baby's name is Mary Killeen. We extend to Marj and her husband our sincere congratulations.

A letter from Al Yarnelle Hanna, in Fort Wayne, Indiana, tells of the birth of a son, Robert C. Hanna, Jr., on March 14th.

Elizabeth Gill was married, on August 1st, to William Hamilton Lathrop at the Gill's summer home in northern Wisconsin. Margaret Woods writes of the wedding: "Gilly and Bill were married in a little shrine improvised of small pine trees set around an altar of birch. Gilly looked lovely, with much tulle and white gladioli, and old lace pieces for her cap and for her wide collar—they were from her mother's wedding dress." The Lathrops are living in Devon, Pa.

The Woods twins, except for going to Gilly's wedding and spending a few days at the Fair, had a quiet and pleasant summer in Iowa City. They have now moved to Cambridge where they are studying Anthropology at Radcliffe and enjoying it very much.

Denise Gallaudet announced her engagement to Carleton Francis, of Philadelphia and Boston, on July 2nd. Plans for the wedding are still uncertain. Denny will continue working for Stokowski this winter. Grace Dewes is engaged to George Stickle Oram, of Rockaway, N. J. Greta Swenson has announced her engagement to Kimberly Cheney, of South Manchester, Conn.

The class wishes to extend its deepest sympathy to Dodo Brown, who lost her sister a few weeks ago, and to Flewellyn McCaw French, whose father died recently.

1933

Class Editor: JANET MARSHALL
112 Green Bay Road, Hubbard Woods, Ill.

It would seem that as soon as the last cars drew away from Bryn Mawr in June, the graduating class spread itself as thinly as possible over all parts of the globe. Even in Chicago, which might have served as a center of affairs this summer, there were not so many visitors registered from 1933.

What little we have gleaned so far is this:

Radcliffe seems to have grabbed a large share of those who intend to continue their studies. Betsy Jackson is working in Biology there. Jo Williams and Becky Taft, when last heard from, were preparing to take work in Economics. And Alice Brues taking some more Philosophy.

Jinny Balough and Margie Collier will both be in and around Bryn Mawr this winter. Jinny is taking her master's degree in Psychology with Dr. Helson, and Margie is helping Miss Grant with the hockey team. Emily Grace and Jeanette LeSaulnier are also planning to work at Bryn Mawr, but so far we haven't found out much about their plans.

Ellinor Collins is the librarian at Penn Charter School for Boys in Germantown. The last librarian was driven away by the behavior of the six hundred students. Nobody seems to know Collie's plans for handling them. Evie Remington is acting as secretary to a church organization in Philadelphia.

Ella Berkeley and Mimi Dodge are both in Macy's, and Mimi sounds a little harrassed. Ella Bella's job has something to do with correspondence, and seems to be more pleasurable. Serena Weld and Kate Lefferts went abroad and hadn't returned when we last heard. Marg Ullom was still wandering about England and the continent with the All-American Hockey Team, and doing special articles for a Philadelphia paper when we heard from her. Tilly McCracken also went abroad, and has returned, but has no definite plans yet.

Sue Torrance is going to study medicine at Johns Hopkins this winter, and Becky Wood will be at Penn, taking architecture. Someone wrote that Carolyn Lloyd-Jones was to teach French at Baldwin, but again, we're not sure.

Betty Edwards plans to stay home in Dallas this winter. Sidda Bowditch is going down to the wilds of the Kentucky Mountains to be a courier in Mrs. Breckenridge's famous Frontier Nursing Service. She assures us that she is not going to "do any doctoring"—just riding around.

Kag Berg has been very ill this summer and is recuperating at home in Portland.

As for the editorial "us," we're working for a magazine here in Chicago, and still going to the Fair.

SCHOOL DIRECTORY

Miss Beard's School

PREPARES girls for College Board examinations. General courses include Household, Fine and Applied Arts, and Music. Trained teachers, small classes. Ample grounds near Orange Mountain. Excellent health record; varied sports program. Established 1894. *Write for booklet.*

LUCIE C. BEARD
Headmistress
Berkeley Avenue
Orange   New Jersey

THE SHIPLEY SCHOOL
BRYN MAWR, PENNSYLVANIA

Preparatory to
Bryn Mawr College

ALICE G. HOWLAND
ELEANOR O. BROWNELL } *Principals*

THE AGNES IRWIN SCHOOL
OF PHILADELPHIA

opened on

SEPTEMBER 21, 1933

at

WYNNEWOOD, PENNSYLVANIA

BERTHA M. LAWS, A. B., Headmistress

The Ethel Walker School
SIMSBURY, CONNECTICUT

Head of School
ETHEL WALKER SMITH, A.M.,
Bryn Mawr College
Head Mistress
JESSIE GERMAIN HEWITT, A.B.,
Bryn Mawr College

WYKEHAM RISE
WASHINGTON, CONNECTICUT

A COUNTRY SCHOOL
FOR GIRLS
FANNY E. DAVIES, *Headmistress*
Prepares for Bryn Mawr and Other Colleges

ROSEMARY HALL
Greenwich, Conn.

COLLEGE PREPARATORY

Caroline Ruutz-Rees, Ph.D.   Head
Mary E. Lowndes, M. A., Litt.D. } Mistresses
Katherine P. Debevoise, Assistant to the Heads

LOW-HEYWOOD
On the Sound ~ At Shippan Point

ESTABLISHED 1865
Preparatory to the Leading Colleges for Women.
Also General Course.
Art and Music.
Separate Junior School.
Outdoor Sports.
One hour from New York
Address
MARY ROGERS ROPER, *Headmistress*
Box Y, Stamford, Conn.

The Kirk School
Bryn Mawr, Pennsylvania

Boarding and day school. Record for thorough preparation for the leading women's colleges. Four-year college preparatory course. One-year intensive course for high-school graduates. Resident enrollment limited to thirty girls. Advantage of small classes and of individual instruction when desirable. Informal home life. Outdoor sports.

MARY B. THOMPSON, *Principal*

BRYN MAWR
ALUMNAE
BULLETIN

FORMAL OPENING OF THE DEANERY

AS THE ALUMNAE HOUSE

December, 1933

Vol. XIII   No. 9

Entered as second-class matter, January 15, 1921, at the Post Office, Phila., Pa., under Act of March 3, 1879
COPYRIGHT, 1933
ALUMNAE ASSOCIATION OF BRYN MAWR COLLEGE

Form of Bequest

I give and bequeath to the ALUMNAE ASSOCIATION
OF BRYN MAWR COLLEGE, Bryn Mawr, Pennsylvania,
the sum of.............................dollars.

PRESIDENT-EMERITUS THOMAS

BRYN MAWR ALUMNAE BULLETIN

OFFICIAL PUBLICATION OF
THE BRYN MAWR ALUMNÆ ASSOCIATION

MARJORIE L. THOMPSON, '12, *Editor*
ALICE M. HAWKINS, '07, *Business Manager*

EDITORIAL BOARD

MARY CRAWFORD DUDLEY, '96
CAROLINE MORROW CHADWICK-COLLINS, '05
EMILY KIMBROUGH WRENCH, '21
ELIZABETH BENT CLARK, '95, *ex-officio*

ELLENOR MORRIS, '27
ELINOR AMRAM NAHM, '28
PAMELA BURR, '28

Subscription Price, $1.50 a Year   *Single Copies, 25 Cents*
Checks should be drawn to the order of Bryn Mawr Alumnae Bulletin
Published monthly, except August, September and October, at 1006 Arch St., Philadelphia, Pa.

VOL. XIII   DECEMBER, 1933   No. 9

The tea at the formal opening of the Deanery, with Miss Thomas herself graciously receiving the some eight hundred and fifty guests, was an occasion that any one who was there will never forget. The beautiful rooms need people and lights and a sense of gaiety to come most fully into their own. All this they had, but underlying the charm of it all was a strong current of emotion that even the least sensitive could not fail to perceive. The alumnae who had been in College under Miss Thomas remembered the innumerable times that they had seen her standing thus, in the characteristic setting that she and Miss Garrett had created, making it, in spite of all its formality, a very personal thing. Younger alumnae, who had never known Miss Thomas, nevertheless, even in the brief moment of greeting her realized that here was one of that splendid generation of women who had fought, fought with high courage and often at great personal cost, for the things that this generation carelessly takes for granted. Both groups were united in a sense of warm gratitude, however, and a hope and a determination to make the gift of the Deanery do for the alumnae and for the College just what Miss Thomas herself has dreamed that it may. One of the most delightful things about the whole occasion was the quick perception, on the part of the undergraduates, of all the implications. These last few years the undergraduates have been discovering the alumnae, and are, one likes to think, feeling a certain pride in them, as an integral part of the College scheme. Nothing has done more to foster this pride than Miss Thomas' attitude toward the alumnae as a group. In the account of the opening of the Deanery which appeared in *The College News*, and is carried elsewhere in this number, the whole feeling about the alumnae is summed up in the sentence: "Miss Thomas' gift to them of her own house is a symbol of their partnership in her love and work for Bryn Mawr." It could not have been better said, and the alumnae humbly, but proudly, accept the tribute.

WHAT THE DEANERY WILL MEAN TO
THE ALUMNAE

The alumnae of Bryn Mawr College, in this autumn of 1933, are convinced that dreams come true and that romance has not vanished from daily life. Just as Aladdin woke one morning to see his palace erected overnight, outside of his window, so are we presented this autumn, from the wealth of Miss Thomas' affection for us and interest in our welfare, with a home that will incomparably enrich the life of the alumnae. We receive the gift reverently, mingled with inevitable sense of loss, knowing as we do that the house can never be the same to us with its presiding spirit away. At the same time we understand that the best expression of our gratitude that we can give to Miss Thomas is to enjoy her gift to the full and show her how our activities will broaden, as she desires them to do, and how much delight and stimulus they will receive under her roof.

What the gift will mean to the alumnae one may easily conjecture. Hitherto we have been the stepchildren of the campus, tucked perforce into vacant corners of the residence halls when we returned to our alma mater. For years the officers of the Alumnae Association have wistfully visited alumnae houses in other colleges and talked of vague plans that seemed to our small association impossible to realize. Miss Thomas, by the generous gift of the contents of her house to the Trustees for the benefit of the alumnae, has splendidly solved our problem. It is her wish, as the Deanery Committee has told us, that "this house shall serve the College and the Alumnae in as many ways as possible, and that the beauty of its rooms and of its garden shall be preserved for their enjoyment."

The arrangement of the house is admirably adapted to both our formal and our individual activities. The great sitting room is perfectly designed for formal entertaining, the small blue room for committee meetings, and Miss Thomas' library on the second floor, a charming retreat with books and easy chairs, is reserved for alumnae only.

The garden of the Deanery, woven into our memory of many commencements, is a magic spot, and the story of its planning, as Miss Thomas tells it, is delightful. It is a green garden, without flowers, except that every year pink tulips, hyacinths and geraniums are planted in succession in the ivy borders, to bloom in spring and early summer. The planting was arranged by John L. Olmstead, of Boston, in 1908. The ground slopes toward a little glade and had to be built up in terraces to lower the effect of the house. The beautiful and unusual decorations have been selected by Miss Thomas from all over the world—the wall fountain is copied from a famous washerwomen's fountain in Assisi; the sixteen bronze fountain figures are exact copies of figures found in Herculaneum; the hundred palm tiles, set in the walls over the two fountains, came from Bagdad—they originally were set in the domes of tombs of Syrian saints and are symbols of immortality; the two stone lions on the stone staircases are from a Mandarin's palace in Manchuria; the three hundred yellow and white glass lanterns that light the garden at night were blown from special designs at Murano, near Venice. For these lamps Miss Thomas, in her

(4)

eagerness to make her gift as complete as possible, has recently ordered a set of dimmers to give a more romantic light.

It is impossible to list the gifts which Miss Thomas has made to us and to which she has added daily. The realization will have to come by degrees as we grow accustomed to seeing and using them, and many, of course, will not show to the transient guest. Her great desire, that has filled these weeks for her with anxious thought, is to do everything in her power to make this venture of the alumnae house a success. She has foreseen many of our needs and forestalled them with her gifts.

To forecast the many ways in which the house will be used by the alumnae one need only consider the program of the first month. From the first day of October there have been a large number of alumnae and their friends visiting the Deanery. In the first twenty-three days over two hundred meals were served and many teas and small after-dinner parties were given. When distinguished lecturers come or when President Park invites the presidents and deans of other women's colleges to meet at Bryn Mawr, they will stay at the Deanery. The engagement book of the House Committee is rapidly filling with board meetings, teas, class suppers and visiting alumnae. The Entertainment Committee has delightful plans for opening the house on Sunday afternoons for some special programs. It is early to say what part the Deanery may play as a refuge for the individual alumna, but one suspects that she will be lured to the campus as a haven of rest, far more often than before. It is easy to predict how much class reunions will be enhanced, and class activities generally will be stimulated.

The great value of the work of the Deanery Committee, of the House Committee, who have worked so hard and successfully to make the house ready, of the Entertainment Committee who are deep in interesting plans, is proved by the success of the opening reception and by the enthusiasm of each one of the eight hundred and fifty alumnae who were present. We take possession thankfully of our palace, which unlike Aladdin's, does not vanish but grows daily in interest and in opportunities to strengthen our alumnae ties with Bryn Mawr.

ANNE KIDDER WILSON, 1903.

MEETING OF BOARD OF DIRECTORS

The Board of Directors of the College met in Philadelphia on Thursday, October 19th. All the Alumnae Directors and the three Alumnae Directors-at-large and the Alumnae member of the Board of Trustees were present. The next meeting of the Board will be held in Bryn Mawr on Thursday, December 21st. Alumnae are urged to communicate with the alumnae members of the Board if they have any matters which they would like to have discussed at that time.

The Alumnae Association wishes to extend its deep sympathy on the sudden death of Anne Morris Scattergood to her husband, Mr. J. Henry Scattergood, Treasurer of the Board of Trustees of Bryn Mawr College, and to her sisters. Evelyn Morris Cope, 1903, and Jacqueline Morris Evans, 1908.

ADDRESS BY PRESIDENT-EMERITUS THOMAS

AT THE TESTIMONIAL DINNER GIVEN FOR HER IN NEW YORK BY THE AFFILIATED SCHOOLS FOR WORKERS, ON OCTOBER 24, 1933

We are dining together tonight with the exhilarating feeling that we are facing the future with a new vision. The United States is at last beginning to organize socially. The NRA codes of President Roosevelt and his advisers are necessary social reforms of great significance. American men and women workers are to be given for the first time, not as a temporary concession but as an inalienable right, some hours of leisure every day, a longer week-end holiday, and fairer, if not yet adequate wages. (Twenty-five workers' education centres listened in.)

Why is it that we are only now just beginning to apply our intelligence, already so gloriously successful in scientific achievements, to organize our community life? Our alarming neighbors, the bees and the ants and all the great insect tribe, have been socially organized for centuries. Each contented insect has its appointed niche and all work for the good of the whole. Indeed so efficiently organized are they that had not scientific research armed us against them they might easily have destroyed the human race. All ancient civilizations in the history of the world seem to have borne within themselves the seeds of decay and miserably to have perished. No one of them seems to have foreseen and provided against the approaching destruction. And now suddenly this same terrifying disintegration seems to be taking place again in our Western civilization. The handwriting is on the wall for all to see. We must reform ourselves drastically and at once or we, too, shall meet the same ruin.

We are delighted that Miss Hilda Smith's unique experience—twelve years in workers' education and eight years in college administration—is to be utilized in organizing this great federal insurance against revolution, the government educational program to be offered to adult workers in their new leisure. Our residential summer schools are now more necessary than ever before. Labor leaders, as well as all other leaders, are desperately needed. We hope that we are developing them. Miss Mary Anderson tells me that the so-called Bryn Mawr group has already made a reputation in labor controversies for initiative and sanity. One-half of our Summer School students are American-born, one-half foreign born; one-half are unorganized, and one-half belong to labor unions. We try to keep this same proportion summer after summer. There is absolute freedom of discussion and no propaganda. The value of the education they receive from this contact which they have with each other and with their professors and tutors in the setting of beautiful and quiet lawns and buildings cannot be overestimated. Whatever may be destroyed in the future, workers so educated will save our schools and colleges. The School managing committee is organized on a fifty-fifty basis, one-half workers or women who have given their time to working for or with workers, and one-half

College and faculty representatives. I have had to preside over many committee meetings in my life, but I do not remember anything so exciting, so touching, so rewarding, as those all-day meetings when in 1921 and 1922 we worked out the curriculum of study for workers.

In the Victorian 1880's and 90's, when girls first began to go to college, and in 1920, when American women first became citizens with votes, we rejoiced in the possibilities of social betterment brought into our national life by those additions of many women voters, as yet uncorrupted politically. But above all we rejoiced because we believed that a splendid new source of leadership had been tapped. No one who is not an early Victorian can, I believe, appreciate the tremendous change in women's outlook and achievement that has already taken place in only thirteen years. Miss Frances Perkins, our Secretary of Labor, a college woman of great ability, integrity and experience, standing four-square as she does for justice to labor, is a splendid example of what we may hope for in the immediate future. As we Victorian women rejoiced in the 80's and 90's over what one or two college women may mean, so we rejoice tonight over what it will mean to the United States when millions of men and women workers enter into their heritage of leisure and more educational opportunities under the NRA codes. They form the majority of voters in the United States, and to a great extent they, too, are not yet financially and politically corrupt, and they also will furnish a great untapped source for leaders. If we could only feel sure that in the next generation there could be even one great leader, man or woman, industrial or white collar worker, or even a rebel son or daughter of the House of Morgan, now nursed on the knees of the gods, we should feel more courage. Such a leader will have at hand scientific knowledge unknown in ancient civilizations. We now know how to limit our population and how to space our industrial work so as to do away with all unemployment, underfeeding and starvation. We know how to eliminate the half-witted and the criminal-minded which are slowly but surely outnumbering our better stocks and giving many nations moron majorities. We shall then be able to have a decent heredity, a good education, a comfortable home, safeguarded by every hygienic device, and ample playgrounds for every child born. We shall also be able to give every adult worker limited hours of daily work and opportunities for relaxation and amusement and more intellectual development throughout life. The new psychology is teaching us how to select boys and girls of genius and those heaven-sent qualities of personality and imagination that have marked every advance of the human race. We shall then be able to give our embryo leaders the best conditions of development which is all that they need. Their genius will do the rest. But it seems too much to hope that our generation can put through this glorious program. We have too many Victorian, Edwardian and Georgian inhibitions. Our hands are not clean. We have permitted the Great War which has killed millions of the youth of the world. But we at least can take now the first comparatively easy steps by giving support to President Roosevelt's codes and his other remedial legislation. Through them we can at once give the younger generation a fairer deal than ever before. If we do our part and support these in the time that the English speaking races may perhaps some day call the second Elizabethan age, the next generation may save our Western civilization from its present disintegration and rebuild for the future a happier and a fairer world.

THE NATIONAL EXPERIMENT IN ADULT EDUCATION

By Hilda W. Smith, 1910

Immediately after the close of the 1933 Bryn Mawr Summer School I came to Washington for a day or two to inquire into the possibilities of Federal grants for our workers' schools. I found that many people here in the Office of Education and in other government departments were discussing the educational needs of adult workers in connection with the present emergency program of the government.

I was asked to work on detailed plans for educational work in connection with the public school system. Having come for only two days, I remained for almost two weeks, trying to develop plans and possibilities for an expansion of the present program of our affiliated schools. At the end of this period we were all delighted to see the announcement in the Federal Emergency Relief Administration's releases that Federal funds were to be used as work relief for unemployed teachers to teach adults to read and write English.

Four and a half million people in the United States can not read and write English. These new funds, given in the form of work relief for teachers, offer an opportunity to change the face of the illiteracy map which is painted black in many sections of the country.

At this point all of us concerned with the workers' education program saw that the next step following the illiteracy classes must be a broad program of adult education comparable to developments in European countries where government funds are used for various types of adult schools and classes.

It was possible that following week to see several people in government departments who expressed a great interest in the work of the affiliated schools and said that they hoped the program developed during the past thirteen years since the opening of Bryn Mawr Summer School could be developed, and that our experience in teaching and in organizing schools and classes could be applied in connection with the new government program. As the result of these numerous conferences the scope of the work relief program was expanded and our suggestion of a general program of adult education was included in the new statement.

As stated in this release, the funds can now be used in the following fields: (1) Unemployed adults who are in need of vocational training or adjustment to make them employable, many of whom are, and will continue to be, unemployable without this training; (2) unemployed adults who are physically handicapped and need additional training in work opportunities, and (3) unemployed and other adults who are in need of further general educational opportunities to fit them to take their part as self-supporting citizens.

Those who have been interested in the progress of the Bryn Mawr Summer School and the other schools and classes, which have grown out of the initial effort on the part of President Thomas to use empty college buildings for workers' education, will rejoice to know that now the way is open ahead for the rapid expansion of adult education in the United States with the support of government funds on the basis of work relief wages.

I have been appointed as "Supervisor of Work Relief in the Field of Education," and have taken up my headquarters in Washington. The need to provide relief for the 80,000 unemployed teachers who are suffering economic distress is urgent. The educational possibilities are overwhelming in all their implications. I have been told that our experience in recruiting workers for an educational program, organizing classes, training teachers, and developing methods of teaching, is needed in order to make this new government plan effective.

The procedure in establishing the new program will be as follows: Each State Emergency Relief Administration is asked to consult the State Board of Education and to present a plan, outlining the scope of adult educational work considered necessary or desirable in each state. These state plans will come to the Federal Emergency Relief Administration in Washington and will be approved or revised in coöperation with the Office of Education.

The next step will be to have the plans as approved sent out to the local superintendents of schools in every city, town and county. We will then, at the request of the state or district school authorities, work directly with the local school superintendent in developing a sound plan of education in this new and pioneer field.

We are already overwhelmed with the scope of our new opportunities. The affiliated schools, through the Board of Directors and the staff in the New York office, will be asked to strengthen its organization, build up local committees for recruiting and for finance work, make sure that the winter budget and the summer budget are secure, and use all the resources of the organization to coöperate with the government when the call comes for coöperation.

There are, of course, many difficulties in the way of developing a sound program of education in an emergency situation. The best that can be done, I suppose, will be to establish certain demonstration centers in localities where conditions are favorable and where the affiliated schools have strong committees to help direct the new venture. It may be that local advisory councils can be organized, using those people in each community who know the problem of workers' education and can adapt its methods to this broader plan. Teachers' training is an essential part of this new plan, as many teachers inexperienced in this field will undoubtedly apply immediately and will be in need of work relief. Materials for classes will be urgently needed and must be written, printed, and distributed. Since Federal funds cannot be used for this purpose, local funds will have to be secured. Grouping plans must be studied through the further development of psychological tests such as have been used at the Bryn Mawr School and in other places. A service of interpretation of these new plans through the labor movement must be carried on by those who are familiar with this movement and can reach organized workers in trade unions and other workers' groups. Already we have requests for teachers for thousands of new union members organized by some of our former students in the shirt makers' locals of the Amalgamated Clothing Workers Union and others.

The Bryn Mawr alumnae who have stood behind the Bryn Mawr Summer School during these pioneer years of laborious effort and experimentation are needed as never before to stand behind the school with courage and determination now that this new opportunity is open before us. Here in this office I would welcome suggestions from any alumnae groups or from individuals as to the educational needs of their own communities and how these educational needs should be met. We shall need the help of every Bryn Mawr alumna to list the needs of her own community, to see that these needs are presented to the local school authorities through the new advisory councils when organized, and to take an active part in helping the government to establish education in this new field. We do not know what the future holds, but we hope that after the emergency funds are exhausted and the relief emergency itself has been met, some sound kind of permanent support for adult education may come from the state funds or from other government appropriations.

In the meantime, we have the opportunity to bring before the whole country the needs of adult workers for education, the lack of present facilities, and the great social purpose which must illuminate the work of students and teachers to analyze and study all the facts of our present economic and industrial society and to take the next steps forward toward a new social order.

UNDERGRADUATE APPRECIATION

(Reprinted from *The College News* of October 25, 1933)

The opening of the Deanery as an Alumnae House last Saturday afternoon had a significance understood only by those who know the traditions of Bryn Mawr. As far as what actually happened is concerned, eight hundred and fifty alumnae passed the receiving line to greet Miss Thomas, Miss Park, Miss Slade, and Mrs. Clark. But even the undergraduates, who have not had the inestimable advantage of knowing Miss Thomas, felt the emotion underlying the return of the alumnae to accept the reward of their work. This official recognition by Miss Thomas of the alumnae as important to the past and future of Bryn Mawr contained not only a tribute for the alumnae as a whole, but an individual meaning for each woman there.

In the eyes of the undergraduates, who have found in the College the tradition of intelligent foresight, scholarship, and loyalty which is their heritage from Miss Thomas, it is apparent that those women who had the good fortune actually to know her must have left College inspired with the love of Bryn Mawr which she herself felt. Miss Thomas' gift to them of her own house is a symbol of their partnership in her love and work for Bryn Mawr. Any undergraduate who talked or listened to the alumnae soon realized the intensity of their gratitude for the gift and the pride which they felt in having been deemed worthy of it. Miss Thomas could have chosen no way of symbolizing this partnership which would have given greater pleasure or satisfaction to the alumnae than the gift of the Deanery. The undergraduates, who were honored to be told by Miss Thomas, when they assembled to cheer her, that she misses knowing them and their ideas more than she misses any other aspect of her college work, feel proud to carry on so glorious and so fittingly rewarded a tradition of working for Bryn Mawr.

PRACTICAL POLITICS AT BRYN MAWR

Gone are the days when the academic denizens of the campus maintained a detached attitude about local politics. Once upon a time a full professor insulted the Governor of the Commonwealth of Pennsylvania by asking him for his credentials when he arrived to take his place in the academic procession forming in the library. Now the village leaders and the college worthies are boon companions.

No doubt Mr. Fenwick's talks on current events started the ball rolling, and to him belongs the credit for actually persuading Marion Parris Smith, 1901, to be a candidate for one of the Lower Merion Township Commissionerships, and Frederick Manning to run for School Director. He himself is familiarly known as the leader of the Montgomery County Brain Trust, and used his influence to have Mrs. Smith appointed Democratic Committee Woman for East Bryn Mawr. Accordingly, as a direct result of Mrs. Smith's and Mr. Fenwick's united efforts there were enrolled among the active working members of the Democratic committees for East and West Bryn Mawr, Marion Edwards Park, Gertrude Ely, 1899, Helen Taft Manning, Eleanor Brownell, 1897, Alice Hawkins, Esther Maddux Tennant, 1909, Lucy Evans Chew, 1918, Elizabeth Norton Potter, 1927, Katharine Peek, 1922, and Elizabeth Forrest Johnson, of the Baldwin School.

On the 23rd of October an unprecedented event took place in the form of a Democratic rally held at the Fire House in Bryn Mawr in the interests of the candidates to be voted for by the residents of East and West Bryn Mawr and Rosemont. All the registered Democrats were invited to a supper provided by the committees and served quickly and quietly by a large corps of waitresses recruited from the College undergraduates and the pupils of the Baldwin and Shipley Schools under the generalship of Gertrude Ely. A large and enthusiastic audience heard rousing speeches delivered by the candidates and by Mr. Fenwick and General Smedley Butler, who has deserted his traditional party to campaign against the abuses of machine politics in Pennsylvania.

As a result of all this activity a complete Democratic ticket for local offices was put in the field—for the first time in many years—and on Election Day the polling places for the two Bryn Mawr precincts—the Fire House and the office of Hart and Hall—had many members of the College community working as watchers or as chauffeurs to transport voters whose hours of work made it difficult for them to exercise their too often neglected right of franchise. It may be said in passing that their duty and their privilege in this connection had been carefully pointed out to them during the preceding weeks through the medium of the best Bryn Mawr vocabularies. All of this oratory and effort should be considered altruistic, as none of the College candidates had the slightest expectation of being elected, although it is whispered that President Park at the last was almost alarmed lest success should somewhat sidetrack some of the more usual campus enterprises.

Actually, the most fantastic hopes were realized when at midnight on Election Day the workers, stiff and reeking of cigar smoke, learned from the returns, which were counted and tabulated under their own weary but still piercing eyes, that the most important candidate on the ticket—running for Judge of the Court of Common Pleas against a sitting judge—had been elected by a respectable majority, and that their other candidates had been defeated by only a slender margin. Rock-ribbed Republican Bryn Mawr was split asunder. When the tally at one precinct showed that the number of *straight* Republican ballots exceeded the number of *straight* Democratic ballots by only twelve, whereas the usual total count is about that number, an old timer who boasted that he had watched at the polls for forty-seven years remarked ruefully: "Well, we have to hand it to you people. You sure are organized."

To appreciate how remarkable the results were, we should call attention to a few pertinent facts. Lower Merion Township has been noted for many years as the richest township in the country, and as the political unit with the highest pro-portion of Republican voters. In the precinct of East Bryn Mawr, for instance, the ratio of registered Republicans to registered Democrats is 11 to 1. Mrs. Smith failed of election only by the ratio of 2½ to 1. Unquestionably the results in these districts are a part of the great Democratic trend throughout the State, which began last year in the Presidential election and culminated this year in the defeat of the Republican machine in Philadelphia and Pittsburgh. However, the campus cannot help boasting that, although the total vote cast was less than in 1932, Mrs. Smith's and Mr. Manning's proportion of that vote was about 10 per cent greater than Mr. Roosevelt's last year.

While concrete gains may seem small, the by-products are not inconsiderable. We pass lightly over the greatly improved appearance of the polling places, thanks to the admirable examples of sartorial and tonsorial elegance, and speak gratefully of the more liberal attitude toward fresh air. A real effort was made to discoun-tenance some time-honoured abuses, such as unnecessary assistance to voters and the dissemination of marked sample ballots. The high moment of the day was perhaps reached in the discomfiture of a member of the bar, who had been flagrantly breaking the law by standing at the very threshold of the room containing the polling booths, and soliciting votes for one of the candidates. He made the mistake of accosting Frederica de Laguna, European Fellow of the Class of 1927, whom he already knew. She listened to him quietly, and then in a low tone, perfectly audible to any one in the building, she replied: "Thank you very much, but I am afraid that I cannot make any promises in response to a request made in this particular location."

A. M. H., '07.

THE UNIVERSITY WOMEN'S CHORUS

A chorus of college women is being organized to meet on Thursday evenings at 7.30 o'clock at the College Club, 1300 Spruce Street, Philadelphia, beginning November 2d.

Mr. Gerald Reynolds, leader of the Women's University Glee Club in New York, will conduct. Two concerts will be given during the season. All college women interested in group singing are cordially invited to join the chorus.

THE COUNCIL AT BOSTON: AN IMPRESSION

Hospitality, at 8 A. M., struck the keynote of the Council meeting in Boston. Biting winds of winter were soon forgotten in the warmth of cordiality that enveloped us, from the opening business session at the home of Mrs. Torbert to the close.

Planned with amazing forethought and skill, the meeting for parents and pupils at the Winsor School reached the top notch of such meetings in the annals of the Council. Interested school girls and their parents filled to overflowing the large assembly room. Whether it was Boston or the depression, the liberal sprinkling of earnest papas, concerned with the education of their daughters, was interesting. President Park, directing her address primarily to the scholars, brought home to them the question they must ask themselves, "Where can I get the most light on what I want to know?"

Following the scholarship conference for Councillors at the home of Mrs. Walcott, the Councillors' reports on the second day furnished at once the thrill and glory of the Council. Useful suggestions from the Councillor-at-large about cultivating the corporate garden of the alumnae, drawn from a study of what alumnae associations of other colleges do, pointed up the reports. The urgent need of the loan fund in these lean years, the health of students, body mechanics and the rigid discipline of dancing, passed in interesting array to terminate in the drama of the Deanery. Mrs. Slade, at the constant beck and call of Bryn Mawr, sketched the gift of the Deanery, the arrangements, the opening party, to a Council so eager and grateful that it telegraphed its appreciation to Miss Thomas.

That evening one hundred and thirty alumnae assembled in the ball-room of the Women's Republican Club, anxious to hear President Park. Despite the present smooth-going year at the College, the danger inherent to women's education in poverty, the danger to private endowment in a world of rapidly dwindling resources and no dividends, must claim the best thought of women. President Park struck the right note in building up the case for service in a new civilization, in which the human mind must think the way out without "prejudice, indulgence, or selfishness."

After the feast of fat things, by all the rules, the last session of the Council ought to be anti-climactic. Not so; more than ever in a cracking world do people cling to memories of other days, of youth on the Bryn Mawr campus. Accordingly the undergraduate point of view, always interesting to alumnae, had a particular interest this year. Dean Schenck's discussion of the Graduate School brought much desired information to the alumnae who, no doubt, as publicity agents of the College, have had to defend the set-up of a graduate school in a small college exclusively for women. The wide spread of other colleges (41) represented in the graduate school counterbalances the presence of 32 Bryn Mawr alumnae in a school of 112. Vigorous insistance that candidates for the Ph.D. degree do not pass all their years of graduate work in Bryn Mawr gives, on the other hand, a wide range to training.

It was with more than regret that the Council disbanded after two happy days of intensive grooming in the affairs of Bryn Mawr, and with the greatest gratitude to the Boston committee which had planned so completely such a pleasant conference.

ELIZABETH LEWIS OTEY, 1901.

THE PRESIDENT'S PAGE

The entering class is larger than the average class at Bryn Mawr, falling short only by five of the college record; at the same time the percentage of non-resident students is hardly increased over last year's and a happy necessity has thus made us open Wyndham again. The class is young—for the first time in history just under instead of just over eighteen. As usual two-thirds of its numbers belong to families of American birth for at least three generations. Again, as usual, stock from the British Isles predominates in both the father's and the mother's lines, but almost every continental nation is represented in the list compiled from the answers to this question. Almost twenty per cent of the class have college trained fathers and mothers and about fifty per cent college trained fathers, and mothers without college training. Harvard and Bryn Mawr predominate on the two sides of the house, respectively.

So far the Bryn Mawr statistics repeat themselves. At three points, however, this year shows something new. The class has a wider geographical distribution than usual. The percentage coming from our private rectangle with New York and Washington for its northern and southern limits and Paoli guarding the west drops from 65 per cent to 45 per cent; New England and the middle west are over their average, and the south, both the nearer and farther southern states, has made a considerable gain. In the second place, variation in the form of admission has increased: 42 girls have come to Bryn Mawr by the old Bryn Mawr process, Plan A, demanding an examination covering every school course for admission; 76 by Plan B, that is, by four examinations taken at one time and just before entrance; 3 presented themselves as special cases under Plan C, the variation of Plan B offered last spring, by which the four examinations may be divided between two years. Three were accepted under the Harvard-Radcliffe plan, i.e., with no examinations, from schools which guaranteed them as outstanding students, but did not regularly prepare for college or were remote from it. In the third place, in addition to the Alumnae Regional Scholarships for freshmen, more scholarships than usual were offered by the college itself, including two new funded scholarships in honour of Amy Sussman Steinhart and Louise Hyman Pollak specifically awarded to a far western and a Cincinnati girl. These three points are connected. They go to show that the college itself, and among us especially Miss Ward, the Alumnae and many schools have been actively and most fruitfully interested in finding girls of unusual promise and suggesting Bryn Mawr to them. The effort has clearly been widespread; though in a number of cases scholarship help has been necessary to bring such a girl to the college, other girls as promising have come paying their own way entirely. All of us were helped by the fact that a late decision to enter Bryn Mawr was made possible by readjustments of the subjects required for entrance, a policy adopted as a temporary measure primarily for non-resident students last spring. A few freshmen were admitted with these readjustments.

The problem of the Admissions Committee as a result of the varying forms of admission was thus more complicated than usual. Common to all alike, however, were the school reports, the recommendations of the heads of the schools and the

(14)

Scholastic Aptitude Test. Further, in all but the three Harvard-Radcliffe plan cases, the same English examination, and in the great majority of cases the same Latin or French examination was at hand for comparison. In many cases examination books were read by the Committee. The Committee worked over its 180 names during four broiling days, with interest, some excitement and, I trust, success.

The entrance record of the students is unquestionably good. In the Scholastic Aptitude Test common to the 124 members of the class, two girls had A in both the verbal and the mathematical divisions, 16 had A in one and B in the other, and 34 girls in all had an A in one of the two. One girl had an examination average of over 90 on a full series of course examinations and two students had the same record on the 4 B Plan examinations submitted to us. Twenty-three per cent of the class entered college with an examination average of 80 or above, and others, whose history we came to know, performed a greater feat in working under difficult conditions of haste and poor early training or ill health, thus proving their intelligence and persistence.

All the college thinks 1937 a promising beginner.

THE MILLION DOLLAR FELLOWSHIP FUND OF THE A. A. U. W.

It is breath-taking to realize that the sale of one million maps would probably complete the Million Dollar Fellowship Fund which is being emphasized in the plans of the American Association of University Women this coming year. The Association has the exclusive sale of this historical map, "The Conquest of a Continent"—a map carefully prepared by one of our members, showing progress across the United States in all its significant features presented in a most decorative manner. The coloring has been designed by experts, and the map makes an attractive picture for the walls of libraries, schools and young people's rooms.

This project is interesting to college women all over the country. In Philadelphia the map is being sold for the Marion Reilly International Fellowship, named after one of Bryn Mawr's eminent graduates, and of added value because of its international designation. The map is on sale at The College Club, 1300 Spruce Street, Philadelphia. The price ranges from $1.00 to $3.75, according to the mounting.

COLLEGE CHOIR TO SING WITH PHILADELPHIA ORCHESTRA

On December 22nd and 23rd, the Choir, with some other groups, will sing Vaughan Williams' *Fantasia on Christmas Carols*. The Friday concert will be broadcast at 2.30, over the Columbia network. (Station WCAU in Philadelphia.)

ERRATUM

The Rockefeller Foundation and The Emergency Committee in Aid of Displaced German Scholars, not the Rockefeller Foundation and the Institute of International Education, as was stated in the November BULLETIN, united to make it possible for the Department of Mathematics to invite Dr. Noether to Bryn Mawr.

SUCCESS OF THE NEW YORK BRYN MAWR CLUB

The Bryn Mawr Club of New York has now been at the Park Lane, 299 Park Avenue, for a year. The experiment of combining the informality and intimacy of a club with the utility of a hotel has proven a great success. Our own rooms are pleasantly reminiscent of the old clubhouse, with much of the same furniture and gay chintzes. There is a quiet room set aside to keep the library intact—with new books added, reading lamps carefully placed, and a great window to the west with plenty of afternoon sun. The L-shaped living room is far larger than anything that the old club boasted, and so convenient is the location and so pleasant the surroundings that it is often full to overflowing. It affords the opportunity for a quiet game of bridge, uninterrupted by noisy, if legitimate, children's games, or by housekeeping worries. In fact, an impromptu game can sometimes be picked up, in the sensible fashion of men's clubs. We continue to feature tea, and have our own maid on duty every afternoon to serve those special teas so dear to all Bryn Mawr hearts. For the suburbanite, whose New York day often lasts from nine in the morning until after theatre at night, there are beautiful modern bathrooms, not at all reminiscent of the dark Victorian relics of the old clubhouse, and a large couch in a well equipped dressing room.

In anticipation of Repeal, the club is ready with a shaker, glasses, and ice, all conducive to the comfort of those who give dinners in the hotel dining room but who find it more sociable to assemble their guests in the club rooms before dinner. The dining room does not segregate Bryn Mawrters like naughty children in a separate corner, but treats them like very distinguished guests, at a moderate price. To entertain a man in so thoroughly civilized a fashion, in one of New York's best hotels, instead of dragging him protesting to a woman's club dining-room, marks another step forward in the equality of the sexes.

The Park Lane supplies the club with bedrooms from which no line need form, to wait, disgruntled, outside a too long occupied bathroom door, and for which we pay a very minimum sum. These bedrooms are available single or double, and husbands need not be checked outside overnight in this delightfully modern club, but may occupy Park Lane bedrooms exactly as if they, too, belonged.

MADELEINE FLEISHER ELLINGER, 1914,
Vice-President.

NOTICE

The Board of Governors of the Bryn Mawr Club of New York will be glad to issue guest cards to anyone interested in seeing the club.

WASHINGTON BRYN MAWR CLUB

The Bryn Mawr Club of Washington, D. C., wishes to learn of any former students of Bryn Mawr who have come to Washington so recently that their names are not on the present secretary's list. The club would like to welcome them to its meetings and urges them to send their names and addresses to Mrs. Gerald Gross, 201 East Thornapple Street, Chevy Chase, Maryland.

COLLEGE CALENDAR

Sunday, November 26th—5 p. m., The Deanery (Tea, 4 to 5)

First of a series of entertainments: Lecture on "Chinese Painting," with slides, by J. Lawrence Binyon, Curator of Oriental Prints at the British Museum and Exchange Professor at Harvard University.

Monday, November 27th—8.20 p. m., Goodhart Hall

Lecture on "The Hopes We Inherit," by Jane Addams
under the Anna Howard Shaw Foundation.

Tuesday, November 28th—8.20 p. m., Goodhart Hall

Lecture on "Our Overdue Renaissance," by James Stephens, poet and novelist, author of "The Crock of Gold," etc. Reserved seats, $1.25; Unreserved, $1.00 and $.50.

Monday, December 4th—8.20 p. m.; Goodhart Hall

Lecture on "Opportunities of the New Day," by Jane Addams,
under the Anna Howard Shaw Foundation.

Friday, December 8th, and Saturday, December 9th—8.20 p. m., Goodhart Hall

Varsity Play, "The Knight of the Burning Pestle," by Beaumont and Fletcher.
Reserved seats: Friday, $1.25 and $.75; Saturday, $1.50 and $1.00.

Sunday, December 10th—5 p. m., The Deanery

Second of the series of entertainments: Reading of her Christmas Play,
"The Lady of the Inn," by Katharine Garrison Chapin (Mrs. Francis Biddle);
Christmas Carols by the College Choir under the direction of Ernest Willoughby, A.R.C.M.

Thursday, December 14th—5 p. m., The Deanery (Tea, 4 to 5)

Informal talk on "The Drama in Poetry," by Hope Woods Hunt.

Sunday, December 17th—7.45 p. m., Goodhart Hall

Christmas Musical Service. Address by the Reverend Leicester C. Lewis,
Rector of St. Martin's-in-the-Field, Chestnut Hill, Philadelphia.

Monday, December 18th—8.20 p. m., Goodhart Hall

Readings from her own poems by Edna St. Vincent Millay.
Reserved Seats, $1.50 and $1.25; Unreserved, $1.00.

MANY GIRLS IN UNIFORMS

BRYN MAWR (Μπράϋυ Μώρ), THE WOMEN'S UNIVERSITY TOWN OF THE UNITED STATES

(Discovered, and translated from a Greek newspaper by Dorothy Burr, 1923)

In the United States, where man can find all he can desire, there he will find something unique in the world—the antithesis of our absolutely male democracy of Athos: the female university of Bryn Mawr.

Not far from Philadelphia, in a place of almost incredible beauty, in the foothills of the Alleghany mountain (ALEGKANY), there is a most charming as well as a strange settlement. In the centre is a colossal, nevertheless not an ungraceful building, before which stretch flowery lawns several meters in length and breadth. Right and left of the two smaller buildings above are the other buildings, each of which include about 200 public and private rooms. Behind the three central buildings and in a wood which covers the side of the foothills of the Alleghanies—are charming little villas, little single dolls' houses, with three, four, or at the most five rooms.

The whole place is surrounded and divided off by lawns, small artificial lakes, gardens, tennis courts, grounds for gymnastics and athletics, for golf or cricket and all such activities, which are necessary to the life of a well-brought-up Anglo-Saxon.

The region of the settlement holds something magic, something not of the world; it is, you think, when you approach, when you see it open before you, such a place as most of the romanticists write about in their universal Utopias. The mythical and fantastic character of the whole place is given by the character of the living beings who infuse life and movement into their incredible colony. There are about 500 girls, girls but not in uniform, the prettiest of little American creatures, who play tennis or cricket, or do rhythmic gymnastics, or two, three, four together walk among the gardens and parks, or sit in a corner, in the shade of a tree a century old, or read. A sight not for mortals!

We are dealing with the largest woman's university in the world, the College of Bryn Mawr in the United States. But because we are dealing with a college, not a university, with the education of the rich girls of the United States, who stay ten months a year and three years in succession, in Bryn Mawr, they are taught—whatever they want. From cooking to higher mathematics, surveys of all the branches of knowledge in such a way that young girls or their parents have nothing to do but choose what they want to study.

The teachers number 100, those who have undertaken to teach these 500 girls, that is—but why quibble?—they are women! Because—no male foot may enter Bryn Mawr as no female foot may enter Athos. With one exception! With the exception of the "Prenuptial Chambers." For they are, in other words, in the central building several rooms, «παρλουὰρ,» into which at their request with the permission of the parents, and of the administration, the young charges of Bryn Mawr may receive the visits of gentlemen—who, nevertheless, in most cases—

there is scarcely an exception with the high approval of the family—are chosen to unite their lives with the charges of Bryn Mawr whom they visit. Once a week such visits are arranged, which, nevertheless, cannot be stretched beyond a half hour. The unhappy-happy inhabitants of the paradise of Bryn Mawr have no more than half an hour a week to exchange oaths of eternal faith and love with their chosen mates. The austerely limited character of the visitors and the significance of the visits gave to the rooms of Bryn Mawr where these visits take place the characterizing name: "Prenuptial chambers!"

THE ALUMNAE BOOKSHELF

Night Over Fitch's Pond, by Cora Hardy Jarrett, 1899. Houghton Mifflin. $2.50.

In *Night Over Fitch's Pond*, besides writing an absorbing tale, Cora Hardy Jarrett has done an atmosphere of dark destiny in a milieu of charming commonplace, and she has drawn at least two characters with extraordinary psychological insight.

The charming commonplace is a lovely spot almost in the wilderness where there are two little summer cabins, each occupied by a professor and his family. No more harmless setting could well be imagined for a somewhat macabre tale, where the characters converse cheerfully around the family-manipulated ice cream freezer and take their swims and paddles in the most every-day fashion. The crash of tragedy comes with that terror which is so true in life, and which is therefore so peculiarly overwhelming.

The two characters who are outstanding are Professor Julius Nettleton and his neighbor's wife, Eloise Deming. They are studies of two kinds of unpleasant people, and as they are types by no means generally unknown, it is the greater triumph that they have been painted with such extraordinary clarity and penetration.

The book is written in the first person, presumably by Julius Nettleton's friend, Walter Drake—but the keenness with which he views the subtle machinations of Eloise and the bitter and indomitable actions of Julius, is distinctly feminine. Only a woman could understand the delicate mental torture that Julius' wife Mary was made to endure; only a woman could comprehend the particular form of revenge Eloise chose to take.

The book is vivid and excellently written, and it has distinct charm; the dramatic personae are three-dimensional; the feeling of doom (cleverly suggested by starting the story at the end) is not inartistically intense, and—delightful for those who love a good tale—there is a real plot and a decided denouement.

HELEN MacCoy, 1900.

BOOKSHOP NOTICE

To those alumnae interested in current French literature, the College Bookshop would like to announce that it has about five hundred paper-bound volumes on hand. These it is selling out at cost, and in the present state of the exchange this means very good bargains. A list of titles will be sent to anyone on request.

Among the authors represented are Barrès, Bourdet, Brieux, Claudel, Cremieux, Daudet, du Gard, Duhamel, France, Gide, Gerbault, Giraudoux, Green, Mauriac, Maurois, Prevost, Proust, Tharaud and Verhaeren.

CAMPUS NOTES

By J. Elizabeth Hannan, 1934

Although the most important event on campus this month, the opening of the Deanery, is of interest primarily to alumnae, the undergraduates have been very inquisitive about just what is in and what goes on at the Deanery. Mrs. Chadwick-Collins satisfied the general interest and curiosity by giving a tea, October 8th, for a number of undergraduates, and later the House Committee allowed the College the use of the Deanery tea-room on three days set aside for the purpose. For those who missed these chances of viewing the collection of precious objects, there is still the possibility of commandeering an alumna friend as camouflage and pursuing the inspection of the Deanery treasures. And then, conferences in connection with the Shaw lecture series will be held there twice a week when conferees may gratify their interest in economics and interior decoration at the same time.

The actual opening of the Deanery was another occasion for the College to gather round in a body. As Miss Thomas drove up to the reception the afternoon of October 21st, she was welcomed by the college cheer from undergraduates who had assembled in the garden to greet her. In response to this enthusiastic salute, she made a short and very flattering speech, assuring her audience that she misses knowing them and their ideas more than she misses any other aspect of her college work. Probably one of the most valuable results of having an alumnae center on campus will be the increased sense of unity of alumnae and undergraduates, who will feel more strongly now than ever before that they all belong to the traditions fostered by Miss Thomas, and now further encouraged by her generous gift of the Deanery to the alumnae. There has been more talk of tradition and the history of the College lately than we have ever heard before, more interest in yesterday and its likeness or contrast to today. This may be because of the establishment of the alumnae on campus, or again it may be due to the prevalent fashion of harking back to Only Yesterday. In her speech over the radio, October 24th, Miss Thomas recalled the work of the feminists in the Victorian period and later, praising their efforts for the education of women, and pointing to the new field, the betterment of workers, that has been opened up to them in the Summer Schools. Although this topic is not absolutely vital to most undergraduates, many listened in over their radios. Unfortunately, college radios are unreliable because they cannot be plugged in on the electric current, so most of them folded up in the middle of the address or gave a fascinating program of static.

However, with the Shaw lectures under way, the radio and newspaper will not be our only way of keeping in touch with world affairs, for these lectures deal with modern economic and political developments. They did not begin as scheduled, because of the illness of Miss Jane Addams, who was to have given the first two. As now arranged, she will not come to Bryn Mawr until November 27th, but perhaps the series of lectures and conferences which are to precede her will prepare us more fully for the privilege of having Miss Addams on campus for two weeks. Mrs. Vera Micheles Dean, Research Associate of the Foreign Policy Association, spoke October 30th on "Fascism or Democracy in Europe." The enthusiastic reaction of her audience may be taken as proof that the College really is interested in hearing good speakers who do more than present a rehashing of some already stale subject. We do not mean to indicate that a Bryn Mawr audience is bored by anything out of touch with the modern age, but that it objects to sitting through a lecture that might easily have been read in half an hour in an elementary text-book. It is quite natural that those who are required to go and those who go of their own free will should be a little disgusted at the waste of time and wary about trusting themselves in Goodhart again. At present it appears that Mrs. Dean has cured the College of its habit of shunning lectures, and has also attracted a large number of undergraduates to her afternoon conferences.

Other speakers, such as Miriam O'Brien Underhill and, under the auspices of the International Club, Dr. Haridas Mazumdar, author of *Ghandi the Apostle*, have already this year disproved the theory that it is impossible to please a Bryn Mawr audience. The former spoke very entertainingly, as usual, on Mountain Climbing, with the inevitable consequence of an orgy of climbing from floor to floor in the halls. Dr. Mazumdar's talk held a quite different interest, that of a rather biased criticism of Western stupidity and ignorance of Oriental psychology. Both were valuable in that they had a new and awakening influence upon their hearers; but probably the only way to discover just how much impression or improvement had been made, and why, would be to send out a questionnaire in the whole campus instead of drawing conclusions from one's own reactions and the satisfaction or dissatisfaction of individuals.

The Bryn Mawr League has started a new system this year, that of having all the Sunday evening sermons on the same general topic—"The Place of the Christian Church in the World Today" or "The Church's Attitude Toward the Problems of Modern Life." This plan will undoubtedly attract a larger attendance at chapel, because it will present a coherent account of this aspect of modern life for those who are interested in it. According to the League's announcement in the *News*, "There is an even more revolutionary plan for the second semester," what including we cannot tell you at present.

The Varsity Dramatics Club, our organ of expression and only purveyor of light amusement within the college walls, is still vague about its plans for the year. Although the date for the fall three-act play has been set for some time after Thanksgiving and a Miracle play is in project before the Christmas holidays, the source of the male leads for the three act, whether Pennsylvania, Princeton, or Haverford, has not been decided. A one-act play, *Atalanta in Wimbledon*, by Dunsany, has been put on already by Sophomores trying out for Players Club, that amorphous subsidiary of the Dramat Board. According to Miss Schwab, President of Dramat, the plan of having applicants for Players demonstrate their interest and ability by presenting a one-act play, or by assisting the regular board in giving the three-act, promises to work out successfully and provide a sound basis for choosing members. To keep our interest in the drama alive, the Hedgerow Players were brought to Goodhart November 14th, when they presented Shaw's *Heartbreak House*. Johnnie Rieser, ex-'31, who is still with the Hedgerow, will thus be returning to the stage where she played in the *Constant Nymph* and other college productions.

The Freshmen are still new enough to attract voluminous comment from the administration. At Miss Park's chapel on freshman statistics several variations from the usual norm were announced. The enrollment from the South has jumped from four to ten per cent. And perhaps as a consequence, since southern schools graduate pupils at an earlier age, this year's class is the youngest ever to enter Bryn Mawr, 17 years and 11 months being the average age. Thirteen Freshmen were under 17 and fifty-nine under 18 on entrance. In commenting on the comparative youth of the entering Freshmen, Miss Park said that opinions of alumnae, who finished at 21 and have had a few years to meditate on the advantages or disadvantages of such an early exit from college, would be of value in deciding upon the right age for entrance.

Physical statistics, as given by Dr. Wagoner and Miss Petts, are equally interesting. Seven of the Freshmen are over five feet ten, and the average height is 5 feet 5.7 inches—although the percentage of smokers is higher than usual! The Infirmary is probably pretty baffled by this successful flying in the face of the laws of nature, but statistics never lie. Not only are they a healthy lot, as confirmed by still more statistics, but their neat and appropriate "college outfits" are setting a new high for the rest of the campus to strive after. Curiously enough, during the lean years the average Bryn Mawr student has improved in appearance until she bears little resemblance to the tattered figures of yesteryear, the excuses for so many *News* editorials.

The *News* is able to take up its burden of informing and reforming the College this year with a calm and untroubled spirit and a large undergraduate subscription, three hundred to be exact. This amazing total was reached, not by means of compulsory subscription, as projected last year, but in a more subtle way. A meeting of Undergrad was called at which the Editor of the *News*, Sallie Jones, and the Business Manager, Barbara Lewis, set forth the distressing state of the *News* finances, and stated that publication would be suspended unless three hundred college subscriptions were forthcoming within the week. The effect of this harsh ultimatum was so great that within a week all that great company of readers but non-subscribers, which has been the despair of former *News* boards, had docilely signed up. And best of all, the word *compulsory* has been avoided.

The Senior Class has also been active at this and that. Hallowe'en Night they gave their annual party to the Freshmen, which turned out to be a scavenging party this year. A wide collection of flotsam-jetsam, including all the campus dogs, a battalion of professors in red ties, mouse traps, and Mrs. Chadwick-Collins in a baby cap, was brought into the Common Room by the eager scavengers. The team of which Hardenbergh and Jackson were members won first prize, and Steinhart, another alumnae daughter, led the team which won second prize. This speaks well for the stamina of the second generation.

The year book of the Senior Class is to be published in the form of an eighteenth century almanack; but, so we are told, the antiquarian spirit will go no deeper than the cover. The board is already seething with ideas for making it the best of all possible year books, and their plans, as so far revealed, sound excellent.

DOINGS OF ALUMNAE

The following account of Anita Boggs', 1910, activities appeared in the September, 1933, issue of *Shoreham Topics,* the monthly publication of the Shoreham Hotel in Washington:

"Dr. A. Maris Boggs, whose Diplomatic Sunday Evening Salons have been the outstanding events of the winter season of the Shoreham since the hotel opened, has been asked to be on the special list of distinguishd speakers of the National Recovery Administration.

"Dr. Boggs received her A.B. from Bryn Mawr; on a graduate scholarship in Economics at the Wharton School of Finance, she finished her scholastic work at the University of Pennsylvania. Dr. Boggs founded and is the Director of the Bureau of Commercial Economics, which since its inception has been affiliated and coöperates with fifty-four major governments of the world to promote international good-will, mutual understanding and international trade among nations.

"In connection with her work, Dr. Boggs travels extensively in the civilized and uncivilized parts of the world, and knows personally practically all the crowned heads of Europe and Asia and the Presidents of the Republics in Europe and South America, as well as the Prime Ministers and leading men of the world. When Dr. Boggs travels abroad she is usually the guest of the government and is afforded unusual opportunities of seeing the country and studying its political and economic life. Her work brings her in intimate contact with all the governments of the world. Her information is first hand.

"Dr. Boggs is internationally known and recognized as an economist. A Fellow of the Royal Geographic Society; member, Academy World Economics; Academy of Political and Social Sciences; she is a fellow or member of many learned societies in America and abroad. Her writings on economics, international finance and trade have been published in the leading economic journals of America, Europe, the Near East and Asia.

"Dr. Boggs has lectured in many countries. She has addressed the Parliaments of several nations, business clubs, scientific and learned associations, women's clubs. with audiences varying from 100 to 8,000. Her familiarity and broad knowledge of her subjects permits her to present them in a non-technical, concise, compact with facts, yet readily understandable manner, seasoned with a sense of humor in a clear, carrying, appealing voice.

"Dr. Boggs, who has recently been decorated with the Order of the White Lion for distinguished services to the Republic of Czechoslovakia, is being considered very seriously for the position of Minister to Egypt, under the endorsements of many national organizations and prominent persons throughout the United States. for her long, successful experience in diplomacy."

FELLOWSHIPS IN THE SOCIAL ECONOMY DEPARTMENT

The Y. W. C. A. is this year financing at Bryn Mawr in the Social Economy Department a fellow, Miss Vesta Sonne, from California, and a Scholar, Miss Helene Coogan, a graduate of the University of North Carolina. The Family Welfare Society of Philadelphia is also giving a fellowship for Maurine Boie, M.A., Bryn Mawr 1933; and Mildred D. Moore, Oberlin, B.A., 1933, has been given the Ella Sachs Plotz Fellowship offered by the National Urban League.

CLASS NOTES

Ph.D. and Graduate Notes

Editor: MARY ALICE HANNA PARRISH
(Mrs. J. C. Parrish)
Vandalia, Missouri

1889

No Editor Appointed.

1890

No Editor Appointed.

1891

No Editor Appointed.

1892

Class Editor: EDITH WETHERILL IVES
(Mrs. F. M. Ives)
1435 Lexington Ave., New York

The class will be grieved to hear that Dr. Frederick M. Ives, husband of the Class Editor of '92 (Edith Wetherill Ives), died on October 27th.

1893

Class Editor: SUSAN WALKER FITZGERALD
(Mrs. Richard Y. FitzGerald)
7 Greenough Ave., Jamaica Plain, Mass.

1894

Class Editor: ABBY BRAYTON DURFEE
(Mrs. Randall Durfee)
19 Highland Ave., Fall River, Mass.

Fay MacCracken Stockwell has been appointed by the Trustees of Vassar College as Field Secretary for the 1934 Summer Institute of Euthenics.

Margaretta MacVeagh Smith, Marie Minor, Elizabeth Mifflin Boyd and Abby Brayton Durfee were at the housewarming party at the Deanery in honor of Miss Thomas.

Mary Harris' address is Alden Park Manor, Germantown, Philadelphia.

1895

Class Editor: SUSAN FOWLER
c/o Brearley School
610 East 83rd St., New York City.

The Class Editor is inclined to abandon handwriting and to buy a typewriter forthwith; it is gall and wormwood to her to read in the Class Notes of the November BULLETIN about Madeline Harris Brown's "very *own*

granddaughter"; what the Editor thought she wrote was very *young*, or perhaps *new*.

(NOTE: The BULLETIN Editor encourages, nay, urges the use of typewriters!)

Caroline Foulke Urie is living now at Yellow Springs, Ohio. She writes: "It was nice to have a sign from you out of that Fourth Dimension that somehow manages to give unity and continuity to one's life in a kaleidoscopic world of changes. As I read your note, the strains of 'Who's Seen Sal Skinner?' came reverberating from the past as freshly as if it were yesterday.

"But when you ask me for news of the intervening aeons, I cudgel my brains for anything in my short and simple annals worthy of your editorial interest.

"Yes—we still have the Valsolda home; though it is now more of an improbably lovely dream than ever. We left it three years ago because our Janet was a student here in Antioch College and we couldn't live with the ocean between us. And now that she has married and left us, we are tied to America by poverty and family complications—so that (if a house exactly on the frontier of almost any two European countries were just now anything but a liability) we ought really to be selling it and renouncing that dream forever. But people aren't buying homes in military zones in the present state of international relations!

"We live on in this little college town because of inertia and because it is an interesting place, a gathering place of some rather unusual people, an experiment station for sundry original ideas. I've been an educational radical ever since I had a child to educate, and that was one of the chief reasons for our coming here to live.

"My days are now mainly filled with the care of an invalid husband and two aged and invalid parents. And the rest of my time and thought goes chiefly to radical pacifism (War Resistance) and socialism; though my only present official connection with either movement is as a member of the State Executive Committee of the Ohio Socialist Party.

"Our Janet has been married for more than a year to an Antioch graduate, a former fellow-student, Stanley Hoerr, now a 'student in the Harvard Medical School; and she is living very busily and happily in Boston.

"I hope you'll have better luck with the rest of '95! I doubt if mere friendly good-will is an adequate motive for offering you such an attenuated *Apologia pro Vita Mea* as the above."

1896

Class Editor: ABIGAIL CAMP DIMON
1411 Genesee St., Utica, N. Y.

Mary Hopkins and Elizabeth Kirkbride drove to Maine early in July to spend a few days with Ruth Porter on Great Spruce Head Island. Here Ruth and James in the summer gather their five children, five grand-children, and friends of the three generations. Eliot has his own house on the island and Nancy built one this summer, so with the farmer's house quite a settlement has grown up.

On their way home Mary and Elizabeth happened upon Clara Farr in her home under the shadow of Crawford Notch, and hunted up Elsa Bowman at New London, New Hampshire. Elsa has a small cottage, where she keeps house for an invalid friend and an invalid dog, and enjoys her Ford and the summer attractions of New Hampshire.

Katharine Cook spent the summer in Norway and Sweden with Marion Taber as her companion most of the time. Katharine prepared herself by studying Norwegian, which she reports is quite unnecessary, as English is pretty generally understood in Norway. The tale, however, was different in Sweden, where they found at their first hotel no one who knew any German or English or French, while they had unfortunately neglected to learn Swedish. Katharine was most enthusiastic about both countries, saying of Norway, "One could spend all the summers of one's life there and not exhaust it." Marion Taber came back to America early, and Katharine intended to end her trip with a few days in Berlin and sail for home from Copenhagen.

Rebecca Darlington spent the summer studying at the University of Perugia, Florence and Siena. She returned to school this fall refreshed and stimulated by her wholly successful and delightful experience.

Abba Dimon lost her position at the Ambler School of Horticulture and is back in Utica, settling down to domestic interests after a happy summer, the last part of which was spent in visits to Bertha Ehlers, Elizabeth Kirkbride, Edith Wyatt, Ruth Porter, and Frieda Heyl. She has joined a night class in Italian in which most of the other pupils are young Italian-Americans, and she hopes to master a little grammar in the course of the winter.

The class will be grieved to hear of the sudden death on September 17th of Christine Openhym, sister of Pauline Goldmark. Christine's house had been next to Pauline and Josephine's in both Hartsdale and St. Hubert's, and the loss of her constant companionship will be a serious one.

Hilda Justice demonstrated her youthful energy and activity this summer by taking a four weeks' pack-horse trip with a party of eight riders, four men, and twenty horses in the Canadian Rockies. She writes: "Everything was in our favor—outfit, weather, company—but we found many places on the trails so blocked with windfalls that our progress was often slow. We made a fine round—down to Assiniboine (over Brewster and Og Passes), three days in camp, just above Sunburst Lake, with Mt. Assiniboine showing through the larches in their fresh green, and carpets of Alpine lilies and chalice cup anemones all around; then by two more passes to Pharaoh Creek and down to the motor road. The trip up Prospectors' Valley to the far end (just at Opabin Pass) was very rewarding, though Wolverine Pass was equally high and magnificent. We finally came around by McArthur Pass and stopped off two days at Lake O'Hara in the bungalow camp."

After the riding trip Hilda and her friend, Miss Ketchun, took train to the coast, and on their way East visited Zion Canyon and Mesa Verde.

A letter to our Class Collector from Eleanor Lattimore, begun last February and sent in June, gives the following account of her two-year-old job in Buffalo: "I have had to devote every single minute to this new task upon which I entered a year and a half ago.

"I am enclosing a bulletin to give you some idea of the multifarious lines of activity involved in evolving a new school of social work in a community in which one is an utter stranger.

"And so many agencies have urged us to expand and to include specialized training— e. g., hospital work and psychiatric social work —for which we are not prepared.

"The job is fascinating and utterly absorbing. I have a full-time teaching program on the campus of the College of Arts, and three regular (just now four) evening classes in addition, down town. Add to these endless committee meetings, conferences with field work students, and agency supervisors of students, tutorial students following individual pursuits, research students, and my assignment of eight Freshmen for whose courses through college I am responsible.

"*Every* one is delightfully coöperative and there has been no friction. Even the Catholic groups are coöperating, in spite of their violent opposition to the academic freedom espoused by the University of Buffalo."

The bulletin referred to in her letter lists Eleanor as Associate Director, Curriculum of Social Work of the University of Buffalo, and describes the curriculum as follows: "The curriculum is divided into three sections, Pre-Clinical, Clinical, and Research. It is expected that the Bachelor's degree will be received at the end of the pre-clinical period. The Certificate in Social Work is granted at the completion of the clinical year. The degree of Master of Arts in Sociology is granted at the completion of the Research Period."

At least two '96 husbands have been honored by the national administration in appointments to aid in carrying out the plans for stabilization and recovery. Gerard Swope is a member of the Committee on Industrial Arbitration, the Committee on Indian Arbitration, and the Committee on Industrial Relations. Henry Waite is Deputy Administrator of Public Works. On October 6th Henry Waite also received the honorary degree of Doctor of Engineering from the University of Cincinnati.

1897

Class Editor: FRIEDRIKA HEYL
104 Lake Shore Drive, East, Dunkirk, N. Y.

The 1st of November finds Anne Thomas in Bermuda, where she is having a few weeks' rest after a very busy summer in Philadelphia.

Mary Fay, who has retired from the Kirk School, is living in New York City this winter at 520 West 14th Street. She is thoroughly enjoying her leisure and reveling in picture exhibitions, etc.

Sue Blake is teaching Physics at Hollins College, Hollins, Virginia, in the mountains near Roanoke.

Frances Arnold in her annual letter from Cornish, N. H., seeking class contributions, adds a few seasonable lines: "Klein has gone down and all the summer folk, and the evenings close in early and the tang of winter is in the air. Next week I go down to New York to vote and see my family."

Ida Gifford is enjoying life in the house she designed for herself in Nonquit, Mass., where she would love to see her friends.

Clara V. Brooks, M. Campbell, S. Hibbard, F. Hand and E. Sedgwick Shaw, with Main Line classmates, represented the class at Miss Thomas' party in the Deanery.

E. Sedgwick Shaw has sent from her Montclair Garden a gift of lily-of-the-valley pips for the Wardens' picking garden, near the little Wyndham greenhouse.

Elizabeth Jackson's second daughter, Margaret, seems to be the only '97 daughter in the Freshman Class. She is occupying her sister's room in Rockefeller. Betsy Jackson is studying at Radcliffe this winter.

M. Campbell and her father spent the summer in Stonington, Connecticut. Mr. Campbell has quite recovered from his serious illness in the spring.

F. Heyl, en route to Bryn Mawr for a few days at the President's House, stopped over in New York with M. Campbell. They lunched with Marion Taber in her Lexington Avenue apartment and were thrilled by her account of her summer in Norway and Sweden, which she is going to write up, we hope, for a later BULLETIN.

Gertrude Frost Packer's daughter, Louise, is following in the footsteps of her sister, who lives in Turkey. Louise was married this summer to Ewart Seager, the brother of her sister's husband, and they sailed in August for Istanbul.

1898

Acting Editor: ELIZABETH NIELDS BANCROFT
(Mrs. Wilfred Bancroft)
615 Old Railroad Ave., Haverford, Pa.

In September, the London *Times Weekly* had the following announcement about Charly Mitchell Jean's daughter: "The engagement is announced between John de Rosier Kent, only surviving son of Mr. and Mrs. C. W. Kent, Fairhurst, East Molesey, Surrey, and Olivia, only daughter of Sir James and Lady Jeans, Cleveland Lodge, Dorking."

Edith Schoff Boericke's daughter, Edith Clara, was married to Mr. Andrew Fell McCandless on the 24th of June, in Fallon, Nevada.

Sarah Ridgway Bruce has established a very pleasant custom by inviting her nearby classmates to a reunion in September at her new home in Columbus, New Jersey. This year was the third time she has opened her house to '98. Unfortunately, only a few could come on September 21st, but Marion Park, Helen Sharpless, Helen Williams Woodall, Mary Sheppard, Mary and Alan Calvert, Betty Nields Bancroft, Sarah and George Howard Bruce enjoyed a delightful luncheon together.

1899

Editor: CAROLYN TROWBRIDGE BROWN LEWIS
(Mrs. H. Radnor Lewis)
451 Milton Road, Rye, N. Y.

Cora Jarrett's book, *Night Over Fitch's Pond*, published by Houghton Mifflin in September, has already gone through two editions, and has been listed as a best seller in a number of cities. This is her first writing to appear under her own name. Heretofore she has written under the name of Faraday Keene. (See p. 19.)

1900

Class Editor: LOUISE CONGDON FRANCIS
(Mrs. Richard Francis)
414 Old Lancaster Road, Haverford, Pa.

Grace Jones McClure spent the summer cruising in waters around Newfoundland as a member of a geological expedition sent out by Yale University. "I was twice at St. Anthony, which is the headquarters of the Grenfell Association, and saw there Harriot Houghteling (Mrs. Charles S. Curtis), whose husband is in charge of the Grenfell work there."

1901

Class Editor: HELEN CONVERSE THORPE
(Mrs. Warren Thorpe)
15 East 64th St., New York City.

1902

Class Editor: ANNE ROTAN HOWE
(Mrs. Thorndike Howe)
77 Revere St., Boston, Mass.

1903

Class Editor: GERTRUDE DIETRICH SMITH
(Mrs. Herbert Knox Smith)
Farmington, Conn.

1904

Class Editor: EMMA O. THOMPSON
320 S. 42nd St., Philadelphia, Pa.

The class desires to express its deep sympathy to Adola Greely Adams, whose husband, the Rev. Charles Lawrence Adams, died on September 11th, after a long period of frail health. Adola has left the rectory at New Canaan to spend the winter with her brother in Honolulu.

Bertha Brown Lambert writes enthusiastically of her visit in Japan with Michi Kawai:

"Michi has, as you can imagine, many exacting outside interests—peace, church, social, educational. She is in constant demand as a speaker by both Japanese and foreigners, and although she resolutely refuses nearly all invitations she is on the go all the time. I never knew anyone could work so hard, but she has a fine constitution and manages to keep afloat, and, more than that, young looking. Do you know she has just written a book? She and I, with her maid to look after us, retired this summer to a distant lake, where she diligently wrote and I corrected and copied. The book (no title yet) is a commission from the N. Y. Central Committee on the United Study of Foreign Missions. It is to be used as a textbook and is an account of the work of Japanese Christian women, but it is far more than that. A background of all the movements, educational, religious, etc., in which Japanese Christian women work is of necessity included. Michi is a famous story-teller, and there is many a picture drawn from life. This will come out next spring. A Mrs. Kubushiro wrote some of it. Do you know anyone who would review it for the BULLETIN?

"Settled in a Japanese home with no tourist urge to distract me, I had time to form friendships with several Japanese women who could speak English. They confided to me how impracticable is the charming but confining Japanese dress, how hot the obi; how tiresome the visits of Japanese friends, who stay for hours and must be entertained every minute, compared with those of Americans, who can be told the dinner hour and left to themselves; how despotic the mother-in-law had been. I visited wealthy Japanese homes to see treasures or attend receptions, through the offices of Michi, of course, and in simple ones no less interesting and more revealing. In vacations I went from the southern island, Kiushu, to the northern one, Hokkaido. Michi took me to the remote village in Ise whence her mother had originally come and where she passed her last years, visited occasionally by her famous daughter. In the low, tile-roofed typical Japanese house that had been her home, in the very room Michi had built for her, with a fine view up the Yamada River, which dashed against the cliff far beneath us, we spent the night, lying on Japanese quilts on the soft matted floor, with a bright moon outside and a fierce wind blowing from up river.

"The Bryn Mawrtyrs in Tokyo have the pleasant habit of giving a party for any visiting B. M. people who happen along, and so one evening we assembled in a charming small Japanese place of entertainment, rather like a private home, for a delicious Japanese feast. Beside Michi and myself, there came from Tsuda College, Ai Hoshino, 1912, its President, Taki Fujita, 1925, who teaches English there, and Miss Anna C. Hartshorne. There were also Ryu Sato Oyaizu, 1917, and May Fleming Kennard, 1907, who also teaches at Tsuda College and elsewhere. Uta Suzuki, 1908, failed to appear, but I saw her several times, and she took me to see a famous Dolls' Festival collection. I stayed a week in the Japanese home of Edith Sharpless, 1905; and in Kyoto took lunch with Michi Matsuda, 1899, at Doshisha Girls' School, from the deanship of which she is now retiring. Viscountess Uchida I saw at a meeting of university women, at which both she and Michi spoke in English of their American days."

1905

Class Editor: ELEANOR LITTLE ALDRICH
(Mrs. Talbot Aldrich)
59 Mount Vernon St., Boston, Mass.

Margaret Nichols Hardenbergh writes the following: "Helen Griffith and Emily Cooper Johnson took a steamer trip to Labrador this summer and stopped off for a short call on us in Intervale, New Hampshire. We had a fine season there, father as well as ever, brother and husband enjoying the good old mountainous vacation, all my four children in one place for the first time in nearly two years."

From Helen Jackson Paxson comes this news: "When 1905 comes to California I shall be delighted to welcome them after December 1st at High Gate Road, Arlington Acres, Berkeley —sounds sniffy, doesn't it? The Realtor had 'vision'! We have gone native and are building an old California type — Spanish or Monterey, as you prefer. Nice patios and loggias, which were unsuited to Wisconsin climate, are in our scheme now, with a touch of modern that I have carried away from the Fair. I traveled to Chicago and back via bus, and my total expense, including two nights at a hotel with room and private bath, was $68. I had a month in Madison for seeing old friends and doing some business."

Ruth Jones Huddleston writes: "Our old Bryn Mawr College Professor Keasby lives in Tucson now and we enjoy many chats. His idle moments are spent with his pedigreed dogs."

1906

Class Editor: HELEN HAUGHWOUT PUTNAM
(Mrs. William E. Putnam)
126 Adams St., Milton, Mass.

1907

Class Editor: ALICE HAWKINS
Taylor Hall, Bryn Mawr, Pa.

We apologize for the belated announcement of the latest honor bestowed on Antoinette Cannon. She and Miss Neva Deardorff (formerly Associate Professor in the Carola Woerishoffer Department of Social Economy) divided a prize of $250 offered for the best paper presented at the National Conference of Social Work, held in Detroit last May. Diligent readers of this column will remember that Tony flew from New York to attend this meeting. In announcing the award, the editorial committee said in part: "Miss Cannon, in *Recent Changes in the Philosophy of Social Workers,* gives us a philosophy of social work, revealing an understanding of human nature so penetrating as to be distinctly scientific." We understand that Tony is using her share of the prize to install a fountain in her backyard garden in Macdougall Street. This, added to the Riveraesque fresco on her living-room wall, now makes her house one of the high spots of Greenwich Village.

The Chicago *Tribune* for October 17th gives a very favorable notice to the opening of the Playwrights Theatre, a new group of amateurs and semi-professional actors. The first produc-

tion was a revival of Alice Gerstenberg's dramatization of *Alice in Wonderland* and *Through the Looking Glass.* This was originally produced in Chicago in 1915 by a professional cast and had a New York engagement that spring. Since that time the text has been widely used in the little theatres of the country. Alice is one of the moving spirits of the Playwrights Theatre.

May Ballin and your Editor recently paid a short visit to Lelia Stokes at her Maryland country place, The Mill. They checked up on the spring planting done by various members of 1907, and found that the summer floods had made the rock garden bloom so luxuriantly that it is hard to believe it had not been there since colonial days, but that the wild garden transplanted from the woods to the sides of the creek had vanished utterly, overwhelmed by the torrents which swept literally truck-loads of sea sand up through Chesapeake Bay and the Susquehanna River to cover the meadow bordering on Deer Creek, and established a new high-water mark on the sides of the mill.

1908

Class Editor: HELEN CADBURY BUSH
Haverford, Pa.

1909

Class Editor: HELEN B. CRANE
70 Willett St., Albany, N. Y.

1910

Class Editor: KATHERINE ROTAN DRINKER
(Mrs. Cecil K. Drinker)
71 Rawson Road, Brookline, Mass.

In a letter written last May from Nanking, Mary Boyd Shipley Mills reports the Mills family as tearing up their roots in China, selling off their furniture, and coming home to America to live. "And it's not because of the depression, for though our salaries have been cut twice, our board hasn't started turning people off; nor because of the Laymen's Report; nor because of Pearl Buck (in whose house we happen to be living this year); nor because we ourselves are dissatisfied with Missions. It's because some years ago we decided that we wanted to make a home in America for our children when they had to come home for school. Sam is to be teaching Bible at the Haverford School, and we shall come back to live there, among family and old friends, and next door to Bryn Mawr.

"We're going around the long way, sailing from Shanghai, June 28th, and reaching Genoa on August 1st. After a little sightseeing in Italy and Switzerland, Sam goes directly on home, while I stay with the children in Vevey for the winter. They'll go to the local schools and we'll travel during vacations; then the next June we'll turn our faces homeward."

On June 21st, last, Marion Kirk received the degree of Master of Laws from the University of Pennsylvania, her thesis being on "Double Jeopardy During the Year Book Period," that is, from approximately 1290 to 1335.

Ruth Cabot, Roxbury, Mass.: "I am working for the Family Welfare Society here as a case-worker—a very stimulating and interesting job. I took a short seminar at Smith College last summer on some of the problems of case-work; and I have joined a drawing class for recreation."

Elsa Denison Jameson is working for a master's degree in Educational Psychology at Teachers' College, Columbia. "It is fascinating work when approached from a psycho-analytical angle, which seems to be the only approach that can reconcile all the various factions, psychiatric, mental hygiene, psychological and philosophical. I hope eventually to teach emotional education in a high school.

"Only one of my three children is at home, the youngest at the Dalton School. My eldest child, Elsa, Jr., entered Bennington College last year, and my son is at school in Lake Placid.

"My most interesting recent experience was seeing Miss Thomas again at the dinner for the Affiliated Schools for Workers, and hearing Jane Smith tell about her new job with the Federal Emergency Relief Organization as field supervisor of their adult education program."

Jeanne Kerr Fleischmann: "We have given up our apartment in New York and stay at the Hotel Chatham when in town. My hobbies are still early American sporting books, due to my husband—and camellias. I spend my winters in Tallahassee, Florida, seeking new varieties to add to my collection, while my husband runs our cotton plantation, and shoots."

Rosalind Romeyn Everdell: "I have spent the past three years moving! Renting our houses that we couldn't afford to live in has kept us on the jump. We are now settled for a while in a little cottage on our place in Manhasset, L. I., and as all the children are away from home in college or boarding school, I find that instead of improving my mind, I am dawdling. . . . Freedom from responsibility of rearing the young has gone to my head."

Juliet Lit Stern has a daughter, Jill Lit Stern, in the Freshman Class at Bryn Mawr.

Ethel Chase Selinger: "I am continuing my work as President of the Board of Trustees of the Froebel League School in New York, but we are now spending the winter as well as the summer in New Canaan, Conn. My two daughters, aged 9 and 6, are in the Community

School of New Canaan, a school for which I am also working, so you see that my interest is in elementary education of a progressive nature."

Emily Storer: "I always stay at Waltham for a short time in the spring and fall, and try to catch up with my friends and fast-growing-up nieces and nephews, and my neglected garden. Then to Washington for the winter, where time is very full with concerts and lectures, Democratic Club, and lots of work at Friendship House, a social settlement. Most of last summer I was at 'Sconset on Nantucket Island, very unique and out of the world."

Gertrude Erbsloh Muller and her two grown sons had tea with your Editor one afternoon last spring. Gertrude, somewhat plumper than twenty-five years ago, when we last met, blonde, smiling, and pleasant as ever, reported herself as living alone in an apartment in New York, her boys both being at Harvard.

Helen Bley Pope writes that she is still teaching Classics at Brooklyn College, Brooklyn.

1911

Class Editor: Elizabeth Taylor Russell
(Mrs. John F. Russell, Jr.)
1085 Park Ave., New York City.

Among the autumn changes of address are the following:

Louise Russell to 353 West 57th Street, New York City.

Julia Chickering to 285 Madison Avenue, New York City.

Mary Case Pevear to 327 East 55th Street, New York City.

Margery Hoffman Smith to 2141 Davis Street, Portland, Ore.

Mollie Kilner Wheeler to 1928 N. W. 31st Street, Portland, Ore.

Alice Channing to 4 Bond Street, Cambridge, Mass.

Kate Chambers Seelye to 96 Maynard Road, Northhampton, Mass.

The latter, when seen by your Editor, was in fine fettle and had placed her children in schools in Northhampton, and was anticipating the winter there with great pleasure.

Margaret Hobart Myers' step-daughter Alice is engaged to Olin Gordon Beall, of Macon, Georgia. Her daughter Rosamund enjoyed a summer camp in the Blue Ridge very much and is headed for B. M. Hoby herself taught most of the summer at Sewanee, demonstration work in drama and pageantry; the course was unusually strenuous, owing to an epidemic of whooping-cough among the actors. Her usual winter routine calls for teaching from 7 a. m. until 2.15 p. m., and again for an hour in the evening. Besides this, she gives a series of teas for the faculty and students, and chaperones the dances at the college. The N. R. A. ought to come in here somehow, we feel.

Anna Stearns, Emma Forster and Emily Caskey were our representatives at the opening of the Deanery. Emily has just returned from a motor trip to Florida.

Mary Pevear's daughter Catherine is teaching at the Dalton School in New York.

At the Affiliated Workers' dinner in honor of Miss Thomas we saw Helen Parkhurst, Pinky Russell and Elsie Funkhauser.

1912

Class Editor: GLADYS SPRY AUGUR
(Mrs. Wheaton Augur)
820 Camino Atalaya, Santa Fé, N. M.

The members of 1912, in and around Philadelphia, had dinner together in the Deanery recently, with Phyllis Goodhart as their guest of honour. Afterwards they sat in the Blue Study, made grim for two of those present by memories of German Orals, and regaled Phyllis with hilarious unpublished *mémoires* of the class.

1913

Class Editor: HELEN EVANS LEWIS
(Mrs. Robert M. Lewis)
52 Trumbull St., New Haven, Conn.

1914

Class Editor: ELIZABETH AYER INCHES
(Mrs. Henderson Inches)
41 Middlesex Road, Chestnut Hill, Mass.

Martha Hobson has gone to Morningside College, Sioux City, Iowa, as head of the Speech Department. She expects to be kept busy there for some time, as she will also work in the summer school in connection with the Conservatory of Music.

1915

Class Editor: MARGARET FREE STONE
(Mrs. James Austin Stone)
3039 44th St., N. W., Washington, D. C.

It was a great shock to all those who saw the Carys when they were in the United States this spring to read of the death of Richard L. Cary, Mary Goodhue's husband, on October 15th in Berlin. Mr. Cary had been for more than two years the representative of the American Friends' Service Committee at the Friends' Center in Berlin. He and Mary had become members of the Society of Friends in Germany and his ashes were interred in the old Quaker Cemetery at Bad Pyrmont, near Hanover. The deep sympathy of the class, I know, is with Mary at this time.

Our sympathy also goes out to Ruth Hubbard, whose father died in September. Ruth is still with the Institute of International Education, in New York, but her home address has changed to 22 Seymour Street, Montclair, N. J. She spent some time in Maine this summer and "had a happy day with Liz Smith, who has two sweet boys and a beautiful house in a perfect setting at Soamesville."

The New York *Sun* of October 20th carried the following item of interest to 1915:

"Miss Susan Brandeis, gifted daughter of Justice Louis D. Brandeis, dislikes notoriety, and therefore her participation in public affairs cannot be measured by her appearance in print. But she does participate, actively, and just now she is busy campaigning for Joseph V. McKee for Mayor of New York.

"A lawyer, admitted to the New York bar in 1921, Miss Brandeis appeared before the United States Supreme Court in 1925—this being the first plea by a woman before that tribunal. The presence of her father on the bench caused her some embarrassment, but he tactfully withdrew. She apparently does not share her father's preoccupation with liberal jurisprudence, mainly intent on being a workmanlike and successful lawyer—which she is.

"Bryn Mawr and the University of Chicago Law School set her on her way. Her first practice involved special prosecutions under the Sherman Act for the United States District Attorney's office in New York. In 1925 she was married to Jacob H. Gilbert. On days off she likes to get up at 4 o'clock in the morning and tramp all day."

1916

Class Editor: CATHERINE S. GODLEY
768 Ridgeway Ave., Avondale
Cincinnati, Ohio

Greetings after a year! Larie has started us off with a dash, and I herewith thank her publicly for making my sabbatical year possible. You probably expect me to return so refreshed by my vacation from gathering evasive news that I will make our column a model of wit and freshness. However, I did not spend the year in leisurely travel and study, which, I believe, is the approved way of using a sabbatical year. I did nothing to brighten my point of view or sharpen my wits, and no pleasant journeys took me within reach of classmates, where I might have picked up a little news, if not "a little scandal and a little misfortune." I stayed right in the home town and grubbed—by day on my job and by night on my home. And my hours of daily and nightly toil were, and are, such that no Blue Eagle will ever hang in my window. But being busy makes the time hurry past; the year is up, and here I am again, determined to have news of you at any cost. Do write to me, even if you have nothing to recount save your technique in keeping the wolf from the door.

True to her promise, Larie has sent me the rest of the notes gathered at Reunion. But before we proceed with the "E's," let's go back to the last "D."

Constance Dowd was married in Saratoga Springs on September 1st to Mr. Albert Grant, of Cincinnati. Mr. Grant is a graduate of Purdue and has his master's degree from the University of Chicago. He came to Cincinnati five years ago to accept the position of statistician in the Psychological Laboratory of the Public Schools. Cedy resigned from her position at the Cornell Medical Center this fall and came to Cincinnati in October. The day after she arrived she began teaching the fifth grade at Mrs. Helen Gibbons Lotspeich's interesting school, which has already progressed beyond the progressive stage. Besides that, she has been appointed Secretary and Treasurer of the Scholarship Committee of the Vocation Bureau, which awards scholarships to needy but promising students in the public high schools. She spends two afternoons each week talking with the boys and girls, who report once a month for their checks. Until the last of June, when Cedy leaves for Camp Runoia, her address will be Sheffield Road, Glendale, Ohio. Both she and her husband prefer country life to the hubbub of the city, and by a stroke of luck they met the owners of an enchanting old white house on a hill who wanted to rent their home for a time. There are fields and woods almost at the doorstep and a creek at the foot of the hill. But in spite of all this rusticity, the house is quite accessible to town.

And now for the "E's" and the "F's," when we had better stop until next time.

-- Engelhard, Margaret—Lives in Winnetka, Ill. Her husband is instructor at Chicago Art Institute. They have twins, a boy and a girl.

Fordyce, Rebecca—Wrote a detective story, *Murder in the Cellar*. Interested in the ladies' board of the Youngstown Hospital.

Fuller, Clara—Has one daughter. Lives in Madison, Wis., where her husband teaches.

1917

Class Editor: BERTHA CLARK GREENOUGH
203 Blackstone Blvd., Providence, R. I.

Apropos of all that is going on in this country at the moment, some of you may find the following excerpt from a letter from Margaret Scattergood of interest (the date was August 25th): "At the American Federation of Labor

we are right at the hub of the busy world of activities centering around industrial codes. It is quite thrilling to be on the staff, getting up briefs for code hearings, attending hearings and getting such a close view of this movement for a new method in industry. Of course, we are up to our ears in work, but it is so interesting that we do not mind and it makes contacts with interesting and worthwhile people.

"I am about to move to the country to live with a friend in a nice country house about five miles from the city. We will have a tennis court and be only a mile from the river for swimming. So it is an ideal home to look forward to. All we need to make it perfect is to have some of 1917 come to visit us."

Caroline Shaw Tatom was made President of the Bryn Mawr Club of Pittsburgh last spring. She had a bad time with an injury to her leg from some pruning shears the end of February. Apparently it was one of those lovely warm days and she was inspired to trim her roses. The result was a sojourn in bed and two months of hobbling around on crutches and canes. During the summer there was some political work to be done preparatory to the September primaries. During the month of August Carrie was back on the job at Hornblower and Weeks, but "things calmed down" and she again joined the leisure class.

Thalia Smith Dole and her three children spent the month of August with her family at Ogunquit, Maine.

1918

Class Editor: MARGARET BACON CAREY
(Mrs. H. R. Carey)
3115 Queen Lane, East Falls P. O., Phila.

The following letter was received from Helen Walker in May, and is printed now with apologies from the Editor—in whose desk it was snowed under during the summer (excuse the paradox): "I am to have two miniatures hung in the National Miniature Exhibition in the Graphic Arts Pavilion of the Century of Progress Exhibition. This is to be the only exhibit of art in the Fair outside of the Art Institute, and inside the actual grounds of the Fair; and required a special release and permit from Mr. Dawes and the Art Institute. There will be some 300 miniatures included from all over the country. I have also been requested to design and execute a mural for the front wall of the exhibit room. Whether I succeed will depend on the time at my disposal between now and the 1st of June. It will have to share the honors with housecleaning and decorators in our apartment."

The Editor had a very pleasant glimpse of Teddy Howell Hulburt at tea one day recently in Washington. She is the same cheer-ful, hospitable Ted of college days, and it was amusing to see her with a large 13-year-old son who was busily practicing on the violin. She reported a successful summer made up of a sail from Annapolis to Camden, Maine, a month there, and another sail back to Maryland. She plans soon to get a studio and go on with her art work, attractive samples of which we saw about the house.

The Editor would much appreciate hearing from those members of the class to whom she has written for news, and from any others who feel moved to contribute.

1919

Class Editor: MARJORIE REMINGTON TWITCHELL
(Mrs. P. E. Twitchell)
Setauket, N. Y.

Elizabeth Besson Rudolphy is the name of Edith Rondinella's little daughter, born Sunday, October 8th.

Ruth Driver Rock sent a snapshot of her most delightful family—thus announcing the arrival of her fourth daughter just a year ago. Mary is the eldest, "very shy for her age, Dodo is tall and weighs a bit more, the only fair one in the crowd," Joan comes next, and then Ruth, Jr. "Last year we took the children up in the mountains back of the Mojave Desert for their first real winter."

Isabel Whittier is teaching history—Europe 1100-1783—at Brooklyn College. This is her fifth year there. She went abroad this sum-mer, visiting Ireland, Scotland and England, particularly the Jacobite regions and cathedral towns.

Fritz Beatty was "in the MacDowell Colony among poets, painters, etchers, composers" dur-ing the summer.

Beany Dubach has "been taking graduate work in bio-chemistry at the University of Colorado Medical School in Denver." Like several other classmates she has put a curb on the Editor's quoting her delightful letter, say-ing, "My school in St. Louis in a recent issue of their Alumnae News printed my obituary. That seemed to me a bit unnecessary, but on the whole I prefer it to publicity of doings not worth recording." (Editors enjoy hearing any-thing and everything!)

Helene Johnson Van Zooneveld wrote of a delightful vacation in Brittany.

Ruth Wheeler Jackson spent the summer in America. Her older boy, 8, was with her. The classmate who sent in that bit of news said "Ruth is just the same—as pretty as ever, not a day older. Tony resembles her and is

very English. We all got a great kick out of his broad English accent. My youngsters gazed upon him as if he were something out of a zoo."

Roberta Ray Mills deserted her entire family for a whole week in July and went to Chicago to visit one of her sisters. Both sisters are now married: they "were just little girls at the time of our graduation." Does that make us feel old? How about returning in June and seeing how young we all really are? Don't forget to begin planning now on a grand Fifteenth!

1920

Class Editor: MARY PORRITT GREEN
(Mrs. Valentine J. Green)
430 East 57th St., New York City

From Polly Chase Boyden—"The end of the Cape has become more and more my habitat. This year I am moving as far as Provincetown, and the children are going with the Portugese to the public school. Maybe New York after Christmas, but my three years there were so over-stimulating that I feel the need of at least three more months' absolute silence in which to collect my wits. I am still plugging ahead with the writing—short stories mostly—which are still being automatically rejected. However—in spite of that—have never been in better spirits."

From Harriet Wolf Rosenau—"My husband, three sons, and address are all the same as in previous reports. As for me, I shall never be the same again after having spent five weeks traveling in U. S. S. R. last summer. No mat-ter what your political beliefs may be, the experience is worth having. It's an incredible country, a really 'Brave New World' which you must see in order to understand. I would love to compare notes with any fellow-enthusiasts."

From Theresa James Morris—"I haven't seen anyone from B. M. for ages, but seem willing to tell about myself again. I seem to be full of activities this year. I am Secretary of the Board of Animal Rescue League; on the Board of the Associated Charities; President of the Madeira School Alumnae of Washington; and plan to shellac braille once a week, as usual. I don't know how I got involved in so much. We had a grand summer; bought an Elco 35-foot cruiser, and spent weeks at a time on it, my husband, my police dog, and myself; and generally we had another couple with us. Ed was captain; I was cook and crew, and the dog—well, you should have seen her go up and down the ladder when we took her ashore in an infinitesimal dinghy."

From Elinor McClure Funk—"I have three children—two boys and a girl, aged 9, 7, and

2½, respectively. This year I am going to art school in Los Angeles, and enjoying it thoroughly."

From Elizabeth Holloway Nesbitt—"I am rather busy keeping up with four daughters, ages 10 to 4—all blondes and very lively. Aside from that, I have just finished being Secretary to our Bryn Mawr Club and another large club here in Indianapolis, and am entering my second year as Recording Secretary to the American Legion. Ours is the biggest post and unit here in town."

From M. K. Cary—"My life wags along so evenly that one year isn't different from another. My work is blood chemistry on ailing infants and experimental animals, which we try to make as sick as our infants, so we will know more about how to treat the next infant. Exciting in prospect; sometimes powerful dull in actuality. Place: Yale Medical School. Travels: between New Haven and Richmond. My hobby is sailing in a small open boat on the Sound from May to October. Get Sloanie to tell you about her cabin boat and cruises on the Chesapeake."

From Katherine Roberts Prew—"I have a girl, Anne, who is 11, and a boy, Neill, who is 10. I am the head of the Whitfield Country Day School, which I started in 1931. This is the most interesting job in the world to me, and keeps me busy directing and teaching French. We love living in Sarasota, and travel only each summer, when we motor north for a visit."

From Peggy Dent Dandon—"I really don't think I have any news of interest to impart, but I am so impressed by the effort you make writing postcards that I feel I must make one too, and you can do what you like with it. I am still doing a little part-time teaching at Bryn Mawr. We have moved to Haverford and like it very much. The children go to the Haverford Friends School, where they are now in the 4th and 2nd grades, respectively. The only '20 I really see is Kitty Robinson, and her cheery smile about the library is a bright spot in an ofttimes dreary world. You knew she is secretary to Miss Schenck, dean of the graduate school."

From Katharine Townsend—"No, I have no job, just being philanthropic with different charities. I had a grand seven weeks in Great Britain this summer, three in London and four weeks touring through Scotland in a Ford, visiting all the golf courses we could."

Betty Brace Gilchrist is in Europe.

The class wishes to send its love and sympathy to Roger and Katherine Clifford Howell, whose four-year-old son, William, died early in November.

We wish to thank all of those of '20 who have responded to our pleas for news.

1921

Class Editor: WINIFRED WORCESTER STEVENSON
(Mrs. Harvey Stevenson)
Croton-on-Hudson, N. Y.

Mary Baldwin Goddard has a second daughter and third child, Faith Baldwin, born July 7th.

1922

Class Editor: SERENA HAND SAVAGE
(Mrs. William L. Savage)
106 E. 85th St., New York City

The class sends its deep sympathy to Emily Anderson Farr, whose mother died suddenly last June.

June Warder was married last summer to Mr. Allen Chester; Mr. Chester teaches English at the University of Pennsylvania.

At the reception given at the formal opening of the Deanery in honor of Miss Thomas, the following members of 1922 were present: C. Baird Voorhis, O. Floyd, E. Pharo, C. Ludington, V. Grace, and Marion Garrison, now Mrs. Byron King. Katherine Peek and Josie Fisher, who are doing graduate work at Bryn Mawr, were also there.

Alice Woodruff was married on September 30th to Mr. George Wright Allen. Her address is 18 Princeton Place, Montclair, N. J.

A very welcome letter from Vinton Liddell Pickens has given us news of 1922 in all parts of the world. Vinton writes from Lausanne, Switzerland, as follows:

"After practically a year of life in a suitcase we shall alight and rest for a few months. . . . We sailed from New York on October 13th of last year for the Orient, and we had a most interesting and pleasant trip, made especially so by the fact that we knew people stationed everywhere and were consequently able to get more than a tourist impression. We left the children in Honolulu and came back after six months to find them brown and healthy, and swimming like Sunny Hobdy and D. Cooke. Dorothea's three children and my two were very good friends by the end of the winter. I can't say enough for all Dorothea and Martha did for Bob and me during the month we spent on the island on our return trip. Dorothea lives on Mamalahoa Road, on the hills above the Honolulu the tourists never see except in passing to take the famous Pali drive. On the way out I saw Katherine Haworth Leicester at San Francisco. She has a husband and two small boys, and is studying medicine at the University of California. After seeing Dorothea, next on my travels I saw Fung Kei. Really, that was interesting! I was the first person from 1922 or any year near it that she had laid eyes on since leaving college. I honestly think I was Exhibit A in her proof to her school children that she really had been in America. I was positively touched by her obvious delight in my going out to visit the school. As you know, a lot of us have been sending her small sums yearly for her work. China is so huge that I felt that her efforts were like those of the lady who tried to scoop up the ocean with a teaspoon. However, I wanted to see what the school was like and whether a Bryn Mawr education could root in the soil of China, so I sent word to Fung Kei one time when I was going to be in Hong Kong. She came down to see me and we got on the boat for the four-hour trip to the island of Macao, the most astonishing town I have ever seen. After having only oriental or very modern buildings before me for so long in the East, I could hardly believe my eyes when I saw rising out of the water before me a little Mediterranean village of rose and tomato and blue-tinted stucco houses—incredibly Portugese on the Asia coast. It's a bewilderingly lovely place, with the gorgeous red and gold and jewel colored Chinese signs and banners in the pastel European streets. Fung Kei still speaks English quite well and teaches it to her children. In my very short visit of two days I did have time to hear some of Fung Kei's ideas on education and serious matters, and I was impressed with the tremendous amount she has accomplished, practically single-handed. She has a very good school, I should judge, by the order, discipline and cleanliness—this last under very difficult conditions—and is really doing good work in giving standards of right and wrong to a lot of children who might, without her teaching, grow up thoroughly confused in the breakdown of the old Chinese ethical system, which is crumbling faster than a new one can take its place. Without being in any way dogmatic, she is imbuing them with the fundamental principles of Christianity—principles that we don't appreciate enough until we see places where they have never been known.

"Bob and I went up to Pekin after my Hong Kong interlude, and there we saw Marnie Speer. She seems to be very content with life. Her house is in the compound at Yenching University. Marnie showed us the summer palace and the other things nearby. In San Francisco, returning home, I saw Sunny Hobdy Hobart with her two children and extremely new baby boy."

After months of no news at all, this letter brings us the best kind of information because it is first hand; I for one would like to ask the author of it to take over our column, for a traveler has opportunities that are forbidden to a very domestic stay-at-home Editor!

1923

Class Editor: HARRIET SCRIBNER ABBOTT
(Mrs. John Abbott)
70 W. 11th St., New York City

Julia Ward is Assistant to the Dean and Director of Admissions at Bryn Mawr. The exigencies of this interesting job are such that she has not yet had time to give us further particulars, but we hope next month to have more information about it.

Eleanor Mathews is taking the first steps toward a master's degree in Political Economy at Columbia. During the past few years she has taken an active interest in politics and has done inconspicuous but apparently effective work for Repeal legislation.

Virginia Miller was married to Mr. Walter Lindsay Suter in June, 1932, in Winnetka, Ill. They have a small son, an apartment filled with delightful things got on a trip abroad, and Mr. Suter is teaching architecture at the Art Institute in Chicago.

After a summer in La Porte, Indiana, Laura Crease Bunch has returned to New York and resumed her bridge classes at the York Club and the Barbizon-Plaza. Her system is Culbertson. She likes to take a busman's holiday and play a social game of an evening.

The following news of Frieda Selligman Yoelson is copied from a Cleveland, Ohio, paper: "Mrs. Frieda S. Yoelson, Supervisor of the Humane Society, will be the instructor in the Child Welfare course of study, one of six courses to be held in conjunction with the Ohio Welfare Conference, October 2nd to 4th. The subject of Mrs. Yoelson's course will be 'The Practice of Child Welfare in the Existing Depression.' Mrs. Yoelson conducted a similar course at the New York State Conference for Social Work last year. She is a graduate of the New York School of Social Work and was formerly with the Child Welfare League of America. While with this latter organization she did survey work in the Indianapolis Orphan Asylum." And Frieda herself writes, "Although working, housekeeping and a husband keep life pretty full for me, I'd still like to hear from any Bryn Mawrters who get out this way."

We had just about decided that our own life is a busy and pleasant one and we were going to write you something amusing about it when a dreary little incident changed all that. Looking what we felt was our best we went to register in order to cast a vote for La Guardia. The clerk took down our answers briskly until she came to "business connection," when she gave us one searching look and wrote Housewife before we could speak for ourself. And that's really all we are. We are still mystified as to the qualifications for looking the part, but the wind is out of our sails.

The class extends deepest sympathy to Elizabeth Gray Vining, whose husband was instantly killed in an automobile accident near Lake Mahopac, New York, October 1st. Elizabeth was seriously injured, but is improving.

1924

Class Editor: DOROTHY GARDNER BUTTERWORTH
(Mrs. J. Ebert Butterworth)
8102 Ardmore Ave., Chestnut Hill, Pa.

This summer, Jean Palmer, with a friend, rented a car in Paris and motored straight over to Heidelberg, Rothenburg, Munich, Salzburg, Innsbruck, Oberammergau, Constance, Zurich, and back to Paris. "In Munich," writes Jean, "Hitler went to the opera with us, but didn't seem to recognize us. His picture is in every shop window, and the Nazi publicity campaign is very similar to our N. R. A. program. The Nazi emblem is seen everywhere and the movies are 100 per cent propaganda. No one slapped my face, much to my disappointment, but I am sure all of the soldiers at the frontier wanted to when they struggled with my German. We went right through Frederichshafen (where the Graf Zeppelin lives), and were just in time to see it depart on its scheduled trip to South America. I was very impressed at a Zeppelin living on a schedule; the charge to Rio is $500, and the trip takes two days and two nights. Every one keeps asking me how conditions were in Germany, and I feel very badly not to have more to report—all the men are in Nazi uniforms of a hideous shade of brown— but they certainly were nice to us. My only regret is that I could not read the German newspapers; it's amazing how little you are affected by political disturbances when motoring. I thought the country was heavenly, the opera horrible, and the weather hot."

1925

Class Editor: ELIZABETH MALLET CONGER
(Mrs. Frederic Conger)
Dongan Hills, Staten Island, N. Y.

See, we've gone suburban—expecting to find the "fast young married set" seen on the stage, with the long cocktail hour and home-wrecking golf professional. We promise to meet and welcome anyone great enough to overcome the Manhattan prejudice and risk the ferry trip. The New Deal has certainly brought prosperity or hope to '25. Everyone seems to be branching out in business, getting married or having babies.

Baldie (Dr. Eleanor de Forest Baldwin) has an office at 16 East 90th Street, where she practices general medicine "by appointment." She is very busy, too, at the gynecology clinic at Bellevue and the Medical Clinic at Presbyterian. (If you have any nice transportable illnesses, take them to Baldie.—Editor's comment.)

Edith Walton was married, on September 30th, to Lombard Carter Jones. Mr. Jones was on the *Harvard Lampoon* and the *Advocate* when he was in college. He is now on the staff of *The Forum*, where Edith has worked with him for several years. After October 20th the Jones' will live at 26 West 9th St., New York City.

(Doctor) H. Potts writes: "I'm expecting to be married, October 28th, to Theodore O. Yoder. He's not medical; got his M.A. last year at Columbia, and is present staff associate at the National Society for the Prevention of Blindness. He spent three years in Cairo, Egypt, at the American University there, and hopes to go back, if the university's finances improve in a few years.

"At present I'm working on some research in the Neuropathological Laboratory (Medical Center) here at the Institute, and I expect to keep on with the work."

Caroline Quarles Coddington had a little daughter on May 14th, Elizabeth Broughton Coddington. Caroline sends news also of Adelaide Eicks Stoddert and her navy husband, who has been transferred to the West Coast. After spending the summer in Seattle, they will move to Long Beach this fall.

Beth Comer Rapp has a six-month-old son, Richard Walther Rapp, Jr., nicknamed "Dick." Beth writes: "Last winter, besides having a baby five weeks old in April, I taught school and took some work in Old French and History at Bryn Mawr. I'm still teaching this year at Holman Prep. French, but I've about decided that I prefer babies to a Ph.D. They seem more worthwhile—at least as far as I'm concerned. I can't see any reason for working any longer for a degree which I shall probably never use."

Our jungle hewer has come back. The Lunns, having abandoned digging for teaching and writing, are spending the winter at Amherst, where Kay (Fowler) has embarked on a book—as well she might. Amherst, we fancy, might be something of a change from African housekeeping. We wonder if Kay would like to transport her gangs of thirty or forty digging boys to hang curtains or help with the tea wagon?

A delightful note from Betty Smith tells news of the Thompsons: "Tommy and I spent a September week-end in Wellsville with the

Holbrooks and had a grand time. George, Jr. (Elizabeth Bradley Holbrook's son) is now 2½ and very attractive, with about the sweetest disposition I've ever seen in a child. (Inherited from his parents.)

"The Thompsons are practically dropped by their non-golfing friends because they're never home. I'm about to suggest that they give prizes to semi-finalists as well as finalists, though. I've got to the semi-finals of four tournaments this summer and lost three of them—will probably lose the fourth next week. Some day I may win and die of the shock."

The rest of this column is just hearsay, but that's life.

Franny Briggs Leuba with her husband and three sons went on a camping trip this summer, but is settled again at Antioch College, Yellow Springs, Ohio.

Kay McBride is still working on Aphasia and is about to burst into print, probably indecipherable to most of us, but print nevertheless.

We hear that Smithy (Helen Lord Smith) took a delightful trip this summer through England and Ireland, where she visited Janet Wiles (her aunt or niece, we never could get that straight). Now she is back at her job with some children in Connecticut.

Maris Constant labors still at Pisa Brothers —only every other week now, because people only like to go abroad every other week these days—you know how it is. Any way, at last Maris is obtainable for lunch—on the national at-home weeks.

Via Saunders Agee worked last winter on *The Symposium*. She and her husband are living at 38 Perry Street, New York.

Chissy (Helen Chisolm) and Calvin Tomkins, after beach-combing the entire Atlantic coast, have found the ideal spot at Nonquit, Mass. They spent their summer in a huddle with architects and builders, and are promising a charming house with at least one guest room that does not look out on the water. (Week-end sailing will not be compulsory, either, if you feel as we do about it.) Dickie has learned to walk!

The class sends very deepest sympathy to Dot Lee Haslam, who lost her mother in July and her father in August.

1926

Class Editor: HARRIOT HOPKINSON
18 East Elm St., Chicago, Ill.

Practically no news of the class has come the way of the Editor recently—and what has come seems to indicate that many of us have reached the point where we continue to do the same things that have been doing for months or even years; which probably proves something very significant, but is not conducive to news.

Two children may have eluded these pages before now—Paula Nan, born July, 1932, daughter of Anna Lingelbach Taylor, and Peter, born last December, brother of Phyllis and son of Eleanor Hess Kurzman.

Polly Kincaid recently attended the American Library Association convention in Chicago. She continues her job of reference librarian at the public library of Akron, O.

Eleanor Follansbee von Erffa and her husband will sail in November for Germany, where he will continue his archeological research in Munich.

Deirdre O'Shea Carr spent a quiet summer in Dorset, Vermont, but will be in New York again this winter, writing.

Charis Denison is back at Radcliffe again.

H. Hopkinson is again in Chicago, on the staff of the Library of International Relations, 86 East Randolph Street, of which Eloise ReQua, '24, is in charge. During the World's Fair, the library has maintained a children's international library called the Story Cove, on the Enchanted Island, the children's section of the Fair, with stories and picture-books from all over the world, story-telling and the celebration of national festivals as particular attractions. It has proved extremely popular and interesting to visitors and workers alike, through these five months, and it is hoped that the children's collection may remain a part of the main library after the Fair closes. Requests for reading lists and information keep coming in from parents and teachers who have visited the Story Cove on the Fair grounds, and as a reference center and reading room the collection seems well worth making permanent.

1927

Class Editor: ELLENOR MORRIS
Berwyn, Pa.

1928

Class Editor: CORNELIA B. ROSE, JR.
57 Christopher St., New York City

The latest "tickler" has brought results from four members of the class of whom we have had no news since they left college. Anne Petrasch Emmons has two children, a daughter 3½ years old, and a son 1½. Since 1930 she has been doing interior decorating with Ethel A. Rewe, Inc., at 17 East 49th Street, New York. Edna Klein Graves (who is now living at 15 West 67th Street, New York City) reports that she has been very busy being married and trying her hand at everything from selling to doing pastel portraits of children for cash. Her husband is a painter and teacher in fine arts at Pratt Institute in Brooklyn. In 1932 they spent the summer in Italy painting and sketching.

Julia Altheimer Stein has three children—a girl, a boy and another girl, 2, 4 and 6 years old, respectively. It is not surprising to have her list as her occupation, "bringing up family," but in addition she finds time to study music, enjoy concerts and galleries in New York, and even managed a trip to Europe in the summer of 1931. Rose Milmine Wolf (1021 Park Avenue, New York City) has a daughter, Charlotte M., aged 8 months.

Two other members of the class have recent arrivals to report—Missy Dyer Flint's daughter, Clarissa Dyer Flint, Jr., was born on July 24th, 1933, and Eleanor Speiden Davico's daughter Paola also was born in July. We expect more news for this department shortly from at least two quarters.

We have been out of touch with Allie Talcott Enders for so long that her second child, a boy, has had time to reach the age of a year and three-quarters before we even knew that he had been born. Her daughter is now 4½. Last winter Allie went to Trinidad. Alita Davis is doing her second term as President of the St. Louis Junior League. Last summer saw her in France and Scotland for the shooting. Helen Tuttle, since leaving college, has done some teaching at country schools, and studied painting in New York at the Art Student's League, in Paris with André Shot (?) and in Cambridge at the Fogg Museum. She now has some water colors on exhibition at 144 West 13th Street, New York City, and at the Grassburger Gallery, in Narberth, Pa.

Ruth Peters received her degree as doctor of philosophy at Radcliffe in June and is now one of the unemployed. Katherine Shepard has done graduate work at Bryn Mawr (1928-30), and at the American School for Classical Studies in Athens (1930-31). In 1931-32 she was a Fellow in Greek at Bryn Mawr, and is now at home in New York working on her dissertation. Christine Hayes did graduate work in Psychology at Columbia for three years, and in the winter of 1930-31 taught at the Edgewood School in Greenwich. She also studied music at the Institute of Musical Art in New York for two years. She has just joined the faculty of the All-Arts Studio in Greenwich, where she will "form classes in ear training and rhythm for small children and give a course in sight reading for those under 16," to quote from a local paper.

The Fair seems to have attracted comparatively few members of the class. Nancy

Pritchett (who has left the Girard and is now with the Peirce Business School), says that she was the only member to have registered in the College Book by September 11. But we know that some others were there: Jean Morgenstern Greenebaum spent the summer in Cleveland with her family, upon whom she deposited her babies while she went to Chicago. "Babies" is Jean's term, but they are practically grown now, since Billy is 3½ and Julian almost 2. Lenore Hollander also took in the Fair on her way to Toronto to see her married sister and her young niece. Eliza Funk was another visitor; Eliza is with Graham Parsons & Co., investment house in Baltimore. Cay and Hal Cherry stayed with Bertha Alling Brown in June. Bertha says that she has had one guest after another for the Fair all summer. Bertha further reports that Ruth Holloway has been in the Berkshires all summer and that Alice Bonnewitz Caldwell is out in Coronado again.

Several people have emulated their Editor's bad example and moved, since last we heard from them. Frances Putnam Fritchman is now at 20 Fourth Street, Bangor, Maine, where her husband is minister of the Unitarian Church. Mattie Fowler Van Doren has taken her family out to 50 Bellevue Avenue, Summit, N. J. Puppy McKelvey and Crina Chambers, '27, have moved from 965 to 785 Madison Avenue, where personal observation enables us to tell you that they are most comfortably situated and will serve you a swell meal. C. Smith and Puppy still carry on the bookshop and now have added Pueblo pottery, hand picked by Elinor Amram Nahm when she was in New Mexico this summer. The stuff is very good—so good, in fact, that they gave some that had been broken in transit to the Natural History Museum, who wanted broken pieces for a display and preferred not to smash any of their own! They plan to add some Navajo jewelry. Martha Ferguson Breasted is living at 5807 Dorchester Avenue, Chicago. Martha confesses to knowing nothing about archeology, and we presume that she is applying herself to some intensive studying.

Just one more new address, and then we'll stop. We have more news, but we have no intention of squandering it rashly, having an eye to the lean months ahead. Jo Young Case will be at 6 Mercer Circle, Cambridge, Mass., this year, working for an M.A. at Radcliffe in the intervals of housekeeping and baby-tending, while her husband writes his Ph.D. thesis at Harvard.

So, good-night, folks. Next month, at the same time, we will be with you again. Be sure to listen in on the cosy Chit-Chat Hour, when Grandma Rose will give you all the latest news, real and fabricated, about your classmates.

1929

Class Editor: MARY L. WILLIAMS
210 East 68th Street, New York City

1930

Class Editor: EDITH GRANT
Rockefeller Hall, Bryn Mawr, Pa.

A long-overdue announcement is that of the marriage of Margaret Mary Cook to John Bertolet, brother of Mary Bertolet. The wedding took place last March. The Bertolets are living in Reading, Pa.

Lois Davis Stevenson has returned to this country and is residing in New Haven. Aside from the fact that she saw Whiz Bang last summer before leaving China, she has told us nothing.

Helen Louise Taylor has definitely embarked on a medical career. We believe that the present scene of her activities is the College of Physicians and Surgeons in New York.

Johnnie Stix Fainsod is doing graduate work, at Radcliffe. Her husband teaches at Harvard.

Our ex-classmate, Martha Gellhorn, was married last summer in Spain, to Bertrand de Jouvenal, son of Henri de Jouvenal.

Mary Elizabeth Edwards continues to run a baby clinic for the Oklahoma City Junior League, and has added to this activity a three-times-weekly trip to the state university, where she is studying Zoology.

The class is represented on the Bryn Mawr campus by Elizabeth Fehrer, Agnes Lake, and ourselves. The first two are living in Radnor and working for their doctor's degrees. Nan has just returned after two years at the American Academy in Rome, absorbing information on archaeology and the classics.

Virginia Loomis has announced her engagement to Bayard Shieffelin. Mr. Schieffelin attended Groton and Yale, 1925. He is employed at the Central Hanover Bank & Trust Co., N. Y.

1931

Class Editor: EVELYN WAPLES BAYLESS
(Mrs. Robert N. Bayless)
301 W. Main St., New Britain, Conn.

1932

Class Editor: JOSEPHINE GRATON
182 Brattle St., Cambridge, Mass.

A. Lee Hardenbergh came back from Europe in August, spent a couple weeks in the White Mountains before going home to Minneapolis, where she expects to take some German and History courses at the university. Dolly Tyler also returned from a winter abroad, spent a month in Banff on the Conference for Pacific Relations, with Hat Moore and the other members of the Institute of Pacific Relations. She is now back in New York working for the Institute. Hat, according to last report, was planning to take her Fellowship this year, and expects to start work at the University of London after Christmas.

Betty Barker has a Scholarship at the University of Pennsylvania this year. Laura Hunter will be studying biology at Bryn Mawr where she has received a Scholarship. Ruth Milliken has gone to Oxford for the year to study philosophy.

A letter from Betty Young enclosed a program of the Litchfield (Conn.) Summer Theatre, in which three members of 1932 figured. Miss Jalna Young (Betty said she had to change her name since "there are 3001 Betty Youngs in this world!") was playing the lead in Martha Madison's *The Night Remembers,* a production staged by Dmitri Ostrov, of *As You Desire Me* fame. Lucy Swift's name appeared beside the title Assistant Stage Manager, and Charlotte Einsiedler's beside that of Treasurer.

Florence Taggart had a half-time position teaching Latin at the Dalton School, but was taken ill before school opened. Isabel Eckhardt is in the Latin Department there. Dolly Davis will be at the Baldwin School again this year. Anne Burnett has a position as apprentice teacher at Shady Hill School in Cambridge, and Nancy Balis is an apprentice teacher at Brearley. Anne and Nancy both spent the summer as councillors at Maskoma Lodge Camp in New Hampshire.

Jo Graton spent the summer driving to California and back with Betsy Jackson, '33, Betty Faeth, '35, and Marion Bridgman, '36, dropping in on all Bryn Mawr friends possible. The only members of 1932 she saw were Marion Hughes Walz, who for two years has been living at the Praesidio in San Francisco where her husband is stationed (they have a baby son); Emma Paxson who is living in Berkeley, California, and studying at the university, and K. Kruse who, after a visit with Sylvia Cornish Allen, '33, on Lake Michigan, returned to her home in Oklahoma to work in her father's office during the winter. From first-hand experience Jo can recommend a couple weeks at a sheep ranch in the redwood belt in California, visits to Lake Tahoe and Glacier National Park as high spots in an ideal summer vacation.

Eleanor Renner was married on Thursday, September 21st, to Mr. Wallace de Laguna. They are living at 6 B Gibson Terrace, Gibson Street, Cambridge, Mass.

1933

Class Editor: JANET MARSHALL
112 Green Bay Road, Hubbard Woods, Ill.

SCHOOL DIRECTORY

Kindly mention BRYN MAWR ALUMNAE BULLETIN

SCHOOL DIRECTORY

Kindly mention BRYN MAWR ALUMNAE BULLETIN

—about Cigarettes

Of all the ways in which tobacco is used the cigarette is the mildest form

YOU know, ever since the Indians found out the pleasure of smoking tobacco, there have been many ways of enjoying it.

But of all the ways in which tobacco is used, the cigarette is the mildest form.

Everything that money can buy and everything that Science knows about is used to make Chesterfields. The tobaccos are blended and cross-blended the right way—the cigarettes are made right—the paper is right.

There are other good cigarettes, of course, but Chesterfield is

the cigarette that's milder
the cigarette that tastes better

Chesterfield

They Satisfy.. just try them